CW00687348

Free Books
Hatfield

THE ECCENTROPEDIA

THE MOST UNUSUAL PEOPLE
WHO HAVE EVER LIVED

By Chris Mikul

Illustrations by Glenn Smith

www.WorldHeadpress.com

CONTENTS

To Cath, who puts up with my books, and me.

INTRODUCTION

he word 'eccentric', which derives from the Greek 'ekkentros' or 'out of centre', first gained currency in England in the last decades of the eighteenth century. Eccentricity was originally conceived as a specifically English quality, as noted by both the English themselves and foreign travellers to Britain. The Russian Nikolai Karamzin, who arrived there in 1789, wrote, 'Other European countries are like well-laid out gardens where the trees are all of the same size, the paths straight, and everything uniform. The English, on the other hand, grow up, morally, like wild oaks, according to the will of fate. Though they are of one stock, they are all different.' That the concept of eccentricity was being defined during the same period as the French Revolution was not a coincidence, for there was a political dimension to it as well. The prevalence of English eccentrics was seen as a by-product of the stability of British society, its representative system of government, and the unique liberties that the British were said to enjoy. For conservatives, eccentricity was a sort of social safety valve that would help to ensure that Britain would never have a revolution of its own. In *Englishness Identified*, historian Paul Langford notes that the various types of eccentric represent exaggerations of traits which are universally accepted as typically English. Thus the Englishman's awkwardness when confronted with the opposite sex finds its purest expression in the figure of Henry Cavendish, who had a second staircase built in his house to avoid the possibility of encountering one of his female servants.

The fashion for eccentrics, which only increased during the Victorian era, saw many magazine articles and compilations of the lives of eccentrics published, while eccentric characters became staples in plays and novels. The definition of eccentricity was, however, rather broader at first than it later became. In James Caulfield's *Portraits, Memoirs and Characters of Remarkable Persons* (1819), figures we immediately recognise as eccentric today, like John Bigg, the Dinton Hermit, rub shoulders with people born with physical deformi-

ties and famous criminals like Dick Turpin the highwayman. Criminals could hardly be held up as exemplars of liberty, however, and it soon became integral to the concept of eccentricity that eccentrics are essentially amiable individuals, immersed in their own peculiar pursuits but incapable of malice or of hurting others. Another attribute of true eccentrics, as they came to be defined, is that there must be an element of innocence or a lack of calculation in their behaviour that sets them apart from others. In other words, anyone who consciously sets out to be an eccentric will fail.

Eccentricity is still particularly associated with the English. Although this book should dispel the notion that they have a monopoly on it, it nevertheless does appear that the concept is stronger in countries with an Anglo-Saxon cultural heritage. (There are exceptions to this, notably Japan, a country which, perhaps not coincidentally, has an innate sense of national superiority similar to that found in eighteenth and nineteenth century England.) Eccentricity provides a template with which unorthodox behaviour can be put into a context and therefore, at least to some extent, understood. While I am sure that all societies have their share of unconventional people, in those societies where eccentricity is celebrated as

a positive quality, such individuals are more likely to be written up in newspaper articles or books or, more recently, on the Internet, so that their fame may spread across the world. A certain level of political freedom is another essential element for this process to take place — repressive regimes have no truck with eccentrics.

Eccentrics would seem to be a fertile field for psychological study, but in fact very little work of this kind has been done, perhaps for the simple reason that eccentrics, believing there is nothing wrong with them, rarely seek out psychologists. The most comprehensive psychological survey of eccentricity remains the one carried out by David Weeks, a neuroscientist at the Royal Edinburgh Hospital, which commenced in 1984. Weeks and his colleagues began by placing small advertisements in shops, pubs and other public areas, asking for anyone who considered themselves eccentric to contact him. The story was taken up by media in the U.K., then the U.S., and Weeks estimated that 140 million people were potentially exposed to the appeal. Weeks and his team whittled the respondents down to just over a thousand individuals who could be considered truly eccentric. They interviewed each of these subjects, and gave them IQ and other psychological tests.

The results did not surprise anyone who had previously taken an interest in eccentrics. Of the fifteen characteristics which Weeks found his subjects shared, the top five were that they were nonconforming, creative, curious, idealistic, and obsessed with one or (usually) more hobbyhorses. Weeks was interested in the link that many psychologists — and indeed people in general — have made between eccentricity and mental illness, particularly schizophrenia, but found that his sample exhibited fewer primary symptoms of schizophrenia than studies of the general population. It also seemed to Weeks (although he admitted it was difficult to be objective about this) that the eccentrics he studied were happier than most people. Based on his study, Weeks estimated that only about one in 10,000 people is a true eccentric (with a margin of error of plus or minus fifty per cent).

While no definition can possibly encompass all the varieties of eccentricity, I tend to divide eccentrics into four broad categories: contrarians, theorists, visionaries and entertainers. These categories are certainly not mutually exclusive, and there are some eccentrics (Emperor Norton of San Francisco, for example) who could be said to straddle all four.

The contrarian is the individual who probably springs most often to mind when people hear the word 'eccentric'. Contrarians are the people who do not give a fig for social conventions and determinedly go their own way, whether it's in their clothing, habits, beliefs, hobbies or living arrangements. Their spiritual father is Diogenes, and they have absolutely no doubt that they are the sensible ones and it is the rest of the world that is out of step. Contrarians, especially in England, are often associated with the aristocracy (who after all, do often have the time and money to be able to live exactly as they please), yet they may come from all walks of life, and indeed, some of the most notable have literally lived on the streets, becoming in the process well known and often well loved individuals. It is the contrarians that John Stuart Mill was thinking of when he wrote in *On Liberty*, 'That so few now dare to be eccentric marks the chief danger of the time.' Mill understood that conformity in a society breeds stagnation. By rejecting conventions, eccentrics demonstrate new ways of thinking and living. Of course, what may seem outrageous or crazy to an eccentric's contemporaries may be judged as eminently reasonable and sensible by later generations (Charles Waterton's early conservation efforts and Victoria Woodhull's tilt at the White House being but two of many examples that could be given).

If the contrarian is often a solitary individual, the theorist craves followers. Theorists may in most respects be thoroughly conventional, but they have become possessed by one grand but unfashionable idea which they believe would, if generally accepted, provide an answer for many if not all of humanity's ills. (The Australian sex reformer William Chidley actually called his theory 'The Answer'.) Some theorists have considerable success in promoting their ideas, like Cyrus Teed (a.k.a. Koresh), who held that we are living *inside* a hollow Earth, lit by an interior sun, and whose community in Florida became one of the most successful of nineteenth century experiments in communal living. Others remain voices crying in the wilderness, like Charles Jackson, doggedly promoting the concept of a flat Earth into the space age. Whatever one may think about their beliefs, the fortitude with which many theorists have faced almost universal ridicule can often be inspiring.

Visionaries may seem to the outside world to be perfectly normal, even dull people, but their heads teem with extraordinary, often religious themed visions which they are driven to render in concrete terms. Perhaps the archetypal visionary artist was William Blake, for whom the natural world was a mere shadow or 'Mundane Shell', compared to the extraordinary, internal world of spirits and angels which he experienced as a daily reality. Blake's visions infused his paintings and illustrated books, to the bewilderment and disdain of his contemporaries. In 1808, when he had a one-man show in London (the only one held during his lifetime), only one newspaper deigned to review it, with the reviewer describing him as an 'unfortunate lunatic, whose personal inoffensiveness secures him from confinement'. Today, Blake is considered the greatest British artist of the eighteenth century.

It would seem that the sort of visions that Blake experienced are not uncommon in children, but the faculty, or whatever you wish to call it, usually disappears as they approach adolescence. Eccentrics in general tend to retain a somewhat childlike view of the world and its possibilities. And while few of the visionaries who have followed Blake have attained the posthumous fame and adulation he did, some of their achievements have been, in their own way, just as remarkable. Their creations may be visible to all, like the cathedral of Justo Martinez or Rodia's Watts Towers, or they may have been meant for the eyes of their creator alone, like the astonishing art and writings of Henry Darger. At first glance, the visions

of these individuals may seem to resemble those experienced by schizophrenics. However, David Weeks makes the important point that schizophrenics are often terrified by their visions, while eccentrics tend to have much more control over them, and find in them a source of delight and, indeed, a reason to live.

My final category, entertainers, are individuals whose behaviour has a strong element of performance about it. Some of them may actually make a living as performers, and it is here that it gets tricky, for it is sometimes difficult to tell the difference between an eccentric who is entertaining, and a person whose eccentricities are simply part of an act. An instructive figure here is the great comedian W.C. Fields, whose life story, eagerly disseminated by studio publicists, was well known to his legion of fans during the thirties and forties. Fields had a childhood of almost Dickensian poverty. After leaving home at the age of eleven, he slept in a hole in the ground and hung around saloons where he learned to play pool and juggle. Entering showbusiness, he took his juggling act from London to India to Pago Pago, performing for all manner of kings, nabobs and potentates. He opened hundreds of bank accounts in false names during his travels, so that he would have money wherever he went. Back

home, he went into the movies, and the persona you saw on the screen was the man himself — the famed curmudgeon who despised women, children, dogs and non-alcoholic liquids. Yet, as Simon Louvish makes clear in his meticulously researched biography, *The Man on the Flying Trapeze*, virtually none of this is true. Fields adopted the cloak of eccentricity to wonderful comic effect. He was a hardworking, hard drinking showman, but apart from a tendency to use pseudonyms like 'Mahatma Kane Jeeves' and 'Otis Criblecoblis' when he wrote screenplays, there was nothing particularly eccentric about him at all.

In deciding who should be included in this volume, I have concentrated on individuals whose eccentricity seems to me to colour and shape their entire lives (and, in the case of those who are also artists, writers or other creative types, their works as well). I have therefore generally steered clear of the many famous people who may have had their foibles (and in some cases, *very* peculiar foibles) but who are generally remembered for their non-eccentric activities. The Marchesa Luisa Casati may have been the only eccentric to have actually said 'I want to be a living work of art', but in the life stories of true eccentrics can be found the sort of unity and coherence, abundance of arresting

detail, humourous moments and, occasionally, tragedy, that we associate with a great novel or play.

I grew up in Sydney, a city with a fine tradition of eccentrics, and in particular, street characters — public eccentrics, if you will. As a boy, I watched Joseph Cindric push his trolley through the streets, and wondered like many others where he had come from and where he was going. I listened as Owen Lloyd, the 'Birdman of Kings Cross', played his fiddle with multi-coloured birds perched on his bow. I was fascinated to read the stories of earlier eccentrics who had graced the city, like the toga-clad Chidley, the Shakespeare-spouting Bea Miles, the 'witch' Rosaleen Norton, and Arthur Stace, who is estimated to have written the word 'Eternity' on its streets over half a million times. I think such characters are an essential part of the fabric of a city, interrupting the monotonous flow of everyday life like a boulder thrown into a stream. They get people talking and speculating, and perhaps even questioning their own lives and assumptions. They may often be loners themselves, yet in strange and unexpected ways they can bring people together.

In researching this book, I have discovered many eccentrics who were previously unknown to me, and I have been constantly surprised by the sheer vitality, creativity and origi-

nality of these splendid individuals. Of course, no work like this can be definitive, and although I believe I have covered most of the really notable eccentrics, I'm sure there are many more out there worthy of inclusion. I am therefore open to suggestions for any future edition, and can be contacted at <eccentropedia@hotmail.com>

ADAMSKI, GEORGE

(1891–1965)
UFO contactee

While he wasn't the first, Adamski was for many years the best known UFO contactee. Born in Poland, he arrived in the U.S. with his family at the age of two, and eventually settled in California. He became interested in eastern philosophy in the 1930s, lectured on the subject, and founded the Royal Order of Tibet. During the 1940s, Adamski and his wife Mary ran a café (often described as a 'hamburger stand') that stood on the road to Mount Palomar Observatory.

In 1947, pilot Kenneth Arnold's sighting of flying objects that flew like saucers skipped across water ushered in the UFO era. Adamski claimed to have seen mysterious objects in the sky prior to that and,

attaching a camera to a telescope, began to photograph them. In 1951, hearing that sightings had been made in the desert areas around Mount Palomar, he began to make regular forays into them.

On the morning of 12 November 1952, Adamski and six companions were out in the desert when they saw 'a gigantic cigar-shaped silvery ship' moving slowly towards them. Saying, 'That ship has come looking for me and I don't want to keep them waiting,' Adamski had one of his companions drive him about half a mile down the road, then asked to be left alone. As he told it, a smaller ship made of translucent metal soon landed nearby, and Adamski saw a figure walking towards him who he realised was 'a man from space'. He had shoulder-length blond hair ('glistening more beautifully than any woman's I have ever seen'), a round face with a high forehead and grey-green eyes 'slightly aslant at the outer corners', and wore a seamless one-piece garment of a colour Adamski couldn't describe. Communicating using telepathy and hand gestures, Adamski learned that this being hailed from Venus. He told Adamski that all the planets of the solar system are inhabited, and the reason for their recent visits was concern about atomic testing, which was sending dangerous radiation into space and would eventually lead to

Earth's destruction. Adamski was invited to inspect the spaceman's ship, but his request for a ride in it was declined.

The spaceship returned on 13 December. On this occasion, Adamski took some remarkably clear photographs. They show an idiosyncratic circular craft with a dome-shaped top, portholes around the edge, and three ball-shaped protruberances at the base. Sceptics denounced them as photos of a model (it was suggested the top section came from a vacuum cleaner) but they convinced many. Adamski's story was included in the British writer Desmond Leslie's *The Flying Saucers Have Landed* (1953), which became a bestseller.

Adamski said that he eventually did get to make several trips into outer space, and described them in a 1955 book, *Inside the Spaceships*. These included a journey around the far side of the Moon, on which he was able to observe cities. Adamski toured the world giving lectures, and was invited to an audience with Queen Juliana of the Netherlands (a rumoured follow-up audience with Queen Elizabeth of England failed to eventuate). He also claimed to have met with Pope John XXIII, and displayed a gold papal coin as proof. In 1962, he announced that he was to attend an interplanetary conference on Saturn.

Adamski's supporters argue that he was genuine in his philosophical beliefs and his efforts to save mankind from itself, and while he charged for lectures, he never tried to make great sums of money from his claimed experiences. After his death he was largely forgotten, but he has a legacy that lives on. He set the template for communication with the kindly aliens generally known as the Space Brothers. He was also one of the first to scour the Bible for references to what might have been UFO sightings, paving the way for Erich von Däniken and various other proponents of the Ancient Astronaut theory. ▨

AHBEZ, EDEN
(1908–1995)
Proto-hippy

eden ahbez (he insisted on his name not being capitalised — only God and Infinity deserve that) was born George Aberle to a poor family in Brooklyn, New York. Like some of his twelve siblings he was adopted out, ending up with a family in Kansas named McGrew. He left them as a teenager and spent the next few years crisscrossing America on freight trains and on foot, finally landing in Los Angeles in 1941. Here he began his musical career playing piano in a raw food restaurant called the Eutrophean.

EDEN AHBEZ

This had been opened in 1917 by two German immigrants, John and Vera Richter, who were advocates of a philosophy called 'lebensreform' (life-reform). This advocated a natural lifestyle, vegetarianism (with food eaten raw), dress reform, nudism, natural medicine and communal living, and those who adopted it were known as Nature Boys.

George McGrew changed his name to eden ahbez. He let his hair and beard grow, and wore a robe and sandals. He married Anna Jacobsen, and they had a son, Zoma. For a while, they lived in a commune in Topanga Canyon. To celebrate his new lifestyle, ahbez wrote a song called 'Nature Boy', which tells of a 'strange and enchanted boy', who had wandered far and found that 'The greatest thing you'll ever learn/Is just to love and be loved in return'. It was written as a tribute to an earlier Nature Boy, Bill Pester, who had arrived from Germany in 1906 and lived in a palm hut near Palm Canyon. (Pester played guitar, practised yoga, wore beads, and has a pretty good claim to being the first hippy.) In 1946, ahbez approached Nat King Cole's manager, Mort Ruby, outside a theatre and gave him the manuscript of the song. Cole included it in his live performances, and audiences responded well. When the decision was made to record it, Ruby was despatched to

locate ahbez and acquire the rights (he eventually found him, according to legend, living with his wife and son in sleeping bags beneath the first 'L' of the Hollywood sign). The song went to number one in 1948, and has since been covered by many other singers, including Frank Sinatra and David Bowie.

The success of 'Nature Boy' made ahbez a minor celebrity, and articles about him appeared in *Time*, *Life* and other magazines. He wrote a few more songs during the 1950s, including 'Lonely Island', which was a minor hit for Sam Cooke, and in 1954 collaborated with the jazz singer and actor Herb Jeffries on an album called *The Singing Prophet*. His lifestyle remained unchanged, however, and he claimed to live on just $3 a week. In one of the anecdotes told about him, a policeman once tried to haul him off to a mental institution. 'I may look crazy, but I'm not,' he told the cop. 'And the funny thing is, that other people don't look crazy, but they are.' The cop is supposed to have thought about this for a while and said, 'You know, bud, you're right.'

In 1960, ahbez (who was known to his friends as 'ahbe'), released a concept album, *Eden's Island*, recorded in the 'exotica' style made popular by musicians like Martin Denny and Les Baxter.

It was a flop, and he afterwards

drifted into obscurity. His wife Anna died in 1964, while Zoma drowned a few years later. He could still be seen on the streets of L.A. occasionally, playing his own compositions on hand-carved flutes, and lived out of an old white Dodge van which contained a bed, his clothes, musical instruments and master tapes of his music. He was recording again in his last years, and some of this music was released posthumously. Sadly and ironically, the 'Nature Boy' died after being hit by a car. ◙

AIRAUDI, OBERTO

(b. 1950)
Mystic

Airaudi, born in Balangero in northern Italy, worked as an insurance broker before moving into more spiritual pursuits. During the early seventies he became a successful psychic healer (or 'pranotherapist') and spiritual medium, and acquired a small group of followers who were attracted to his teachings, an optimistic blend of paganism, Gnosticism, theosophy and other beliefs usually found intermingling in so-called New Age philosophy. In 1975, he leased some land in the Valchusialla Valley, about thirty miles (forty-eight km) from Turin, and founded the community of Damanhur (an Atlantean word, according

to Airaudi, meaning 'City of Light'). He believes that human beings must work together to attain self-enlightenment, and conceived Damanhur as nothing less than a separate, spiritual nation. Beginning with a couple of dozen 'citizens', its population now exceeds 800. It has its own constitution, currency, daily newspaper, supermarkets, schools and university. Its citizens, who adopt the names of animals when they join — Auraudi is known as Falco (Falcon) — live in groups of ten to fifteen in eco-friendly houses, and run a variety of businesses to support themselves as they seek their inner 'Master'.

While Damanhur would be notable simply as a successful experiment in communal and alternative living, it is the incredible underground temples Airaudi and his followers created — the Temples of Humankind — which have made it the greatest New Age showpiece in the world. Work on these began in 1978 when the first excavations were made into the side of a mountain. Over the next few years, a system of nine major temples on five levels, all connected by hundreds of metres of corridors, was created deep below the Earth. Airaudi says that his intention was to recreate the exotic temples he had visions of as a young boy, and which he took to be memories of a past life in a perfectly enlightened world. The temples 'demonstrate that it is

possible to bring dream into matter', and that 'dreams can be shared'. They were made by the Damanhurians using little more than picks and shovels, but perhaps the most extraordinary thing about them is that their existence was kept a secret from the outside world for so long. It was not until 1992, when a disgruntled former Damanhurian mounted a lawsuit against the community, that the Italian authorities learned of their existence. A state prosecutor accompanied by police arrived at Damanhur, threatening to blow up the temples — which had of course been built without planning permission — unless he was allowed to see them. The prosecutor and three of the policemen were taken through the old wooden door which hid the entrance to the temples, and emerged hours later in a state of shock.

It's a terrible cliché to say it, but the Temples of Humankind must be seen to be believed. Each temple has a theme — the Hall of Mirrors, the Hall of the Earth, the Hall of the Spheres and so on. They are decorated with hundreds of statues, murals, mosaics, carved pillars, stained glass windows and domes. Stylistically, Graeco-Roman, Egyptian and Celtic and what might be called 'late Hippy' influences predominate, and everything is meticulously detailed and vividly coloured. There are also hidden doors and passageways, a labyrinth and an alchemical laboratory to which all parts of the structure are connected with copper wires. Symbols from many ancient cultures are incorporated into the designs, and the structure as a whole is designed to be symbolic of the nature of the universe and humanity's part in it. While some of the decoration veers into kitsch, the sheer scale of the temples, and the high quality of the workmanship throughout, make them an astonishing achievement, whatever you might think of the philosophy behind them.

On discovering this phantasmagorical creation, the first reaction of the local government — with the backing of the Catholic Church — was to order that it be destroyed. After a public outcry and a court case lasting four years, the temples were given retrospective planning permission, and work on them resumed. The Damanhurians say that they are still only ten per cent complete, which means that much of Auraudi's dream, and the dreams of his followers, are still to be realised. ◙

ALINGTON, JOHN
(1795–1863)
Priest

Alington was educated at Oxford and ordained in 1822. In 1830, he inherited estates in Letchworth,

Hertfordshire, from his maternal grandfather. Out of courtesy, the local vicar, Samuel Hartopp Knapp, invited the new lord of the manor to conduct some of the services in his church. Alington was soon insisting on taking all the services (apart from the funerals) and his preaching style was far from conventional. He jettisoned the normal order of service, and his readings weren't restricted to passages from the Bible. Knapp was horrified and complained to his bishop, who banned Allington from conducting further services.

Undeterred, Alington started his own church. His services, held at Letchworth Hall, now resembled an early version of a rock concert. He was often roaring drunk, and wore a leopard skin instead of traditional vestments. He preached from a hollowed-out log, sang bawdy songs, and propelled himself up and down the aisle on a four-wheeled vehicle of his own devising, offering random worshippers snuff from a jar. He sometimes ended his impassioned if often incomprehensible sermons by throwing his wig at the congregation.

Some of the income of his now sworn enemy, Knapp, derived from tithes on Alington's estates. Alington therefore delighted in making them unproductive, assigning his workers to pointless tasks like digging then filling in holes, or erecting columns of flint stones. Otherwise he was an enlightened employer who cared about the education of his workforce, and often read to them from Shakespeare and the Bible. In 1851, when the Great Exhibition was being held at the Crystal Palace in London, he decided his men would benefit from a visit to it. He was concerned that they might lose their way between King's Cross train station and the exhibition, though, so had them construct an enormous road map of London out of logs. The men spent a week practising the journey on this, wearing hay bands around their right legs for the trip from the station, and around their left legs for the trip back. In the end, Alington decided they just weren't up to it and abandoned the idea. During the Crimean War, he had them construct a model of the fortifications of Sebastapol so they could better follow the progress of battle. His most ambitious educational scheme involved the construction of a model of the world in a pond. Alington took his men on trips through it in a rowing boat, pointing out interesting geographical features as they went along.

Alington liked to be carried around his estate in an open coffin, explaining that he was preparing for the end. Growing ill at the age of sixty-eight, he refused to take the medicine his doctor had prescribed until his gardener had taken it for three days. When the three days were up, he decided to down a glass of brandy instead, and dropped dead. ▣

ANDREWS, STEPHEN PEARL

(1812–1886)
Political philosopher & linguist

Andrews, known as Pearl to his friends, was born into a Baptist family in Templeton, Massachusetts. At the age of eighteen he moved to Louisiana where he established a law practice, and in 1835 married Mary Gordon, with whom he had three sons. He became an ardent abolitionist, and moved to Texas where he promoted a plan to end slavery by purchasing all the slaves and freeing them. This did not endear him to most Texans, and in 1843 an angry mob descended on his home and the family was forced to leave the state. Andrews went to England, where he attempted to raise funds for his plan. He received a sympathetic hearing from many, including members of the government, but in the end they declined to help him for fear of provoking war with the U.S.

While in England, Andrews discovered Pitman's shorthand, and became fascinated by it. He had long been interested in languages (he would eventually have a reasonable knowledge of thirty of them) and with the grandiosity which characterised all his thinking, he saw phonetic spelling as the basis of a new 'Single Grand Planetary Language' that would solve the problem of illiteracy and unite mankind. On his return to the U.S., he went to New York where he wrote several textbooks on phonography (shorthand), and published journals printed in phonetic type. He continued to campaign against slavery and, coming under the influence of the pioneering American anarchist, Josiah Warren, helped to establish a utopian commune on Long Island, called Modern Times. This was organised according to Warren's economic ideas, with the price of goods determined by the time spent producing them. Individual freedom was the ideal, and when Andrews began to espouse the doctrine of 'free love', the concept was enthusiastically adopted by commune members.

Modern Times attracted all sorts of crackpots, and despite early success eventually disintegrated. Andrews set up a more modest commune, Unity House, in several brownstone houses in New York City. He moved into this in 1856, along with his second wife Esther (née Hussey), Mary having died the previous year.

Andrews believed his greatest

contribution to humanity was the philosophy he called Universology, which would bring all knowledge into a unified whole and reconcile all intellectual differences among human beings. He outlined it in a book, *The Primary Synopsis of Universology* (1871), of which one reviewer wrote, 'Possibly Mr. Andrews may understand what he means to say.' Applying the principles of Universology to politics, he advocated the establishment of a world government called the Pantarchy, of which he would of course be the leader, or 'Pantarch', as well as a New Catholic Church, of which he would be pope. Meanwhile, Andrews and the small but enthusiastic band of Pantarchists he had gathered around him were beavering away at his long dreamed-of universal language, to be called Alwato, which was based on the idea that all the sounds used in speech had inherent meanings which had been forgotten.

In 1870, Andrews paid a visit to the notorious women's rights campaigner, stock broker and future presidential candidate, ☞ Victoria Woodhull, declaring, 'I have many things of immense importance which I want to communicate.' She invited him to contribute to her newspaper, *Woodhull & Claflin's Weekly*, and he ended up writing much of it, using it to promote his Pantarchist ideas. He also contrib-

uted to Woodhull's downfall by helping to write the article attacking Henry Ward Beecher for adultery which saw her imprisoned and her presidential campaign scuttled.

In his later years, Andrews founded the Normal University of Universology, of which he was the sole professor, while its only students were his followers, who never numbered more than about twenty. He continued to churn out books and pamphlets which few if anyone could understand. At the age of seventy-four, he decided to announce to the world that he was the reincarnation of Jesus Christ, but was persuaded against this by his faithful follower Theodora Spencer, with whom he often corresponded in Alwato. He was working on the proofs of his dictionary of the universal language when he died. It was eventually published by his sons and, like many of Andrews' undoubtedly well-meaning but deeply obscure ideas, was greeted with universal indifference. ▨

ARAKAWA
(1936–2010)
Artist & architect

Shusaku Arakawa, who used only his surname, was an artist who declared war on death. Along with his wife and close collaborator,

Madeline Gins, he developed a philosophy called Reversible Destiny. 'We have decided not to die,' they declared. 'Death is old-fashioned.'

Arakawa was born in Nagoya, Japan, and studied at the Musashino Art School in Tokyo, where he was associated with a group of neo-Dadaists. His preoccupation with death was evident in one of his earliest exhibitions, entitled 'Another Cemetery at the Muramatsu Gallery', which consisted of a number of wooden 'coffins' containing cement sculptures laid out on expensive fabrics. In 1961, he moved to New York, arriving with, he said, $14 and (Dada founder) Marcel Duchamp's phone number in his pocket. He met Gins while studying at an art school in Brooklyn, and they married in 1965.

After working on poems, paintings and installations, the pair moved into architecture. In 1998, they won a competition to design a seventy-five acre (thirty hectare) housing development in Tokyo. They planned to turn this into the 'City of Reversible Destiny', but in the end only nine apartments were built. Their architecture is based on the idea that a building should be disorienting and confusing, full of odd angles and potential pitfalls. Living in such an environment made a person's relationship to the world less comfortable and more 'tentative', which they said was good for the immune system and would ward off death. The ultimate expression of these concepts was the project Arakawa spent the last ten years of his life working on, Bioscleave House (Lifespan Extending Villa) in Long Island, New York. It has lumpy, undulating floors, oddly placed windows and light fittings, and poles extending from floor to ceiling which can be held onto if one becomes too disoriented, all painted in dozens of dazzling colours. 'It can take five hours to get from one side of the room to another,' Arakawa and Gins boasted. Helpfully, they provided a training manual for the house, which includes instructions like 'Try to maintain two (or more) separate tentativenesses, that is, two (or more) distinct areas of indeterminacy'.

Arakawa and Gin made the mistake of investing their money with the notorious Bernie Madoff, and when his fraudulent investment empire collapsed at the end of 2008, like thousands of others they lost everything. They were forced to close their office and lay off staff. Arakawa died after a week in hospital. Gins was philosophical, saying, 'this mortality thing is bad news,' but vowed to redouble her efforts to prove that 'ageing can be outlawed'. ▣

THE ECCENTROPEDIA

BACH, DR. CHARLOTTE (KAROLY HAJDU)

(1929–1981)

Transsexual evolutionary theorist

Dr. Charlotte Bach was one of the oddest figures on the fringes of British academia during the 1970s. A former lecturer in psychology at Budapest University, she was a tall, heavily built woman with a booming voice and a strikingly original take on evolution. Drawing on studies of animal behaviour, she argued that all creatures have an inborn desire to become the opposite sex. Some human beings reject this desire, others accept it, and it is the resulting tension that produces human creativity. Homosexuality, transvestism and other activities often dismissed as abberations therefore acquired a new and previously unsuspected significance. For Bach, sexual devia-tion was the engine that powered evolution.

Bach wrote a massive book, *Homo Mutans, Homo Luminens*, outlin-ing her theories, which she was convinced made Darwin and Freud obsolete, but this failed to find a publisher. Her ideas were neverthe-less taken up by a few writers, and she became something of a cult figure. She gave weekly talks which she advertised in newspapers and magazines, and was invited to speak at academic institutions including Cambridge University. She was also very popular with gays and lesbians — after all, according to her, they were on the cutting edge of evolu-tion. Growing ill towards the end of her life, Bach refused to see a doctor, and eventually succumbed to liver cancer. The autopsy revealed that she was a man.

'Charlotte Bach', it transpired, was one of several identities ad-opted by a Hungarian named Karoly Hajdu. The son of a Budapest tailor, Mihaly Hajdu, and his wife Roza, he was largely self-educated, and began to experiment with cross-dressing as a teenager. Hadju escaped from Hungary in 1948 and was accepted into Britain as a refugee.

He was at this point posing as an aristocrat, Count Carl Hajdu, with appropriate dress and man-ners. He married a British woman, Phyllis, who had a son, Peter. After

DR. CHARLOTTE BACH
(KAROLY HAJDU)

the Soviet Invasion of Hungary
in 1956, Count Hajdu founded the
Committee for the Assistance of
Hungarian Freedom Fighters, which
raised £2,000 in donations. When it
became clear that he had pocketed
most of this money, Count Hajdu
bowed out, and Hajdu adopted a
new identity, Michael Karoly, and
a new career as a goatee-bearded
psychologist and hypnotherapist.

Despite his lack of qualifica-
tions, he was quite successful in his
new career. He wrote a column for
a monthly magazine and a book on
hypnosis. At one point he arranged
an interview with ☞ Alexander
Thynne, who received him at
Longleat. The future Marquess of
Bath wasn't at all pleased when a
newspaper reported that the interview had been part of a pioneering
study Karoly was undertaking into
the psychology of the peerage, and
refused to have anything more to do
with him.

Kajdu's relationships with other
women took a heavy toll on his
marriage, and he was also secretly
dressing as a woman. He separated
from his wife during the early sixties, and started up a group called
Divorcees Anonymous, the main
purpose of which seems to have
been to attract lonely women whom
he could seduce.

He was nevertheless devastated
when Phyllis died suddenly in 1965

and his stepson was killed in a car
crash a few weeks later. He retreated
to the flat he had shared with Phyllis
and barely left it for months. He
took to wearing her old clothes, immersed himself in the study of psychology, biology, history, mysticism
and other subjects, and over the next
few years mutated into Dr. Charlotte
Bach (while she also had a sideline
for a while working as a dominatrix
named Daphne Lyell-Mansell).

When the truth about Charlotte
Bach was revealed after her death,
most of her supporters were genuinely astonished, but many were also
amused. After all, she had only been
putting her theories into practice. ◉

BACKHOUSE, SIR EDMUND
(1873–1944)
Fantasist

Backhouse was born into a family of
Quaker high achievers — his father
was a director of Barclay's Bank and
one of his brothers became First Sea
Lord of the British navy. He studied
at Oxford but failed to graduate,
and ran up huge debts which forced
him to leave England. He went to
China where his remarkable facility
for languages led to a job translating
for George 'Chinese' Morrison, the
Times correspondent in Beijing. In
1910, having gained a reputation as

one of the best-connected English-men in China, with many friends in officialdom and the court, Backhouse was appointed an agent for the John Brown shipbuilding company, charged with selling battleships to the Chinese government.

Also in 1910, Backhouse and a journalist, J.O.P. Bland, published *China Under the Empress Dowager.* This was the first inside account of the court of the wily Empress Dowager, who had maintained her grip on power for forty years until her death in 1908. Its centrepiece was a lengthy excerpt from the diary of a court official, Ching-shan. While doubts were raised about the authenticity of this, the book was generally hailed as an important contribution to Chinese scholarship. Backhouse's scholarly reputation was further enhanced when, in 1912, he sent the first of several shipments of rare Chinese books and manuscripts to the Bodleian Library at Oxford. He would go on to send thousands of volumes to the library, generally asking only for shipping expenses. One of his motivations was that he was angling for the chair of Chinese at Oxford, but this was eventually given to someone else.

In 1915, the British Government, desperate for arms to fight the war, thought they might be found in China. The country was neutral, any arms deals would have to be secret,

and it was decided that Backhouse would make the perfect agent. He was soon sending detailed reports about large caches of rifles and ammunition he had negotiated to purchase. Back in London, the War Office, and Lord Kitchener in particular, were growing increasingly excited, and £2 million was earmarked to pay for the weapons. Backhouse reported that a flotilla of ships was assembled to transport them to Hong Kong. After various setbacks they set out, but were diverted to Canton. Fearing that the deal was about to fall through, Sir John Jordan, the British Minister in Peking, paid a visit to the Chinese President, Yuan Shih-kai. To his astonishment, the President denied all knowledge of the shipment. The War Office concluded that Backhouse had been duped by his contacts, but Jordan eventually realised that the flotilla with its cargo of weapons had never existed.

After lying low in Canada for a while, Backhouse indulged in two further elaborate frauds. Acting as agent for an American banknote printing company, he negotiated a contract with the Chinese government for the supply of millions of banknotes, while he also sold them a number of ships on behalf of his old employer, John Brown & Co. Both deals were illusory. Backhouse made little or no money from any of these schemes. It

seems that his main motivation was the construction of intriguing plots in which he could be a central character.

When Backhouse returned to Britain in 1920, he had a long black beard and wore silk robes. While word of his dubious dealings in the East had not reached England, his relations with the Bodleian now soured. He had promised a further large shipment of books and manuscripts, and the library had paid him for their shipping, but only a small portion of the material arrived (and some of that was found to be forged). Backhouse also fell out with his family when they learned he was attempting to raise money on a non-existent pearl necklace. He quietly slipped out of England.

Backhouse spent the rest of his days in China. Living as a hermit and avoiding westerners (although those who did have dealings with him found him as charming and beguiling as ever). In his last years, he was befriended by Dr. Reinhard Hoeppli, the honorary Swiss consul in Peking during World War II, who urged him to write his memoirs. Backhouse delivered two long manuscripts dealing with his life in England and early years in China. In these, he claimed to have been on intimate terms with just about every well known person of the day — Oscar Wilde, Paul Verlaine, Winston Churchill, Lord Roseberry, Sarah

Bernhardt, Tolstoy, to name but a few — and to have had sex with many of them, especially the men. He also claimed to have been the frequent lover of the septuagenarian Empress Dowager. All of this was described in graphic and extended detail. Realising he could not publish such a pornographic work, but believing it all true, Hoeppli held onto the manuscripts for decades. They eventually fell into the hands of the British historian Hugh Trevor-Roper, who determined that they were almost entirely fantasy. He also determined that Ching-shan's diary, on which Backhouse's scholarly reputation rested, was a forgery, probably carried out by Backhouse himself.

While many individuals have led lives which were largely fantasy, few have drawn as many important and intelligent people into their imaginings as Sir Edmund Backhouse. ▪

BACON, DELIA
(1811–1859)
Anti-Stratfordian

To question the authorship of the plays and poems attributed to William Shakespeare, an English cultural icon since the early eighteenth century, is to take on the full might of the literary establishment — an irresistible challenge to some. Several thousand books have been written in an attempt to prove that the plays were the work of Francis Bacon, Christopher Marlowe, the Earl of Oxford, Sir Walter Raleigh, a host of lesser Elizabethans or a combination of the above. Such speculations thrive because so little is known about the historical Shakespeare, an actor and shareholder in the Globe Theatre in London. The plays demonstrate considerable learning, but no one knows how Shakespeare, the son of a tradesman, acquired such learning. Moreover, the brief biographical glimpses we do have of the man, who in his forties gave up acting and returned to his birthplace of Stratford-upon-Avon to concentrate on business, hardly fit the picture most people have of the 'Immortal Bard'.

The first anti-Stratfordian (as those sceptical about Shakespeare's authorship are called) was probably James Wilmot, a clergyman who spent time in Stratford in the 1770s, attempting to research a Shakespeare biography. Having found few memories of him among the locals, he scoured the area for books or papers that might have come from his library, but found nothing. Wilmot decided this man could not be the author he was looking for and, casting about for another candidate, settled on the brilliant scholar and Machiavellian politician Sir Francis Bacon.

Wilmot was too shocked by his discovery to publish anything, and it was left to an American woman, Delia Bacon, to become the first prominent anti-Stratfordian. She was the daughter of a missionary, David Bacon, whose attempt to found an ideal city in Ohio ended with his bankruptcy. Delia, who was six when he died, was adopted by a rich woman and given a progressive education at a school run by the Beecher Sisters (one of whom, under the name Harriet Beecher Stowe, would go on to write *Uncle Tom's Cabin*). Delia became a writer and educator who specialised in giving flamboyant lectures on historical subjects. At some point she also became convinced that Shakespeare, or 'that booby' as she called him, could not have written the plays, and that Francis Bacon probably had. With the financial support of a banker and Bacon enthusiast, Charles Butler, she travelled to England in 1853 to gather evidence. Her first thought was to have the tomb of Bacon opened, believing it would contain evidence of his authorship of the plays, but failed to get permission from the church or Bacon's descendants.

Delia was a very charming woman, and one of the people she befriended in England was the writer Nathaniel Hawthorne, who

was serving as an American consul. He agreed to supply a preface for the book she was writing. As it approached completion, Delia decided to move to Stratford to get the final proof for her theory — this time by opening Shakespeare's tomb. He had clearly foreseen such an occurrence, for an inscription on it reads in part, 'Blest be the man that spares these stones; And cursed be he that moves my bones.' Delia reasoned that she was exempt from this, being a woman. She succeeded in having herself locked alone in Stratford church for several hours, with a shovel in hand, but her resolve deserted her at the last minute.

Hawthorne wrote the promised preface, in which he praised the author's many talents, but could not bring himself to endorse her theories. Delia rejected it out of hand. Hawthorne nevertheless (without her knowledge) funded the publication of her book, *The Philosophy of the Plays of Shakspere* (sic) *Unfolded*, which appeared in 1857. He thought he was doing her a favour, but this was really the end of her. The book, in which she argued that the plays were the work of a band of literary insurgents, led by Francis Bacon, intent on spreading philosophical ideas too radical to be published under their own names, was densely written and often very

obscure. The critical drubbing it received was a heavy blow for Delia, whose grip on sanity had sometimes been tenuous. She suffered a complete mental breakdown and was placed in an asylum. A nephew eventually rescued her from this and paid for her passage back to America, where she died two years later.

Delia Bacon may have been mocked for her beliefs, but she ignited a controversy that smoulders to this day. Inspired by her, Ignatius Donnelly, an American Congressman chiefly remembered for his writings on Atlantis, produced *The Great Cryptogram* (1888), in which he used complex mathematical formulae to reveal some singularly unconvincing messages Francis Bacon supposedly encrypted in the plays. Many other anti-Stratfordians have followed. The current consensus — if you can have consensus among a group as disparate as this — would seem to be that the plays were the work of a group of writers, just as Delia Bacon believed. ▨

BAGENAL, BEAUCHAMP
(1735–1802)
Duellist

Called 'the handsomest man in Ireland', Bagenal was a respected parliamentarian, prodigious womaniser and famously hard drinker, but was best known for his passion for challenging other men to duels.

Bagenal lived at Dunleckney Manor, County Carlow. As was customary for gentlemen of his time, he commenced his adult life with a Grand Tour of Europe. In his memoirs, *Personal Sketches*, Sir Jonah Barrington records that during his tour Bagenal

had performed a variety of feats which were emblazoned in Ireland, and endeared him to his countrymen. He had fought a prince, — jilted a princess, — intoxicated the Doge of Venice, — carried off a Duchess from Madrid, — scaled the walls of a convent in Italy, — narrowly escaped the inquisition at Lisbon, — concluded his exploits by a duel in Paris; and returned to Ireland with a sovereign contempt for all continental men and manners, and an inveterate antipathy to all despotic Kings and arbitrary governments.

Bagenal was unrepentant about his habitual duelling. 'Respect will only be accorded to character,' he wrote. 'A young man must show his proofs.' His favourite spot for a duel was the nearby Killenane Cemetery. This was useful for taunting his opponent (he would ask him to choose a grave before the duel began) but also meant that Bagenal, who had a lame leg (the legacy of a

previous duel), could lean against a tombstone as he blasted away.

On one occasion, he challenged his godson, Beauchamp Harvey Bagenal, to a duel. After the younger man had fired his first shot, Bagenal roared, 'You damned young villain! You had like to have killed your godfather… I only wanted to try if you were brave. Go to Dunleckney and order breakfast. I shall be home directly.'

Dinners at Dunleckney Manor were famously drunken affairs, with Bagenal keeping a pistol handy to ginger up guests who weren't pulling their weight. In 1782, he threw a party to celebrate the Irish Parliament gaining legal independence from England. Jonah Barrington recalled that afterwards 'the park was like a field of battle, strewed over with prostrate bodies'.

Bagenal was elected to the Irish Parliament in 1768, and served in it until 1783. He fought his final duel at the age of sixty, after challenging a neighbour whose pigs had wandered onto his land. Having grown infirm, Bagenal requested that he be allowed to engage in combat in the afternoon, while sitting in an armchair. Thus seated, he severely wounded his opponent, who only managed to hit the chair. Bagenal himself was unscathed, and honour was satisfied.

BARKER, COLONEL VICTOR

(1895–1960)
Male impersonator

The tall, strapping figure of Colonel Victor Barker was well known to British war veterans during the 1920s. Having fought at Mons (an experience he described vividly), he started an organisation for other veterans of the battle, and was immensely popular with them. 'The finest type of officer and gentleman anyone could hope to meet' was the summing up of one ex-sergeant major. Barker's problems began when he opened a café in London that lost money. When he failed to turn up to court for a bankruptcy examination in 1929, he was traced to the hotel where he was working as a reception clerk and arrested. 'It is the end for me,' Barker was heard to say as he was taken off to Brixton prison. Here, about to undergo a medical examination, he took a doctor aside and admitted to being a woman.

Barker was born Lillias Irma Valerie Barker on the island of Jersey. Valerie, as she was known, was a robust girl who loved horses, cricket and boxing. Signing on as a nurse at the start of World War I, she ended up breaking in horses for the front.

After a brief marriage to an Aus-tralian soldier named Arkell-Smith, she joined the Women's Royal Air Force and trained as a driver, but the war ended before she saw active service. Without bothering to get a divorce, she married another Aus-tralian, Ernest Pierce Crouch, and they had two children, a boy and a girl. For a while they ran a farm in Surrey, but Valerie did most of the work, Pierce Crouch having turned out to be a lazy and sometimes violent alcoholic. Valerie was by now habitually dressing as a man, and could be seen sauntering around the village of an evening, wearing a din-ner suit and puffing on a cigar.

In 1922, she left Pierce Crouch, and the children were placed with foster parents. She also made a mo-mentous decision. From now on she would live as a man — and not just any man, but a gentleman, a baronet and a war veteran. Enter Sir Victor Barker, DSO.

The transformation was ef-fected more easily than Valerie had expected. She told her closest friend, Elfrida Haward, that she had always been a man, and amazingly, Ethel be-lieved her (although Barker's reason for the deception — war wounds — was not altogether implausible at the time). Barker checked into a Brighton hotel and lived the high life on the proceeds from selling the farm and Valerie's jewellery. He courted Elfrida and they married in

COLONEL VICTOR BARKER

1923. (Elfrida's parents, having also been persuaded that the person they had known as Mrs. Pierce Crouch was a man, had pressed for an early wedding so their daughter's reputation would not suffer!)

Colonel Barker, his funds running low, tried his hand at various jobs — actor, farmer, labourer and, in an ill-advised political move, became for a time secretary to one of the leading officers in the British Fascisti, before setting up his veterans' organisation and the café that led to his downfall.

Barker was appalled by the sensationalistic press coverage that followed his arrest. He didn't consider himself abnormal, and hadn't he always tried to be the perfect gentleman? The public mood demanded that he be charged with something, but no one was quite sure what it should be. Eventually, the charge was 'knowingly and willingly entering a false statement in a register of marriage'. Barker dressed as a man during the trial, while the crowds that flocked to the courtroom to watch it were mostly women.

Barker was convicted and served nine months in Holloway. After his release, his notoriety made it impossible for him to find regular work. For a while, he exhibited himself in a sideshow in the seaside town of Blackpool. Punters paid twopence to see the infamous 'Man-Woman'

lying on a bed, his 'wife' in another bed beside him. In real life, Barker had acquired a new wife, although little is known about her.

Barker served in the Home Guard during World War II, and was devastated when his son (who appears never to have known the truth about his 'father') was shot down over France. He suffered from ill health in his later years, becoming so obese he could barely walk, and died in obscurity. ▨

BARRETT, JOHN
(1753–1821)
Scholar

'Jackie' Barrett was educated at Trinity College, Dublin, and spent virtually his entire life within its walls. One of the most renowned scholars of his day, he had a remarkable memory and was fluent in Greek, Hebrew and a host of Oriental languages, yet his English was almost incomprehensible and punctuated by involuntary explosions of swear words (today, he might have been diagnosed with Tourette's Syndrome), making his lectures extremely popular with students.

Barrett was a great miser. He hoarded his salary, supplementing it by saving and selling candle ends, and kept it in a stocking. A small, stooped man with a grimy

Mr. Punch face, he wore ragged, greasy clothes, a tattered professor's gown, and an old pair of leather slippers far too big for his feet. He refused to buy a wig — the natural accoutrement of all gentlemen of the day — and when the occasion demanded it, powdered his own hair (afterwards combing the powder out onto a piece of paper for later use). He lived on bread and milk during the day, and took his evening meals in the commons room because they were free. He lived in a dingy apartment with little more than piles of books in it. During winter, he refused to light a fire, and snuck down to the college's kitchen to warm himself there, until the kitchenhands objected to his shabby appearance and he was barred. The students nicknamed him 'Sweep'.

His lack of knowledge of the outside world was legendary. On one of his rare excursions into the country, he was baffled by the sight of a herd of sheep, and delighted to learn he was looking at 'live mutton'. After being taken to see the sea for the first time, he described it as 'a broad, flat superficies, like Euclid's definition of a line expanding itself into a surface, and blue, like Xenophon's plain covered with wormwood'. He was also notoriously impractical. According to one story, he kept two cats, and had holes cut into the bottom of his door so they could go in and out.

When asked by a visitor why two holes were needed, he replied that the bigger cat could obviously not get through the smaller hole. The visitor pointed out that the smaller cat could, however, go through the bigger hole. Barrett exclaimed, 'I never thought of that!'

For all his peculiarities, Barrett attained the post of vice provost of Trinity. On his death he was found to have accumulated £86,000, which he left in his will 'to feed the hungry and clothe the naked'. ◉

BARRETT-LENNARD, SIR THOMAS
(1826–1919)
Animal lover

Barrett-Lennard could not bear to see any animals killed on his estate, Belhus in Essex, and had his servants set down bowls of water for the rats. He was master of the local hunt, but used to lay false trails so that the foxes would escape. When horses, dogs and cats on the estate died, they were given a funeral service by the vicar of Avely, and buried in the Barrett-Lennard family plot.

Barrett-Lennard had little concern for his personal appearance, and his shabby clothing meant he was often mistaken for a servant or grounds keeper. On one occasion, having left Brentwood mental hospital where he had just chaired a meeting of the Essex Asylum Committee, he was accosted by a policeman who took him to be an escaped lunatic and returned him to the hospital in handcuffs.

BATES, DAISY

(1859–1951)
'The White Queen of
the Never-Never'

Bates was born Margaret Dwyer in Tipperary, Ireland. At the age of eighteen, she left Ireland, apparently fleeing from a scandal (a young man whose family had engaged her as a governess had killed himself). She arrived in Australia in 1882 and, over the next fifteen months, managed to marry three men. The first of these was Harry 'Breaker' Morant, the sometime 'bush poet' who would later, famously, be executed by the British army during the Boer War. She ditched Morant quickly after he failed to pay for their wedding, and married a cattle drover, Jack Bates, with whom she had a son, then another man named Baglehole. She never bothered to divorce any of them.

She returned to the UK in the 1890s, worked as a journalist, and possibly married again. Back in Australia, she approached the West Australian government, saying she had been commissioned by the *Times* of London to investigate the living conditions of the Aborigines (something she may have invented). She spent most of the rest of her life studying, writing about and often living with tribal Aborigines in remote areas of western Australia and South Australia. Despite having no formal anthropological training, she recorded their lifestyles, customs and languages in meticulous detail, and published hundreds of articles in newspapers and magazines. She lived for years at a time in a tent equipped with the complete works of Dickens, and endured temperatures of forty-degrees Celcius or more wearing full Edwardian dress — long skirt, jacket, high-collared blouse, hat and gloves.

Bates had varying degrees of government support for her activities. She applied unsuccessfully for the position of Protector of Aborigines in the Northern Territory, but was later made an honorary protector in South Australia. She denounced the treatment of Aborigines by white Australians, and worked hard to improve their welfare (although she had no time for half-castes). She said that the Aborigines of western Australia called her 'kabbarli', meaning grandmother. Yet, despite her closeness to the people she called 'my natives', she remained convinced that the Aborigines were

a backward race who would die out soon, and the chief task of whites was to 'soothe the dying pillow', beliefs outlined in her 1938 book, *The Passing of the Aborigines*. She infuriated anthropologists with accounts of widespread cannibalism and infanticide among the Aborigines, which they said were greatly exaggerated or completely spurious. She grew more cantankerous in her old age, and her image wasn't helped by her endorsement of Hitler and other dictators during the 1930s.

Bates was once feted as a great Australian hero, and was appointed a Commander of the Order of the British Empire in 1934. Her reputation declined sharply after her death, with her legacy denounced by anthropologists and, later, a new generation of politically active Aborigines.

Ironically, it is only in recent years that Daisy Bates' real worth to the Aborigines has become apparent. The copious records she kept have become an invaluable resource for Aboriginal people making land rights claims in which they must prove an unbroken connection to the land. Some of her work was used as evidence by the Noongar people who, in 2006, were successful in claiming native title over 6,000 square kilometres of land, including the West Australian capital of Perth and its surrounds. ▨

BEAN, JUDGE ROY

(1825?–1903)
'The Law West of the Pecos'

This disreputable but entertaining character was born Phantly Roy Bean Jr. in Mason County, Kentucky (his odd first name, which he quickly dropped, was possibly a corruption of Fauntleroy). His early years were checkered, to say the least. He shot and killed a man in Mexico circa 1848, fled back to America and settled in San Diego, California, where he wore fancy Mexican outfits, gained a reputation as a ladies man, and was imprisoned for duelling with a Scotsman. After escaping (having dug through the prison wall using knives smuggled into his cell hidden in tamales) he moved to San Gabriel. Here he worked as a bartender in a saloon owned by his brother, Joshua, who shortly afterwards became the first mayor of San Diego. In 1854, Bean became romantically involved with a girl who was engaged to a Mexican officer, shot the officer dead, and was promptly hung from a tree by the murdered man's friends. They left before all the life was squeezed from him, though, and the girl was able to cut him down. Bean sported a rope burn on his neck for the rest of his life.

He then moved to New Mexico,

where another brother, Sam, was a county sheriff and ran a general store and saloon. Bean helped out with the business and developed a sideline smuggling guns through the Union blockade during the Civil War. In 1866, he married a young Mexican girl, Virginia Chavez, with whom he had a tempestuous relationship and four children. They lived in a poor area of San Antonio which became known as Beanville. Bean supported his family by running various dubious businesses, including selling watered-down milk and stolen firewood.

In 1882, a railroad was being built from San Antonio to El Paso, Texas. With good money to be made servicing thirsty railroad workers, Bean left Beanville (he had already separated from Laura) and set up a saloon in a tent city near the Pecos River called Vinegaroon. With law scarce in those parts and drunkenness and gambling rife, some of the locals called on the county authorities to take action. Bean, perhaps on account of two rather more respectable brothers, was appointed a justice of the peace in 1882.

Armed with a copy of the *Revised Statutes of Texas* (1879 edition — he would ignore all subsequent ones), Bean moved to a hot and dusty spot called Langtry in the Chihuahuan desert west of the Pecos River, where he established a saloon-cum-courtroom. While the town had been named after a railroad boss, Langtry had a particular resonance for Bean as he had become enamoured of the British actress Lillie Langtry (whose photo he kept in his wallet). He gave his establishment Langtry's nickname, 'the Jersey Lilly', and put up signs above the porch saying 'ICE BEER' and 'LAW WEST OF THE PECOS'.

The judgments handed down by Bean, who was usually drunk (as indeed were his jurors) were famously idiosyncratic. When an Irishman named O'Rourke was accused of killing a Chinese worker, Bean thumbed through his law book for a while, declared he could find nothing in it about the killing of Chinamen, and dismissed the case. Another anecdote, this time probably apocryphal, has it that he once issued a judgment stating 'the Mexican shouldn't have gotten in front of the gun my friend happened to be firing'. As Langtry had no jail, most cases were settled with a fine (the fine usually coinciding with the exact amount of cash the convicted man had on him). Once, when a passing stranger fell down dead outside the Jersey Lilly, Bean searched the body and found a gun and forty dollars. He immediately fined the deceased forty dollars for carrying a concealed weapon.

While Bean may not always have

followed the letter of the law, his judgments where usually respected, and he was known for his generosity to the townspeople. It seems that his reputation as a 'hanging judge' is also underserved. His own experience with the noose may have encouraged leniency here, for although he sentenced a few men to hang, all were apparently allowed to escape. When Bean wasn't dispensing justice or whisky, he could usually be seen sitting on the porch of the Jersey Lilly, a rifle by his side, and his pet bear tethered to a nearby mesquite tree.

The Jersey Lilly burnt down in 1896. Bean had it rebuilt, and across the street from it built a house which he named the Opera House. He told people that when Lillie Langtry came to visit — as he was sure would happen one day — she would perform there. Bean never met his idol, but according to some sources they corresponded, and she once sent him a present of two pistols.

Bean died the morning after going on a bender in Del Rio. Ten months later, his greatest dream came true, too late for him, when Lillie Langtry stopped off at Langtry while en route to San Francisco. The townsfolk regaled her with tales of Bean, and she later wrote in her autobiography, 'It was a short visit, but an unforgettable one.' ▣

BEALE, EDITH EWING BOUVIER
&
EDITH BOUVIER BEALE

(1895–1977) & (1917–2002)
'Big Edie' & 'Little Edie'
of Grey Gardens

Edith Ewing Bouvier (later known as 'Big Edie') was one of five children of John Vernou Bouvier Jr., a prominent American attorney and later judge, and his wife Maude, the daughter of a wealthy wallpaper manufacturer. In a family history he had privately printed called *Our Forebears*, John claimed that the Bouviers were the descendants of French nobility. In fact, the first of the clan in America, Michael Bouvier (John's grandfather), was a former soldier in Napoleon's army who arrived shortly after the battle of Waterloo. A cabinetmaker by trade, he did extremely well in his adopted country, and even sold furniture to the White House.

The young Edith was a playful and headstrong girl, a fine pianist and an accomplished singer. In 1917, she married Phelan Beale, who worked in her father's law firm, and the couple had three children — Edith ('Little Edie'), Phelan Jr., and Bouvier. In 1923, they moved into a lavish, fourteen-room mansion called

EDITH EWING BOUVIER BEALE
& EDITH BOUVIER BEALE

Grey Gardens in East Hampton. Edith continued to pursue a singing career, hiring an accompanist and performing at functions. After Edith and Phelan separated in 1931, she stayed on at Grey Gardens, where she threw parties for her friends, mainly writers, artists and musicians. Other visitors to the house included the daughters of Edith's brother, John Vernou Bouvier III — Jacqueline (who would go on to marry John F. Kennedy), and Lee (later Lee Radziwill). Edith's father was increasingly displeased by her bohemian lifestyle, especially when she arrived late for her son Bouvier's wedding wearing an opera dress, and essentially disowned her. When he died in 1948, he left her only a small trust fund in his will.

Edith's daughter, Little Edie, was every bit as flamboyant as her mother. A striking, statuesque blonde, she was a much sought-after society girl in her twenties. She dated ☞ Howard Hughes, and reportedly turned down a proposal of marriage from J. Paul Getty. She was intent on a career of her own though. In 1947, she moved to Manhattan, where she worked as a model and tried to break into showbusiness. She always said she was just on the verge of being signed by the Broadway producer Max Gordon when, in 1952, she was summoned home by Big Edie, who could no longer afford to

send her living expenses.

Over the next few years, mother and daughter led an increasingly hermetic existence in Grey Gardens. While they still had visitors, Big Edie did her best to ward off any suitors who might take Little Edie away. They were unable to afford upkeep on the large estate, which rapidly fell into disrepair. The walls and garden became massively overgrown. The plumbing failed. The house was infested with cats and raccoons, and rooms were piled high with empty cat food tins and other rubbish. A tree grew in Big Edie's original bedroom. In 1971, after numerous complaints from neighbours, the local authorities declared the place unfit for human habitation and ordered the Beales out, but they refused to budge.

The story was soon taken up by the media, and Jackie Onassis and Lee Radziwill agreed to pay for the house to be refurbished. The roof was replaced, walls and plumbing repaired, and a huge amount of garbage hauled away.

In 1973, David and Albert Maysles (who had made the Rolling Stones documentary *Gimme Shelter*) began filming a documentary on the Bouvier family, but quickly realised that the two Edies were far and away its most interesting members, and switched the focus to them. The result, *Grey Gardens*, released in 1975, is a mesmerising portrait of two supremely odd but effortlessly entertaining women. Big Edie, crippled with arthritis and mostly confined to her bed, sings (beautifully) some of the songs of her youth. Little Edie, wearing an array of fancy scarves, bathing suits and various improvised but strangely stylish outfits, sings (not so beautifully) and dances like an overexcited teenager. The house has again been overrun by cats (not to mention the raccoons in the cellar, which Little Edie is seen feeding with white bread and Cat Chow). Mother and daughter constantly bicker and talk over the top of each other, spouting dialogue that would have made Tennessee Williams feel pleased with himself. Little Edie says that she still feels like a little girl when she's in the house and yearns to escape. She regrets all the things she didn't do in her youth. ('Everything's good that you didn't do,' says Big Edie sagely. 'At the time you didn't want it.') Grey Gardens itself, looking like the archetypal haunted house, emerges as a character in its own right. The two Edies were thrilled with the finished documentary, which was screened at film festivals around the world and garnered much acclaim.

In 1978, the year after Big Edie's death, Little Edie was invited to perform for eight nights at a cabaret nightclub called Reno Sweeney's in Greenwich Village. She sang and danced, and afterward wandered through the audience greeting everyone graciously. Sadly, it was the beginning and end of her performing career. She sold Grey Gardens two years later, and afterwards lived in various places, eventually settling in Florida where she died of a heart attack or stroke at the age of eighty-four.

The gothic comedy of life at Grey Gardens has been the subject of books, a Broadway musical and more recently a film. If the two Edies were thwarted in their career ambitions during their lifetimes, the Maysles' documentary transformed them into icons. ▣

BECKFORD, WILLIAM
(1760–1844)
Writer & folly builder

Beckford was the son of a former Lord Mayor of London who made a fortune from sugar plantations in Jamaica. He was educated at home, and at the age of six received music lessons from a nine-year-old Mozart. His father died when he was ten, leaving him a fortune of around £1 million, an almost unfathomable sum at the time.

When he was nineteen, Beckford met William Courtney, known as 'Kitty', the future Earl of Devon, who was ten. They began an intense (though probably not sexual) relationship which led to much gossip. Having had a very insular childhood, Beckford now became a much more sociable creature, and threw wild parties at his home at Fonthill in Wiltshire, one of which lasted three days. He travelled to Italy, wrote a book about his experiences there, and at the age of twenty-one, produced (in French) his masterpiece, *Vathek*. A product of Beckford's fascination with the East, it tells the story of the Caliph Vathek, whose quest for supernatural knowledge leads him to damnation in the realm of Eblis, the Muslim Satan. A tour-de-force of sensuality and decadence, it was published in an English translation in 1786 and remains an undisputed masterpiece of gothic fiction. Byron called it his Bible.

With rumours of debauchery and even black magic swirling around Beckford, his mother persuaded him to marry Lady Margaret Gordon in 1783, and by all accounts they were happy together. But the following year, he was openly accused of having an improper relationship with Courtney. He and Margaret moved to Geneva where, in 1786, she died giving birth to two daughters (both of whom survived).

Beckford spent the next few years travelling around the continent, particularly Italy, Spain and Portugal.

He took with him an enormous retinue including a valet, doctor, cook, footmen and twenty-four musicians. No expense was spared and once, while on an extended stay in Portugal, he had a flock of English sheep imported so that he could gaze at them from his window. Of the many sights he saw, he was particularly impressed by the magnificent gothic monasteries of Alcobaça and Batalha, which he visited in the company of the Portuguese Prince Regent.

Returning to England, he settled on a new passion for building. Having erected a wall around his Fonthill property, his first thought was to build a half-ruined convent on it (such ready-made 'ruins' were all the rage amongst British aristocrats at the time). Then he became much more ambitious. He commissioned an architect, James Wyatt, to design an enormous, ramshackle, gothic building which would end up looking like a sort of demented cathedral, with a central octagonal tower almost 300 feet (ninety-one metres) high.

Beckford was a notoriously impatient man who constantly changed his plans and wanted everything done as quickly as possible. Hundreds of workmen laboured day and night on Fonthill Abbey, bribed to work harder with extra rations of alcohol so that they were often drunk. As no proper foundations were laid and inferior building materials were used, the inevitable happened and the tower collapsed soon after it was finished. Beckford had it built again. The interior of the abbey, painted mainly in red, purple and gold, was full of corridors higher than they were wide, and numerous poorly ventilated bedrooms which remained empty (although other rooms housed his vast collection of books and artworks). Beckford lived at Fonthill with a small retinue, including his doctor, his Spanish dwarf Piero, and his pet dogs, among them Viscount Fartleberry, Mrs. Fry, Caroline and Tring.

Beckford served in Parliament three times and had hopes of obtaining a peerage, but the taint of scandal still clung to him. He only entertained guests on a grand scale at Fonthill Abbey once, when Lord Nelson, his mistress Lady Hamilton and their party came to visit. They were treated to a lavish banquet and Lady Hamilton took part in the entertainment herself, posing in one of her famous 'attitudes', just as she had done years before in ☞ James Graham's Temple of Health.

Beckford's fortunes dwindled in the early nineteenth century, and he was forced to sell Fonthill in 1823. Despite having spent over twenty years of his life building the abbey, which was still unfinished, he expressed little sadness at having to leave it. Three years later the tower collapsed a final time (it was made of such flimsy materials that it was said to have fallen almost silently). He moved to Bath, where he built another, smaller tower, which still stands. In his last years he could be seen riding on a grey pony through the streets of Bath, dressed in old-fashioned finery and accompanied by three footmen and his faithful dwarf, a figure as exotic and enigmatic as his own Vathek. ▧

'Some people drink to forget their unhappiness. I do not drink, I build.'
WILLIAM BECKFORD

BEEFHEART, CAPTAIN,
see Don VAN VLIET ☞

BENTHAM, JEREMY
(1748–1832)
Philosopher

Bentham was one of the chief proponents of utilitarianism, which teaches that society should strive for 'the greatest happiness for the greatest number'. A child prodigy, he studied at Queen's College, Oxford, and trained as a lawyer, though he never practised. He was an ardent social reformer, advocating the abolition of slavery, freedom of speech, equal rights for women, free trade, an end to corporal punishment and a host of other ideals now generally accepted throughout the western world.

One of Bentham's most cherished projects was the building of a radical new prison he had designed called the Panopticon. This was a circular building with a central tower, constructed so that the cells radiated out from the tower like the spokes of a wheel. The advantage of this was that a single jailer, situated inside the tower, would be able to observe all the prisoners (without himself being seen), thus saving a great deal of money on guards. Bentham offered to make the scheme even more economical by acting as the jailer himself, without pay. He spent years and much of his fortune trying to make the Panopticon a reality. At one point, Parliament sanctioned the purchase of some land on which to build it, but a new administration scotched the plan in 1811.

Another one of Bentham's hobbyhorses was the idea that the bodies of the deceased should be put to practical use. He suggested that family portraits be abandoned, and instead, the mummified heads of the deceased should be retained. (Several generations, he said, could be stored in 'a moderate sized cupboard'.) Alternatively, the entire body could be mummified and turned into an 'auto-icon'. Instead of trees lining the roads to stately mansions, these auto-icons could be erected, a permanent reminder to the young of their revered ancestors.

Practising what he preached, Bentham left precise instructions in his will for his own body to be dissected, mummified and dressed in his best clothes, and purchased a pair of glass eyes to be placed in his head when the time came. After his death, his closest friends gathered to watch the dissection, which took place during a violent thunderstorm. The surgeons performing it botched the head, so this was replaced with a wax replica. In 1850, the mummified body was presented to University College London, an institution which had been founded along Bentham's principles, its doors open to students of all races, creeds and political persuasions.

The UCL put the esteemed utilitarian on display in a glass-fronted cabinet. His real head was originally stored in this cabinet too, tucked between his feet, but after being repeatedly stolen by college students (who once held it for ransom, and on another occasion played football with it), it was locked away elsewhere. Bentham is still to be found in the South Cloisters of the college, dressed in his smart black coat, a cane in his hand and a large straw hat on his head. He once received a change of underwear, thanks to his fan ☞ Charles Kay Ogden. On special occasions he is brought to meetings of the College Committee, where he is recorded in the minutes as being 'present but not voting'. ▣

BERNERS, GERALD TYRWHITT-WILSON (LORD)

(1883–1950)
Composer, artist & writer

Lord Berners was an eccentric of many parts. He was born Gerald Tyrwhitt, the only child of a naval officer, Hugh Tyrwhitt, who had married Julie Foster, the daughter of a wealthy industrialist (for her money, according to their son). Tyrwhitt Snr. was often away at sea, and the young Gerald, a solitary boy with a talent for art and music, had little in common with his humourless, philistine mother. He was sent to a boarding school where he was subject to the usual humiliations, then Eton where he developed crushes on several other boys. Deciding to enter the diplomatic

service, he spent most of the next few years on the continent, learning French and German, while continuing to dabble in sketching and composing. He failed to pass the diplomatic exams twice, but in 1910 was accepted as an honorary attaché, and was posted to Constantinople, then Rome. Here he hobnobbed with the aristocratic circle gathered around the British ambassador, Sir Rendell Rodd, which included ☞ the Marchesa Luisa Casati. He also met Picasso, Cocteau and Stravinsky, who became a firm friend and would later declare that he was the most interesting British composer of the century. He remained in Rome for the duration of World War I.

In 1918, after the death of an uncle, Tyrwhitt inherited the title Lord Berners and a considerable estate. He left the diplomatic service the following year to concentrate on composing, and had a considerable success with a ballet, *The Triumph of Neptune*, produced by Diaghilev in 1926. He also took up painting, and wrote whimsical novels like *The Camel*, about a camel which turns up on the doorstep of a vicar. He divided his time between Rome and his home of Faringdon in Berkshire, which he filled with fine art, curios and kitsch. He delighted in practical jokes, and often wore masks (saying he grew bored with his own face). He had the pigeons on his estate dyed vibrant colours, and attempted to persuade the farmers on neighbouring properties to dye their cows purple. When his friend Penelope Chetwode visited with her white Arabian mare, Moti, he liked to entertain the horse in his drawing room. He also built the last great English folly (at the time of writing, at least), a tower almost 100 feet (thirty metres) high, despite the objections of some locals. (When a town council committee looked into the matter and decided they could not see the point of it, Berners responded, 'The great point of the tower is it will be entirely useless.') Berners prevailed, and placed a sign at the entrance to it reading, 'Members of the Public committing suicide from this tower do so at their own risk.'

Berners entertained a constant stream of guests at Faringdon — artists, writers, socialites, indeed anyone who interested him. They included Churchill, George Bernard Shaw, John Betjeman, the Marchesa Casati (who arrived once with a boa constrictor in a glass case) and ☞ Salvador Dalí. It was Berners who procured the diving suit that Dalí wore when he gave his famous lecture at the International Surrealist Exhibition in 1936. He was also one of the people who worked frantically to remove the helmet, which was bolted on, when it became apparent the surrealist inside it was suffocating.

Having sailed painlessly through World War I in Rome, Berners, who was politically naïve, failed to see World War II coming. It hit him hard — in fact, he had a nervous breakdown. In a novel published in 1941, *Far From the Madding War*, he has a character clearly based on himself say, 'I believed it was the end of everything and certainly of people like me.' He recovered somewhat, and developed a new sideline writing music for films.

Berners was a homosexual, but not a very determined one. Robert Heber Percy, an exuberant bisexual thirty years his junior and known as the 'Wild Boy', was his chief companion from 1932 onwards. Heber Percy usually refused to sleep with him though, and Berners did not mind. But then Berners, as he freely admitted, was not really passionate about anything. His health declined after the war, and he died of heart failure. On his gravestone is a self-penned epitath (below). ▣

Here lies Lord Berners
One of life's learners,
Thanks be to the Lord
He was never bored.

BESWICK, HANNAH

(1680–1758)
'The Mummy of Manchester'

The fear of premature burial is an ancient one, but began to increasingly occupy European minds from the mid-eighteenth century onwards. This was no doubt related to an increase in the use of wooden coffins (prior to this, most people had been buried in shrouds) which provided a dank, dark, enclosed space in which a person might find themselves interred alive and start screaming. Doctors hotly debated the most reliable methods for determining death, and newspapers were full of lurid stories about coffins being opened to reveal the battered and bloodied corpses of those who had tried to escape their early graves. A number of devices where invented to prevent such occurrences, including the Bateson Life Revival Device, which enabled a person to ring a bell from inside their coffin. Its inventor, George Bateson, became so consumed by the fear of premature burial that he ended up pouring linseed oil over himself and setting himself on fire rather than risk it.

Hannah Beswick was another person with a mortal fear of premature burial (perhaps understandably, for her brother was said to have nar-rowly escaped it). She was a spinster who lived in a large manor house, Birchwood Bower, in Manchester. In her will, she left £25,000 to her doctor, Charles White, on the condition that she be kept above ground for 100 years, and that White, accompanied by two other reliable persons, would inspect her body every year for signs of life.

White, who was one of the most famous surgeons of his day and the author of an influential treatise on childbirth, had the body embalmed with bandages and tar, leaving only the face exposed. He kept it in an old grandfather clock case in an upper room of his house, along with other natural curiosities including a stuffed hedgehog and a starfish hanging from the ceiling. He was diligent about carrying out Hannah's final request, and sometimes showed his unusual patient off to visitors (among them the young Thomas de Quincy). White would lead them to the clock case, which was kept upright, open a door at the top of it, lift a little curtain of cloth and reveal Hannah's face, which was said to look perfectly lifelike. All this attention made Hannah something of a celebrity.

After White's death in 1813, the famed mummy was moved to the Manchester Museum of Natural History, where it was put on public display. In 1868, when the museum

was moving to new premises, its
trustees decided to finally bury Hannah Beswick. After one final check
for vital signs, she was interred in
Harpurhey Cemetery. ▣

BIGG, JOHN

(1629–1696)
'The Dinton Hermit'

Bigg was an educated man who had
acted as a clerk to Simon Mayne,
one of the judges who sentenced
Charles I to death. Shortly after
the restoration of Charles II, Bigg
retired to a cave in Dinton, Buckinghamshire, and stayed there for
the next thirty-five years or so.

Some said he felt remorse for his
part in the king's death (there was a
rumour that he had been one of the
hooded executioners), while others
thought he was depressed about the
return of the monarchy. Whatever
the reason, Bigg became a popular
fixture in Dinton, and the locals kept
him supplied with food and drink.

He was most famous for his
extraordinary clothes, which were
made of innumerable scraps of
leather nailed together. In fact, the
only thing Bigg ever begged for
was more leather to nail onto them.
James Caulfield's *Portraits of Remarkable Persons* (1794) has a marvellous
engraving showing the result, with
Bigg resplendent in patchwork

jerkin and trousers, a cloak with a
horned hood, and enormous shoes.
The latter were made of hundreds
of pieces of leather, ten layers deep.

After his death, one of the
shoes was souvenired by a local
gentleman and remained in Dinton,
while the other found its way to the
Bodleian Library at Oxford. They
were finally reunited for an exhibition at the Ashmolean Museum in
September 2003. ▣

BILLINGS, CORNELIUS

(1861–1931)
'Horseback Billings'

Billings was a wealthy industrialist whose family owned a Chicago
utilities company. He retired at the
age of forty, and thereafter devoted
himself to leisure pursuits, principally yachting and horse racing. He
acquired a twenty-five acre (ten
hectare) estate in northern Manhattan, on which he built a magnificent
Louis XIV style mansion, Tryon
Hall, with stables large enough
to house thirty-three horses and
twenty-two carriages.

To celebrate the completion of
the stables in 1903, Billings held a
celebrated dinner at Sherry's restaurant in New York City. One of the
restaurant's ballrooms was decorated as a garden, with imitation
grass on the floor and an artificial

JOHN BIGG

moon hanging from the ceiling. The thirty-six dinner guests, in formal dress, were all on horseback, with the horses facing each other in a circle. They dined on pheasant from trays attached to their saddles, and drank champagne from their saddlebags through rubber tubes (the horses had to make do with oats). It was the talk of New York society for years. 🔲

BLAKE, WILLIAM

(1757–1827)
Poet, painter & visionary

Had Blake been born a century or two earlier, the visions which shaped his life might have seen him accepted as a genuine prophet. By the late eighteenth century, however, to see such things meant being marked as deluded or insane, and this is how many of his contemporaries judged him.

Blake was one of five children of a London hosier, James Blake, and his wife Catherine. They were Dissenters (i.e. members of a non-mainstream Protestant sect, but which one is not certain) and Blake grew up to be profoundly religious but contemptuous of all established churches. An unworldly, headstrong boy, he was indulged by his parents, who did not send him to school. Instead he was educated at home

by his mother, her lessons supplemented with his own wide reading, although the Bible was and would remain by far the most important influence on him.

He is reputed to have had his first vision at the age of four, when he saw the face of God through a window, and this was followed by visions of angels in trees and the Prophet Ezekiel.

Blake studied drawing from the age of ten, and at fourteen was apprenticed to an engraver. One of the tasks he was given was to make a series of drawings of the tombs of kings in Westminster Abbey. The assignment instilled in him a love of the Gothic, and a profound sense of the reality of the past, and of mortality. In 1779, having completed his apprenticeship, he was accepted into the recently established Royal Academy Schools, where he consolidated his artistic skills but railed against the fashionable oil painters of the day like Sir Joshua Reynolds (then the Royal Academy's president), preferring the strong, clean lines of classical and Renaissance artists. He also set himself up as a commercial engraver, a trade he would practice for the rest of his life. In 1782, he married Catherine Boucher. She was illiterate, but he taught her how to read and write, and she became an assistant in his work and devoted companion to the end. Blake's younger brother, Robert, his favourite among his siblings, also worked as his assistant until his death in 1787. Blake, at his deathbed, saw his spirit rise through the ceiling, and after that, conversed with Robert every day.

Blake was a man of forthright opinions and radical sentiments, who believed that men and women were equal, as were people of all races. Keen to express these ideas in images and poetry, in 1789 he produced his first major 'illuminated book', a collection of poems aimed at children called *Songs of Innocence*. This was produced using a process he had refined called 'relief etching'. He would first paint his design (combining words and pictures) directly onto a copper plate which was then treated with acid to leave a raised image. This was then printed and hand coloured, meaning every copy of the book was slightly different. In subsequent illuminated books, such as the *Marriage of Heaven and Hell* and *The First Book of Urizen*, he developed a complex mythology peopled by figures like Orc, the rebel, and Urizen, the lawgiver, a sort of parallel to the Bible which, while it owed something to the writings of mystics such as Swedenborg, Paracelsus and Boehme, was almost entirely of his own invention. Blake made no distinction between the body and soul, and thought that the established churches served to stifle physical pleasure on Earth. 'What are called vices in the natural world,' he wrote, 'are the highest sublimities in the spiritual world.' He was interested in sexual magic, and his unpublished drawings are littered with images of hermaphrodites and outré sexual practices. He also indicated that wives should be shared (although there is no indication that he put any of these ideas into practice).

In 1790, Blake and his wife moved to a new house in Lambeth, where they could sometimes be seen relaxing naked in their back garden (one of his patrons, Thomas Butts, recounted how he had visited them one day to be greeted by Blake's cheery cry, 'Come in, it's only Adam and Eve, you know!'). He was making a reasonable living in these years from commercial commissions, although he developed a reputation for delivering work late. Partly to blame were his visions, as powerful, if not more powerful, than they had been when he was a child. He wrote, 'my abstract folly hurries me often away while I am at work, carrying me over Mountains and Valleys, in a Land of Abstraction where Spectres of the Dead wander.'

In 1800, Blake and his wife moved to Felpham, Surrey, to be near a new patron, the now-forgotten poet Thomas Hayley. He

THE EGGENTROPEDIA

WILLIAM BLAKE

laboured for the next three years for Hayley, who admired his talent but could also be condescending. It was now dawning on Blake that his own work was not going to bring him the recognition he craved, and illustrating the inferior poetry of Hayley became increasingly galling. The period at Felpham ended dismally for Blake when he was accused by a soldier of uttering seditious remarks about the King. He was eventually acquitted of the charges, but badly shaken by the ordeal.

Returning to London, Blake and Catherine moved into smaller lodgings. Still struggling to have his work seen by the public, he held an exhibition in his brother's hosiery shop in 1808. In the prospectus, he asked that 'those who have been told that my Works are but an unscientific and irregular Eccentricity, a Madman's Scrawls, I demand of them to do me the justice to examine before they decide'. Few people came to the exhibition though, and no pictures were sold.

In his last years, Blake withdrew further from the world. He laboured incessantly despite failing health, both on commercial work and his own projects. These included a large painting, *The Last Judgment* (now lost), and his final illuminated prophetic book, *Jerusalem*, in which he painted a dark vision of an England where war, Newtonian science and indus-

trialisation had brought about conformity and sterility. On the last day of his life, he took up a pencil and made a drawing of his wife, saying, 'You have ever been an angel to me,' then began to sing songs and hymns. He died a few hours later.

Blake's art was considered crude and 'wild' according to the refined tastes of his day, and he was only known to a small circle of friends during his lifetime. Even some of those failed to appreciate his true worth as an artist (while it seems that no one understood his poetry). Blake predicted his neglect in his own time would be 'Execrated in Future ages'. He was right.

BLAVATSKY, MADAME HELENA
(1831–1891)
Occultist

The remarkable, rambunctious Helena Petrovna Blavatsky, responsible more than anyone else for the occult revival in the West, was born Elena Von Hahn in what is now the Ukraine. Her father, Baron von Hahn, was a soldier, her mother, after whom she was named, a romantic novelist who died when Elena was eleven. She was an impulsive, imaginative girl who liked to tell her younger sister fantastical stories in which she was the heroine. At the age of sixteen she married Nikifor Blavatsky, who was in his early forties and a vice governor in Erevan (now the capital of Armenia), but ran away from him three months later.

Blavatsky spent the next twenty-five years wandering around the world having adventures which included (if her account is to be believed) touring as a concert pianist, riding bareback in a circus, fighting with Garibaldi's troops, practicing as a spirit medium, serving as Princess Eugénie's decorator and getting shipwrecked off Greece. Most famously (and dubiously) Blavatsky claimed to have spent seven years in Tibet, a country then almost inaccessible to outsiders. Here, she said, she was the guest of the Great White Brotherhood, also known as the Masters, a group of all-wise beings who can astral travel and dematerialise at will. Most of the Masters were former human beings who had attained a state of spiritual perfection, including Jesus, Buddha, Plato, Lao Tzu, Caglisotro and the Comte de Saint-Germain, along with various other lesser known individuals such as Koot Hoomi (who had materialised in front of Blavatsky in London and invited her to Tibet).

In 1873, at the behest of the Masters, Blavatsky travelled to the United States, where she sought out a lawyer and spiritualist named Henry Olcott. He was mightily impressed by Blavatsky's mediumistic skills, and the fact that she seemed to have far more control over her spirits than other mediums.

The pair became inseparable, although their relationship remained non-sexual (Olcott designated them as 'chums'), and they moved into adjoining apartments in New York. Blavatsky's apartment, which became known as the 'Lamasery', was crammed with exotic oddities she had picked up in her travels, along with a large collection of stuffed animals including a baboon dressed as a man and clutching a copy of *The Origin of Species*.

Blavatsky was a stout, forceful woman with slightly bulging, mesmerising eyes and crinkly hair. She smoked constantly, laughed easily and was always determined to get her own way. She and Olcott gathered around themselves a group of like-minded individuals, and in 1875 formed the Theosophical Society ('theosophy' means 'divine science'). As eventually formulated, the society had three aims: the formation of a universal brotherhood; the study of comparative religion, philosophy and science; and the investigation of paranormal phenomena.

In 1877, she produced an enormous book, *Isis Unveiled*. The first half is basically a broadside against Darwinism and materialistic science, the second an exposition on religion in which she argued that all faiths derived from a single ancient source. According to Blavatsky the book was not written in the normal fashion but 'precipitated', which means some of it was dictated to her by the Masters, while other sections simply appeared spontaneously on paper. Blavatsky had also astral travelled to Tibet, where she consulted books in the Masters' vast library. Letters from the Masters, precipitated in a similar fashion and addressed to the society's members, became Blavatsky's chief means of keeping her troops in line.

Despite gaining a lot of publicity when it arranged for the cremation of one of its deceased members, a certain Baron de Palm (cremation being a controversial practice at the time), the society attracted few members in its first two years. Olcott and Blavatsky decided to move to India, a bold decision which made some sort of sense given that in her writings Blavatsky gave short shrift to Christianity compared with Hinduism and Buddhism. They arrived in Bombay (now Mumbai) in 1879, and three years later moved the society's headquarters to Adyar in Madras (now Chennai), where it remains to this day. It flourished in India, attracting members from the European expatriate community and native Indians.

Branches (or 'lodges') also opened in England, Australia, Sweden and other countries over the next few years. But with the larger-than-life Blavatsky around, it wasn't all going to be smooth sailing.

In addition to being the accredited mouthpiece for the Masters, Blavatsky's occult performances included all sorts of tricks reminiscent of other mediums — spirit forms in darkened rooms, objects appearing out of nowhere and so on, and even some of her supporters suspected that some of it was fraudulent (Blavatsky would simply laugh off such suggestions). In 1884, while she was in London, this became a full-blown scandal when her disgruntled housekeeper, Madame Coulombe, threatened to release letters Blavatsky had written to her unless she was paid by the society. These revealed that Coulombe had helped Blavatsky in her deceptions, while the shrine-room in the Adyar headquarters, in which all sorts of objects were prone to materialise, had a secret back entrance leading to Blavatsky's bedroom. When the society's officials refused to pay up, the letters were published in an Indian Christian newspaper, and an investigator sent from London by the Society for Psychical Research wrote a report in which he labeled Blavatsky 'one of the most accomplished, ingenious and interesting

MADAME HELENA BLAVATSKY

impostors of history'. Many society members resigned. On her return to India, Blavatsky wanted to sue Coulombe, but Olcott persuaded her not to, which caused a falling-out between them.

Blavatsky, or HPB as she was usually known to her followers, had now grown morbidly obese and was suffering from a variety of ailments. She went back to Europe (she had to be lowered onto the ship with a rope and pulley) and eventually settled in London, where she became head of the society's 'Esoteric Section'. She produced one more vast book, *The Secret Doctrine*. Supposedly a commentary on *The Book of Dzyan*, a work Blavatsky had read in Tibet (in its original language of 'Senzar'), it traced the evolution of humanity through a series of 'root races', each of which is more corporeal than the last (we are part of the fifth root race). It was generally poorly received, although there was one unexpected rave review by a prominent social reformer and friend of George Bernard Shaw, Annie Besant. Previously a campaigner for rationalism, socialism, women's rights, birth control and a host of other worldly causes, she now became an ardent Theosophist. She invited Blavatsky to live in her house, and after HPB's death, succeeded her as head of the Esoteric Section. She would go on

to become president of the society in 1907.

Blavatsky may have succumbed to her many illnesses in 1891, but the synthesis of eastern and western philosophies she pioneered has lived on. Her hidden Masters have proved particularly resilient, popping up in some form or another in innumerable belief systems throughout the twentieth century and beyond. If evidence for the physical existence of these superhuman beings has been hard to come by, the idea that they are out there, somewhere, working behind the scenes to help humanity, remains an irresistible concept for many. ▣

BOCK, IOR

(1942–2010)
Transmitter of the 'Bock Saga'

Bock became famous in his native Finland during the 1980s, after he began making public a body of folklore he said had been passed down orally through his family for many generations. The 'Bock Saga', as it is known, is a vast chronicle of people and places stretching back tens of thousands of years, which takes in the origins of human language and the roots of Finland's pre-Christian, pagan culture.

Bock's own life was almost as convoluted and eventful. He was brought up as the adopted son of Bror Svedlin and his wife Rhea, but claimed that his real father was Rhea's father, Knut Victor Boxström. Aged eighty-one and desperate for a male heir, Boxström impregnated his daughter, then died a month after Ior was born.

Bock left school early and his first job was lighting technician in a Helsinki theatre. In 1962, he was present when his brother Erik was killed by a gunshot wound to the chest. Bock told the police that he had thrown a loaded pistol at his brother which had accidentally gone off. He was convicted of involuntary manslaughter and given a suspended sentence (he maintained that his brother committed suicide). After that, he became a tour guide at the island fortress of Suomenlinna in Helsinki, where he remained until 1984.

It was after the death of his mother in 1984 that Bock, who claimed to be a direct descendant of the ancient Finnish god Lemminkäinen, began to make recordings of what would become the Bock Saga. He said that, between the ages of seven and twenty-seven, he sat with his mother every day as she passed on the Boxström family's traditions, and in her will instructed him to share them with the world. The saga traces the history of humanity back to the Ice Age, when

Atlantis was to be found in southern Finland. It goes on to record the histories, cultures and bloodlines of the various tribes who have lived in Scandinavia down the centuries.

Because so much of the traditions depend on the learning and interpretation of sounds, they can only be properly transmitted orally, which is why Bock chose to record them on tape (although some of the material has now been published in book form). His most striking claim about the customs of the early pagans is that men ritually ingested their own sperm (or 'water of life'), while women would also ingest their vaginal secretions, and those of others (using a straw).

The Bock Saga has attracted a number of enthusiasts, many of whom have noted its similarities to Tolkien's *Lord of the Rings* and related Middle Earth stories, usually arguing that Tolkien was working from the same sources. They practise yoga (which always comes in handy if one is trying to achieve autofellatio). In the late 1980s, Bock and his followers busied themselves searching for the lost Temple of Lemminkäinen, which he said was an ancient treasure trove hidden behind a stone slab. A slab was located on the side of a mountain in Sipoo, and permission was obtained from the town council to excavate behind it. The group began to raise funds to

accomplish this, but their activities were curtailed when Bock was arrested and charged with possession of marijuana in 1990.

Bock was attacked by a man at his sister's apartment in Helsinki in June 1999, and stabbed in the back several times. He survived, but the attack left him a quadriplegic. On 23 October 2010, Bock was the victim of a second stabbing attack, which proved fatal. ▣

BODENHEIM, MAXWELL

(1891–1954)
Poet

Bodenheim was born dirt poor in Mississippi and, after a stint in the army, landed in Chicago in 1912, defiantly self-educated and determined to be a poet. He was just in time for the city's much-vaunted cultural 'renaissance', and joined forces with one of its literary luminaries, Ben Hecht. They wrote plays and indulged in pranks. The most famous of these took place after they had been invited to give a debate at a snooty literary club. As the audience took their seats, the subject of the debate was announced: 'Resolved: That People Who Attend Literary Debates Are Imbeciles.' Hecht got things rolling by saying 'The affirmative rests', to which Bodenheim replied, 'You win.' Having already

pocketed their fees for this performance, the pair headed for the exit, pursued by irate literati.

Bodenheim fell out with Hecht after the latter lampooned him mercilessly in a novel, *Count Bruga*, which became a bestseller. He and his wife Minna moved to New York.

He took up residence in Greenwich Village, where he cemented his reputation as a poet with a number of well-received collections, and became known as 'King of the Bohemians'. He supplemented his poetical income by writing 'realistic' (for which read 'salacious') novels with titles like *Naked on Roller Skates* and *Replenishing Jessica*.

Bodenheim was a handsome young man with long golden hair and pale eyes. He affected an air of world weariness, as he thought befitted a poet, and wore a widebrimmed hat and a cape. He was an inveterate womaniser, and many women were in turn besotted by him. Bodenheim's troubles began when they started to kill themselves over him.

In 1928, eighteen-year-old Gladys Loeb presented Bodenheim with a sheaf of her poems for his consideration. He told her they were rotten. Devastated, Gladys clasped a signed photo of Bodenheim to her bosom and put her head in a gas oven. Luckily, her landlady smelled the gas, and police broke down the door in time to save her. Bodenheim was denounced by Gladys' father and mobbed by reporters.

A few weeks later, twenty-four-year-old Virginia Drew presented Bodenheim with several boxes of her compositions, but his verdict was as negative as the one he had given to Gladys Loeb. Virginia became hysterical, attacking the poet, pulling his hair, screaming that if she could not write as well as him she would kill herself. Bodenheim tried to persuade her against this, he said, to no avail — she left his hotel and threw herself into the East River. Her body was found three days later. Bodenheim, knowing what was coming, had gone into hiding. The newspapers went into a frenzy. *The New York Times* commented, 'A rebel against the canons of poetry and life, the poet by his absence has enmeshed himself in a case as bizarre as any of his own books.'

Reporters tracked Bodenheim down to a shack in Provincetown. He was questioned by police, but released when it became apparent that Virginia Drew had committed suicide. The headlines had barely died down when a dancer and former flame of the poet, Aimee Cortez, decided to adopt the Gladys Loeb method — head in oven, picture of Bodenheim in hand. Unlike Gladys, she succeeded.

Bodenheim was hit hard by the Depression, his literary career grinding to a halt. He peddled books he had stolen from shops and his friends, and wrote poems for the price of a drink. His only steady income was $35 that Hecht sent him every week for years.

He still wore his cape, but it was now a shabby thing. He could be found in the San Remo bar of an evening, a glass of gin in his hand, reciting his poetry and his troubles to anyone who would listen. 'I have a malady of the soul' was his constant refrain. By the early 1950s he was a beggar living on the streets.

He met a waif-like twenty-nine-year-old named Ruth Fagin, who had a university degree and a history of mental instability. She became the last woman to fall for Bodenheim's charms. He quickly dragged her down to his level, and they slept on park benches or in abandoned buildings. He mocked her and sometimes beat her, but she remained doggedly by his side. They married in 1952.

Ruth was friends with an unbalanced ex-convict named Harold Weinberg. On a bitterly cold evening in February 1954, she and Bodenheim took refuge in Weinberg's room in a cheap hotel near the Bowery. Weinberg passed a bottle of whisky round, then started to make love to Ruth. When Bodenheim objected, Weinberg picked up a gun and shot him twice in the chest. Ruth attacked Weinberg, they scuffled, and he stabbed her to death.

Friends of the Bodenheims gathered in the San Remo bar the following evening, and ceremoniously smashed Bodenheim's favourite gin glass. ▣

BOVAR, ORIC

(1917–1977)
Mystic

Bovar was an actor and opera coach who began a mail order astrology business in the 1960s, and became known for the accuracy of his predictions. By the early seventies, he had attracted around 200 followers in New York and California, including a number of celebrities. He advocated an austere lifestyle — no alcohol, drugs or sex outside marriage — and forbade his followers to consult doctors.

Around 1975, Bovar returned from a trip to Italy, having suffered some sort of breakdown there. He had lost a lot of weight and his previously red hair had turned white. He told his followers that he was the reincarnation of Christ, and that they should celebrate Christmas on his birthday, 29 August. He also said that he could now survive for a year without going to the bathroom. He

tried to exert greater power over them, and to arrange marriages between them. Many left the group.

In October 1976, one of Bovar's followers, Stephanos Hatzitheodorou, died from cancer in his New York apartment at the age of twenty-nine. Bovar announced his intention of bringing the young man back to life, and persuaded five followers to help him. They spent the next two months praying and chanting over the body (Bovar paid the rent on the apartment during this time so they would not be disturbed). In December a woman calling herself Mary Magdalene rang the police to inform them of the situation. They raided the apartment and arrested Bovar and the others, charging them with violating health regulations and not reporting a death.

Like that other intriguing but enigmatic mystic, ☞ Rodney Collin, Bovar fell to his death. He jumped from the tenth floor of his New York apartment the day before he was due to appear in court, apparently believing that he would be resurrected in time for the hearing, with a much stronger case to make. ▣

BRONNER. E.H

(1908–1997)
Soap maker

Bronner became famous for the

lengthy philosophical and religious musings which he printed on the labels of his soap products. He was born Emmanuel Heilbronner in Heilbronn, Germany, into a family which had been making soap since the mid-nineteenth century. As a young man, he was more interested in Zionism than soap, however, and after a quarrel with his father emigrated to the United States in 1929. After the Nazis came to power, he urged his family to follow him there. His sisters eventually did but his parents stayed behind. Both perished in concentration camps.

Bronner (born Emanuel Heilbronner, but dropping the 'Heil' from his name after 'Heil Hitler' became ubiquitous in Germany) settled in Milwaukee, and married Paula Wolfahrt in 1933. They had three children, Ellen, James and Ralph. The family moved to Chicago in the early 1940s, and Paula, who had been ailing for a long time, died in 1943.

Bronner left his children in the care of friends, and began to spend more time on his efforts to save the world. These had begun with numerous telegrams to President Roosevelt, and he would go on to send hundreds of messages to world leaders. Bronner called his philosophy the 'Moral ABCs'. He called for humanity to unite and live in peace, and worship at the

altar of an 'All-One-God-Faith'. He also railed against communism and fluoridation. In expressing his beliefs, Bronner was not always entirely coherent, and some people thought he was crazy. In 1946, he was attempting to convert students at the University of Chicago to his beliefs when the Dean called the police. Bronner was carted off to a mental institution where he was given electroshock therapy. After a couple of unsuccessful attempts, he managed to escape, and made his way to Los Angeles.

It was here that Bronner began to put his family's soap-making secrets to good use, mixing his first soap products by hand using vegetable oils and natural scents. Dr. Bronner, as he was now calling himself, realised that he could combine commerce and philosophy by including messages on his labels. These were quite brief to begin with, but he was soon cramming in thousands of words in tiny lettering. The messages, which he revised endlessly, are characterised by idiosyncratic punctuation, frequent obscurity and undeniable enthusiasm. The one on bottles of Dr. Bronner's 18-in-1 Hemp Lavender Pure-Castile Soap reads in part:

Only hard work can save us, but if we teach only our clan? We're all hated then! So, we must teach friend and enemy, the

whole Human race, the full-truth, hard-work, free speech, press-&-profitsharing Moral ABC's All-One-God-Faith, lightning like, 6 billion strong, for we're All-One or none! All-One-God-Faith, as teach the African shepherd-astronomers Abraham and Israel, for 6000 years, since the year 1: "Listen Children Eternal Father Eternal One!" — We're One! All-One! Exceptions eternally? None!! Absolute none!!

Bronner married again and moved to Escondido, where he set up an office in a bedroom of his house, and a small factory where his soap was mixed and bottled by hand. In the 1960s, Dr. Bronner's Magic Soaps, famed for their lathering properties and multitude of uses, from brushing your teeth to washing your pets, caught on among the hippies. Soon, his products were sold in health food shops across America, despite the fact that he spent nothing on advertising.

Bronner was blind for the last twenty years or so of his life, for which he blamed the shock therapy he had been subjected to in the 1940s. He rejected all overtures from the corporate world to expand his company, and was known to conduct business meetings wearing his leopard skin bathing suit. Today, the business is run by his sons, Ralph and Paul. It is worth about $7 million, ships its products worldwide,

and has donated millions to worthy causes. Yet it is still run out of the bedroom and manufacturing and packing are still done by hand, by a small workforce who share in the profits. The only difference is that Dr. Bronner is no longer around to rewrite the labels, which have remained the same since his death. ▨

BROOKS, WILEY
(b. c.1920s)
Breatharian

Brooks is, after ☞ Jasmuheen, the most prominent recent advocate of Breatharianism, the idea that a human being may live without eating. He first came to the attention of the American public with a 1981 appearance on the television show *That's Incredible!*, in which he appeared to lift over 1,000 pounds (454 kg), or ten times his body weight. He said that he had been a Breatharian for ten years, and claimed to sleep only one hour a night. Brooks' Breatharian credentials took a battering in 1983 when it was widely reported that he had been seen leaving a 7-Eleven store in California carrying a hot dog, a Slurpee and a packet of Twinkies.

Since then, Brooks and his organisation, the Breatharian Institute of America, have varied their message somewhat. He now spends a

WILEY BROOKS

lot of time promoting what he calls 'Earth Prime', a five-dimensional version of Earth which has recently come into being and which is much more peaceful and beautiful than our three-dimensional one, as well as being 'a full member of the RA/Pleaidean Confederation (the federation of positive planets of the Universe)'. Earth Prime is now crying out for immigrants — but the only people eligible to go are Breatharians who have managed to make their bodies five-dimensional. Brooks offers two methods by which you can do this. The first is to meditate for at least thirty minutes a day using the 'five magical words' — Jot naranjan, Omkar, Rarankar, Sohang and Sat Nam.

The second is to follow this meditation with a meal consisting of a McDonald's quarter-pounder with cheese and a Diet Coke ('in the plastic bottles only'), while also avoiding water, fruits and fruit juice. The benefits of the quarter-pounder, Brooks explains, derive from the fact that cows are actually five-dimensional beings, and hence beef is a five-dimensional food, while Diet Coke (but only in conjunction with the plastic bottle) contains 'liquid light'. Such dietary advice might appear to contradict Brooks' Breatharian message, but he now acknowledges that living without food is only possible if one has the purest of air to breathe, and living in cities makes this virtually impossible. In any case, he wrote on the Breatharian Institute's website, 'If you are reading this, You are already natural, true Breatharians. So stop trying to be something you already are and get on with the process of returning to your true home, which is the 5d Earth.'

In 2006, Brooks posted the following message on the website:

I am committing myself to doing 5 Empowered Ascension Initiation workshops within the next few months which will be for Billionaires only. The cost will be $1,000,000.00 USD for the 5 days of initiations. If you are approved to participate in one of these workshop [sic] *there will be no refunds of the prepaid cost under any circumstances. These workshops will be for the first 5 prepaid persons who have been approved by me. This offer ends September 1, 2006. After this date the cost of the workshops go up to $10,000,000.00. NO EXCEPTIONS.*

Brooks was true to his word (about the increase in prices, that is). The asking price for the full Breatharian course hit $25 million in 2008, but is back to a manageable $1 million as of writing.

On 11 November 2008, Brooks announced on his website that he had become 'Kuthumi, Chohan of the Golden Ray of Love and Wisdom'.

BUCKLAND, WILLIAM

(1784–1856)
Scientist & omnivore

Buckland was a pioneering geologist and palaeontologist, the first person to describe the fossil of what would later be known as a dinosaur, and an early convert to the theory that many geological features were formed by glaciers. His expertise in geology, or 'undergroundology' as he called it, was said to be such that he could taste a sample of soil and tell where in the British Isles it came from.

Buckland began to collect fossils as a young boy. He was educated at Oxford, where he was ordained as a priest and also appointed reader in minerology. His wife, Mary, whom he married in 1825, shared his interests, and they spent their honeymoon touring geological sites in Europe.

Buckland's lectures were famously lively affairs. One former student recalled him rushing around, brandishing the skull of a hyena at the class and demanding to know 'What rules the world?' The correct answer was the stomach. 'The great ones eat the less,' he explained, 'the less the lesser still.' Buckland

knew about such things firsthand, taking pride in the fact that he had eaten his way through much of the animal kingdom. The worst thing he had ever eaten was mole, he said, but that was only until he tried bluebottle. Guests for dinner at the Bucklands' house might find themselves treated to such delicacies as hedgehog, crocodile, panther and mouse.

Buckland's omnivorous tendencies went further than the animal kingdom. On one occasion, he was visiting his friend, Edward Harcourt, the Archbishop of York, at Harcourt's family seat of Nuneham in Oxfordshire. Harcourt had been in France during the revolution, and had somehow managed to purchase the heart of King Louis XIV.

When he produced the relic, which he kept in a small box, for his guest to inspect, Buckley declared, 'I've eaten many things, but never the heart of a king,' and scoffed it down before he could be stopped.

Buckland's son, Frank, inherited his father's adventurous eating habits. He was a famous naturalist and the author of the celebrated work, *Curiosities of Natural History*. He was also a co-founder of the Society for the Acclimatisation of Animals in the United Kingdom, which encouraged the introduction of exotic animals to provide new sources of food. At one society

dinner in 1862, the menu included sea-slug, kangaroo, wild boar and curassow. Not all Frank Buckland's culinary experiments were successful, however. Having cooked up several slices of porpoise head one day, he reported that the results tasted like 'a broiled lamp wick'. ▣

BURROUGHS, WILLIAM S.
(1914–1997)
Writer

Burroughs was born in St. Louis, Missouri. His grandfather, William S. Burroughs, Snr, invented the first adding machine, but lost control of the company he founded to manufacture it, and most of the accompanying riches. His parents, Mortimer and Laura, were nevertheless comfortably well off and part of the city's high society. The young Burroughs was a sickly looking, slightly built boy, aware of his homosexuality from an early age. He became obsessed with guns and explosives (at fourteen, he almost blew his hand off while playing with chemicals). In 1929, he was sent to Los Alamos, a ranch school in New Mexico designed to transform the delicate sons of the rich into strapping young men. He loathed it, and at the age of sixteen swallowed a quantity of chloral hydrate ('to see how it worked')

which almost killed him. He eventually persuaded his parents to let him leave the school (which was taken over by the U.S. Government during the war and transformed into the facility where the atom bomb was developed).

Burroughs graduated from Harvard in 1936. After a period in Europe (during which he studied medicine in Vienna) he briefly returned to Harvard, but decided that an academic life was not for him. His parents were paying him an allowance of $200 a month but still expected him to work, and he took several jobs, including an eight-month stint as a pest exterminator in Chicago, which he enjoyed.

Moving to New York, he met Allen Ginsberg, Jack Kerouac and his girlfriend Edith Parker, and Parker's flatmate Joan Vollmer, who was married to a soldier and had a young daughter. Their circle — the nucleus of the Beat Generation — was joined by two of Burroughs' friends from St. Louis, David Kammerer and Lucien Carr. Kammerer was infatuated with the younger Carr, who was still a student, and followed him everywhere. In August 1944, during a drunken fight in a park, Carr stabbed Kammerer to death. Burroughs was arrested as a material witness, but was bailed out by his parents.

Burroughs was attracted to

Joan Vollmer's intellect, and though he was mainly homosexual, didn't mind having sex with women, so they became a couple. By now, he was addicted to heroin, and Joan to Benzedrine. Having fantasised about being a criminal since he was a child, Burroughs dressed like a hood, indulged in petty crime, dealt narcotics and was arrested for forging prescriptions. He and Joan, along with Joan's daughter, moved to Texas, where she gave birth to his son, William Burroughs III, then to New Orleans, where he was busted for possession of drugs. Facing two years in jail, he fled to Mexico with Joan and the children.

On the evening of 6 September 1951, he and Joan were at a party in Mexico City. Burroughs had brought along a gun, a .380 automatic, that he intended to sell. At a certain point, for reasons he could never fathom, he announced, 'Well, I guess it's about time for our William Tell act.' Joan placed a glass on her head and Burroughs, a crack shot and sitting just a few feet away, aimed at the top of the glass. The bullet hit her in the head, and she died almost immediately. Burroughs, who had an almost medieval view of the world and believed that nothing happened by chance, thought that an evil spirit had entered into him. He was nevertheless wracked with guilt for the

rest of his life. He always said that killing Joan was what turned him into a writer, although by this time he had completed his first book, *Junkie*, which had been published (under the pen name William Lee) in America to complete indifference.

Shooting your wife dead was not such a big deal in Mexico. Burroughs was released from jail after posting a bond, and left the country. He spent the next few years wandering more or less aimlessly round the world. In South America, he sought out a hallucinatory plant extract called yage, which he had become convinced was the ultimate drug (when he finally found a medicine man who would give him some, he hallucinated being able to change his sex at will). In Tangier, still an international city of almost limitless freedoms when he arrived in 1954, he savoured Spanish boys and completed the bulk of his next book, *Naked Lunch*.

Moving to Paris, he became reacquainted with the Swiss-born painter Brion Gyson, whom he had first met in Tangier. He and Gyson practised meditation and mirror-gazing, the latter involving staring at a mirror for hours until visions appeared.

In July 1956, Maurice Girodias of the Olympia Press, a renowned publisher of 'dirty books' (as well

WILLIAM S. BURROUGHS

as works by writers like Beckett and Nabokov) agreed to publish *Naked Lunch*. The text was hurriedly finalised, with sections sent off to the printer in no particular order. In the end, this order was maintained in the published book. This element of randomness foreshadowed the infamous 'cut-up' technique which Burroughs now adopted (at the prompting of Gyson). He would take his own writings, articles from newspapers and the works of other writers, cut them up and mix them together. Although many found the resulting texts unreadable, Burroughs thought that the technique opened up writing to unconscious and psychic influences, and produced works that could even be prophetic. He used it extensively in his next few books.

When *Naked Lunch* was published in the U.S. in 1962, several booksellers were charged for selling an obscene work, but in 1966 the Massuchusetts Supreme Court declared that it was not obscene, effectively signaling the end of literary censorship in America. Burroughs had spent most of the previous year in New York, cementing his reputation as a hero of the counter-culture. With his three-piece suits and gentlemanly manner he was a far cry from the average hippy, but the theme of control — and how to break free of it — that runs through

all his works chimed perfectly with the times.

During the late sixties and early seventies Burroughs lived in London, where he joined the Church of Scientology and became obsessed with its auditing process, but left after tiring of its authoritarianism. He had long been interested in various alternative ideas and therapies. In the forties, having undergone extensive psychoanalysis and becoming disillusioned with it, he had latched on to the theories of ☞ Wilhelm Reich, and for the rest of his life liked to spend part of each day sitting in one of Reich's orgone boxes.

In 1974, he returned to America permanently, and settled in New York. Here he lived in 'the Bunker', a windowless, white-painted space which had formerly been the locker room of a gym, and found a new source of income giving readings from his works in his rusty, robotic voice. Burroughs was, if anything, even more revered by the punks than he had been by the hippies, and musicians, artists and other celebrities visited the Bunker to pay homage.

He became hooked on heroin again during these years, but in 1981 made a decisive break with his past by moving to Lawrence, Missouri. He spent his last years there in rural isolation, completing the 'Red Night' trilogy of novels in which he returned (sort of) to conventional narrative. He also combined his love of guns and art with a series of paintings produced by firing at cans of paint placed in front of wooden boards.

Burroughs was a unique individual, both in his personality and his writings. He had no direct literary forebears, and his books, which teem with aliens, mutations, drugs, viruses, violence and explicit homosexual sex, offer one of the bleakest visions of life produced in the twentieth century. Nevertheless, in 1983, he received the literary establishment's ultimate accolade when he was inducted into the American Academy and Institute of Arts and Letters, and afterwards wore its rosette on his jacket lapel. Having been subjected to more than a few drug searches in his time, he noted that an award like this 'gets you respect from customs agents'. ■

BUTLER, ELEANOR & SARAH PONSONBY

(1739–1829) & (1755–1832)
'The Ladies of Llangollen'

Butler, the daughter of an Irish lord, and Ponsonby, an Englishwoman with aristocratic connections living in Ireland, met around 1774 and fell in love. As they feared that their respective families were planning to marry them off to men they had no interest in, they decided to run away together. In 1780, they settled into a house called Plas Newydd, near the town of Llangollen in Wales. Here they lived in glorious isolation with a maidservant, a dog named Flirt and a cat named Mrs. Tatters. They always wore men's clothing, and many of their possessions, including china and books, bore the initials E.B. and S.P.

In truth, their lives were entirely quiet and uneventful. They were largely self-sufficient, growing vegetables, raising chickens and making their own bread and wine, and spent their spare time reading and sketching. After they moved into Plas Newydd, neither ever spent a night away from it. And yet, they were a subject of enormous fascination for their contemporaries. Among the illustrious personages who made the trip to Llangollen to visit them were the poets Wordsworth, Byron and Shelley, Sir Walter Scott, Josiah Wedgwood and the Duke of Wellington.

'The Ladies', as they were known, are often cited as pioneering lesbians, but whether their relationship was a sexual one is not known. Plas Newydd survives and is now a museum. ■

CARBONE, GIORGIO

(1936–2009)
'His Tremendousness'

In 1963, Carbone, a former market gardener and doctor, was elected Prince Giorgio I of the small and picturesque Italian village of Seborga (having received 304 out of a possible 308 votes), and declared it a sovereign state, independent of Italy. His claim was based on the fact that Seborga had been a principality from 1079 to 1729, when it was sold to the King of Sardinia. Carbone maintained that this sale was invalid, and the village had never been part of the Kingdom of Italy created in 1861. 'Seborga has existed for 1,000 years,' he told a reporter in 1999, 'Italy for a mere 130. It is not Italy that should recognise Seborga, but vice versa.'

Carbone assumed the title of 'Sua Tremendita' ('His tremendousness').

The principality has its own flag, designed by Carbone, a motto (Sub Umbra Sede, or 'Sit in the shade', which seems eminently sensible), stamps and currency (the Liguino). Seborga has been recognised by some twenty states, including Burkina Faso, although not by the State of Italy, which largely ignored Carbone's princely shenanigans (the villagers continue to pay their taxes to the Italian government). The bearded, chain-smoking Carbone was not paid for his services, but there were other perks to his job, including free ham and cheese from the village shop. Many of his ministers doubled as town councillors, with the two arms of government happily co-existing.

In 2006, Carbone announced that he would be retiring when he reached the age of seventy, but changed his mind when a potential rival to his throne emerged. This was a woman who called herself Princess Yasmine von Hohenstaufen Anjou Plantagenet, who claimed descent from Frederick II, a thirteenth century Holy Roman Emperor. Princess Yasmine wrote to the Italian president, magnanimously offering to hand over Seborga to Italy.

Carbone was scathing about her claim, calling her an 'Internet princess'. The good people of Seborga were happy to stay with the prince they knew.

CARSTAIRS, JOE

(1900–1993)
'The Queen of Whale Cay'

Marion 'Joe' Carstairs, who was born in London, traced her life from the moment when, aged about four, she was thrown from a bolting camel and acquired the nickname 'Tuffy'. Her mother was a serial-marrying alcoholic and heroin addict, but more importantly the heir to an oil fortune, which meant that her daughter was wealthy enough to make up her life as she went along. She served as a driver during World War I, and afterwards started an upmarket car hire company with a crew of female chauffeurs. She was by now calling herself Joe, dressing in men's clothes and busily seducing women (her lovers would go on to include Greta Garbo and Marlene Dietrich). She also took up the new sport of motorboat racing, won trophies in England and the U.S., and became known as 'the fastest woman on water'.

The pivotal point in Carstairs' life came in 1925. She was on holiday in Switzerland when a girlfriend presented her with a doll in the shape of a man, thirteen inches tall,

with a leather face and beady black eyes. She dubbed him Lord Tod Wadley and he became her constant companion, alter ego and muse. She dressed him in imported clothes, provided him with a full set of miniature possessions, wrote poems to him and, while she wouldn't risk him on a motorboat, took him everywhere else.

As the 1920s drew to a close, Carstairs' boat racing career was faltering. She also found that the press were turning against her. In the years following the war — in which so many women had served with men — masculine women like Carstairs had been seen as a novelty. But the controversy surrounding Radclyffe Hall's novel *The Well of Loneliness* generated something of a moral panic over lesbianism. Carstairs' tattoos, swearing and chain smoking, previously seen as amusing affectations, now seemed rather more sinister.

In 1933, after reading a news-paper advertisement, Carstairs purchased a small island called Whale Cay in the Bahamas for $40,000. Prior to her arrival it was inhabited by a solitary black couple, but she quickly set about establishing a kingdom. She had roads laid and a harbour dredged. She built a lavish, five-bedroom house (which became the scene for many wild parties for her guests from Europe and the

U.S.), a store, a church, a school and even a radio station. She also built a museum to herself, filling it with her racing trophies, knife collection, the heads of animals she had bagged and a life-size model of Wadley. Eventually some 200 islanders were living and working on Whale Cay. Carstairs ruled her island with a firm hand (she was known to sentence adulterers to be bullwhipped). Her subjects called her 'The Boss'. They believed she had magical powers, and that Wadley was her idol. Church services were handled by the Reverend Julian Henshaw, a gay priest (or, in Carstairs' words, 'a very, very gay priest') who liked to open his robes at parties to show that he was wearing nothing underneath.

Carstairs was genuinely interested in the welfare of the native people, and wanted to see the economic success she had brought to Whale Cay spread to other islands. She set up the Coloured League of Youth, which provided the means for people to set themselves up as farmers. This brought stiff opposition from the white aristocracy in Nassau, who made money by importing goods and had no desire to see the natives self-sufficient.

Carstairs nevertheless faced increasing resentment from the islanders during the 1960s. Out of fashion again, she sold Whale Cay in 1977 — a traumatic event. She spent most of her remaining years in Florida, continuing to financially support a host of ex-girlfriends and others she had met over the years. After her death at the age of ninety-three, Lord Tod Wadley was cremated with her. ▣

CASATI, MARCHESA LUISA
(1881–1957)
Aristocrat & muse

The remarkable Marchesa was one of the most flamboyant and exotic personalities of the early twentieth century. Born Luisa Amman in Milan, she was the youngest daughter of Comte Alberto Amman, a cotton magnate, and his Austrian-born wife Lucia, both of whom died when Luisa was in her teens, leaving her a vast fortune. A slightly built girl with large, expressive green eyes, she was painfully shy when young.

In 1900 she married the Marchese Camillo Casati, a cavalry officer and scion of one of Milan's oldest aristocratic families, and they had a daughter, Cristina, the following year. Luisa soon became bored with her husband, who spent most of his spare time hunting, and began to develop new interests, including fast cars and the occult.

In 1903, she caught the roving eye of Gabriele D'Annunzio, notorious decadent poet and novelist, and keen seducer of other men's wives. D'Annunzio was forever on the lookout for his ideal woman, and the Marchesa actually exceeded his expectations. (He would later write, 'She was, in fact, the only woman who ever astonished me.') They began a passionate affair that would continue intermittently for years. Camillo turned a blind eye to it, perhaps because Luisa brought much more money into their household than he did, and they led essentially separate lives after this (although they would not be divorced until 1924). She began to alter her appearance, dying her naturally brown hair red in emulation of Sarah Bernhardt, wearing clothes that emphasised her thinness, applying white makeup to her face and accentuating her eyes with thick applications of kohl (later, she took to putting drops of poisonous belladonna in them to dilate the pupils). The Marchesa soon attracted a coterie of artists entranced by this striking new image, and a portrait by Guiseppe Boldini, showing her wearing a long black satin gown decorated with a spray of violets, with her black greyhound at her feet, caused a sensation at the 1909 Paris Salon.

D'Annunzio also introduced her to the splendours of Venice. In 1910, the Marchesa bought the sprawling but dilapidated eighteenth century Palazzo Venier on the Grand Canal. She had the interior sumptuously renovated, with black, white and gold the dominant colours, but the crumbling appearance of the exterior was retained. Renamed the Palazzo dei Leoni (Palace of the Lions), it became the scene for the Marchesa's legendary parties and masked balls, where she appeared in ever more fantastical outfits designed by Léon Bakst, who also designed the costumes for Diaghilev's Ballets Russes. The Palazzo's landscaped gardens were home to flocks of white peacocks and albino blackbirds, and these were joined over the next few years by a veritable menagerie of creatures including cheetahs, apes, parrots, ocelots and tigers. In her travels around the world, Luisa was often accompanied by her pet boa constrictor (when it wasn't coiled around her arms, it would be ensconced in a satin-lined box), and she was known to wear a live gold-painted snake as jewelry.

Luisa was soon the most talked about person in Venice. She became known for walking through the Piazza San Marco at night, wearing a fur cloak under which she was naked, leading two cheetahs on jeweled leashes and accompanied by a huge Negro servant bearing flaming torches. So regular were her nocturnal expeditions that tourists used to look out for her.

In need of a new audience, the Marchesa made frequent visits to Paris, where the parties she threw were just as extravagant as those in Venice, and no less an expert on flamboyancy than ☞ Robert de Montesquiou dubbed her 'a goddess'. She commissioned dozens of portraits of herself from well known painters, and her narcissism reached delirious heights. She even had a realistic wax mannequin of herself made (fashioned from a full plaster cast of her body, it was said). Her dinner guests might find themselves sharing the table with this mannequin, dressed in identical clothes to their flesh and blood hostess.

After the outbreak of war in 1914, the Marchesa fared rather better than many other sirens of the Belle Epoque, who quickly faded from view. She associated herself with younger avant-garde artists such as Marinetti and the Futurists, and was photographed by Man Ray (his triple-exposed portrait of her, in which she appears to have three sets of eyes, became a Surrealist icon). After the war, she travelled extensively, and continued to throw lavish theme parties. She experimented with costumes incorporating electric light bulbs, on at least one occasion almost electrocuting herself.

In the mid-twenties, years of eye-watering extravagance finally began to take an appreciable toll on the Marchesa's fortune, and she was forced to sell most of her Italian properties, including the Palazzo dei Leoni. Meanwhile D'Annunzio, still her intermittent lover, was undergoing his own decline. After becoming a national hero during the war, then briefly the proto-fascist dictator of Fiume (an Italian city assigned to Yugoslavia in the postwar settlement) he fell from a window in mysterious circumstances in 1922, fracturing his skull. He ended his days as a semi-recluse in a house on the shores of Lake Garda, obsessed by death and the occult, surrounded by an extraordinary array of objects and curiosities he had collected over the years, including a biplane he had flown during the war (which hung from the ceiling) and the gloves of numerous former lovers.

Luisa's main residence was now a pink marble mansion called the Palais Rose, about an hour's drive from Paris and formerly owned by Robert de Montesquiou. She decorated it in her usual fashion, and hung over 100 paintings of herself on its walls, but her extravagant parties were starting to fall flat, and increasingly scurrilous rumors were circulated about her. Her debts continued to rise, but the Marchesa was constitutionally unable to rein

MARCHESA LUISA CASATI

in her spending. The crunch came in 1934, when she was forced to sell almost all her remaining possessions.

With debtors still clamoring for payment in France and Italy, she moved to England, where she survived with the help of a few old aristocratic friends, the painter Augustus John, and her daughter Cristina. (During the Marchesa's wildest years, Cristina had been confined to a strict Catholic boarding school in France, and had gone on to marry an English aristocrat.) Most of her last two decades were spent in a state of wretched poverty, her once fabled menagerie dwindled to a few Pekinese dogs. Still rail-thin, she moved around London clad in tattered black velvet and leopard skin, a wraithlike reminder of her glory days, but she reportedly never lost her spirit, or her ability to startle. ■

'I want to be a living work of art.'

THE MARCHESA LUISA CASATI

CASLEY, LEONARD

(b. 1925)
Prince Leonard of the Principality of Hutt River

Casley, the son of a fireman, was born in Kalgoorlie, western Australia, and married another West Australian, Shirley Butler, in 1947. The pair worked in a number of farming and mining ventures, and had seven children. In 1969, the family purchased a 7,500 hectare (18,525 acre) property around the Hutt River, about 517 km (321 miles) north of Perth, where they intended to grow wheat. They produced a bumper harvest in their first year, but then the Wheat Quota Board imposed what Casley said was an absurdly low quota on them, which would have doomed their business to failure. He appealed the decision, but found that no appeals were allowed. He wrote to the state and federal governments, to no avail. Casley, trying another tack, filed for compensation. He then learned that a bill had been introduced into Parliament which would have allowed the government to reclaim rural lands from their owners. Fearing that the bill was directed at them, the Casley family made a momentous decision.

On 21 April 1970, they served notice on the West Australian Premier and Governor, the acting Prime Minister and the Governor-General, that they were seceding from Australia (although they were happy to remain under the sovereignty of Her Majesty, Queen Elizabeth).

It would be fair to say that the Casleys' declaration took the various levels of the Australian government by surprise. The West Australian government asked the Federal government to intervene in the matter, but the Governor-General declared that it would be unconstitutional for it to do so. Nevertheless, Casley was threatened with prosecution. Looking to the law to bolster the claims of Hutt River Province, as the new nation was called, Casley found a clause in the *Treason Act* (since removed) which said that anyone hindering a de facto prince from attaining his office could be charged with treason. The Casleys promptly declared Hutt River a principality, and Leonard Casley assumed the title His Royal Highness Prince Leonard of Hutt.

Remarkably, this seems to have done the trick. Since then the Australian government has largely left Prince Leonard and his nation to its own devices (although, angered by the government's refusal to allow the country to have its own airline, Hutt River briefly declared war on Australia in 1977).

In its heyday, up to twenty tourist buses a day rolled into Hutt River Province, where they were usually greeted by Prince Leonard or his wife, Her Serene Highness Princess Shirley. Having received their visas, the tourists could wander among the handful of cement buildings which comprise the nation's capital, Nain,

admire the carved slab commemorating the nation's independence, and buy Hutt River T-shirts and other items at the souvenir shop, staffed by members of the Casley family. The nation has its own national anthem, a flag featuring a stylised bull's head incorporating an eagle and the scales of justice, and issues stamps, coins and bank notes (the Hutt River dollar is tied to the Australian dollar) which are eagerly collected. It also issues passports to its citizens which are accepted around the world.

While Hutt River Province has never had more than about thirty permanent residents, Prince Leonard has granted citizenship to many others, while appointing various ambassadors and other representatives around the world. This process began to greatly accelerate in the 1980s, when he appointed Kevin Gale, a flamboyant Queensland businessman (with, as it later transpired, a somewhat shady past) as Prince Regent. Prince Kevin created hundreds of knights, earls, dukes, barons, marquesses and lords. He talked of purchasing an island in the Pacific and registering it with the United Nations, and of Hutt River having its own Olympic team. He also raised a fortune selling Hutt River stamps and banknotes, with little of the money making its way back to Prince Leonard. Just as

it was becoming clear that Prince Kevin was in fact planning to usurp the throne, he died suddenly in 1995.

Since this unfortunate episode, Hutt River Province (which officially changed its name to the Principality of Hutt River in 2006), has featured less in the news, and visitors to it have dwindled. It continues to be ruled by Prince Leonard, with his son, Crown Prince Wayne, in line to succeed him. While Prince Leonard, with his elaborate ceremonial robes and glittering insignia, remains a fairly well known figure, particularly to older Australians, few realise that he actually achieved what he set out to do. The residents of Hutt River have paid no income taxes to the Australian government since independence was declared. It really is a separate country. ▨

CAVENDISH, HENRY

(1731–1810)
Scientist

Cavendish was one of the most respected British scientists of his day, famed for his discovery of hydrogen and for accurately measuring the density of the Earth. He was also, as one acquaintance put it, 'shy and bashful to a degree bordering on disease; he could not bear to have any person introduced to him, or to be pointed out in any way as a remarkable man.'

He came from an extremely wealthy family but, for reasons that are not quite clear, his father kept him on a strictly limited income for the first fifty years of his life, and he lived in converted stables.

When attending Royal Society dinners, he was allowed to take the cost of the meal — five shillings — and no more. After coming into his inheritance, he remained completely indifferent to his wealth. He went about in faded clothes that were fashionable decades earlier, and dined every night on the same meal of a leg of mutton. On one occasion, when his bankers became concerned about a sum of £80,000 that was sitting in an account instead of being invested, they sent a man to his house to discuss the matter. Cavendish was aghast. 'If it is any trouble to you,' he said in his high-pitched voice, 'I will take it out of your hands. Do not come here to plague me.'

Cavendish lived in a large house in Clapham filled with scientific equipment — a laboratory in the drawing room, a forge in the adjoining room, an astronomical observatory upstairs, and numerous thermometers, rain gauges and other instruments scattered about the place. He rarely entertained visitors, and the local people thought he was a wizard. He had a particular aversion to women and, like William John Cavendish-Scott-Bentinck, lived in fear of encountering his own servants. After one unfortunate brush with a maidservant on the stairs, he had a second staircase built. A Mr. Tomlinson recalled how one evening, while dining at the Royal Society, someone noticed a very pretty girl in a house across the street. One by one the diners left the table to have a look at her. 'Cavendish, who thought we were looking at the moon, bustled up to us in his odd way, and when he saw the real object of our study, turned away with intense disgust, and grunted out Pshaw!'

Apart from attending Royal Society meetings, Cavendish rarely mingled with his fellow men. In order to affect any communication with him at all, his contemporaries were forced to perfect the art of addressing him as if they were speaking to empty air. If they did this well enough, they might elicit a response. On one occasion, Cavendish had been persuaded to attend a gathering at Sir Joseph Banks' house, where he was introduced to an Austrian gentleman then visiting London. This gentleman proceeded to heap praise upon Cavendish's head, saying that meeting the great scientist had been his principle reason for coming to the city. Cavendish stared at the floor uncomfortably until,

spying an opening in the crowd, he made a bolt for his carriage outside and was quickly driven home. He always took his exercise of an evening, walking in the middle of the road to avoid meeting people.

On his death, he left an enormous fortune to his cousin, Lord George Cavendish (to earn it, he had been obliged to visit Henry every year — for half an hour exactly). He also left behind masses of unpublished papers. Examined years after his death, they were found to contain numerous discoveries that had by then been attributed to other scientists. ▨

CAVENDISH, MARGARET
(1623–1673)
Writer

Margaret Lucas was the last of eight children born into a wealthy, staunchly royalist family in Essex. Her father, Thomas Lucas, died when she was two, and the running of his estate was taken over by her mother, Elizabeth, who became a strong role model. Although Margaret received only the rudimentary formal education then normally given to girls, she supplemented this by reading, joining in intellectual discussions with her siblings, and studying nature or, as she put it, 'making the world my book'. She had absolutely no interest in the domestic duties of spinning, needlework and the like that were supposed to occupy women. She wanted only one thing, to be a writer — despite the fact that women writers were all but unknown at the time. Acutely aware of the limitations society placed on women, she saw writing as her only chance for immortality. 'Though I cannot be Henry the Fifth, or Charles the Second,' she later wrote, 'yet I endeavour to be Margaret the First.'

The Lucas family's fortunes inevitably suffered during the English Civil War, which broke out in 1642. St. John's, their principle home in Essex, was ransacked by a mob and the family was dispersed. Margaret became a Maid of Honour to Queen Henrietta Maria, and accompanied her into exile in France. She hated the vacuousness of courtly life, and escaped it by marrying the dashing William Cavendish, the Marquess of Newcastle. Cavendish, who was twenty-five years older than Margaret, had distinguished himself as a soldier, swordsman and equestrian, but he was also a poet and scholar whose friends included some of the most brilliant men of the day. After their marriage they went to live in Antwerp.

Like most royalist exiles, Cavendish was cut off from the income from his British estates, and he and Margaret lived precariously on the goodwill of creditors. In 1651, she returned to England to petition the government to be allowed to receive income from her husband's estates (such petitions were often granted to royalist wives, but Cavendish was considered such an arch-royalist her petition was eventually denied). While waiting for a decision, she put together her first book, *Poems and Fancies*, which was published in 1653, with her name on the title page.

Margaret had already attracted attention among London society because of her unconventional dresses (which she designed herself), but the book's appearance cemented her reputation for eccentricity. Even among the male courtly poets who were her writing peers, publication was considered ungentlemanly, and those who did publish usually did so anonymously. In issuing a book in her own name, Margaret risked accusations of dishonour. Moreover, she tackled traditionally masculine subjects — science, philosophy, war. Her book, not surprisingly, attracted considerable interest. Many who read it were appalled by Margaret's clearly materialist worldview, while others doubted that a woman was capable of writing it at all.

Margaret was certainly ambitious in her writings. In *Philosophical Fancies* (1653) and other works, she proposed a complete theory of the universe. She believed that all matter was alive, or 'innated', and in constant motion. There were six principle motions which produced all physical phenomena (light, air and water, for example, were produced by spinning motions). In addition to her scientific works, she wrote short stories, essays in the form of letters on numerous subjects, many plays far too long to perform, an autobiography, a biography of her husband, and an odd, proto-science fiction novel called *The Description of a New World, Called the Blazing World* (1666). This tells the story of a woman who travels to another world joined to ours at the North Pole, where she quickly becomes Empress. She engages in long philosophical discussions with the bear-men, worm-men, bird-men and other beings who live in this world, and meets the soul of none other than Margaret Cavendish. They get on so well that they become 'platonic lovers'.

Margaret wrote obsessively, her brain a constant ferment of ideas. Although she could be defensive about her lack of formal education, she firmly believed that it was best to come up with one's own ideas rather than copying anyone else, and her ideas were certainly original, if not always coherent. Adding to the problem was her terrible handwriting and (even for her time) erratic

spelling, which meant that numerous errors crept into her books (she refused to read proof pages because she thought seeing her old ideas would hinder her from having new ones).

Margaret and William returned to England after the Restoration. William was made the Duke of Newcastle for his services to the Crown, and was eventually able to claw back most of his estates. Margaret, with her forthright opinions and idiosyncratic costumes, continued to be an object of amazement for London society. In 1667, she arrived at the opening night of William's play, *The Humorous Lovers*, wearing a classical style dress which left her breasts bare (with her nipples painted scarlet for added effect). The diarist Samuel Pepys became obsessed with her, writing, 'The whole story of this lady is a romance,' and spent weeks trying to get a glimpse of her.

Since her sudden death at the age of fifty, Margaret's reputation has waxed and waned. To the Victorians, she was a faintly ludicrous figure, 'Mad Madge' (although it seems that her contemporaries never used this nickname). They considered much of her work coarse, and when her poetry was reprinted it was often bowdlerised. In the early twentieth century, Virginia Woolf did her no favours, dismissing her as 'hare-brained, fantastickal'. Since then, her reputation has recovered significantly, and she is now studied as a unique and fascinating literary figure — just as she always wanted.

'I have made a world of my own: for which nobody, I hope, will blame me, since it is in everyone's power to do the like.'

MARGARET CAVENDISH

CAVENDISH-SCOTT-BENTINCK, WILLIAM JOHN (LORD)

(1800–1879)
'The Tunnelling Duke'

The magnificently named Lord William John Cavendish-Scott-Bentinck, the Fifth Duke of Portland, was apparently quite a normal fellow in his younger days. He was keen on horse racing, served in the army and was briefly a Member of Parliament. By the time he succeeded to the dukedom in 1854, however, he had developed an extraordinary aversion to seeing, or being seen by, other people.

On the rare occasions when he ventured outside his family home, Welbeck Abbey in Nottinghamshire, the Duke (whose regular attire on such occasions was a two-foot tall top hat, a brown wig and three frock coats) carried a large umbrella to shield himself if anyone else came into view. He never invited anyone to his home, and his servants and tenants were under strict instructions to never acknowledge his presence if they saw him. Only his valet was allowed to be in the same room with him. Should he require a medical examination, his doctor was forced to carry it out from the next room. Every day, a servant pushed his lunch — half a roast chicken — through his door. His dinner — the other half of the chicken — followed in the evening.

Whenever he was forced to go to London on business, the Duke travelled in his carriage (with curtained widows) to the local train station. This was then lifted onto a flatbed railway carriage for the journey to London. On arrival, it was driven to a house he owned in Cavendish Square, where the servants hid until the Duke was safely ensconced in his study. There were inevitably rumours that he had some sort of facial deformity or skin condition (leprosy was even suggested) but nothing like this is evident in photographs.

The Duke occupied only four rooms in his mansion. He ordered all the rest stripped of furniture and decorations (but had lavatories installed in them), and the walls painted pink. He spent most of his time overseeing extensive building works on his estate, almost all of which were underground. These included a ballroom 174 feet (fifty-three metres) long, with room for 2,000 people. It was illuminated during the day by dome-shaped skylights, and at night by gas jets, and was serviced with a hydraulic lift. Among the other underground developments were a glass-roofed observatory, a billiard room large enough for twelve billiard tables, and several libraries. A network of tunnels was dug which is said to have totalled fifteen miles (twenty-four km). One tunnel, connecting the estate to the nearest village, was wide enough to accommodate two carriages travelling side by side. The Duke's above-ground projects included a huge riding school with mirrored walls, chandeliers, and room in the stables for 100 horses. As the Duke never had visitors, the ballroom, the riding school and all the other structures were never used.

The Duke was employing 15,000 men by the end of this life. He paid them well and presented each of them with a donkey and an umbrella (although anyone who acknowledged his presence was instantly sacked). Like that other inveterate tunneller ☛ Joseph Williamson, the Duke was sometimes said to be motivated by philanthropy — he just wanted to provide work for his men. He was certainly known to be a generous soul who gave to worthy causes and tossed coins to children from behind the curtained windows of his carriage. Yet, with his uniquely retiring personality, it's hard to believe he was being purely altruistic in creating his underground world.

The Fifth Duke of Portland's curious life had a curious sequel when, seventeen years after he died, a woman named Anne Maria Druce came forward with the claim that her father-in-law, T.C. Druce, a shopkeeper, had actually been the Duke in disguise. She said that T.C. Druce's funeral in 1864 had been a sham, and her son was in fact the heir to the Portland estate. Although the claim was roundly mocked, the fact that the Duke had spent so much of his life out of the public eye meant the idea that he amused himself masquerading as another man was at least possible. The tale became even more tangled when a man arrived from Australia claiming to be G.H. Druce, the long-lost son of T.C. Druce. These various claims tied up the courts for years, until a judge finally put an end to them in 1907 by ordering that the body of T.C. Druce be exhumed.

The real Duke had of course

been dead and buried for decades. He had asked for shrubs to be planted around his grave in Kensal Green Cemetery, so he could get some privacy.

CERUTTY, PERCY
(1895–1975)
Coard

The hyperactive Cerutty was born into a working class family in Melbourne, Victoria. As a youth he showed some promise as a runner, but poor health forced him to abandon athletic ambitions. He married a local girl and got a job with the post office, but in 1939 suffered a nervous breakdown.

Taking leave from work, Cerutty embarked on a rigorous programme of mental and physical rejuvenation. He read poetry and philosophy, studied the movements of animals to see how their muscles worked, and exercised constantly, swimming, diving, running, weightlifting. He ran marathons, and in his late forties began to break records. He abandoned his post office career, and became an athletics coach.

He bought some property by the beach at Portsea, and set up the International Athletics Centre in a shack. Cerutty called himself a 'Stotan' — a cross between a Stoic and a Spartan. His system called

for punishing runs through rugged terrain and up impossibly steep sandhills, and swimming in the ocean all year round. He taunted athletes he thought weren't pushing themselves hard enough, telling them, 'Thrust against the pain. Pain is the purifier.' If any of his athletes collapsed from the strain, the others were forbidden from helping them up. He thought it was important for athletes to spend part of every day naked so that their bodies would become immune to the cold. He abhorred cooked vegetables, red meat and milk (he said milk made boys 'mother-drawn', and called for dairies to be closed). He encapsulated his ideas in a series of books, including *Be Fit! Or Be Damned!* and *On Greatness.*

For Cerutty, the most important factor in achieving greatness — in sport or any other endeavour — was emotion, and advised his athletes to feed their emotional life 'on art, music, sculpture, architecture, even on tragedy'.

His methods may have been harsh, but they got results. His greatest protégé was Herb Elliot, who beat the world 1,500 metre record at the Rome Olympics in 1960. Others who benefited from the Cerutty treatment included John Landy (the second man to run a mile in under four minutes), world champion boxer Jimmy Carruthers, and four-time Olympic gold medallist Betty Cuthbert.

Cerutty loved publicity. He once appeared on a television panel show, and when he didn't like the chairman's line of questioning, challenged him to a fight. 'I'll pull your nose for you,' he declared. 'It might be the first time on television, but I'll do it.' On another occasion, bored at a garden party in Ireland held in honour of Herb Elliot, he stood on his head in the middle of the lawn. When asked why, he answered, 'I like to be different.'

Cerutty believed that women were unsuited to sport, and once said, 'Their efforts are ridiculous and sometimes lowering when compared to men.' (He would later relax this attitude after meeting Betty Cuthbert.) He nevertheless made no secret of his attraction to women, and his ardour did not fade as he grew older. At the age of seventy-seven, he developed an unlikely obsession with Germaine Greer, the feminist and author of *The Female Eunuch*. He began to collect newspaper cuttings about her, and wrote in a notebook that 'the picture of her, her face and expression, is with me most of my waking hours heightened, no doubt, by rereading her book most days'. He wrote to her, and a brief correspondence ensued. In one letter, he called her 'the greatest female mind

who has ever lived', and urged her to meet him. Greer was eventually forced to distance herself from her over-eager septuagenarian admirer.

Cerutty was sure he would live to be 100, and declared on his eightieth birthday, 'I am more alive than ever.' He died a few months later from motor neuron disease. He was survived by his second wife, Nancy, whom he married in 1958. ▣

* * *

'I hope I'll be convicted of adultery at 100.'
PERCY CERUTTY

* * *

CHAND, NEK

(b. 1924)
Creator of the Rock Garden
of Chandigarh

Nek Chand Saini was born in the small village of Barian Kalin in what is now Pakistan, where his father had a farm. During Partition in 1947, Chand's family, who were Hindu, moved to India, and Chand and his wife settled in Chandigarh, where he had secured a job as road inspector with the Public Works Department (PWD). Chandigarh was a city essentially being built from scratch as a new capital for the states of Punjab and Haryana, with much of it designed by the French architect Le Corbusier.

Like  Ferdinand Cheval, Chand had a fascination with rocks and stones. Around 1959, he began to clear a spot of ground behind the PWD stores, in a gorge near Lake Sukhna on the northern outskirts of the city. He gathered interesting looking rocks from the surrounding area, and deposited them in this spot, which was on land the government had set aside as a forest reserve. He also began to stockpile many other items he found among the villages demolished to make way for the new city — bits of broken pottery and ceramics, bottles, rags, pieces of metal, plastic dolls…

During the mid-sixties, Chand expanded the garden and began to lay down pathways. Working mostly at night, he erected the first small buildings, and statues made of rocks and reinforced concrete covered with pieces of broken crockery. It seems that he pilfered cement and other building materials from the PWD stores, and even directed road workers he was in charge of to work on it.

Fearing that he would lose his job if the garden was discovered, Chand decided to reveal his secret to M.N. Sharma, Chandigarh's chief architect, in 1969. Sharma went to see the garden, and although it was illegal, was so impressed that he agreed to keep it secret. It was not until 1973, when a group of malaria research workers stumbled onto Chand's domain, that it became generally known what he had been up to for so many years. While there was some talk of demolishing it, the authorities realised its potential and authorised Chand to keep going. They also assigned fifty workers to help him, and collection points were set up in the city so that people could donate materials for use in its construction. The city's chief commissioner, M.S. Randhawa, named it the 'Rock Garden', but Chand has been quoted as saying, 'It's a child's dream and not a garden of cold rocks… it is my poetry with rocks.'

Today the garden covers some forty acres (16.2 hectares), and features many buildings (some made to look like ruins), streams and waterfalls, and thousands of statues of humans and animals, including a fabulous array of macaque monkeys amassed on a pottery covered hillside. Thousands of people visit it every day, and it has been called the most significant Indian artistic creation since the Taj Mahal.

CHANNELL, IAN
see WIZARD OF
NEW ZEALAND

CHEN, HON-MING

(b. 1955)
Cult leader

One of the most entertaining cult leaders of recent times, Chen became famous when he predicted that God would announce the end of the world on television in 1998.

Born in Chiayi, Taiwan, Chen was a social scientist who worked for a pharmaceutical college. An atheist in his youth, he began to have visions of 'golden balls of light', and came to believe that God was sending messages to him. In 1992, he joined the Association for Research on Soul Light, which taught that individuals could increase their 'spiritual light energy' through meditation and other techniques. Chen soon left to form his own group, which went by several names including God's Salvation Church and God Saves the Earth Flying Saucer Foundation, but was usually known as Chen Tao ('Right Way').

Chen predicted that, on 11 February 1996, all the 'Gods and Buddhas' in heaven would descend on the Taiwanese village of Pei-Pu. His followers rushed there to build a 'gathering place', but the Gods and Buddhas failed to appear. Chen then decided that they should all move to the United States (despite the fact that he spoke no English). In 1997, accompanied by twenty-five followers, he settled in Garland, a suburb of Dallas, Texas (which he apparently chose because it sounded like 'Godland'). The group eventually grew to about 150.

Chen had developed a complex mythology combining elements of Buddhism, Taoism, Taiwanese folk religion, apocalyptic Christianity and UFO lore. He predicted that the next 'Great Tribulation' would begin in 1999, when China would attack Taiwan. All nations would become involved in a nuclear war that would end the world. The only survivors — about twenty per cent of the population — would be in America, where God would rescue them in flying saucers.

In his first book, *The Practical Evidence and Study of the World of God and Buddha*, Chen claimed that Jesus Christ had been reincarnated and was living in Canada. This new Jesus was six feet tall, aged about thirty, and looked like Abraham Lincoln. The group went to some lengths to locate him, even putting personal ads in Canadian newspapers, but the Canadian Jesus proved elusive. They had better luck with the reincarnation of Buddha who, Chen revealed, was already with them in the form of a ten-year-old boy named Chi-Jen Lo.

Chen's next book, the delightfully named *God's Descending on Clouds (Flying Saucers) to Save People* contained his most startling prophecies yet. At 10 a.m. on 31 March 1998, God would descend from the heavens in a flying saucer and land on the lawn of 3513 Ridgedale Drive, Garland (i.e. Chen's house). He would look exactly like Chen, speak all languages, and have the ability to walk through walls, become invisible and replicate himself endlessly. As if that wasn't enough, six days prior to this, at 12:01 a.m. on 25 March, God would appear on channel 18 on television sets across the United States, and announce his imminent arrival.

In March 1998, thirty-nine members of the Heaven's Gate cult committed suicide in California. Some feared that Chen Tao was heading down the same path. Chen called a press conference on 12 March to allay these fears, and gave reporters a tour of some of their houses.

On 24 March, Chen Tao members performed rituals in preparation for the coming miracle, with about twenty men shaving their heads. Meanwhile, police were erecting barricades around the area, and reporters and television broadcast trucks surrounded Chen's house. As midnight approached, his followers, wearing mostly white clothes and white cowboy hats, gathered in his backyard.

Midnight came, and Channel 18 showed only static.

After twenty-five minutes, Chen emerged. Speaking through an interpreter, he said, 'Even though the image doesn't show on the television, I don't have any reason to doubt the existence of the supreme being, God.' He also added, with admirable candour for a prophet, 'Because we did not see God's message on television tonight, my predictions of March 31 can be considered nonsense.'

Chen regained some of his élan over the next few days. On 31 March, police and reporters gathered for the second instalment of his prophecy. Chen told them he would give a demonstration of his divinity, and stared at the sun for a few moments, which didn't impress anyone.

He then said that anyone who wished to stone him to death or crucify him in the next ten minutes was free to do so, but there were no takers. When 10 a.m. had passed with no sign of God's spaceship, Chen declared, 'The Kingdom of God has descended and God has already changed into human beings. You yourself are God.' He also suggested that, as everyone was now God, they could ask themselves — and answer — their own spiritual questions.

Chen moved to New York, taking some of his followers with him (the remainder, their visas having expired, had to return to Taiwan). By March 1999, the group had dwindled to about thirty. Chen was now teaching that God had postponed the 1999 tribulation to give human beings time to advance spiritually, one of the signs of which would be an immunity to AIDS and cancer. He offered his services to pharmaceutical companies as a guinea pig for the development of a spiritual vaccine.

Chen fell out with some of his followers in 2002 and was forced to leave. His current whereabouts are unknown. ▣

CHERRY SISTERS, THE

Ella (1854–1934),
Lizzie (1857–1936),
Addie (1859–1942),
Effie (1867–1944)
& Jessie (1871–1903)
Vaudeville act

The Cherry Sisters were an act famed for their complete lack of talent and the derision and occasional violence they provoked in audiences. They were farm girls from Marion, Iowa, left orphans when their father died in 1888 (their mother had died earlier, while their brother Nathan mysteriously disappeared after travelling to Chicago in 1885). After struggling with the family farm for

a while, they decided to supplement their income by taking to the stage. Their first performance, a mix of songs and skits, took place in their hometown in 1893 and was given a polite reception. Their second performance, in the town of Cedar Rapids, was far more representative of their subsequent career, with the audience hurling anything that came to hand at them and the reviews scathing. 'They couldn't sing, speak or act,' reported the *Cedar Rapids Gazette.*

They spent the next few years touring the Middle West, their notoriety growing. Their performances were drowned out by hoots and catcalls, and vast quantities of eggs, fruit, tin cans and other objects were aimed at them (although it may be a myth that they used to perform behind wire meshing). Performances occasionally descended into real violence. During an appearance in Dubuque a heavy washbasin among other objects was hurled onstage, and one sister briefly appeared brandishing a shotgun, before the concert broke up and the sisters fled to their hotel, pursued by a rowdy mob.

In 1896, the impresario Oscar Hammerstein engaged the Cherry Sisters to play at his recently opened Olympia Music Hall on Broadway. Hammerstein was in a dire financial situation after a string of quality

THE CHERRY SISTERS

shows had flopped, and thought he had nothing to lose. His decision paid off as the sisters played to packed and jeering houses for six weeks. Their act, entitled 'Something Good, Something Sad', began with the sisters singing their theme song as Jessie banged out the rhythm on a bass drum.

Cherries ripe, boom-de-ay!
Cherries red, boom-de-ay!
The Cherry Sisters
Have come to stay!

There followed more songs, in-cluding Jessie's signature tune, 'Fair Columbia', which she sang draped in an American flag, and various skits and spoken word pieces, mostly of a highly religious and morally uplifting nature, for some of which the sisters donned male clothes. It culminated with a tableau in which Jessie appeared as Christ, hanging from a cross. Offstage, the sisters were just as moralistic, and during their time in New York, it was said that they refused to visit Coney Island because they did not want to see women in bathing costumes.

Newspaper critics tried to outdo

themselves writing damning reviews of the sisters. In 1898, the editor of the *Odebolt Chronicle*, Billy Hamilton, penned one which read in part:

Their long skinny arms, equipped with talons at the extremities, swung mechanically, and anon were waved frantically at the suffering audience. The mouths of their rancid features opened like caverns, and sounds like the wailing of damned souls issued therefrom.

This was reprinted in many papers, including the *Des Moines Leader*, which the sisters decided to sue for libel. They eventually lost the case, which set a precedent for the right of critics to criticise without fear of offending their subjects.

The sisters continued to tour for several more years, but retired after Jessie, the youngest of them, died suddenly from typhoid in 1903. They went back to the farm, and later ran a bakery in Cedar Rapids. In the 1920s, Effie twice ran for mayor of the town on an anti-alcohol, anti-tobacco ticket, and lost. Occasionally she and Addie took the show on the road again, but as they grew more elderly, the effect was more sad than good. The accounts of the money they had made in their heyday (including stories of their earning $1,000 a week during their New York run) were greatly exaggerated, and their last years were spent in dire poverty.

The Cherry Sisters, who remained defiantly unmarried until the end, have recently come in for something of a reappraisal as proto-feminists who took on the male-dominated theatre industry. And if they were deluded about their own talents, they were also extremely brave in facing down endless derision (and physical threats), and promoting their highly moral view of the world to audiences who didn't want to know about it.

The theatre historian Peach Pettinger has noted how much these homely, mostly middle-aged women, who appeared on stage in modest dress and without makeup, differed from the voluptuous, flirtatious women who had become staples of burlesque theatre. Certainly the outrage exhibited by their (overwhelmingly male) audiences seems to have been much more than a negative reaction to some lousy singing and acting. Ultraconservative country bumpkins they may have been, but when the curtain rose on the Cherry Sisters, they were subversives. ▣

CHEVAL, FERDINAND
(1836–1924)
Builder of the Palais Idéal

In 1879, a French postman named Ferdinand Cheval was on his mail route when he stumbled on a stone. Looking down, he saw it was an oddly shaped and particularly beautiful stone. He put it in his pocket and took it home. Returning to the area the following day, he found more of these amazing stones lying around. After that, he collected stones every day. At first he carried them home in his pockets, then (after his wife complained about having to constantly mend his pockets) in baskets, and finally in a wheelbarrow. As he went along his mail route during the day, he marked interesting stones, and returned for them that night. He began to forego sleep, devoting all his time to stone gathering.

Cheval lived in the small town of Hauterives in the Drone region of southeast France. It is an area that was once under the sea, and is particularly rich in fossils and unusual formations of limestone. Cheval's neighbours, seeing his obsessive stockpiling of stones, thought he had gone mad. Then in 1888, after retiring from the post office, he began to build with them. He said that, years before, he had dreamed of building a fabulous palace, filled with exquisite gardens, grottoes and sculptures. Stumbling on those oddly shaped rocks had re-awakened that dream. 'Since Nature provided me with sculptures,' he had said to himself, 'I shall become an architect and a mason.'

Cheval spent some thirty-three years building his 'Ideal Palace'. He often worked through the night with a candle attached to his hat. The result of his labours is an extraordinary walled structure of lime, cement and wire. Three giant, elongated figures dominate the east façade, supporting a tower from which sculptures of palm trees sprout. The west façade features miniature versions of various religious temples, including a mosque (which has a sign over the door saying 'Entrance to an imaginary place'). Inside the walls, the palace is a tangle of different architectural styles (some of Cheval's own invention), incorporating columns, grottoes, tunnels, spires, gardens and numerous statues and carvings of animals, human beings and gods. There is detail everywhere you look — faces peeping from openings, rocks carved into flowing lines, and hundreds of chiselled inscriptions and snatches of poetry.

In the evening after dark
When man is resting
I work on my palace
No one will ever know
How hard it was.

Cheval had little formal education. Prior to his employment as a postman, he had been a baker, and he had no previous experience in building. His palace was constructed without plans — Cheval simply started it one day and it grew from there. Because some of the structures show an Arabian influence, there is speculation that he spent some time in Algiers, but there is no proof of this.

Cheval had originally intended that he and his wife would be buried in the palace, and dug two deep pits in which he placed stone coffins. He was forced to abandon this plan, possibly because civic authorities objected, and instead built himself an elaborate tomb in the local cemetery. He completed the palace to his satisfaction in 1922, then set to work writing his autobiography. He finished it in 1924, and died two days later.

After initially ridiculing the palace's creator, the people of Hauterives soon realised its potential as a tourist attraction. It was declared a national monument in 1963, and is today open to the public. One of the objects on display is Cheval's wheelbarrow, which bears the inscription, 'My partner in pain.' ▣

CHIDLEY, WILLIAM JAMES

(1860?–1916)
Sex reformer

Abandoned as a baby, Chidley was one of five children adopted by

British immigrants to Australia, John James Chidley and his wife Maria, who lived in Melbourne. Chidley Snr. was at various times a toy shop owner, publisher and photographer. A strict vegetarian, he was also an inventor, and during the 1870s built a flying machine from imported Chinese bamboo which, alas, failed to fly.

Chidley, who was largely self-educated, worked as an itinerant photographer and portrait artist during the early 1880s, then joined a travelling repertory company based in Adelaide. Here he met an actress named Ada, who was estranged from her husband, a violent criminal. Although they never married, Chidley and Ada lived together on and off for the next few years.

Both of them drank heavily, and the relationship was a turbulent one. (After their final separation in 1893, she gave birth to a boy Chidley believed was his son.)

Around 1885, Chidley faced a crisis when he was diagnosed with tuberculosis. He cured himself — or at least he believed he had — by switching to a diet of fruit and nuts, and abstaining from sex. Chidley had always been confused and guilt-ridden about sexual matters, as he made clear in his autobiography, *The Confessions of William James Chidley* (which was not published until 1977). A pivotal event occurred

WILLIAM JAMES CHIDLEY

around this time when he was lying in bed with Ada one night. The couple had not intended to have intercourse, but Chidley realised that his un-erect penis had somehow found its way into Ada's vagina. This curious event, never repeated, assumed a monumental significance in Chidley's mind. He had always had a nagging feeling that the ills of humanity were linked to sex, and expounded his unique solution to the problem in an early version of his pamphlet, *The Answer*.

The old theory I wish to explode is that an erection is necessary for coition. The new theory I wish to introduce is that Natural coition takes place by means of the UN-ERECT penis of the male being first drawn by suction or pressure of air into the erect and distended vagina of the female; that we have fallen into our present mode of coition through TAMPERING ignorance, and crude first theory; that our present unnatural mode of coition is the cause of the vanity, crime, disease, lust, misery, madness, deformity, and degeneracy generally of the Human race.

In his autobiography, Chidley recalled Ada's reaction to this new theory — 'What, do you mean that what people have been doing for thousands of years — is unnatural? You have discovered that?' His friends laughed at him, but Chidley

was now a man on a mission, and told everyone who would listen about his discovery. This caused him few problems until he published the first version of *The Answer* in 1911. He was arrested several times by the police in Melbourne, who also put pressure on booksellers who were stocking the pamphlet. This prompted him to move to Sydney in 1912, but he found the police there even less tolerant.

Chidley's recipe for saving humanity was threefold: vegetarianism, natural coition and dress reform. Nudity was the ideal, but if clothing must be worn it should be as light as possible. Chidley had now adopted his famous outfit of a Roman-style tunic of white silk, under which he wore cotton underpants. Many found this costume indecent, although he was never prosecuted for it. He was prosecuted — repeatedly — for talking about sex in public (never mind the fact that adopting his ideas would virtually guarantee an end to sex). When magistrates, usually more tolerant than the police, kept letting him off with small fines (which were often paid by his supporters), the authorities decided on a different strategy. In August 1912, after being lured to Darlinghurst Gaol on a pretext, Chidley was detained, charged with insanity and sent to Callan Park mental asylum. To the credit of the people of Sydney, there was a huge outcry about this. While his theory of natural coition had few takers, many found his ideas about dress eminently sensible (at a time when three-piece woolen suits were still standard garb during a sweltering Australian summer). There was a debate in the New South Wales parliament, and a few months later Chidley was quietly released on condition that he dress normally and cease to address the public. But Chidley's compassion for the people he saw around him, their faces clearly showing the results of the 'shocks' of unnatural coition, meant he could never agree to this.

The last four years of Chidley's life fell into a dismal cycle of arrest, incarceration in prison or asylum, a release engineered by his supporters, followed by another arrest. Inevitably, Chidley was worn down by it all. In September 1916, while being held in another asylum, he apparently doused his clothes with kerosene and set himself on fire. The flames were extinguished before he was too badly burned, but those who saw him towards the end say that all the spirit seemed to have gone out of him. A few months later this strange, tormented man died suddenly while talking to another inmate of Callan Park, probably of a heart attack.

'There has never been such a grave miscarriage of justice as my conviction for lunacy.'
WILLIAM JAMES CHIDLEY

CHU, FRANK

(b. 1960)
Protestor

Frank Chu, sometimes called 'the 12 Galaxies guy', has been baffling and entertaining San Francisco since the early 1990s. His dedication to protesting was recognised by the *San Francisco Bay Guardian*, which declared him the city's 'Best Protestor' in 2000.

That no one can quite work out what he is protesting about has only added to his fame.

Chu, who lives in Oakland, can be seen on the streets of San Francisco almost every day, bearing one of his trademark signs. His protests, at least in the early years, were chiefly directed at President Clinton whom he believes is, like other presidents, under the control of the '12 galaxies'. In most accounts, Chu's major grievance is said to be that he and his family were secretly filmed for a television show, 'The Richest Family', and he is demanding payment for it. Chu's signs

WHITESTONE

TUCKROVILLIONS OF POPULATIONS

BBC:WATROSTRENIKOL NETCASTS

VICRODRENICAL

CENSORSHIP CIRCUMSTANTIVE

SATROCRENIKUL

FRANK CHU

usually feature six or seven rows of neat lettering in fluorescent colours on a black background. The early signs, which always included the phrase '12 Galaxies', usually called for Clinton's impeachment, e.g.

IMPEACH
CLINTON
12 Galaxies
Guiltied to a
ALTAtronic
Rocket Society

Chu changes the signs every day. They bristle with long words of Chu's own devising, and recently the number of galaxies which seem to be causing all the problems has grown exponentially. In a photo posted on his MySpace site in 2008, Chu holds a sign proclaiming:

GOUGH
9,569,000,000 GALAXIES
ABC: KUTRODRENIAL
BROADCASTS
RETROWDRENIAL
PRELIMINARY
RENOVATIONS
BRUTCHOSTENIAL

Little is known about Chu's early life, although there was an unfortu-nate incident in 1985 where he re-portedly held eleven members of his family hostage in his home and fired a gun at a police officer. This belies the more peaceful image he has as a protestor. While he has been known to rant, he is always polite to people who speak to him, and many San Franciscans have questioned him about his beliefs, though few have come away any the wiser. (Asked to explain the 12 Galaxies, he replied, 'Well, those might have been some Quintronic populations that were kept top-secret behind closed doors in Washington.') Chu also actively seeks out television news crews, eager to get his message on the air.

Chu inspired the 12 Galaxies Bar in San Francisco, where he regularly expounds his beliefs in spoken word performances (likened by some who have heard them to beat poetry). Like ☞ Emperor Norton a century and a half earlier, he is often given free meals in the city's restaurants. Lately he has been supplementing his income (which derives mainly from social security payments) by selling advertising space on the back of his signs. ▣

CINDRIC, JOSEPH

(1906–1994)
The 'Trolleyman'

The Trolleyman, as he was usually

known, was one of the most familiar sights on the streets of Sydney for decades. A hunched, gnomic, taciturn figure with a red motorcyclist's helmet planted on his head, he could usually be seen in the area surrounding Hyde Park, pushing before him a battered metal cart containing all his wordly possessions, like a slow but unstoppable force of nature. The subject of what might be in the cart was the cause of much speculation among Sydneysiders, and once, when the question was put to him by a reporter from the *Daily Mirror*, he replied, 'Things to fix it with.'

After his death, it was revealed that he was Joseph Cindric, a Croatian (some accounts say Polish) World War II refugee and former shipwright who had lived to the ripe old age of eighty-eight. And in his cart? His shipwright's tools, and letters from his lost son. His final cart (he had several over the years) is now in the collection of the Powerhouse Museum, and had pride of place in the 'Sydney Eccentrics' exhibition held at the New South Wales State Library in 1999. ◙

COATES, ROBERT 'ROMEO'
(1772–1848)
Actor

Coates, born in Antigua in the West Indies, was the son of a wealthy sugar planter and merchant. As a young man, he developed two passions. The first was for fancy clothes, often decorated with diamonds. The second was for acting, for which he had no talent whatsoever, and in particular the role of Romeo. His two passions were brought together in his costume for Romeo, which he never travelled without.

After his father's death in 1807, Coates inherited his fortune and moved to England. He settled in Bath, where he was encountered breakfasting in a hotel by a Mr. Pryce Gordon. Hearing Coates reciting Shakespeare 'with a tone and gesture striking to both the eye and ear', Gordon offered to introduce him to a local theatre manager. A performance of *Romeo and Juliet* was arranged for 9 February 1810, and English audiences were treated to their first glimpse of Coates, resplendent in a spangled blue cloak, a hat with white feathers, and diamonds on his shoe buckles. By his later standards, it was a subdued performance, with a minimum of catcalls and orange peels thrown. It was only terminated in the fifth act when Coates attempted to open Juliet's tomb with a crowbar, causing an uproar.

Coates now took his unique style on the road, appearing in

JOSEPH CINDRIC

Brighton and other towns. He billed himself as 'the Amateur of Fashion' or 'the Philanthropic Amateur' (the latter because his performances were often for charity). During one performance, having delivered Romeo's exit line 'Oh let us hence, I stand on sudden haste', Coates failed to exit, and began crawling about on all fours instead. When the prompter called for him to get off, he replied that he was looking for a lost diamond buckle.

'In the school of Coates,' wrote a reviewer in *The Scourge*, 'dignity is denoted by strutting across the stage in strides two yards long; agony by a furious stamp of the feet at the end of every second line.' Reviews like this made London's theatregoers eager to see the new prodigy.

'Romeo' Coates made a suitably splashy arrival in London, travelling in a chariot, or curricle, in the shape of an enormous scallop (earning him another nickname, 'Curricle' Coates). His London debut was in the role of the seducer, Lothario, in Nicholas Rowe's *The Fair Penitent* at the Haymarket Theatre. The audience included dukes, earls and various other species of nobility, and thousands had to be turned away on the night. Coates' costume this time was of silvery white silk encrusted with diamonds, and his performance was everything that could have been expected.

Alas, the play had to be halted halfway through due to persistent crowing from the audience (yet another of the actor's nicknames was 'Cockadoodle' Coates, thanks to his crest, which showed a rooster with outspread wings and the motto 'While I live, I'll Crow'). The reviews next day were predictably scathing. Coates replied with a rather dignified letter to the *Morning Herald*.

In regard to the innumerable attacks that have been made upon my lineaments and person in the public prints, I have only to observe, that as I was fashioned by the Creator, independent of my will, I cannot be responsible for that which is out of my control.

Despite, or because of, this debacle, Coates continued to tread the boards for several years. He was known for changing the words of plays at will, interrupting the action to converse with friends in the audience, threatening hecklers with his sword (if the role had demanded one), and adopting various improbable stances designed to show off the admirable symmetry of his legs. Many actors refused to perform with him because of the ever-present threat of violence from the audience, while those who did often forgot their lines, adding to the merriment. Audiences that allowed a play to continue to its end might be treated to one of Coates' specialities — his death scene. He would begin by polishing a spot on the stage with his handkerchief, carefully lay the handkerchief out, place his hat on it, then, after some final histrionics, fall down dead (sometimes on the hapless Juliet). On at least one occasion, his death drew so much applause that Coates gave an encore.

For all the absurdity of his performances, contemporary accounts suggest Coates took his art seriously. His reverence for Shakespeare was apparently genuine, too (as much as he liked to 'improve' on the Bard's lines). When visiting Shakespeare's birthplace in Stratford-upon-Avon, Coates exclaimed to his companion, 'The Pride of Nature has been in this room! I must kneel. Leave me! I don't like people to see me cry.'

Coates gave few performances after 1815. He seems to have been worn down by the relentless ridicule, while a slave revolt in the West Indies severely reduced his income and ability to mix with high society. He married in 1823 and lived in France for a while, but later returned to London. At the age of seventy-five, while running back to a theatre for some opera glasses he had left behind, he was hit by a carriage and killed.

COIT, LILLIE HITCHCOCK

(1842–1929)
'Firebelle Lil'

Lillie was the only child of Charles Hitchcock, a U.S. army doctor, and his wife Martha. Born in West Point, she grew up among soldiers and became a feisty and free-spirited tomboy. When she was eight-years-old the family moved from West Point to San Francisco. Lillie went fishing with the local boys and helped them catch rats. She also developed a fascination with fires and firefighters, and began to tag along with fire engines as they made their way to burning buildings.

Lillie was an intelligent girl with an aptitude for languages and mathematics, and grew into, as one contemporary put it, 'the most dashing belle San Francisco ever knew, with her gay spirits and spectacular independence'. When the Civil War broke out, Lillie and her mother, who hailed from Virginia and had Confederate sympathies, were forced to leave the city. They went to Paris, where they became regulars

at the court of Princess Eugénie, and Lillie was given the task of translating documents sent to France by the Confederate government.

After two years, they returned to San Francisco, and Lillie resumed her firefighting activities. Her parents, who were now hoping to marry her off to a suitable husband, did all they could to deter her, but eventually admitted defeat. In October 1863, Lillie was made an honorary member of Knickerbocker Engine Company No. 5. She wore her gold No. 5 badge at all times, and signed her name 'Lillie Hitchcock 5'. (Later, when she married, she became 'Lillie Hitchcock Coit 5'.) After big fires, she liked to treat her beloved firemen to meals in fancy restaurants, and during parades, could be seen riding on top of Engine No. 5, a fire helmet on her head, acknowledging the cheers of the crowd. San Francisco had embraced her as one of its many characters.

Despite being a member of the city's social elite, Lillie was the opposite of snobbish and entirely unconstrained by expectations of feminine behaviour. She smoked cigars and wore trousers, and was said to dress as a man so she could sneak into gambling dens, which were forbidden to women. Her husband, the handsome and

wealthy Howard Coit, whom she married in 1868, tried to curb some of her excesses, with little success. When he objected to her dying her naturally dark hair blonde, she shaved her head and wore a succession of wigs, alternating between black, blonde and red. She eventually proved too much for Coit and they separated, but remained on good terms. Lillie went to live on an estate in Napa Valley which her father had paid for.

Coit died in 1885, leaving Lillie $250,000. She returned to San Francisco and established herself in a suite in the Palace Hotel. She had stopped chasing after fire engines by now, although she continued to take an interest in the welfare of firemen, visiting them when they were ill and sending wreathes to their funerals. Otherwise, her lifestyle remained as unconventional as ever. One day, wanting to see a boxing match (another pastime forbidden to women), she arranged for one to be held in her hotel suite. Lillie watched it from a chair planted on a table. After several rounds, the referee asked her if she wanted the fight stopped, but she said no, she was keen to see a knockout.

In 1904, a tragic event forced Lillie to leave San Francisco again. She was having tea in her sitting room with a friend, Major McClurg, when an employee and distant cousin, Andrew Garnett, who had become deranged, burst in and shot McClurg. He almost shot Lillie, too, but she talked him out of it. McClung died the following day, and Garnett was put into an asylum. A traumatised Lillie fled to Europe, and did not return until after Garnett's death in 1924.

Lillie, who was now eighty-two, had found in San Francisco a city willing to indulge her foibles. Wishing to repay the debt, she made inquiries about buying Telegraph Hill and presenting it to the city, but found that others had already done this. Shortly afterwards, she suffered a cerebral haemorrhage which left her paralysed and unable to speak. She died four years later, and was buried wearing her No. 5 badge. In her will, she left a third of her fortune 'to be expended in an appropriate manner for the purpose of adding to the beauty of the city which I have always loved'. After much debate, Coit Tower was erected on Telegraph Hill in her memory. ▨

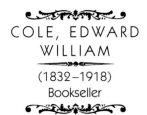

COLE, EDWARD WILLIAM
(1832–1918)
Bookseller

Cole was a bookseller who had no equal in Australia, and possibly the world. The son of a labourer, he was born in Kent, England, and after a stint in South Africa, arrived in Australia in 1852 to make his fortune in the goldfields of Victoria. He wasn't cut out to be a miner, though, and instead made a living selling lemonade. Later, he moved to Melbourne where he had a pie stall.

Cole had received little education as a child, but read voraciously in the public library. He was very interested in religion, and dreamed of synthesising all the best features of the world's religions into one universal faith. He planned to write a series of books on the subject, beginning with *The Real Place in History of Jesus and Paul*. Finding no publisher in Melbourne or Sydney willing to publish it, he printed part of the text as a pamphlet himself and sold it door-to-door. This got him interested in the business of book selling, and he opened a secondhand bookstall in Melbourne's Eastern Market in 1865. His business soon expanded, mainly due to his flair for advertising. He eventually gained the lease on the entire market, and opened his first book arcade in Bourke Street.

Advertising had been such a boon for his business that Cole, who was very shy, decided he would use it to find a wife. On 3 July 1875, the following appeared on the front page of *The Herald*.

*A GOOD WIFE WANTED
TWENTY POUNDS REWARD
POSITIVELY BONA FIDE
I, EDWARD WILLIAM COLE
of the
BOOK ARCADE
BOURKE-STREET
wish to obtain a person for a wife with the
following characteristics:-
SHE MUST BE A SPINSTER
of thirty-five or six years of age, good
tempered, intelligent, honest, truthful,
sober, chaste, cleanly, neat, but not
extravagant or absurdly dressy…*

The ad continued down the page, listing further qualities Cole was seeking. Reading the replies he received, Cole found only one, from Miss Eliza Jordan, that seemed serious. He met her, married her, and they had six children and a long and happy life together.

In 1883, Cole opened a new, much grander book arcade in Bourke Street, which became one of the wonders of Australia. The 'Palace of Intellect' as he called it, was three storeys high, and grew to be 600 feet (183 m) deep. It featured an enormous rainbow on its façade, and beneath this two little mechanical men dressed as sailors turned a series of boards featuring advertisements and Cole's philosophical

mottoes. Inside, the galleries were supported by 140 brass pillars, and the interior was decorated with mirrors and pictures. The roof was of arched glass, and the upper gallery, where books would have faded from the sun, housed a large collection of china and household ornaments. Among the arcade's attractions were a cage full of live monkeys, funfair-style trick mirrors, and a mechanical hen which dispensed 'golden eggs' (made of tin and containing toys or sweets), while a band played every afternoon. It may not have contained two million books, as Cole claimed, but it was certainly the largest bookshop in the world. No one was ever pressured to buy a book, however. Indeed, people could spend all day sitting in the chairs provided, reading without buying if they wished to, while a blind eye was generally turned to book thefts (Cole reasoned that he made up for these losses with the sales of crockery upstairs). This easygoing philosophy generated enormous public goodwill. Cole opened bookshops in other cities and his business thrived, even during the depression that hit Australia in the 1890s.

Like many Victorians, Cole kept scrapbooks, and from them assembled a number of books, most famously *Cole's Funny Picture Book*, which first appeared in 1879. A collection of cartoons, riddles, jokes and puzzles intended mainly (but not exclusively) for children, it was hugely popular for decades. Its most famous image is probably 'Coles Patent Whipping Machine', a steam-driven affair featuring a revolving drum equipped with numerous canes, capable of whipping four naughty schoolboys at a time.

Cole continued to publish pamphlets on diverse subjects. He despised racism, pointing out that all human beings were ultimately related, and was an early opponent of the 'White Australia' immigration policy which existed at the time. He also believed that dark skins were caused by tropical climates, and if black people moved to temperate climates they would grow pale. At one point, the Book Arcade actually employed a 'Black Man Who Turned White'. He was a Portuguese named Samuel Gabriel whose skin had become white over the years, for unknown reasons. He worked as a turnstile attendant, and Cole placed a sign next to him urging his customers to question Gabriel, then write down what they thought his nationality might be in a book provided. He later published the list in a newspaper, gleefully noting that no one had guessed the truth. Cole's anti-racism brought him attention in Japan. He was invited to visit the country and, accompanied by his wife and two of his daughters, spent six months there in 1903.

Cole retired at the age of eighty, but continued to produce quirky books. After his death, his successors displayed little of his business acumen, and Cole's Book Arcade closed its doors less than ten years later. ▣

COLLIN, RODNEY
(1909–1956)
Mystic

Collin is a minor figure in the labyrinthine history of twentieth century occultism, but an intriguing one. He began as a disciple of the Russian esoteric philosopher P.D. Ouspensky, who was in turn a disciple of ☞ G.I. Gurdjieff. Ouspensky spent the last year of his life in England where he had a house in Lyne, Surrey. Collin worshipped him, believing him to be the most spiritually advanced person in the world. When Ouspensky died in 1947, Collin locked himself in the room where he had died and refused all offers of food and drink. He emerged six days later, apparently believing that his teacher's spirit had entered him.

Ouspensky's group split into factions after his death, and Collin and his wife Janet moved to Mexico where they set up a community in Tlalpan near Mexico City. Collin was,

like ☞ Harry Crosby, a worshipper of the sun, and set about building the Planetarium of the Tetecala, an ambitious, semi-underground structure (never completed) with a central opening to capture the sun's ray's during the summer solstice. He had moved away from the practical system of spiritual teaching espoused by Gurdjieff and Ouspensky to a mysticism of his own devising. He believed that the world was about to enter a new stage of harmony in which he was to play a central part, and came up with a unique cosmology he set forth in *The Theory of Celestial Influence* (1952).

Collin and his wife befriended a Mexican spiritualist medium, a Catholic woman who was instrumental in his making an unexpected conversion to Catholicism. Collin's take on it was, not surprisingly, an unusual one, and he increasingly saw himself as a Christlike figure with a spectacular fate awaiting him. He was right.

In May 1952, in Cuzco, he found a crippled boy named Modesto begging on the streets. Collin made a show of publicly washing him, gave him clothes, and promised God that he would give up his body in return for Modesto being healed, then changed his mind. The following day, he climbed the bell tower of the city's cathedral, at the top of which Modesto lived, apparently intending

to tell the boy he would instead pay for an operation on his leg. There is some dispute over what happened next, but Collin either jumped or fell, plummeting to the square below, his arms outstretched in the shape of a cross.

COLLYER BROTHERS, HOMER & LANGLEY
(1881–1947) & (1885–1947)
Hoarders

The Collyers, whose name became shorthand for the obsessive accumulation of junk, began life with high prospects. Their father, Herman Collyer, was a prominent New York gynaecologist, their mother, Susie Gage Frost, a former opera singer. Both brothers studied at Columbia University. Homer specialised in law, and was admitted to the bar in 1905. Langley took a degree in chemistry and engineering, but then set his sights on a career in music. He was an accomplished piano player who performed at Carnegie Hall, and let his hair grow long.

In 1909, with Herman's practice prospering, the family moved into a lavish, four-storey brownstone terraced house at 2078 Fifth Avenue in Harlem. Herman conceived the idea of turning it into a sanatorium, and when Susie refused, he moved out.

He died in 1923, leaving his books, medical equipment, furniture and other possessions to his wife. All of it was delivered to 2078 Fifth Avenue.

During the late 1920s, Homer worked as a lawyer (his speciality was real-estate law, not admiralty law as some sources state). Susie died in 1929, and some time around 1933 Homer became blind (possibly after a stroke). He also suffered from rheumatism which eventually paralysed him. Langley took it upon himself to care for his brother, devising a diet to cure his blindness which had him eating 100 oranges a week.

In the years since the Collyers first moved there, the once prosperous white district of Harlem had suffered a steady economic decline, and many African Americans had moved in. People tried to break into the brothers' house after rumours spread that it was filled with valuables, and kids threw stones at their windows. The brothers developed a siege mentality, and Langley boarded up the windows. Homer never left the house now, and Langley only ventured out at night to go shopping. On his way back, he would pick up all sorts of things in the street and bring them back to the house. As their gas and electricity had been cut off, they relied on a kerosene heater for warmth. Langley tried to convert the engine of a Model T Ford kept in their basement into an electrical generator.

Their rooms began to fill inexorably with junk, and part of the reason for the mad accumulation seems to have been fortification. Langley opened a maze-like series of tunnels between the piles of newspapers and packing cases that towered above head height, and set booby traps. Any burglars who managed to break in would not get far.

Stories about the Collyers, or the 'ghosty men', as they were known locally, began to spread. In 1942 a *New York Herald Tribune* reporter interviewed Langley, and asked him about the piles of newspapers in the house. 'I am saving newspapers for Homer,' he replied, 'so that when he regains his sight he can catch up on the news.'

On 21 March 1947, a man phoned the police and told them that there was a dead body in 2078 Fifth Avenue. The police were unable to get into the house through the front door, and an officer eventually managed to gain entry through a second-storey window. After two hours of crawling through masses of junk, he found the emaciated body of Homer lying on the floor in a foetal position. A doctor determined that he had only

been dead for about ten hours, so he could not be the source of the stench filling the house.

The police began the daunting task of emptying the house. They found baby carriages, dress makers dummies, musical instruments including fourteen pianos and a clavichord, an X-ray machine and other medical equipment from Herman Collyer's surgery, Susie Collyer's hope chests full of linen, an enormous quantity of unused fabric, old bicycles, guns, clocks, lampshades, many gramophone records, pictures, thousands of books and innumerable newspapers and magazines. As the roof leaked badly, just about everything was damp and rotting. It was estimated that around 103 tons of rubbish was eventually removed from the house.

Nineteen days after the cleanout began, a workman came upon the decomposing and rat-chewed body of Langley, just ten feet from where his brother had been found. It seemed that he had fallen victim to one of his own booby traps and been buried in rubbish. Unable to fend for himself, Homer had died of dehydration a few days later.

Disposophobia, the fear of throwing anything away, is now also known as Collyer Brothers Syndrome. And New York fire fighters, called on to extricate someone from a rubbish-packed home, look at

each other ruefully and say, 'It's a Collyer.' ▣

COOKE, ADOLPHUS
(1792–1876)
Landowner

Cooke was the illegitimate son of Robert Cooke, who owned a large estate in County Westmeath, Ireland. After serving as a soldier in Wellington's army, he inherited his father's estate (both his legitimate half-brothers having already died). Cooke treated his tenants and employees with a mixture of kindness and military style discipline. Men starting work with him were presented with a wheelbarrow and a collection of tools, each of which had their initials on them. Anyone who mislaid any of the tools was instantly dismissed.

Most of the stories about Cooke's eccentricities involve his idiosyncratic attitude to animals. He believed that human beings were reincarnated as animals, and that a turkey cock in residence on his farm was his late father (his employees were therefore instructed to show it great deference at all times). Believing that he himself was going to return as a fox, he instructed his men to dig deep foxholes across his estate, which would provide him with the means to escape from future hunters. Not surprisingly, he tended to treat animals as human beings. Once, when he learned that one of his bullocks was drowning in a river, he ordered all the other cattle on his estate taken to the spot so they could observe it and learn not to make the same mistake.

Cooke's favourite dog, a red setter named Gusty, had an unfortunate tendency to wander off and associate with inferior dogs. Gusty was given an ultimatum — stray no more or face death by hanging. When the recalcitrant dog did stray again, Cooke ordered a trial to be held, with witnesses called and some of his tenants acting as jurors. The verdict was Guilty of Misbehaviour and Cooke, as judge, pronounced a sentence of death. No one was eager to carry out the execution, however, until a man with the unlikely name of 'the Bug Mee' volunteered. He carried Gusty away to the appointed place for the hanging, but returned with the dog still alive, explaining that, as he had put the noose around its neck, it had started to speak in some strange language. Cooke, realising that Gusty was the reincarnation of a foreigner, gave the dog a reprieve.

Cooke bred horses, but rarely bothered to have them broken in, so most just ran wild. The crows on his estate also fared well. Cooke believed them to be the best and

strongest crows in the area, and forbade his men to cut down trees and
thus deprive them of resting places.
At one point, he had the men
gathering twigs and weaving nests
for them, but the crows turned up
their beaks at such prefabricated
dwellings.

In his last years, Cooke built a
magnificent, forty-foot (twelve metre) tall marble vault, furnished with
a marble chair, table, fireplace and
bookshelves — he wanted to be interred sitting upright in front of the
fire. In the end, though, the local
vicar refused to accede to this wish,
and he was buried in the beehive-
shaped tomb where his father lay. It
may still be seen at the St. John the
Baptist church in Reynella. It gave
rise to the absurd story that Cooke
thought that he was coming back as
a bee, when of course, as we have
seen, it was actually a fox. ▣

COOMBS, FREDERICK

(fl. 1830s–1860s)
'George Washington II'

During his reign as Emperor of
the United States and Protector of
Mexico, ☞ Joshua Norton's great
rival in eccentricity in San Francisco
was Frederick — sometimes known
as Willie — Coombs. Born in New
York, he first came to public attention when he travelled throughout
the West during the 1830s, giving
lectures on phrenology, reportedly accompanied by a giant and a
dwarf, and publishing a book on the
subject in 1841. After several years
in Europe, where he failed to interest investors in his invention of a
prototype electric train, he returned
to the U.S. and began a new career
as a professional photographer.

He landed in San Francisco in
the early 1860s. According to one
version of events, so many people
told Coombs that he looked like
George Washington, possibly as a
joke, that he came to believe he was
the president. He dressed accordingly, wearing a tricorne hat and
uniform of tanned buckskin, and
issued presidential proclamations.
He took up residence in Horton
and Martin's saloon, where he could
be seen of an evening poring over
maps and documents as he re-
fought the War of Independence.

It was never going to be easy
for two such strong-willed, self-
possessed and splendidly garbed
individuals as Coombs and Joshua
Norton to get along together within
the confines of one large city. A
feud between them broke out when
Norton, no doubt resentful of the
newspaper coverage his rival had
been getting, began tearing his posters off the walls. George Washington II, as he was now known,
complained to the police, who said

they were powerless to act. He then went to the *Alta California* newspaper to complain, saying that Norton was 'jealous of my reputation with the fair sex'. (Despite being short, fat and balding, Coombs thought himself highly attractive to women, and sometimes went about the streets carrying a sign identifying himself as 'the Great Matrimonial Prospect'). After the newspaper made fun of both of them, and Norton issued a proclamation demanding that the police throw this 'seditious and turbulent fellow' into a lunatic asylum, some of the wind seems to have gone out of Coombs' sails, and he left San Francisco.

Mark Twain encountered him in New York in 1868. 'This serene old humbug still infests the eastern cities,' Twain wrote.

A year ago he was looking very seedy, but latterly his lines have fallen in pleasanter places, and he crops out occasionally in his fullest San Francisco bloom, and displays his legs on the street corners for the admiration of the ladies. In Baltimore, Philadelphia, Washington and New York, he drives a brisk trade in the sale of his own photographs at twenty-five cents apiece — especially in New York, where nothing whatever is totally unsalable, I think.

Twain noted that Coombs had once proposed to ask Congress to give him the Washington Monu-

ment. No fan of the monument ('that lumbering thing'), Twain thought that Congress should agree to his request. ▣

COPE, HENRY

(d.1806)
'The Green Man'

Cope, who came from a wealthy family, lived in Brighton, England, and could often be seen promenading in its streets wearing a splendid costume entirely of green — green pantaloons, waistcoat, frock coat, gloves and cravat. The walls of his room were painted green, his carriage, furniture and all his other possessions were the same colour, and he was said to eat nothing but green fruit and vegetables. Some said that he dyed his hair and whiskers green as well, although this is not apparent in the marvelous picture of him in the collection of the National Portrait Gallery.

One morning, Cope was seen to leap from the window of his lodging house, make his way across the street to a cliff, and jump off it, landing twenty-feet (six metres) below on the beach. It seems that he survived the fall, at least for a short time, but was afterwards confined in a straightjacket, though presumably not a green one. ▣

CORVO, BARON

see Frederick ROLFE

CRAVAN, ARTHUR

(1887–1918?)
Poet & boxer

Arthur Cravan, literary provocateur and force of nature, was born Fabian Avenarius Lloyd in Lausanne, Switzerland. His father, Otho Lloyd, was the brother of Oscar Wilde's wife Constance, making Cravan Wilde's nephew (although he sometimes claimed to be his son). He was educated in Switzerland and England, and in his teens embarked on extensive travels, visiting Germany, Italy, Australia and America. In 1909, he arrived in Paris. Six feet four inches (193 cm) tall and powerfully built, Cravan adopted the persona of a brash American with criminal intent (he boasted of having carried off some great jewel heist in Switzerland) and became a boxer, winning France's light heavyweight title by default (after his opponent failed to show up for a fight).

In 1912, Cravan began to publish a 'literary journal', *Maintenant*, which he sold from a wheelbarrow in the streets. It featured poems, essays and reviews, all written by Cravan under various pseudonyms.

Among its most notorious pieces were 'Oscar Wilde Lives!', an interview supposedly conducted thirteen years after Wilde's official death (this created a bit of a stir, and was even reported in the *New York Times*); and a review of the 1914 *L'Exposition des Independents* in which he managed to abuse most of the leading avante garde figures in Paris. For Cravan, pugilism and literature were inseparable. He would begin boxing matches by shouting out his credentials — 'Hotel thief, muleteer, snake-charmer, chauffeur, ailurophile, grandson of the Queen's chancellor, nephew of Oscar Wilde, sailor, gold prospector, poet with the shortest hair in the world.' He loved to create a stir, whether it was by dancing the tango wearing colourful outfits, or firing a revolver during a literary lecture.

Owing allegiance to no nation, he left France to avoid being drafted and, travelling with a false passport, made his way to Spain. In 1916, he had the biggest fight of his career in Barcelona, going head to head with the legendary black American boxer Jack Johnson, who knocked him out in the sixth round. The money he made from this bout enabled him to book passage on a steamer for America (one of his fellow passengers was Leon Trotsky, who recorded their meeting in his autobiography). Arriving in New York,

Cravan was adopted by the city's small clique of modernists. In April 1917, Marcel Duchamp and Francis Picabia arranged for him to give a lecture as part of the Independent Artists Exhibition. Cravan arrived for it drunk (some said Duchamp and Picabia had arranged this, too).

He began by falling forward onto the speaker's table with a loud thump, then started to take his clothes off while shouting abuse. As the mainly socialite audience began to leave, he was manhandled away by security and narrowly escaped jail. 'What a wonderful lecture,' Duchamp declared.

Shortly after this, Cravan met the poet Mina Loy. The diminutive and beautiful Loy was initially wary of the hulking, sullen, obscenity spouting Cravan, but the two eventually became inseparable. With America having joined the war, however, Cravan was again facing the draft. He fled to Newfoundland, then Mexico, where he persuaded Loy to join him. They lived among a ragbag group of American bohemians and draft-dodgers known as the 'slackers', and Cravan supported them by teaching boxing at a physical culture school, but lost his job after a disastrous bout with a local fighter. With no money to buy food, Cravan suggested suicide, but Loy remonstrated, 'How can we die when we have so much to talk about?'

They married, and Loy fell pregnant. Realising that they had to get out of Mexico, they went to Salina Cruz on the Pacific Coast. There are various versions of what happened next, but it seems that the pair had decided to go to Chile. Because of Loy's delicate condition, she would go on a passenger ship, while he would make his way in a boat. Whether Mina Loy caught the ship first, or he left in the boat as she waved him goodbye, depends on which version you choose. However it happened, Arthur Cravan was never seen again.

'I will state once and for all, I will not be civilized.'

ARTHUR CRAVAN

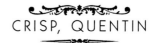

CRISP, QUENTIN

(1908 – 1999)
'The Stately Homo of England'

He was born Dennis Pratt in Surrey, one of four children of Charles Pratt, a dour solicitor, and his wife Harriet. As a child, he loved dressing up as a woman, and was picked on by other children for being a sissy. At eighteen, he moved to London to study journalism, but soon abandoned this. He met other

QUENTIN CRISP

homosexuals for the first time, and briefly became a prostitute. Having suffered all his life for his effeminate speech and manner, he had learnt that the best strategy was to exaggerate them and invoke laughter. In his early twenties, he decided that he was going to live openly as a homosexual (when sex acts between men were, of course, still illegal). He changed his name to Quentin Crisp, dyed his shoulder-length hair with henna, and wore sandals to show off his painted toenails. The effect on England was akin to an incendiary device landing in the street. Crisp faced constant abuse from strangers and was regularly beaten up.

When Britain declared war on Germany, the first thing Crisp did was stock up on henna. He was found unfit for military service on the grounds that he was 'suffering from sexual perversion', and supported himself by working as a commercial artist and artists' model. He found that people were somewhat more accepting of him during wartime, but he was nevertheless arrested at one point and charged with soliciting after two policemen saw him talking to men in the street (they were acquaintances). Crisp defended himself by asking the magistrate, 'Who could hope to solicit anyone in broad daylight in a crowded London street looking

as I do?' The case was dismissed. It was also during the war that Crisp entered the only long-term relationship of his life, living for three years with a working class man he nicknamed 'Barn Door' because of his size. The chief piece of advice Crisp gleaned from this experience was 'Never get into a narrow double bed with a wide single man.'

When the relationship ended, Crisp moved into a one-room bedsit (he could never see the point of a second room) in Chelsea, where he lived for the next thirty years. He was famously indifferent to matters of domestic hygiene, remarking, 'After the first four years the dust doesn't get any worse. It's just a question of not losing your nerve.'

After the war, when Crisp was accused of dying his hair red to hide his age, he switched to blue (thus entering his 'blue period'). He spent the fifties and early sixties living his largely solitary life, continuing to work as a model, and attempting to get a literary career off the ground with little success. Things began to turn around for him when a radio interview led to an offer from a publisher for his autobiography. *The Naked Civil Servant* appeared in 1968 and was a bestseller. When it was made into a television film in 1975, with a brilliant performance by John Hurt, Crisp became an international celebrity and gay icon. But Crisp was never going to be a representative for anyone but himself, and infuriated many gay activists with comments like 'Homosexuality is a curse and I wouldn't wish it on anyone.'

He developed a one-man show, *An Evening with Quentin Crisp*, with which he toured the world. The first half consisted of his observations on style and other matters close to his heart; in the second half he answered questions from the audience. He wrote more books, became a regular on television and acted in films, most notably *Orlando* (1992), in which he played Elizabeth I.

Crisp fell in love with New York on his first visit. He moved there permanently in 1980, at the age of seventy-two, and took up residence in a one-room flat which was soon as squalid as his Chelsea bedsit had been. His number was listed in the phone book, and he would usually go out for dinner with anyone who invited him (they were expected to pay, but would be richly recompensed with a stream of Crisp's well-honed quips and anecdotes). He continued to make headlines with his often outrageous comments, such as his assertion that AIDS did not exist, or that Princess Diana 'was trash and got what she deserved'. Fame had come so late for him that he found it difficult to refuse any offer of work ('If we

wish to be totally free from blame for our anonymity we must never say no to anything.') and he died in Manchester at the age of ninety, on the eve of another tour. ▣

'I have entered the profession of being.'
QUENTIN CRISP

CRISWELL
(1907–1982)
Psychic

Criswell was a television psychic known for his fanciful, doom-laden predictions. He also appeared in some of the films made by his friend, ☞ Edward D. Wood, Jnr., notably *Plan 9 from Outer Space*, in which he portentously declares, 'We are all interested in the future, for that is where you and I are going to spend the rest of our lives.'

Born Jeron Criswell Konig (he later changed his surname to King) in Indiana, Criswell began his television career in the early 1950s as a newsreader on a Los Angeles station, then began to host a segment called *Criswell Predicts* which brought him some local fame. 'The Amazing Criswell', as he billed himself, cut a striking figure, with his shiny tuxedo and elaborately coiffed hair complete with spit-curl. He claimed to sleep in a satin-lined coffin.

Criswell was great friends with  Mae West, who used to cook meals for him and send them over in her chauffeur-driven limousine. He predicted that she would be elected President of the United States on a pro-space flight ticket, and they would travel to the moon together, accompanied by ☞ Liberace, in 1965. His wife, a former burlesque dancer who used the stage name Halo Meadows, was an eccentric in her own right. Charles C. Coulombe, who lived in a house owned by Criswell in the 1960s, recalled, 'His wife was quite mad. Mrs. Criswell had a huge standard poodle (named "Buttercup") which she was convinced was the reincarnation of her cousin Thomas. She spent a great deal of time sunbathing — which, given her size, was not too pleasing a sight.' Mrs. Criswell used to turn up at the legendary Friday dinners her husband organised at the Brown Derby for years, frequented by Ed Wood and a host of Hollywood outsiders, and dance on the table in a bikini. Coulombe also recalled seeing her in a vacant lot one day, on all fours, eating grass.

Criswell claimed to have been making predictions since he was at school, and that they were eighty-six per cent accurate. He wrote several books, including *Criswell Predicts: From Now to the Year 2000*, which appeared in 1968. Among this volume's startling revelations:

- ❖ Fidel Castro will be assassinated (by a woman) in 1970.
- ❖ A scientist will invent an 'aphrodisiacal fragrance' that will turn many into sex maniacs between 1988 and 1989.
- ❖ London will be destroyed by a meteorite in 1988.
- ❖ Denver Colorado will be enveloped in a 'jellylike substance' in 1989.
- ❖ On Wednesday, 18 August 1999, the world will be covered by a 'jet-black rainbow' that will suck all the oxygen out of the air and kill everybody.

To give Criswell his due, some sources claim that during an appearance on *The Jack Paar Show* in March 1963, he predicted that John F. Kennedy would not seek re-election because something was going to happen to him the following November. ▣

CROSBY, HARRY
(1898–1929)
Poet & sun worshipper

The brilliant, erratic and doomed Crosby was born into one of

CRISWELL

Boston's wealthiest families. He was the son of an investment banker, Stephen Van Ransellaer Crosby, and his wife Henrietta (née Grew), and the nephew of financier John Pierpont Morgan. Henrietta was a kindly, pious woman who instilled in her son the habit of reading the Bible every day. As a student at the exclusive St. Mark's School, Crosby was an indifferent scholar and sportsman, and showed little interest in literature (other than a love for *The Rubaiyat of Omar Khayyam*). When war broke out, he was eager to take part, and on his graduation in 1916, joined the American Field Service Ambulance Corps.

Crosby and his colleagues had the task of transporting often horrifically wounded soldiers from the frontline to field hospitals. The first flowerings of his literary talent came in the hundreds of letters he sent back to his family, in which he vividly described the carnage around him. The pivotal event in Crosby's life took place on 22 November 1917, during the Second Battle of Verdun, when a shell exploded near the ambulance he was driving, obliterating it. Crosby should have been killed but escaped without a scratch. He believed it was a miracle — he had been saved by God. For the rest of his life he had no fear of death and, indeed, actively courted it.

When Crosby returned to America he enrolled at Harvard, as his father had wanted, but it was soon clear that he was not going to slot into the expected role of lawyer or banker. Having begun to drink while in France he kept it up, and his behaviour grew more reckless and impulsive. He painted his fingernails black. Worse, he fell madly in love with Polly Peabody, a married woman seven years his senior. Polly (who had the distinction of inventing a wireless brassiere while a teenager) was married to Richard Peabody, whose chief interests were drinking and watching buildings burn down (the fire department would alert him to interesting examples), and with whom she had two children. Crosby pursued her relentlessly, saying that he would commit suicide if she wouldn't marry him (although a double suicide would be acceptable as well). Richard graciously agreed to a divorce, and in the face of fierce opposition from the Peabody family, most of Crosby's relatives and Boston itself, they were married in 1922.

Crosby, Polly and her children moved to Paris, where he had taken up a position at a bank co-owned by J.P. Morgan, but soon quit. He was hardly in need of the money, owning enough stocks (courtesy of his parents) to finance a comfortable lifestyle. He and Polly (who had changed her name to Caresse) had decided to become poets.

Crosby approached his new vocation with great seriousness. He began a rigorous programme of self-education, reading widely in literature and philosophy, and was heavily influenced by French poets like Rimbaud and Baudelaire, and Wilde's A–Z of decadence, *The Picture of Dorian Gray*. Believing that madness was a shortcut to genius, his life became a constant search for new and more intense experiences. He gambled recklessly, drank heavily and smoked hashish and opium. He abandoned Christianity for his own religion, a somewhat confused but undoubtedly passionate worship of the sun. He took many lovers, a situation Caresse was forced to accept (she took lovers too, with less enthusiasm). They hosted wild parties, and attended the legendarily orgiastic Four Arts Ball in Paris every year from 1923 to 1929. (In 1926, when the ball had an Incan theme, Harry arrived coated in red ochre and wearing three dead pigeons around his neck, while Caresse, bare breasted and sporting a turquoise wig, won a prize of twenty-five bottles of champagne after being carried around the ballroom by a papier-mâché dragon propelled by art students.) At one point, Crosby fired off a telegram to his long-suffering father reading, 'PLEASE SELL $10,000 WORTH OF STOCK. WE HAVE DECIDED TO LEAD A MAD AND EXTRAVAGENT LIFE.'

Amidst all this chaos, Crosby laboured daily at his poetry. It was full of the sun and suicide, for he still thought the latter a great necessity, especially for a poet. He set a date on which he and Caresse would end their lives — 31 October 1942 — and, should it happen earlier, always carried on him instructions for how their bodies were to be dealt with after death. To get their poems into print quickly, he and Caresse published them themselves, and in 1927 founded the Black Sun Press. Under this imprint, they would go on to produce elegant volumes by modernists like Lawrence and Joyce.

Crosby's father wrote to him, 'You will be a dismal failure and a laughing stock if you take writing poetry seriously,' but he found an ally in his older cousin Walter Berry, a lawyer and man of letters who lived in Paris. When Berry died in 1927, he left Crosby the bulk of a fabulous library of 10,000 volumes. Crosby spent the rest of his life giving them away, pressing rare first editions into the hands of acquaintances, or marking them with low prices and leaving them in booksellers' stalls. He was just as generous with his money.

Crosby liked to ask his girlfriends if they would commit suicide with him. The one who said 'yes' was a free-spirited Boston socialite named Josephine Rotch, whom he met in Paris in July 1928. They embarked on an affair intense even by Crosby's standards. Josephine then returned to Boston where she married her fiancée, Harvard student Albert Bigelow, but five months later, when the Crosbys were visiting America, she was keen to resume the affair. Crosby arranged to meet her on 10 December 1929 at the studio of his friend, the painter Stanley Mortimer, on the ninth floor of the Hotel des Artistes in New York.

Crosby had an appointment to meet his mother, Caresse and J. Pierpont Morgan that evening at 5 p.m. When he failed to arrive, Mortimer was dispatched to the studio. Finding the door bolted on the inside, he had the building superintendent break it down with an axe. They found the corpses of Harry and Josephine lying on the bed facing each other. He had a bullet hole in his right temple, she had one in her left temple, and clasped in his right hand was a .25 automatic engraved with an image of the sun.

All the evidence suggests that Crosby did not intend suicide when he stepped into Mortimer's studio that afternoon (he had purchased tickets for his and Caresse's return trip to Europe just hours before). Perhaps Josephine, whose letters

to Crosby show that she bought wholeheartedly into his dream of suicide, made him an offer he couldn't refuse. It is generally assumed that he shot her, then himself, but the possibility remains that she could have shot herself and left him to deal with the consequences. Whatever happened, the forensic evidence suggested he died two hours after she did. He left no suicide note, but probably felt there was no need.

'I shall cut out my heart take it into my joined hands and walk towards the Sun without stopping until I fall down dead.'

HARRY CROSBY

CROWLEY, ALEISTER

(1875–1947)
Occultist

Crowley is a figure almost as misunderstood by his supporters as his detractors. For the latter, he is a charlatan of the highest order, the 'Wickedest Man in the World' of newspaper headlines. The excesses that provoked these headlines — his occult beliefs, bisexuality and (admittedly prodigious) drug-taking seem much less shocking today, and Crowley's followers now vastly outnumber the few he had in his lifetime. Yet, ironically, many of them seem to be attracted to the notorious newspaper image rather than the complex man Crowley actually was.

Edward Alexander Crowley was born in Warwickshire, England. He was the son of Edward Crowley, whose father made a fortune brewing beer, and his wife Emily, both of whom were members of the stern Plymouth Brethren sect. The Bible was virtually the only reading material allowed in their house, and the young Crowley read it constantly, but found himself drawn to figures like the Scarlet Woman and the Great Beast. It was Crowley's mother, who seemed to foresee exactly the sort of person he would become, who first bestowed on him the name of 'the Beast'. He idolised his father, a lay preacher, and was devastated when he died suddenly when Crowley was eleven. He underwent a crisis of faith, but instead of rejecting the tenets of Christianity, he decided to go over to Satan's side, and embraced the idea of sin. Once, to test the idea that a cat has nine lives, he caught one and killed it in nine different ways, including gassing it, stabbing it, drowning it and eventually throwing it from a window.

Crowley spent three years at Cambridge, where he changed his first name to Aleister, but failed to take a degree. Having been a keen seducer of women for several years, he discovered he was bisexual, and also developed an interest in alchemy and the occult. He briefly considered becoming a diplomat or chess player, then set his sights on poetry, and self-published several volumes including the homoerotic *White Stains* (issued under a pseudonym). In 1898 he joined the Hermetic Order of the Golden Dawn, a secret occult society founded in 1887 by William Wynn Westcott and S.L. MacGregor Mathers. He had two rooms in his London flat set up as temples for white and black magic, and installed a human skeleton in the black temple which he fed with blood in an attempt to bring it back to life.

Crowley was only active in the Golden Dawn for a couple of years. He was disliked by some of the other members, including the poet William Butler Yeats, who preventing him joining the society's inner circle, despite the support of Mathers, now living in Paris. He quit in disgust and spent the next four years travelling, visiting Mexico, America, Ceylon and India, and studied yoga and Buddhism. His other great passion was mountain climbing. With a friend, Oscar Eckenstein, he climbed mountains in Mexico, and in 1902 they made the first attempt to climb K2 in the Himalayas, the second highest peak in the world.

Returning to Britain in 1904, on a whim Crowley married Rose Kelly, the sister of a friend. After their wedding, they fell madly in love, and went on an extended honeymoon which took in Egypt. It was here that the pivotal events of Crowley's life took place. According to his own account, over three days in April, an entity named Aiwass, emissary of the Egyptian god Horus, dictated a text to him which would be published as *The Book of the Law*. Crowley was adamant that he had no part in its composition, and claimed to not understand some of it. Through Aiwass, Crowley learned that a 'New Aeon' had begun, and he was to be its prophet, while *The Book of the Law* would become the central document in his new religion of Thelema.

Its most notorious sentence, 'Do what thou Wilt shall be the whole of the Law', is often assumed to be a licence for people to do anything they want (and given Crowley's limitless self-indulgence, that's hardly surprising). But it actually means something more subtle — that people should determine what their 'True Will' or nature is, and live their lives accordingly.

In 1904, Rose gave birth to a girl Crowley named Nuit Ma Ahathoor Hecate Sappho Jezebal Lilith. The following year, he and four other mountaineers, accompanied by native porters, set out to climb Kangchenjunga, the third highest mountain on Earth and considered a tougher climb than Everest. The preparations for this had been perfunctory, Crowley trusting that his clairvoyant powers would see them through any difficulties. The expedition was soon bogged down by terrible weather, and the men were unhappy with Crowley's leadership. On 1 September, three of them announced they were abandoning the attempt, and were making their way back down the mountain when a Swiss named Alexis Pache and three porters were buried in an avalanche. Crowley, still in his tent, could hear the cries of the survivors, but did not go to help, damning him in the eyes of mountaineers forever. After this disaster, Crowley resumed his travels, taking Rose and their baby daughter on a potentially perilous journey through China. Rose and the baby were heading back to England when the latter, still not yet two, died in Rangoon from typhoid. Rose began drinking heavily after this, and Crowley eventually divorced her.

Crowley formed his own occult society, the A∴A∴, and received his first real publicity in 1910 when Mathers took him to court to

ALEISTER CROWLEY

prevent him publishing the Golden Dawn's secret rituals. He decided to capitalise on this by holding a series of theatrical performances with music entitled *The Rites of Eluesis*. Although these were fairly innocuous, Crowley was attacked in the press for blasphemy and his alleged sexual proclivities. In 1912 he was invited to join an organisation (probably) founded in Germany several years earlier, the Ordo Templii Orientis (O.T.O.), and became its leader in England, and eventually its world leader. The O.T.O.'s ultimate secret was the use of sexual magic, which Crowley had been practising for years with the aid of a succession of 'Scarlet Women' (and a few scarlet men).

Crowley spent the war years in America. He had by now frittered away most of his inheritance, mainly on producing lavish, limited editions of his books which few wanted to buy (today they are worth small fortunes).

In America, his main source of income was writing for a pro-German magazine, leading to accusations of treason. Crowley countered by saying that he made the articles so ludicrous as to be counter-productive, while it's true that he offered his services to British Intelligence, who didn't want him. In 1915, Crowley decided that his occult progress entitled him to the appellation 'Magus', and adopted the name 'To Mega Therion' (Greek for 'the Great Beast').

In 1919, Crowley met a school-teacher, Leah Hirsig, who would become his most important Scarlet Woman. (In his autobiography, *The Confessions*, he describes how she had been introduced to him by her sister. 'Without wasting time on words, I began to kiss her. It was sheer instinct. She shared it and equalled my ardour.') In the same year, Crowley engaged in sexual magic with Kate Seabrook, the wife of ☞ William Seabrook, with his approval. In 1920, Crowley and his ménage, including Hirsig, the daughter she had borne him (who soon died), and another American woman, Ninette Shumway, moved to a villa in Cefalù, Sicily. He renamed it the Abbey of Thelema, and decorated its walls with obscene and blasphemous paintings. Various disciples arrived at the Abbey over the next three years to undergo magical training, and in 1923 one of them, Raoul Loveday, died of enteritis after drinking spring water. The English newspapers were full of lurid stories about the goings-on in Cefalù, and the Sicilian authorities quickly booted him out of the Abbey.

Crowley spent his next few years wandering about the world, finding and losing more Scarlet Women, living at various times in Tunis, Paris

and Berlin. In 1929, he married a Nicaraguan woman named Maria Sanchez, but they separated after a year. He had been using all manner of drugs in his rituals for years, but had now become (to his shame) addicted to heroin and, to a lesser extent, cocaine. He was always short of money, relying on contributions from disciples around the world. Back in England in 1933, he brought a libel suit against the writer Nina Hamnett for referring to him as a black magician in her memoir *Laughing Torso*. The trial was a famously entertaining one for all involved, with Crowley having great fun in the witness box. (When asked to explain his title of 'The Beast 666', he replied that it 'only means sunlight. You can call me Little Sunshine.') He lost the suit, but never paid costs as he was declared bankrupt the following year.

Despite his fearsome reputation, Crowley seems to have been accepted during these years as an essentially harmless character. He could be seen swanning around London in sometimes outrageous costumes (he believed he could wear anything anywhere, having mastered the ability to make himself invisible). He sported the shaven-headed look seen in the famous photo of him which later popped up on the Beatles' *Sgt. Peppers* sleeve, and those who met him variously described his

skin as yellow, mud-grey or green. His breath reeked of ether, and he carried with him a heady aroma of civet, musk and ambergris which he rubbed on his body, convinced it made him irresistible to women. Crowley did indeed retain his powers of seduction, and one of his favourite gambits was to ask women if they wanted to receive the 'Serpent's Kiss'. If they said yes, he would bite them on the lip or wrist with his unusually sharp upper incisors, drawing blood.

During the war Crowley again offered his services to British intelligence, and for a while there was a plan (dreamed up by Ian Fleming of James Bond fame) to use him in an operation directed at Hitler's deputy, the occult obsessed Rudolf Hess, but this was aborted when Hess made his bizarre parachute drop into Scotland.

The self-styled 'hell of a Holy Guru' spent his final years as a frail, asthmatic old heroin addict living in a guest house in Hastings, trying to keep the sometimes unruly members of the O.T.O. around the world in line through letters. He had mellowed considerably, and was popular with the local children.

Crowley certainly had his faults — monumental egotism, selfishness and occasional cruelty to name a few — but he could also be generous and loving, and while he expended much energy separating people from their money, he genuinely believed in Magick (as he spelled it) and its importance for humanity. He was an odd character, not so much for his debaucheries (equalled if not exceeded by any number of rock stars), but for how traditional he was in many ways. Despite the fact that he wanted to overthrow Christianity, he never freed himself from the concept of sin and a childish desire to shock, which (as he eventually realised) prevented people from taking his religion of Thelema seriously. Many of his attitudes, including his misogyny and racism, were rooted in the nineteenth century, and in retrospect Thelema can be seen as yet another 'theory of everything' along the lines of theosophy, communism and psychoanalysis.

Towards the end of his life he gave a description of how a Thelemic society might work, with a bureaucracy of experts determining each individual's 'True Will'. It all sounds as naïve and impractical as the most idealistic of utopias.

> '*I have never grown out of the infantile belief that the universe was made for me to suck.*'
>
> ALEISTER CROWLEY

CURTIS, JAMES

(fl. 1820s)
Court reporter

Curtis was a court reporter for the *Times* of London, and to say that he enjoyed his job would be an understatement. He prided himself on the fact that he never missed a session at the Old Bailey (apart from those days when he had an execution to attend). What's more, he was there from the opening of proceedings until the end, and transcribed every word of every trial, even if he was not reporting it (he was a famously fast shorthand writer who wrote a book on the subject). He often befriended criminals who had been condemned to death, visited them in their cells and accompanied them to the scaffold, where he might be the last person they saw as the nooses were placed around their necks.

Curtis was an insomniac who slept only a few hours a night if at all (as an experiment, he once went 100 days without getting into bed). He was also a prodigious walker who refused to travel any other way. If he had slept, he would rise at 4 a.m. and set off for the Old Bailey, taking a circuitous route and often doubling back on his tracks so that he had walked eight miles or so by the time he reached the courts.

In 1828, England became transfixed with the case of Maria Marten, who had been murdered by her lover, William Corder, in Polstead, Suffolk. Almost a year after Maria disappeared from the village, having supposedly gone to London with Corder, her stepmother claimed to have dreamt that she was buried in a local barn (the notorious 'Red Barn'). Maria's father went to investigate and found her body. Corder was arrested in London and brought back to Suffolk for trial. Curtis, sensing the importance of the case, walked (of course) the fifty miles (eighty km) to Polstead, where he stayed for two weeks, talking to witnesses and visiting the scene of the crime.

Thousands flocked to Bury St. Edmunds for the trial, which was a suitably sensational affair. Corder was accused of stabbing, shooting and strangling Maria (he would later admit to shooting her accidentally) and at one point her head was introduced as evidence. Curtis, who had befriended the accused in his usual fashion, stood in the dock with him. (One newspaper artist mistook him for the accused, and his picture appeared on the front page, billed as William Corder. Curtis was delighted by the mistake.) Corder was found guilty and an enormous crowd gathered to watch his execution three days later. Afterwards, his body was partially skinned by the county surgeon, George Creed, and put on public display.

Curtis used the notes he had gathered to write *An Authentic and Faithful History of the Mysterious Murder of Maria Marten*, considered to be the first modern true-crime book. One very special copy of it was made by Creed, which is today one of the most popular exhibits in Moyse's Hall Museum in Bury St. Edmunds. It is bound in Corder's skin.

CUTTER, BLOODGOOD
(1817–1906)
'The Poet Lariat'

Bloodgood Haviland Cutter was a wealthy farmer and landowner who owned extensive properties in the villages of Plandome and Great Neck in New York State. He was a devout man who could often be seen walking the streets with an open Bible in his hand, urging passersby to read certain passages. He was also an inveterate poet. He would print his poems on long strips of paper, with an engraved portrait of himself at the top, which he gave away to anyone who would take them.

In 1857, 'the Long Island Farmer Poet,' as he called himself, embarked on a five-month tour of the Holy Land on the ship *Quaker City*. Fortuitously, one of his fellow passengers was Mark Twain, that great connoisseur of cranks, who recorded his experiences on the trip in his first book, *The Innocents Abroad*. Twain dubbed Cutter 'the Poet Lariat' and wrote that he 'gives copies of his verses to consuls, commanders, hotel keepers, Arabs, Dutch — to anybody, in fact, who will submit to a grievous infliction most kindly meant'. In the notebooks he kept on the voyage, Twain expanded on Cutter's character and his compulsion to write when the muse was upon him. 'Many's the time,' Cutter told him, 'I've had to leave my dinner and many's the time I've had to get up in the night when it came on me. At such time as that, I can't any more talk without rhyming than you could put fire to powder and it not go off.' Cutter, in turn, recorded his impressions of Twain.

One droll passenger there was on board,
  The passengers called him 'Mark Twain',
He'd talk and write all sort of stuff,
  In his queer way, would it explain.

Despite the fact that Twain poked fun at him in the book, Cutter never tired of telling people that he was 'the Poet Lariat', and proudly included the epithet on the title page of his self-published collec-tion, *The Long Island Farmer's Poems* (1886). It's a hefty volume of almost 500 pages, with the first 100 pages or so taken up by poems composed on the *Quaker City*. There is much along the lines of:

Gibraltar Rock soon came in sight;
  With glasses at it we did gaze;
How wonderful it seemed to be,
  Exceeding it did us amaze.

The remainder of the volume covers a wide variety of subjects, from Civil War battles to fairs and the completion of a new barn.

Whenever anyone gave Cutter a present, or did anything that pleased him, he would dash off a poem for them. He even used poetry to obtain civic improvements, calling on the directors who controlled the tollgate on Jackson Avenue to dig a well there.

We pay you twenty cents a day,
  That is enough, I really think;
When traveling on your great highway
  To have cold water as free drink.

Anyone who believes that poetry has no practical purpose would do well to read the follow-up poem.

At my request you dug a well
  For that, I will now write a spell;
And will endeavor thus to show,
  The gratitude I to you owe.

He goes on to compare the directors to Christ curing the lepers, and is thrilled that they named it Cutter's Well, calling it a monument 'Better than the pyramids of stone'.

Cutter lived in a large house at Prospect Hill, every room of which was crammed with art objects and curios brought back from his travels in Europe and Asia — oil paintings, statues, clocks, glassware — mixed in with broken furniture and other rubbish, and all in glorious disarray. After his death, most of his considerable estate went to the American Bible Society. ▩

DALÍ, SALVADOR

(1904–1989)
Surrealist

Dalí, who said 'the only difference between me and a madman is that I am not mad', was born in the Catalonian city of Figueres in Spain. He was the second son of a public notary, freethinker and Catalonian nationalist, Salvador Dalí Cusí, and his wife Felipa (née Ferrés). He was born nine months after the death of their first son, also named Salvador, who had died at the age of twenty-two months, and believed himself to be a reincarnation of his deceased brother. Possibly as a result of the earlier tragedy, his parents spoilt him terribly, and he threw tantrums when he didn't get his way. Each year, the family spent some of their holidays in Barcelona, where the young Dalí was hugely impressed by

☞ Gaudí's Park Güell.

He began to paint around the age of ten, developed a love for the Renaissance painters, and later fell under the spell of the Impressionists. In 1922, he arrived in Madrid to study at the San Fernando School of Fine Arts, and became friends with the future film director Luis Buñuel and the charismatic poet and playwright Federico García Lorca (who would try to seduce him). Dalí had been dressing as a dandy since the age of sixteen, and cut a striking figure with shoulder-length hair and long sideburns, flowing neckties and velvet jackets, and gilded cane and pipe (which he never lit). Yet the main characteristic that his contemporaries remembered was his shyness. Dalí discovered the writings of Freud, who would become a major influence on his work. In 1926, on his first visit to Paris, he met his other great idol, Picasso.

After engineering his expulsion from the San Fernando School by refusing to take an exam, Dalí returned to Figueres where he worked on a series of paintings in which masturbation was a recurring theme (he was a compulsive, lifelong practitioner). Up to this point, he had been alternating between realistic and (under the influence of Picasso) Cubist painting styles, but was increasingly attracted to Surrealism, a movement led by the French writer André Breton.

He first publicly declared himself a surrealist in 1928, and developed his celebrated (if somewhat obscure) 'paranoiac-critical method', which he defined as 'a spontaneous method of "irrational knowledge" based on the critical and systematic objectivisation of delirious associations and interpretations'.

In 1929, he collaborated with Buñuel on the short film *Un Chien Andalou*, which features the notorious shot of a man slicing a woman's eyeball with a razor. (Dalí appears in it as one of two bemused Marist Brothers attached to grand pianos topped with rotting donkeys who are dragged across the floor by the film's protagonist.) It had a successful run in Paris, somewhat to the surprise of Buñuel and Dalí, who had expected more outrage. (They fared better with the follow-up, *L'Age d'or*, which caused a scandal and was banned.) Soon after the premiere, Dalí met and became infatuated with Gala Éluard, the sexually voracious, financially ambitious Russian-born wife of the poet Paul Éluard. If his autobiography *The Secret Life of Salvador Dalí* is to be believed, the painter adopted some unusual courtship methods, including wearing his trousers inside out, a shirt with a hole cut out to reveal one nipple, a geranium behind his ear, and a perfume he had made from fish glue,

SALVADOR DALÍ

aspic and goat manure. Whatever he did, he was successful, for Gala left Éluard for him.

In 1931, he had an exhibition in Paris which included The Persistence of Memory, the first of his paintings to include his most famous image — the soft watch. It was bought by art dealer Julien Levy and exhibited in New York, causing a stir and paving the way for Dalí's first visit there. Accompanied by Caresse Crosby, the widow of Harry Crosby, who acted as their assistant and translator, Dalí and Gala arrived in New York in November 1934. Reporters were fascinated by the artist, a one-man show mounted by Levy was a huge success, and surrealism was suddenly all the rage. The visit culminated with a party thrown by Crosby, where guests were asked to come as their favourite recurring nightmare. Dalí turned up with his head swathed in bandages and a glass case attached to his chest containing a pink bra. He made just as big a splash in England, where he had found a new and generous patron in Edward James. In the wake of the International Surrealist Exhibition held in London in 1936, he gave a celebrated lecture on the benefits of immersion in the subconscious while clad in a diving suit and helmet. (When he began to suffocate inside this, it fell to James

to frantically search for a spanner to release him.)

Dalí's earlier timidity had now vanished, and his ego was ballooning like the oversized head of 'the Great Masturbator', a figure who appears in the painting of that name and many others.

Dalí stayed out of Spain during the civil war, refusing to publicly back the Republican side as his fellow surrealists had. His relations with Breton were strained by his ambivalent attitude to Hitler, and the break between them became final in 1939. Dalí and Gala fled Paris when the Germans invaded, and made their way to the U.S., where they remained for the next eight years. On arrival, Dalí told reporters that, while he remained the only true surrealist, he was now moving towards 'classicism'. Few critics saw much difference in his paintings, although they did note he was becoming repetitive, using again and again certain motifs — crutches, ants, eggs, lobsters, empty beaches and, of course, soft watches. As well as painting, he worked on other projects, including his fanciful autobiography *The Secret Life*, and designing the dream sequence for Hitchcock's psychoanalytical thriller *Spellbound* (a short animated film he worked on with Walt Disney was eventually abandoned). He supplemented his income by doing society portraits, and was now a wealthy man. His perceived avarice (which, to be fair, was largely due to Gala, his ruthless business manager) inspired Breton to dub him 'Avida Dollars' (an anagram of Salvador Dalí). Dalí thought this was hilarious.

In 1948, Dalí and Gala returned to Spain, where he waxed lyrical about Roman Catholicism and the Franco government, to the disgust of many former colleagues. Since the first atomic bombs were dropped, he had been incorporating scientific concepts into his paintings (he called this 'nuclear mysticism') and now began to use religious imagery as well, with Gala standing in for the Virgin Mary. Other obsessions he developed during the fifties included DNA and rhino horns, and his paintings became full of optical tricks which most critics dismissed as gimmicks.

Dalí and Gala lived at Port Lligat, one of his childhood haunts where he had built a sprawling house, although they spent part of each year in Paris and New York. The insatiable Gala was still taking younger lovers into her seventies, with Dalí's consent, and in 1969 he bought her a medieval 'castle' in Púbol, where she was free to carry on her affairs in private (he took a masochistic delight in the fact that he was only allowed to visit if she gave him written permission).

Dalí also gathered around himself a coterie of young, good looking men and women, although being quite impotent now (something he associated with all great men) his sexual involvement with them was confined to voyeurism. The most colourful of them was undoubtedly the transsexual model and future disco star Amanda Lear, who had been born Alain Tapp. Dalí met her in the mid-sixties, after her sex change operation, which fascinated him (hermaphrodites were another obsession), and she was his regular companion for years.

In the 1960s, Dalí found a lucrative new source of income in selling signed reproductions of his works. By the 1970s, he was signing blank pieces of paper by the thousand, without a care for what would be printed on them. The practice eventually became a scandal which damaged the painter's reputation.

Dalí's health went into a sharp decline after 1980, and his condition was not helped by Gala giving him large doses of tranquillizers and other prescription drugs. His right arm shook so badly that painting was almost impossible, and the later works attributed to him are probably largely the work of assistants. Relations between Dalí and his muse grew strained in their final years, with Gala continuing to spend enormous sums of money on her lovers, but when she died in 1982 he fell into a deep depression. He refused to eat so that his carers were forced to insert feeding tubes in his nose, and his speech became almost incomprehensible. He reverted back to the spoilt child of his early years, making life almost impossible for his staff. In 1984, a fire broke out in his bedroom at Púbol, where he had been staying (probably started by an electrical fault after Dalí had overused the button that summoned his nurses) and he was badly burned. In 1988, he was hospitalised with heart problems. Ever the egotist, he had a television installed in his room so he could watch the reports of his impending death, and was thrilled to receive a visit from King Juan Carlos (he had become a staunch monarchist). He lingered on till the following year, though. He is buried at his Theatre-Museum in Figueres, where his first public exhibition had been held in 1919. ▣

DANCER, DANIEL
(1716–1794)
Miser

Dancer came from a long line of misers, but it was left to him to turn penny pinching into something approaching a science. When his father died in 1736, he inherited an estate which gave him a comfortable in-come of £3,000 a year. He devoted the rest of his life to not spending it.

Dancer lived in a rundown shack on a farm in Harrow Weald, Middlesex, with his sister, who served as his housekeeper and was perfectly attuned to his miserly ways. Every Sunday she cooked a piece of meat and fourteen dumplings which would feed them for the rest of the week. They must have thought all their Christmases had come at once when they chanced upon the rotting carcass of a sheep in a field one day. They dragged it back to the farm and cut it up to make mutton pies upon which they feasted for a fortnight.

Dancer hated spending money on clothes, and wore his shirts till they fell away in rags. Soap, too, was an impossible luxury. When he bathed, which was infrequently, he would go to a nearby pond and scrub himself with sand. He spent his days wandering around the countryside, on the lookout for bones, firewood and cow dung which he would stuff into his pockets. Whenever he saw an acquaintance he would cadge a pinch of snuff, deposit it in his snuffbox, and when it was full, exchange it for a candle.

Dancer was on friendly terms with his neighbour, Lady Tempest. As a treat, she once sent over one of his favourite dishes, trout cooked in claret. This put Dancer in a quandary — the dish was quite cold, yet he did not wish to waste precious wood lighting a fire to warm it. He solved the problem by putting the trout between two pewter plates and sitting on it until it was warm enough to eat.

Dancer's chief love was his dog, Bob, which he addressed as 'my child'. Yet even Bob was not immune from his master's obsession. Fearful that Bob, who had taken to chasing sheep, would catch one and Dancer would be forced to compensate its owner, he had the unfortunate animal's teeth broken. His sister fared little better. When she lay on her deathbed in 1766, Dancer refused to fetch a doctor, declaring, 'Why should I waste my money on wickedly endeavouring to counteract the will of providence? If the old girl's time has come, the nostrums of all the quacks in Christendom cannot save her — she may as well die now as in any future period.' Outside his family circle, though, Dancer was less harsh. He could be generous to his friends, and paid his servant Griffiths, whom he hired after his sister's death, well enough that he had a better standard of living than his own.

Not surprisingly, thieves were often after the famed miser's money (once a group of them suspended him by the neck until he told them where some of it could be found).

He naturally tried to outwit them by hiding money in all sorts of unlikely places. After his death, £2,500 was found inside a dunghill.

Towards the end, Lady Tempest came to visit him. She found him lying on a filthy bed, the shack where he had lived for over half a century falling down around him, wearing only a sack. 'I came into this world without a shirt,' he told her, 'and I'm determined to go out in the same manner.' By his own exacting standards, Dancer lived a full and exemplary life. ▨

DARGER, HENRY

(1892–1973)
Artist & writer

Darger, who created a vast body of work meant for his eyes alone, is perhaps the most intriguing 'outsider artist' of the twentieth century. He was the son of a German immigrant, Henry Darger Sr., a tailor who settled in Chicago, and his wife Rosa. When he was four-years-old, Rosa died giving birth to a girl (who was immediately put up for adoption). Darger's father, who was crippled, found it increasingly hard to look after him, and in 1900, he was placed in a Catholic boys' home. He was a troubled youth, occasionally violent and given to making involuntary noises and gestures. In 1905, he was

unceremoniously deposited in the Lincoln Asylum for Feeble-Minded Children, where he could easily have spent the rest of his life, but managed to escape in 1908.

Back in Chicago, he found work as a cleaner in a Catholic hospital. He was drafted into the army in 1917, but was discharged after less than a year. He lived in rented rooms, attended Catholic mass most days, and continued to work in hospitals as a cleaner or dishwasher until his retirement in 1963. As far as the external details of his life go, that's about it.

Darger's real life was the one he lived inside his own head, a fantasy life that he was driven to document in astonishing, sometimes disturbing, detail. He dated the genesis of this to around 1911. He had begun to collect clippings from newspapers, and one day realised that he could not find a certain clipping from a Chicago paper — the photo of a five-year-old girl named Elsie Paroubek, who had been abducted and strangled. Darger searched desperately for it. He prayed to God to let him find it, and went through the first of many spiritual crises when God failed to answer his prayers.

Darger's early experiences in institutions left him deeply affected by the mistreatment of children by adults. They also left him emotionally stunted and terribly naïve. Around

the time he was fretting about Elsie Paroubek's photo, he made inquiries about adopting a child (it's been suggested that he was so ignorant of sexual matters that he thought this was the only way to obtain one). He also seems to have identified Elsie with his lost sister, whom he mourned for and whose name he never knew. Whatever the reasons (and nothing about Darger is straightforward) he now embarked on a prose epic entitled *The Story of the Vivian Girls, in What is known as the Realms of the Unreal, of the Glandeco-Angelinnian War Storm, Caused by the Child Slave Rebellion*. He continued to work on it for decades, and the complete manuscript, which is typed, runs to 15,145 pages. It may be the longest piece of fiction ever produced by a human being.

In the Realms of the Unreal is set on an unnamed planet which has Earth as its moon. It tells the story of the children of the Christian country of Abbieannia, who have been enslaved by the evil, godless Glandelinians, led by one John Manley. The central characters, the Vivian girls, are seven princesses of Abbieannia who are leading figures in the rebellion. They are aided by the Blengigomeneans or Blengins, serpent-like creatures with large, colourful wings, which can assume human form. Much of the narrative is taken up with detailed descriptions

of battles, and of the apocalyptic cruelties inflicted on young girls by the Glandelinians, who strangle, burn and disembowel them by the thousand. Darger enters the action in various guises, including a general fighting on the side of the children, while Elsie Paroubek appears as Annie Aronburg, whose assassination triggered the rebellion.

Darger adopted a semi-journalistic style to describe the child slave rebellion (which overall has a distinctly Civil War flavour to it — Darger was a Civil War buff), and although his writing is full of misspellings and stylistic oddities, as you might expect, his vocabulary was amazing for a man of such limited education. While he clearly had no intention of any of it being published, he worked hard to make his storytelling effective, and there are even a few comic interludes to balance the horrors.

Darger felt compelled to provide illustrations for his epic. He couldn't draw, but developed various techniques to overcome this. He used collage extensively, and from his meagre wages paid to have images he found in newspapers and magazines photographically enlarged. Having completed a drawing using these components, he painted it with watercolours. In this way, he produced hundreds of extraordinary, often beautiful paintings, many on

sheets of paper twelve feet (3.7 m) long, which he bound into three enormous books. Undoubtedly their most unusual feature, and the subject of endless speculation by psychoanalysts and others, is that young girls in them, who are often depicted nude, usually have male genitals. This may have been due to an ignorance of anatomy, but again, no one can be sure.

In addition to all this, Darger produced another work of fiction featuring the Vivian sisters (set in a haunted house in Chicago), which runs to 10,000 pages, a weather diary (weather was another obsession), and an autobiography. The latter begins with a reasonably straightforward, 206-page account of his life, then suddenly turns into a description of a destructive tornado called 'Sweetie Pie' which runs for almost 5,000 pages.

All through the years that he was producing these works (which he apparently never showed to anyone else) Darger was working diligently at his hospital jobs. He only ever had one close friend in his life, a man named Schloeder who died in 1959.

From 1932, Darger lived in a rooming house at 851 Webster Avenue. The other lodgers thought him odd but harmless. They often heard him in his room conducting conversations with imaginary females (he would provide their voices). After being forced to retire, Darger retreated even further into his imaginary world. He roamed the streets, collecting newspapers and other rubbish which he accumulated in his room until it reached the ceiling. As a diary he kept shows, he was a spiritually tormented man in his last years, his frequent outbursts of rage against God (which he called 'tantrums') punctuated by trips to the confessional.

Darger's health declined in his last years (like his father, he became lame). In 1972, no longer able to walk, he asked to be taken to a Catholic nursing home. His landlord, Nathan Lerner, discovered his paintings and writings in his room. By an incredible stroke of good fortune, Lerner was a photographer and art educator who immediately realised their importance. When told in the nursing home that his paintings had been found, Darger simply said, 'It's too late now.'

Today, the paintings of this strange, solitary man sell for large sums. Books have been written, exhibitions held, and the meaning of his work will no doubt be debated for years to come. There is certainly scope for further investigation — *In the Realms of the Unreal* is so long that it is possible no one person will ever read it all. ▩

DAVIDSON, HAROLD
(1875–1937)
The Rector of Stiffkey

Davidson's father, Francis Davidson, was an Anglican clergyman, as were many other members of his family. For a while it looked like he would buck this trend by becoming a professional actor. He spent several years during his twenties touring with various acting companies, performing mostly in comedies, and on several occasions appeared alongside Sarah Bernhardt. He eventually gave up acting, took holy orders, and was appointed the Rector of Stiffkey, Norfolk, in 1905. He married a woman named Molly the following year.

During weekends, Davidson performed his clerical duties at Stiffkey diligently, and was very popular with most of his flock. On weekdays, though, he could generally be found in London pursuing what he saw as his higher calling — the saving of fallen (or about to fall) women. Davidson supposed, reasonably enough, that the younger and prettier the woman, the greater danger she was in, and tailored his ministry accordingly. He was particularly concerned about the young women who worked as waitresses in tea shops, and after a while was barred from entering some of them. During the 1920s, he befriended a young prostitute, Rose Ellis, and began to support her financially.

In 1930, one of Davidson's parishioners complained to the ecclesiastical authorities about his constant absences, and a detective was hired to trail the rector in London. He interviewed a large number of women, among them Rose Ellis, who made statements implicating Davidson in improper behaviour (but retracted these the following day). The story reached the press, and Davidson defended himself from the pulpit. In 1932, a church disciplinary trial was held in Westminster, which culminated with the production of a photograph apparently showing Davidson with a barely clad young girl. He was found guilty on all charges and defrocked. There are those who believe that the trial was rigged against Davidson, and that the photograph was a fake.

Davidson continued to protest his innocence, but in a typically theatrical way. He signed up with the Blackpool showman Luke Gannon, whose attractions included Daisy Winterbottom, 'the Ugliest Woman in the World,' and various men and women who were paid to sit in barrels and (supposedly) go without food for ten days or more. Davidson, in clerical garb, also appeared in a barrel, accompanied by a 'half-naked bird' (actually a budgerigar without feathers). He also became one of the 'starvers', and in 1935 was arrested and charged, rather absurdly, with attempting suicide, but was found not guilty. He later successfully sued for damages.

In 1937, Davidson was appearing in a cage with a lion named Freddie at an amusement park in Skegness. On 28 July, apparently after he tripped on Freddie's tail, the lion turned around and mauled him, tearing a wound in his neck and breaking his collarbone. He died in hospital two days later. Three-thousand mourners attended his funeral in Stiffkey, at which his widow wore white, saying she wanted it to be a celebration of his life. ▣

DAY, THOMAS
(1748–1789)
Writer & philanthropist

Day was an early British disciple of Jean-Jacques Rousseau, who believed that human beings are born in a state of natural goodness but are then corrupted by society. He was one of the earliest advocates for the abolition of slavery, and co-wrote the first literary attack on it, a poem called 'The Dying Negro'. During his lifetime, he was most famous for a children's book, *The History of Sandford and Merton*, which promoted

Rousseau's ideas about education.

When it came to finding a wife, Day put these principles into practice. Having proposed to several ladies who rejected him, he decided that the only way he could be sure of finding an ideal wife was to raise her himself. To this end, he adopted two orphan girls, aged eleven and twelve (adopting two of them doubled his chances of success). He gave them new names — Lucretia and Sabrina — and in order to remove them as far as possible from the corrupting influence of society, took them to live in Avignon, France. Day began their education with high hopes, but the girls' constant bickering drove him to distraction, and he took them back to England after a year. Lucretia, he had come to realise, was simply not intellectually equipped to be his ideal wife, and he apprenticed her to a milliner. He persevered with Sabrina for a while longer, but concluded that she was not made of stern enough stuff. (This is hardly surprising, given that his tests to determine Sabrina's strength of character included dripping candle wax on her arm and firing an unloaded — although she was not to know it — pistol at her petticoats). Ironically Sabrina went on to marry Day's friend, the lawyer James Brickman, who had collaborated with him on 'The Dying Negro', and helped organise the girls' adoption.

Day continued to champion noble if unpopular causes. He wrote pamphlets calling for improved wages and conditions for labourers, and defended the rights of the American colonists in their revolt against the British.

His quest for a wife continued, but his ideals remained an obstacle. He was a wealthy man, but to express his solidarity with the working classes he insisted on leading a very simple lifestyle. It was not until he met Esther Milnes that he found a partner who shared his principles and was willing to live by them. They married and moved to a farm in Essex, where Day wanted to set an example by treating their workers well. He insisted that he and Esther lived as they did — she even had give up her beloved harpsichord. 'We have no right to luxuries when the poor want bread,' he said. Alas, the farm's soil was poor and the enterprise failed.

Day and his wife went to live on his country estate in Surrey, where he completed the first part of *The History of Sandford and Merton* in 1883. It tells the story of Tommy Merton, the spoilt son of a slave owner in the West Indies who eventually comes to appreciate the virtues of an honest day's work. The book became enormously popular, and was regularly reprinted until the late nineteenth century.

Day's kindness extended to the animal kingdom, and it was this that killed him. He was on his way to visit his mother, riding on a horse he had attempted to break in without beating it, when it threw him on his head. Esther fell into a deep depression after his death, rarely left her bed, and died two years later. ▣

DEAMER, DULCIE
(1890–1972)
'The Queen of Bohemia'

Born in New Zealand, Deamer had a rather charmed if poor childhood, and would go on to have a rather charmed if poor life. As a young girl she took to sneaking off into the wilderness by herself, skinny dipping in the local creek and experiencing nature as a mysterious and awesome 'Presence'. At the age of seventeen she won a short story competition run by an Australian magazine with 'As It Was In The Beginning', a lusty little tale about the mating habits of cavemen. ('Then the Strong Man sprang, lion-like, and struck her down, and stifled her first scream as it was born.')

Deamer was herself conquered in the same year, although not quite so brutally, by aspiring theatrical producer Albert Goldie. She spent the next decade and a half touring the world with him and acting in his productions. She learned jazz dancing in Los Angeles, was caught up in a riot in Colombo, watched the ritual immolation, or suttee, of a twelve-year-old bride in India, and had six children along the way. As Albert's productions made little money, she began to write romantic novels with historical settings which were considered quite raunchy in their day. Her most successful book, *Revelation* (1921), a story of forbidden love between one of King Herod's dancers and a disciple of Christ, was published in America and serialised in William Randolph Hearst's newspapers, gaining a huge readership.

She landed in Sydney in 1921, minus Albert and happy to let her mother look after the children (two had died in infancy). She soon fell in the with the Noble Order of I Felici, Litterati, Conoscenti e Lunatici (the Happy, Literary, Wise and Mad), a loose group of writers, eccentrics and hangers-on led by Sam Rosa, sometime editor of the scurrilous newspaper *Truth*. Every Saturday they met in a café to drink red wine, eat exotic (for the times) dishes like spaghetti, and perform absurd rituals dreamed up by Rosa, the 'Grand Master'. Deamer's duties included kissing male members as they were initiated, dancing to jazz records and doing the splits for the edification of all. In 1923, wearing a

ELOISE BARONESS WAGNER
DE BOSQUET

ragged leopard skin and a string of dog teeth around her neck, Deamer made a well publicised appearance at the Artists' Ball, an annual and legendarily drunken event held within the staid confines of Sydney Town Hall. In 1925, she was officially crowned 'the Queen of Bohemia' in a ceremony presided over by the Order's resident wizard, a Lancastrian bricklayer and acolyte of ☞ Aleister Crowley named Frank Bennett.

Meanwhile, Deamer maintained a precarious existence as a freelance writer. She wrote chatty columns for women's magazines, poems, symbolist plays and even some serious journalism (one of her more famous exploits was visiting an abattoir — then barred to women — in the guise of a visiting male Argentine vet).

Like all good bohemians, Deamer believed that her bohemia — the bohemia of the 1920s — was the most fabulous of all. She called it 'the Golden Decade', and described it vividly in an autobiography which was published posthumously as *The Queen of Bohemia*. In it, she recalled a number of other larger-than-life, now almost forgotten characters, including Geoffrey Cumine, an impoverished poet who had 'To Let' tattooed on his forehead, signifying he would write for anyone; and Lala Fisher, another poet and exponent of incomprehensible sexual theories,

who believed that 'mating should only occur every seventh spring', and ended her days in a mental institution.

Deamer was still doing the splits well into her seventies. She spent her last years in the same nursing home as ☞ Bee Miles. ▣

DE BOSQUET, ELOISE BARONESS WAGNER
(1887?–?)
The Baroness of Floreana

The details of the flamboyant Baroness' early life are as sketchy as her ultimate fate is mysterious. She was probably born in Vienna, claimed to have been a spy during World War I, and was married at least four times, once to a Baron Wagner, and lastly to a French airforce officer named Bosquet, with whom she lived in Paris in the 1920s. In her forties, the Baroness was a buxom, bucktoothed, peroxided creature who dressed exotically and could still take pride in her powers of seduction. Around 1930, she left Bosquet for a young German, Rudolph Lorenz, who owned a gift shop in Paris.

During these years, many in Europe had become fascinated by the story of a German dentist and physician, Dr. Friedrich Ritter, and his partner Dore Strauch, who in 1929 had gone to live on the small, rocky island of Floreana, part of the Galapagos group. Ritter, a vegetarian, nudist and follower of Nietzsche, believed that by living simply and naturally a human could live to be 140. Tales of the 'Adam and Eve of the Galapagos' appeared in German newspapers, and a number of people made the journey to Floreana to have a look at them — to Ritter's annoyance. To his even greater annoyance, in 1932 a German family, Heinz and Margret Wittmer and their son Harry, came to stay.

The Baroness, having become the manager of Lorenz's shop (and quickly bankrupting it), decided that she too would make the long journey to Floreana. She arrived with Lorenz and another young lover, Thomas Philippson, bringing with her some mail for the Ritters and Wittmers which she had obviously opened and read. Arriving at the Wittmers' house, she further antagonised them by having Lorenz wash her feet in the spring they used for drinking water.

The Baroness announced that she was building a luxury hotel on Floreana, to be called Hacienda Paradiso, which would be a haven for American millionaires. The finished hotel, a one-room corrugated shack with carpets hanging on the walls, was less impressive than promised. She lived in it with her two lovers, who were clearly competing for her affections. In the end, it was Phillipson who won. Lorenz, ill with tuberculosis, was increasingly harassed and assigned menial tasks.

The Baroness treated Floreana as her personal domain. She roamed it wearing long boots and riding breeches, a revolver in her belt and riding crop in her hand, occasionally terrorising visitors to the island who displeased her. To Dr. Ritter's fury, her fame around the world soon far outstripped his own. When he and Heinz Wittmer wrote to the Governor of the Galapagos to complain about her high-handed behaviour, the Governor decided to come and see the situation for himself. He ended up granting the Baroness title to a large parcel of land, then went on holiday with her for several weeks.

One of the people who came to Floreana around this time was a Danish adventurer, Hakon Mielke. He visited the Hacienda and left a vivid picture of the Baroness and Phillipson, or 'Baby' as she called him.

Nestling with dreamy, half-closed eyes in a corner of the divan, the Baroness — quite unasked — related her romantic story, the gospel of her life, as she called it, while Baby stroked her hands and arranged the cushions behind her.

Lorenz had by now been reduced to a pathetic, ragged figure

whose screams could sometimes be heard at night as he was apparently beaten by Phillipson. In March 1934, he took refuge in the Wittmers' house. It is at this point that events on Floreana become murky. According to Margret Wittmer, the Baroness and Phillipson came to her house looking for Lorenz. When told that he wasn't there, the Baroness made a startling announcement — she said that friends of hers had arrived in a yacht, and she had decided to leave Floreana with them and travel to Tahiti. When told of this, Lorenz feared a trap, but two days later mustered the courage to go to the Hacienda. He returned to say that it had been abandoned.

The Ritters and Wittmers threw a party to celebrate the departure of their nemesis. Ritter, who seemed certain that she would never return, bought some of the property at the Hacienda from Lorenz at nominal prices. (Dore Strauch noticed that the Baroness had left behind some of her most treasured possessions, including her favourite book, *The Picture of Dorian Gray*.)

In July, Lorenz left Floreana on a boat owned by a Norwegian fisherman. It never reached its destination, and months later the bodies of the two men were found on Marchena, another Galapagos island, which has no fresh water. There was no sign of their boat. Another tragedy

followed when Dr. Ritter died, apparently after eating spoiled chicken meat. As it was clear to the other islanders that he and Dore had come to loathe each other, and the account she later wrote of his death differs markedly from Margret's, some have suspected she had a hand in it.

The biggest mystery, of course, is the fate of the Baroness and Phillipson. Nobody else saw the yacht that supposedly took them from the island, and it is inexplicable that the Baroness left her favourite possessions behind. It is also inconceivable that someone like her could have arrived anywhere else without making a splash. She and Phillipson were almost certainly murdered, but who among the odd group gathered on Floreana was responsible will probably never be known. 🔳

DE HORSEY, ADELINE

(1825–1915)
The Countess of Cardigan

Adeline had an appropriate surname, being a keen horsewoman all her life and a niece of Admiral Henry Rous, a leading authority on thoroughbred racing who was known as 'the Dictator of the Turf'. A great beauty, at the age of thirty-two she caught the eye of James Brudenell, the Earl of Cardigan, who was sixty. Cardigan,

the commander of the Light Brigade when it made its ill-fated charge, was a blustering reactionary and notorious womaniser. He had created a scandal when he separated from his first wife, Elizabeth Tollemache, in 1847. (Elizabeth had gone to live with Lord Colville. When Collville asked Cardigan if he wanted to fight a duel over her, Cardigan declined, saying that relieving him of Elizabeth had been 'the greatest service one man may render to another'.) Adeline's father naturally objected to her relationship with this ageing roué. As Cardigan passed by Adeline's house in Mayfair each day on his way to ride in Hyde Park, she would lower a piece of string weighted with a lump of coal, and he would attach a love letter to it.

Adeline soon defied her father and ran off with Cardigan, and they lived together openly for a year until his first wife died in 1859. They married a few months later. Polite society was appalled by such behaviour, and Queen Victoria refused to have Adeline at court. Not that Adeline gave a fig about polite society.

In 1868, Cardigan died from injuries he received from falling off his horse. Adeline took a second husband, a Portuguese count, the Conde de Lancastre, in 1873, yet she continued to live in the Cardigan family home of Deene in Northamptonshire. She lived extravagantly (at one

point almost bankrupting the family), and remained as outrageous as ever. She organised steeplechases through the local graveyard, and could be seen riding a bicycle through the village wearing a leopard skin cape and Cardigan's red military trousers. She was convinced that Deene was haunted by the ghost of a nun, and liked to dress up as the ghost and scare her guests.

She was fascinated by the idea of her own death, and for years kept her coffin in the ballroom. She would often lie in it and ask people how she looked.

For others who liked to have their coffins around them, see ☞ John Alington, ☞ Timothy Dexter and ☞ Jemmy Hirst. ▣

DE MONTESQUIOU, ROBERT
(1855–1921)
Dandy

The slender, elegantly dressed, impossibly effete figure of the Comte Robert de Montesquiou-Fezensac was one of the most recognisable — and caricatured — in Paris during the Belle Époque. Montesquiou, who traced his ancestry back to medieval kings, was a handsome fellow with wavy black hair and a fine moustache. He was famed for his impeccably tailored, brightly

coloured suits (the colour always chosen to match his mood).

Montesquiou wafted through the highest levels of society, usually with a throng of adoring if apparently misguided ladies in tow. He was also popular with writers (if only because he provided such good subject matter). He fancied himself a writer too, and published several volumes of Symbolist verse in small, sumptuously bound editions.

For Montesquiou, conversation was a performance art. His talk, peppered with obscure allusions and fine turns of phrase, was accompanied by florid hand gestures. His chief subject was himself, and one acquaintance dubbed him 'the world's most laborious sayer of nothing'. Having made his point, he would clap his hand to his mouth as if to suppress a shrill laugh (but probably to hide his teeth which were quite black, something else he had in common with his fellow aesthete Oscar Wilde). He boasted that he had posed for photographers 199 times, and commissioned numerous artists to paint his portrait. His vanity knew no bounds. Once, when about to take his seat at a dinner party, he remarked, 'The place of honour is where I find myself.'

During the 1890s, Montesquiou lived in a fabled suite of rooms at the top of his father's house in the Quay d'Orsay. Entered via a tapestry

lined tunnel, the rooms were decorated in faux Japanese and Arabian style. In one room, everything was a shade of red, in another, everything was grey, even the flowers (when he could find grey flowers). Two other rooms were furnished as a monk's cell and the cabin of a yacht, and the library featured a veritable forest of bonsai trees. His bed took the form of a dragon carved out of ebony, while his wardrobe had a glass front and internal lighting, the better to display his collection of 100 neckties. Every room was crammed with expensive china, mounted butterflies, exotic musical instruments, peacock feathers and all sorts of oddities. He was a keen collector of relics of the rich and famous, and among the items he acquired were the butt of a cigarette smoked by George Sand, a tear shed by Lamartine, the bullet that killed Pushkin and a bedpan used by Napoleon after the Battle of Waterloo.

Montesquiou was widely believed to be homosexual and may have had physical relationships with the composer Edmond de Polignac, and with his secretary, a South American named Gabriel Yturri (whom he was buried beside). Nevertheless, he had a brief love affair with the legendary actress Sarah Berhardt. The aftermath of this was unfortunate, however — Montesquiou is supposed to have vomited for a week.

If Montesquiou never achieved the respect he craved as a writer, he managed to insert himself into more than a few books. Among the characters said to be principally modelled on him are Des Esseintes in J.K. Huysman's novel *À rebours* (*Against Nature*), the book which became almost the bible of the aesthetes, and Baron Charlus in Marcel Proust's *À la recherche du temps perdu* (*In Search of Lost Time*).

'The place of honour is where I find myself.'
ROBERT DE MONTESQUIOU

DENSHAM, F.W.

(1870–1953)
Clergyman

In 1931, Reverend Frederick W. Densham arrived in the small, isolated and close-knit farming community of Warleggan in Cornwall, to take up the post of rector in the parish church. It seems that the townsfolk took an instant dislike to the new arrival. Densham was perceived to be authoritarian, and his ignorance of rural matters was demonstrated when he bought a litter of puppies which, the locals predicted, would soon be attacking their sheep. When these predictions proved correct, Densham tried to rectify the situation by building an eight-foot (2.4 metre) high barbed wire fence around the rectory to keep the dogs in.

By now, most of the parishioners had ceased to attend church services. Densham, in a misguided attempt to lure them back, and without telling anyone what he planned to do, painted the interior of the church bright shades of red, yellow and blue. The remnants of the congregation turned up for mass the following Sunday and were aghast. Complaints about this and other matters went to the Bishop of Truro, Walter Frere, who travelled to Warleggan to hold a conciliation meeting in 1933. This came to nothing. Henceforth, Densham would be conducting services in an empty church.

Densham professed indifference to his lack of worshippers. 'They all come to me in the end as I conduct all the funerals,' he said. 'They won't come to church on their feet but they have to come in their black carriages.' He had the barbed wire fence raised higher. He rarely left the rectory, a large building of thirteen rooms, almost entirely unfurnished and without electricity or running water. He had food and other supplies delivered fortnightly, and lived mainly on porridge. The vegetation around the rectory grew wild and impenetrable. He allowed visitors, but only if they wrote to him beforehand, and anyone who arrived even a minute later than arranged would incur his displeasure.

Denshan continued to hold services and meetings of the church council, of which he was the sole member. He took to writing the names of previous rectors on cards that he would place on the church pews and preach to (according to some accounts, he made cardboard cut-outs of them).

He dutifully filled out the church register after each service or meeting, writing comments like 'No rain, no wind, no sun, no congregation.' He did make some efforts to attract people back to his church. He once bought a slide projector and advertised a night of mythological scenes, but nobody came to see them. Advised that he should concentrate on the young, he bought sweets to hand to children, and had an elaborate playground built. But the parents of Warleggan instructed their offspring to steer well clear of the rector, and no children ever played on the swings or the merry-go-round.

The fame of the clergyman without a flock slowly spread, and at the beginning of 1953, a reporter from a regional newspaper arrived at the rectory with, rather more surprisingly, a reporter and photographer from *Life* magazine in tow. Who knows what international recognition would have meant to Warleggan and its rector? Alas, two days after the visit, Densham collapsed on the stairs on his way to his bedroom and died. It was some time before his body was discovered.

After his death, red crosses were found painted on doors inside the rectory, with each room assigned a biblical place name. He had, it seemed, attempted to transform the cold and empty building into a model of the Holy Land. A new rector took over and the building was quickly whitewashed, but traces of Densham's paintwork may still be seen. Today, the building is said to be haunted.

DERING, GEORGE
(1831–1911)
Inventor

George Edward Dering was a prolific inventor, chiefly of electrical and telegraphic devices. Some of these were on show at the Great Exhibition in London in 1851. In the following year, the Bank of England began to use a needle telegraph he had designed. Dering was an obsessive collector of books and pamphlets on electricity, leaving behind some 35,000 of them on his death. They were eventually donated to the Massachusetts Institute of Technology.

Dering had other interests, however, not the least of them being tightrope walking. He was a friend of the famed French tight-rope walker Blondin, who stayed at Dering's home, Lockelys in Welwyn, Hertfordshire, just prior to his celebrated walk across Niagara Falls in 1859. Blondin practised for this feat on a rope stretched across the nearby Mimram River (Dering had earlier suspended electrical wires over the same spot). The inventor helped out, sitting in a wheelbarrow which Blondin pushed along the tightrope (while blindfolded).

Dering worked mostly at night. He was easily distracted by noise, and the shutters of his house were kept permanently closed to block it out. Farmers were forbidden to have new-born lambs in the fields around his house, lest their bleat-ing disturb him, and he once built a section of public road at his own expense to divert traffic from his property.

During his last three decades, Dering spent most of his time away from Lockelys, only returning for a few days every Christmas to attend to business and check his mail. His whereabouts during the rest of the year were a complete mystery to his family, servants and other employ-ees. Only after his death did the

truth come to light. He had been living under an assumed name in Brighton, where he had married and had a daughter. His wife and daugh-ter, in turn, knew nothing about his life in Hertfordshire. His daughter was most surprised to learn that she had inherited Lockelys and a considerable fortune. ▣

DEXTER, TIMOTHY

(1747–1806)
'Lord Dexter'

Dexter, the ultimate self-made man, was born in Malden, Massachusetts. Having had little schooling, he was sent to work on a farm by his father, and at sixteen became apprenticed to a leather dresser. Moving to Newburyport, he married a rich widow, Elizabeth Frothingham, who was nine years his senior, in 1770. He started several businesses and invested in land. His unlikely path to fame and fortune began during the War of Independence, when he bought up a great many state bonds. As it was widely believed that these would never be redeemed, they were selling at a fraction of their face value. In 1790, when treasury secretary Alexander Hamilton persuaded the federal government to honour the debts of the states, Dexter was suddenly a very wealthy man indeed. He had two ships built

and began to trade with Europe and the West Indies.

To his contemporaries, Dexter seemed as bereft of commonsense as he was of education, and many resented his good fortune. They took great delight in suggesting to him harebrained schemes that must surely lose him money. Dexter invariably followed their advice, and somehow he always came up trumps. When he sent a shipment of bed warming pans to the West Indies, they were snapped up for use as molasses ladles. Loads of woollen mittens and Bibles to the same destination proved just as profitable. Most famously, Dexter was the man who 'sold coals to Newcastle' (his ship arrived at the city in the middle of a miners' strike). Such tales of his uncanny good luck made him a legend, although some recognised a businessman who operated instinctively. The tale of Dexter and the whalebone is probably instructive here. Apparently after a misunderstanding (some say he thought whalebone was necessary for the construction of ships, others that he had heard whales were dying out) he instructed his agents to buy all they could of it in Boston, Salem and New York. What he ended up doing, however unwittingly, was cornering the market on the stuff, which he was then able to sell at a premium to corset manufacturers eager to supply the latest fashions.

Dexter was generous with his money, and donated to many worthy causes, yet it seems fair to say the worthiest cause was himself. In 1798, he purchased a large estate in Newburyport. He built minarets topped with golden balls on the roof, and a Roman arch in front of the door. In the gardens, he erected over forty life-size painted wooden statues of presidents, generals, philosophers, goddesses, Indian chiefs, four lions and, of course, one of himself. He assumed the title of Lord Dexter, rode about in a coach emblazoned with a coat of arms of his own devising, and employed a poet laureate to sing his praises.

Wishing to impart his wisdom to the world, in 1802 Dexter published a book called *A Pickle for the Knowing Ones or Plain Truth in a Homespun Dress*. He had never learned to spell, and the book is completely free of punctuation. It begins as it means to go on:

IME the first Lord in the younited States of Americary Now of Newburyport it is the voise of the peopel and I cant Help it and so Let it goue Now as I must be Lord there will foller many more Lords pretty soune for it dont hurt A Cat Nor the mouse Nor the son Nor the water Nor the Eare…

The book proved a great hit, although some complained that the lack of punctuation made it a little hard to follow. Dexter brought out a new edition which included a page of punctuation marks so that the reader 'may peper and solt it as they plese'. *A Pickle* was often reprinted during the nineteenth century. Its flaunting of conventions and un-abashed self-glorification led Oliver Wendell Holmes to compare Dexter to Walt Whitman.

Dexter had a tomb built in his garden, and a magnificent ma-hogany coffin with silver handles that he kept in his hallway. Curious about his funeral, he staged a dress rehearsal. Three thousand people turned up to hear his eulogy and watch his coffin carried off (he was most displeased that his wife, with whom he had a strained relationship, put on an insufficient display of sorrow). Dexter died for real at the age of sixty, having spent most of his last years drunk. A believer in re-incarnation, he confidently predicted that he would return as a dragonfly, 'to see houe you goue on.' ▓

'I am the First in the East, the First in the West, and the greatest philosopher in the Western World.'
TIMOTHY DEXTER

DIOGENES

(c. 404–323 BC)
Cynic

Diogenes was the original model of a particular kind of eccentric, the individual who raises a middle finger to convention and lives life as he or she pleases, quietly — or not so qui-etly — believing others to be mad. A person who by turns annoys, appals, bewilders and inspires.

He was born in Sinope in what is now Turkey, where his father ran the town's mint. After a murky episode in which his father, or perhaps Diogenes himself, 'debased the coinage' (a phrase later used to describe Diogenes' flouting of con-vention), he fled to Athens. Here he became the best known exponent of cynicism, a school of philosophy derived from Socrates that stressed the importance of living a simple, virtuous life.

Diogenes taught that one should look to dogs as an example. They live in the present, eat what they find, sleep where they can, are free of worries and incapable of guile, and have no embarrassment about their bodily functions. (The word 'cynic' is generally supposed to have derived from the Greek 'ky-ron' for dog.) Diogenes lived just as simply and spontaneously, relishing

his own poverty. His diet consisted mainly of onions and the occasional bit of raw meat. He is said to have lived in a barrel or tub next to the temple of the Earth goddess Cybele, and to have thrown away one of his few possessions, a cup, when he saw a boy drinking water from his cupped hands. Insulted by another guest at a dinner party one night, Diogenes cocked his leg and urinated on him. He thought nothing of social conventions, and defecated and masturbated in public. On the subject of masturbation, he said, 'If only I could soothe my hunger by rubbing my belly in the same fashion.'

He is believed to have written books, though none have survived. Many anecdotes about him have come down to us, though, and some of them may even be true. Some stories have him engaged in intellectual jousting with Plato (Diogenes had no more time for abstract philosophy than a dog). In others, he gets the better of Alexander the Great. The most famous tale told of Diogenes is that he roamed the marketplace in daylight with a lamp or torch in his hand, 'looking for an honest man'. (A fruitless task.)

Towards the end of his life, Diogenes is supposed to have been captured by pirates while on a sea voyage and sold into slavery (he expressed the desire to be sold to a man who required a master). He ended up being bought by a Corinthian named Xeniades, and spent his last days tutoring Xeniades' sons. Whatever the truth of all that, he did die in Corinth (some said from holding his breath). In his honour, the Corinthians erected a fine marble statue of a dog.

DIVINE (HARRIS GLENN MILSTEAD)
(1945–1988)
Actor & singer

The outrageous actor, unlikely disco diva and heroine to drag queens everywhere was born Glenn Milstead into a conservative, Baptist family in Baltimore. An only child, he was indulged by his parents and bullied by his schoolmates. He experimented with cross-dressing and dreamed of becoming a movie star like his idol, Elizabeth Taylor. When he was twelve, the Milstead family moved to a new house just six doors away from the future underground filmmaker John Waters, perhaps the only person in the world equipped to make young Glenn's movie star dreams come true.

Waters christened him 'Divine' (a Catholic thing, the director later explained), and began to use him in his early films. It soon became ap-

parent that Divine was the most talented of the Baltimore misfits who made up Waters' acting troupe, the Dreamlanders, the one who would help him take his trash aesthetic to the world. During these years, Divine was working as a hairdresser and living a life of parties and extravagance far beyond his means, with his still-doting parents usually footing the bills.

In *Multiple Maniacs* (1970), Divine played Lady Divine, the proprietor of the Cavalcade of Perversions, a travelling show which features acts like the 'puke eater' and 'actual queers' kissing. Becoming bored, Lady Divine kills some of the show's patrons and goes on the run. After various adventures, including receiving a 'rosary job' in a church at the hands of a religious lesbian, she is raped by a giant lobster, goes completely mad and is shot down by the National Guard. *Multiple Maniacs*, which also featured the debut of another Waters discovery, ☞ Edith Massey, was a hit in Baltimore, as the earlier films had been. Word of Waters' unique sensibility was by now spreading across the country, and Divine, feeling that stardom was imminent, abandoned his hairdressing career.

Planning his next 'celluloid atrocity', Waters said to Divine one day, 'Would you eat some dogshit for real in the next film?' Divine replied, 'Sure.'

For *Pink Flamingos* (1972) Divine was given a striking new look by Van Smith, Waters' resident makeup artist and costume designer. Smith shaved the star's eyebrows and hairline back to the top of his scalp, applied enormous cartoon eyebrows and a blonde wig, and sewed his now 300-pound (136 kg) frame into a series of figure-hugging dresses, creating a character part Jayne Mansfield, part monster.

The film's plot revolves around Divine and her depraved family, who live in a trailer, and their war with baby farmers Raymond and Connie Marble for the title of filthiest people alive. It culminates with the infamous scene in which Divine spots a poodle defecating in the street, scoops the deposit up and eats it, then turns to the camera for the ultimate 'shit eating grin'. As Waters later noted, 'It's a first, and probably last, in cinema history.'

After Waters secured a distribution deal with New Line Cinema, *Pink Flamingos* became an underground hit in New York, then around the world. Divine was an instant celebrity, rubbing shoulders with the likes of Liza Minnelli and Grace Jones at Studio 54, and appearing on stage with Elton John. He starred in a number of off-

DIVINE
(HARRIS GLENN MILSTEAD)

Broadway plays including *Women Behind Bars*, then found a new and lucrative career on the gay disco circuit. Initially, his act consisted of little more than abusing the audience, but they loved it. He went on to record a number of disco singles, some of which became hits in America, Europe and Australia, including 'You Think You're a Man', which went to number sixteen in the UK, and spent much of the 1980s touring the world endlessly. Thanks to the conniving of various record industry types, he made very little money from his recordings, but continued to live extravagantly, to the despair of his British-born personal manager, Bernard Jay (who nevertheless went on to write an affectionate biography of his often infuriating charge).

Divine never considered himself to be a transvestite. He was an actor and the drag a costume. His greatest ambition was to be taken seriously as a character actor, and he almost got his wish. He was widely praised for his performances in Allan Rudolph's *Trouble in Mind* (1985), in which he played a man, and Waters' *Hairspray* (1988), and was ecstatic when he secured a role in the Fox network sitcom *Married… With Children*. The night before he was due to start filming on it, he died in his sleep from heart failure. ▣

DONNITHORNE, ELIZA

(1826–1886)
The original Miss Havisham?

Eliza Emily Donnithorne was born in India, where her father, James Donnithorne, was an East India Company judge and Master of the Mint. James was devastated by the deaths of his wife and Eliza's two sisters during an outbreak of cholera in Calcutta in 1832. After his two sons joined the army, he decided to retire and move to Australia, taking ten-year-old Eliza with him.

They arrived in 1836, and took up residence in a fine Georgian mansion, Camperdown Lodge, in what is now the innercity suburb of Newtown.

James Donnithorne prospered in Australia, investing in farms and real estate. A generous and liberal man, he was active in the New South Wales Benevolent Society and a keen fundraiser for worthy causes. When Eliza came of age, he attempted to have her married off to various suitable partners, but she was as stubborn as he was, and insisted she would only marry for love. Rejecting the suitors her father proposed, her eyes fell upon an English shipping clerk, George Cuthbertson. James, who was known for his hot temper, was completely opposed to the match, and ordered Eliza to stop seeing him. The lovers continued to meet secretly, however, often in nearby Camperdown Cemetery. James eventually relented and allowed Cuthbertson to court his daughter openly. When Cuthbertson proposed to her, James summoned the young man to his study, and made it clear that any bad behaviour on his part after their marriage would not go unpunished.

Lavish preparations were made for the wedding. When the day came, coaches lined the street in front of the Donnithornes' house, ready to take the guests to St. Stephen's church for the ceremony. A magnificent wedding feast was laid out on the long table in the dining room. Eliza, wearing a fashionable wedding dress and attended by her bridesmaids, was in her bedroom awaiting the groom's arrival. But there was no sign of Cuthbertson. As the hours went by, the guests began to quietly slip away. Eliza came downstairs, saw some of them helping themselves to the food, and shouted at them to stop. She became hysterical and was taken back to her room, where she remained for several weeks. At her request, the wedding feast was left intact and the dining room locked. Eventually it became apparent that Eliza was pregnant to Cuthbertson. After she

gave birth the baby was spirited away and given to a servant to raise so as to prevent a scandal.

Eliza remained in the house, refusing to see any of her friends. She still held out hope that her errant fiancé would appear, and at night the front door was left slightly ajar, fastened by a chain, with a candle burning just inside it. Cuthbertson never reappeared. It is not known why he abandoned Eliza, although it may be surmised that James Donnithorne was a daunting prospect as a father-in-law. (Cuthbertson reportedly ended up in India and died there in 1858.)

James Donnithorne died in 1852, and Eliza inherited most of his estate. After his death, she became even more reclusive. She had all the shutters on the windows of the house nailed up, and dismissed all but two of her servants, Sarah and Elisabeth Bailey, relying on them to conduct all her business with the outside world. She continued to wear her wedding dress, and the dining room with its uneaten feast remained locked. She was, nevertheless, as generous a soul as her father had been, and gave freely to worthy causes. Destitute people who turned up at her door rarely left empty handed.

Charles Dickens' *Great Expectations* was first serialised in 1860, and published as a book the following

year. Many in Sydney immediately assumed the character of Miss Havisham, with her faded wedding dress and mouldering wedding cake, had been modelled on Eliza. While it has never been proved, this may have been the case (Dickens certainly had contacts who could have passed the story on to him). Camperdown Lodge now became something of a tourist attraction. Local children, perhaps inevitably, thought that the permanently shuttered house was haunted, a belief no doubt encouraged by the fact that Eliza could sometimes be seen walking in its overgrown gardens late at night.

After her death, Eliza Donnithorne was buried beside her father in Camperdown Cemetery, the scene of secret trysts with her lover years before. Sydney has never quite forgotten this strange soul. In 2004, when vandals knocked over her marble headstone, breaking it in two, the story received wide coverage in the media. Donations from the public ensured that the headstone was swiftly restored. ▧

DUFF, JAMIE

(d. 1788)
'Bailie Duff'

Duff was one of the great street characters of Edinburgh during the mid-eighteenth century. Tall, scruffy, inarticulate and somewhat grotesque and Mr. Punch-like in appearance, he was often portrayed in popular prints. He first came to the attention of the public when he entered himself in a horse race at Leith, as his own horse, and proceeded along the course barefoot, whipping himself to a furious pace as he went (although, needless to say, he came last).

He was most famous, however, in his self-appointed role as a bailie (the Scottish term for a bailiff or magistrate). He adopted the dress of a bailie — cocked hat, wig and a brass (in place of gold) medal and chain around his neck — and made it his business to attend every funeral in Edinburgh, usually walking at the head of the funeral party as they made their way to the cemetery. On these occasions he would don black crape and a black cravat, and if it was a notable person's funeral, he took care to have his black hat freshly dyed. Eventually his presence at funerals came to be expected, and it became customary to pay him a shilling or half a crown for his services.

One day, Duff was drawing water from a well in the street when he was horrified to see a funeral procession which he had not heard about. Despite the fact that he was not wearing his normal funerary attire, he quickly joined the head of it — carrying the buckets he had been filling with water. Strangely, the procession did not follow any of the normal routes. It continued on its way, Duff resolutely out in front, and eventually arrived at the seaside town of Queensferry, nine miles (fifteen km) away. It was only then that Duff realised that a trick had been played on him.

Duff lived with his widowed mother and was very faithful to her. If invited to dinner by someone, he would sit at the table, but refrain from eating. At the end of the meal, he would gather up his serving and deposit it in his pockets, not making a distinction between solid and liquid food. He would then go home and present it to his mother, who was not invariably pleased to receive it.

Duff depended on the generosity of people in the street to survive, but at one point became paranoid about accepting silver coins from strangers, lest he be tricked into joining the army by taking 'the King's shilling'. This threatened to severely curtail his income. It was Duff's mother who came up with the solution — his young nephew was assigned to walk with Duff as he made his perambulations through the city, accepting coins on his behalf. ▣

EGERTON, FRANCIS

(1756–1829)
Dog lover & shoe collector

Francis Henry Egerton, the eighth Earl of Bridgewater, lived in Paris for over thirty years, and seemed to spend most of his time there proving to the French just how eccentric a British aristocrat could be. He never bothered to learn French, liked to serve his unfortunate dinner guests such British delicacies as boiled beef and potatoes, and imported foxes so that he and his companions, wearing the traditional pink jackets, could stage miniature fox hunts in his garden.

He far preferred the company of dogs to people, and kept fifteen of them in his house. He dressed them as human beings, in fashionable clothes and handmade boots. When they needed exercise, they were

driven to the Bois de Boulogne in a carriage drawn by four horses, seated comfortably in the back on silk cushions. Once there, footmen would shield them with umbrellas if it rained. Egerton's two favourite dogs, Bijou and Biche, regularly ate at his table, with napkins around their necks and footmen standing behind their chairs ready to serve them.

Egerton was as well dressed as his dogs, and had a particular obsession with shoes. He wore a pair only once, after which they were carefully stored by a valet in the order in which they had been worn. The shoes were not cleaned, so Egerton could consult them and tell from the various marks and stains on them what he was doing and what the weather was on a particular day.

Growing too old to indulge in another favourite pastime, shooting, Egerton solved the problem by stocking his garden with 300 rabbits, along with numerous pigeons and partridges with clipped wings. He would totter out to the garden, propped up by a servant, and blast two or three of them, and these would later be served at dinner.

Egerton's father had been the Bishop of Durham, and he himself had been ordained in his youth, but he showed little interest in religious matters during his lifetime. Perhaps to make amends, he left £8,000 in his voluminous will to pay for

the writing and publishing of a work 'On the Power, Wisdom and Goodness of God, as manifested in the Creation'. Eight authors were eventually engaged to accomplish this, and the resulting works were known as the 'Bridgewater Treatises'. Rationalists, of course, scorned them, dubbing them the 'Bilgewater Treatises'. ▣

EGLINTOUNE, SUSANNA (LADY)
(c.1689–1780)
Beauty

Susanna Kennedy was Edinburgh's most celebrated beauty during the early eighteenth century. Suitors pursued her, amateur poets wrote verses to her and, if the chronicles are to be believed, men fought duels over her. She spurned all their advances. Then one day she was walking in her garden when a hawk alighted on her shoulder. Attached to it were some bells bearing the name of Lord Eglintoune, and Susanna took this as an omen that she would marry him. He happened to be married to his second wife at the time, but she obligingly died soon afterwards, and Susanna, who was twenty, married Eglintoune, who was forty-nine. She bore him seven daughters — said to be almost as beautiful as their mother — fol-

lowed by three sons. The procession of mother and daughters being carried on sedan chairs to the Assembly Rooms was one of the sights of the city.

Lord Eglintoune died when Susanna was forty, and she retired to the family estate at Auchans, where she frequently entertained guests. She retained her beauty into old age, her still-youthful complexion attributed to her habit of regularly bathing her face in sow's milk. Dr. Johnson and James Boswell paid her a visit when she was eighty-five, and were captivated. 'Her figure was majestick,' wrote Boswell, 'her manners high-bred, her reading extensive, and her conversation elegant.'

Although she had a long and happy life (she died aged ninety-one) it seems that she grew disenchanted with human beings in her later years, commenting that four-legged creatures showed more gratitude. She was particularly fond of rats, which lived in great numbers behind the wainscoting of Auchans. At meal times, she would tap a panel on the wainscoting, and a dozen or so of her favourites would emerge and join her at her table where they fed on scraps. When the meal was completed, Her Ladyship would give a signal, and the rats would file dutifully back to their abode within the walls. 🔳

ELLERTON, SIMEON
(c. 1702–1799)
Stone gatherer

Ellerton lived in Durham, England, and made his living running errands for the local gentry, which often involved him walking long distances, including trips to London. Like the French postman ☞ Ferdinand Cheval, he took to picking up stones as he walked and carrying them home (in Ellerton's case, on his head). Unlike the Frenchman, he was content to build a cottage with them rather than a palace. Having finished it, he continued to carry stones on his head, saying that they made walking more comfortable. Whenever anyone asked him about it, he would reply "Tis to keep on my hat.'

Ellerton's obituaries stated that he lived to 104, but there is a record of his baptism taking place in 1702, suggesting he may have been only ninety-seven. That's still a pretty good advertisement for walking around with a stone on your head. 🔳

ELWES, JOHN
(1714–1789)
Miser

Elwes was a British Member of Parliament famed for combining extreme miserliness with great gen-

erosity of spirit. He was born John Meggott, the son of a Southwark brewer named Robert Meggott, who died when he was four. Despite the fact that Meggott left a considerable fortune to John and his mother Amy, she was said to have starved herself to death (an event which his contemporaries believed clearly presaged his own miserliness).

John Meggott's early years were typical of a well-to-do young man of the time. He was educated at Westminster School, where he studied the classics and proved himself a talented scholar (yet after leaving it, he apparently never read another book). He spent some time in Geneva, where he enjoyed gambling and the high life, met Voltaire, and gained a reputation as a horse rider. It was upon his return to England that his miserly ways set in. He had the best possible tutor in the subject in the form of his reclusive maternal uncle, Sir Harvey Elwes, who had a fortune of £250,000 but lived on less than £100 a year.

Meggott, determined to become his uncle's heir, proceeded to butter him up. Before visiting him he would stop at an inn where he changed into ragged clothes like those his uncle wore, and ate a hearty meal, thus fortifying himself for the meagre dinner that Sir Harvey invariably served.

The two men would then spend the evening sharing a single small glass of wine and railing against the extravagance of other people, before retiring to bed (without wasting money on the lighting of a candle). Sir Harvey was thrilled to find a kindred tightfisted spirit within the family, and in 1863 Meggott became the sole heir to his estate (one of the will's stipulations being that he change his surname to Elwes).

A curious thing happened, though. John Elwes, having put on the pretence of being a miser, now became an even greater one than his uncle, adopting the sort of rigorously self-denying lifestyle associated with other celebrated misers like ☞ Daniel Dancer. He refused to light a fire even if he had arrived home soaked with rain, ate whatever rotten meat was left in his cupboard rather than spend money on food, and let his country mansion fall into ruin around him. Yet in other ways, he was an unusual miser. He continued to enjoy gambling, and though he would walk many miles to save a few pennies, thought nothing of losing thousands of pounds while playing cards. In financial matters he was just as reckless. He never kept proper accounts, and invested in all sorts of dubious schemes that lost money. He could also be amazingly generous, lending large sums to people he barely knew. He was firmly of the belief that a gentleman should never ask another gentlemen for money, and as a consequence of this, many who owed him money were never made to pay up.

One anecdote sums up the amiability that made him many friends. He was out shooting with an inexperienced companion who could barely hit a target. At one point, this companion fired through a hedge and hit Elwes in the cheek. Far from being angry, he exclaimed. 'My dear sir, I give you joy on your improvement — I knew you would hit something by and by.'

In 1772, Elwes was elected to Parliament, and served in it for the next twelve years. While he gave no speeches, he took his responsibilities seriously, showed great independence of mind when voting, and became renowned for his integrity. He was, however, appalled when he heard there were moves to make him a peer — which would have forced him to buy a carriage and engage servants better dressed than he was.

Elwes owned many houses in London. In his last years he moved around constantly, living in whichever of them happened to be vacant. His furniture, according to his biographer Captain Topham, consisted of 'a couple of beds, a couple of chairs, a table and an old woman'. One day, a friend who went in search of him found him in one of these houses, lying unconscious in one room. The old woman, who had apparently died two days earlier, was in another. On this occasion Elwes was revived.

Elwes never married, but prior to inheriting Sir Harvey's fortune he had fathered two sons, John and George, with his housekeeper. He loved them, but refused to pay for them to be educated, saying that 'putting things into people's heads is the sure way to remove money from their pockets'. At the end of his life he was living in John's house, and growing increasingly delusional. One night, another guest woke to find Elwes scrabbling around in his room in the dark. 'I have been unfortunate enough to be robbed,' the old man told him, 'of all the money I have in the world — of five guineas and a half — and half a crown!' His real wealth, closer to a million pounds, was left to his sons. ▣

ERDOS, PAUL

(1913–1996)
Mathematician

Erdos was born in Hungary, but had no real country other than the worldwide community of mathematicians. He was constantly on the move for most of his life, skipping from one university or conference to the next, dependent on the hospitality of colleagues for a meal and

a place to sleep. They were always glad to see him though, for he was one of the most brilliant mathematicians of the twentieth century, always brimming with ideas and keen to share them with others.

He was born in Budapest, the son of two Jewish mathematics teachers, Lajos and Anna Erdos. He was their only child, two daughters having died from scarlet fever prior his birth. His parents soon realised they had a mathematical prodigy on their hands. He studied mathematics at university, receiving his doctorate in 1934. With the Hungarian government developing close ties with Nazi Germany and anti-Semitism on the rise, Erdos went to England, where he took up a post-doctoral fellowship in Manchester. He continued to make regular trips to Hungary until 1938, but with the outbreak of war imminent, moved to America.

His first American posting was at Princeton, but he was soon on the move, settling into the pattern that would characterise his career. He had no home, no bank account and few possessions. He travelled with a suitcase containing some items of clothing and his notebooks, and when he made any money he usually gave it away.

After the war, Erdos found out that his father and many relatives had been murdered by the Nazis, but his mother had survived.

He made frequent trips back to Hungary to visit her, which raised suspicion among U.S. authorities in a period of anti-communist paranoia, and in 1954 he was refused a re-entry permit. The ban on travel to America, or 'samland' as he called it (after Uncle Sam), remained in place until 1963. During these years he spent much of his time in Israel.

Erdos was a mathematician who posed and solved problems. Arriving at the home of a colleague, he would invariably have a few ideas to kick around, and most of the 1,500 papers he wrote — more than any other mathematician in history — were in collaboration. Erdos' speciality was number theory, but many of the proofs he came up with had applications in other fields, particularly computer science. He liked to imagine that God (whom he called the Supreme Fascist) had a book which contained the fundamental laws of mathematics, and would describe any particularly elegant proof as 'one from The Book'.

Erdos was showered with honorary doctorates in his final years. He never married or had children, and admitted to having an aversion to sexual pleasure. He maintained his hectic schedule to the end, fuelled by coffee and amphetamines, and died while attending a conference in Warsaw. ▣

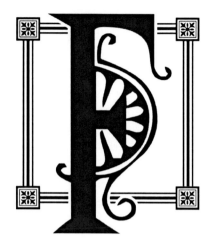

FABYAN, GEORGE

(1867–1936)
Cloth merchant & cryptologist

Fabyan, who was born in Boston, was the son of George F. Fabyan of Fabyan, Bliss & Co., a major manufacturer and distributor of cotton goods. As a young man he ran away from home and was disinherited, but later went to work for the company as a salesman under an assumed name. He notched up such an impressive sales record that his supervisor introduced him to the head of the company — which was, of course, his father. The prodigal son was welcomed back, and when his father died in 1907, he inherited $3 million and was made head of the Chicago office. Fabyan was also on the military staff of Illinois governor Richard Yates, and served as a military diplomat under President Theodore Roosevelt, helping to negotiate the treaty which ended the Russo-Japanese War.

In 1905, Fabyan and his wife Nelle bought a farmhouse and six acres (2.4 hectares) in Geneva, Illinois, which eventually grew to an estate of 300 acres (121 hectares) called Riverbank. He had the house remodelled by Frank Lloyd Wright, and his other additions to the property included a full-sized Dutch windmill, a lighthouse, sculptures, a Japanese garden, and a menagerie featuring bears and monkeys (in winter, the monkeys slept in the main house, in a room with a tin floor). Fabyan, a science enthusiast, also made the estate available for military research, and went on to fund a host of other projects.

Around 1912, Fabyan met Mrs. Elizabeth Wells Gallup who, like ☞ Delia Bacon, was convinced that Sir Francis Bacon had written the plays attributed to Shakespeare. Bacon had invented the 'bilateral cipher', a method of encoding messages within texts using thick and thin letters, and Mrs. Gallup believed this had been used in the original printed versions of the plays. Fabyan, who had a particular interest in codes and ciphers, invited her to continue her work at Riverbank, and recruited a number of cipher experts to help her.

In 1916, a movie producer

named William Seligman, who had filmed a series of Shakespeare plays, went to court to stop Fabyan publishing a book claiming that Bacon was the real author. Several of Fabyan's experts testified, and the judge, Richard S. Tuthill, ruled that he had been convinced by them that Bacon had indeed written the plays, as well as the works of Edmund Spenser and others. The story made the papers in London, but the whole thing had in fact been cooked up as a publicity stunt by Fabyan, Seligman and Tuthill, who were all friends. Tuthill was later reprimanded by his superiors for the frivolous ruling.

As part of the great Shakespeare project, Fabyan purchased a number of Bacon's works. One of them included a design for a levitation machine, which Fabyan decided to build. It consisted of wooden tubes connected by strings, the vibrations of which would supposedly cause one of the tubes to rise. As its success depended on the strings being correctly tuned, he hired a number of acoustics experts, including Wallace Sabine, a physics professor at Harvard University, to work on the project. While the levitation machine never worked, Fabyan was so impressed by Sabine that he set up a laboratory for him at Riverbank. Sabine went on to design the Symphony Hall in Boston, and is today acknowledged as the father of architectural acoustics.

Fabyan decided to set up a Department of Genetics at Riverbank, and hired a young graduate of Cornell University, William Friedman, to head it. Friedman fell in love with Mrs. Gallup's assistant, Elisabeth Smith, and they married. He also became interested in their decoding work, found he had a natural aptitude for it, and was made head of the Department of Ciphers as well. Alas, the department was making little headway in proving Bacon was Shakespeare, and Fabyan was considering disbanding it when, in 1917, America entered the war. He offered its services to the U.S. government (which had no such department of its own). Fabyan and Friedman trained army officers in code-breaking, and Riverbank proved an invaluable asset to the war effort. Friedman went on to become one of the world's most respected cryptologists (in fact, he coined the word 'cryptology').

Today, Fabyan's house has become the Fabyan Villa Museum, where visitors can inspect the fabulous collection of art objects and curios that he and his wife collected, while the Riverbank Acoustic Laboratories are still in operation nearby. Fabyan may have had some wild notions, but he also had a unique knack for making them pay off. 🕮

FIRBANK, RONALD

(1886–1926)
Writer

Firbank, who was born in London, was the son of a former railway man and later Labour MP, Sir Thomas Firbank, and his wife Harriet. As a youth, he idolised Oscar Wilde, dressed like a dandy and decorated his rooms at Cambridge with paintings, ornaments and flowers. He was a tall, slender figure who moved in an undulating manner, the epitome of camp before the word was invented. In the wake of Wilde's trial and disgrace, such an open display of homosexuality was risky, but those who knew Firbank noted a certain steeliness beneath his effete exterior which commanded respect. (As Lady Parvula, one of the characters in his novel *Valmouth* remarks, 'I suppose that none but those whose courage is unquestionable can venture to be effeminate?')

Many anecdotes are told about Firbank's almost crippling shyness. In a restaurant one day, he was so terrified by the sight of the headwaiter that he hid under the table, and during a two-year stay in Oxford it is said that he only spoke to two people — his charwoman and the guard on the train to London. According to one of his few friends,

Lord Berners, it was almost impossible to have a normal conversation with him. Even asking a simple question, such as where someone lived, would elicit an evasive answer followed by nervous laughter and a coughing fit. He ate very little (he suffered from some sort of constriction of the throat which made swallowing difficult) and, invited to dinner once by a friend, consumed nothing but a single pea.

Firbank's first book, *Odette d'Antrevernes* (1905), was a Wilde pastiche. The first of his eight novels, *Vainglory*, appeared in 1915, and as with subsequent novels Firbank paid for its publication himself. They are witty, rarefied concoctions, almost plotless, peopled by exotic characters — kings and queens, aristocrats and priests — and consisting largely of dialogue and fragments of dialogue. Firbank wrote them on large blue postcards, and in their original editions they teem with idiosyncratic spelling, grammar and punctuation, including a profusion of italics and exclamation marks (after his death, sadly, meddling editors removed many of these idiosyncrasies). Critics have often dismissed the books as inconsequential, but Firbank has been championed by many other writers, including Evelyn Waugh and W.H. Auden.

Firbank spent much of his life

BOBBY FISCHER

travelling, often going to places on a whim. (He once sent a telegram to a friend which read, 'Tomorrow I go to Hayti. They say the President is a Perfect Dear.') He had a habit of travelling to a country, conceiving a novel to be set there, then going to another country to write it. Wherever he went, he took a small collection of things — pictures, books, figurines, and a palm tree — to make him feel at home. While staying in a flat in Chelsea for a time, he engaged a gardener to water the palm tree twice a day. Firbank was very pleased with this fellow, who wore a green apron and spoke with a country accent. When he moved to another flat in Piccadilly, he continued to engage the gardener, but insisted that he walk to Piccadilly and back again every day, wearing his apron and carrying a green watering can.

Firbank was in Rome (where the last of his novels to be published in his lifetime, *Concerning the Eccentricities of Cardinal Pirelli*, is set) when he died suddenly from pneumonia at the age of thirty-nine. Lord Berners was in Rome at the time and organised his funeral. Not knowing that Firbank had converted to Catholicism, Berners had him buried in the Protestant cemetery, but his body was later moved to a Catholic one. ▦

FISCHER, BOBBY

(1943–2008)
Chess player

Fischer, who was born in Chicago, became obsessed with chess at the age of six. He painted a board on the ceiling of his bedroom so he could play imaginary games on it. 'All I want to do, ever,' he said, 'is play chess.' In 1958, at the age of fourteen, he became the youngest ever U.S. champion, and the following year, the youngest ever grandmaster. During the 1960s, Fischer cemented his reputation as a player of genius, coldly logical rather than intuitive, running through countless moves in his head before making a decision. At the same time, he became known for petulance and making unreasonable demands. He dropped out of a tournament in 1967 and went into semi-retirement for eighteen months. He had also joined an apocalyptic religious sect, the Worldwide Church of God, founded by Herbert W. Armstrong in 1933, and gave much of his earnings to it.

Fischer made a triumphant return to chess in 1970. He won a string of victories against other grandmasters, and set himself up for a shot at the world championship, held by the Soviet Union since 1937. Fischer had previously played against the current champion, Boris Spassky, but had not yet defeated him.

The possibility that he might do so electrified the chess world and transformed it into a new Cold War battlefront. Fischer, fiercely anti-communist, declared himself eager for the task, but then he stalled. He complained about the venue, the board, the chess pieces, the prize money. At one point, Henry Kissinger rang him, begging him to play. Most of Fischer's demands were eventually met, and the match began in a sports hall in Reykjavik, Iceland, in 1972. Spassky won the first game. Fischer, complaining about the television cameras, withdrew from the second game and almost the match, only agreeing to continue if the remaining games were played in a back room, away from cameras. Fischer went on to defeat Spassky convincingly. He was hailed as an American hero, and chess dominated the front pages of the world for the first and probably last time. Little did anyone realise that Fischer's career was effectively over. He refused to play any more tournaments, and in 1975, when he was due to defend his title against a new challenger, Anatoly Karpov, he presented chess' governing body with a list of sixty-four demands. They agreed to sixty-three of them but baulked at one, and Fischer resigned his world title.

He spent the next twenty years as a virtual recluse. At first he lived in a luxury apartment in Pasadena, provided by the Worldwide Church of God, but eventually fell out with it. After that he stayed in a series of cheap hotels. The once lean, immaculately groomed, impeccably suited grandmaster became an overweight, bearded, scraggy haired figure. At one point, he was arrested after being mistaken for a bank robber and held in jail for two days.

He became best known for espousing virulently anti-Semitic conspiracy theories (although his mother, and quite possibly his biological father, were of Jewish descent). He thought the communists were after him, too, and had the fillings in his teeth removed to stop the KGB from bugging them. In case they tried to poison him, he carried a suitcase full of alternative medicines (he rejected western medicine), including Chinese remedies and 'Mexican rattlesnake pills'. He accused the media of poisoning the public mind against him. 'They constantly use the words eccentric, eccentric, eccentric, weird. I am boring. I am boring!'

In 1992, he burst back into public consciousness with the news that he was to play a reunion match with Spassky in Yugoslavia. With the

Balkan war still raging, this was in defiance of U.N. sanctions. Fischer appeared at a press conference and spat on a letter from the U.S. Treasury Department warning him not to take part. He went on to win the match and over $3 million in prize money. Over the next few years he spent much of his time in Japan where his girlfriend, Mayoko Watai, was president of the Japanese Chess Association. After being told of the 9/11 attacks, he declared on Filipino radio, 'This is all wonderful news… It's time to finish off the U.S. once and for all.'

In 2004, he was arrested trying to leave Japan (his American passport had been revoked without his knowledge), and remained in custody for nine months while the U.S. tried to extradite him to face charges of sanction breaking. Then Iceland, where he was still considered a hero, came to his rescue by granting him citizenship. He spent his last years there, trying unsuccessfully to persuade the chess establishment to adopt a new form of chess he had devised, where pieces are arranged randomly at the beginning of a game. He died after refusing treatment for kidney failure. For all his idiosyncrasies, many believe he was the greatest chess player in history.

FLYING PIEMAN
see William KING ☞

FOMENKO, MICHAEL
(b. 1930)
Australia's Tarzan

Fomenko, born in Soviet Georgia, was the son of Daniel Fomenko, a university lecturer, and Princess Elizabeth Machabelli, a member of Russia's pre-communist aristocracy. The family moved to Australia via China and Japan, and Fomenko's father secured a job as a teacher at the exclusive Shore school in Sydney. Michael became a student at the school, and it was here that he first acquired a reputation for toughness. At one point, he engaged in a fight with a fellow pupil, Tim Bristow, who would later become a notorious private detective and enforcer. The fight went on for hours and ended with Fomenko thoroughly beaten. The next day, Fomenko, his face swathed with bandages, approached Bristow. He was accompanied by his father, who asked if he could referee a rematch. 'We are Cossacks,' he explained. 'We never give up.' Bristow said he would rather shake hands, which he and Michael did.

Fomenko never felt a part

MICHAEL FOMENKO

of Shore, where he was the only foreigner among 900 boys. He was a poor student but became a star athlete, and almost secured a place in the Australian team for the 1956 Olympics.

At the age of twenty-four, after a brief period working as a shipping clerk, he set off for the wilds of far north Queensland, and found a new home for himself in the rainforests between Wujal-Wujal and Cook-town. He lived in close proximity to the local Aborigines, hunted wild pigs for food, and covered his body with ash to ward off mosquitoes. In 1958, he carved a dugout canoe from a cedar log and set off on an epic 398 mile (640 km) journey from Cooktown to Thursday Island, making his way through the treacherous reefs of the Torres Strait, a trip that some said he would not survive. Arriving in Thursday Island, he decided to continue on to New Guinea, and this leg of the trip almost did kill him. He ended up in Merauke, suffering from malnutrition and dysentery, and without a passport. His father, who sympathised with his son's adventurous spirit, arranged for him to be brought back to Australia, and the exploits of 'the Wild Man of Wujal Wujal' made headlines around the world.

Fomenko settled back into his isolated existence. He wasn't always popular with local landowners, however, and in 1964 he was tracked down by police and arrested on charges of vagrancy, robbery, and indecent behaviour (i.e. wearing a lap-lap). He was sentenced to six months jail, but then, at the instigation of his mother (his father had died in 1960), was declared insane. He was placed in a barred railway carriage and taken to a mental institution in Ipswich, where he remained for two years and was given electric shock treatment. Finally released in 1966 with a certificate declaring him to be sane, he returned to the jungle.

Since then, Fomenko has made occasional reappearances. Proud of his local nickname, Tarzan, for years he wore nothing but a pair of leopard skin underpants and sandals. Journalists eagerly wrote up his experiences, which included fighting off sharks with his bare hands. He would hint to them about his liaisons with Aboriginal women, telling one of them, 'Let's just say I'm up to scratch in every possible way.' He had little knowledge of the outside world, and was most surprised to be told in 1996 that the communists no longer ruled Russia.

In recent years, it has been reported that Fomenko now occasionally travels by bus or taxi, and some of his neighbours have expressed fears for his health. Tracked down

by the *Courier Mail* in 2003, Fomenko brushed aside those fears. 'I am still young,' he declared. 'They are concerned about nothing and you should not worry about that talk.'

Nevertheless, he has made a few concessions to the modern world, and can now be seen wearing football shorts, runners and a tattered shirt. He also occasionally books himself into a local hotel for an overnight stay and his favourite meal of fish and chips, a soft drink and a tub of vanilla ice cream.

FORESTIERE, BALDASSARE

(1879–1946)
Creator of the
Underground Garden

Forestiere was born in the village of Filari in Messina province, Sicily. After a quarrel with his father, he migrated to America where he was set on making his fortune. He bought, sight-unseen, seventy acres of land in Fresno, California, intending to start a citrus farm, but soon realised that its hard, dry earth was totally unsuited to farming. He was also taken aback by the heat of the Californian summer. Recalling the delicious coolness of cellars in his homeland, he began to dig, and found that the earth beneath the hard surface could be worked

relatively easily.

Over the next forty years, Forestiere kept digging, creating an extraordinary maze of subterranean tunnels and chambers covering over ten acres (four hectares). He had no overall plan, and often worked at night, using little more than a pick and shovel to break through the earth. He constructed walls and arches from mud bricks, so that the completed tunnels look something like the Roman catacombs. He created bedrooms, a kitchen, a living room with fireplace, a chapel, and a courtyard with a fishpond. And he even managed to grow fruit trees and grape vines down there, making openings in the ground above them to let in the sunlight. Forestiere was occasionally helped in his labours by his brother, and used a couple of mules to drag out the earth as he excavated it, but otherwise the Underground Garden was his work alone.

Why Forestiere devoted almost his entire life to such a project (apart from the obvious fact that he created a very pleasant space in which to live) remains a mystery, although he once remarked to a newspaper reporter that 'The visions in my mind overwhelm me', and there is certainly a spiritual dimension to the way the structure is laid out. He died before he could extend the garden to twenty acres (eight hectares), as he had planned. Afterwards, it fell into disrepair, but it has since been restored by members of Forestiere's family and is open to the public. It remains a wonderful place to visit on a scorching hot day in Fresno. 🕲

FORT, CHARLES
(1874–1932)
Anomalist

Charles Hoy Fort was born into a family of wholesale grocers in Albany, New York State. His father, Charles Nelson Fort, was a strict disciplinarian who regularly beat and locked up the young Fort, which no doubt encouraged the healthy spirit of anti-authoritarianism that characterised his life and work. As a boy, Fort was an inveterate collector of stamps, minerals, birds and bird eggs, seashells and other specimens. At seventeen he became an apprentice newspaper reporter, but soon abandoned journalism to spend two years travelling. He crisscrossed America and spent time in England and South Africa, collecting experiences. Back in America, he married a childhood friend, Anna Filing, in 1896.

The couple moved into an apartment in New York's East Side. Fort now had his sights set on being a writer, and wrote a quirky autobiography which failed to find a publisher. He had a little more luck writing mostly humourous stories for magazines, and acquired a literary champion in the novelist Theodore Dreiser, who became his closest friend. Dreiser helped organise the publication of Fort's novel *The Outcast Manufacturers* (1909). Throughout these years, Fort and his wife lived close to poverty.

Fort haunted the New York Public Library in search of material for stories, and found himself drawn towards accounts of strange phenomena — mysterious appearances and disappearances, odd coincidences, unexplained sightings and the like. He used some of this material in two books, *X* and *Y*. In *X*, Fort suggested that life on Earth was controlled by a civilisation on Mars, which used rays to influence the way people behaved (while giving them the illusion of free will). In *Y*, he postulated the existence of a 'complementary civilisation' to our own at the North Pole. He apparently intended these ideas to be taken seriously. Dreiser was enthusiastic about the books, but no publisher wanted them, and Fort eventually destroyed the manuscripts.

If *X* and *Y* had been published, Fort might be remembered today as a crank along the lines of Ignatius Donnelly, the champion of Atlantis, but he was destined to use the odd material he had been gathering in far more interesting ways. In 1916, after the death of his uncle, he came into an inheritance that ended most of his financial woes. He and Anna moved into a better apartment, and Fort was able to spend as much time as he wanted in the library.

He ploughed through newspapers and scientific journals, making notes on small rectangular pieces of paper which he filed away, accumulating tens of thousands of them. They became the basis of *The Book of the Damned* (1919), which Dreiser practically blackmailed his publisher into bringing out. It begins:

A procession of the damned. By the damned, I mean the excluded.

We shall have a procession of data that Science has excluded.

Battalions of the accursed, captained by pallid data that I have exhumed, will march. You'll read them — or they'll march. Some of them livid and some of them fiery and some of them rotten.

Fort's mature style is by turns arch, oracular, mocking, amusing and self-deprecating. He parades his carefully annotated data before the reader — strange lights in the sky, rains of blood, falls of frogs and fish from the air, frogs found within solid rock — sometimes without comment. At other times, he mocks the explanations that science gives for these phenomena, such as the theory that frogs and other objects that are seen to fall in showers have been collected by whirlwinds. ('Whirlwinds we read of over and over — but where and what whirlwind? It seems to me that anybody who had lost a pond would be heard from.') And sometimes he comes up with theories of his own, such as the idea that there is another dimension, a 'super-sargasso sea', where things lost from the Earth end up. But Fort did not actually believe in these theories. They are satirical in intent, no more or less fanciful than, as he saw it, the orthodoxies of science. Fort's overarching theme — among several — is that the universe is a vast collection of parts connected in ways we cannot imagine, and by studying individual bits of it separately, scientists cannot hope to get at the truth. Yet, despite his broadsides aimed at science, Fort was a confirmed materialist, and had no truck with religion.

The Book of the Damned sold quite well but reviews were mixed. Some found Fort's attacks on science ludicrous, but for others, his writings were a revelation (writer Ben Hecht declared, 'Henceforth I am a Fortean'). Fort would follow it with three more weighty compen-

diums of strangeness — *New Lands* (1923), *Lo!* (1931) and *Wild Talents* (1932).

Fort and his wife spent much of the1920s in London, where he could be found most days collecting notes in the Reading Room of the British Museum. Returning to America at the end of the decade, they settled in an apartment in the Bronx. In 1930, one of Fort's most enthusiastic fans, ☞ Tiffany Thayer, decided to found a Fortean Society. Fort wanted nothing to do with it and had to be tricked into attending its inaugural meeting. His health was declining now — he was probably suffering from leukaemia but refused to see doctors. No longer going to libraries, he continued to write copious notes, but these were now about his deteriorating physical condition, his surroundings and his own thoughts. He died the day after he was shown one of the first copies of *Wild Talents* to come off the press.

Fort has proved a very influential writer, and his books remain in print. The word 'Fortean' today has a variety of meanings. It is applied to the sorts of anomalous phenomena that Fort gleefully collected, but is also used to describe someone equally willing to question science and mysticism. ▣

'I cannot say that truth is stranger than fiction, because I have never had acquaintance with either.'

CHARLES FORT

FULLER, JOHN

(1757–1834)
'Mad Jack'

Fuller was a British parliamentarian and philanthropist, but was best known for the architectural follies he built. The son of a clergyman, at the age of twenty he inherited the estate of Rose Hill in Brightling, Sussex from his uncle, Rose Fuller. The Fuller family had grown immensely wealthy from iron founding and sugar plantations in Jamaica.

Fuller was a hearty, down to earth fellow who weighed in at twenty-two stone (140 kg), wore his powdered hair tied in a pigtail, and was nicknamed 'Hippo' or 'Mad Jack' (though he preferred 'Honest John'). He began his parliamentary career at the age of twenty-two, serving one term as Member for Southampton, and was Member for Sussex from 1801 to 1812. He was a vigorous performer in Parliament, and was once ejected for referring to the Speaker as 'the insignificant

little fellow in the wig'. He was as generous as he was rich, being a major patron of the Royal Institute and endowing two professorships which continue to this day. He presented the town of Eastbourne with its first lifeboat, and paid for a lighthouse on Beachy Head. When hard economic times set in, he had a wall built around his estate just to provide local men with work.

Fuller's follies include a sixty-five-foot (twenty metre) high obelisk, known as the Brightling Needle, and a thirty-five-foot (10.5 metre) high tower — Fuller's Tower. After making a bet that the conical spire of St. Giles church in Dallington could be seen from his house (then returning home to find it could not), Fuller had a full-sized replica of it built in a nearby meadow to win the bet. A Greek-style rotunda built on a hill in the grounds of his estate was said to have had a more practical purpose, being the scene of card parties and (according to more scurrilous rumours) orgies. All of these structures survive. Fuller was also responsible for the survival of the magnificent medieval castle of Bodium, which he bought after learning there were plans to demolish it and recycle the stones for roads.

Long before his death, Fuller erected another folly, a pyramid in the churchyard at Brightling which would be his mausoleum. According to a widely reported legend, Fuller was interred in his pyramid upright and fully clothed, with a glass of claret and a chicken dinner in front of him, but during restoration work in 1982 the tomb was opened and this was found not to be the case (he had been buried beneath the floor).

A marble bust of Fuller, done in the Roman style, stands in Brightling church, with the inscription *'Utile nihil quod non honestrum'* — 'Nothing is of use which is not honest.'

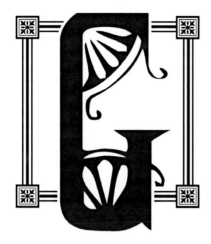

GABE, FRANCES

(b. 1915)
Inventor of the
self-cleaning house

Millions of women (and the occasional man) have complained about housework over the centuries, but few have done anything, really done anything, about it. Frances Gabe is one woman who did do something about it. She was born Frances Arnholtz in Idaho, and as a young girl wanted to be an artist. Discouraged in this by her mother, she instead became interested in the work of her father, a building contractor. She studied at the Girl's Polytechnic College in Portland, Oregon, and, after the war, married an electrical engineer named Bateson. They started a building repair business and had two children. Gabe resented having to do housework that kept her away from the kids. 'Housework is a thankless, unending job, a nerve-twangling bore,' she said. 'Who wants it? Nobody! With my jaw set hard I was determined that there had to be a better way!'

Gabe spent the next forty years designing and building a prototype self-cleaning house in Newberg, Oregon. It is made from cinder blocks, with the interior walls, floors and ceiling coated in waterproof resin. The house contains numerous devices invented by Gabe (who has applied for sixty-eight patents over the years). On the ceiling of each room is a device which, at the flick of a switch, sprays soapy water over the room, rinses it with clean water, then blow dries it. The floor is at a slight tilt so that excess water drains away (Gabe invented adjustable joists so the tilt can be maintained if the ground beneath the house subsides). All the furniture is covered in waterproof fabric, and there are transparent protector boxes to safeguard books, papers and other vulnerable items. The kitchen cupboard acts as a dishwasher, while the closets wash and dry the clothes inside them. The sinks, bathtub and toilet are self-cleaning, and the fireplace automatically disposes of its ashes. Gabe built the house entirely by herself at a cost of about $15,000.

Not everyone could see the benefits of the self-cleanng house, however. Tired of being ridiculed by her neighbours, its inventor started to use the name Gabe (sometimes written as 'GABe') to protect her family, but she has received much praise from her fellow inventors as well. She continued to live in the house until 2007, when she went into care. Her family were reported to be looking for someone who would buy the house and maintain it. 🖾

GAILLARD, SLIM

(1916–1991)
Jazz singer

The irrepressible Bulee 'Slim' Gaillard was probably born in Detroit, Michigan, although he sometimes said it was Cuba. His father was a ship's steward who occasionally took the young Slim on voyages, and (according to Slim) accidentally left him behind in Crete when he was twelve. He worked his way back to the United Stated as a merchant seaman, picking up at least a smattering of Greek, Arabic and various other languages in the process. Back in Detroit, he tried his hand at boxing, and worked as a bootleg liquor runner for the evocatively named Purple Gang.

Deciding to become an entertainer, Gaillard moved to New York and worked the clubs on 52nd Street. His specialty was playing guitar while tap-dancing, while he also played piano, vibraphone, drums and other instruments. He teamed up with a bass player, Slam Stewart, and as Slim and Slam they began to play a regular breakfast radio broadcast from the Criterion Theatre, alongside the likes of Woody Herman and the Andrew Sisters. When Decca approached them with the offer of making a record, Gaillard presented them with the first song he had written, 'Flat Foot Floosie (With a Floy Floy)'. Decca objected to the word 'floosie', and with the title changed to 'Flat Foot Floogie', it became a huge hit.

Gaillard was quite a talented musician (he could, for example, knock out a reasonable piano solo with his hands upside down, and play 'Jingle Bells' on a snare drum), but his real gift was for language. He invented his own, which he called Vout, ('vout' being a word which could mean anything really).

A variation of the Negro 'jive talk' of the day, it was characterised by a liberal use of suffixes like 'oreenie' and 'oroonie', bursts of rapid-fire Spanish, and flights of surreal fancy involving unlikely Gaillard obsessions such as avocado seeds. Food is a running theme in songs like 'Potato Chips', 'Dunkin' Bagels' and 'Fried Chicken O'Routee', while 'Yep Roc Heresy' is an Armenian restaurant menu put to music.

SLIM GAILLARD

Slim and Slam had another hit with 'Tutti Frutti' and made an appearance in the anarchic 1941 film comedy *Hellzappopin'*, but the partnership ended when Gaillard was drafted in 1943. He served as a radio operator in the airforce. After his discharge, he teamed up with another bass player, Bam Brown, and had a big hit with 'Cement Mixer, Putti-Putti' (a song Gaillard composed on the spot when he heard a cement mixer outside the recording studio), appeared on the radio, and scored a residency at Billy Berg's nightclub in Hollywood. In 1946, when Charlie Parker and Dizzy Gillespie began to play there, Billy Berg's became the epicentre of the bebop revolution in jazz. Gaillard went on to record with both musicians, and became a hero to the Beat Generation, receiving the ultimate Beat accolade with a guest appearance in Kerouac's *On the Road*.

Gaillard's music went out of fashion during the 1960s. He dropped out of the business for a while, managed a hotel in San Diego, then an apple orchard in Washington state. After that he drifted into acting and had roles in television series' like *Mission: Impossible*, *Charlie's Angels* and *Roots: The Next Generation*. In the early 1980s, Dizzy Gillespie persuaded him to play some European jazz festivals. He ended up moving to London where

he performed regularly, made his first recordings in decades and even wrote for commercials. A mooted autobiography never appeared, but in 1989 the *Arena* television programme broadcast a four-part documentary on his life called *Slim Gaillard's Civilisation*. The producers went to considerable lengths tracking down people from the singer's colourful past, and even found the last two surviving members of the Purple Gang.

Gaillard dispensed his last 'oroonie' two years later, having succumbed to cancer. ▣

GALTON, SIR FRANCIS
(1822–1911)
Scientist

Galton was one of the great polymaths of Victorian science, lauded in his time but today mainly remembered as the proud father of the discredited science of eugenics. Born in Birmingham, the son of a wealthy banker, he was a child prodigy, able to read Latin and Greek at the age of five. He initially studied medicine but, after his father died in 1844, leaving him a fortune, he abandoned his studies and spent the next few years travelling and enjoying himself. Joining the Royal Geographical Society, in 1850 he embarked on a

two-year expedition in southwestern Africa (in what is now Namibia) and returned with the first proper maps of the region.

Galton was obsessed with counting, measuring and comparing — he couldn't sit for a portrait without counting the number of brushstrokes the artist made — and channelled these obsessions into many different areas of study. He pioneered the use of questionnaires, came up with the first weather map, devised new methods of statistical analysis, and developed the first system for categorising fingerprints. Some of his other achievements were more dubious. He once spent two months conducting experiments designed to produce the perfect cup of tea, and wrote a paper on 'The weights of British noblemen during the last three generations'. As the latter suggests, he was fascinated by physical characteristics. He used to walk the streets with a piece of paper in his pocket divided into three sections, and a thimble with a needle attached to it on one of his fingers. Whenever he passed a girl he made a hole in the paper, its placement depending on whether the girl was beautiful, average looking or ugly. The aim here was to create a 'Beauty Map of Great Britain'. Although the map was never completed, preliminary results suggested that the most beautiful girls were to be found in

London, and the ugliest in Aberdeen.

Galton was a half-cousin of Charles Darwin, and was hugely impressed by his theory of natural selection. He believed, however, that the evolution of humans was too important to leave to nature, and formulated the principle of eugenics (he coined the term in 1883). According to this, superior people, the strongest, most intelligent and adaptable, would be encouraged to marry and have children, while those deemed inferior would remain childless. For this to be accomplished, it was necessary to accurately measure and evaluate human stock. Galton's attempts to do this led him down some interesting paths (he was the first person to study twins separated at birth, for example). In his quest to identify various types of human being, he combined the photographic images of individuals from specific groups (criminals, Jews and so on) in an attempt to reveal their inherent characteristics, and thus invented composite photography. These efforts were ultimately a failure, as indeed were all Galton's attempts at quantifying what made a human being superior.

Eugenics nevertheless gained many followers in the late nineteenth and early twentieth centuries, some of them embracing it with an almost religious fervour. It led to programmes of forced sterilisation in some countries, including the U.S., and, ultimately, the horrors of Nazi Germany. Galton could not have foreseen this, but in promoting eugenics, it is true that he never ruled out the idea that coercion might be involved. (In Galton's defence, it might be noted that there were many Jewish supporters of eugenics during his lifetime, and Galton himself admired the Jews, seeing in their strict laws about whom they could marry an example of eugenics in practice.)

Towards the end of his long life, Galton decided to encapsulate his ideas in a novel, *Kantsaywhere*, which depicted a society run on eugenic lines. Although parts of it survive, much of it was burnt by his niece (who apparently objected to the love scenes). Galton thought eugenics was his greatest achievement, the one that he wanted to be remembered by. He got his wish, and damned his reputation. 🔲

'I often feel that the tableland of sanity upon which most of us dwell, is small in area, with unfenced precipices on every side, over any one of which we may fall.'

SIR FRANCIS GALTON

GAUDI, ANTONI

(1852–1926)
Architect

Gaudí was born into a family of metalworkers in or near the town of Reus in southern Catalonia, Spain. As a youth, he was fascinated by the natural world, and studied the forms of animal and plant life which would infuse so much of his work. He and his two closest companions explored archeological sites around Reus, and hatched a grand scheme to restore a ruined medieval monastery at Poblet. It was perhaps while drawing up plans to do this that Gaudí first saw his future as an architect. In 1868, he went to Barcelona, where he studied at the University and later the School of Architecture. As a student, he was forced to work within the staid neoclassical style favoured by his teachers, but supplemented his classes by poring over the school's extensive archive of photographs of 'exotic' architecture from around the world. His natural idiosyncrasies had begun to emerge, and on his graduation in 1878, one of his professors declared, 'Gentlemen, we are here today either in the presence of a genius or a madman.'

Soon after Gaudí began his professional career, two events took place which would shape the rest

of his life. The first was meeting a wealthy and cultured industrialist, Eusebi Güell, who would become his principal patron. The second was to be named director of public works for the Sagrada Familia cathedral. Construction on it had begun in 1882, but its chief instigator and fundraiser, Bocabella, had fallen out with his original architect, and took a chance giving the job to the relatively inexperienced Gaudí. No one could have guessed that he would spend the next forty-two years of his life working on it.

Barcelona's economy was booming during these years, with money flowing in from Spain's colonies. Catalan nationalism was also on the rise. The Catalans saw themselves as culturally distinct from — and superior to — the Castilians who governed the country from Madrid. Businessmen like Güell were interested in commissioning buildings that reflected this new spirit, and Gaudí, a fervent Catalan nationalist, was the ideal man for the job. He was also, like Güell, a devout Catholic.

During these years, the ambitious young architect was known as a dandy. He wore impeccably tailored suits, white kid gloves and made-to-measure black silk top hats. He enjoyed the theater, and went around town in an open-topped carriage, from which he would direct the

work on his various building projects. In his private life, he was an abstemious vegetarian who lived mainly on a diet of bread, nuts and lettuce splashed with milk or olive oil. In his late twenties, he is reported to have asked a schoolteacher to marry him, but was rebuffed. After that, he seemed to give up all interest in women, and he may well have died a virgin. All of Gaudí's energies were directed to his work.

Gaudí's chief source of inspiration remained what he called 'the Great Book of Nature'. His stunningly original buildings are rich in natural forms — the spirals of seashells, columns like trees or bones, a roof in the shape of a dragon and not a right angle in sight. Because nature was colourful, Gaudí believed that buildings should be colourful, too. He often achieved this using intricate tilework, and was a particular fan of *trencadis*, in which fragments of pottery and glass are laid over a new surface, creating a collage-like effect. This is best seen in the famous serpentine bench in Park Güell, the large park (originally intended to be a housing estate) which Gaudí built for his patron on the outskirts of Barcelona. Like Gaudí's other works, the bench (which was overseen by his assistant Jujol) is full of hidden Catalan and Catholic symbolism.

Construction on the apartment

block which is perhaps Gaudí's
greatest building, the Casa Milà, began in 1906. The overal inspiration
was a mountain or rockface (it has
always been known by Barcelonians
as 'La Pedrera' or 'the Quarry'). It
has windows that open up like eye
sockets in skulls, and balconies of
twisted metal inspired by seaweed.
Its undulating roof, which echoes
the mountains behind it, is topped
with chimneys and air ducts in the
form of abstract, totemic figures.
Like many of Gaudí's buildings,
though, it was not finished according to his original plan, in which
it was to have been topped by a
gigantic bronze statue of the Virgin
Mary. However, 1909 saw the 'Tragic
Week', when anti-clerical mobs went
on an orgy of destruction in Barcelona, burning churches, murdering
priests and digging up the corpses
of nuns. The man who had commissioned the Casa Milà decided that a
statue of the Virgin on top of his
house wasn't such a good idea.

On its completion, Casa Milà
was roundly mocked and lampooned.
Gaudí's architecture was well out of
fashion by then, and he spent the
last two decades of his life working
almost exclusively on the Sagrada
Familia. After the initial decades of
enthusiasm, the funds for this had
dried up and progress was slow.

Gaudí grew ever more pious
over the years. The one-time dandy
became a shrunken figure in a worn-
out black suit, his white hair and
beard often long and unkempt. He
took to asking passersby for pesetas
to contribute to the Sagrada Familia,
and people would cross the road to
avoid him. In 1926, he was hit by a
tram and severely injured. Nobody
recognised the dishevelled figure
with empty pockets, and he was
taken to the public ward of a hospital where he died three days later.

Construction on the Sagrada
Familia has proceeded in fits and
starts since then. For a long time, it
looked like the building would never
be finished, but work has acceler-
ated in the last few years (particularly
thanks to contributions from Japan
— the Japanese love Gaudí), and
2030 is now mentioned as a possible completion date. The project
remains controversial, however. In
1936 anarchists broke into the Sagrada Familia's crypt and destroyed
all of Gaudí's working papers and
models, so no one is sure exactly
how he wanted the finished building
to look. ▩

GOULD, GLENN
(1932–1982)
Pianist

Gould, who was born in Toronto,
had an upbringing much like that
of ☞ Percy Grainger. Both had

ANTONI GAUDI

dominating mothers who believed their sons were destined for musical greatness, and made them spend endless hours practising piano. If they faltered, Grainger's mother used a whip, Gould's a ruler over the knuckles. And both became child prodigies who went on to have idiosyncratic performance styles (as well as a host of other peculiarities).

At the age of ten, Gould went to study at the Royal College of Music in Toronto, and gave his first public performance in 1945. He always played sitting on a little wooden adjustable chair his father had made for him, which left him chest-high to the keyboard (it has been surmised that this recreated his experience as a child, when he had been forced to reach up to the keys). As he played, his body swivelled back and forth and he hummed along to the music. Sometimes his humming was audible on recordings, which infuriated the purists. Despite the oddity of his style, he was known for his ability to play fast, intricate passages with perfect clarity. His recording of Bach's *Goldberg Variations*, released in 1955, caused a sensation in the classical music world, and is still revered by many.

Gould recorded extensively for television and radio, and gave many concerts over the years, at one point touring Russia. He loathed performing live, though, and gave it up for good in 1964. After that he concentrated on recording, and lived on the proceeds of an unexpected mastery of the stockmarket.

Gould hated being touched, avoided shaking hands, and always wore gloves when he wasn't at the piano. He was a hypochondriac who took vast amounts of pills for imagined ailments, and always wore several thick layers of clothing, even at the height of summer. He was once arrested after being mistaken for a vagrant (the same thing had happened to Percy Grainger). While Gould had a number of relationships with women, the longest lasting several years, he was essentially a loner who conducted his friendships mainly over the phone. Every morning, between 2 and 3 a.m., he emerged from his apartment in Toronto to walk to a nearby diner for the same meal of scrambled eggs.

One of Gould's biographers, Peter F. Ostwald, described meeting him towards the end of his life. He had become a bloated and stooped figure. 'His skin, which had always been on the pale side, had acquired an unnatural greyness, roughly the color of steel, due probably to the lack of sunlight.' Gould suffered a stroke in 1982, and died soon after. Since then, a veritable industry has sprung up around him. His recordings have been reissued and many books and memoirs about him have appeared. The little wooden chair on which he sat as he played may be seen in a glass case in the National Library of Canada. ▣

GOULD, JOE

(1889–1957)
'Professor Seagull'

One of the most recognisable, exuberant and malodorous denizens of Greenwich Village for decades, Joseph Ferdinand Gould was ☞ Maxwell Bodenheim's chief rival for the title of 'King of Bohemia'. Born into a wealthy family in Boston, he was the son of a respected physician, and was educated at Harvard (where his classmates included T.S. Eliot). His father wanted him to be a doctor, too, but Gould was constitutionally unfit for this occupation, or indeed any occupation. Instead he developed an interest in eugenics, and spent several happy months in North Dakota measuring the heads of thousands of Chippewa Indians.

In 1916, Gould moved to New York, and worked as a police reporter on a newspaper, but threw it in after a year. After that, he survived by begging (or rather, by asking for contributions to 'the Joseph Ferdinand Gould Fund'). He slept on trains or in flophouses, wore cast-off clothes that were usually too big for him, and rarely bathed. He was a short, skinny, gnomelike fellow, bald on top, with a scraggly, nicotine-stained beard usually adorned with bits of food. If he was a bum, though, Gould was a superior bum. He smoked the butts he found on the street in a cigarette holder, and if he stuffed newspapers into his shirt to stave off the cold, he made sure they were pages from the *New York Times*.

The legendary status that Gould acquired was largely due to an enormously long book he was supposed to be writing, to be called *An Oral History of Our Time*. This would mainly consist of conversations he had overheard and written down, interspersed with his own commentaries. He was rarely without a tattered cardboard portfolio which held the school exercise books in which he was writing this great work. By the mid-thirties, he was telling people he had written over seven million words (the figure later grew to eleven million). The book would only be published after his death, and he predicted that 'some of it will live as long as the English language'. He was, nevertheless, rather careless with the exercise books in which his magnum opus was taking shape, and often left them behind in cafés and flophouses.

Despite his grimy appearance, Gould was a frequent guest at Greenwich Village parties, and was known for two party turns. The first, called the Joseph Ferdinand Gould Stomp, involved him stripping to the waist and performing an exuberant dance, featuring much stomping and hand clapping, which he said he had learned from the Chippewa. The second was his famed impersonation of a seagull, which had him squawking and flapping his hands. Gould claimed to understand the language of seagulls and once translated one of his rival Bodenheim's poems into it (hence his nickname, Professor Seagull).

He occasionally recited his own poems, and delivered the following brief but memorable piece during a meeting of the Raven Poetry Circle devoted to religious poetry.

In the winter
I'm a Buddhist
And in the summer
I'm a nudist.

A number of writers became fascinated by Gould, including the novelist William Saroyan. He had been much impressed by Gould's essay 'Civilisation', which appeared in the literary magazine *The Dial* in 1929. In this, Gould had attacked the modern world, calling skyscrapers 'bric-a-brac' and cars 'unnecessary'. On a visit to Greenwich Village, Saroyan tracked Gould down. Gould later said that the novelist was so intent on discussing the *Oral History* that he could barely get a word in (although he did manage to ask Saroyan, his 'disciple', to buy him a pair of false teeth, or 'store teeth' as Gould called them).

Gould's health eventually deteriorated, and he spent the last four years of his life in an institution on Long Island, occasionally doing his seagull impression for the edification of other patients. After his death, Gould enthusiasts went in search of the *Oral History*, but only a few small fragments were ever found.

'I have a delusion of grandeur. I believe myself to be Joe Gould.'
JOE GOULD

GRAEFF, TOM
(1929–1970)
Filmmaker

Graeff is mostly remembered as the creator of one the greatest pieces of fifties schlock cinema, *Teenagers from Outer Space*, but he was an intriguing

and charismatic individual. The son of a mining engineer, he grew up in Los Angeles and studied film-making at UCLA. After completing a couple of short films, he made a feature-length colour comedy, *The Noble Experiment*, in which he played an amateur scientist who invents a pill that makes people 'get-along'. It had its premiere in 1955, but sank without trace.

Graeff was then hired as an assistant by B-movie mogul Roger Corman for his latest project *Not of This Earth* (he also appears in the film briefly as a car park attendant). Inspired by Corman, Graeff set out to make his own science fiction epic, from a script he had written called *Killers from Outer Space*. Having scraped together a budget of $14,000, Graeff shot the film in 1956. It stars his lover at the time, Chuck Roberts (billed as David Love), as an alien named Derek, who takes pity on the human race when his fellow aliens attempt to flood Earth with flesh-eating monsters called Gargans. Graeff, who plays a reporter in the film, had trouble paying off all the debts he incurred making it, and was forced to sell it to Warner Brothers. It was eventually released under the title *Teenagers from Outer Space* in 1959. The film, which became a staple on television during the sixties, is most famous for the scenes involving an

alien raygun (the 'focusing disinte-grator ray') that turns living creatures into skeletons.

The failure of the film, which received poor reviews and was screened mostly in drive-ins, hit Graeff hard and triggered a personal crisis. By all accounts a sensitive and intelligent young man who was concerned about the state of the world, in 1959 he took out a full-page ad in the *Los Angeles Times*, in which he proclaimed himself to be the reincarnation of Jesus Christ. A second ad, which listed churches where he would be preaching, was pulled by the newspaper, and an attempt by Graeff to have his name legally changed to Jesus Christ II was unsuccessful.

Following this debacle, Graeff moved to Pennsylvania where he enrolled at Pendle Hill, an educa-tional centre run by the Quakers. They didn't take to Graeff's claims to be Christ and tried to expel him, but he resisted. He ended up in jail, then a mental institution (where he may have been subjected to electroshock therapy). Released in 1964, he returned to Los Angeles and worked as an editor on another science fiction atrocity, *Wizard of Mars*. Graeff's last attempt to make it in the movies came in 1968, when he placed an ad in *Variety*, offering a script he had written entitled *Orf* for the princely sum of $500,000. The story was taken up by a *Variety* columnist, Joyce Haber, who mocked Graeff and wrote about his earlier breakdown, effectively killing his career.

During his last years, Graeff started a mail order business called the Evolutionary Data Foundation. Through this, he sold an LP record of a lecture he had given, featuring a painting of Jesus on the cover, entitled *Homosexuality is Naturally Stronger in Man than is Heterosexuality*. In December 1970, his body was found in a car parked in a garage in La Mesa, San Diego. The coroner found that he had died of carbon monoxide poisoning, and ruled the death a suicide.

Graeff was quite open about his homosexuality during an era when this was still a dangerous thing to do, and some latter day admirers have dubbed him 'the gay Ed Wood'. Much about his life remains mysterious.

GRAHAM, JAMES
(1745–1794)
Quack

Graham was one of the most exuberant and entertaining quacks of the eighteenth century. The son of a saddler, he was born in Edinburgh where he studied medicine but failed to qualify as a doctor. He

then travelled to America, where he practised as an eye specialist in Philadelphia. It was in America that he discovered the wonders of electricity, which he decided was the cure for all mankind's ills.

Moving to London, the newly electrified 'doctor' Graham soon had aristocrats queuing up to sit in his 'magnetic thrones' and 'electrical baths'. In August 1779, Londoners were struck by the sight of two huge men, dressed in splendid livery and nicknamed Gog and Magog, walking through the streets distributing handbills advertising the opening of Graham's Temple of Health. Occupying a house in the Adelphi district, facing the Thames, it was, said the handbills, a 'Magical Edifice... where wit and mirth, love and beauty — all that can delight the sound and all that can ravish the senses, will hold their Court, This and every Evening this Week, in chaste and joyous assemblage.' And it must be said that Graham's establishment lived up to the hype. The rooms on the lower floor were sumptuously decorated, with oil paintings on the walls and numerous marble statues. Scented candles filled the air with perfume, and soothing music played on hidden wind instruments. Upstairs, the rooms contained an extraordinary array of electrical and chemical apparatus. As well as availing themselves of Dr. Graham's various electrical treatments, visitors could listen to his lectures, peruse his treatises, and purchase an array of pills and potions formulated to settle the nerves and purify the blood.

While the focus of the Temple was health, the subtext of it all was sex. Standing among the statues, striking elegant poses, were pretty, often scantily clad young women known as the 'Goddesses of Health and Beauty'. (One of the most popular was sixteen-year-old Emma Lyon, who would go on to become Lady Hamilton, the mistress of Lord Nelson.) And the centrepiece of it all, although not available for inspection by casual visitors, was the famous 'Celestial Bed'. Measuring twelve feet by nine feet (3.7 m by 2.7 m) and richly decorated and gilded, the bed was guaranteed to cure impotence and sterility in those who slept in it. It had a mattress stuffed with 'straw mingled with balm, rose leaves, lavender flowers and oriental spices', and was topped with a dome on which stood automata playing miniature musical instruments. It was equipped with magnets and, beneath the mattress, a device that generated static electricity. Those wishing to sample the commodious delights of the Celestial Bed had to book ahead in writing and pay a fee of £50 for one night.

Inevitably, the novelty of the Temple and the Celestial Bed wore thin, the crowds ceased to come, and Graham was forced to close its doors. He opened a new 'Temple of Health and Hymen' in Pall Mall where, along with electrical treatments, the efficacy of mud baths was promoted. This was good news for the aspiring poet George Dyer, who loved to read his works out loud, and found Graham's patients, up to their necks in mud, to be the perfect captive audience. While the new Temple had a profitable sideline in gambling for a while, Graham was forced to close it in 1784. He continued to promote mud baths, and there is a wonderful description of a demonstration he gave in Newcastle in 1791. Graham and an attractive female companion, having stripped off their clothes, 'were each interred up to the chin, their heads beautifully dressed and powdered, appearing not unlike two fine, full-grown cauliflowers.' They remained like this for six hours.

Graham went through a religious period after this, founding the New Jerusalem Church and adopting the title 'Servant of the Lord, O.W.L. (which stood for 'Oh! Wonderful Love!'). The last — brief — chapter in the life of this remarkable mountebank came when he embraced inedia, the idea that one may live without food (and today

PERCY GRAINGER

the province of Breatharians like ☞ Wiley Brooks).

He wrote a treatise entitled *How to Live for Many Weeks or Months or Years Without Eating Anything Whatsoever*, and shortly afterwards died unaccountably at the age of forty-nine. 🖾

GRAINGER, PERCY
(1881–1961)
Pianist & composer

One of the most successful musicians of the early twentieth century, Grainger is now mostly remembered for his many peculiar beliefs, hyperactive libido and love of flagellation. Born in Melbourne, Australia, his education was overseen by his strong-willed mother, Rose, who believed he was destined for greatness. She sat beside him as he practised at the piano, and if his attention wandered, she was not afraid to get the whip out. The whippings seem to have worked. After his first public performance at the age of twelve, Grainger was hailed a child prodigy. The following year, Rose took him to study in Germany. It was here that he developed racial ideas that revolved around the superiority of the Nordic race. He immersed himself in Scandinavian myths and legends, which Rose also adored, and de-

cided that Germans and Italians had far too much influence on music. It was up to the Scandinavians and Anglo-Saxons — with Grainger at their head — to develop a revolutionary Nordic music.

Grainger toured the world and was a hit wherever he performed, both for his musical talents and his eccentricities. He was a striking looking fellow with piercing blue eyes and a shock of orange hair, and his energy was phenomenal. He liked to be in a state of exhaustion before giving a concert, and would run for miles beforehand, bursting onto the stage at the last minute (in London, he acquired the nickname 'the Jogging Pianist'). He rarely wore a hat, or an overcoat even in winter, and when travelling on trains liked to sleep upright in his seat rather than book a sleeping carriage. After touring New Zealand, and being impressed by Maori culture, he took to wearing brightly coloured shirts and shorts that his mother made for him out of towelling. His diet mainly consisted of rice pudding, nuts, cereals and oranges.

Granger's upbringing left an indelible mark on him, and his greatest pleasure was to whip women and be whipped in return. He indulged his passion with several female friends, but his intense relationship with his mother, who continued to control every aspect

of his life, prevented him taking a wife.

Grainger and his mother settled in the U.S. in 1915. While Rose remained a handsome looking woman, she was suffering from the effects of syphilis, contracted from her philandering husband years before. Her mental health began to decline, and rumours that her relationship with Percy was an incestuous one proved too much for her to bear. In 1922, she threw herself from the eighteenth floor of a building in New York, leaving a note denying it all. Grainger was devastated by her death, but kept up his manic schedule.

Grainger went on to marry a Swedish painter and poet, Ella Viola Strom, who came of approved blue-eyed Nordic stock. She had been apprised of the flagellation situation before their wedding (which took place during a concert at the Hollywood Bowl). For Grainger, flagellation was absolutely central to his creativity. He spent a great deal of time analysing his own sexuality and sharing his thoughts on it with friends. In one letter he wrote, 'Everything that deals with sexual matters absolutely knocks me over. I love to simply wade and swim in a sea of overwrought, ceaseless sexual thought… That is how I live, following my lusts, composing now and then on the side.'

Grainger's racial beliefs led him to develop what he called 'blue-eyed English', in which words which did not have Anglo-Saxon roots were eliminated. For him, a composer was a 'tone-smith', while he replaced the Italian terms traditionally used in music scores with phrases like 'louden lots bit by bit'. As a racialist, though, Grainger was as contradictory as ever, having many Jewish friends, championing negro causes and hailing Duke Ellington as a genius.

Grainger's music fell out of favour after World War II, and he returned to Australia. He spent his last years constructing machines that would play a new form of music he called 'free' or 'beatless', based on natural sounds. At night, he and Ella roamed the streets looking for junk to incorporate into these machines. One of them, called 'the kangaroo pouch free music machine', was nine feet tall and incorporated two large rolls of carpet. None were ever completed.

Grainger was one of the first musicians to take an interest in folk music, and his setting of an old English folk tune which he called 'Country Garden' was hugely popular around the world. He grew to loathe it, but it's the only piece of his music that has lasted. His legacy lives on in the museum devoted to himself which he gave to an aston-

ished University of Melbourne. As well as his musical memorabilia, it contains hundreds of photos that Grainger took of himself and his wife after flagellation sessions, as well as eighty-three whips, crotch protectors and a pair of blood-stained shorts — though not, as he had requested, his skeleton. 🕮

'Apart from sex I am not such a bad fellow.'
PERCY GRAINGER

GREEN, HETTY

(1834–1916)
'The Witch of Wall Street'

America's most celebrated miser was born Henrietta Howland Robinson in Bedford, Massachusetts. Her father, Edward Mott Robinson, was a member of a Quaker family which had made a fortune from whaling. Hetty (as she was always known) began acquiring business knowledge literally at her father's knee — he had her reading the stockmarket figures to him when she was six — and she also absorbed the family's natural sobriety and frugality, to a perhaps alarming degree.

When her father died in 1864, Hetty inherited cash and investments worth approximately $7.5 million. The following year saw the death of her aunt, Sylvia Ann Howland, who left Hetty half of her estate of $2 million, with the other half going to charity. Hetty contested the will (in an earlier version she had inherited the entire estate), and produced a document to support her claim which was alleged to be a forgery. She eventually lost the case, which caused much bitterness within the family.

In 1867, having spurned numerous suitors as fortune hunters, Hetty married the independently wealthy Edward Green (after he signed a prenuptial agreement foregoing any claim to her money). The couple moved to London, where Hetty invested heavily in bonds issued by the U.S. government after the Civil War ended. Other investors had been wary of them, but she made a huge profit. She also gave birth to two children — Edward (known as Ned) and Sylvia. Returning to the U.S., the family settled in Edward's home state, Vermont. Hetty continued to keep her financial activities separate from those of her husband, a wise move as he lost most of his money when a financial house he was involved in collapsed in 1885. Hetty left him and moved to New York with the children.

Hetty Green was an extraordinarily astute investor. She made a killing during the stockmarket

crash of 1873, buying up stocks which quickly regained their value. Much of her money went into solid investments like real estate and railroad companies, and she always took care to maintain large cash reserves. She became one of the bona fide tycoons of the day, fit to rub shoulders with the likes of John D. Rockefeller and J. P. Morgan. In 1907, when a financial crisis threatened to bring the U.S. economy down and Morgan called an emergency meeting to discuss the situation, Hetty was the only woman invited.

Her business savvy was matched only by her extreme stinginess. She lived with the children in cheap hotel rooms, moving around frequently between New York City, Hoboken and New Jersey so as to avoid paying state taxes. She refused to turn on heating and spurned hot water. Not wanting to waste money renting an office, she conducted most of her business in a space allocated to her by the Chemical Bank, where the bulk of her funds were deposited. She wore a single long black dress, and as she only ever washed the hem, it eventually turned a shade of green. She is said to have lived mostly on oatmeal and onions. Some of the stories told about her are probably apocryphal, such as the one about her spending a whole night searching for a two-cent stamp. But there's no doubt about the most appalling one of them all. One day, when Ned was still a child, he dislocated his knee while sledding. Hetty attempted to treat the injury herself, and when that failed, took him to Bellevue Hospital where she tried to have him admitted as a pauper. She was recognised though, and when the hospital demanded payment, she refused and took the boy away. When Edward Green heard what was going on he offered to pay for treatment immediately, but by then it was too late. Ned had to have his leg amputated, and afterwards got around on an artificial one made of cork.

Hetty suffered badly in her later years from a hernia, but refused to pay $150 for an operation to fix it. When she died at the age of eighty-one, after suffering a series of strokes which left her in a wheel-chair, she was widely reported to have been the richest woman in the world, with an estimated fortune of $100 million.

She left it all to her children, who reacted against her parsimony in different ways. Ned lived extravagantly, indulging in numerous interests ranging from stamp collecting to auto racing, while Sylvia became a philanthropist of legendary generosity.

GREEN, STANLEY

(1915–1993)
'The Protein Man'

For a quarter of a century, Green kept up a lonely campaign against the immoderate eating of proteins — and the passions he was convinced that this aroused.

Born in London, Green served in the navy during World War II, and later worked as a civil servant, storeman and gardener. He began his campaign in 1965, and from then on could be seen walking up and down London's busiest shopping strip, Oxford Street, on most days, carrying a large placard which originally read: 'LESS LUST FROM LESS PROTEIN: MEAT FISH BIRD: EGG CHEESE: PEAS BEANS NUTS. AND SITTING.' (Later, he changed 'LUST' to 'PASSION'.) He also sold a pamphlet called *Eight Passion Proteins with Care*, which he printed himself on a clanking old press in his council flat in Northolt. He is supposed to have sold an astonishing 87,000 copies of this passionate (in an acceptable way) work. An extract:

At some point in our twenties, when the body comes to adult perfection and size, we cease to require protein for body building, and so passion gets a bonus of protein, if we do not eat less of protein, correspondingly. During late youth, energetic games would help to keep the passion gentle and help to develop the growing body, too. Yet, even a growing youth could eat more protein than the body required for health and development, and thus, by having more passion, it might be very hard to be well behaved with a sexual friend, and to be headstrong in one's lonely bed: HARD to follow a responsible moral-code, in the unmarried years.

Use your unaided will, for as long as you can, to develop your character; but do not let passion defeat you, ALONE, nor with a sexual friend.

Green didn't like it when he was mistaken for, as he put it, 'a religious nut.' Sometimes people spat at him too, which led him to wear a pair of green overalls. After his death his placards and other paraphernalia went to the Museum of London.

GURDJIEFF, GEORGE IVANOVITCH

(c. 1880–1949)
Guru

Gurdjieff kept much of his early life obscure, starting with the date of his birth (he gave it as 1866, but it was likely up to twenty years later). He was born in Alexandropol in what is now Armenia, close to the Russian-Turkish border, a region

teeming with different languages, cultures and religions. His mother was Armenian, his father a Greek carpenter and storyteller, a preserver of oral traditions. He was also, according to his son's account, a harsh disciplinarian who exposed the young Gurdjieff to snakes and other terrors in order to make him fearless.

Gurdjieff characterised his teachings as ancient wisdom that he had gleaned from various enlightened individuals while travelling extensively during the first four decades of his life. He gave an account of them in his lively if not entirely factual book, *Meetings with Remarkable Men.*

Whatever the real extent of his travels, which he claimed included visits to Egypt and Tibet, he enters undisputed history in Moscow in 1912, the persona of imperious, exotic, hypnotically powerful guru already firmly established. In 1915, he met his most important disciple, the Russian journalist P.D. Ouspensky (1878–1947), who was enormously taken by Gurdjieff's 'system'. While this eventually grew to include an elaborate psychological theory and a preposterous cosmology, Gurdjieff's basic idea was a simple one. Human beings, he taught, are so deadened by habits and routine that they are like robots, literally asleep. Gurdjieff's goal was

to jolt them awake. To achieve this he prescribed hard work, breathing exercises, fasting, chanting and the performance of incredibly complicated physical routines. He also liked to keep those around him off guard by making contradictory and outrageous demands, throwing tantrums, causing conflicts and summarily rejecting them (it seems to have been the lot of every Gurdjieff disciple to be rejected at some stage). Ouspensky could never decide how much charlatanry lay behind Gurdjieff's façade. He later tried to distance himself from the teacher while retaining many of the teachings, but, as others would find, this was not an easy thing to do.

Gurdjieff moved his band of followers to Finland briefly in 1916, then spent the next few years in somewhat perilous journeyings across civil war-torn Russia. After brief sojourns in Constantinople, Germany and England, he moved to France in 1922, leased a mansion in Fontainebleau, and established the Institute for the Harmonious Development of Man, also known as the Prieure. Here his followers, mainly poor Russian exiles, rich British spiritual dabblers and members of his own family, put Gurdjieff's system, otherwise known as 'the Work', into practice. And work it was. Expected to surrender their will completely to their master,

GEORGE
IVANOVITCH GURDJIEFF

they lived a punishing routine of household chores, pointless tasks, like digging holes, and the usual mind-bogglingly difficult exercises, punctuated by spontaneous, lavish banquets. Many seemed to benefit, at least temporarily, from this lifestyle. Gurdjieff's experiment gained considerable publicity around the world, and celebrities such as D.H. Lawrence went to investigate. The New Zealand writer Katherine Mansfield, dying of tuberculosis, spent her last three months at the Prieure (as well as joining in the hard work, she was ordered to spend several hours each day in the stables, where Gurdjieff said she would benefit from the cows' breath).

Perhaps it was all going too smoothly for Gurdjieff, who seemed to want to make his own life as precarious as those of his followers. In 1924, he was involved in a mysterious car crash (staged, according to his detractors) while driving back to Fontainebleau from Paris. Found alone beside his crashed car, apparently seriously injured yet covered with a blanket and with a pillow beneath his head, he quickly recovered, but expelled most of the Prieure's inhabitants shortly afterwards. It continued for several years, but Gurdjieff seemed to have lost interest in it, and devoted most of his time to writing.

Gurdjieff spent the 1930s living a bohemian life in Paris, teaching smaller groups of disciples and making occasional forays to America in search of money. He remained in Paris during the war, securing by his considerable wits a remarkably comfortable existence during the occupation. After the war, many of his British and American disciples returned to see him, and there was talk of setting up another institute. But in 1949, the formerly robust guru sprang his last surprise on them by sickening rapidly and dying. In the following year they arranged the publication of his lengthy book, the monumentally puzzling *Belzebub's Tales to his Grandson*. Gurdjieff was no writer, however, and the spirit of the man survives not in his books, but in the anecdotes told about him by his hapless disciples, many of them extremely funny. ▣

GWYER, JOSEPH

(1835–?)
Potato seller & poet

Gwyer, the son of a farmer and proud resident of Penge in southeast London, has been called England's answer to ☛ William McGonagall. He was inspired to write poetry while in hospital recovering from an abscess.

The doctor gave me orders, too,
No more hard work I should do,
So what to do I did not know,
When poetry began to flow.

The subject of my first attempt
Was Irish Church, by Gladstone met;
Since then many rhymes I've wrote,
On subjects varied made a note.

He shared many of these subjects with McGonagall, including royalty, shipwrecks, state visits and temperance. (Gwyer was, by his own account, a bit of a tearaway as a youth, with an inordinate fondness for beer, skittles and street pranks, until he became a Methodist and saw the light.) To these he added his own pet subject — potatoes, which is not surprising given that Gwyer made his living selling them.

In Ivy Cottage, Hawthorn Grove
Your humble servant dwell
I traffic not in gold or gems
But to the public sell –

Potatoes, which stand next to bread
The staff of life to man
So if the chance presents itself
Buy of me if you can.

I travel with my horse and van
For twelve miles round or more
With Ware Potatoes for the high,
The low, the rich, the poor

My goods as such I think will vie
With any salesman round
Their cheapness and their worth combined
Will you I'm sure astound.

Gwyer bombarded Queen Victoria and other royal personages with samples of his verse. He was proud of the curt letters sent by private secretaries acknowledging their receipt, and reprinted them in his books. Like some of the other celebrated bad poets, he exhibited a curious blindness to criticism couched in ironic or facetious terms. In his self-published *Life of Joseph Gwyer, (Potato Salesman); with his Poems, (Commended by Royalty)* (1876), Gwyer happily included several reviews of this kind, the highlight being a hysterical three page overview of his career reprinted from *The World* magazine. ('Long have we watched in vain for the advent of a genuine new poet, but at last we have the unspeakable happiness of hailing that auspicious event.')

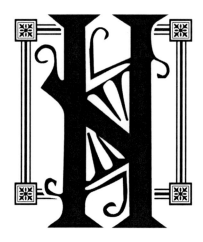

HAJDU, KAROLY
see Dr. Charlotte BACH

HAMILTON, ALEXANDER

(1767–1852)
Aristocrat

Alexander, the 10th Duke of Hamilton, was the most titled man in Scotland, having inherited several dukedoms, baronetcies, earldoms and other titles after his father's death in 1819, and had such an intense belief in the importance of these things that he was known as 'the proudest man in Britain'. He was a member of the House of Commons for several years, holding various official posts, including that of Lord High Steward at the coronation of Queen Victoria and, later, Trustee of the British Museum, and

was also a noted dandy. Nicknamed 'El Magnifico', he remained a fabulously dressed creature into old age, his fingers covered with gold rings. He married Susan Euphemia Beckford, a great beauty and the second daughter of ☞ William Beckford. Their home was Hamilton Palace in South Lanarkshire, the largest non-Royal residence in Britain.

Hamilton was a friend of the Egyptologist Thomas Pettigrew, who used to entertain his dinner guests by bringing out mummies and unwrapping them. Hamilton decided that he would like to be mummified when he died, and engaged Pettigrew to carry out the task. He bought what was supposed to be the sarcophagus of an Egyptian princess, originally intended for the British Museum, to serve as his coffin, and built an elaborate domed mausoleum 120 feet (thirty-six metres) high in the grounds of Hamilton Palace to house the first nine dukes, and himself when the time came.

One thing played on his mind, though — he wasn't sure that the sarcophagus would prove to be big enough, and his last words on his deathbed were said to have been 'Double me up! Double me up!' Pettigrew performed the mummification as requested but, alas, the Duke's fears had been well founded, and he did not fit inside the sar-

cophagus. Instead of doubling him up, though, they cut his feet off and laid them beside him. ▣

HAMPTON, JAMES

(1909–1964)
Throne maker and visionary

Hampton was an African-American janitor who lived in Washington D.C. A month and a half after his death from stomach cancer, Meyer Wertlieb, who owned a garage that Hampton had rented for years, opened its door and beheld an amazing sight.

The interior had been transformed into an ornate, glittering throne room. The centrepiece was the throne itself, and arranged symmetrically on each side of it were other objects, some looking like church furniture — altars, pulpits and the like — and many, like the throne, equipped with wings which can also resemble eyes. In all, there were about 180 objects, each wrapped in silver or gold foil. And while it all looked solid enough, it was made of such flimsy materials that a stiff wind would have blown much of it away.

The creator of *The Throne of the Third Heaven of the Nations' Millennium General Assembly*, as he called it, was born in Elloree, South Carolina. His father, also named James Hampton,

abandoned his wife and four children to become an itinerant Baptist preacher. In 1928, Hampton went to Washington D.C. where he lived with his brother Lee and worked as a cook. He served in the army for three years during World War II, and at one point was stationed on Guam. Back home, he worked in various jobs before securing a position as a janitor with the General Services Administration.

Hampton made at least one of the smaller objects in the throne room in Guam, but it is believed that he began working on it in earnest around 1950. He bought furniture in secondhand shops, and scavenged through the streets looking for materials to incorporate into it — foil, light bulbs, electrical cord, tin cans, cardboard tubes — and assembled them using tacks, pins and glue. He finished his janitor's shift at midnight and worked in the garage until dawn. He told few people about what he was doing, although at some point someone took a photo of him, dressed in a dark suit and tie as would befit a minister, standing stiffly in front of his creation.

The words 'Fear not', a quote from the Bible, appear above the central throne, and Hampton wrote numerous inscriptions on the objects, including references to biblical passages, particularly passages from Revelation. Tacked

onto a notice board on the wall was a quotation from Proverbs: 'Where there is no vision the people perish.' Adding to the mystery are the other writings that Hampton left behind in the garage. Some of them are notes in English in which he apparently recorded various visions he had over the years, including one which states, 'This is true that on October 2, 1946, the great Virgin Mary and the star of Bethlehem appeared over the nation's capitol.' Most intriguing of all is a 112-page notebook, *St. James: The Book of the 7 Dispensation* [sic], which is written in code. Nobody has been able to decipher this as yet, although linguists believe that it is indeed a coherent language.

The throne and its trappings are clearly saturated with symbolic meanings, and although their precise nature may never be known, it seems clear that the structure as a whole refers to the end of the millennium. The throne could therefore represent the one that, according to Revelation, Christ will occupy on his return — or did Hampton intend it be the actual throne? Another suggestion is that Hampton wanted to be a preacher like his father, but he was too painfully shy (it appears that his brother was the only close friend he ever had). It may be that he wanted his throne to do the talking for him.

Meyer Wertlieb sold Hampton's creation to two men who donated it to the Smithsonian Institution. It is now recognised as one of the great masterpieces of American visionary art.

For other secret creators, see ☞ Henry Darger and ☞ A.G. Rizzoli. ▣

HANKS, FLETCHER
(1887 – 1976)
Comic book artist

Hanks was only active in the American comic book field for about three years from 1939 to 1941, but in that time he produced some of the strangest works ever issued by commercial comics publishers. His artwork is crude, almost amateurish, but the images he conjures up are so surreal — a gigantic spider stinging an elephant to death, all the policeman of New York suspended in the air, humans and beasts fleeing gigantic disembodied flaming hands — that the overall effect is oddly compelling.

Hanks was working at the very dawn of the superhero era (Superman having debuted in 1939), before its conventions were fully worked out. The chief heroes of his strips are Stardust the Super Wizard ('the most remarkable person ever known'), a square-jawed fellow with

unfeasibly large shoulders; and Fantomah, the Mystery Woman of the Jungle, a glamorous blonde whose face turns into a skull when she is angry. They possess various super powers, secret rays and the like, and are pitted against a succession of grotesque criminals. The basic set-ups are thus similar to other superhero comics. But Hanks' criminals are not interested in anything so mundane as kidnap or bank robbery — they're more intent on wiping out whole civilisations. Their extravagant plots include destroying gravity so that all Earth's inhabitants float into space, setting fire to Mars, and causing Venus and Earth to crash into each other. And the treatment they receive when these plots are foiled is correspondingly cruel, even sadistic. Some of the punishments meted out by Stardust include the following:

- ❖ A gang of criminals are left hanging in the air, with the skeletons of their victims dangling beside them.
- ❖ A criminal is transformed into an enlarged head, which Stardust carries into space and hurls at 'the Headless Headhunter… the hugest giant in the universe'. The head lands on the Headhunter's shoulders and is absorbed into its body, crying out as it sinks, 'Help! Help!'

- ❖ A criminal is placed in a 'floating prison of eternal ice' with Stardust declaring, 'In your frozen condition, you'll live forever — to think about your crimes!'

These violent, dreamlike (or rather nightmare-like) tales appeared in various small-circulation comic books, and for years were known only to a small band of collectors. Almost nothing was known about their creator's life until the artist and writer Paul Karasik tracked down his son, Fletcher Hanks Jr., who had distinguished himself as a pilot during World War II. The younger Hanks told Karasic that his father, the son of a Methodist preacher, had grown up in Oxford, Maryland, and was a violent alcoholic who physically abused his wife and sons (at one point, he threw Fletcher Jr. down a flight of stairs, causing a head injury that left him unable to speak properly for five years, and he once punched his wife so hard that bones in her face were broken). Around 1930, when Fletcher Jr. was ten, his father simply abandoned them, and the family had little to do with him after that. In January 1976, Fletcher Hanks was discovered by police, frozen to death on a park bench in New York.

Stardust couldn't have handled it better.

HARDEN-HICKEY, JAMES

(1854–1898)
Prince James I of Trinidad

The flamboyant Harden-Hickey was born in San Francisco according to most accounts. His father, E.C. Hickey, was of Irish extraction, and his mother was French. She took him to France at an early age, and he was educated at a Jesuit school in Belgium, and later the French military academy of Saint Cyr. Harden-Hickey absorbed the heady atmosphere of Paris during the Second Empire, with the economy booming and the theatres packed every night. He also became an ardent royalist, throwing in his lot with those who wished to restore the Bourbon monarchy.

Graduating from the military academy, he emerged as an expert swordsman, but chose not to join the army. Instead he followed a more bohemian path, frequenting the Latin Quarter, dabbling in journalism and penning a number of swashbuckling novels. In 1878, he married the Countess de Saint-Pery, and they had two children. He started an inflammatory, pro-Bourbon newspaper, *Triboulet*, which attracted many lawsuits and saw Harden-Hickey fighting numerous duels in the Bois de Boulogne. He was also an ardent Catholic, and for services rendered to the Church was made a baron of the Holy Roman Empire.

After his newspaper folded in 1888, he went to London where he boarded an English merchant ship, intending to travel around the world. One of the places it stopped at was the small, rocky island of Trinidad, 700 miles (1,127 km) off the coast of Brazil (and not to be confused with the much larger island of Trinidad in the West Indies). While the British had claimed it years before, and a small group of Portuguese had occupied it for a time, it was then uninhabited. It was impossible to land on for much of the year, the seas around it being so rough, but Harden-Hickey managed to, and took the opportunity of claiming it for himself, after running up a flag he had designed.

He continued on his world trip, and stayed for a year in India after becoming interested in Buddhism. Back in Paris, he met an American girl, Annie Flagler, the daughter of John H. Flagler, an iron and steel magnate, and they married in New York in 1891. While Flagler had objected to the marriage, he actually rather liked his son-in-law, and showed considerable tolerance for his mad schemes over the next few years. This affection was not returned by Harden-Hinkley, who thought of himself as a gentleman

from an earlier era, and believed Flagler to be tainted by his involvement in business. He was happy enough to take his money though, and used it to buy cattle ranches and mines in Califonia, Texas and Mexico.

He also proclaimed himself James I of the Principality of Trinidad, and issued a prospectus to attract settlers to his island. This emphasised the money that could be made from its turtles, birdlife and guano deposits, and also noted it was reputed to have buried treasure. He commissioned a crown from a firm of jewellers, and appointed his friend, the Count de la Boissiere, as his minister of foreign affairs. He also inaugurated a new order of chivalry, and issued postage stamps.

Harden-Hickey was perfectly serious about his venture. He engaged hundreds of Chinese labourers who began to build docks and houses on Trinidad. It was all going wonderfully, when the British came along and spoiled the party. In the midst of laying an undersea telegraph cable to Brazil, they found that Trinidad made an excellent cable station, and reclaimed it. De la Boissiere fired off a letter of protest to the U.S. Secretary of State, requesting that the U.S. recognise the Principality of Trinidad as an independent state and come to its aid. The Secretary of State promptly handed the letter over to the press, which had great

sport with it.

The loss of his kingdom hit Harden-Hickey hard. He began to plan an invasion of Trinidad (in a nod to his Irish roots, this was to be mounted from Ireland) and asked his father-in-law to fund it, but Flagler declined. In an attempt to maintain his lavish lifestyle, he tried to sell off some of his properties, including a large tract of land in Mexico, but could find no buyers. He had also grown estranged from his wife, so the prospect of further funding seemed distant.

A few years earlier, Harden-Hickey had written a book called *Euthanasia, or the Ethics of Suicide*. He argued in this that 'it is of greater moment to live well than to live long, and that often it is living well not to live long', and detailed numerous suicide methods (accompanied by his own illustrations). Taking his own advice, he booked into a hotel in El Paso, Texas, and swallowed a fatal dose of morphine. His crown was found in a trunk beside him. ▣

HARTLEY, KELVER
(1909–1988)
Academic & recluse

Born in Adelaide, South Australia, Hartley was the only son of a clerk, Frank Hartley Jones, and his wife Clara (the family, who clearly had social ambitions, would later drop the surname Jones). They spent several years in Britain during the 1910s, Clara believing (erroneously) that she had wealthy relatives there. Back in Australia, Hartley studied for a Bachelor of Arts at Sydney University, and did so well at French that he was awarded a French government scholarship to study in Paris for two years. During his stay there, he became involved in right-wing politics, and attained a doctorate with a study of the French influences in Oscar Wilde's work.

Back from France, Hartley taught at various schools around New South Wales, and in 1955 was appointed Senior Lecturer in French at Newcastle University College. When this became the University of Newcastle in 1965, he was made the inaugural Chair of the French Department. He was a dedicated if somewhat idiosyncratic teacher, who would interrupt his lessons with tales of taking part in street protests during his Paris days, demonstrations of fencing, or anecdotes about witchcraft, medieval torture methods and other interesting arcana. His most notable characteristic, though, was his incredible shyness, especially in front of female students. He always took care to be in a classroom long before anyone else had arrived, and used to hide in the lavatory between lessons. Where

he lived was a mystery to everyone at the university — if another staff member gave him a lift home, he insisted on being dropped off some distance from it. Inevitably, rumours sprang up about his private life, with some maintaining he had a sideline writing sexy novels.

On retiring in 1969, Hartley made the unusual request that his $30,000 in entitlements be paid in cash. It was delivered in an armoured truck, and Hartley carried it away in a suitcase. Few of his colleagues ever heard from or saw him again. He bought a small flat in Sydney, and seems to have devoted most of his time to writing fiction. He wrote a number of science fiction tales and sent these off to American magazines, but only one was ever accepted.

Although Hartley's academic career had been a respectable one, and he had published papers in several journals, he clearly believed he had never reached his full potential. Perhaps to make up for this, he conceived a plan to turn his savings into a million dollars, which he would leave to the French Department of the University of Newcastle, on the condition that it be used to fund students who wished to study in France. Having written a will to this effect, he made the odd decision to move to Mexico. He sold his flat, used the proceeds to buy more

KELVER HARTLEY

shares, and set off in 1984, but the Mexican authorities refused to grant him residency.

He returned to Sydney and rented a $25 room in a boarding house in Glebe. He rarely spoke to the other tenants, although they knew from his mail he had once been a professor. All his efforts were devoted to raising that million dollars. He wore a threadbare suit and plastic sandals, lived mostly on oranges, and walked everywhere rather than pay for public transport. Thanks to his frugality, his assets rose above the million mark, but then disaster struck, with the 1987 share crash reducing it to about $950,000. For Hartley, whose health had been failing, this seems to have been one disappointment too many. He swallowed a handful of barbiturates washed down with alcohol, and died.

Afterwards, the manuscripts of two books were found in his room. The first was a long, almost incomprehensible political essay called *Optimism*, written in the forties, in which he denounced democracy and called for society to be ruled by scientists (he was so convinced of the importance of this work that dates in it are expressed in terms of the half life of radium). The second was a novel with autobiographical elements, *Remus Leaping*, apparently completed in the seventies, and dealing with spiritualism, sex and murder.

The share market soon rallied, making Hartley's assets worth considerably more than a million dollars, and the Hartley Bequest Program paid for the first student to travel to France in 1997. It has also arranged for the publication of several volumes of 'Kelveriana', including a memorial book featuring fond reminiscences of Hartley by former students, *Remus Leaping* (issued under the title *The Haunting of Dr. McQuaig*) and a collection of his science fiction stories. ▨

HARTMANN, SADAKICHI

(1867–1944)
Poet & art critic

Hartmann, born in Nagasaki, Japan, was the son of a wealthy German coffee merchant, Otto von Hartmann, who married a Japanese woman, Osada. After the death of his mother, he and his older brother were sent to Germany. He was educated in private schools and briefly enrolled in a naval academy, which he hated and ran away from. His father, who had remarried, decided that the best place for the boy would be the United States, and booked his passage on a steamship. He arrived in 1882, and went to live with relatives in Philadelphia.

Hartmann worked in menial jobs, read voraciously in his spare time,

and set his sights on a career in the arts. He befriended the ageing poet Walt Whitman and published a small booklet recording his conversations with him (Whitman objected to it, claiming he had been misquoted). He made several trips back to Europe where, thanks to contacts he had made through Whitman, he was able to hobnob with some of the leading musicians, artists and poets of the day, including ☞ Algernon Swinburne in London and Stéphane Mallarmé in Paris. He began writing for newspapers and literary magazines, and founded a short-lived journal, *Art News*, in New York in 1896. He was also writing symbolist poems and dramatic works, and created a stir in 1893 with the play *Christ*, which one reviewer called 'absolutely the most daring of all decadent productions'. Most copies of it were burnt and Hartmann was thrown in jail for a week.

His reputation as an art critic was cemented in 1901 with the publication of his two-volume *History of American Art*, which became a standard work. Hartmann discovered many young artists, and was also the first critic to take photography seriously as an artform. He travelled around the country giving lectures and promoting artists he liked. He was also quick to point out what he didn't like, and made many enemies. Once, while attending a performance by Moriz Rosenthal of Lizst's 'Hungarian Rhapsody', he objected to the pianist's variations on the score by shouting 'Is this necessary?!' As he was escorted from the concert hall he commented, 'I am a man needed but not wanted.'

If Hartmann revered genius when he saw it in others, his favourite genius was himself. Convinced that the world owed him a living, he was a consummate sponger, adept at wheedling his way into the houses of the rich until, inevitably, he outwore his welcome and was forcibly ejected. During the 1910s, he lived in Greenwich Village, where his rollicking lifestyle led to him being dubbed 'King of Bohemia', a title later assumed by ☞ Maxwell Bodenheim.

Hartmann's career began to decline after 1920, with his chronic asthma and increasingly heavy drinking taking their toll. He moved out to California, where he latched onto Douglas Fairbanks and scored his only acting role as a court magician in Fairbanks' 1924 epic *The Thief of Baghdad*. When he grumbled about having to be on set, wearing his character's elaborate and heavy headdress, while lights and camera were readied, Fairbanks assigned a look-alike to take his place. It is believed that this was the first use of a stand-in.

By the late 1930s, Hartmann was living in a shack on an Indian reservation in Banning, California.

He was now a decrepit if still striking figure, over six feet (182 cm) tall and stick thin, with a wizened face and a shock of grey hair. He was suffering from a scrotal hernia which he refused to have treated, and wore a bulky, homemade truss which gave him a somewhat priapic outline. It was at this point that he was adopted by a hard drinking band of Hollywood veterans which included W.C. Fields, John Barrymore, the writer Gene Fowler and the artist John Decker (who once attracted the attention of the F.B.I. when he painted several caricatures of Eleanor Roosevelt which, when turned upside down, resembled a certain part of the female anatomy).

The group, which met in Decker's studio in Bundy Avenue, was entertained by Hartmann's oracular pronouncements, tales of carousing with the likes of Mallarmé and Verlaine, and lively dancing (hernia notwithstanding). For Barrymore, he was 'the last of the Pharoahs, and nicely mummified at that', although Fields was a dissenting voice, calling him 'a no-good bum'. Fowler was prevailed on to write a biography of the old rascal, which he did in a way, producing an amusing book called *Minutes of the Last Meeting*, which is as much about the Bundy Avenue gang's hijinks as it is about Hartmann (who had advised Fowler at the beginning of the project, 'Be careful that you do not fall in love with your subject — in love with my wonderful character and genius.')

When America entered the war, Hartmann, with his German/Japanese background, inevitably came within the sights of the F.B.I. Most of his remaining friends dropped him and he spent his last days in fear of being interned. In late 1944, he went to visit one of his daughters in Florida (Hartmann was married twice and had, by his reckoning, thirteen children). This unusual specimen, in equal parts gifted and preposterous, died in her house, while sitting on a chair.

'I have symptoms of immortality.'

SADAKICHI HARTMANN

HASTINGS, HENRY

(1551–1650)
Squire

Hastings is the earliest recorded example of a certain eccentric archetype, the sports-mad, animal-loving English country gentleman who would reach his full flower in the form of ☞ Jack Mytton. He was a younger son of the Earl of Huntingdon, and became the squire of Woodlands in 1587. He was a squat, red haired fellow who always wore green, and he loved to hunt anything that moved. He lived on a large estate with many fish ponds, in a house full of hawks, dogs and cats, with fox skins adorning the walls and bones scattered about the floor. At dinner, three or four cats would be at his table, and he kept a white stick by his plate to keep them away from the choicest bits of meat. He used the pulpit of one of the house's chapels to store his beef, venison and bacon, being the best place to keep it from the dogs.

Hastings had an eye for the ladies and, according to a contemporary account, when he wasn't hunting or fishing he would 'caress his neighbours' wives and daughters, there being not a woman in all his walks, of the degree of a yeoman's wife, or under, and under the age of forty, but it was her own fault if he was not acquainted with her'. He ate oysters twice a day, every day (presumably for their supposed aphrodisiac qualities), was still riding horses in his eighties, and lived to be ninety-nine.

HAWKER, ROBERT STEPHEN
(1803–1875)
The Vicar of Morwenstow

Hawker, the son and grandson of clergymen, was born in Plymouth, England, and grew up in Cornwall. He was a high-spirited youth who became known for his practical jokes, which included impersonating a mermaid and painting the local doctor's horse with zebra stripes. He studied at Oxford, wrote poetry, and at the age of nineteen married forty-one-year-old Charlotte I'ans. After graduating he took holy orders, and, in 1834, he was assigned the parish of Morwenstow, a desperately bleak and isolated spot on the Cornish coast, prone to fierce storms and the scene of numerous shipwrecks.

The people of Morwenstow, mostly farmers and labourers living in or close to poverty, had been without a vicar for over a century. Hawker set about gaining their trust. He was a compassionate man and often used his own income to help the poor. He remained shocked by their often brutish ways (while acknowledging that these were the result of poverty), and did his best to civilise them, discouraging them from looting the wrecks (a favourite pastime for centuries) and urging parents to send their children to school. On the whole, he preferred the company of animals and birds to human beings. He kept numerous cats and dogs which were always welcome in his church during services (although there may be no truth in the oft-told tale that he ex-

communicated one of his cats after it caught a mouse on Sunday).

Hawker detested black clothes, the usual attire of Anglican clergymen, and as a young curate could be seen wearing a purple velvet cape, a stole embroidered with gold, and scarlet gloves. In later years, he wore a claret or purple coat, blue fisherman's jumper, knee-high boots and a variety of unusual hats. This colourful attire was in marked contrast to his often grim duties, which included retrieving and burying horribly mutilated corpses washed up after shipwrecks. While the sea could be terrifying to Hawker, it could also be inspiring. Using timber salvaged from wrecks, he built a little hut into the cliff below his church. Here he would sit, looking out on the vast Atlantic and writing poetry.

Hawker read few contemporary books and had little time for the modern world. He was essentially medieval in outlook, and lived in a world where the supernatural was never far from the surface. He was fascinated by local folklore, and firmly believed in ghosts, angels, demons, pixies and brownies, having seen a few of them himself. At some point, probably in the 1850s, he developed an opium habit, and it may have been under the influence of the drug that he wrote his finest poem, *The Quest of the Sangraal*, an Arthurian epic in blank verse which

was admired by Tennyson.

Hawker's wife Charlotte died in 1863, and the following year he married Pauline Kuczynski, the daughter of a Polish exile. Again there was an age gap, although this time it was the other way round — Hawker was sixty and Pauline twenty. Like his first marriage, however, it was a genuine love match, and he and Pauline had three daughters. In his last years, illness and financial worries contributed to a mental decline, and he became increasingly paranoid, believing that others were working to undermine him. On his deathbed, he converted to Catholicism.

Hawker's life of splendid isolation, charity, hard work and old-fashioned mysticism caught the imagination of the Victorians, and after his death, many apocryphal stories about him circulated. The little wooden hut he built survives, and is the smallest structure registered with the National Trust. ▓

HEAVISIDE, OLIVER
(1850–1925)
Scientist

Heaviside was a brilliant, mainly self-taught scientist who made major contributions to electrical engineering and telegraphy, although the importance of many of them was not appreciated until after his death.

He was born in Camden Town, then a very rough, working class area of London. His mother ran a school for girls, which he also attended for a while, and his sense of being an outsider increased when a bout of scarlet fever left him almost deaf. He was an extremely shy boy, and remained socially awkward all his life.

He left school at the age of sixteen, but continued to educate himself. Encouraged by his uncle, Sir Charles Wheatstone, who had been one of the inventors of the telegraph in the 1830s, he studied telegraphy, as well as several languages including Danish. This enabled him to take a job with a telegraphy company in Denmark, the only paid work he had in his lifetime, but quit when he was twenty-four. He retired to his parents' house to devote himself to mathematical and scientific studies. One of his greatest achievements was to produce a much simplified version of the equations developed by James Clerk Maxwell to predict the movement of electromagnetic waves. He was also one of the first scientists to predict the existence of the ionosphere.

Heaviside rarely left his room. His family would leave meals outside his door, but he was very fussy about what he ate, and sometimes went for days consuming nothing but milk. Like an earlier scientist, ☞ Richard Kirwin, he had a morbid fear of the cold, and went around swathed in blankets. Later, he would rack up huge heating bills which he could not afford to pay.

Heaviside published numerous scientific papers, but they acquired a reputation for being difficult to understand, and many of his ideas were ignored, including his suggestion for using induction coils to reduce distortion in telegraph and telephone lines. (It was later patented by an American scientist named Pupin who made a fortune from it, a bitter blow to Heaviside.) In 1889 he received the highest praise of his life when Lord Kelvin, the incoming president of the Institution for Electrical Engineers, called his work in telegraphy the best in the field. Soon after this, Heaviside moved to Devonshire with his parents. After their death in the mid-nineties, he moved into a house in the village of Newton Abbot. His peculiarities soon became known to the villagers, and the local boys would stand outside his house chanting 'Poop-poop-poopin!' (a reference to the American who, as Heaviside was keen to tell people, had stolen his ideas).

Heaviside's behaviour grew stranger in his last years. He replaced the furniture in his house with granite blocks, and took to painting his fingernails pink. His sense of inferiority increased, and he signed letters with the initials

W.O.R.M. He died at the age of seventy-four after falling from a ladder while attempting to help a workman repair his roof. ▣

HERVEY, FREDERICK

(1730–1803)
The Earl-Bishop of Derry

The aristocratic Herveys were an English family so associated with wild and unpredictable behaviour during the eighteenth century that it was said that 'God created men, women and Herveys'. Frederick Hervey, the 4th Earl of Bristol and Bishop of Derry, was perhaps the wildest and most unpredictable of them all.

Hervey took holy orders at the age of twenty-four. In 1867, thanks to the influence of his brother the 2nd Earl, who was briefly Lord Lieutenant of Ireland, he was appointed the Bishop of Cloyne, and a year later was promoted to the much richer bishopric of Derry.

He immediately embarked on an ambitious building programme. He declared that all churches in his diocese should have spires, and built roads and the first bridge across the Foyle River. These activities earned him the nickname 'the Edifying Bishop'. He also built three massive residences, Downhill and Ballyscullion in Ireland, and Ickworth in the

family seat of Suffolk in England, which was the most impressive of them all (although he never actually saw it, being too busy travelling on the continent in his later years).

The English bishop was popular with his Irish flock thanks to his extremely liberal political and religious views. He was a supporter of both the Americans in their war of independence, and of the nationalist Irish Volunteer movement. He also believed that all religions should be treated equally, and his theological views were so idiosyncratic — and his conversation so blasphemous — that some doubted he was a Christian at all. While in many ways he was a diligent (albeit often absent) bishop, it's fair to say that he did not take his ecclesiastical duties entirely seriously. He once organised a horse race between Protestant and Presbyterian clergy on the seashore near Downhill. A contemporary account noted that, 'The established clergy being rather portly men who were more accustomed to drive in their carriages than to ride on horseback, tumbled from their horses — while the Presbyterians, being leaner men, kept their seats.' On another occasion, he arranged for his fattest clergymen to take part in a running race, the prize being a desirable appointment. As part of the course went through a bog, none were able to complete it.

Hervey was also famed for his ostentatious dress. He arrived at an Irish Volunteers convention one day wearing 'episcopal purple, white gloves with a gold fringe around the wrists and golden tassels and diamond buckles on his knees and shoes', having been 'drawn through the streets in an open Landau by six horses caparisoned with purple ribbons'. Hervey repeatedly bowed to the enthusiastic crowd, and was rewarded with cries of 'Long live the Bishop!'

Hervey married Elizabeth Davers in 1852, and they had four sons and three daughters whom he treated rather shabbily. He would write to them from abroad, urging them to economise, while he was spending large sums on paintings and statues. He travelled endlessly through Italy, Germany, Switzerland and Spain in an enormous carriage, with two cooks riding ahead so they could prepare his dinner wherever he happened to be staying that night.

In the last eleven years of his life, Hervey did not bother to return to Britain at all. He spent much of his time in Rome, and his colourful costumes meant he was often mistaken for a Catholic bishop — to the great annoyance of the Vatican. He was romantically linked to a number of them, including Countess von Lichtenau, former mistress of Frederick William II of Prussia. He used to keep a picture of her around his neck, in place of a cross.

He was taken ill while riding in Italy one day in 1803, and carried to a peasant's outhouse, where he died. His body was shipped back to Britain the following year. As sailors in those days were superstitious about having corpses on board their ships, it was put into a box and labelled 'antique statue'. ▨

HEYBOER, ANTON
(1924–2005)
Artist

Heyboer was born in Sabang in the Dutch East Indies (now Indonesia). He was the son of a mechanical engineer, and his family moved around constantly during the 1920s and thirties, living at various times in the Netherlands, New York and Curaçao. They were in Haarlem in the Netherlands when World War II broke out. In 1943, Heyboer was transferred to a forced labour camp in Berlin, where he almost died.

In 1951, Heyboer admitted himself into a psychiatric hospital in Bloomendaal, but left after a year, determined to become an artist. Working at a furious pace, he began to create artworks characterized by primitive figures, geometrical shapes, scribbled texts, mystical symbols and splashes of simple colour. At first he concentrated on etchings, but later started painting. He dismissed other artists because they did not live their art. 'My life is Art and I don't create it,' he wrote. 'In that life I touch things which consequently become Art.' At first, he sold his works in the street, but in 1961 he moved into a barn in Den Ilp were he started his own gallery.

Heyboer was one of the most prolific artists of the twentieth century, turning out works by the thousand. In the Netherlands, however, he was probably more famous for his lifestyle than his art (although for him, of course, the two were inseparable). He lived with three, later four 'brides' — Maria, Lotti, Marike and Joke. His barn, the exterior of which was painted in vivid colours and decorated with all manner of religious statues, figures of animals, giant flowers and other odds and ends, became a tourist attraction.

He died in his sleep aged eighty-two. 'He was not ill but exhausted,' one of his brides was quoted as saying. 'I don't know any artist who made as many works as he did. He gave everything he had.' ▣

HIRST, JEMMY

(1738–1829)
'The very genius of eccentrics'

James 'Jemmy' Hirst was born on

a farm in Rawcliffe, Yorkshire. As a small boy, he attracted attention with his 'queer sayings', which made his parents think he would make an excellent clergyman, and he was packed off to a boarding school with this in mind. After a few years, however, his constant pranks caused him to be expelled. These included riding around on an old sow owned by the school's parson using a piece of string as a bridle, and teaching a hedgehog to follow him around. Returning to Rawcliffe, Hirst was apprenticed to a tanner, and fell in love with the tanner's daughter, Mary. He was devastated when Mary died from smallpox, and took to his bed for several weeks, suffering from 'brain fever'.

He recovered, and took over the family farm on the death of his father. Wanting to make more money than the farm would bring, he began speculating in agricultural produce, and made a fortune from it. This allowed him to concentrate on leisure pursuits, many of which involved animals. He rode in fox hunts on his bull, Jupiter, which he had trained to jump over small fences (he also attempted to train pigs to act as foxhounds, with less success). His best friends were said to be an otter and a fox, and he also owned monkeys and a bear named Nicholas, all of which were allowed free entry into his house. (Lest it be

thought that Hirst was an animal lover in the modern sense, it should be noted that one of the bear's functions was to be regularly baited by Hirst's hounds.)

Hirst was, literally, a colourful character. His hunting dress consisted of a red coat with blue sleeves, a multicoloured waistcoat and breeches, yellow boots and a lambskin hat with a brim nine feet (2.7 m) in diameter. His formal attire included a rabbitskin coat, a waistcoat of duck feathers, and red and white stockings. He had an extraordinary carriage of multicoloured wickerwork built, equipped with a double bed, a wine cellar and a device he had built to measure mileage. It was initially drawn by Jupiter, and later by a team of four mules. At one point he equipped it with sails, until a change of wind made it crash into a shopfront in Pontefract. As can be seen from all this, Hirst had an inventive frame of mind, and also designed a windmill to cut up turnips.

The exploits of the colourful Yorkshireman reached the ears of King George III, who invited Hirst to visit him in London. Hirst was rather astonished by this, and wrote back saying he didn't owe the King anything that he knew of, and was busy teaching an otter to fish (which was true — although getting the otter to relinquish its catch was actu-

ally the hard part), but he had always wanted to see London so would come in a few weeks. He eventually made the journey, wearing his usual colourful regalia and enormous hat, and with his carriage freshly painted. As it approached the palace, the carriage had to make its way through a huge crowd which had gathered to gawp at it. On seeing Hirst, the Duke of Devonshire began to laugh so hard that Hirst, saying that he must be having a fit, threw a glass of water in his face and shook him by the nose. He was then presented to the King, but instead of bowing and kissing the royal hand in the usual manner, shook it firmly and said he was pleased to see that the King was as plain-looking a gentleman as he was, causing much laughter in the court. The King took all this with admirable good humour and presented Hirst with some bottles of wine from the royal cellars to replenish his carriage. Hirst spent a week in London, visiting the sights and being feted by high society, but was relieved to get back to his house and animals.

Hirst liked to entertain the local people. During winter he had the boys and girls over to his house one night a week, and the old women over on another. He summoned them by blowing a horn, gave them dinner, then played the fiddle as they danced. He also wrote doggerel

poetry, which he published himself, and an autobiography.

This 'very genius of eccentrics', as his chronicler Tomlinson called him, made his own coffin, equipped with folding doors, peepholes and a bell inside. It stood against a wall of his house for years. Male visitors were made to pay a penny for the privilege of standing in it, while women had to give up a garter, which Hirst would then tie around his armchair. He left instructions in his will that at his funeral, the coffin was to be followed to the grave by twelve old maids, accompanied by a fiddler and piper playing happy songs. In the event, the vicar would only allow the piper to play solemn music, and banned the fiddler altogether, displaying just the sort of dreary attitude that Jemmy Hirst had fought against all his life. ▨

HODGES, ROBERT

(b. 1942 or 1662)
'Prince Mongo'

The colourful Mr. Hodges, better known as Prince Mongo (or occasionally King Mongo or Saint Mongo), has been a local identity in Memphis, Tennessee, since the mid-1970s.

He claims he is over 330-years-old, and an alien from the planet Zambodia, which is nine light years away. He says that his first human identity was as a Blackfoot Indian, and that since then he has had thirty-three wives (all now dead). 'I'm from another planet, there's no doubt about that,' he said in 2000.

I'm here on a mission to save Earthlings, and I will in due time. The Earth is self-destructing and when the time comes I will save a few people and take them with me. People don't realize how much I've already saved them from. I saved them from the earthquake, tornadoes, hurricanes. I've used my energies to divert those things.

Known for his outlandish outfits, constantly changing hair and permanently bare feet, he first came to the attention of the public as the owner of a pizza restaurant called Prince Mongo's. Since then he has owned a number of bars and nightclubs in Memphis, including Prince Mongo's Planet and the Castle, which have often been subject to allegations of underage drinking and public nudity. In 2000, Prince Mongo appeared at a hearing at the city's council chambers, after the beer licence for the Castle had been revoked. Mongo, who was wearing bug-eye sunglasses, a long grey wig and a military style coat, denied that dancing took place at the Castle, which did not have a dance permit. Instead, his nightclub was a place of religious atonement where patrons did 'exercises' to

'cleanse their bodies and souls to rid themselves of demons'. He then gave a demonstration of this, letting out a few barks and yells before dancing — or 'exercising' — his way out of the building.

Nobody knows where Mongo gets his money from, but he's clearly well off, owning a number of properties including a $2 million house in Fort Lauderdale, and a yacht. The walls of his house are decorated with his own paintings, along with record covers and other pictures, all hung at odd angles. In 2002, Mongo was given a court order to clean up the front yard of his house, which was littered with old toilet seats, mannequin heads, umbrellas, lampshades and other junk. He arrived at court to protest the order wearing goggles, with his face painted green and a rubber chicken hanging around his neck. He was charged with contempt of court, fined nearly $14,000, and spent ten days in prison.

Mongo has often stood for public office, and first campaigned to be the mayor of Memphis in 1978. (He ran again in 2007, but was disqualified because of unpaid state fines.) He now spends most of his time in Florida. With his rubbish-filled properties and antics, like standing on his roof to bay at the moon, he can certainly be a nuisance (particularly if you live next to him).

Nevertheless, he is known to be very generous, particularly to homeless people. In 2006, he told reporter Bob Norman that he never locked the doors of his house. 'Anybody can come in here anytime and take what they please. I don't care. I'll give anything away. People are always walking off with my TVs. I don't mind. I have a terrible phobia about throwing things away. Why throw things away when you can give it away?' ▣

'I don't need money. I live off the stars and the earth and the energy of the sun.'
ROBERT HODGES
a.k.a. PRINCE MONGO

HUGHES, HOWARD
(1905–1976)
Billionaire

Hughes was the son of a hard-living oil man, Howard Robard 'Bo' Hughes, who married a neurotic Texan socialite, Allene Gano. When Howard was four, his father invented (or at least patented) a new kind of drill bit which could penetrate bedrock. It revolutionised oil drilling and made him a fortune. Hughes Jr. excelled in mathematics and physics

at school and was a natural engineer, building his own radio transmitter at the age of eleven. As a teenager, he acquired the two passions that would dominate his life — aviation and the movies.

Hughes was cosseted by his mother, who worried about his health and turned him into a hypochondriac (he appears to have faked a bout of infantile paralysis at the age of fifteen). She died during an operation in 1922, and his father died of a heart attack two years later. An instinctive businessman, Hughes declared himself an adult at the age of nineteen, bought up the stock his relatives owned in the Hughes Tool Company, and took control of it. As part of the negotiations with his relatives, he agreed to get married. His bride was a former schoolmate, Ellla Rice, although he barely knew her.

Hughes had no interest in running a tool business. In 1925 he arrived in Los Angeles, intent on becoming a film producer. He certainly made a splash, spending up big on cars and clothes and bedding actresses by the dozen. He made a couple of films that were quite successful, then combined his two great loves by producing and directing the World War I flying epic *Hell's Angels*. Begun as a silent picture he had much of it reshot with sound, and replaced the original leading

lady with newcomer Jean Harlow. He organised a lavish premiere at Graumann's Chinese Theatre, with fifty planes flying in formation overhead. Audiences gasped at the film's spectacular aerial scenes (three men had died filming them and Hughes had been badly injured) but it failed to recoup its $4 million budget.

Hughes produced a few more films, including the gangster classic *Scarface*, but in 1932 temporarily abandoned movies for aviation. He hired a brilliant aeronautical engineer, Glenn Odekirk, who designed for him a fast, lightweight plane, the H-1. In 1935 Hughes broke the airspeed record in it, although the attempt almost ended in disaster when the plane's engine cut out (it transpired that someone had sabotaged the fuel line, but the culprit was never found). In 1938, Hughes completed a round-the-world flight in a Lockheed plane which took him ninety-one hours and made him one of the most famous men in the world.

It was during these years that Hughes' personal eccentricities became more marked. He began going deaf as a teenager (due to a hereditary condition), and was incapable of hearing most conversations, but refused to wear a hearing aid. He became extremely fussy about his food — his regular evening meal consisted of a steak, potatoes and peas, and he measured each pea carefully,

rejecting any that were too large. He inherited his mother's phobia for germs. Having caught syphilis from one of his many lovers, he decided his clothes were infected and had his vast and expensive wardrobe burned. When guests came to dinner at his house, the plates they ate off were later smashed. He also took to disappearing for weeks at a time, wearing workman's clothes and travelling incognito. At one point, he applied for a job with American Airlines, and worked there for three months as a baggage handler and trainee pilot until he was recognised.

Ella had filed for divorce during the making of *Hell's Angels*, and throughout the thirties Hughes cut a swathe through Hollywood's most famous actresses. His most intense relationship, lasting four years, was with Katherine Hepburn, to whom he was introduced by his close friend Cary Grant (some biographers allege Hughes had a sexual relationship with Grant, too, although others dispute this). While seeing Hepburn, Hughes found time for dalliances with Ginger Rogers, Bette Davis and many others.

As the Depression ended, the profits of the Hughes Tool Company soared. In 1939, Hughes fulfilled another ambition, buying a controlling interest in Trans World Airlines, which he equipped with a fleet of advanced Constellation airliners.

The following year, he returned to movie making with a sex-charged western, *The Outlaw*. Ostensibly the story of Billy the Kid, it soon became apparent that the real focus was on the breasts of its leading lady, Hughes' latest discovery, Jane Russell. Concerned that the seams of her bra were showing through her blouse, he worked late into the night designing a new bra that would further accentuate the actress' assets (the result was so uncomfortable that Russell only pretended to wear it). Hughes spent many months obsessively editing the film, but refused to make cuts demanded by chief censor Joe Breen. After a limited release in 1943, it was re-released with a provocative ad campaign in 1946, causing a sensation and paving the way for more sexually explicit cinema.

Hughes obtained several lucrative government contracts during the war, including the development of a spy plane and a huge wooden aircraft to transport troops, but he secured some of the contracts by bribery. The F.B.I. began to take an interest in his activities, and put him under surveillance. In 1943, he set out on a test flight of an amphibious plane without checking it properly. It crashed in Lake Mead, and two of the other men on board died. This was only the latest in a series of plane and car crashes which had left Hughes with head injuries.

His love life was as complicated as ever, with Lana Turner and Yvonne De Carlo among the women he was stringing along. In late 1944, he suffered a breakdown, and spent the next eight months moving aimlessly around the country, staying mostly in hotels and, at one point, being arrested as a vagrant.

By the time he emerged from his wanderings, the war was over. Hughes was still keen to complete his two greatest wartime projects though. In July 1946, he was test-flying his spy plane, the XF-11, when he lost control and crashed into houses in Beverly Hills. He was pulled from the wreckage with terrible burns and most of his ribs broken. He fared better with the transport plane, the H-4 Hercules, which had a wingspan as long as a football field. In October 1947, a crowd gathered at Long Beach, California, and watched as Hughes got the enormous plane, nicknamed the 'Spruce Goose', into the air for a minute. It was, nevertheless, completely obsolete and never flew again.

Having survived a Senate investigation into his wartime contracts and needing something to do, Hughes purchased RKO Studios. The Senate hearing had made him obsessed with security. He took to hiring Mormons as his aides (he liked the fact that, like him, they didn't drink or smoke),

and employed a veritable army of security men. They were kept busy with the dozens of young, would-be actresses he had spotted, signed up, and installed in houses around Los Angeles. They had to follow rigid daily schedules, and were assigned drivers who ferried them between acting, singing and dancing lessons and took them out to dinner. Hughes' relationship with most of these women was platonic, but they were forbidden to see other men, and their phones were bugged. Some lived like this for years, waiting for promised film roles that failed to eventuate.

Hughes' aircraft company made enormous profits from military electronics during the fifties, but his increasingly erratic behaviour and indecisiveness were bankrupting both RKO and TWA. He became much more paranoid about germs and toxins, and refused to touch anything until he had wrapped his hands in tissues. He wrote lengthy memos to his staff to ensure that nothing he came into contact with had been touched or contaminated (the instructions on how to open a can of peaches ran to three pages).

Hughes often proposed to women he was pursuing (he found it an excellent way to get the recalcitrant ones into bed). In 1957, worried that his subordinates were planning to have him certified and believing that

having a wife would make this more difficult, he married the actress Jean Peters in a secret ceremony in Nevada. After their honeymoon, they moved into separate bungalows in the Beverley Hills Hotel where they mainly communicated by phone and memo. He promised Peters that they would one day live in a dream home together, but it never happened.

Hughes had now entered his notorious twilight years. He spent his days in darkened hotel rooms, often naked, his hair down to his shoulders and his nails uncut and curling. He was still wracked with pain from injuries sustained in the 1946 plane crash, and was administered massive daily doses of codeine, Valium and other prescription drugs. When he wasn't stupefied by the drugs, he watched movies or wrote rambling memos.

In 1966, Hughes and his entourage moved to Las Vegas, where they took over the top floor of the Desert Inn. Over the next few years, he bought up hotels and casinos at a furious pace, until he owned a quarter of the city. He even bought the local television station, so he could make it run his favourite movies through the night.

In 1970, Hughes suddenly left Las Vegas without telling many of his closest associates or his now estranged wife where he had gone. Newspapers reported that he

had been kidnapped or murdered, but he had actually gone to the Bahamas. The following year, the reclusive billionaire was flushed out of hiding to some extent when McGraw-Hill announced it would be publishing his memoirs, based on interviews given to the writer Clifford Irving. Hughes, who hadn't spoken to a reporter in fourteen years, was forced to give a phone interview with seven of them. He denounced the book as a hoax and Irving ended up in prison. Although Hughes sounded lucid during the interview, there is little doubt that he was essentially a prisoner of his aides in his last years. They kept him under control with drugs, and persuaded him to sell the Hughes Tool Company in 1972, enriching themselves greatly in the process.

The old Howard Hughes had one last hurrah in London in 1973, when he took to the skies again, making several flights in a Hawker-Siddeley aircraft (he insisted on piloting the plane naked, though). Shortly after this, he broke his hip in a fall and was bedridden for the rest of his life. He died either in Acapulco, or in a plane taking him to Houston. The second richest man in America (after J. Paul Getty), Hughes had a stomach swollen from malnutrition, and a body so emaciated his elbows and knees had broken through the skin.

ICKE, DAVID

(b. 1952)
Conspiracy theorist

Icke was born in Leicester, England, and his first career was in professional football. At the age of fifteen he was signed as an apprentice by Coventry City, and showed great promise as a goalkeeper, but was plagued by painful swellings of his elbow and knee joints. At the age of nineteen he was diagnosed with rheumatoid arthritis, which put an end to his sporting career. He then tried his hand at sports journalism, writing for a local newspaper before being picked up by the BBC. He proved to be a popular presenter, and hosted the BBC's flagship sports programme *Grandstand*.

Icke, his wife Linda and children Kerry and Gareth moved to the Isle of Wight in 1984. He be-gan to dabble in politics, joining the Liberal Democrats briefly before switching to the Green Party. He became their national spokesman, and there was talk of him becoming their first MP, but this ultimately came to nothing. Meanwhile, he was embarking on a new and far stranger career.

It began when he went to see a Brighton-based psychic, Betty Shine, seeking treatment for his arthritis. In 1990, Shine told him that she had been in contact with various notables on the other side, including Socrates, and they had told her that Icke had been put on Earth to accomplish a great mission — nothing less than saving humanity. Icke accepted the responsibility with enthusiasm, and spent the next few years travelling around the world, studying esoteric and spiritual matters. He met a British-born heiress, Deborah Shaw, who lived in Canada and shared his interests. Shaw (who later changed her name to Mari Schawsun) became his travelling companion.

On 27 March 1991, Icke held a press conference in London, accompanied by Schawsun, his wife Linda (who was now calling herself Michaela after the archangel Michael), and their daughter Kerry. All four wore turquoise tracksuits (turquoise being, Icke explained, the colour of love and wisdom).

As the jaws of the gathered journalists dropped, Icke announced that he was 'a messenger of the great Godhead'. He proceeded to list a host of natural disasters that were about to occur around the world, including earthquakes, floods, volcanic eruptions; predicted that the Channel Tunnel would collapse before its opening; and warned that, should people not change their ways and begin treating each other with love, the world would end in 1997. A few weeks later, when Icke appeared on a chat show hosted by Terry Wogan and described himself as 'the Son of God', he was ridiculed mercilessly by the British media.

Undeterred, he outlined his views on the true nature of reality in a series of books, beginning with *The Robots Rebellion* (1994), which meld the political conspiracy theories of the last two centuries with the contemporary self-actualisation movement. They are full of arcane detail about the usual suspects said to be secretly in control of world affairs — the Masons, quasi-government organisations like the Bilderberger Group, the Trilateral Commission and so on. His message, however, is that we should not hate the members of these groups, but love them, for they are people like ourselves, and many don't even realize the part they are playing in humanity's subjugation. Most people have been reduced to robots by the mind control techniques of the Global Elite or Illuminati, and the only way to combat them is for individuals to release positive energy and break their shackles.

While in the past most conspiracy theorists blamed the ills of the world on simple greed or lust for power on the part of politicians, bankers and industrialists, for Icke the true culprits are negative entities which have been around since the time of Atlantis. These entities, which he also calls 'the Prison Warders', are responsible for all the political and religious dogmas that plague society. Because the Prison Warders literally feed on negative energy, it is in their interests to promote hatred, violence, misery and war. In *The Biggest Secret: The Book that Will Change the World* (1999) Icke finally revealed the identity of the Prison Warders — they are reptilian creatures from the constellation of Draco. These creatures have bred with human beings to form hybrids which can shift between reptilian and human form. Reptilian blood has coursed through the veins of the upper classes for millennia, and today's closet lizards include the Queen and other members of the Royal Family, George Bush (both Snr. and Jr.), Henry Kissinger, Hillary

Clinton, many world leaders and (rather more puzzlingly) the actor and singer Kris Kristoffersen. The reptilians also drink blood, and *The Biggest Secret* has a description of the Queen, having shapeshifted into a lizard, stabbing and ripping into the flesh of a victim. Icke's is, without a doubt, the wildest alternative reality on offer since the heyday of ☞ Richard Shaver.

Icke has often been accused of anti-Semitism. In *...and the Truth Shall Set You Free* (1995) he refers to the notorious forgery 'The Protocols of the Elders of Zion' as an outline of the Illuminati plan. Icke counters that the villains of the piece are reptilian and therefore not human, let alone Jewish. He has accused several anti-racist organisations of being Illuminati fronts.

Icke continues to live on the Isle of Wight with his second wife, Pamela. He travels the world constantly, giving lectures and promoting his many books and videos. He is a brilliant, charismatic speaker who can talk for hours and is adept at drawing even a skeptical audience into his worldview, if only momentarily. ▣

JACKSON, MICHAEL
(1958–2009)
Entertainer

Born in the heavily segregated industrial city of Gary, Indiana, Jackson was the seventh child of Joe Jackson, a steelworker who played in an R&B band, and his wife Katherine, a devout Seventh Day Adventist. From the age of five, Jackson was performing with his brothers Jackie, Tito, Jermaine and Marlon. Joe's musical career had failed to take off, but he was determined that his children would find fame and fortune within the industry. He made them rehearse constantly and, Michael and some of his siblings would later claim, resorted to physical abuse in his quest for musical perfection. As unpleasant as Joe's methods may have been, they got results. The Jackson 5 signed to Motown

MICHAEL JACKSON

in 1969 and were an instant, huge success. Their first single, 'I Want You Back,' went to number one on the Billboard chart, as did its three follow-ups. The focus of the group was undoubtedly Michael, whose almost preternatural talents as singer and dancer belied his age.

The group continued to have hits during the seventies, while Michael also released a number of solo records. In 1978, he appeared in the musical film *The Wiz*, and met its musical director, Quincy Jones, who produced his first mega-selling solo album, *Off the Wall*. Jackson was determined to make his next album even bigger, and succeeded. *Thriller*, released in 1982, spawned seven hit singles and remains the highest selling album of all time. The following year, Jackson gave a now-legendary performance of 'Billie Jean' during the Motown twenty-fifth anniversary television special, unveiling his signature dance move, the Moonwalk.

In 1984, Jackson made headlines for quite different reasons when he was hospitalised after his hair caught fire during the filming of a Pepsi commercial. It was around this time that Jackson's musical achievements began to be overshadowed by the peculiarities of his lifestyle, such as the fact that he shared his bedroom with his pet chimp, Bubbles.

For a while, Jackson's public relations people collaborated in the process, issuing the (false) stories that he slept in a hyperbaric oxygen tank (in the belief that this would enable him to live to 150), and that he had tried to buy the skeleton of John Merrick, the Elephant Man. Such stories gained Jackson the tabloid appellation 'Wacko Jacko', but he would later distance himself from them.

Meanwhile, strange things were happening with Jackson's face. He first underwent rhinoplasty in 1979 after breaking his nose while rehearsing a dance routine. Jackson had always been self-conscious about his appearance (his family used to tease him and call him 'Big Nose'), and now that he had discovered plastic surgery his face continued to change through the eighties (causing a corresponding increase in the surgery bills of Michael Jackson impersonators the world over). For a while, he bore an uncanny resemblance to Diana Ross, whom he idolized, but he soon went beyond this. He had his cheeks redefined, his eyes widened, and a cleft added to his chin, while his nose, after endless tinkering, became a sad, upturned, vestigial point. The net effect of his surgery (which he mostly denied having) was that the top half of his face became more feminine looking, and the bottom half more masculine, giving him an almost alien appearance. Then there was the matter of his skin, which kept getting paler. The official explanation was that he suffered from lupus and vitiligo, and Jackson emphatically denied that he was bleaching his skin because he was ashamed of his blackness. Yet other African Americans were entitled to ask — if he was disguising the patches of pale skin typically caused by vitiligo — why would he chose to whiten his skin rather than darken it?

In 1988, Jackson bought a 2,800 acre (1,134 hectare) property in Santa Barbara, California, and built the Neverland Ranch (named after the place in the Peter Pan stories where children never grow old). The ranch had its own zoo, theme park, full-size Ferris wheel, steam train, merry-go-round which played 'Like a Virgin', and theatre stocked with children's films, and Jackson often had children there as his guests. He explained that, having been immersed in showbusiness since the age of five, he was merely trying to recapture a childhood he had missed.

While Jackson's relationships with individual children would be his undoing, it seems his concern for children in general was heartfelt. He gave enormous sums to children's charities, and his videos and performances make it clear that he saw himself as a Christlike figure who could save the world through its children. Another indication of

Jackson's self-image is a large painting he commissioned which hung at Neverland. It shows him in the company of the Mona Lisa, Washington, Lincoln, E.T. and Einstein, with all of them wearing Jackson's trademark sunglasses and single jewelled white glove.

In 1993, Jackson was accused of molesting thirteen-year-old Jordan Chandler at Neverland. Other children who had been guests there denied anything untoward had happened to them. While Chandler's mother did not believe the charges, police searched the ranch and Jackson was subjected to a humiliating examination and photographing of his genitals. He made an out-of-court settlement with the Jordan family in January 1994 (a figure of $26 million is often mentioned). A few months later Jackson married Lisa-Marie Presley, a union many believed was a sham. After his death, Presley denied this, writing in a blog, 'It was an unusual relationship, yes, where two unusual people who did not live or know a "normal life" found a connection, perhaps with some suspect timing on his part.' The marriage lasted seventeen months.

In 1995, Jackson released a double album, *HIStory: Past, Present and Future, Book I*. Its launch was celebrated with enormous statues of the singer in military style costume

erected in various European cities (the London statue was sent down the Thames on a barge). While in Australia for the HIStory World Tour, Jackson married his dermatological nurse, Deborah Rowe, who went on to bear him two children, Prince Michael and a daughter, Paris. They divorced in 1999, with Rowe giving up all custodial rights to the children. Jackson had a third child in 2002 (the surrogate mother has never been named), Prince Michael II (known as 'Blanket'). Having been out of the headlines for a few years, Jackson caused a furore when, on a visit to Berlin, he briefly dangled Blanket over a fourth-floor balcony.

In an attempt to repair his reputation, Jackson agreed to take part in a British documentary, which aired in February 2003. This was a disaster for Jackson who, under questioning by the programme's host, Martin Bashir, admitted that he had slept with many young boys in his bed at Neverland, although he denied that anything sexual had happened. Shortly after it screened, Gavin Arvizo, a boy seen holding Jackson's hand in the documentary (the singer had paid for his cancer treatment), accused Jackson of abusing him.

He was arrested and charged with four counts of molesting a minor, plus various other charges. His close friend, Elizabeth Taylor, came out in his defence, saying she too

had shared a bed with Jackson. They had spent the time watching Disney movies, and 'there was nothing odd about it'. The trial ended in June 2005, with Jackson acquitted on all counts.

After the trial was over, Jackson moved to Bahrain in the Persian Gulf, where he was spotted shopping wearing a woman's black abaya and veil. He was the guest of Sheik Abdullah bin Hamad al-Khalifa, the second son of Bahrain's king, who was keen for Jackson to record songs he had written, but the two eventually fell out, and Jackson later lived in Dubai and Ireland. His record sales had been in steep decline for many years, but he had never curbed his extravagant spending and was hundreds of millions of dollars in debt, which had necessitated closing the main house at Neverland. His main source of income was now the Beatles' song catalogue, which he had bought for $47 million in 1985.

Jackson returned to America in 2008, and announced a world tour beginning with fifty concerts in England, the first scheduled for 13 July 2009. Jackson's health had been deteriorating for years, though. He was underweight and addicted to prescription drugs, and many doubted he would have the stamina for the concerts. He was in the middle of rehearsals when he suffered a cardiac arrest and died. According

to Lisa-Marie Presley, he had always feared he would 'die like Elvis'.

The autopsy found that he had died after being injected with lorazepam and propofol, the latter being a powerful anaesthetic generally used on patients undergoing surgery, which Jackson had been taking as a cure for his insomnia. ▣

'Why not just tell people I'm an alien from Mars.'
MICHAEL JACKSON

JAMES, EDWARD
(1907–1984)
Arts patron & folly builder

James was one of the last great British folly builders. That he chose to build his follies in the middle of the Mexican jungle only added to his eccentric lustre.

He was the son of William James, whose father, Daniel, was an American steel and railroad magnate. William, born in England, married Evelyn Forbes, who was rumoured to be the illegitimate daughter of the Prince of Wales (the future King Edward VII). Edward certainly believed this was the case. He was William and Evelyn's fifth child, following four daughters, and his

birth was the cause of fireworks and days of festivities at the family's vast estate, West Dean in Sussex. James inherited it when his father died just five years later, and his fortune was greatly increased after the death of an uncle in 1928.

James studied at Oxford and briefly embarked on a diplomatic career, for which he had no aptitude. He fell in love with an Austrian dancer and artist, Tilly Losch, and they married in 1931, but the marriage was clearly based on a misunderstanding. Losch had believed it to be a marriage of convenience to cover up James' homosexuality, and was shocked when he tried to consummate it on their wedding night. James eventually realised she had married him for his money, and there was an acrimonious divorce in 1934.

James was an amateur poet and lifelong patron of the arts, particularly surrealism. During the thirties, he became the foremost collector of surrealist works, bankrolled ☞ Salvador Dalí for two years, and put René Magritte up in his London home. He worked closely with Dalí decorating Monckton House at West Dean, with the furnishings including the artist's famous Mae West sofa. He also made guest appearances in several iconic surrealist works. In Magritte's *La Reproduction Interdite*, he's the fellow who stares into a

mirror and sees the back of his head in it.

James travelled extensively through Europe and the Americas, overseeing his business interests. In 1944, while in Mexico, he engaged a young man named Plutarco Gastulum to act as a guide and travelling companion. He was apparently searching for a spot to grow orchids, another passion. Gastulum led him to Xilitla, a village set in a mountainous rainforest area about nine hours drive from Mexico City. According to James' account, Gastulum had stripped off to bathe in a river near the village, and was reclining by its bank when hundreds of butterflies descended on him, covering his body. This surreal moment convinced him that the spot, with its lush vegetation, waterfalls and natural pools, was a special place.

James spent decades and several million dollars transforming the site into Los Pozas ('the Pools'), a maze-like garden of stunning strangeness and beauty. With Gastelum as overseer, hundreds of local men were employed to clear land and plant almost 30,000 orchids. They built an intricate network of walkways, arches, staircases, bridges, gates and a private zoo. Dotted throughout are some forty large structures or follies, designed by James and made from reinforced concrete. There are buildings in gothic and Egyptian styles,

looming towers, giant flower-like forms and fleur-de-lis, and abstract sculptures that defy interpretation. The influence of surrealism is obvious in many of these creations, which have names like 'The House with a Roof Like a Whale'. The overall effect of the site, which covers over forty acres (sixteen hectares), is of an alien city which is at the same time completely in harmony with its natural surroundings.

James visited Los Pozas as often as he could, sometimes staying for months at a time (he loved to bathe naked there, and liked his workers to do the same). His last visit was in 1983. He suffered a stroke the following year, and died in a French nursing home. Unfortunately, he made little provision for Los Pozas in his will. Gastelum's family looked after it as best they could, but the concrete structures became mildewed and overgrown. It looked like the jungle would absorb James' surreal creation, but in 2007 a consortium including the local government, bankers and a cement company bought the site and set about restoring it. ▨

JANDEK

(b. 1945)
Singer

Jandek is one of the most contrary

and enigmatic figures in rock music, although to label most of his output 'rock' is to stretch the term so far as to make it almost meaningless.

It is generally agreed among Jandek fans that his real name is Sterling Smith (in which case the birth date given above is correct) and he resides in Houston, Texas. Other than that, virtually nothing is known about his personal life, and that's how he wants to keep it.

The first Jandek album, *Ready for the House*, appeared in 1978 on the Corwood label. It was initially credited to the Units, but then Jandek discovered there was already a band of that name. All subsequent albums, which have followed at the rate of one or two a year since 1981, have been credited to Jandek. The covers invariably feature a photo, sometimes a blurred, seemingly accidental shot of part of a room or the exterior of a house; sometimes of Jandek himself at various ages, usually looking pale and expressionless. The back of the sleeve has the album's title and track listing, along with a post office box address in Houston for Corwood Industries. No further information is ever given.

The early records feature what might be called the classic Jandek style, with the artist performing solo, singing in a soft, mournful voice, and accompanying himself in rudimentary fashion on an untuned (or at least not conventionally tuned) acoustic guitar. The lyrics are often melancholy and personal; the songs primitive, repetitive and usually devoid of melody. Later, Jandek began to use other musicians, a drummer or a second guitarist perhaps, and some tracks feature guest singers, including a woman named Nancy (at least, she appears on a track called 'Nancy Sings'). There was a period when the albums became 'rockier', and at one point he dropped instruments altogether and released three spoken word albums in a row. Throughout the recordings, there are echoes of blues, folk and pop, but they are faint indeed.

Jandek sent his early records to radio stations. Deejays occasionally played them, and word spread so that a (very) small cult developed. People who wrote to the post office address would often receive a whole box of records. Later there was a deal where you could buy twenty-five for $50. Rumours began to spread about this strange person churning out records hardly anybody wanted.

Then in 1999, journalist Katy Vine from the *Texas Monthly* managed to track him down (or thought she had — he certainly looked like the photo on the record covers). While he would not acknowledge that he was Jandek, he invited her to go for a beer, and offered some

fragmentary information — that he had travelled widely, and had some sort of white collar job. When she asked if he wanted people to 'get' Jandek's music, he replied, 'There's nothing to get,' and steered clear of music questions in general. He finished by saying that he never wanted to be contacted by a fan or a journalist about Jandek ever again. The only proper interview Jandek has ever given remains a phone interview with John Trubee of *Spin* magazine which took place in 1985. During this, he volunteered the information that he came up with his pseudonym one January day when he was to talking on the phone to a man named Decker.

In October 2006, Jandek stunned fans by playing at a music festival in Glasgow, Scotland (he had appeared on the condition that no advance publicity was given for the gig). This solved at least one mystery — for the first time it was confirmed that the man pictured on the albums was Jandek. Since then he has performed several times a year in Europe and America. He usually plays with local musicians backing him, having had one rehearsal with them, and the shows are mostly improvised. Corwood continue to release Jandek albums (there are now over fifty of them) with the earlier ones available on CD. Despite this flurry of activity, Jandek remains almost as much of a mystery as ever. Hardcore fans note that it is not even certain that the name 'Jandek' refers to the individual rather than his project, and therefore prefer to call him 'the representative of Corwood'. As rock fans, they must be unique in allowing the object of their devotion the privacy he has requested. ▣

JASMUHEEN

(b. 1957)
Breatharian

Jasmuheen, whose real name is Ellen Greve, claims to have not eaten a meal since 1993. The daughter of a Norwegian couple who migrated to Australia after World War II, she married and had two children, but separated from her husband after seven years. During the 1980s, she held down a lucrative job in the financial sector as a mortgage broker, but after losing this in 1992, embarked on a quite different career.

Jasmuheen claims to be in contact with the Ascended Masters, that merry band of all-wise, non-corporeal beings who have been a fixture of western occult and alternative beliefs since introduced by the redoubtable ☞ Madame Blavatsky. In 1993, while meditating, the message came through from St. Germain that food is not essential for survival, as nourishment can be derived from light (or 'Pranic light' as Jasmuheen puts it, 'prana' being the Hindu term for 'lifeforce'). A vegetarian prior to this, she began to radically reduce her food intake until she said she was consuming little more than two cups of herbal tea a day and the occasional chocolate biscuit (to satisfy stubborn taste cravings).

She began to sell books and tapes outlining her Breatharian beliefs over the Internet, and was soon claiming to have 5,000 followers, mostly in Germany (although no proofs for this claim have been forthcoming). Journalists who travelled to the luxurious home in Brisbane which she had bought with the proceeds of Breatharianism were both charmed and baffled by this pretty, still youthful-looking blonde woman who claimed not to eat. She was always happy to show them her fridge, which was full of food, but said this belonged to her partner Jeff, a vegan.

Jasmuheen gained considerable notoriety during the late 1990s when her beliefs were linked to three deaths around the world. A German kindergarten teacher, Timo Degen (thirty-one) was the first, dying twelve days into a fast inspired by her writings in March 1997. In July 1998, a Brisbane woman, Lani Morris (fifty-three) survived for fourteen days without food before dying of a stroke caused by dehydration (the elderly couple who had charged her $700 to oversee this process were later found guilty of manslaughter and jailed). Finally, in September 1999, Australian-born Verity Linn (forty-eight) headed into a remote area in the Scottish Highlands with a copy of Jasmuheen's book *Living on Light*, intent on following the twenty-one-day course which she advocates for beginning Breatharians (seven days without food or water, followed by fourteen days on fruit juice). Her near-naked body was later found some distance from her tent. Her diary showed she had lasted twelve days.

Jasmuheen denied any responsibility for these deaths, saying the victims had not been spiritually or mentally prepared to take her course. A month after Verity Linn's death, she agreed to take part in a trial of her beliefs to be filmed by the Australian television programme *60 Minutes*. The trial began in a Brisbane hotel room, but after two days Jasmuheen complained that the air was too polluted for her to receive the nutrients she needed, and was moved to a country retreat. After a further two days, with Jasmuheen showing definite signs of dehydration, the doctor supervising the trial said that she faced kidney failure if she continued, and the trial was called off.

With no further deaths from

Breatharianism reported, Jasmuheen faded from the headlines. She continues to travel the world, selling books and giving seminars, promoting an idea which, as she is at pains to point out, is a logical solution to the problem of world hunger. ▣

JENKINS, FLORENCE FOSTER
(1868–1944)
Singer

Florence Foster Jenkins was to singing what ☛ William McGonagall was to poetry and ☛ Robert Coates to acting. All three had absurdly inflated opinions of their own talents, and were laughed at when they performed. Yet when people laughed at McGonagall and Coates, the laughter was tinged with derision. When they laughed at Jenkins, they often took care to mask it with wild applause. Jenkins may have been unable to hit two consecutive notes in an aria, but audiences loved her.

This unlikely soprano was the daughter of a lawyer and banker, Charles Dorrance Foster, and was born in Wilkes-Barre, Pennsylvania. She learned the piano as a child, showed a prodigious musical talent, and performed in public. At the age of seventeen, she begged her father to let her study in Europe, but he refused. She promptly eloped with a doctor named Frank Thornton Jenkins, and they went to live in Philadelphia. Florence's father cut off all financial support, and she scraped a living giving piano lessons.

Florence and Jenkins were separated by 1902, although they may never have divorced. In 1909, her father died, and the inheritance she received allowed her to resume her musical career. She moved to New York where she joined numerous women's clubs, often in the role of musical director, and in 1912 started her own musical society, the Verdi Club. She met a British-born actor, St. Clair Bayfield, who became her common-law husband and right-hand man. He helped her organise performances, which ranged from her own piano recitals to full-blown opera productions.

At some point, Jenkins suffered an injury to her arm which prevented her from playing the piano, and she switched to singing. She took lessons, and began to give invitation-only recitals, including an annual performance at the Ritz-Carlton in New York. For six years from 1928, her regular accompanist was a talented pianist, Edwin Macarthur, until Macarthur made fun of her on stage one night. After that, his place was taken by the engagingly named Cosmé McMoon. (Many have assumed this was a pseudonym, and it was long rumoured that

FLORENCE FOSTER JENKINS

McMoon was actually Macarthur. In fact, McMoon was a Mexican-born composer and musician whose real name was McMunn.) Her repertoire ranged from selections from opera — including pieces which are famously difficult to sing — to popular tunes of the day, as well as a few songs for which she wrote the words and McMoon the music. Whatever the song, the result was invariably dire, and soon people were clamouring for tickets. One of her biggest fans was Cole Porter, who attended every concert he could.

Part of Jenkins' appeal was her flamboyance, the sheer gusto with which she took to the stage. Now in her sixties, matronly and full bosomed, she went through several changes of costume during a recital, favouring elaborate gowns, hats and wigs. One of her signature tunes was Valverde's 'Clavelitos' ('Carnations'), which she sang dressed as a Spanish señorita and carrying flowers which she threw into the audience to cries of 'Olé!' (Afterwards, it fell to McMoon to go around the hall collecting the flowers so they could be re-used at the next performance.)

Jenkins — who liked to be addressed as 'Lady Florence' — recorded a number of songs which were released on five 78 rpm records. She loved to listen to them, and play them for others. Sometimes she would play her version of a song alongside versions by other singers, and ask her guests which they liked the best (she was rarely disappointed with their verdicts). The question has often been asked — *what was Florence Foster Jenkins thinking?* Was she having people on, or was she deluded? The truth seems to be simpler — she was completely tone deaf, and thought she sounded terrific.

The culmination of Jenkins' career came when she hired Carnegie Hall for a performance on the evening of 25 October 1944. Three-thousand tickets sold out almost immediately, and 2,000 people had to be turned away on the night. She performed 'Clavelitos' and other favourites and the audience went berserk. The following day, the critics were mostly scathing, although Robert Bagar, writing in the *World Telegram*, struck a more balanced note. 'She was exceedingly happy in her work,' he wrote. 'It is a pity that so few artists are, and the happiness was communicated as if by magic to her hearers, who were stimulated to the point of audible cheeriness, even joyous laughter and ecstasy by the inimitable singing.'

A few weeks later, Jenkins suffered a heart attack, and died on 26 November. Some have suggested that she was crushed by the negative reviews of her Carnegie Hall concert, and this contributed to her death. Others point out that she had seen bad reviews before, and maintain that she died happy. Since her death her fame has, if anything, increased. He recordings were issued on LPs, then CDs, and several plays have been written about her.

'*People may say I can't sing, but no one can ever say I didn't sing.*'

FLORENCE FOSTER JENKINS

JOHNS, JAMES

(1797–1874)
Self-publisher

Writers have been publishing their own work since the invention of the printing press. In America, the late nineteenth century saw the birth of the amateur journalism movement, where writers who could not break into professional publications edited their own journals, which they would circulate to each other. In the 1930s, science fiction fans, taking advantage of cheap copying methods like mimeographing, began to produce the first 'fanzines' containing criticism, stories and artwork. Shortened to 'zine', the word was applied to any primitively produced, small-circulation publication which focused on extremely specialised or arcane subjects. The ubiquity of photocopiers led to an explosion in the number of zines published during the 1980s and nineties (although since then many writers have turned to the Internet). In the annals of self-publishing, however, it is doubtful that there has ever been a more industrious individual than James Johns.

Johns, who was born in Huntington, Vermont, was a prolific writer from the age of thirteen, turning out a stream of poems, essays and short stories. A slim volume of his verse, *Green Mountain Muse*, appeared in 1828, but few copies were sold. Johns blamed the publisher for this, and resolved that he would henceforth publish all of his writings himself. He began to issue broadsides and pamphlets, including *A Brief Record of the Fatal Accidents Which Have Happened in Huntington* and other chronicles of local history. His most famous publication was a daily newspaper, the *Vermont Autograph and Remarker*, which first appeared in 1834. It covered local events like births and marriages, unusual happenings and the weather (a pet topic of Johns), while he wasn't afraid to attack local politicians he thought were corrupt. Surviving copies show that it was a nicely produced publication, excellently printed. The most interesting thing about it, however, was that it was not printed. Johns wrote it all

out by hand, in a style which made it look like printing (sometimes called pen-printing). It took him half a day to complete a single issue, which would then be made available to the eager readers of Huntington.

In 1857, Johns bought a printing press which he used for some of his productions, but he continued to handwrite the *Autograph*, issuing it daily from Monday to Friday, and kept it up for forty years. He only ceased to write eight months prior to his death. ▨

JOHNSON, CHARLES K.

(1926 –2000)
Champion of the flat Earth

'The spinning ball thing makes the whole Bible a big joke,' Johnson declared. During the 1960s, the former aircraft mechanic began to correspond with the president of the American branch (well, the only branch really) of the Flat Earth Society, Samuel Shenton. Like many flat Earthers, Johnson had come to his beliefs via the Bible, which states clearly that the Earth has four corners. The Flat Earth Society had its roots in the Universal Zetetic Society ('zetetic' being a word derived from Greek meaning 'to find out for one's self'), which was founded by an Englishman, Samuel Rowbotham, in 1832. When Shenton died in 1971,

the leadership of the society passed to Johnson.

The society's headquarters were a spare room in Johnson's house, which stood in the middle of an expanse of satisfyingly flat desert in Hi Vista, California. Johnson and his Australian-born wife Marjory lived there with a large collection of dogs, cats and chickens, but no running water or electricity. 'Marjory has always known that the Earth is flat too,' Johnson told a reporter. 'As far as she knew, everyone in Australia knew it. She was rather shocked when she arrived here and found people speaking of Australia as "down under". It really offended her.' Marjory became the society's secretary. As other flat Earthers before them, the Johnsons conducted various experiments that convinced them of the soundness of their beliefs.

Anyone who sent Johnson $10 received a magnificent Flat Earth Society membership certificate signed by him and Marjory, a flat Earth map — basically the same map, with the north pole at its centre, used as the symbol of the United Nations (flat Earthers find this a dead giveaway) and a subscription to the society's spirited publication, *The Flat Earth News*. 'The International Flat Earth Society is the oldest continuous Society existing in the world today,' wrote Johnson in his manifesto.

'It began with the Creation of the Creation.' Johnson believed that the moon landings were a hoax scripted by Arthur C. Clarke, an assertion that struck a chord with many conspiracy minded Americans.

According to Johnson, the society's membership rose to 3,500, but in 1995 his house burnt down. Johnson managed to get Marjory, who was by then an invalid, out in time, but all the society's archives and records were lost. The Johnsons had no insurance, and were forced to move into a battered old trailer. Marjory died the following year.

Johnson, who sported a magnificent grey beard worthy of a biblical prophet, worked hard to rebuild the society, and by the time of his death had recruited around 100 members. Believing in a flat Earth, he once said, 'makes you kind of a loner. Everyone likes to be liked, but you can't be liked. You have to make up your mind to do without that.'

The idea of the flat Earth still awaits another champion with the strength of character of Charles Johnson.

'Reasonable, intelligent people have always recognised that the Earth is flat.'
CHARLES K. JOHNSON

KEELER, HARRY STEPHEN
(1890–1967)
Crime writer

Keeler was undoubtedly the most unusual crime fiction writer of the twentieth century. He was a lifelong denizen of Chicago, a city he loved and celebrated as 'the London of the West', and which forms the backdrop of most of his strange, convoluted, unrealistic and — for those attuned to his idiosyncratic style — highly entertaining novels.

Keeler's father died when he was eighteen months old. His mother married again, but her second husband turned out to be a chronic gambler who ended up committing suicide. She was forced to take in boarders, many of them theatrical types, giving Harry an early expo-

HARRY STEPHEN KEELER

sure to flamboyant characters.

What was undoubtedly the most formative experience of his early years came when, at some point, probably when he was around twenty, his mother had him committed to an insane asylum. The details of why she did this and the length and nature of his treatment remain unclear, but he had been discharged by 1912, when he was working as an electrician in a steel mill. He later wrote about the experience of being committed in the novel *The Spectacles of Mr. Cagliostro* (1926).

Keeler sold his first short story to a magazine in 1913, and never looked back. Between 1917 and 1940, he also edited a fiction magazine, *10 Story Book*, which became increasingly risqué over the years. With photos of scantily clad girls its main selling point, Keeler was given free reign to publish all sorts of odd stories, as well as plugs for his own books and illustrations by his wife, Hazel Goodwin, whom he married in 1919.

Keeler's first novel, *The Voice of the Seven Sparrows*, was published in 1924. Like many of his subsequent novels, it was a 'webwork', Keeler's term for a book featuring a large cast of characters drawn into a complicated plot full of improbable coincidences. Further novels poured from his typewriter in quick succession throughout the 1920s

and thirties, including *The Amazing Web*, *The Face of the Man from Saturn*, *The Riddle of the Traveling Skull*, *The Skull of the Waltzing Clown*, *Finger, Finger!* and *The Man with the Magic Eardrums*. As the titles of two of these suggest, Keeler had something of an obsession with skulls (other obsessions included safes, wills with absurd clauses, physical deformities and anything Chinese). His characters often have ridiculous names (Dr. Maclingo Summerdyke, Tuddleton Trotter, Piffington Wainright, Pfaff Kusswurm, to pick a few from thousands). Two of Keeler's most interesting books, *The Marceau Case* and *X Jones — of Scotland Yard* are 'documented' novels, with the story told through newspaper clippings, telegrams, letters, drawings and photographs (including one of Keeler himself). Yet for all the absurdity of his books, Keeler was a craftsman. His plots, while outrageous, are meticulously worked out, and he almost always pulled off a genuine surprise ending.

Astonishingly, it seems that few critics, or indeed anyone else at the time, noticed that Keeler was doing anything unusual. His books sold quite well in America and Britain, and one of them, *Sing Sing Nights*, was twice adapted for the movies. However, Keeler's American publisher, Dutton, grew increasingly exasperated by the enormously long manuscripts he was turning in. (*The Box From Japan*, with 765 pages of very small type in the original edition, is reckoned to be the longest mystery ever written, while some other works had to be split into several books for publication.) Having published thirty-seven of his novels, Dutton dropped him in 1942. Keeler secured a deal with a small publisher, Phoenix, which brought out a further nine titles in America, the last in 1948. His British publisher issued his last book there in 1952.

Although the market for his work had almost completely dried up, Keeler continued to produce novels at a rapid rate. Some of them were published in translations in Spain and Portugal (where he had small but devoted followings), but the remainder would not appear in any form until after his death. Keeler often complained about the agonies he suffered writing his books, but he was clearly addicted to the process, and never lost the belief that what he was doing was somehow important.

He did stop writing for a while after Hazel's death in 1960. They had been a devoted couple, and her passing left him a broken man. Three years later, however, he married Thelma Rinaldo, who had been his secretary back when he was editing *10 Story Book*, and started writing again. His last novel, *The Scarlet Mummy*, was finished the year before he died.

Keeler was completely forgotten at the time of his death, but a revival of interest in his work began in the 1970s. This has gathered steam, helped along by the advent of the Internet and the founding of a Harry Stephen Keeler Society in 1997. ◙

KELLOGG, JOHN HARVEY
(1852–1943)
Physician

Kellogg, born in Tyrone, Michigan, was the son of John Prescott Kellogg and his second wife Anne. When he was still a young boy, the family moved to Battle Creek, Michigan, where his father started a broom factory. They were devout members of the Seventh Day Adventist Church, which was formally established in Battle Creek in 1863, and at the age of twelve, Kellogg went to work as a 'printer's devil' in the Adventist publishing house.

One of the leading Adventists, Ellen G. White, had a keen interest in health issues, and in 1866 founded the Western Health Reform Institute in Battle Creek, which specialised in hydrotherapy (water cures). The young Kellogg had impressed Ellen and her husband James, and they encouraged him to study medicine. He obtained his medical degree in New York in 1875, and the following year was appointed superintendent of the institute, which was renamed the Battle Creek Sanitarium. It had only twenty patients when Kellogg took over, but over the next few years he transformed it into one of the best-known medical institutions in the country.

As an Adventist, Kellogg had been brought up a vegetarian, and a proper diet was central to his thinking. He believed that most diseases could be traced to bacteria in the body, the result of eating meats and other harmful foods. For Kellogg, the ideal diet was chiefly composed of grains and nuts. He was fanatical about the importance of regular enemas — he had one himself every morning — and thought there were few ills that could not be alleviated by several gallons of water swished through the bowels, followed by half a pint of yogurt.

Kellogg's ideas on sex were greatly influenced by those of Sylvester Graham (1794-1851), who had also advocated dietary reform, and became famous during the early decades of the nineteenth century for a spirited campaign against masturbation. For Kellogg, who set out his sexual theories in the book *Plain Facts for Old and Young*, the 'solitary vice' was one of the great scourges of humanity, leading to epilepsy, cancer, insanity and a host of other unhappy consequences. He advocated various techniques for discouraging masturbation, including circumcision for boys (he stipulated that this should take place without anaesthetic, so as to have 'a salutary effect on the mind'), while women might benefit from an application of carbolic acid to the clitoris. Sexual intercourse was almost as bad as masturbation, and it was best to abstain from it altogether unless you wanted an offspring.

Kellogg certainly practised what he preached, and never consummated his marriage to Ella Eaton, whom he wed in 1879 (it is said that he spent part of his wedding night working on *Plain Facts*). While he and Ella obviously could not have children of their own, they raised dozens of orphans in their home, and formally adopted at least seven of them.

Patients at the sanitarium were subjected to a battery of treatments. They sat in tubs of cold water, soaked up the rays of artificial sun-baths, and exercised in the open air to aid their digestion. The sanitarium had a famously high 'cure' rate, but then, Kellogg refused to take in anyone seriously ill. Whatever the efficacy of his various treatments, none were harmful, and it seems clear that most of his patients benefited from simply having a rest in congenial surroundings.

To make his beloved grains and nuts more palatable, Kellogg experimented endlessly with new foodstuffs. He producing the first nut-based meat substitutes and a kind of peanut butter, but is today mostly remembered as an unwitting pioneer of breakfast cereals. Early in his career at the sanitarium he produced a concoction of oats and corn meal (which became Granola), and later developed shredded wheat and cornflakes. With his younger brother, Will, who looked after business affairs at the sanitarium, he set up the Sanitas Food Company, then, in 1906, the Battle Creek Toasted Corn Flake Company. Will was much more entrepreneurial than his brother, quarrelled with him over the issue of adding sugar to the cornflake recipe, and eventually gained control of the company. This caused a rift between the two brothers which lasted the rest of their lives.

Kellogg had boundless energy and an unshakable faith in the correctness of his ideas. When the sanitarium burned down in 1902, he quickly rebuilt it on larger scale. He also had a falling out with the Adventists at this time, but this had no ill effects on the sanitarium. Soon thousands of patients were being treated there each year, and the staff included thirty physicians. Kellogg's energy hardly flagged in his later years. He kept two secretaries employed full time, and performed some 22,000 operations for which he did not charge — his income came from the almost fifty books that he wrote. He was planning further expansions to the sanitarium when the Great Depression hit. Business declined precipitously after this, and the main building was sold to the government in 1942.

John Harvey Kellogg died the following year, aged ninety-one. Will, who had eclipsed his brother in cornflake fame, died in 1951, having reached the same age. ▣

'Is God a man with two arms and legs like me? Does He have eyes, a head? Does He have bowels? Well I do, and that makes me more wonderful than He is!'

JOHN HARVEY KELLOGG

KING, SIR GEORGE

(1919–1997)

UFO contactee

George King, a former fireman and taxi driver and a keen practitioner of yoga, found his true vocation one seemingly unremarkable day in 1954. He was washing the dishes in his London flat when a disembodied

voice boomed out, 'Prepare yourself! You are to become the voice of interplanetary parliament.'

The speaker, King learned some time later, was the Master Aetherius, who lived on Venus and was 3,456-years-old. He was just one of several 'Cosmic Masters' who began to channel messages through King (whom they dubbed the 'Primary Terrestrial Mental Channel'). The others included Mars Sector 6, Buddha, Krishna, the Lord of Karma and, most controversially, Jesus Christ. King hired a public hall and gave live transmissions from outer space. As with other UFO contactees of the time, many of the messages concerned the threat posed to human beings by nuclear war. King attracted much ridicule, but a few followers as well, and in 1956 he founded the Aetherius Society to help spread the word.

The Cosmic Masters announced through King that, in order to boost the Earth's spiritual energy, they would be sending a spaceship, called Satellite No. 3, to orbit it for a few months each year and beam energy upon us. Between 1958 and 1961 King and a small band of enthusiastic followers carried out Operation Starlight. They travelled around the world, climbing eighteen mountains in the United Kingdom, France, Switzerland, America, Australia and New Zealand. Upon reaching the summit of each, King performed a ceremony that directed the energy from the Masters' spaceship into it.

Many of the activities of King and his followers revolved around using this precious spiritual energy efficiently. He developed a number of inventions, including the Spiritual Energy Radiator and the Prayer Battery. The latter is a compact device made from gold, quartz crystals and other materials, which is charged by Aetherius Society members praying over it. The energy stored inside is then available to be fired off in short sharp bursts to prevent or alleviate the effects of wars, famines, earthquakes and other disasters. The Aetherius Society is nothing if not a practical organisation.

As he travelled around the world, King gave lectures, appeared on television, and opened new branches of the society. In 1959, he moved to America permanently. The Society made its headquarters in Los Angeles, where it rubbed shoulders with numerous other contactee groups.

Over the years, King was showered with honours. Buddha made him a Knight Templar, the Liberal Catholic Church made him an archbishop, and he received a knighthood from the Byzantine Royal House (whoever they may be). He remained to the end a cheery, down to earth, typically British fellow, always keen to throw himself into

another 'operation' to help the world. Since his death in 1997, the society has carried on his good work. It has Spiritual Energy Radiators in its London, Los Angeles and Auckland centres that are regularly switched on in times of crisis, with the results duly posted on its website. ▣

KING, WILLIAM

(1807–1873)
'The Flying Pieman'

King was one of the most recognisable characters in Sydney during the mid-nineteenth century. He was born in London, where his father, who worked in the Treasury at Whitehall, tried to set him up in business as a stockbroker. Far too high-spirited for such a staid occupation, he migrated to Australia, arriving in 1829. (It has been suggested that he was a 'remittance man', which means that his family, finding his presence embarrassing, had paid for his passage to Australia, then continued to support him there by sending funds.) After working as a private tutor in New South Wales, he moved to Sydney where he began to sell pies from a brightly coloured cart on the corner of King and Pitt streets.

It was at this point that he became known for his remarkable pedestrian feats. These included walking from Campbelltown to Sydney (a distance of sixty-five miles or 105 km) and back in twelve and a half hours, and walking 1,615 miles (2,600 km) in thirty-nine days, in almost constant rain. On such walks, he was often handicapped with weights, and at various times could be seen lugging a heavy pole, a dog, a boy and a live goat. He liked to race against mail coaches, and it was said that he would sell pies to passengers boarding the ferry leaving Circular Quay in Sydney for Parramatta (some sixteen miles or twenty-five km away), then meet them at their destination to unload his remaining stock.

As the Flying Pieman's fame spread, people began to issue increasingly elaborate challenges to him — which he never refused. One challenge saw him picking up 1,000 corn cobs, each set three feet apart, which he managed to do in fifty-five minutes. On another occasion he ran a mile, walked a mile, wheeled a barrow for half a mile, pulled a carriage with a woman in it for half a mile, walked backwards for half a mile, picked up fifty stones, then jumped over hurdles for fifteen minutes. In the 1840s, he left Sydney and lived in various places around the country, continuing to perform amazing athletic feats. In 1848, in Maitland, he accepted a wager to walk 1,000 quarter miles in 1,000 quarter hours. On the ninth day, he had to ask to be horsewhipped as an incentive, but he won the bet.

King grew stout in his later years, and may have suffered from dropsy which curtailed his pedestrian activities. He took to wearing a top hat and carrying a long staff, both decorated with coloured streamers, and, back in Sydney, appointed himself the city's town crier (although his proclamations were not always comprehensible). His last years were spent in poverty, and he died in a home for destitute men.

KINGSBOROUGH, EDWARD KING (LORD)
—————
(1795–1837)
Antiquarian

Kingsborough was an Irish aristocrat who devoted his life to proving that the Mayans were one of the Lost Tribes of Israel. He first became obsessed with the idea after being introduced to the 'Codex Mendoza', a famous Mayan manuscript which had found its way to the Bodleian Library in Oxford, by his friend, the fanatical book collector ☞ Sir Thomas Phillipps. After that, he spent years scouring libraries throughout Europe for other early Mexican documents. He never thought to actually visit Mexico (and, stranger still, never went to Spain, where the majority of Mexican documents in Europe were

to be found).

Kingsborough attempted to prove his theory by tracing similarities between the ancient Israelites and the Mayans. He found, for example, that both cultures practised circumcision and prohibited the eating of pork, while sacrifice was a central concept in both their religions. He published the results of his researches in eight huge volumes entitled *Antiquities of Mexico* (the final two were issued posthumously). They were extremely lavish productions, with many hand-coloured illustrations and engravings of Mexican manuscripts. Kingsborough was praised by scholars for making so much of this rare material available. He received less praise for his theories, which were generally dismissed as poorly argued and unconvincing.

The books sold badly and Kingsborough gave away many sets. As rich as he was, their publication ended up bankrupting him. Unable to pay his debts, he was arrested and thrown into the Sheriff's Prison in Dublin, where he quickly contracted typhus and died age forty-two. ◻

KIRWAN, RICHARD
—————
(1733–1812)
Scientist

Kirwan was the second son of land-owners Martin and Mary Kirwan of

Cloghballymore in County Galway, Ireland. He received part of his education in France, and in 1757 married Anne Burke. She died eight years later, leaving him with two daughters, and he never remarried. He briefly studied for the priesthood, then practised as a lawyer, but after 1768, when his elder brother was killed in a duel and he inherited the family estate, he devoted himself to science. His interests were wide, and he wrote extensively on chemistry, geology, meteorology, philology and other subjects. He was one of the last defenders of the existence of phlogiston, a substance supposedly contained within combustible materials which made them burn. He was very well known and respected in his day, and was elected president of the Royal Irish Academy in 1799.

If Kirwan's scientific reputation has faded, the tales of his eccentricities have kept him alive. He was a highly cultured man who spoke several languages and loved to talk. He entertained guests at his home twice a week, and, like everything else in his life, these gatherings ran to a very orderly pattern. At 7 p.m. a servant removed the knocker from his front door, an indication that no further guests would be admitted, and at 9 p.m. Kirwan removed his shoes, a signal for his guests to leave.

Kirwan liked to walk around his estate, Clegg Castle, accompanied by his six large dogs, and with an eagle perched on his shoulder. He suffered from a condition which made it difficult for him to swallow and he always ate alone, his diet consisting mainly of ham and milk. He had a terrible fear of catching a cold, kept a roaring fire going in his house at all times, and always wore a hat and coat indoors. If he had to go outside, he would first stand before the fire with his coat open, soaking up its heat, then wrap himself in scarves. Once outside, he moved through the streets at a furious clip, his mouth shut tight lest any of the precious heat escape. One of the duties of his manservant, Pope, was to enter his master's bedroom several times a night and pour hot tea down his throat to top up the internal fires. Despite such measures, Kirwin caught a cold at the age of seventy-nine. He treated this by the approved method of starving it, and so expired. 🔲

KLIMA, LADISLAV
(1878–1928)
Philosopher

Klíma, the son of a lawyer, was born in Domažlice, Bohemia (now the Czech Republic). 'As a child', he wrote in an autobiographical essay, 'I hated everyone, every caress made me want to vomit... If I analyse my

memories — it was already in the first few years that I felt myself and humanity to be like two warring parties, and I instinctively belittled the enemy, considering him as nothing.'

At the age of seventeen, Klíma was expelled from school after writing an essay in which he called the Hapsburgs 'a dynasty of swine'. He underwent no further formal education. His philosophy, heavily influenced by Schopenhauer and Nietzsche, was essentially an extreme form of subjectivism. Klíma believed that the world was an illusion created by individuals as they perceive it. Each individual is, or at least has the potential to be, the God of their own world, to achieve, as he called it, their 'deoessence'. Klíma presaged postmodernism by declaring that all truths are relative — 'At one moment lunacy seems to one like reason, at another, reason seems like lunacy.'

It was essential that such a philosophy be put into practice. If Klíma was God, he was going to act like God. He rejected all conventional morality and the expectations of society. He turned up his nose at the idea of a career or regular employment, preferring the pursuit of truth to a full stomach and material comforts. He would have no truck with practical matters — 'Everything practical is dishonourable.' In his twenties, he scraped by on an inheritance, and then on the proceeds from occasional publications, odd jobs, and the generosity of his friends (who, despite his war on humanity, do not seem to have been in short supply).

Klíma lived in a rigorously spartan manner. Later in life, he occupied an unheated hotel room almost devoid of furniture in Prague — he wrote while lying on the floor. He prided himself on never becoming ill, and liked to test his own body, almost taunting it to fail. He spent nights out in the open during winter, wearing only light clothes, and drank water that he knew was contaminated. He lived on raw foods — vegetables, eggs, meat — and wasn't particular where they came from. 'Once,' he wrote, 'I stole a bitten-into mouse from a cat and gobbled it down, just like it was, with the fur and bones — as if I were eating a dumpling.' He drank prodigious amounts of spirits for most of his life, but boasted that he never suffered any after-effects. The only time he felt physical pain, he said, was when his shoes pinched his feet. He occasionally had sex, but had no interest in taking a wife. Most of his sex life, he admitted, was conducted in his head, and he dreamed of discovering 'about twenty "perversities" unknown until now'.

Klíma set out his main philosophical ideas in *The World as Consciousness and Nothing* (1924). After

that he concentrated on spreading his view of the world in a series of fantastic, often grotesque and obscene fictions. Most were not published until after his death, and he destroyed many manuscripts. Some of Klíma's fellow philosophers were offended by his antics, but there was a grudging respect for the uncompromising way he led his life. After his death, from tuberculosis, the playwright and novelist Karel Čapek said, 'Next to Klíma, Diogenes in his barrel was a homeowner.'

Klíma's novel of sadomasochism and transcendence, *The Sufferings of Prince Sternenhoch*, is the only book of his so far translated into English. ■

'My whole life has been one big divergence from everything reasonable, living only for myself from the very beginning... so that I don't know that anyone could find such an example in all of history (leaving aside forgotten history).'

LADISLAV KLÍMA

KNIGHT, LEONARD

(b. 1931)
Creator of Salvation Mountain

Knight, who was born in Vermont,

spent his early years working on the family farm and avoiding school as much as possible. He was drafted into the army during the Korean War, but it ended ten days after his arrival in Korea. Back in Vermont after his discharge, he worked in a car dealership and taught himself to play guitar, becoming proficient enough to give lessons to others.

In 1967, he was visiting his sister Irene in San Diego. Irene was a Christian but Knight had never had a religious bone in his body. Tiring of her attempts to convert him, he went and sat in his van where, for reasons that he could never explain, he began to repeat a prayer –'Jesus, I'm a sinner, please come upon my body and into my heart.' He repeated it for twenty minutes, and has been a Christian ever since. His faith is of a cheerful and uncomplicated kind — he believes anyone who accepts Jesus will be saved.

Three years later, Knight was in Burlington, Vermont, watching people's reactions as a hot air balloon flew overhead, when he conceived the idea of a balloon emblazoned with the words 'God Is Love'. He spent ten years praying and attempting to raise funds for it, then realised he would have to make it himself. He began to buy up odd scraps of balloon material and stitched them together on an old sewing machine. His attempts

LADISLAV KLIMA

to inflate his balloon always failed, however, and when he was forced to leave it out in the open one winter, it began to rot. In 1984, he moved to a hot and dusty spot on the outskirts of Slab City, California. (Slab City is a former World War II Marine base. It's now home to squatters and itinerant 'snowbirds' who come down from the northern states to spend the winter there.) Knight took his balloon with him, but it had rotted beyond repair and he was forced to abandon it. Before leaving the area, he decided to build a small monument on a ridge overlooking the highway. He fashioned it using half a bag of cement, painted it white and added the words 'God Is Love' in red. Having completed it, he changed his mind about leaving. He had conceived a project far bigger than a hot air balloon.

The small cement monument was the beginning of Salvation Mountain. Knight kept adding to it, incorporating junk, like refrigerators and tyres from the local dump, covering it with cement and painting it.

Because he had little money to buy cement, he mixed a lot of sand in with it, making the structure unstable. Three years after work on it commenced, it all came down. Undeterred, just thankful nobody had been hurt in the collapse, he immediately began rebuilding.

For his new mountain, Knight experimented with adobe mixed with straw and found it a much sturdier material. He laboured incessantly, sometimes working at night to avoid the day's heat. As word of Knight's project spread, more people arrived with donations, especially of acrylic paint. The structure grew to about fifty feet (fifteen metres) tall and 150 feet (forty-five metres) wide. It is surmounted by a cross, and decorated with religious slogans and biblical quotations, images of flowers and an American flag, all vividly coloured, the colours changing as Knight adds more and more layers of paint.

In 1994, having taken soil samples which they said contained dangerous levels of lead, the county authorities announced their intention of demolishing Salvation Mountain and shipping it off to a toxic waste dump in Nebraska. There was a local outcry, and supporters of outsider art from around the world began a letter writing campaign. When independent tests which Knight commissioned showed the soil did not contain hazardous chemicals, the county authorities backed down. In 2002, Salvation Mountain was declared a national treasure.

Leonard Knight continues to live and work on the site. Rather than making it any bigger, he now

concentrates on adding paint, reasoning that the more he adds the longer the structure will last. He lives in a small house built on the back of an old fire truck which is decorated in the same simple and colourful style as his mountain. He has no electricity or running water, and washes himself in a hot spring. He loves receiving visitors and encourages them to take photos, but never tries to force his religious beliefs onto them, and is self-deprecating about his achievement. 'I always kinda figured that God scraped the bottom of the barrel to have me work on that mountain,' he once said. 'Maybe he just wanted to prove that he could pick somebody that really couldn't do it and then make him do it.' ▣

'I let my mountain do my talking.'
LEONARD KNIGHT

KYSELAK, JOSEF
(1799–1831)
Autographist

Kyselak, who worked as a clerk in the court of the first Austrian emperor, Franz I, has been called the father of 'tagging'. Some time in the early 1820s, he made a bet with friends that in three years his name

would be known throughout the Austrian empire. He immediately began to write it, or 'Kyselak war hier' ('Kyselak was here'), in bold black letters everywhere he went. He put his name on walls, churches, castles, bridges, stones, trees and, being an avid mountaineer, the tops of mountains. In 1925, accompanied by his pet dog, he spent two months wandering and autographing throughout the empire, and recorded his travels in a book, *Journey on Foot through Austria, Styria, Carinthia, Salzburg, Berchtesgaden, Tyrol and Bavaria to Vienna* (1829).

Kyselak's friends were forced to concede that he had won the bet, but having won it, he continued to sign his name at every opportunity. According to one story (possibly apocryphal, but a lovely story nevertheless), he was once summoned to be reprimanded for his activities by the emperor himself. Kyselak acted suitably chastened, but after he left, his name was found on the emperor's desk.

Kyselak died during an epidemic of cholera in Vienna. It is said that he persisted in eating fresh fruit despite the risk of contracting the disease from it, and after falling ill, refused medical attention. Some of his original autographs survive, including two on obelisks in Vienna's Schwarzenberg Park. ▣

LANGLEY, EVE

(1904–1974)
Writer

Eve Langley was born on a cattle station in New South Wales. Her mother, Mira Davidson, came from a family with extensive land holdings in Gippsland, Victoria, but had been disinherited when she married Eve's father, Arthur Langley, a labourer. The family, including Eve's younger sister June, moved around New South Wales for several years before settling in the small town of Crossover in Gippsland, where Mira managed a hotel owned by her brother. Shortly after their arrival, when Eve was eleven, Arthur Langley died.

Although her education was patchy, Langley was an avid reader, especially of mythology and poetry. Growing up among the rough, bearded, hard drinking bushmen who frequented the Crossover pub, she and June became tomboys. This was hardly surprising, but Eve's gender confusion went deeper. Haunted by the image of her late father, she believed that she was carrying his spirit in her body, and that she should have been born a man. Yet, while she had infatuations with women, she fell in love with men. Her most intense relationship in her early years was, however, with her sister.

The years 1925 to 1928 were the happiest of Langley's life. Eve and June, who wore men's clothing and went by the names Steve and Blue, spent most of this time picking peas and hops in Gippsland, and living in a bark hut. Their male attire sometimes attracted the attentions of the police, but they were generally accepted by local people, who nicknamed them 'the Trouser Women', because they were such hard workers. Meanwhile, Langley was involved in her first and most important romantic relationship with a drover, Mackinnon Howlett (known as Macca).

In the end, Langley could not square the idea of marriage with her artistic ambitions, and ended her relationship with Macca. In 1929, she crossed the Victorian Alps on horseback, an arduous trip rarely attempted — another incident which entered her personal mythology. At the end of it, she rejoined June in Eurobin, but their relationship had started to break down. June was the prettier of the two, more outgoing and popular with boys, and Eve was increasingly jealous. In 1930, June married an Englishman and they moved to New Zealand, taking her mother with them.

Langley began a relationship with an ex-jockey named Johnston and went into a sharefarming venture which failed. In 1932, she made the reluctant decision to leave her beloved Gippsland and join her sister and mother in New Zealand. She stopped wearing men's clothes (in favour of peasant dresses) and began to forge a literary career, having numerous poems, short stories and articles accepted by newspapers and magazines. She had a passionate affair with an Italian named Rinaldo, became pregnant, and gave birth to a daughter who died after a few weeks. She then fell in love with a young art student, Hillary Clarke, who had a studio in a windmill, and pursued him relentlessly. For once, she was keen to get married, and Clarke, against his better judgment (and after learning she was pregnant) agreed.

The marriage was a disaster. Clarke had no desire to give up his bohemian artist lifestyle and was often away from home. Langley was incapable of keeping a house or looking after children. A daughter,

Bisi, was soon followed by a son, Langley, who was nicknamed Adolf (Eve, who had only the vaguest understanding of politics, adored Hitler). They were desperately poor. Yet during this period, Langley wrote her first novel, *The Pea-pickers*, which recreated with almost hallucinatory intensity the golden summers she had spent with Blue and Macca in Gippsland. It won an Australian literary prize worth £100 in 1940, and was published in Australia and America. It is considered an Australian classic, and has been reprinted several times, most recently in 2002.

Langley's triumph was short-lived. She had long been exhibiting signs of mental instability, and her condition was not improved by another pregnancy (the child, born on Labour Day 1941, was given the unlikely name of Karl Marx). Clarke enlisted in the army in 1942, and believing Langley incapable of looking after herself, had her committed to Auckland Psychiatric Hospital, where she remained for seven years. The children ended up in an orphanage.

After her release, Langley worked as a bookbinder at Auckland Public Library, and had a second novel, *White Topee*, published in 1954, which continued the adventures of Steve and Blue. In a publicity photo on the back cover, Langley is wearing a typical outfit — white topee hat, long fur coat and canvas shoes, and holding an elephant gun (because, she explained, it went with the hat). The novel's oddest passage comes when Steve remembers her birth and describes the soul of Oscar Wilde entering her body. This was much more than a literary fancy. After years of wrestling with the idea that she was a man trapped in a woman's body (she had resumed wearing men's clothes during her marriage), she resolved the problem with the belief that she was Oscar Wilde re-incarnated. In 1954, she changed her name by deed poll to Oscar Wilde.

She returned to Australia in 1956, travelled extensively, and even went pea-picking in Victoria again. She continued to write manically, transforming her journals from the thirties and forties into a series of 'novels', but these were all rejected by her publisher. Langley was ter-rified by the passage of time, and her writings were a doomed attempt to regain her past and the men she had loved, like Macca, who in her mind assumed the status of Greek gods. In 1965, she managed to organise a trip to Greece, a land she had dreamed of since a child, but it ended with Langley losing most of her possessions and living rough on the streets of Athens until a return fare could be raised by friends back in Australia.

She spent the last years living reclusively in a four-roomed shack

she dubbed 'Iona Lympus' in bush-land in the Blue Mountains, west of Sydney. Her chief companions were dolls. She died in early June 1974, but her body was not found for several weeks. ▣

LAWSON, ALFRED W.

(1869–1954)
Lawsonomist

Lawson had no doubt he was one of the greatest men, if not the greatest man, who had ever lived. In middle age, having, as he saw it, conquered the worlds of baseball and aviation, he could surely have rested on his laurels. Instead, he devoted the rest of his life to the development of Lawsonomy, a science so revolu-tionary and all-encompassing that it would advance humanity to the next evolutionary level.

The 'First Knowledgian', as he styled himself in his last years, was born in London, the sixth child of Robert and Mary Lawson. Three weeks later, the family moved to Canada, then to America, and settled in Detroit. According to his own account, Lawson was a rebellious child, and left school — and home — at the age of twelve. Two years later his parents persuaded him to return and take an industrial course, the only other formal education he received.

Lawson took up baseball at the age of eighteen. He pitched for various teams, and was later a manager and promoter. Despite the fact that he billed himself as 'the Magic Man of Baseball', he only had middling success in the sport. Midway through this period, he took stock of his life, and gave up smoking, drinking and eating meat. He penned a strange utopian novel, *Born Again* (1904), where he described an ideal society in which people abandoned selfishness and all property was shared. It was the first inkling of Lawsonomy.

In 1908, after almost two decades in baseball, Lawson switched to an entirely different field — aviation. He published the first popular magazine devoted to the subject, and became an effective booster for the fledgling air travel industry. His predictions about the future of air travel were typically grandiose. He claimed that the ability to fly would eliminate national boundaries, and even postulated that by the year 3000 a new, more highly evolved human, called 'alti-man', would live permanently in the skies, and become the natural ruler of the 'ground-men' below. In 1917, he founded the Lawson Aircraft Corporation, and two years later built the world's first airliner (a word Lawson coined), with seating for sixteen passengers. With Lawson in

the pilot seat, the plane went on a barnstorming tour of America, generating enormous publicity. Lawson, now known as 'the Columbus of the Air', envisioned a fleet of airliners crisscrossing the country daily. Alas, the money he raised from private investors was insufficient to realise this dream, and when his second, larger airliner crashed on its first flight, the company folded.

While Lawson would make further attempts to set up an airline in the late 1920s, he began to focus most of his energies on developing Lawsonomy, which would replace conventional physics, biology and any number of other sciences. Lawson declared that energy is a myth. He believed that the universe is composed of various substances, including what we think of as matter — solids, liquids and gases — but also sound, light, electricity and so on. All substances have different densities, and it is the nature of the higher density substances to penetrate the lower ones, resulting in pressure and suction. It is these two forces that keep everything in the universe in constant, complex motion, which Lawson characterised in the memorable phrase 'zig-zag-and-swirl'. Moreover, the universe is literally alive, teeming with mental organisms or 'menorgs', which work to maintain Earth at an equilibrium between the forces of pressure

and suction, and also drive human evolution. Lawson claimed to have discovered the basic principles of Lawsonomy while watching dust motes in the air at the age of four. Interestingly, his notion of a universe alive and in constant motion bears a marked resemblance to the theories dreamed up by that other great self-taught scientist, ☞ Margaret Cavendish, almost three centuries earlier.

The Great Depression prompted Lawson to adapt his new insights to economics, which he did in the book *Direct Credits for Everybody* (1931). Lawson believed that the great enemies of the people were the financiers, who accumulated money for themselves, while the fact that money was tied to the gold standard artificially reduced the amount of 'real money' in the economy. His solution was to abolish the gold standard, private banks and interest on loans. The government would determine the amount of money based on the total productivity of the economy, and divide this fairly among individuals in the form of 'direct credits'. In 1931, Lawson founded the Direct Credit Society. Anyone could join, and although members were encouraged to donate to the cause, there were no dues. It was a considerable success, attracting over two million active or passive members. They

wore uniforms, marched in parades and attended meetings where they sang songs in praise of Lawson, whose new epithets included 'the People's Coach' and 'the Man of Destiny'. Lawson loved giving stirring speeches to his followers. However, his refusal to speak on radio, or advertise in newspapers or magazines (which he believed were in the hands of the financiers), meant his movement remained confined to the midwestern states, and in the end it had no influence on American politics.

As the 1930s wore on and the New Deal came into effect, Lawson lost interest in direct credits, and concentrated on setting out the principles of pure Lawsonomy in a series of books. He now declared that he was one of the prophets that God sent along every 2,000 years. In 1943, he bought the site of the defunct Des Moines University in Iowa and founded the Des Moines University of Lawsonomy. In practice, this was more like a commune than a normal university, with its students — usually no more than a few dozen at a time — living according to austere Lawsonian principles. They 'studied' Lawsonomy, which basically involved learning the master's books by heart.

In 1948, the logical culmination of Lawson's career came with the incorporation of the 'Lawsonian

Religion'. His movement was in a steep decline by now. The university, which had been treated with great suspicion and sometimes antagonism by the local people, was forced to close in 1954 after it was revealed that it had bought a large amount of war-surplus machinery, supposedly for educational purposes, then sold most of it at a large profit. Lawson died two weeks later. His memory was kept alive by a dwindling band of believers, but for all his undoubtedly prodigious efforts, the world soon forgot the name of Alfred Lawson.

'I sometimes think that I was born ten or twenty thousand years ahead of time.'

ALFRED W. LAWSON

LAY, BENJAMIN

(1677–1759)
Abolitionist

Lay was a fabulous little bundle of moral indignation who liked nothing better than to make the lives of slave owners a misery. Born in England and a seaman in his youth, he first encountered slavery in Barbados, where he set up a shop with his wife, Sarah, around 1730. Lay and his wife, who were Quakers, were deeply affected by the conditions in which the slaves lived. He began to denounce slavery publicly, earning the enmity of the plantation owners. He and Sarah eventually decided to leave and moved to Philadelphia, where they were shocked to find many of their fellow Quakers were also slave owners.

Lay was a hunchback about four feet six inches (137 cm) tall. His arms were almost as long as his legs and he had a white beard that grew down to his waist. In Philadelphia, he lost no time denouncing the slave owners, and often turned up at Quaker meetings, sometimes wearing sackcloth. Ejected from one meeting, he lay at the front door so that the congregation had to step over him as they left. He invaded another meeting wearing a military uniform with a sword, and carrying a hollowed out book (to represent the Bible) in which was concealed a bladder containing pokeberry juice. Declaring that enslaving a man was no better than stabbing him through the heart, he drew the sword and plunged in into his 'Bible', spattering those nearest him with the red juice. He once sat outside a meeting in the middle of winter with one bare leg deep in the snow. When passersby expressed concern, he said, 'You pretend compassion for me, but you do not feel for the poor slaves in your fields who go all winter half clad.' He was not afraid of taking direct action, and once went so far as to kidnap a slave owner's three-year-old child, so he would know how it felt to lose a loved one.

Lay wrote a number of anti-slavery tracts, some of which were printed by Benjamin Franklin. On receiving the manuscript for *All Slave-Keepers That Keep the Innocent in Bondage, Apostates*, Franklin flicked through the pages and saw that they were unnumbered and in no order whatsoever. Lay told him to print them however he liked.

In addition to his stand against slavery, Lay was a strict vegetarian and a vociferous opponent of alcohol and tea. In emulation of Jesus, he once attempted to fast for forty days, but was persuaded to give up after twenty-one days by his wife and others. He made all his own clothes rather than risk wearing a product of slavery. He spent the last years of his life living in a cave.

Lay was on his deathbed when word came through that the Quakers had voted to reject slavery. 'I can now die in peace,' he cried, and did so shortly afterwards. The little man who had been such a thorn in the side of the Quakers became, after his death, one of their heroes, and his picture was a common sight in Quaker homes for many years. ▣

LEADBETTER, CHARLES WEBSTER

(1854–1834)
Theosophist

Leadbetter told as many tall tales about his early life as his guru, ☞ Madame Blavatsky. He claimed to have grown up in South America, where his father was the director of a railway company, and where his adventures included finding Inca gold and fighting with rebel Indians who murdered his brother. In fact, he was an only child, and his father was a railway clerk in Stockport, England, who died when Charles was eight. His widowed mother could not provide much of an education for him, but family connections saw him ordained as an Anglican priest in 1878.

Leadbetter's real interests lay in the psychic and occult, and he found the perfect niche in the Theosophical Society, founded by Blavatsky and Henry Olcott in 1875. Impatient to advance within it, he made contact with Blavatsky. She must have been impressed with him, for a letter soon arrived from one of the Masters of the Great White Brotherhood — the benevolent, enlightened, non-corporeal beings who lived in a secret underground location in Tibet, and with whom Blavatsky claimed to be in daily contact.

The letter authorised Leadbetter to travel to the society's headquarters in Adyar, India, to undergo spiritual training. He did so, and was soon in regular contact with the Masters, something which did not altogether please Blavatsky, who liked to keep them to herself.

After three years teaching in a school set up by Olcott in Ceylon (now Sri Lanka), Leadbetter returned to England in 1889 with a young Sinhalese boy, Jinarajadasa, in tow. The following year he met Annie Besant, Blavatsky's successor, and the attraction between them was as immediate as it was unlikely. As a rule, Leadbetter could hardly bear to be alone with a woman, and refused to shake hands with one lest it impair his 'purity'. Yet he and Besant were devoted to each other, and she came to rely on his easy communication with the Masters and his many other psychic powers. He quickly became one of the leading Theosophists, touring the world giving lectures and writing numerous books, either alone or with Besant. He was fascinated by reincarnation, and compiled a vast work detailing the past lives of his fellow Theosophists going back thousands of years. (They all turned out to have been related to each other in various permutations during each incarnation, had frequently changed sex, and a few had lived on

other planets.)

Leadbetter's meteoric rise within Theosophy was brought to an abrupt halt when scandal broke out. As suggested by his close relationship with Jinarajadasa, his weakness was an inordinate fondness for young boys, and in 1906 he was accused of teaching boys in his care to masturbate, and worse. There were angry calls for his expulsion from the society, and Besant was eventually forced to act on them. However, after she became president following the death of Olcott in 1907, he was allowed back into the fold.

Besant had great plans to expand Theosophy. She shared with Leadbetter a love of colourful costumes and elaborate rituals, and was soon creating all sorts of different orders and sections within the society to indulge these whims. Not all of this went down well with the more straightlaced members, but Leadbetter's suggestion that a great World Teacher was about to appear on Earth caught the imaginations of many. In his quest for this Teacher, Leadbetter began to keep an even closer eye on young boys than usual. In 1909, he was back in Adyar when he saw an Indian boy bathing in the sea and was struck by his powerful aura. The boy, Jiddu Krishnamurti, happened to be the son of a Theosophist, and Leadbet-

ter also determined that he had a fabulous set of past lives. Under the older man's spiritual tutelage, he was soon communing with the Masters.

Besant persuaded Krishnamurti's father to allow the boy to be taken to England. Here, Leadbetter continued to oversee all aspects of his education and life — including his bathing habits, and of course strictly forbade him from having any intimate dealings with women. Krishnamurti, who was no scholar, chafed under his strict discipline and the stifling company of other Theosophists, and missed his home terribly, but nevertheless began to grow into the role assigned to him. That the World Teacher was apparently among them electrified the Theosophists, and worldwide membership rose to 45,000 in 1920.

By then, Leadbetter, who continued to be the subject of fierce attacks by other Theosophists, had moved to Australia. He was ordained into the Liberal Catholic Church, a tiny, eccentric offshoot of the Catholic Church which — importantly for Leadbetter — retained its costumes. After eight days he was made a bishop, and adopted the requisite purple robes and amethyst ring. He still played a role in Theosophy, but scandal continued to dog him, the Australian police were investigating him, and during a convention in Sydney he was attacked on all sides. When he refused to step down, many members resigned.

After that, Leadbetter and a group of loyalists occupied themselves building a grandiose amphitheatre on Sydney's Balmoral Beach where the World Teacher would speak. Perhaps inevitably, it was popularly believed that they expected this to be the setting for the Second Coming, with Christ advancing across the waters of Sydney Harbour in triumph.

Leadbetter died in 1934, five years after Krishnamurti renounced Theosophy and indeed all forms of organised religion, declaring instead that it was up to the individual to find their own path to enlightenment. He went on to have an impressive career as a speaker and writer on spiritual and philosophical issues. He attended the funeral in Sydney of Leadbetter, the man who had plucked him from obscurity, but refused to enter the church. ▣

LEATHERMAN, THE
(c.1824–1889)
Pedestrian

The Leatherman was a well known figure in Connecticut and New York State, famous for walking a well-defined, 360 mile (580 km) circular route through the rural areas between the Connecticut and Hudson

THE LEATHERMAN

THE ECCENTROPEDIA

rivers, a route that took him exactly thirty-four days to traverse. He did this for thirty-two years.

His name derived from his remarkable outfit. Like ☞ John Bigg, he wore only leather clothes, including a round leather hat with a brim, leather coat, jerkin and trousers, and high leather boots with wooden soles. Like Bigg, he would happily accept donations of pieces of leather (while Bigg used to nail these pieces onto his outfit, the Leatherman sewed them on with leather thongs). He wore this outfit all year round, and during summer it was said to squeak as he walked.

What was notable about him, apart from his clothing, was his supreme regularity. People who lived along his route knew that he would reappear every thirty-four days without fail. Sometimes they would put food aside to give to him. He would never enter anyone's house, and usually ate while sitting by their front door. At night, he slept in caves, or in makeshift lean-tos.

The Leatherman spoke fluent French but only a few guttural words of English, so it was assumed he hailed from France. He was sometimes identified as Jules Bourglay, a name which appeared in newspaper accounts and was put on his tombstone, but there is no proof of this. He refused to answer questions about his past. As with any mysterious public character, stories about his origins arose to fill the vacuum. According to one popular tale, he was born in Lyons, and fell in love with the daughter of a leather merchant. Employed by the merchant, he made bad investments (or perhaps started a fire) that almost ruined the business. Forbidden to marry the daughter after that, he journeyed to America where he wore leather as penance. Others said he was a war veteran.

In 1888, the Leatherman almost froze to death during a blizzard, and was taken to a hospital, but escaped from it soon after. The following year, he was found dead in one of his caves, having succumbed to mouth cancer. A French prayer book was found in the leather sack he always carried, along with his leather-working tools. His clothing, which weighed sixty pounds (twenty-seven kg), went on display in the Eden Musée in New York. ▣

LEEDSKALNIN, EDWARD

(1887–1951)
Builder of the Coral Castle

Leedskalnin was born in Riga, Latvia, and migrated to America when he was about thirty. After working as a logger in various places, he contracted tuberculosis, and moved to Florida City where he bought a

plot of land and began work on the extraordinary monument he initially called Rock Gate Park. This was essentially an open air house, constructed entirely of blocks of oolite limestone (not coral), some of them weighing over thirty tons, which were apparently quarried, carved and moved into place by Leedskalnin working entirely alone.

Just how he managed to achieve this prodigious feat has been the subject of much speculation. Leedskalnin was a small man, four feet eight inches (361 cm) tall. He always worked at night, behind a high stone wall, and initially used tools he had fashioned from the parts of an old car. In 1936, he decided he had chosen the wrong spot for his monument, hired a truck and — again apparently single-handedly — moved the whole lot ten miles (sixteen km) away to Homestead, near Highway 1, where it was completed and renamed the Coral Castle.

The precision of some of his handiwork is astonishing. Most famous is the door to his domain, a nine-ton slab of rock so perfectly balanced on its centre of gravity that it revolves at the touch of a finger. Leedskalnin hinted that he had rediscovered the engineering secrets that allowed the ancients to build the Pyramids and other monuments, and stories circulated that he had mastered the art of levitiation and could make enormous rocks float around like balloons. Nevertheless, there are photos of him using pulleys to move blocks of stone, so his methods would seem to have been conventional if exceptionally ingenious. He was also a keen amateur scientist who published a number of pamphlets outlining his unusual theories about magnetism and electricity.

According to Leedskalnin, he built his rock monument in honour of a sixteen-year-old girl who had jilted him in Latvia just before their wedding was to take place. The 'house' he built was intended to tempt her to join him in America. It came complete with furniture, including rocking chairs, beds, a cradle, a bathtub, couches and tables, all hewn from solid rock. Other features of the structure include a two-storey tower in which he lived and worked; a forty-foot (12.2 metre) obelisk; a twenty-two-ton (22.4 tonne) block of stone sculpted into a crescent; and 'Repentence Corner', a sort of pillory in which a misbehaving child (or indeed wife) could be restrained. Leedskalnin wrote repeatedly to his former fiancée, whom he always referred to as his 'Sweet Sixteen', but she never replied.

In addition to his electromagnetic treatises, Leedskalnin produced a small volume called *A Book in Every Home*. This is largely concerned with advice for parents on how to raise their daughters and keep them safe from the depredations of 'fresh' young men. It also has a brief section on politics, which unsurprisingly reveals Leedskalnin to have been a rugged individualist.

Nobody can eat for you and so it is that if you want the things to eat you will have to produce them yourself and if you are too weak, too lazy, lack machinery and good management to produce them, you should perish and that is all there is to it.

Every right-hand page in the booklet is blank so that, as Leedskalnin puts it in a note, the reader may 'write your own opinion opposite it and see if you can do better'.

In his first few years constructing the Coral Castle, Leedskalnin was very reclusive, but he later allowed visitors in to admire his handiwork, giving them guided tours for a dime. In 1951, feeling ill, he placed a note on the front gate which read 'Going to the hospital'. He died in a Miami hospital three days later from stomach cancer.

The Coral Castle remains a popular tourist site, while many alternative science publications and websites continue to speculate about how Leedskalnin mastered gravity. In 1980, a group of Latvian visitors told the site's manager that the name of Leedskalnin's 'Sweet

Sixteen' was Agnes Skvust. It turned out that she was still living in Latvia, aged eighty-three. An invitation to visit the Coral Castle was sent to her, but she declined it, just as she always had. ▣

LEGENDARY STARDUST COWBOY, THE
(b. 1947)
Singer

'The Ledge,' as he is known to a small but devoted band of fans around the world, was born Norman Carl Odam in Lubbock, Texas. Walking down the street one day, aged seven, he decided that somehow he was going to be famous, and later came up with the name Legendary Stardust Cowboy (the 'stardust' deriving from his love of outer space). At fourteen, he began to develop his unique vocal style, practicing rebel yells, Indian whoops (being part-Shawnee), bird calls and other noises. He began to play guitar, bugle and kazoo, and gave impromptu performances at school in the (forlorn) hope of attracting girls. Sometimes he performed on top of his car, a Chevy Biscayne on which he had spray painted 'NASA presents the Legendary Stardust Cowboy'. He sang original compositions like 'My Underwear Froze to the Clothesline' and 'My Baby's Shaped Like an Ironing Board', and people often threw things at him. He managed to get a few club dates, and on one occasion had his guitar smashed by an audience member who thought he was making fun of country music.

In 1968, the Ledge set off for Los Angeles, determined to score a guest spot on the *Johnny Carson Show*. Stopping off at Fort Worth on the way, his talents were noticed by a couple of vacuum cleaner salesmen who took him into a recording studio where he recorded his signature song, 'Paralysed'. The young recording engineer T. Bone Burnett (who went on to become a highly respected singer and songwriter) played drums, while the Ledge did his usual thing. The resulting cacophony is, depending on your point of view, either one of the worst records ever made, or a wild burst of spontaneity and freedom. Five hundred copies of it were pressed, and it became a hit on regional radio. The Ledge acquired a manager, Major Bill Smith, who secured a deal with Mercury Records. Re-released, 'Paralysed' entered the Billboard top 100, and before he knew what was happening, the Ledge was performing it on the then wildly popular television programme *Laugh-In*, also the chief showcase for ☞ Tiny Tim.

There were offers from other programmes, including the *Ed Sullivan Show*, but then fate intervened in the form of a musicians' strike. By the time it was over and live music was again allowed on television, the Ledge's moment had passed. When he learned that Major Bill Smith had made off with a tape containing fifty of his songs, he stole it back and destroyed it by unravelling it in the street.

The Ledge released his first solo album, *Rock It to Stardom*, in 1984. In the liner notes he lists Sinatra as his favourite singer and Henry Mancini as favourite composer, although it's fair to say that these influences are not apparent on the album — despite being recorded with a band, it is just as chaotic as ever. Several more albums followed, and he has continued to give notoriously shambolic live performances. He has been hailed as a pioneer of the musical genre 'psychobilly', and gained some influential fans, not the least of them being David Bowie. The story goes that, after being signed by Mercury at the beginning of the seventies, Bowie was given a batch of the company's records including 'Paralysed', fell in love with it, and adopted part of the Ledge's name for his 'Ziggy Stardust' persona. In 2002, he repaid his debt to the wild Texan by including a cover of his song 'I Took a Trip (on a Gemini Spaceship)' on the *Heathen* album. ▨

LENKIEWICZ, ROBERT

(1941–2002)
Artist

Lenkiewicz's parents were Jewish refugees who fled to England from Germany and Poland, and after the war, opened a hotel in London. Lenkiewicz grew up among its residents, many of them Holocaust survivors, and some, as he put it, 'a little unhinged.' When he began to paint, they were among his first subjects.

Lenkiewicz studied at the Royal Academy, but his figurative style was totally at odds with the all-conquering abstract expressionism of the day, and the art establishment would treat him as a marginal figure to the end. Lenkiewicz, in turn, did not see himself as a conventional artist, but as 'a painter who produces sociological inquiry reports by visual means'. He painted society's outcasts — the homeless, the addicts, the crippled and mentally ill — and opened the doors of his Hampstead studio to them. His neighbours were unimpressed. He was forced to leave the suburb in 1964, and eventually settled in Plymouth.

He continued to provide a haven for the homeless, organising squats in nine empty warehouses, which were nicknamed the 'Cowboy Holiday Inns' (and mostly tolerated by the Plymouth authorities).

Dozens of his paintings of tramps formed the basis of his first great project, the Vagrancy Project, in 1973. The paintings were accompanied by a book which recorded the thoughts of the vagrants themselves. A Plymouth councillor was invited to the opening night and gave a speech in which, as Lenkiewicz had anticipated, he noted the city's good fortune in not having a problem with homelessness. The artist gave a signal and over seventy mostly drunken vagrants poured into the exhibition, causing chaos.

His closest friend among the vagrants was a man named Edwin Mackenzie. Lenkiewicz dubbed him 'Diogenes' after learning that he lived in a concrete cylinder reminiscent of the original ☞ Diogenes' barrel. In 1984, when Diogenes died, Lenkiewicz had his body embalmed (having earlier asked his permission). His original plan was to have the old tramp placed in a glass case in his library. 'To have someone one happens to have a deep affection for, and who is quite dead, running parallel with one's daily activities has always interested me,' he said. 'Glancing at him from time to time in my library would, I hope, encourage me even more to work and enjoy the moment.' Lenkiewicz was forced to hide the body, however, when Plymouth's health authority got wind of it. When officers raided his studio,

found a coffin and prised it open, Lenkiewicz jumped out of it bearing a sign reading 'Habeas Corpus'. Health inspector Michael Fox vowed that he would find the body, 'even if it takes ten years,' and Lenkiewicz noted that they were taking far more interest in the tramp now than they ever had when he was alive. As it happened, Diogenes was only found (in a chest of drawers in Lenkiewicz's studio) after the artist's death.

The Vagrancy Project was followed by others, equally ambitious. Some of the subjects — Old Age, Death, Suicide — led to accusations that Lenkiewicz was obsessed by death, but he maintained that he was more interested in the anxiety surrounding it. (In 1981, he faked his own death so that he could see the reaction to it.) Other projects — Love and Romance, Jealousy, Orgasm — tackled sexuality. Lenkiewicz believed that the theme connecting all of them was addiction. A person could become addicted to love, or to irrational ideas, just as they could become hooked on drugs. The ultimate aim of his art, he said, was to explain fascism — the tendency to treat other people as property.

Lenkiewicz was an extremely prolific artist, producing some 10,000 paintings and drawings. He often worked on a grand scale — as a student he did a painting 360 feet long — and his most famous works are probably two huge murals he painted on the Barbican in Plymouth. His love life was equally prodigious (he fathered eleven children and claimed to have bedded 3,000 women). He suffered from a heart condition and died suddenly, leaving his last project, Addictive Behaviour, unfinished. He was found to have £12 in cash, no bank account, and debts of £2 million. Many of his paintings, and his fabulous library (25,000 books on psychology, the occult, sex, death and other subjects) were sold to pay the debts. ▨

LEPPARD, TOM

(b. 1935)
'The Leopard Man'

Tom Leppard was for two decades probably the best-known hermit in England and a worthy successor to the likes of ☞ John Bigg and ☞ James Lucas. That he was tattooed from head to foot with leopard spots only added to his appeal.

Leppard, whose real name is Woodbridge, was evacuated from London during World War II and educated (and mistreated) in a convent school in Devon. He joined the Royal Navy at the age of fifteen, and later spent time in the army and the SAS. Always something of a loner, he was never really happy in the armed services. He resigned after twenty-eight years and moved to London, but he didn't like life there much better.

Throughout his years in the armed forces, he had never acquired a tattoo, but now made up for this in a big way. Over the next three years, three tattooists worked on him, covering 99.2 per cent of his body with leopard markings, and tattooing green cat's eyes on his eyelids. Changing his name to Leppard, he made a little money by giving interviews and exhibiting himself to photographers (he had a special set of fang-shaped dentures for such occasions), and was for a while listed in the *Guinness Book of Records* as the most tattooed man in the world.

After becoming involved in a fracas in an attorney's office (a marriage of convenience to a Turkish girl, the sister of one of his friends, had gone wrong), he spent four months in jail. On his release, he decided to leave London — and people — behind, and moved to the island of Skye in the Scottish Hebrides. Here he lived in a ruined stone cottage, bathed in a stream and cooked his meals on a camping stove. Every two weeks he paddled to the mainland in a kayak to pick up his pension cheque and buy supplies, including food for the birds that were his most constant companions. He was generally happy to receive visitors,

and they were invariably impressed by how contented he seemed. 'As far as I'm concerned, if there is a paradise on Earth, I'm in it,' he once told a reporter. 'You're welcome to what you've got. I'll keep this.'

One of Leppard's more unusual visitors was a sixteen-year-old German girl named Manuela, who was on a working holiday in Britain. After her return to Germany, she married a man named Daniel Ruda. The couple, who claimed to be vampires, gained considerable notoriety in 2001 for the 'Satanic' murder of a friend of theirs, Frank Hackert, whom they hit with a hammer then stabbed sixty-six times. When asked about Manuela, Leppard recalled that she had visited him several times and watched him as he went about his daily routine, but there didn't seem to be anything remarkable about her.

In 2008, with his health declining and the kayak trips becoming particularly arduous, Leppard decided it was time to leave his remote home. He collected his possessions in two plastic bags and moved to the village of Broadford, where a friend had offered him a room in his house. Here he had electricity and a proper bed for the first time in many years, but had no desire for a television or radio. 'I'm not really that interested in what else is going on outside,' he said. ▣

TOM LEPPARD

LIBERACE

(1919–1987)
Pianist

Wladziu Valentino Liberace, who
was born in Milwaukee, Wisconsin,
emerged from the womb with a caul
on his head, traditionally an omen
of greatness. His father, Salvatore,
was an Italian immigrant with a fiery
temper. He played French horn in
various bands and, considering himself an 'artiste', was reluctant to take
other work, which meant the family
was often poor. He insisted that all
four of his children have music lessons. His mother, Frances, of Polish
extraction, protested.

It was soon apparent that 'Wally',
as he was known, was a prodigy.
According to family lore, he was
playing pieces by ear at the age of
three, and was working professionally before his teens. His idol was
Paderewski, the flamboyant pianist
and Polish nationalist, whom he
met backstage after a concert when
he was eight or so. He was a typical
'Mama's boy' who loathed sport but
loved cooking and sewing, and he
was already a fancy dresser. Picked
on by other boys as a sissy, he
learned the trick of exaggerating his
differences to make people laugh.

To the disgust of his father, he
was as happy playing popular tunes
and jazz as classical pieces. As a teenager, he played in theatres, saloons,
strip clubs and even at stag parties, where he provided the musical
accompaniment for pornographic
films. In 1939, he hit upon a new
gimmick, playing pop songs like
'Three Little Fishies' in the manner
of various classical composers. He
continued to hone his act during
the forties, mixing the classics with
boogie-woogie, and concentrated
on playing intimate venues where
he could exercise his considerable
charm on the audience. He was now
going by the single name Liberace
(which he took care to emphasise in
publicity materials was pronounced
'Liber-AH-chee'). A brilliant self-pub-
licist, he acquired a huge, gold leafed
Blüthner grand piano for $25,000,
which he billed as 'the world's most
priceless piano'. It weighed 1,700
pounds (771 kg) and he took it
wherever he was performing. He
also adopted the candelabrum as an
essential stage prop.

Liberace moved to Los Angeles,
and by 1950, when he played at the
White House, he was a major star.
His television show debuted on a
local L.A. station in 1952, then was
syndicated across the country. It
mixed sophistication (his tuxedos
and candelabra) with folksy humour and family values (his brother
George conducted the orchestra,
his mother was usually sitting in
the front row). The critics gagged,

accusing him of schmaltz and 'momism' (excessive mothering), but his mostly female audience lapped it up, and Liberace was, as he put it in his most famous quip, 'crying all the way to the bank'. In 1953, he moved into his first celebrity house, built to his own specifications and replete with piano motifs, including a large, piano-shaped swimming pool. The following year, he played to a sold-out house at Madison Square Garden, earning $138,000 and eclipsing his hero Paderewski. He continued to mix musical styles with adandon. In 1955, he appeared on the *Ed Sullivan Show* performing ☞ Slim Gaillard's 'Cement Mixer, Putti Putti', accompanied by the opera singer Risë Stevens.

Meanwhile, the robust scandal magazines of the day were beginning to print stories about his secret homosexual lifestyle. During a triumphant tour of England in 1956, William Conner, a columnist for the *Daily Mirror*, who wrote under the name 'Cassandra', penned a legendary tirade against the star, calling him 'the summit of sex — Masculine, Feminine and Neuter… this deadly, winking, sniggering, snuggling, chromium-plated, scent-impregnated, luminous, quivering, giggling, fruit-flavoured, mincing, ice-covered heap of mother love…' Liberace sued for libel and eventually won, but the case dragged on for

years. To counteract the homosexual rumours, he was often seen out with women, but some of his partners, such as ☞ Mae West (already ensconced as a gay icon) and the famous transsexual Christine Jorgenson, can hardly have helped matters.

Liberace's career went through a slump in the late fifties. His record sales fell and a lucrative contract to play at Las Vegas was not renewed. Believing that the stories about his sexuality were to blame, he toned down his act considerably, but this only made things worse. He clawed his way back through live performances, playing in hundreds of cities and small towns across America, and in 1963 he was invited back to Las Vegas. He had thrown the switch to excess again, and each year his costumes became more outrageous, such as the red-white-and-blue hot pants suit and jacket with streamers he wore in 1971, and the $35,000 fur coat he sported two years later, for which 100 Danish minks lost their lives. 'Mr. Show-manship,' as he was now calling himself, took to being driven on stage in a Rolls Royce. In 1975, he topped this by flying onto the stage suspended by wires, wearing a cape of white ostrich feathers. In the mid-seventies he moved into a new house in Las Vegas (actually two houses which he had joined together to make an enormous if low-ceil-

LIBERACE

inged residence). Its kitsch opulence — all mirrors, marble, gilt and furniture which would have made Louis IV proud — became an integral part of the Liberace image. Its centrepiece was the master bedroom, as large as a small house. It had a huge canopied bed with an ermine bedspread, and a ceiling painted in the style of the Sistine Chapel, with Liberace in there amongst the cherubs. It can be seen in all its glory in his delirious 1986 coffee table book, *The Wonderful Private World of Liberace*.

Off stage, Lee, as he was known to friends, continued to lead a promiscuous homosexual lifestyle, although he had several long-term relationships, too. The most important was with Scott Thorson, who was eighteen when they met in 1978. After they had been together for a year, Liberace encouraged him to have plastic surgery so that he would resemble him. Thorson had his nose lengthened and his round face made more heart shaped, and after that was sometimes mistaken for Liberace's son. (For a while, the pianist considered adopting him.) The relationship eventually soured, and in 1982 Thorson sued Liberace for millions of dollars in 'palimony'. The case, which received considerable publicity, would not be settled until just before Liberace's death.

In 1984, Liberace fulfilled his final ambition by playing a series of sold-out concerts at Radio City Music Hall, a feat achieved by no other artist. His career had undergone another resurgence in the eighties, and he even gained some grudging respect from the New York critics who had always dismissed him. He sold out Radio City Music Hall again in 1985 and 1986, by which time his body was clearly showing the ravages of AIDS. As emaciated as he was, he still flew onto the stage on wires, and danced enthusiastically with the Rockettes.

In his later years he made self-deprecating jokes clearly referring to his sexuality, but he never admitted to being homosexual or having AIDS, blaming his weight loss on a 'watermelon diet'. He died six weeks after his final television appearance on the *Oprah Winfrey Show*. Many of his costumes and other memorabilia can be seen in the Liberace Museum in Las Vegas.

'I'm a one-man Disneyland.'
LIBERACE

LICK, JAMES
(1796–1876)
The richest man in California

Lick, who was born in Pennsylvania, was trained as a carpenter and cabinetmaker by his father. As a young man, he fell in love with a mill owner's daughter named Barbara Snavely, who became pregnant. Lick asked her father, Henry, for permission to marry Barbara, but the apprentice carpenter was soundly rebuffed. 'When you own a mill as large and costly as mine,' Snavely told him, 'you can have my daughter's hand, but not before.' Lick stormed off after launching a parting shot: 'Some day I will own a mill that will make yours look like a pigsty!'

Lick's unlikely path to riches began with a piano-building business in New York. Having received many orders from South America, he decided to move to Buenos Aires, and ended up spending most of the next three decades in South America. At one point, he returned to the United States with his pockets full of cash, hoping to finally marry Elizabeth Snavely, who had given birth to their son, John, but found that she had married someone else.

Although he prospered there, Lick never took to life in South America. In 1846, he decided to return to the United States for good, and it was now that he made his shrewdest move. Lick could see that a war between Mexico and the U.S. was looming, and guessed that it would result in Mexico

losing California. Having wound up his South American businesses, he arrived in what was then the tiny township of San Francisco in January 1848, with a chest containing $30,000 worth of gold. He immediately began to buy up all the land he could. Within a month of his arrival, two events had taken place: Mexico, having lost the Mexican-American War as Lick had predicted, ceded California to the United States; and gold was discovered at Sutter's Mill, triggering the Californian Gold Rush.

The value of Lick's land soared, and as others raced off to the hills to dig for gold, he bought even more. Despite the vast wealth that he had amassed, he lived very simply. He was known for his shabby clothes, and for sleeping on an old door. A keen horticulturist, he preferred the company of plants to people, and planted orchards on many of his properties. He liked to test the loyalty of his workers by ordering them to do absurd things like plant trees upside down.

In 1855, Lick completed the construction of an extraordinary mill in San Jose which cost him $200,000. Entirely constructed of expensive woods like mahogany, polished to perfection, it was dubbed 'the Mahogany Mill' or 'Lick's Folly'. Its purpose, of course, was to make good on his taunting of Henry Snavely almost forty years earlier. He also made contact for the first time with his son John, who came out to California. Lick commenced building a massive twenty-four-room mansion for them to live in, but they didn't get on, and the mansion went unfinished. Lick used the empty rooms to dry fruit he had grown in his orchards.

Lick suffered a stroke at the age of seventy-seven. He never fully recovered from this, and went to live in the lavish hotel, called Lick's House, which he had built in San Francisco (he had helped lay some of the intricate, inlaid floors himself). Link was now the richest man in California, and the stroke made him think about how he would dispose of his fortune. He first thought of erecting enormous statues of himself and his parents, then conceived the idea of building a pyramid in San Francisco larger then the Great Pyramid of Egypt. Then Lick's friend George David-son, an astronomer and President of the California Academy of Sciences, persuaded him to spend the bulk of it building an observatory with the world's most powerful telescope. Lick died three years after his stroke, and the Lick Observatory, built on the top of Mount Hamilton, was completed in 1887. Lick is buried beneath it. 🔳

LLOYD, OWEN
(1907 – c.1988)
'The Bird Man of Kings Cross'

One of the most agreeable street sights in Sydney during the 1970s was an ageing, white-haired busker who usually sat by a fountain in the red light district of Kings Cross. He played a strange upright fiddle with a horn attached to it, while a host of multicoloured and highly obedient birds perched on his bow. Few of the people who paused to watch him could have realised they were witnessing the tail end of a fascinating showbusiness career.

Owen Lloyd was born in the mining town of Buningyong, Victoria. His earliest memories were of watching miners shooting pigeons for recreation. He would search for wounded birds and try to nurse them, but they always died. As a young man, he became an apprentice engineer, but lost his position shortly before the depression. He was working on a ship when he noticed another crewman entertaining people with a homemade fiddle. Inspired, he went home and constructed his own instrument, finishing it off with a gramophone horn he found in a dump. He learned a few simple tunes and, unable to find any other work, hit the streets with his fiddle.

He met a well known card sharp and magician, Dr. Richard Rowe, and his wife, Mystic Mora, and provided the musical accompaniment for their performances. Keen to expand his repertoire, he learned sword swallowing from a visiting British practitioner, and later added fire eating to his talents. He bought an old Model T Ford and spent years driving around Australia in it, performing in the streets or in carnivals, and sleeping in the car. At one point he acquired a wife and two children and tried to settle down with them in Melbourne, but he had the wandering spirit of the true showman and was rarely home. The marriage did not survive.

One day, while driving along a country road, a small brown bird alighted on the seat next to him. He saw that it reacted to his music, and was happy to sit on his bow as he played. His audiences loved it. Soon afterwards he inherited a cage full of budgies, lorikeets and rosellas from an old man he found dying in a pub. He discovered he had an uncanny ability to communicate with them, to make them stand or turn simultaneously, and even play dead.

Lloyd teamed up with a showman and boxer, Dave Meekin, whose roster included Abdullah the Indian Fakir, the Five Legged Horse and a band of pygmies. Billed as Captain Lloyd, he expanded his act to include illusions like the Electric Girl and the ever-popular Sawing a Woman in Half. With his face blacked and a turban on his head, he was Prince Ranji, master of the Indian Rope Trick. And as the Atomic Healing Wizard he told people's fortunes. During World War II, he joined a Special Services Unit and travelled around Australia entertaining the troops. They loved him, but an officer told him to cut out the sword swallowing. 'They'll shortly be facing the Japs,' he said. 'The less they think of swords going down their bellies the better.'

After the war, Lloyd was persuaded to go to Africa by Dave Meekin (who was after some more pygmies). He stayed in Africa for a while, working as a master of ceremonies for Pagel's Circus, but had mixed feelings about the continent, and worried that people took his magic tricks to be real. After his precious fiddle was stolen in Zanzibar, he decided to move on again, this time to New Zealand. He fell in with a group of Maoris, became fascinated by their culture, and eventually married a Maori woman and had seven children with her. Always interested in natural remedies. He gained a reputation as a healer among the Maoris after reviving a girl who had almost drowned. Sick people began to turn up at his performances, and he was denounced

from church pulpits as an agent of the devil.

Lloyd returned to Sydney to look after his ailing parents, but they died soon afterwards. Losing his taste for life on the road, he opened a secondhand shop and spent his nights busking in Kings Cross. In 1979, he entered ABC TV's Busker of the Year competition. When another busker won, so many people rang to complain the Lloyd was given a special prize.

After a bout of illness, Lloyd sold his shop and returned to his family in New Zealand, where he died. Kings Cross has never been the same without him. ▣

LOLE, WILLIAM

(1800–1874)
'The Old Hermit
of Newton Burgoland'

Lole was a resident of the hamlet of Newton Burgoland in Leicestershire, and despite the fact that he was a perfectly sociable fellow, insisted on styling himself 'the Old Hermit'. This was, he explained, because 'True hermits, throughout every age, have been the firm abetters of freedom'. Lole, who did resemble the traditional hermit by sporting a long beard, was most famous for his fantastical clothes and hats, which were decorated with various emblems,

symbols and embroidered mottoes. Each of his hats — he had at least twenty — was given a name, and a motto usually inspired by its shape. Thus, the hat called 'Bee-hive' bore the legend 'The toils of industry are sweet: a wise people live at peace', while 'Helmet' declared 'Will fight for the birthright of consciences, love, life, property and national independence'. Each hat was usually paired with a particular suit.

Lole's most famous outfit was called 'Military', after its resemblance to army uniforms of years past, and came with a particularly fine hat. According to a contemporary account, 'It was a large conspicuous article, a composition between the old-fashioned cocked hat, and that worn by military commanders; but instead of the military plume, it had two upright peaks on the crown, not unlike the tips of a horse's ears. This hat, which he asserts cost five pounds, was the pride of his heart.' Alas, one day a group of rowdy youths knocked it off his head, played football with it, and tore it to pieces. Lole long mourned its passing.

Lole lived in a cottage with a neat and pretty garden arranged on symbolic lines. Like his hats, it featured numerous emblems and mottoes, here spelled out in flowers and coloured pebbles, along with effigies of the apostles and other decorative

touches. A fierce anti-papist, Lole once hung a figure of the Pope from a model scaffold in his garden, and railed against him from his makeshift pulpit — a large tub.

Although he sometimes charged people for tea parties in his garden, and sold printed pamphlets in the streets, Lole was a very poor man. Where he got the money to pay for his amazing wardrobe was quite a mystery to his neighbours. ▣

LOVECRAFT, H.P.

(1890–1937)
Horror writer

Howard Phillips Lovecraft was born in Providence, Rhode Island. His father, a commercial traveller, died when Lovecraft was seven, and he was raised by his mother, two aunts and maternal grandfather. He was reading books on mythology from an early age, and later recalled that by seven or eight he had become a 'genuine pagan' who erected altars to Pan and Apollo. He read through the books in his grandfather's library, developing a fondness for eighteenth century writers, and came to believe that he had been born in the wrong time — he would have been much more at home in a periwig and breeches. He also thought the War of Independence had been a thoroughly bad thing, and once

when visiting Richmond, Virginia, refused to enter the church where Patrick Henry uttered the words, 'Give me liberty or give me death,' on the grounds that he was 'a loyal subject of the King'.

The young Lovecraft had a vivid imagination, and was plagued by nightmares featuring terrifying creatures that he called 'night-gaunts'. By the age of thirteen, he had rejected all religions, and adopted a materialist, pessimistic, 'cosmic' outlook partly derived from his enthusiasm for astronomy. Gazing through his telescope at the night sky, he had grasped the physical insignificance of human beings amid the vastness of the universe, and came to the conclusion that we are just as insignificant in every other way — that life is essentially meaningless. He planned on becoming a professional astronomer, but in his final year at college, realised that he wasn't good enough at mathematics to achieve this. Shortly after this realisation, in 1908, he suffered a breakdown. Lovecraft had always been of a nervous disposition, prone to facial tics and seizures, but this episode was more serious. He gave up plans to attend university and became a virtual recluse for the next decade or so.

He eventually dragged himself out of his torpor by becoming involved in the then thriving

H.P. LOVECRAFT

amateur journalism scene, and in 1917 wrote his first mature horror stories. Lovecraft's best-known tales belong to the 'Cthulhu Mythos' (a term coined after his death). They postulate the existence of a race of aliens, sometimes called the Great Old Ones, and various other extraterrestrial beings who dwelt on Earth aeons ago (and continue to live beneath the Earth and the sea). Fragmentary memories of them remain, so that they continue to be worshipped by various cults around the world. Some have wondered how a confirmed rationalist like Lovecraft could have conceived such a mythology, but his point was that the Old Ones are physical beings, although very different to us. The geometry of their architecture, even their colours, are incomprehensible to us, and the sight of one of them is often enough to drive someone mad. Their very existence makes a mockery of our supposed supremacy in the universe (in the short novel, *At the Mountains of Madness*, it is revealed that they created life on Earth). In short, Lovecraft had stared into the abyss, and he wanted his readers to stare into it, too.

Lovecraft had virtually no interest in women or sex. 'What is a beauteous nymph?' he asked in a 1919 letter. 'Carbon, hydrogen, nitrogen and, a dash or two of

phosphorus and other elements — all to decay soon.' His friends were therefore astonished when, in 1924, he married a spirited woman named Sonia Greene, whom he had met through amateur journalism. He went to live in her apartment in New York, but events conspired against them. Sonia lost her job and had to move to another state to take up another one. Lovecraft was unable to find any work whatsoever. He came to loathe New York, and after two years moved back to his beloved Providence. The experiment in marriage was over.

Despite the image of a recluse that clings to him, Lovecraft was quite gregarious in New York, and remained so during the last two decades of his life. He had a large circle of (mostly writer) friends and made extensive trips through the eastern states in search of antiquities. It is true, though, that most of his friendships were conducted through voluminous correspondence. The Lovecraft scholar S.T. Joshi has estimated that he penned over 85,000 letters in his lifetime, some as long as thirty or forty pages (Lovecraft, as a gentleman, felt he could never let a letter go unanswered). Some believe these highly literate and engaging letters were his greatest work.

Lovecraft was self-taught in science and philosophy. He held racist views that were all too common at the time, and they emerge in his fiction, with its revulsion at the physical appearance of alien beings. He was much more flexible in his political beliefs, beginning as a crusty conservative but espousing a mild form of socialism by the end of his life.

Lovecraft never held anything like a steady job, and scraped by on occasional story sales and editing the work of others. He refused to tailor his own work to the sensational demands of the pulp magazines — the main market for his fiction — and spent most of his life in more or less dire states of poverty. His poor diet probably contributed to the intestinal cancer that killed him. After his death, two of his correspondents, Donald Wandrei and August Derleth, founded Arkham House to publish his stories in book form. He was on the way to being hailed the pre-eminent American writer of weird fiction of the twentieth century.

Many continue to find Lovecraft's strange character as fascinating as his stories. The iconoclastic French novelist Michel Houellebecq (whose works are not as different to Lovecraft's as they may first appear) wrote a perceptive book about him. 'No one ever once saw him angry; nor crying; nor laughing out loud,' wrote Houellebecq. 'His was a life pared down to the bare minimum whose only animus was literature and dreams. An exemplary life.'

LUCAS, JAMES

(1813–1874)
'The Hermit of Redcoat Green'

Lucas was born into a wealthy family in Hertfordshire, and was pampered as a young boy by his indulgent mother. After the death of his father, a merchant, in 1833, he inherited the bulk of his estate. Lucas' younger brother and three sisters resented this, and there was a falling out between them. Lucas lived alone with his mother in a house in Redcoat Green, and they grew even closer, especially after his love for a local girl, Isabella Amos, went unrequited.

Lucas' mother died in 1849. He was devastated by her death, and kept her embalmed body in the house for three months until forced to bury it. Apparently fearing that the other members of his family wanted to kill him, Lucas shut himself in his house — and remained there. He dismissed the servants and lived in the kitchen, preparing his own meals there and rarely leaving it. The kitchen had no furniture, but he kept the fire burning day and night, and slept on the ash from it. As this was never removed, his ash 'bed' reached halfway up the wall by the time he died. In 1853, his brother tried to have him declared insane, but the Commissioners of Lunacy declared him to be 'a man of the most acute intelligence' and quite able to look after himself.

He communicated to the world through a barred window, and ate mostly bread, cheese, eggs and herrings, which he kept in a basket hanging from the ceiling to protect them from rats, and drank milk mixed with gin. He never washed or cut his hair, and wore nothing but a blanket.

He became, naturally enough, an object of curiosity, and many people made a visit to his house to get a look at him. Lucas was usually happy to receive them, though he enjoyed the company of tramps more than the upper classes. He arranged for his bank to deliver £25 in coins to him every month, which he distributed to needy visitors. Like ☞ James Robertson, the 'Daft Highland Laird', he was a confirmed Jacobite, and refused to accept paper money because it had Queen Victoria's face on it. Every Good Friday he hosted a party for the local children, handing out coins, sweets and glasses of water and gin to them.

Described as timid and softly spoken by those who met him, this strange but essentially kindly man died from what was described as apoplexy (possibly a heart attack or stroke) at the age of sixty-one. ▨

LUDWIG II

(1845–1886)
'The Mad King of Bavaria'

The gold standard for unhinged monarchs, Ludwig Friedrich Wilhelm was the son of Maximilian I of Bavaria and Princess Marie of Prussia, and grandson of Ludwig I of Bavaria, who had been a great patron of the arts and lover of women (his mistresses included the notorious actress and dancer Lola Montez). His parents showed little affection for him, and his childhood was rather bleak. His greatest joys were the times he spent at Hohenschwangau Castle, a magnificent medieval edifice restored by his father, and the works of the composer Richard Wagner, which he discovered at the age of fifteen.

Ludwig was eighteen when he ascended to the throne in 1864. Almost the first thing he did was order that Wagner be located (he was hiding from debtors in Austria) and brought to him in Munich. Ludwig paid off Wagner's debts and became his patron. His ministers were suspicious about Wagner's politics, and when the composer caused a scandal by fathering an illegitimate child with a married woman, Cosima von

Bülow (whom he later married), he was forced to leave Munich. Ludwig was so upset he almost abdicated.

Ludwig had little interest in politics, and his painful shyness made him avoid state functions and public appearances. With pressure on him to produce an heir, an engagement to his cousin, Duchess Sophie, was announced in 1867, but Ludwig kept postponing the wedding and eventually called it off. Most of Ludwig's close friendships were with men, and it is generally assumed that he was homosexual.

In 1871, Bavaria and the other German states united to form the German Empire under Kaiser Wilhelm, formerly the King of Prussia. Ludwig withdrew even further from politics after this, and began to concentrate on an extravagent new hobby — the building of fantastic castles and palaces. These included Neuschwanstein, the ultimate fairytale castle (yet built with cutting edge technology including electricity and heating systems); Herrenchiemsee, a sprawling palace modelled on Versailles and built on an island in the middle of Bavaria's biggest lake; and Linderhof Castle, the only one of the three completed during Ludwig's lifetime, which was also inspired by Versailles. It has an underground grotto (through which Ludwig liked to be rowed in a shell-shaped boat) and an enormous bed-chamber modelled on Louis XIV's. Ludwig was besotted by the image of Louis XIV, the lavishness of his court and the absolute power he wielded. If Louis had been 'the Sun King', however, Ludwig, who slept during the day and came out at night to play, styled himself 'the Moon King'. Ludwig's other architectural follies included installing a lake and artificial gardens on the roof of the Residenz Palace in Munich.

Ludwig used his own money for these projects (albeit money paid to him from the civil list), and by the early 1880s had fallen heavily into debt. He was urged to curb his spending but refused. He planned ever more grandiose projects including a Byzantine palace built of marble and gold, and attempted to solicit loans from other European rulers. His ministers (whom Ludwig now refused to meet face to face) grew increasingly concerned, and resolved to depose him on the grounds of insanity. Ludwig's uncle, Prince Luitpold, agreed to cooperate — and assume the throne — if this could be proved. A report on the King's mental state was commissioned from the eminent psychiatrist Dr. Bernhard von Gudden and three others. It painted a picture of a childish man, prone to fantasies, hallucinations, and paranoia, who threw parties where his male servants were forced to strip naked and dance in front of him. It claimed that insanity ran in his family (Ludwig's younger brother Otto had gone mad), that he beat up his servants, and even criticised his sloppy eating habits. How much of the report was true and how much was based on hearsay will never be known, but it was enough for Luitpold. Ludwig was arrested on 12 June 1886 and taken to Castle Berg on the shores of Lake Starnberg, where he was placed in the care of Dr. Gudden.

'How can you declare me insane?' he asked Gudden on meeting him. 'After all, you have never seen or examined me before.'

The following evening, Ludwig asked Dr. Gudden to accompany him on a walk around the lake. When they failed to return, a search party was sent out, and their bodies were found floating in the lake. Gudden had a head wound, and an autopsy showed that he had drowned. The fate of Ludwig was less clear. The official verdict was suicide, but others have theorised that he was killed during an escape attempt, or that his family, wanting him out of the way for good, had ordered his assassination. The truth will probably never be known, but Ludwig's legacy remains. The castles that his ministers feared would bankrupt them are today some of Bavaria's top tourist attractions. ▣

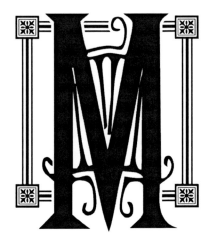

MACINTYRE, F. GWYNPLAINE

(1948–2010)
Writer & fabulist

The details of MacIntyre's early years were shrouded in self-imposed mystery, and his real name is unknown. According to his own version of events, he was one of twins born in Perthshire, Scotland. He had a congenital defect which caused his parents to place him in an orphanage, and he was later sent to Australia where he worked in a 'child labour camp'. He despised his parents because of this, and had no contact with them. As a youth, he worked as a jackaroo, and became familiar with Aboriginal culture (which he later incorporated into some of his stories). Returning to England in the 1960s, he broke into the television industry, and worked on the cult series *The Prisoner*. He also claimed to have been married twice, and to have had two adopted children, but no trace of them could be found after his death.

By the early 1980s, he was living in Bensonhurst, a working class neighbourhood in New York City, and going by the name of Fergus Gwynplaine MacIntyre. 'Gwynplaine' probably derived from a character in the Victor Hugo novel *The Man Who Laughed*. (Conrad Veidt's portrayal of this character in a 1928 silent film version is said to have been the inspiration for the Joker in *Batman*.) He also used other names — he was Timothy C. Allen to the taxman, and had Paul G. Geoffrey on his passport. He began to write science fiction, and had some success in the field, his stories and poems appearing in various magazines, including *Asimov's Science Fiction* and *Weird Tales*, and his 1994 novel *The Woman Between the Worlds* received favourable reviews. He worked nights at a printers, and spent much of his days researching in the New York Public Library.

MacIntyre became a familiar figure at science fiction conventions. He was a shambolic, garrulous, friendly bear of a man, with red hair, bushy sideburns and sometimes a full beard. He favoured Victorian-style clothing, tweed suits and the like, or a kilt and sporran, and always wore gloves. He told some people that this was because he had webbed fingers, hence his nickname 'Froggy'. (Another explanation was that his fingernails had been pulled out by Idi Amin's henchmen during a visit to Uganda.) He loved regaling people with tales of travelling to exotic places and meeting famous people.

Another MacIntyre enthusiasm was cinema, particularly silent film, and he contributed many reviews to the Internet Movie Database. These included reviews of some films considered lost, such as the 1926 Louise Brooks vehicle *A Social Celebrity*, written in a way that suggested he had recently seen them. When people contacted him to ask for more details, he would usually reply that he had viewed a rare print owned by a private European collector who wished to remain anonymous. Many cineastes were outraged when MacIntyre's deceptions (which he never explained) came to light.

MacIntyre lived in a one-room, third-floor apartment crammed with papers, manuscripts, rejection letters and all sorts of junk accumulated over the years or, as he put it, 'the fragments of time that other people throw away.' Nobody ever visited this apartment, and only one other person who lived in the building ever knew he was a writer.

MacIntyre's last years were troubled. In 2000, in a fit of madness, he kidnapped the fifty-five-year-old woman who lived in the apartment opposite his, shaved her head and spray painted her black. He was lucky to escape with a conviction for third-degree misdemeanour assault. He lost his printers job and complained that he couldn't find other work. In June 2010, he sent a group email to friends which disturbed one of them enough to call emergency services. Six policemen arrived at his apartment, and it took all their strength to get him out of there and to a hospital. Discharged, he set two fires in his apartment the next morning, and died in the flames (thankfully no one else in the building was hurt).

Five men spent two days clearing the apartment of its detritus, including the charred manuscripts of numerous unpublished stories. ▣

McGONAGALL, WILLIAM

(c. 1825–1902)
Poet & tragedian

McGonagall was a handloom weaver and occasional actor who lived in the city of Dundee, Scotland. In his autobiography, he described how the urge to write poetry came upon him one day in 1877.

… I seemed to feel as it were a strange kind of feeling stealing over me, and remained for about five minutes. A flame, as Lord Byron has said, seemed to kindle up my entire frame, along with a strange desire to write poetry; and I felt so happy. So happy that I was inclined to dance, then I began to pace backwards and forwards in the room, trying to shake off all thoughts of writing poetry; but the more I tried, the more strong the sensation became. It was so strong, I imagined that a pen was in my right hand, and a voice crying 'Write! Write!'

Casting about for a subject, McGonagall thought of his good friend, the Reverend George Gilfillan, and immediately put pen to paper.

Rev. George Gilfillan of Dundee
There is none can you excel;
You have boldly rejected the Confession
    of Faith,
And defended your cause right well.

The first time I heard him speak,
'Twas in the Kinnaird Hall,
Lecturing on the Garibaldi Movement
Loud as he could bawl…

McGonagall's poem was published in a newspaper, and he was off on an illustrious, if impecunious, poetical career. He gave up the hand loom, let his hair grow, adopted a poet's garb of wide-brimmed hat and cloak, and hit the streets of Dundee, hawking broadsheets of his works for a penny each. His

WILLIAM McGONAGALL

favourite themes were shipwrecks and other natural disasters, current events, temperance, and stirring odes to royalty and other eminent persons. (He was particularly devoted to Queen Victoria, and once spent days walking from Dundee to Balmoral Castle, where the Queen was in residence, only to be turned away at the gatehouse with the words 'they cannot be bothered with you'.) One of his most famous works is his glorious ode to the Tay Bridge.

Beautiful Railway Bridge of the Silvery Tay!
With your numerous arches and pillars in so grand array,
And your central girders, which seem to the eye
To be almost towering to the sky.
The greatest wonder of the day,
And a great beautification to the River Tay…

Sadly, the Tay Bridge proved to be about as well constructed as one of McGonagall's poems, and collapsed one stormy night in 1879 as a train was passing over it, causing great loss of life. McGonagall immediately stepped in with 'The Tay Bridge Disaster'. After darkness comes the dawn, however, and our poet went on to pen 'An Address to the New Tay Bridge' which, he was pleased to note, had

… side screens along your railway
Which will be a great protection on a windy day
So as the railway carriages won't be blown away…

McGonagall's dramatic readings of his works were legendary — and occasionally dangerous. During the patriotic 'Bruce of Bannockburn' he would fling himself about the stage brandishing a huge sword, threatening furniture and the closest spectators. These performances often resulted in him being pelted with everything from rotten eggs to green peas ('Gentlemen if you please, stop throwing peas'), although more appreciative audiences would sometimes attempt to carry the poet off in triumph on their shoulders. So rowdy did these scenes become that the Dundee authorities eventually banned him from live appearances.

Yet despite all the rejections, constant poverty (it was not easy supporting a wife and four children on the proceeds of poetry) and the jeers of ruffians in the street, McGonagall never lost faith in himself and his genius. Who knows what he would have thought of the appellation commonly bestowed on him now, 'the World's Worst Poet'? But the fact remains that his poems are still in print, while any number of his more conventional contemporaries are forgotten.

McINTYRE, JAMES

(1827–1906)
'The Cheese Poet'

McIntyre was born in Scotland, and emigrated to Canada at the age of fourteen. He settled in Inger-soll, Ontario, where he became a successful furniture maker with a sideline in coffins. An inveterate clubman, he was always ready on social occasions to stand up and deliver an impromptu poem on any given subject. He wrote about many aspects of his adopted land, but it is his remarkable series of 'dairy and cheese odes' which have kept his name alive.

The ancient poets ne'er did dream
That Canada was land of cream,
They ne'er imagined it could flow
In this cold land of ice and snow,
Where everything did solid freeze,
They ne'er hoped or looked for cheese.

Yet cheese there would be — aplenty. McIntyre sang of the great dairy pioneers, the cheese making achievements of Oxford county, where he lived, and the greatest cheese of all (or at least the greatest one with which he was personally acquainted), a 7,000 pounds mon-ster immortalised in 'Ode on the Mammoth Cheese'.

We have seen thee, queen of cheese
Lying quietly at your ease,
Gently fanned by evening breeze,
Thy fair form no flies dare seize.

All gaily dressed soon you'll go
To the great provincial show,
To be admired by many a beau
In the city of Toronto.

Cows numerous as a swarm of bees,
Or as the leaves upon the trees,
It did require to make thee please,
And stand unrivalled, queen of cheese.

After a few more stanzas de-scribing this truly enormous cheese, McIntyre concluded with an unfor-gettable image.

We'ert thou suspended from balloon
You'd cast a shadow even at noon,
Folks would think it was the moon
About to fall and crush them soon.

Cheese was not the only arrow in McIntyre's poetic quiver. He could rise to numerous other sub-jects, and I am particularly fond of his poem 'The Wooden Leg', which lists the advantages to the man who has such an appendage. Among these:

In mud or water he can stand
With his foot on the firm dry land,
For wet he doth not care a fig,
It never hurts his wooden leg.

McKINNEY, JOYCE

(b. 1949)
Kidnapper

God's gift to tabloid newspaper editors, Joyce McKinney was born in Avery County, North Carolina. Her father was a school principal, her mother a teacher. She was a bright girl, a 'straight A student' who loved entering beauty contests, and was Miss Wyoming (a state she had never visited) in the 1974 Miss U.S.A. competition. After staying with a Mormon family, she converted to Mormonism and moved to Utah, where she enrolled at Brigham Young University. Almost all the students at BYU were Mormons who dressed conservatively, eschewed alcohol and stimulants like coffee, and would not think of having extra-marital sex. In this staid atmosphere, McKinney, with her blonde hair, impressive bosom, revealing clothes and persimmon coloured Chevrolet Corvette (bought for her by her father), caused quite a stir. 'Call me Joy,' she used to say, 'like the hymn, Joy to the World.'

McKinney moved into an apartment block owned by the Osmonds, the squeaky clean Mormon singing group then enjoying international success, and set her mind on marrying one of them. She managed to strike up a friendship with Wayne Osmond, but then he announced his engagement to another girl. McKinney transferred her affections to a young Mormon student named Kirk Anderson. Just why Anderson, an average looking fellow who weighed eighteen stone (114 kg) and played the trombone, ignited such a passion in McKinney remains a mystery (she said it was because he showered two or three times a day, so was very clean). Anderson succumbed to McKinney's charms enough to have sex with her once, and three days later she told him she was pregnant (she would later claim to have had a miscarriage). After speaking to his bishop, Anderson decided to have nothing more to do with her. She began to stalk him, slashing his tyres and chasing him in her car. He moved to another state to escape, and when the time came to do his compulsory two-year missionary service, asked to be sent to England.

McKinney was undeterred. In August 1977, two years after her relationship with Kirk ended, she and a young trainee architect named Keith May, who was clearly besotted by her, arrived in London under false passports. On 14 September, May and McKinney, armed with imitation revolvers, kidnapped Anderson from the Mormon headquarters in Epsom, Surrey, and drove him to a rented cottage in Devon.

Four days later, Anderson was

released in London and went to the police. He told them that, on the second day at the cottage, he had been chained to a bed, and on the third day, shackled spreadeagled to it. McKinney had torn off his pyjamas and his 'garment' (the tight, one-piece undergarment, embroidered with mystical symbols, which Mormons wear to protect their chastity) and forced him to have sex with her, three times. She told him that he would only be released when he had made her pregnant. McKinney and May were soon arrested.

The case had British journalists salivating, and McKinney obliged them by asking that the usual reporting restrictions be lifted. She maintained that everything with Anderson was consensual, and that, having been brought up in a repressed Mormon family, he could only have sex while tied up. She accused the Mormon church of keeping him away from her. On her way to hearings at Epsom magistrate's court in a police van, she held up messages she had written on the pages of her Bible, including 'Please get the truth to the public. He made it look like kidnapping,' and 'Ask Christians to pray for me'. Some observers questioned whether Anderson could have been raped as he claimed. Detective Chief Inspector Hucklesby, in charge of the initial investigation, probably spoke for

millions when he said, 'I've never been lucky enough to have anything like that happen to me.' At a hearing on 6 December, McKinney gave a stellar performance during which she uttered the immortal words, 'I loved Kirk so much I would have skied down Mount Everest nude with a carnation up my nose.'

After three months in Holloway Prison, McKinney was released on bail. She and May gave a number of bizarre interviews to journalists, then fled the country. Posing as deaf mutes on their way to join a mime troupe in Canada, they made it to Ireland, then back to America. British journalists could not bear to see such lucrative prizes escape, and one of them managed to track the pair down to Atlanta, Georgia, where they were hiding out in a hotel disguised as nuns (Joyce really was the gift that kept on giving). Then McKinney's self-proclaimed image as an innocent, God-fearing girl was blown away by the revelation that, between first seducing Kirk Anderson in Utah and arriving in England, she had worked in Los Angeles as a call girl specialising in bondage, and posed nude for porn magazines.

McKinney made headlines again in 1984 when she was arrested in Salt Lake City after being seen lurking outside the office where Kirk Anderson worked. Her lawyer explained that she was researching

a film script about her life, and all charges were eventually dropped. She briefly resurfaced in 1994, when she claimed to have been abducted by armed men who beat her so badly she was confined to a wheelchair.

She dropped out of sight again after that, apparently for good. Then, in August 2008, newspapers around the world reported that an American woman, Bernann McKinney, had paid South Korean scientists $53,000 to produce five clones of her pet dog Booger, a pit bull which had died two years earlier. British journalists with long memories noted the surname, examined the photos and put two and two together. McKinney initially denied she was the woman at the centre of the 'Mormon Sex-Slave Case', then in a tearful phone call to Associated Press admitted it was true. 'I thought people would be honest enough to see me as a person who was trying to do something good,' she said, referring to the cloning. 'My mother always taught me, "Say something good or say nothing at all."' ▣

McPHERSON, AIMEE SEMPLE

(1890–1944)
Evangelist

Aimee, who was born in Canada, wanted to be an actress but her devout parents forbade it. At eighteen, she married a preacher, Robert Semple, and they sailed to China as missionaries, a plan aborted when Semple died from dysentery. Aimee returned to the U.S. and married a man named McPherson, but she wasn't cut out for housework. She began to travel around America and Canada, preaching in tents and mission halls, acquiring hundreds of followers. Basing herself in Los Angeles she built Angelus Temple, which had seating for 5,000 and its own radio station. Aimee, known to her followers as 'Sister', cut a striking figure at services, dressed in expensive gowns, her dark hair piled on top of her head. Her rousing sermons were illustrated by costumed extras re-enacting biblical scenes on a stage behind her. Some of her fellow ministers were incensed by her publicity stunts — she was known to preach from aeroplanes and ride up to her pulpit on a motorbike — but the Temple's membership soon topped 10,000. All financial matters were handled by her domineering mother, Mildred Kennedy.

But it was Aimee's mysterious disappearance that brought her the most fame. On 18 May 1926, she went to Venice Beach with her secretary, Emma. Having made some notes for the following week's sermon, she went for a swim and was not seen to emerge from the

water. Emma raised the alarm and the news spread quickly. Thousands of Aimee's followers flocked to the beach and the Temple, where her mother led the service that night. 'Sister is gone,' she tearfully told them. 'We know she is with Jesus.' There were hysterical scenes at the beach for days afterwards. Planes flew overhead, divers scoured the ocean floor, and two men lost their lives searching for the body. Meanwhile, the newspapers were full of theories — she had been kidnapped by slave traders or rum-runners; she had quarrelled with her mother over money; she was suffering from exhaustion and had gone away to rest. The most persistent rumours linked Aimee to a former radio operator at the Temple, Kenneth Ormiston, who had recently separated from his wife. He popped up in Los Angeles on 27 May, long enough to answer police questions and deny everything, before disappearing again. The following night, a reporter saw him in his car, a woman in a floppy hat beside him.

Mrs. Kennedy dismissed these stories, as she dismissed a note from kidnappers demanding $500,000. On 20 June, an all-day memorial service was held at the Temple, where she told the estimated 70,000 mourners that her daughter's body had not been found because Jesus had taken it up to heaven.

Two days later, thirty-six days after her disappearance, an apparently dazed and exhausted Aimee stumbled into the Mexican town of Agua Prieta. She told police she had been kidnapped by two men and a woman who had tricked her into a car, drugged her and held her captive in a house. Later, she was moved to a one-room adobe hut in the desert from which she had managed to escape.

Fifty-thousand people greeted Aimee at the train station on her return to Los Angeles, but cracks in her story had appeared. She had supposedly walked twenty miles through harsh desert country after her escape, but her dress was neither torn nor stained with sweat. Her descriptions of the kidnappers were vague, and no shack resembling the one she had described could be found — despite the fact that she joined the police search for it.

Aimee repeated her story to a Grand Jury, which found no grounds for indicting any kidnappers. Soon after this, police learned that a man resembling Ormiston had rented a bungalow in the resort town of Carmel, and stayed there during the disappearance with a woman several witnesses identified as Aimee. The evangelist furiously denied these allegations, claiming that the police, the prosecutors, the press and anyone who doubted her story were the tools of the devil (or at least Catholics). She rejoiced when a woman, Lorraine Wiseman, came forward claiming that it was her sister who had been seen with Ormiston. When reporters discovered Wiseman had a history of mental illness and compulsive lying, she was arrested and confessed that she had been hired by the Angelus Temple. The district attorney issued indictments against Aimee, her mother, Ormiston and Wiseman. 'As I expect to meet my maker,' declared Aimee, 'my story is as true today as the first time I told it.' The preliminary hearing lasted five weeks. Aimee gave her followers at the Temple highly coloured accounts of it each night, accompanied by ever more spectacular tableaux of martyrdom and suffering. The D.A. eventually dismissed the charges on the grounds that the State's chief witness, Wiseman, had changed her story so often her evidence was worthless.

Shortly afterwards, Aimee and her mother fell out, and Mrs. Kennedy left the Temple, claiming it was corrupt. Aimee continued to preach, but some of her spark was gone. She died from an overdose of sleeping pills in 1944. The people of Los Angeles, in a fitting return for all the entertainment she had provided them, gave her a huge funeral.

MARTINEZ, JUSTO GALLEGO

(b. 1925)
Cathedral builder

Since 1961, Martínez has been almost single-handedly building his own cathedral in the small Spanish town of Mejorada del Campo near Madrid. The cathedral, dedicated to Nuestra Señora del Pilar (Our Lady of the Pillar), occupies 8,000 square metres (26,000 square feet) of land, and has a dome almost forty metres (131 feet) high.

As a youth, Martínez joined the Trappist monks, but was forced to leave the order eight years later after he contracted tuberculosis. He began to build the cathedral almost immediately, on a block of land he had inherited from his parents. Like that other obsessive builder, ☛ Ferdinand Cheval, Martínez had no previous experience in construction work, and has never drawn up any plans. 'I'm a labourer, not an architect,' he told one interviewer. 'I never put anything on paper. That's a waste of time — the land is what mattered. I just levelled the earth and then mapped out the ground-works.' The cathedral is built from recycled or donated materials which Martínez has used ingeniously (window arches were moulded from old tires, columns from petrol drums). He

has occasionally been aided in his labours by his nephews (they helped raise the dome using pulleys after he was unable to borrow a crane), and he hired a full-time assistant a few years back, but otherwise, Martínez has done all the work. In addition to the main structure (which has a crypt beneath it), he has also built several smaller chapels, cloisters and a library.

Martínez has never applied for planning permission or a building permit, and he and the local authorities have little time for each other. Despite the fact that the cathedral is the only thing Mejorada del Campo has that remotely resembles a tourist attraction, the town refuses to promote it. Martínez has had a similar lack of support from the Catholic Church (to which he has bequeathed the cathedral). He has often been ridiculed by the townspeople, who dubbed his creation 'la catedral del loco'. Yet Martínez, who is known locally as Don Justo, has carried on undeterred. 'I'm doing it for my mother who always wanted me to work for the church,' he says.

In 2005, Martínez received some much-needed publicity when he was featured in a television advertisment for Aquarius soft drinks. He became famous across Spain and suddenly hundreds of people were coming to visit the cathedral every day. Their donations, and the money he received from Aquarius, have allowed him to buy more materials. He still believes that he may be able to finish the cathedral before he dies, and is sure that it will be consecrated one day. There is some doubt about the structural integrity of the building, however (it has never been properly assessed by an engineer), and it is possible that, upon Don Justo's death, it might all be demolished.

MARZIALS, THEO
(1850–1920)
Poet & songwriter

Theophile-Jules-Henri Marzials was born in France, and came to England with his family in 1857, when his father was made the pastor of a French Protestant church in London. In 1870, he became a library assistant at the British Museum. He was a handsome young man, with long blond hair and a flowing moustache, and an aspiring poet. Several of his fellow employees at the museum were also poets, among them Edmund Gosse, later an influential critic (and, some believe, Marzials' lover). Marzials was not cowed by the competition, and was once overheard by the librarian's supervisor declaring in a high-pitched tone, 'Am I or am I not the darling of the

Reading Room?'

Marzials had a beautiful singing voice, and it was as a singer that he first began to make a name for himself. He also wrote songs, often setting the words of other contemporary poets to music, and one of his compositions, 'Twickenham Ferry', was immensely popular on both sides of the Atlantic.

Marzials owes his current fame, such as it is, to a single poem, 'A Tragedy'. This first appeared in his only verse collection, *A Gallery of Pigeons* (1873). Most of the poems in this are firmly in the 'Art for art's sake' tradition, originally associated with the French poet Théophile Gautier, and known as 'aestheticism' in England. They are pretty and rather vapid celebrations of feminine beauty and nature. In a few poems, however, Marzials experimented with form and subject matter. 'A Tragedy' is one of these experiments, in which Marzials attempted to capture the thoughts of a girl who is contemplating suicide by throwing herself into a river. It seems safe to say, though, that the effect was not what Marzials intended. The poem begins:

> *Death!*
> *Plop.*
> *The barges down in the river flop.*
> *Flop, plop,*
> *Above, beneath*

> *From the slimy branches the grey drips*
> *drop,*
> *As they scraggle black on the thin grey sky,*
> *Where the black cloud rack-hackles*
> *drizzle and fly*
> *To the oozy waters, that longue and flop*
> *On the black scrag piles, where the loose*
> *cords plop,*
> *As the raw wind whines in the thin*
> *tree-top.*
> *Plop, plop.*
> *And scudding by*
> *The boatmen call out hoy! And hey!*
> *And all is running in water and sky*
> *And my head shrieks — "Stop,"*
> *And my heart shrieks — "Die."*

It continues on in this vein for a while, with the girl cursing a friend who has betrayed her, and concludes:

> *And my head is as empty as air –*
> *I can do,*
> *I can dare,*
> *(Plop, plop,*
> *The barges flop*
> *Drip, drop.)*

> *I can do, I can dare!*
> *And let myself all run away with my*
> *head,*
> *And stop.*

> *Drop*
> *Dead.*
> *Plop, flop.*

> *Plop.*

The poem has its defenders as a bold attempt to break away from the strictures of Victorian verse, but it would be fair to say that most people can't get past all the plopping and flopping.

In 1882, Marzials resigned from the British Museum, and afterwards spent several happy years in Italy and France. He returned to England in the early 1890s and had two poems published in the iconic aesthetic journal *The Yellow Book*, but afterwards he largely dropped out of sight. He became addicted to chlorodyne, a patent medicine containing extracts of opium and cannabis mixed with chlorine. Many thought he had suffered a breakdown, but Gosse, who encountered him in 1900, was happy to report that, 'Those people who say that he is incoherent, off his head, and so forth, must be misled by the rapidity of change which has always characterised his talk.'

Marzials spent his last years in Devonshire, staying in a rented room on a farm and rarely leaving his bed. A man named F.B. Skinner used to visit him there, and painted a vivid picture of the scene. The air was thick with the smell of chlorodyne, while on a bedside table there was invariably a saucer of beetroot in vinegar. 'During conversation,' wrote Skinner, ' he would often fish out a slice of beetroot on the end of a fork and drop it into his mouth most elegantly — it was almost a joy to watch him.' He also noted that Marzials could often be seen wandering in the garden at night, singing to himself, occasionally bending to kiss a flower and murmur, 'O my pretty!'

By the time Marzials died, in 1920, most of the people who knew him thought he had been dead for decades. 'A Tragedy' lives on, however. Some argue that it is the world's worst poem, even eclipsing the achievements of ☞ William McGonagall. On the strength of it, Marzials was finally given an entry in the *Oxford Dictionary of National Biography* in 2007, three years after McGonagall made it in. 🖾

MASSEY, EDITH
(1918–1984)
Actress

Edith, known as Edie to her friends, found fame late in life as one of the most grotesque yet endearing characters in the notorious underground films of John Waters. She was born Edith Dornfield in New York, and grew up in an orphanage in Denver, Colorado. Placed in a foster home as a teenager, she ran away from it after the two daughters of the family treated her badly. She went to Los Angeles, hoping to break into

the movies, but ended up selling pencils, razor blades and the like in a sidewalk booth.

She spent the next few decades travelling around the country, sometimes in freight trains. She worked as a dancer and 'b-girl' (hostess) in bars, and did a stint as a madam in an Illinois brothel. She was married once, to a soldier named Massey, in 1946, but the marriage ended in the early fifties. She eventually landed in Baltimore, where she worked for fifteen years on 'the Block', a seedy stretch of strip clubs and sex shops. In 1968, she was working behind the bar at Pete's Hotel, where Waters discovered her. He was so taken by the unfailingly friendly and chatty 250-pound (114 kg) barmaid, with her missing teeth, nasal voice and long brown hair piled on top of her head 1940s style, that he cast her as herself in his next film, *Multiple Maniacs*. She followed this with her most iconic role as ☞ Divine's mother, Mama Edie, or the 'Egg Lady', in Water's never-to-be-topped masterpiece of filth, *Pink Flamingos* (1972). Dressed in a bra and girdle and sitting in a playpen, she spends most of the movie wondering when her beloved eggman will make his next delivery. ('It's ten-thirty! Babs! Babs! Why isn't the eggman here? I'm starving to death for some eggs!')

Massey used the money she

made from her film appearances to open a thrift shop called Edith's Shopping Bag, which she kept open till midnight, eager to hear the story of anyone who walked in and offer advice. She became one of Baltimore's most recognisable and beloved characters, happy to attend any party or event she was invited to, and went to every screening of her films that she could, greeting the often bemused cinemagoers as they arrived (Waters advised her that it would be better to wait until after the screening, so they would know who she was). She appeared in several more of Waters' films, including *Female Trouble* (1974) and *Desperate Living* (1977), and further capitalised on her fame by starting her own punk band, Edie and the Eggs. She appeared on stage wearing the tight, revealing S&M leather outfit she had worn in *Female Trouble*, and released a single, 'Punks, Get Off the Grass' b/w 'Big Girls Don't Cry'.

When Baltimore's winters became too punishing for her, she moved to Venice, California, where she opened another thrift shop. She died of a cancer shortly after appearing in a schlock science fiction film, *Mutants in Paradise*.

Massey told (and re-enacted) her life story in the short film *Love Letter to Edie* (1975). ▣

MATAYOSHI, MITSUO

(b. 1944)
'The Only God Mitsuo Matayoshi
Jesus Christ'

As the reincarnation of Jesus Christ, Matayoshi believes it is his task to usher in the end of the world as we know it. Unusually, he has chosen to do this by political means.

This Japanese perennial candidate ran a private school during the 1970s, and later joined a Pentecostal sect where he honed his preaching skills. He founded the World Economic Community Party in 1997, which advocates an end to international trade and a return to an economy based on agriculture. He has a three-step plan to take control of the world. First, he will become the prime minister of Japan. Second, he will reform Japanese society. Third, the world will be so impressed by the results of this that he will be offered the post of secretary general of the United Nations. Having obtained political power, he will exercise his spiritual power, raise the dead and embark on the Last Judgment. So far, he is stalled on the first step, but that hasn't stopped him being a candidate in numerous elections since 1997.

Matayoshi, who is depicted on his political posters with the sacred heart of Jesus glowing on his chest, campaigns in a van equipped with loudspeakers (although that's not unusual for a Japanese politician). In his role as Jesus, he clearly leans towards the Apocalyptic Christ of the Gospel of Matthew, and looks forward to casting those he finds wanting into the fires of Hell. He is also famous for urging his political opponents to commit hara-kiri (ritual disembowelment).

MATHEW, GEORGE

(d. 1736)
The perfect host

The Irish are famous for their hospitality, but few have gone to such hospitable lengths as George Mathew, who inherited the estate of Thomastown, in Tipperary, at the beginning of the eighteenth century. Mathew immediately conceived the idea of an enormous house, equipped with forty apartments for guests, set amidst 1,500 acres (607 hectares) of beautifully landscaped gardens. To ensure that he had adequate funds for the project, he moved to the continent for seven years, lived frugally there, and poured his remaining income into the house. It was completed around 1812, and Mathew began to issue invitations.

When guests arrived, Mathew showed them to their apartments,

which were equipped with all conveniences, saying, 'This is your castle; here you are to command as absolutely as in your own house. You may breakfast, dine, and sup here whenever you please, and invite such of the guests as may be most agreeable to you.' Guests could also dine together at a large table in the parlour if they chose, and each was provided with a servant (whom they were forbidden to tip). Mathew was very clear on one point, though. He was not to be treated as the host by anybody, but as a fellow guest.

Thomastown had its own coffeehouse, attended by waiters and equipped with newspapers, chessboards, backgammon tables and everything else normally found in such an establishment. Mathews was an abstemious man, but to cater for guests who liked to drink he had set up a tavern away from the main part of the house, as fully equipped as the coffeehouse. Here guests could order whatever they liked (without having to pay, of course). There were billiard tables and a bowling green, while those wishing to hunt or fish were supplied with all the necessary equipment. The only activity that Mathew expressly forbade was gambling — so intent was he on his guests having a good time that he could not bear the thought of them losing money.

One of Mathews' frequent guests was Dr. Thomas Sheridan, a close friend of Jonathan Swift, the author of *Gulliver's Travels*. Sheridan persuaded the notoriously prickly and cynical Swift to spend a fortnight at Thomastown. On arriving, Swift was so astonished by the size of the place and the number of people there that he almost turned back immediately. He spent the first three days of his stay in his apartment, but eventually curiosity drove him to the dining room. After heaping praise on Mathews' head, he declared, 'And now, ladies and gentlemen, I am come to live among you, and it shall be no fault of mine if we do not pass our time agreeably.' He ended up staying three months.

While such a staggeringly generous set-up as Thomastown may seem like a recipe for financial ruin, Mathew was so careful with the running of his estate, and employed such honest staff, that his fortune only grew. He married twice, and had a daughter who died before he did. After his death, his estate passed to a relative, and the entertainment ceased. ▨

MATURIN, CHARLES ROBERT
(1782–1824)
Writer

Maturin's *Melmoth the Wanderer* (1820)

was one of the last great works of gothic fiction. It tells the story of the doomed Melmoth, who has sold his soul to the Devil in exchange for an unnaturally long life, and wanders the world, searching for someone who will take the bargain off his hands. It is a wonder that this vast and fearsome novel ever appeared, for the author, in his typically disorganised way, delivered the manuscript to his publisher in the form of thousands of unnumbered, disorderly pages.

Maturin was a Dublin clergyman with a sideline as playwright and novelist. He had one great commercial success with the play *Bertram* in 1816, which allowed him to do up his house in style, with painted ceilings and ornate furnishings. He married a singer and noted beauty, Henrietta Kingsbury, and insisted she wear only the most fashionable clothes. Even when the money ran out, as it eventually did, his last penny would go to keeping Henrietta in her finery.

Maturin was a man of many contradictions. He had a phenomenal memory, and was able to produce apt quotations from works he had read long ago at will, but was also notoriously absentminded, and could be seen walking around Dublin with a shoe on one foot and a boot on the other. During the day, while socialising, he was the life of the party, and loved dancing, especially French dances like the quadrille (the forerunner of the square dance). At night, when he did his writing, he was gloomy and introspective. If the muse was upon him, he would affix a wafer to his forehead, indicating that he did not want anyone to speak to him. He could, if necessary, write amidst company, but at such times would spread a paste of breadcrumbs and water over his lips to remind him not to speak.

He often stayed up until 3 or 4 a.m., and it was during the early hours of the morning that the morbid fantasies of *Melmoth* were woven. Unlike other Gothic works, where terror derives from thunderstorms, ghosts and clanking chains, the horrors of Maturin's masterpiece are man-made — torture, cannibalism, death by fire. When the ecclesiastical authorities learned he was the author of this and other unsavoury works, they prevented his advancement in the church, and he remained a curate. Although admired by Sir Walter Scott and Byron, his literary career proved no more successful, and his last years were marred by periods of poverty. Once elegantly dressed (he favoured tight pantaloons that showed off his long legs), he was one day spotted in the street wearing an 'extraordinary double-belted and treble-caped rug of an old garment'.

He fantasised about suicide, which was of course forbidden by his faith, and when he died aged forty-two, there were rumours, never substantiated, that he took his own life. He died a failure, but *Melmoth* has lived on. Balzac admired it so much he wrote a sequel called *Melmoth Reconciled*, while ☞ H.P. Lovecraft described it as the work 'in which the Gothic tale climbed to altitudes of sheer spiritual fright which it had never known before'.

Oscar Wilde was Maturin's great nephew. In exile in France after his release from prison, Wilde adopted the pseudonym Sebastian Melmoth. ▨

MEEK, JOE
(1929–1967)
Record producer

Meek, one of four children of George and Biddy Meek, was born in Newent, Gloucestershire. His mother, expecting him to be born a girl, dressed him as a girl for his first four years, and he grew up preferring the company of girls. He became interested in electronics, and spent hours tinkering with bits and pieces of equipment in his grandmother's garden shed. His other great passion was for music. He amassed a large collection of records, and made a little extra money

playing them in dance halls. He was a shy boy but, like his father, who had suffered 'shellshock' in World War I, he was prone to uncontrollable rages.

After a stint in the RAF and working as a television repairman, Meek moved to London, where he scored a job as a sound engineer with the Independent Broadcasting Company (IBC). He began by recording shows for Radio Luxembourg, then graduated to working on records. Meek was not just in love with music, he was in love with sounds. He heard amazing sounds in his head, then did whatever he could to realise them on tape. Recording techniques were primitive in those days (there was no multi-track recording yet), and some of the other engineers were appalled at the unorthodox methods he used — twisting dials to places they weren't meant to go, recording in bathrooms, placing microphones in dustbins and inside instruments. From the start, his records had a distinctive sound — vibrant and echo-laden, they leapt out of the speakers at you. Anne Shelton's martial pop song 'Lay Down Your Arms' became the first Meek-engineered record to go to No. 1 in 1956. A perfectionist, Meek was also temperamental and difficult to work with, and he was already paranoid about others stealing his ideas.

Quitting IBC, Meek put together

JOE MEEK

a state-of the-art studio for jazz impresario Dennis Preston, and became the first man in Britain to combine the roles of producer and engineer. He was writing songs too — unable to read music or play an instrument, he used to hum his tunes (badly) into a tape recorder. Falling out with Preston, he sought work with other studios, but his reputation made them reluctant to hire him. Meek used the spare time to record what may be the world's first concept album, *I Hear a New World*. Reflecting his obsession with outer space and aliens, it depicts life among various creatures on the Moon. The songs have titles like 'The Dribcots Space Boat' and 'Love Dance of the Sarooes', and Meek wrote sleeve notes explaining each of them ('Once again we find the Sarooes in a sad mood as they twist and turn in this almost eastern dance'). Meek made use of an early electronic keyboard, the clavioline, in recording the album, which features speeded-up singing and spacey sound effects (achieved by such simple methods as running a fingernail down a comb). Only a handful of copies of the album were pressed, though it would be re-released years later on CD.

In 1960, Meek co-founded a record label, Triumph, which released a few near-hits but was crippled by distribution problems.

Then, bankrolled by an entrepreneur, Major Wilfred Banks, he set up his own studio in a flat above a leather shop at 304 Holloway Road, Islington. Meek had total control over its recordings, which would be licensed to major labels. His studio was a cramped and chaotic tangle of wires and sometimes homemade equipment, but the sound he achieved in it was extraordinary. The first hit for the new company, RGM Sound, came in 1961, when 'Johnny Remember Me' by John Leyton was No. 1 for five weeks. With an insistent beat and ethereal female chorus, the song was about a man's former girlfriend calling him from beyond the grave. It was written by Geoff Goddard who was, like Meek, a keen spiritualist. Meek's interest in such matters had been spurred by a curious incident which took place in January 1960. He was participating in a séance when a message came through that Buddy Holly would die on 3 February. Meek was a great Holly fan, and when the singer toured Britain a few weeks later, Meek managed to meet him and pass the message on. Holly survived that year, but was killed in a plane crash on 3 February the following year. After that, Meek often conversed with Holly during séances, and believed the late rock legend helped out with his songwriting.

Everything came together for

Meek in July 1962 when, inspired by the launch of a communications satellite called Telstar, he came up with a tune one night. He had it recorded by members of a backing band he had formed, the Tornadoes, with Geoff Goddard playing clavioline. 'Telstar', which begins and ends with some of Meeks' most striking space-age effects, was an enormous worldwide hit, becoming the first record by a British group to reach No. 1 in the U.S.

Meek was looking unstoppable, and then the Beatles came along and turned popular music on its head. With beat groups springing up all over Britain, Meek's records suddenly sounded old hat. The record companies stopped buying his output, and the funds that should have been flowing in from sales of 'Telstar' were frozen when a French composer sued for plagiarism. Desperate for more hits, Meek worked round the clock, fuelled by amphetamines and antidepressants, and his naturally sweet demeanour was increasingly overtaken by volcanic rages. The slightest thing could set him off, and he would be hurling furniture and recording equipment while musicians ducked for cover. Once, unhappy with the way drummer Mitch Mitchell (later a member of the Jimi Hendrix Experience) was playing, he pointed a gun at him (an interesting studio technique also

used by the man to whom Meek is most often compared, Phil Spector). He still thought that others were trying to steal his ideas, and that his studio was bugged. He began to communicate by writing notes.

Meek's promiscuous homosexual lifestyle was also causing him grief. In November 1963, when he was convicted for importuning in a public toilet, the incident was reported in one of the London papers, making him a target for blackmailers. His already healthy paranoia increased when the dismembered limbs of a young man he had known were found in a couple of suitcases in Sussex. Police suspected a homosexual murder, and it was reported that they would be interviewing all known sex offenders in North and West London. To add to his woes, gangsters (the Kray twins, no less) were attempting to take over the Tornados, about the only act on Meek's books still making money.

Events came to a crescendo on 3 February 1967. Meek spent part of the morning burning papers, and later asked his office assistant, Patrick Pink, to summon his landlady, Mrs. Violet Shenton. An argument took place in his office, almost certainly about the flat (the lease had expired, and Meek believed that Shenton and her husband wanted him out).

As she left the office and started to walk down the stairs, he shot her

in the back. She fell on top of Pink, and probably died in his arms. He made it up to the office in time to see Meek put the gun to his head and pull the trigger. It was probably no coincidence that it was the anniversary of Buddy Holly's death.

Meek was virtually forgotten after his death, but interest in him began to revive in the 1980s. His recording techniques have been rediscovered by new generations of producers, and almost his entire output has been released on CD. He is probably better known now than he was in his heyday, and his best records still sound as intriguing and original as he was.

MERHAN, SIR ALFRED

(b. 1942)
Airport dweller

Merhan Karimi Nassiri, who later called himself Alfred Merhan, was born in Masjed Soleiman, an oil company town in Iran. His father, Abdelkarim, was a doctor who worked for the company, and he had four brothers and two sisters. As a young man he was passionately interested in politics, and at one point was detained by the Shah's dreaded security agency, Savak, after taking part in anti-Shah demonstrations, but it seems that his claims to have been tortured are not true (much of

Merhan's past remains murky, with members of his family disputing his own accounts). In 1973, with the help of his brother Cyrus, a businessman living in England, he enrolled in a course of Yugoslavian studies at Bradford University, but failed to complete this.

Merhan lost contact with his family in the late seventies. He applied for refugee status in several European countries including West Germany, the Netherlands and France without success, but was eventually accepted by Belgium. However, he had come to believe that his mother had been a Scottish nurse, and decided that his true home was Britain. He intended to fly to London from Paris, but on his way to the airport was mugged in Gare du Nord station and the bag containing everything he owned — including his papers — was stolen. He still caught his plane, but on his arrival in London, was refused entry to Britain, and sent back to Charles de Gaulle Airport. And there he stayed.

Merhan ended up living in the airport for eighteen years. He slept on a red bench in Terminal One, surrounded by a growing number of boxes and bags containing his possessions, including clippings of the numerous articles about him that had appeared in the world's press. He washed in the airport toilets and

ate in fast food outlets. He spent his days writing a copious diary, reading newspapers and chatting to people who had read or heard about his situation. He survived on donations, and occasionally made a little money acting as a translator. At one point, he received a letter from British authorities which began, 'Dear Sir, Alfred…' and so he became Sir Alfred Merhan.

He engaged the famous human rights lawyer Christian Bourget to help with his case. Attempts were made to have the Belgian authorities reissue the papers confirming his refugee status, but here Merhan faced a Catch-22 situation — he had to apply for them in person, but under Belgian law those granted asylum who left the country voluntarily were not allowed to return. In 1995, the Belgian authorities relented and said he could return, but Merhan turned down the offer. It seems he had become used to his life in the airport, despite the bright lights and constant announcements which made it difficult to sleep.

Merhan's residence in Terminal One finally came to an end in 2006, when he fell ill and was taken to a hospital. He was allowed to remain in France, and at the time of writing was living in obscurity in Paris.

In 2004, Merhan published an odd, fragmented memoir, *The Terminal Man*. His story was the basis of the Steven Spielberg film *The Terminal*, released in the same year (in which the Merhan character, played by Tom Hanks, became an eastern European trapped in an American airport). Spielberg reportedly paid Merhan $250,000 for his story, which has also inspired several other films, and even an opera. ▣

MILES, BEE

(1902–1973)
Bag lady

The rotund, cantankerous and free-spirited Bee Miles was a familiar figure on the streets of Sydney, Australia, for decades. Born Beatrice (she preferred to shorten it to 'Bee'), her father, William John Miles, was a confirmed nationalist, atheist and controversialist, and Bee inherited most of his forthright opinions. She attended an exclusive girls' school and, briefly, university, but dropped out after a bout of 'sleeping sickness'. A tall, pretty and athletic young girl, she first came to the attention of the public riding around on a men's bike wearing a shirt and scandalously short white shorts, or in full evening dress, blowing a police whistle. She also liked to cling to the sides of trams, or jump onto the running boards of moving cars to hitch a free ride.

All of this proved too much for

her father, who had her committed to a series of psychiatric institutions. (She was eventually released after a newspaper campaigned on her behalf.)

Growing too fat to fit on the running board of a car (she would eventually hit twenty stone, or 127 kilos), Bee turned her attention to taxis, which she believed should be free to the public. Sydney's taxi drivers had something to be very afraid of as Bee perfected the art of depositing her stout frame in the seat of a taxi, often while it was moving, and occasionally while someone was already sitting there. Faced with a usually irate driver, Bee's favourite comeback was to twist the taxi's door back on its hinges, sometimes breaking it off.

By the 1940s, Bee was living on the streets, and was said to be better known in Sydney than the prime minister. She could usually be seen wearing a green tennis eyeshade and an army greatcoat, with a bag over her shoulder containing books by her favourite authors — Shakespeare, H.L. Mencken, Nietzsche. Bee was often arrested by the police for minor offences, but always kept a little money pinned inside her clothing so they could never get her on a vagrancy charge. Her court appearances, during which she invariably defended herself, were legendary. 'I admit I use the words

"bloody" and "bastard",' she told one magistrate, 'but I do not use a word starting with "F", or coprophiliac words, but when I'm annoyed, I have the tongue of a taipan.' She liked the cinema, and would sit in the front row, puffing away on one of her ever-present cigarettes, and shout things like, 'Don't kiss with your mouths open, you dirty swine!' at the characters on screen.

Bee's father had left her a small share portfolio in his will, and she supplemented the income from this with money she made by reciting the works of Shakespeare (she knew almost all of them by heart) and Australian poets. She wore a sign around her neck that read 'Shakespearean poetry and prose recited. Rational talks on many subjects.' By living rough, Bee could save her money for occasional extravagances. Her most famous exploit came in 1956, when she took a taxi from Sydney to Perth, on the other side of the continent. Every hundred miles or so, she took a £5 note from her bag and handed it to the driver. The journey took nineteen days. Bee said she made the trip because she wanted to pick flowers.

Bee's health began to fail in the early sixties, and she found a place in an aged care home run by the Little Sisters of the Poor. She spent a lot of her time comforting other patients who were dying, sometimes

praying with them, but held true to her own atheist beliefs. On the day before her death from cancer, she told the resident priest, 'I've never been blessed and I won't be blessed now.' ▣

'*I am an atheist, a true thinker and speaker. I cannot stand or endure the priggery, caddery, snobbery, smuggery, hypocrisy, lies, flattery, compliments, praise, jealousy, pretense, conventional speech and behaviour on which society is based.*'
BEE MILES

MILINGO, EMMANUEL

(b.1930)
Archbishop out of control

Milingo was born into a poor family in a village in eastern Zambia. He studied for the priesthood, was ordained in 1958, and served as a parish priest in Chipata during the sixties. In 1969, at the relatively young age of thirty-nine, he was appointed Archbishop of Lusaka by Pope Paul VI. Soon after this, reports began to reach the Vatican of wild scenes at Milingo's services. The Archbishop was whipping congregations into frenzies with talk of witchcraft, practicing faith healing and exorcising demons by the score.

In 1983, Milingo was summoned to the Vatican to answer his critics. He found some supporters there among Catholics allied to the Charismatic Movement, and while he was forced to stand down as Archbishop of Lusaka, Pope John Paul II eventually gave him permission to continue his 'mission of healing faith', as Milingo called it. He travelled through Europe, performing healings and exorcisms, and gaining a huge following, to the consternation of more conservative Catholics. He was also fiercely critical of the Church, and gave an inflammatory speech at a conference in 1996, accusing high-ranking clergy of being in the service of Satan and condoning homosexuality. When an Italian Cardinal, Silvio Oddi, called him a clown and a sorcerer, Milingo replied, 'You only have to get yourself exorcised to avoid spending eternity next to Satan.' During these years, Milingo also opened up a dialogue with the Korean Reverend Sun Myung Moon's Unification Church (which, as its names suggests, aims to unite all Christian faiths).

Another Milingo hobbyhorse is his opposition to compulsory celibacy for priests. In 2001, even seasoned Milingo-watchers were stunned when he took part in a

'Moonie' mass wedding ceremony in New York. It was presided over by the Reverend Moon who, in his usual fashion, picked out a bride at random for Milingo — a forty-three-year-old acupuncturist named Maria Sung. Milingo, not surprisingly, was hastily summoned back to Rome. When he dropped out of sight for a while, rumours spread across Zambia that he had been imprisoned there in chains, and the Vatican was forced to issue a denial to the Zambian government. Milingo emerged to announce that he was renouncing his marriage and severing ties to the Moonies. Maria Sung promptly arrived in Rome and went on a hunger strike in protest.

Milingo was then bundled off to Argentina, where he spent a year praying and meditating in a Capuchin monastery. In 2003, against the wishes of local bishops, he visited Zambia, where he continues to be hugely popular. He issued a public apology for his behaviour during the previous three years (but also told a television interviewer that he had 'never disappointed God'). Back in Rome, he lay low for a while, but in July 2006, he turned up at the National Press Club in Washington D.C. to announce the formation of a group called Married Priests Now!, and in September ordained four married men as bishops. Milingo had finally gone too far, and two

days later the Vatican announced that, because of this action, he and the four bishops had been excommunicated.

Today, Milingo is back together with his wife, living in Italy and still celebrating mass every day. Amidst his busy schedule, he has found the time to write several books, and even issued two albums featuring his singing, the first of which, *Gubudu Gubudu* ('The Drunkard') appeared in 1996. In 2008, he published an autobiography, *Confessioni di uno scomunicato* ('Confessions of an Excommunicated Catholic'). Fans of the irrepressible cleric eagerly await his next move.

MILKOVISCH, JOHN

(1912–1988)
Creator of the 'Beer Can House'

Milkovisch, the son of Austrian immigrants, was a native of Houston, Texas, and spent most of his working life as a railway upholsterer. He lived in a white weatherboard bungalow in the Houston suburbs with his wife Mary, whom he married in 1940. While he had never considered himself any sort of artist, in 1968 he began to decorate his garden with wood and concrete blocks in which he inlaid marbles, stones and pieces of metal. He eventually paved over the entire front and back yards

of the house (explaining 'I got sick of mowing the lawn').

A beer drinking man who generally put away a six-pack a day, Milkovisch now began to put the empties, which had been accumulating by the thousands in his garage, to good use. He sliced off the tops and bottoms of the aluminium cans, flattened them, and rivetted them to the sides of the house. He strung the tops, bottoms and ring pulls on wires and hung them in shimmering curtains from the eaves and over the driveway. Mary tolerated it all as long as he left the interior of the house alone. Some 40,000–50,000 cans later, the humble house had been transformed into a glittering, tinkling thing of wonder.

The house soon attracted the attention of local folk art enthusiasts. Milkovisch always claimed to be bemused by this. 'I had no idea that people would be so interested in beer cans,' he said. 'Now me, I wouldn't go around the block to see it.' He wasn't making art or sculpture, he maintained, he just didn't like to throw things away (while his idiosyncratic aluminiun cladding helped keep down air conditioning costs). Yet he also said, 'sometimes I lie awake at night, trying to figure out why I do it.'

Milkovisch wasn't the only amateur creating naïve architectural wonders in Houston during these years. Beginning in 1956, postman Jeff McKissac spent twenty-five years building an extraordnary, maze-like structure of iron, wood and concrete, incorporating numerous found objects, painted statues and other decorative flourishes, on a plot of land near his house. It was all in honour of McKissac's favourite fruit, the orange. After his death in 1980, a nonprofit organisation was formed to buy the Orange Show, as it is called, and today runs it as an artistic centre and venue for live events. The Orange Show Centre for Visionary Arts also owns the Beer Can House, which it purchased after Mary died, and spent seven years restoring it to its former glory. It was opened to the public in May 2008. ▣

MISHIMA, YUKIO

(1925–1970)
Writer

Mishima, whose real name was Kimitake Hiraoka, was the son of a government official, Azusa Hiraoka, and his wife Shizue, who lived with Azusa's parents in Tokyo. His upbringing was hijacked by his domineering, neurotic grandmother, Natsuka, who raised him as a girl and rarely allowed him to leave the house or play with other children. He became obsessed with fairytales, and in particular with the idea of dying violently at a young age — the most beautiful way to die, he thought.

He had his first orgasm while looking at an image of St. Sebastian pierced with arrows. (He would later famously recreate this pose for a photograph.)

At high school, Mishima was a brilliant student who remained a loner. He read widely, both Japanese classics and, unusually for the time, works by western writers like Oscar Wilde and Raymond Radiguet. He wrote poems which astonished his teachers, and completed his first major work, *The Forest in Full Bloom*, on the eve of the attack on Pearl Harbour. During the war he joined a nationalist literary group which worshipped the Emperor and glorified death and destruction. He assumed, like others his age, that he would die in the war, and welcomed the fact, yet noted that when air raid sirens went off he ran as fast as anyone else. Drafted in February 1945, he reported for duty suffering from a bad cold. The doctor examining him thought he had tuberculosis, and Mishima, flustered, gave answers which reinforced this diagnosis. He was declared unfit and sent home.

When *The Forest in Full Bloom* was published in 1944, it was credited to Yukio Mishima, (a name coined by one of his teachers), partly because his father opposed his literary career.

After the war, Mishima studied law at university, then took a job at the Ministry of Finance. Throughout this period he continued to write, and his stories began to appear regularly in magazines. To his father's disgust, he quit his ministry job, and the publication of the autobiographical novel *Confessions of a Mask* in 1949 made him the most famous young writer in Japan. During the fifties, his consolidated his reputation with a string of novels, short stories, plays and essays, some of which were translated into English and other languages. He was touted, both in Japan and the West, as a future Nobel Prize winner.

In 1958, Mishima wed Yoko Sugiyama, the daughter of a painter, in an arranged marriage. He had been in few if any relationships with women prior to this, and it is generally assumed that he was homosexual. His writings, which are often misogynist, contain loving descriptions of the male body, and he was known to frequent gay bars. Having grown up a puny, sickly boy, he began weight training in the mid-fifties, and developed a powerful physique which he liked to show off in photographs. He deplored the disdain most intellectuals had for the body.

Mishima's literary career faltered in the early sixties, with sales of his books falling dramatically. He began

a sideline in acting, and starred in a violent yakuza (gangster) movie. He also began to espouse political views for the first time since the war. Mishima had always been vaguely associated with the left, but he now revealed himself to be firmly on the right, denouncing the westernisation of Japan and declaring a somewhat confused but passionate devotion to the Emperor. He also became obsessed with the '2-2-6 incident', a failed coup by ultra-nationalist soldiers in 1936 which ended with some of them committing suicide. He wrote a short story, 'Patriotism', about a soldier on the fringes of the coup who commits harakiri, the ceremonial suicide practised by the Samurai which involves cutting the belly open with a sword. The story contains a lovingly detailed description of this scene, and when it was filmed in 1966, Mishima played the soldier.

'My aim is to revive the soul of the Samurai in myself,' Mishima wrote in a magazine essay. According to ancient tradition, a Samurai should devote himself equally to art and action, and it would seem that Mishima planned the last few years of his life to attain this ideal. On the 'art' side, he embarked on his most ambitious literary work, a tetralogy of novels entitled *The Sea of Fertility*. On the 'action' side, in 1967 he obtained permission to

train with the Japan Self Defence Forces. The following year, he went one better by forming his own private army or militia, which he named the Tatenokai or Shield Society. Mishima paid for their uniforms and led them on exercises and parades. The society attracted about eighty members, mainly students who had the spare time to devote to it, including Masakatsu Morita, who became Mishima's right-hand man. It was Morita who first suggested that the Tatenokai mount a coup, but the idea clearly meshed with Mishima's intentions.

On the morning of 25 November 1975, Mishima left the large western style house in Tokyo where he lived with his wife and two children, having placed the manuscript of the final section of *The Sea of Fertility* in an envelope addressed to his publisher. Accompanied by Morita and two other young Tatenokai members, he drove to the headquarters of the Eastern Army in Ichigawa. There, they took its commander, General Kanetoshi Mashita, hostage in his office, and demanded that the garrison's 1,000 soldiers be assembled outside so Mishima could address them.

Mishima stepped onto the balcony and began to speak, calling on the soldiers to rise up and assert Japan's national honour. His voice was drowned by the helicopters circling

overhead, and the soldiers, who had no idea what he was talking about, heckled and jeered. Giving up after a few minutes, Mishima went back inside to complete the plan. As the astonished general watched, Mishima stripped to a loincloth, knelt on the floor, and picked up a dagger, while Morita stood behind him with a long Samurai sword raised. Mishima shouted a salute to the Emperor, plunged the dagger into the left side of his belly and drew it slowly to the right. Morita brought the sword down to behead him but missed twice, cutting into his back instead, and another Totenokai member, Koga, finished the job. Morita then made a half-hearted attempt at hara-kiri, and Koga beheaded him, too.

The Japanese had considered Mishima's private army the indulgence of an increasingly vain and erratic individual, and most were baffled by his suicide. Was he insane? Was there a homosexual component to it? (It is generally believed that he and Morita were lovers.) Some admired the patriotism behind the act. Yet, while Mishima had framed his bloody demise in political terms, it seems clear that it was mostly about himself and his narcissism. He was forty-five, his body was showing signs of age. He was running out of time to attain the beautiful death he had dreamed of since he was a child.

MONBODDO, JAMES BURNETT (LORD)
(1714–1799)
Proto-evolutionist

Monboddo was a Scottish judge who became better known for his pioneering linguistic theories and his belief that human beings are related to apes. Many of his ideas anticipated the evolutionary theories of Charles Darwin.

Having closely studied a number of primitive languages, including Tahitian, Eskimo and Algonquin, Monboddo became convinced that languages had evolved over time as societies became more advanced. This in itself was a radical notion, it being commonly held that language had been given fully formed to Adam and Eve by God (while a deeply religious man, Monboddo thought the story of Adam and Eve was an allegory). Having developed an idea of evolution through his linguistic studies, he applied it to other areas, and realised that all animals had to adapt in order to survive. He was particularly fascinated with apes, referring to them as 'the brother of man', and toyed with the idea that apes and humans shared a common ancestry (although such speculation made the religious side of him uncomfortable). He believed that orang-utans would learn to speak in due course, when their society demanded it.

If Monboddo was a remarkably modern scientist in some respects, he also harked back to a more credulous era. He lapped up tall tales brought back by sailors and travellers about giants, mermaids, chimpanzees who could play musical instruments and human beings born with tails. Monboddo thought that the latter in particular were quite common, and began to suspect a conspiracy among midwives, who secretly removed the tails from babies as soon as they were born. It was this suggestion more than any other that brought Monboddo ridicule in his lifetime, and he was often shown in caricatures with a tail.

Interestingly, for someone whose ideas encompassed evolution, Monboddo did not believe that human beings were getting any better. He was very firmly of the view that human society — and language — had peaked with the ancient Greeks. He claimed to be the only man alive who knew how to pronounce ancient Greek correctly, and once asked his friend, Samuel Johnson, why he had bothered to compile a dictionary of such an inferior language as English. He shunned any technology not known to the ancient Greeks, refusing to travel in a carriage, and would only allow ploughing on his farm by oxen, as

the ancients did.

Other tales told about Monboddo emphasise his unworldliness. Despite his interest in linguistics, he was partially deaf and, in his later years, shortsighted. One day he was sitting in Kings Court, a guest of the London judges, when it seemed that the roof was about to collapse. Everyone inside rushed in a panic to the doors except for Monboddo, who continued to sit calmly on the Bench. When later asked why, he said that he had supposed he was watching some ancient annual custom peculiar to the English judges which he, as a Scotsman, had no interest in.

In retrospect, Monboddo's most important contribution to science was to act as a punching bag for evolution. By the time Darwin published *The Origin of the Species*, the jokes about men with tails had worn thin.

MONGO, PRINCE
see Robert HODGES

MOONDOG

(1916–1999)
'The Viking of 6th Avenue'

This extraordinary musician, avant-garde composer, street dweller and modern-day Viking was born Louis Hardin Jr. in Kansas.

MOONDOG

He was one of three children of Louis Hardin Sr., an Episcopalian minister, and his wife Norma, a schoolteacher. The family moved around a lot during his early years, at one point living in Wyoming where Reverend Hardin had been given the unenviable task of trying to convert the Arapaho Indians. Young Louis was much taken with their dancing and drumming, and became a drummer himself. In 1933, when he was sixteen, he was playing with a detonator cap he found on a railway line when it exploded in his face, blinding him.

With doctors giving him no hope of regaining his sight, Hardin decided to devote himself to music. He attended the Iowa School for the Blind where he studied piano, violin and viola, and learned to write music in Braille. He let his hair and beard grow long, and began to make his own clothes, fashioning ponchos and other garments from squares of cloth and leather. He had a habit of falling in love with his music teachers, and married one of them in 1943, but the marriage lasted only a few weeks. He took the bold step of moving to New York, where he knew no one. He soon fell in with a circle of bohemians, and was befriended by the New York Philharmonic Orchestra, which allowed him to sit in on rehearsals. He began to compose

music and changed his name to Moondog (after a dog he once had which howled at the moon). In 1948, he set out for New Mexico, aiming to live among the Native Americans there, but they failed to accept him as he expected. After drifting around the U.S. for a couple of years, he returned to New York and began to live on the streets where he became a familiar sight, a caped figure playing his homemade percussion instruments which included the trimba, the tuji, the uni, the utsu and the oo. In 1952 he married Suzuko (Mary) Whiteing. The marriage lasted eight years and produced a daughter, June.

Moondog's music, which is heavily percussive and often employs odd time signatures, encompasses many genres — primitive, classical, oriental, avant-garde, Latin and jazz. His first EP, *Moondog on the Streets of New York*, was released in 1953 (he had previously issued some 78s). It was well received by the critics, as were subsequent releases, but did not sell in large numbers. He nevertheless received considerable press coverage, and was championed by the likes of Duke Ellington and Benny Goodman. For a while, a promoter had a plan to send him on a long tour which could have made him a star, but he pulled out, opting for the relative safety of the small income

he could bring in by begging.

In 1955, he sued the disc jockey Alan Freed, who had adopted the name 'Moondog' and was playing 'Moondog Symphony' at the beginning of his radio programme without accreditation. Moondog was eventually awarded several thousand dollars in damages, and used some of the money to buy a small plot of land in upstate New York, to which he periodically retreated.

During the 1960s, Moondog became increasingly serious about composing. He wrote many orchestral works, madrigals, rounds, canons and even a ballet, although he found it difficult to get them performed. Having abandoned Christianity after being blinded, he developed an intense interest in Norse mythology, prayed to Thor, and adopted his famous Viking look. He could now be seen most days standing on his favourite spot at the corner of 6th Avenue and 54th Street, wearing a horned helmet, a red woolen tunic, cape and leather shoes, all handmade, and holding a spear and a hollow antler to collect donations. He raised money by selling various publications, including a series of 'yearbooks' containing his poetry and music, a 'Perpetual Calendar' (which made it possible to determine the day of the week for any date between 44 BC to 3200 AD) and a new runic alphabet

called 'Inglish'. While Moondog occasionally played on the same bill as ☞ Tiny Tim in the early sixties, he was far too cantankerous and individualistic to be easily co-opted into the counterculture, as the fey singer of 'Tip-Toe Thru The Tulips' would be.

In 1969, CBS offered him a recording deal which saw the release of an ambitious album recorded with an orchestra, *Moondog*, which sold quite well. Its follow-up sank without trace though, and Moondog retired to his upstate retreat for over a year. Then an invitation arrived from Germany for him to take part in a live radio broadcast with other contemporary composers. Having always wanted to visit Europe, the fifty-seven-year-old Moondog set off in January 1974, and apart from one trip back to the U.S., would remain there the rest of his life. In Germany, he was befriended by a young woman, Ilona Goebel, and adopted into her family. Goebel became his business partner, and when she married, he went to live with the couple in Munster.

Moondog entered his most creative period during the decade and a half he spent in Europe. He released a series of records, wrote hundreds of pieces, including his longest work, *The Creation* (which has never been fully recorded or performed), and played acclaimed

concerts in Germany, France, Sweden and Britain. (When conducting musicians, he insisted on sitting beside them, beating out the time on a drum.)

Moondog's place in twentieth century music is still being debated. Some see him as a minor figure who gained the attention he did because of his oddity, while others, such as the minimalist composer Philip Glass (who put Moondog up in his New York apartment for a while in the late sixties), cite him as a major influence. Many of his compositions have not yet been transcribed from the Braille they were written in.

MOORE, JULIA A.

(1847–1920)
'The Sweet Singer of Michigan'

Moore, one of America's most celebrated bad poets, was born Julia Ann Davis. She was the daughter of a Michigan farmer, and had little formal education. As a teenager she wrote her first poem, 'William Upson', which commemorated the death of a local man who died during the Civil War. It begins:

Come all good people far and near,
Oh, come and see what you can hear,
It's of a young man true and brave,
Who is now sleeping in his grave.

Now William Upson was his name –
If it's not that it's all the same –
He did enlist in the cruel strife,
And it caused him to lose his life.

The poem goes on to say how William's mother has been comforted by the return of his body in a coffin, and yet:

She knows not that it was her son,
His coffin could not be opened –
It might be some one in his place,
For she could not see his noble face.

The poem belonged to a mawkish genre of 'mortuary poetry' which was popular at the time. Moore followed it with many more in the same vein. Her favourite subject was the death of children, of whom 'Little Libbie' may be taken as representative.

While eating dinner, this dear little child
Was choked on a piece of beef.
Doctors came, tried their skill awhile,
But none could give relief.

She was ten years of age, I am told,
And in school very high.
Her little form now the earth enfolds,
In her embrace it must ever lie.

Moore's first collection, *The Sentimental Song Book* (many of her verses were intended to be sung to popular tunes) appeared in 1876

and became an unlikely hit. Newspaper critics competed with each other writing facetious reviews of it, and Mark Twain was captivated. It had, he wrote, 'the touch that makes an unintentionally humourous episode pathetic, and an unintentionally pathetic one funny.' Twain based the character of Emmeline Grangerfold in *The Adventures of Huckleberry Finn* on the Michigan poetess.

Moore has often been compared to ☞ William McGonagall. Like the great Scottish tragedian, she was a passionate advocate of temperance, and was often inspired by disasters, penning poems about the Chicago fire of 1871, a yellow fever epidemic in the South, and the collapse of the Ashtabula Bridge.

Have you heard of the dreadful fate
Of Mr. P.P. Bliss and his wife?
Of their death I will relate,
And also others lost their life;
Astabula Bridge disaster,
Where so many people died
Without a thought that destruction
Would plunge them 'neath the wheel
of tide.

Yet Moore lacked the armourplating of egotism that McGonagall and many of the other great bad poets had. In 1878, she gave a performance of her work at the Grand Rapids opera house which was greeted by laughter and jeers.

At the end of it, she told the audience, with considerable dignity, 'You have come here and paid twenty-five cents to see a fool; I receive seventy-five dollars, and see a houseful of fools.'

In her second and last collection, *A Few Choice Words to the Public* (1878), Moore replied to her critics. 'I was very foolish, I admit, in signing my name to that little book, when a ficticious [sic] name would have done just as well. And another foolish act was when I told where I resided.' She admitted that some of her poems could have done with a little more work, or 'filling' as she put it, but then, 'Literary is a work very difficult to do.'

After that, Moore's husband Frederick forbade her from publishing any more poetry. She continued to write poems for friends, and published a novella, *Sunshine and Shadow*. She lived quietly, running a store. After Frederick's death in 1914, she was plunged into a deep depression. When she died six years later, numerous obituaries were published. Her work may have been risible, but there is no question that it was deeply felt. ▨

———➤●◄———

Kind friends, now I close my rhyme,
And lay my pen aside,
Between me and my critics
I leave you to decide.

———➤●◄———

MYTTON, JOHN

(1796–1834)
Hellraiser

The phrase 'larger than life' hardly does justice to 'Mad Jack' Mytton, the squire of Halston. He remains the epitome of a certain type of rollicking, roaring, roistering, devil-may-care aristocrat that Britain periodically throws up, a man who took life in both hands, pummelled it, gave it a drink, then rode his horse over it.

Mytton's father died before he was two, which no doubt contributed to the complete lack of discipline he displayed throughout his life. As a boy, he was thrown out of two schools for fighting, and a stint at Cambridge only got so far as his sending 2,000 bottles of port ahead of him. He changed his mind and went travelling in Europe, and in 1816 joined the British army of occupation in France. Here he bemoaned the end of hostilities, Napoleon having been defeated the year before at Waterloo, and spent most of his time drinking and gambling. On returning to his ancestral home of Halston in Shropshire, he inherited a huge fortune.

Mytton had an iron constitution and a complete lack of fear. His friend and biographer Charles Apperley, known as 'Nimrod', wrote that 'scarcely a day passed over his head in which he did not put his life to the hazard'. His chief pleasures were riding, hunting, brawling and drinking — he usually consumed eight bottles of port a day, until his last years, when he switched to brandy, and was known to drink eau de cologne at a pinch. He was impervious to cold, and would go out in the middle of winter wearing little more than an open waistcoat, thin stockings and flimsy shoes. He was once seen crawling across an ice-covered pond, stark naked, in pursuit of ducks.

Mytton's most famous exploits usually involved animals, of which he was inordinately fond (at one point, it was said that he owned 2,000 dogs). He loved to test the mettle of his horses by urging them to jump over fences or across ditches that no other rider would think of attempting — and often when the horse had a carriage attached. One day he was riding with a friend in a gig (a one-horse carriage) when the friend remarked that he had never been upset in such a vehicle. 'What?' roared Mytton. 'What a damned slow fellow you must have been all your life!' He promptly overturned the gig, throwing them both onto the road. Mytton also owned a bear named Nell, and caused pandemonium at one of his dinner parties when he appeared in

the dining room in full hunting gear, mounted on Nell's back. He then made the mistake of digging his spurs into the bear's flanks, causing it to bite him in the calf.

As the last anecdote suggests, Mytton was not someone who thought that animals should be kept outdoors. One of his earliest pranks as a boy had been to lead a pony upstairs to his tutor's bedroom, where it spent the night, and he once put a drunken horse dealer to bed with two bulldogs and Nell the bear. His favourite animal was his one-eyed horse, Baronet, which he had ridden during his time in the army (Mytton had farewelled his fellow soldiers by riding Baronet over a mess table in the middle of a meal). After a long day of hunting and fighting, he and Baronet would relax by the fire, both of them sipping mulled port.

Mytton was forever falling drunkenly off his horses and breaking bones, but he was usually back in the saddle the following day. He was as generous as he was fearless, and simply gave away much of his money. Ignoring the advice of his friends to try and live within his means, he was eventually forced to flee a rising tide of creditors, and went to Calais. It was here that, in the midst of a persistent bout of hiccups, he thought to frighten them away by setting fire to his

nightshirt. Two gentlemen who were luckily nearby were able to douse the flames, but he was badly burned. (He was nevertheless able to exclaim, 'The hiccup is gone, by God!') He insisted on going out to dinner the following night, swathed in bandages.

Mytton returned to England in 1832, and spent the last two years of his life in and out of debtors' prison. He died in his cell, in the throes of delirium tremens, a sad end for a man as kind as he was wild. 3,000 people turned up to his funeral. ▣

NAKAMATS, DR. YOSHIRO

(b. 1928)
'Japan's Edison'

Dr. Yoshiro Nakamatsu, or NakaMats as he prefers to spell it, is perhaps the world's most eccentric inventor, and certainly its most prolific. He holds over 3,000 patents (almost three times as many as that slacker Edison was granted) and intends to double the figure by the time he dies at the age of 144.

NakaMats' inventing career began at the age of five, when he modified a model plane so that it would fly further. His chief (serious) claim to fame as an inventor is that he came up with a prototype floppy disk. As he tells it, he was in his second year at the University of Tokyo's Engineering Department, and listening to his favourite piece of music, Beethoven's Fifth Symphony, on a 78 rpm record. Thinking he could devise a better recording medium, he designed a floppy disk and data reader which he patented in 1952. He says that he licensed a number of his patents to IBM in 1979, but the details of the arrangement are confidential. While all of this is just a tad hazy, IBM has acknowledged that it has an 'ongoing relationship' with Dr. NakaMats. Other everyday items which NakaMats claims as his own include the digital watch, retractable landing gear on aircraft, the taxi meter and the automatic pachinko machine.

Among the good doctor's less serious innovations are PyonPyon shoes equipped with springs that allow the wearer to bounce; improved golf clubs; an aphrodisiac spray called Love Jet; an anti-ageing spray called Young Again and Dr. NakaMats Condoms. He is a firm believer in the connection between good nutrition and intelligence, and markets various dietary supplements like Dr. NakaMats' Yummy Nutri Brain Snack. He has taken a photograph of every meal he has eaten since the age of forty-four (the idea being that, should he later have a particularly brilliant idea, he will have a record of the meal that inspired it). He limits himself to four hours sleep at night, between midnight and 4 a.m., and during the day takes twenty-minute power naps while sitting in a Cerebrex chair (another invention of his which emits special sound frequencies designed to improve blood circulation and increase synaptic activity in the brain). He swims every day and believes that many of his best ideas come to him while he's underwater (he keeps a waterproof notepad with him to record them). 'I don't need relaxation because I relax all day,' says NakaMats. 'I don't need to drink alcohol in the evening or go to nightclubs. Instead of that, I'm thinking and creating inventions all the time.'

Dr. NakaMats' Innovation Institute employs over 100 scientists who help develop his ideas. In 2005, he finished building his new house, a four-storey concrete structure in an upmarket Tokyo suburb, with a front door shaped like a floppy disk. It has thirty guest rooms, and he boasts that it is energy self-sufficient, being equipped with an 'antenna' that collects cosmic rays, which are then converted to electricity. It is filled with gadgets, as an inventor's house should be.

Dr. NakaMats has also been dabbling in politics. He first ran for governor of Tokyo in 1995, and has been a regular participant in elections since then. NakaMats is scathing about most Japanese politicians, as he is about the conformity that is ingrained in Japanese society. 'Genius lies in developing complete and perfect freedom within a human being,' he says. 'Only then can a person come up with the best ideas.' ▣

'I'm like a time machine, always about ten or twenty years ahead of others.'
DR. YOSHIRO NAKAMATS

NEILD, JOHN CAMDEN
(1780–1850)
Miser

Neild's father, James Neild, made his fortune as a goldsmith in London, and later became a magistrate, prison reformer and public benefactor. When he died in 1814, John inherited his entire estate of £250,000. Those who hoped he would follow in his father's benevolent footsteps were sorely disappointed, for he was soon exhibiting the classic symptoms of miserliness.

He lived in a large house in Chelsea almost devoid of furniture (he slept on a wooden board), waited on by two female servants whom he paid a pittance. He wore old, ragged clothes and preferred to go cold in winter rather than buy a greatcoat.

He spent much of his time travelling around the various properties he had inherited, often on foot, and stayed whenever he could with his tenants. It was during one visit that, having apparently just heard that the value of his stocks had suffered a sudden decline, he attempted to slit his throat. He was saved by the quick actions of Mrs. Neal, his tenant's wife.

As the lessee of the rectory in New Marston, Buckinghamshire, it was Neild's responsibility to repair the lead roof of the church. To save money, he instructed his workmen to replace the lead with painted strips of calico, saying, 'It will do for my time.' He sat on the roof all day watching to make sure they worked hard.

Neild was little-known during his lifetime, but caused a sensation after his death when it was learned that in his will he had left almost his entire fortune, which had doubled to £500,000, to 'Her Most Gracious Majesty, Queen Victoria, begging Her Majesty's most gracious acceptance of the same, for her sole use and benefit, and her heirs, &c.' Hundreds of curious people turned up for his funeral, which took place in New Marston Church.

Accepting Neild's generous bequest, the Queen used some of the money to repair the church roof — this time with lead. She also provided for Neild's housekeeper of twenty-six years (he had left her nothing), and arranged an annuity for his one-time saviour, Mrs. Neal. ◉

NIYAZOV, SAPARMURAT

(1940–2006)
Dictator

The death by heart attack of Saparmurat Niyazov in 2006 brought to an end the world's most eccentric dictatorship. The 'President for Life' of the former Soviet republic of Turkmenistan — a predominately Muslim nation, rich in gas and oil on the border of Iran and Afghanistan — Niyazov constructed a personality cult that would have made Stalin blush.

Niyazov was brought up an orphan, his father having been killed during World War II, while his mother and most of the rest of his family died in an earthquake in 1948. He joined the Communist Party in 1962, rose through the ranks, and in 1985 was appointed Turkmenistan's leader by Mikhail Gorbachev. After it gained independence in 1991, Niyazov was elected president, ditched communism (calling it a 'social disease') and embraced ultranationalism, renaming himself Turkmenbashi ('father of all Turkmen'). Some 10,000 statues of him

were erected around the country. The largest, in the capital, Ashgabat, was covered in gold leaf and revolved slowly during the day to face the sun. 'I'm personally against seeing my pictures and statues in the streets,' said Niyazov, 'but it's what the people want.'

Niyazov encapsulated his wisdom in a 400-page book, *Ruhnama* ('Book of the Spirit'). Not only was every citizen expected to own a copy of this hymn to the Turkmen soul, they were to learn it by heart and kiss it upon entering a mosque or church. Questions about it were even included in the country's driving test.

Niyazov renamed a city, a meteorite, a flower and the month of January after himself (while April and bread were renamed after his mother). He issued dozens of bizarre edicts, including bans on circuses, gold teeth, car radios, smoking, lip-syncing to songs, long hair and beards on young men, opera and video games. He declared the second Sunday in August a national holiday in honour of the country's melons, saying, 'The Turkmen melon is the source of our pride, its taste has no equal in the world, the smell makes your head spin.' Other holidays he introduced celebrated the horse, carpets and, of course, Turkmenbashi himself.

Niyazov used the money that flowed into the country from sales of gas and oil to fund many architectural follies including marble and gold palaces and a giant ice-skating rink. He also commissioned the world's largest handwoven carpet, which measured 300-square metres and was named 'the Twenty-First Century: the Epoch of the Great Saparmurat Niyazov'. Meanwhile millions of Niyazov's subjects faced poverty and food shortages. He treated dissidents harshly, imprisoning thousands and forcing many others into exile, while an alleged assassination attempt in 2002 resulted in show trials reminiscent of Stalin.

Also like Stalin in his last years, Niyazov took a great dislike to doctors. In 2004, he closed all hospitals outside the capital and sacked 15,000 medical personnel, replacing them with untrained conscripts. They pledged allegiance to Niyazov rather that taking the Hippocratic Oath, and studied *Ruhnama* instead of medical books. Not surprisingly, the country's mortality rate took a sudden turn for the worse (Niyazov reacted to an outbreak of bubonic plague by banning it). Had these events not taken place, the dictator's own doctors may have been more solicitous in treating the heart condition that eventually took Turkmenbashi the Great away. ▣

NORMAN, RUTH E.

(1900–1993)
'The Archangel Uriel'

Ruth Norman was the Barbara Cartland of UFO cults. With her glittering capes and gowns, elaborate hairdos, sparkling jewels, heavy makeup and cheery personality, she was the public face of the California based Unarius Academy of Science until well into her eighties.

Born Ruth Nields in Chicago, she founded Unarius with her third husband, Ernest Norman, in 1954. Ernest was a psychic in regular contact with beings from other planets and dimensions, and Unarius was formed to share the messages he received with others. Throughout the 1950s and sixties, the Normans gave lectures and held meetings in their home. Reincarnation was an integral part of their beliefs: Ernest thought he had been Jesus Christ in one past life, while Ruth eventually recovered memories of hundreds of lives, including Queen Elizabeth I, Socrates and Krishna. It was all rather low key until 1971, when Ernest died and Ruth took over as leader.

Ruth blossomed in her new role. With her second-in-command, Charles Spiegal (known as Antares), she began to channel messages from the Space Brothers, as they called the higher beings who live on the other planets. In 1975, she and Antares shared a vision of a grand wedding ceremony on the planet Eros, in which Ruth married the Archangel Michiel (whose previous lives had included Leonardo da Vinci). Ruth was henceforth known as the Archangel Uriel.

Under Uriel, membership grew steadily, and in 1975 Unarius moved into new headquarters in a shopfront in El Cajon, San Diego. Members spent much of their time recalling and transcribing their past lives, building up a complex mythology which they would re-enact in 'psychodramas'. They came to believe that the Space Brothers were about to return to Earth in thirty-three spaceships and usher in a new era of peace and harmony. Unarius purchased some land near their centre for the landing site. Ruth in particular often received messages indicating their imminent arrival, and would lead bands of her followers out to the landing site for all-night vigils. In 1975, she and some of the other Unarians placed bets totalling several thousand dollars with the British bookmaker Ladbrokes that the Space Brothers would be landing that year.

Ruth's flamboyant public image was largely the creation of a young artist named Stephen Yancoskie, who joined Unarius in 1977 and

RUTH E. NORMAN

took on the name Arieson. He designed Ruth's fabulous outfits, decorated the Unarius centre with murals, and also designed the costumes Unarians wore in their psychodramas and annual pageant. Videotapes of the psychodramas, usually featuring Ruth and full of cheesy special effects, were sold by mail order. Ruth became a fringe celebrity. She often featured in the press, and made appearances on television, including a celebrated 1982 guest spot on *Late Night with David Letterman*.

Arieson was eventually expelled from Unarius for his drinking and rampant homosexuality (behaviour frowned on by the Space Brothers, it seems). He proceeded to bitch about his former boss Uriel in public, claiming that she had begged him to marry her. He said she kept over a dozen wedding dresses in her wardrobe and liked to re-enact her marriage on planet Eros. Arieson was later accepted back into Unarius, but died of AIDS during the 1990s.

After repeated disappointments, the Unarians decided that the Space Brothers would not be coming until 2001. Ruth Norman did not live to see the day. Her health declined, and in February 1993, she summoned the Unarians to her bedside. She gave them her blessing, presented them with headbands, and sprinkled them with rose petals. She died in her sleep five months later. ▨

NORTON, JOSHUA

(c.1819–1880)
'Emperor of the United States'

Joshua Abraham Norton was probably born in England (some sources say Scotland) and spent most of his early years in South Africa. Having received an inheritance of $40,000 after the death of his father, he moved to San Francisco, became involved in real estate and importing, and turned his initial capital into $250,000. In 1852, when a shortage of rice had seen its price soar, Norton and several other businessmen attempted to corner the market by buying up all existing stocks, but then several ships laden with rice arrived in San Francisco and the price plummeted. Unable to extricate himself from the deal, Norton was forced to declare bankruptcy in 1858.

He left San Francisco for several months. By the time he returned, he was telling people that he was the Emperor of the United States. On 17 September 1859, the *San Francisco Bulletin* published, without comment, the following proclamation.

At the peremptory request and desire of a large majority of the citizens of these United States, I, Joshua Norton, formerly of Algoa Bay, Cape of Good Hope, and now for the last 9 years and 10 months past of S. F., Cal., declare and proclaim

*myself Emperor of these U. S.; and
in virtue of the authority thereby in me
vested, do hereby order and direct the
representatives of the different States of
the Union to assemble in Musical Hall,
of this city, on the 1st day of Feb. next,
then and there to make such alterations
in the existing laws of the Union as may
ameliorate the evils under which the country
is laboring, and thereby cause confidence
to exist, both at home and abroad, in our
stability and integrity.*

Further proclamations and decrees followed. In October, Norton
formerly dissolved Congress, and
when Congress wilfully failed to
obey his order, sent the army in.
With the Civil War looming, he was
forced to dissolve the Union, and
when war broke out, offered to me-
diate between Abraham Lincoln and
Jefferson Davis. The Emperor did
not confine himself to American affairs, though, and on being informed
that Mexico was also in dire straits,
adopted another title, 'Protector of
Mexico.' He wore a blue military
uniform with brass buttons, and
gilt epaulets presented to him by
some army officers, and a military
cap with red trim (the cap was later
replaced by a tall beaver hat with
peacock feathers and a rosette).

He always carried a sword by his
side, and a cane or umbrella depending on the weather.

Norton picked the right city

in which to declare himself Emperor, for San Francisco has always
cherished its eccentrics. During the
years of Norton's rule it boasted a
particularly rich crop, including a
flashily dressed liniment salesman
who went by the evocative title of
the King of Pain (and who once
gave Norton a suit), the inimitable
☞ Oofty Goofty, and Norton's
arch enemy ☞ Frederick Coombs.
But it was Emperor Norton that
the city took to heart. He ate in
the finest restaurants without being
asked to pay, and had seats reserved
for him at the opening nights of
plays and other performances. He
printed his own currency (run off
for free by local printers), his notes
having a face value of up to $10,
and these were generally accepted
by shopkeepers. When an overzeal-
ous young policeman made the
mistake of arresting him on the
grounds that he was insane, there
was a public outcry. The police
chief, Patrick Crowley, ordered the
Emperor's release, declaring that 'he
had shed no blood; robbed no one;
and despoiled no country; which is
more than can be said of his fellows
in that line'. After that, policemen
saluted him in the street. When his
uniform began to wear out, the city's
Board of Supervisors voted to buy
him a replacement. In gratitude, the
Emperor made them all noblemen.

Norton accepted the fact that his

various proclamations and decrees were ignored with equanimity. He was a hands-on ruler who wandered the streets endlessly, inspecting building works, checking that cable cars were running on time, and generally ensuring that all was well. His bearing was always impeccably regal, and he was most kind and solicitous to children. He is credited with once quelling an anti-Chinese riot by standing in front of the rioters and reciting the Lord's Prayer. It must also be said that some of his decrees were eminently sensible. He called for the building of a bridge and tunnel between San Francisco and Oakland, both of which were later built (the bridge bears a plaque dedicated to him). In another decree, he called for the formation of a League of Nations.

On 8 January 1880, Norton fell in the street. A policeman called for a carriage to take him to hospital, but he died before it arrived. A group of businessman paid for a rosewood coffin and a fine funeral, and up to 30,000 people lined the streets to pay their last respects to Norton I, who sadly left no heirs.

NORTON, ROSALEEN

(1917–1979)
'The Witch of Kings Cross'

Norton was born during a violent thunderstorm in Dunedin, New Zealand, emerging from the womb with a strip of extraneous skin stretching from her right armpit to her waist, and other physical peculiarities which she later identified as 'witch's marks'. She was the third daughter of a British-born merchant seaman, Albert Norton, and his New Zealand-born wife Beena. In 1925, the family moved to Sydney. The young 'Roie', as she was usually known, had a vivid imagination and artistic talent. She loved horror stories and, age fourteen, was expelled from a Church of England girls' school for her drawings of vampires, werewolves and the like.

She held down various jobs such as kitchen-hand and waitress, studied art for a couple of years, and was briefly a cadet journalist at *Smith's Weekly*, a famously irreverent publication of the day. She also worked as an artist's model, posing for Norman Lindsay among others (Lindsay would be a major influence on her work). In 1935, she married Beresford Conroy, who was also seventeen, and they spent time hitchhiking around Australia and working in odd jobs, but the marriage did not last and they divorced in 1951. In the late forties, she met a poet, Gavin Greenlees, who became her soul mate and collaborator in her work.

Norton began to study the occult seriously in the 1940s. She

ROSALEEN NORTON

studied the works of Jung as well as occultists like Aleister Crowley and Dion Fortune, and experimented with self-hypnosis, drugs and sex magic. On entering a trance state, she had visions of Pan and other gods, demons and elemental beings, and depicted them in vibrant, erotic and occasionally grotesque paintings and drawings. She first came to the attention of an extremely conservative Australian public in 1949, when police raided an exhibition of her paintings at the Rowden-White Gallery at Melbourne University. They seized four works and Norton was charged with obscenity. At her trial, several academics spoke in her defence, and the charges were dropped. A triumphant Norton told the *Daily Telegraph*, 'Obscenity, like beauty, is in the eye of the beholder. This figleaf morality expresses a very unhealthy attitude.' Further scandal ensued in 1952 with the publication of a book, *The Art of Rosaleen Norton*, featuring Norton's paintings and Greenlees' poems. Its publisher, Walter Glover, was charged with obscenity and fined, and two pictures were ordered to be excised from all unsold copies of the book.

Norton and Greenlees lived in Kings Cross, Sydney's red light/bohemian district, in a dingy basement flat equipped with an altar, black candles and other occult paraphernalia, along with cats, rats and other animals (Norton had a deep spiritual connection to animals). She was dubbed 'the Witch of Kings Cross' by newspaper reporters who could always rely on her for lurid headlines — 'A Warning to Australia: Devil Worship Here!,' 'Orgies of Sex,' 'Satanists in Weird Kings Cross Ritual.' While Norton had gathered around her a group of like-minded people who participated in rituals in her flat, the accusations that she was running some sort of Satanic cult were certainly wide of the mark. Part of the reason she made good copy was her appearance. With her black hair, arched eyebrows, pointed ears and sharp teeth (she had them filed), she looked, well, just like a witch.

Norton clearly rather enjoyed her notoriety, and sailed blithely through the scandals which periodically engulfed her. Not everyone in her orbit escaped so easily. The most badly burned was Sir Eugene Goossens, conductor of the Sydney Symphony Orchestra, who was a regular, secret participant in the rituals at Norton's flat. In 1956, several letters written by Goossens, describing his participation with Norton in sex magic, fell into the hands of a reporter, who passed them on to the Vice Squad. (They had probably been stolen from her flat, like the photos of Norton naked and taking part in 'unnatural' sex acts with

Greenlees, which a couple of petty criminals had offered for sale to the *Sun* newspaper the year before.) When Goossens returned from a trip to England, police were waiting at the airport to search his bags, and found various banned books, masks and a large number of pornographic photos. His career was ruined.

Norton's notoriety slowly faded during the sixties and seventies. Her artistic powers also waned, and her later paintings are nowhere near as powerful as her work from the forties. Diagnosed with colon cancer, she entered a Catholic hospice in 1979, and died there shortly afterwards. Three years later, Walter Glover reissued *The Art of Rosaleen Norton*, and an exhibition of her paintings was organised to coincide with this. Another retrospective was held in a small gallery in Kings Cross in 2000, but it seems fair to say that Norton's work, some of which is remarkable, has never been accepted into the canon of Australian art. 🔲

'I have been described as eccentric, decadent, exhibitionist, crank, genius, witch, freak and so on, both in public utterances and private conversations. Yes, I am all of these things and glad of it.'

ROSALEEN NORTON

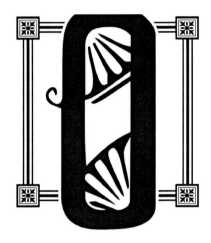

OGDEN, CHARLES KAY
(1889–1957)
Linguist

Ogden is best remembered as the inventor of Basic English, a distillation of 850 words that would serve as a universal language (if only anyone had wanted it), but he had enough careers and interests to keep several people occupied. He was a philosopher, magazine editor, bookseller, art dealer and inveterate collector.

Ogden was educated at Cambridge, and never really left it. As a student, he become known for various quirks, such as his penchant for smoking a fake cigarette with a tiny red bulb on the end that glowed. In 1912, he founded the *Cambridge Magazine*, which evolved into a journal respected for its coverage of international affairs. He went on to write for and edit various publications. His contributions to philosophy included an influential book, *The Meaning of Meaning*, written with I.A. Richards, which appeared in 1923. Ogden also ran a number of small bookshops in Cambridge, and was apparently very popular with visiting Americans. One millionaire was so grateful for Ogden's philosophical guidance that he presented him with a large and expensive collection of clothes.

Ogden's Basic English found an enthusiastic supporter in Winston Churchill. In 1943, having been secretly whisked to America, Churchill gave a speech on Anglo-American relations at Harvard University in which he recommended that Basic English be adopted across the globe. (Roosevelt was not so convinced, writing to Churchill, 'I wonder what the course of history would have been if in May 1940 you had been able to offer the British people only blood, work, eye water and face water, which I understand is the best that Basic English can do with five famous words.') In the wake of Churchill's speech, reporters flocked to Ogden's door, only to be greeted by the linguist wearing a selection of masks. (Ogden was a great fan of masks, and believed that people should wear them while arguing, so as to remove personality from the argument.) Churchill set up a Cabinet Committee to look into

the introduction of Basic English, but Ogden, no lover of bureaucrats, tried to have as little to do with it as possible.

Ogden never went to sleep until dawn. He spent his nights writing, or roaming the streets in search of friends who might also be awake. He thought fresh air was dangerous, kept the windows of his flat shut when he was inside it, and utilised an 'ozone machine'. He was also a keen member of the Anti-Noise League, which briefly flourished during the 1930s, until it was overwhelmed by the noise of World War II.

Ogden collected all manner of things. Every inch of his flat was crammed with shoes, music boxes, automata, clocks and especially books. He had many thousands of them, arranged on his shelves according to strange systems of his own devising (he liked the first letters in titles to spell out words, for example). He owned many books relating to the utilitarian philosopher ☞ Jeremy Bentham, which were bought by University College London after Ogden's death. UCL had been the proud custodian of Bentham's mummified body since 1850. In 1950, Ogden had persuaded its administrators that, after 100 years, it was time to give the old boy a clean-up and a change of underwear. ▣

ONODA, HIROO

(b. 1922)
Soldier

Onoda is probably the most famous of the Japanese soldiers, known as 'holdouts', who remained in the jungle after the end of World War II, refusing to surrender. He certainly held out the longest — almost thirty years — and he fought right up until the end.

Onoda joined the Japanese army at the age of twenty. Three years later, after training in intelligence gathering and guerrilla warfare, and gaining the rank of lieutenant, he was sent to the Philippine island of Lubang, where he was to conduct sabotage operations. The orders given to him by his divisional commander, Major Tanaguchi, could not have been clearer. 'You are absolutely not to die by your own hand,' he was told. 'It may take three years, it may take five, but whatever happens, we'll come back for you. Until then, so long as you have one soldier, you are to continue to lead him. You may have to live on coconuts. If that's the case, live on coconuts!'

Soon after his arrival on Lubang, the Allies retook the island. The Japanese split into groups and retreated into the mountains. Onoda was left with three men in his guerrilla cell — Shoichi Shimada, Kin-shichi Kozuka and Yuichi Akatsu. On October 1945, they came upon their first leaflet telling them that the war was over and calling on them to surrender. They decided it was an Allied trick. Further leaflets followed, including one from General Yamashita ordering them to surrender, and these too were ignored, but in 1949, Akatsu quietly left the group and gave himself up. He later wrote a letter to his former comrades, urging them to surrender, too. Onoda and his two remaining companions looked at each other and shook their heads — another trick.

The men lived mainly on boiled bananas and coconuts. They occasionally stole rice and other goods from villages, and every few months killed a cow, which they butchered, enjoying fresh meat for a few days, and drying the remainder. They built makeshift shelters during winter, and slept in the open the rest of the year. Despite the harshness of their lives, Onoda later recalled that he had rarely been sick during all his years on Lubang. Meanwhile, they continued their guerrilla activities, often firing on villagers (whom they believed to be enemy spies) and were sometimes involved in shoot-outs with Filipino police. Shimada was killed during one of these in 1954.

Onoda and Kozuka continued

to evade search parties sent to find them over the next two decades. But in 1972, during a raid in which they intended to torch a village's stockpile of rice, Kozuka was shot dead. Convinced that Onoda must be alive (he had officially been declared dead in 1959), more search parties were sent out, but Onoda evaded them for another year and a half.

Onoda's apparent survival was widely reported in Japan (in 1972, another holdout, Shoichi Yokoi, had been brought back there, famously declaring 'It is with much embarrassment that I have returned alive'). A college dropout, Norio Suzuki, who was about to embark on a trip through several Asian countries, told his friends that he was 'going to look for Lieutenant Onoda, a panda and the Abominable Snowman'. Amazingly (when it came to Onoda, at least) he succeeded. He struck up a rapport with the ageing guerrilla, but Onoda still refused to surrender until ordered to by his commanding officer. Suzuki returned to Japan with photos of Onoda. Major Tanaguchi, who now owned a bookshop, was tracked down and travelled to Lubang.

On 9 March 1974, Onoda, wearing the remains of his dress uniform, sword at his side, rifle in hand and even some ammunition to spare, was ordered to stand down

by Tanaguchi. In his autobiography, *No Surrender: My Thirty-Year War,* Onoda described his reaction to the news of Japan's surrender: 'We really lost the war! How could they have been so sloppy?'

Onoda officially surrendered to President Marcos, who pardoned him (he and his men had killed some thirty Filipinos over the years). Returning to Japan, he was hailed a hero, but grew uncomfortable with this (while he was unhappy with the meagre backpay he received from the government). He moved to Brazil and became a cattle rancher. In 1996, however, after a trip to Lubang, where he donated money to a school, he returned to Japan. Believing that the Japanese had become weak, he set up a 'nature school' where he teaches philosophy and the survival skills he learned in the jungle. ▣

OOFTY GOOFTY

(?–1896)
Human punching bag

The real name and background of this engaging if somewhat pitiable figure remain a mystery. He first turned up in a San Francisco freak-show in the mid 1800s, his body covered in tar and horsehair, billed as 'the Wild Man of Borneo'. He sat in a cage eating chunks of raw

meat pushed through the bars by an attendant and emitting a cry of 'Oofty goofty! Oofty goofty!', which gave him his stage name. Alas, the tar prevented him from sweating and he became seriously ill. He was taken to a hospital where, according to Herbert Asbury (whose 1933 book *The Barbary Coast* is the chief source of information about him) doctors were unable to remove the tar without removing his skin as well. Eventually they poured solvent over him and left him on the hospital roof, where the sun completed the process.

After that, he briefly performed a comedy act in a beer hall in which he would sing a terrible song, then be forcibly ejected from the place, landing with a thud on the pavement outside. It was supposedly at this point that Oofty Goofty made the startling discovery that he was impervious to pain, and he embarked on a new career — charging his fellow San Franciscans to pummel him. For ten cents, you could kick him; for twenty-five cents, hit him with a stick; and for fifty cents you could lay into him with a baseball bat. He even carried a bat with him, and would approach men in bars or in the street and ask, 'Hit me with a bat for four bits, gents?'

He must have been as strong-boned as he was pain-free, for he kept this up for some fifteen years. He finally met his nemesis in the form of bare-knuckle boxing champion John L. Sullivan, who hit him on the back with a pool cue, breaking two vertebrae. After that, Oofty Goofty walked with a limp, and the slightest blow caused him agony. With his livelihood and claim to fame gone, Oofty Goofty faded into obscurity. ▣

ORSINI, PIER 'VICINO'

(1523–1583)
Creator of the
'Park of the Monsters'

Pier Francesco Orsini, who was known as Vicino, was the son of the Duke of Bomarzo, Bomarzo being a small town in the Lazio region of central Italy. In 1541, he married Guilia Farnese, daughter of the Duke of Latera and a relative of Alessandro Farnese, who had become Pope Paul III. He fought with the papal forces in the Italian War of 1551–1559, part of a long and confusing series of conflicts in which various European powers squabbled for dominance over the Italian states. After spending some time as a prisoner of war, he returned to Bomarzo, where he devoted himself to artistic and literary pursuits.

Orsini was an Epicurean and hedonist, a lover of food and sex

who described himself 'like a dry straw before the flames of lust'. His experience during the wars had made him question Christianity, and he was also fascinated by the other intellectual currents which had influenced the Renaissance, including hermeticism, which drew on what were supposed to be the beliefs of the ancient Egyptians, and various eastern philosophies. It was quite risky for an Italian nobleman to entertain such unchristian ideas at the time, the Italian Inquisition having been established in 1542.

In 1547, Orsini began the construction of a park on a rocky hillside near his house. He began by damming a stream to create an artificial lake, and used the water from it for fountains and decorative rivulets. Unlike other parks created during the Renaissance which were laid out on neat, symmetrical lines, echoing the orderliness of God's creation, Bomarzo's park grew into a chaotic jumble of enormous statues and odd architectural fragments and follies which he continued to add to for almost forty years. Many of the statues were carved out of the bedrock, the shapes of the rocks having suggested their subject matter. There has been some speculation about who created the sculptures, but no one is really sure. As some of the workmanship is quite primitive, it is likely that local

stonemasons as well as professional sculptors worked on them.

The park, which Orsini named the 'Bosco Sacro' or Sacred Wood, was clearly intended to dramatise the philosophical ideas which preoccupied him. At the entrance he placed two sphinxes, which in ancient Egypt acted as the guardians of holy places. Beneath the first is an inscription which translates as 'Whoever is not astonished by this park would not even admire the seven wonders of the world', while the inscription beneath the second asks whether the wonders it contains 'were made as trickery or as art'. Many other, often cryptic inscriptions are scattered throughout the park.

Among the sculptures, there are numerous figures from Roman mythology, including Janus, Venus, the three-headed dog Cerberus and the winged horse Pegasus. Others depict an oriental dragon attacked by two lions, one of Hannibal's elephants carrying a Roman legionnaire in its trunk, and a gigantic tortoise with a female figure representing Fate on its back. The identity of many of the other sculptures is uncertain. A muscular giant tearing a man in two is usually identified as Hercules, but he may be Orlando, the hero of Ariosto's epic poem *Orlando Furioso*. An imposing, bearded figure seen rising from water is of-

ten assumed to be Neptune, but has also been identified as the King of the Underworld. Behind the head of a woman, thought to represent Demeter, are two figures with insect wings holding a boy upside down. The significance of these, along with many other features, has been lost.

Perhaps the park's most famous sculpture is the grotesque face with a gaping mouth so large that a person may stand inside it with arms upstretched. This is the Gate of Hell, with an inscription around the mouth reading 'Abandon thought all ye who enter here'. Inside the mouth is a small grotto with a stone bench and chairs, which is paradoxically a pleasant refuge on a hot day. At the park's highest point, Orsini built a temple dedicated to his wife Giulia, who died in 1560.

After Orsini's death, the park fell into disrepair. It was shunned by the local villagers, who thought it an evil place, and called it the 'Park of the Monsters', a name which has stuck. It became overgrown with vegetation, which fortunately preserved many of the sculptures. Among the first to rediscover it in the twentieth century was ☞ Salvador Dalí, who visited in 1938 and made a short film about it. In 1954, the park was bought by Giovanni Bettini, who began the task of clearing away the vegetation and

restoring the statues and stonework. It is now open to the public, and remains as mysterious and haunting as it must have been in Vicino Orsini's day. ▣

ORTON, ARTHUR

(1834–1898)
The Tichborne Claimant

Orton, born in Wapping, London, was one of seven children of a butcher. As a boy, he sailed on a merchant ship to South America, but deserted it in Chile. After returning briefly to England, he made his way to Australia, where (having possibly indulged in various illegal activities including sheep stealing) he assumed the name Thomas Castro. He married and had two children, and settled in the New South Wales country town of Wagga Wagga, where he took up his father's trade.

In 1865, a Wagga Wagga attorney, Walter Gibbes, noticed an ad in a newspaper which had been placed on behalf of Lady Henrietta Tichborne of Hampshire in England. Lady Tichborne's son, Roger Charles Tichborne, had apparently been lost at sea after his ship, the *Bella*, sailed from South America in 1854. She had never given up hope that he would turn up alive, and placed ads in newspapers around

the world seeking information. Gibbes, who suspected that Castro wasn't the butcher's real name, and had heard him talk about being in a shipwreck, asked him if he was really Roger Tichborne, and he admitted he was. The attorney persuaded him to write to Lady Tichborne, who sent enough money for Orton to get to Sydney, where he met a former servant of the Tichbornes, Andrew Bogle. Despite the fact that Roger had been a thin, sickly looking boy with black hair, and the Claimant was a rough, burly fellow with brown hair, Bogle recognised him immediately.

After raising more funds, the Claimant and his family travelled to England, arriving on Christmas Day, 1886. A few days later, he went to Paris to meet Lady Tichborne, who was overjoyed to have her son back. Some of Roger's former friends also recognised him, and he proved a great hit with the gentry of Hampshire thanks to his good humour and prowess in shooting and fishing. Most of the Tichborne family rejected him outright, however. They sent an agent to Australia to investigate his background, and people soon came forward who identified him as Arthur Orton. To raise money for the trial by jury which would settle the matter, the Claimant's solicitor had the brilliant idea of issuing 'Tichborne Bonds',

redeemable when he came into his inheritance. Some £40,000 was thus raised.

The most notable aspect of the trial, which began in May 1871, was the Claimant's almost complete ignorance of anything to do with Roger Tichborne. Roger had known French, Latin and Greek; the claimant knew not a word of them and wasn't much better with English. Furthermore, he clearly hadn't bothered to check even the details of Roger's life which were on the public record, like the school he went to. Yet, despite intense questioning by the chief counsel for the family, the increasingly exasperated Sir John Coleridge, he remained completely unflappable (he blamed his lapses of memory on the privations he had suffered after being shipwrecked). The trial became the biggest news story in Britain, endlessly discussed and the subject of songs, burlesques and illustrated booklets. The Claimant, who now tipped the scales at twenty-six stone (169 kg), had become a celebrity.

Then, seven months into the trial, Coleridge's first witness, Lord Bellew, made the startling claim that Roger had several distinctive tattoos, including the initials 'R.T.C.', which the Claimant clearly did not have. This was enough for the jury to declare him an impostor, and he was arrested and charged with perjury.

However, the fact that it had taken so long for such apparently conclusive evidence to surface made many suspicious.

To raise the money for his defence, the Claimant went on tour, giving rousing speeches to enthusiastic crowds across the country. The working classes were firmly behind 'good old Sir Roger' now, seeing a conspiracy by the upper classes to deprive a common man of his rightful inheritance. (Of course, if the Claimant was telling the truth, he was actually an aristocrat and therefore a strange choice for working class hero, but very little about the Tichborne case makes sense.) Just weeks before the trial was to begin, the Claimant's supporters secured Edward Kenealy to act as his barrister. Kenealy was almost as odd as the Claimant himself. A fiery Irishman with radical tendencies who loved unpopular causes, he also wrote religious books in which he strongly hinted that he was the next Messiah. In the trial, Kenealy attempted to prove an elaborate conspiracy against the Claimant by the Government, the Tichborne family and the Catholic Church, and took the unusual step of arguing that his client was too stupid to have planned his imposture. The Claimant, who seemed thoroughly bored by it all now, made no objection, and spent most of the trial drawing caricatures of others in the courtroom.

Lasting 180 days, the trial became the longest in British history (and would remain so until the celebrated McLibel Trial of the 1990s). At the end of it, Chief Justice Cockburn made a damning assessment of Kenealy and his arguments, and Orton was found guilty. The authorities had feared rioting would break out at the announcement of this sentence, but in the end the crowds took it quietly.

Orton was released from prison in 1884. He resumed his public speaking tours, but now spoke mostly in music halls and circuses. In 1886, he made a disastrous trip to America in search of funds, but ended up working as a bartender. He returned to England where he sold a confession to a newspaper, then retracted it. He died on April Fool's Day 1888, and was buried in a coffin with 'Sir Roger Charles Tichborne' on its lid. ▨

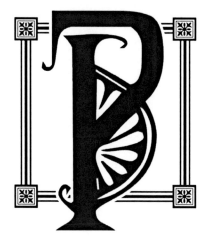

PAGET, HENRY

(1875–1905)
'The Dancing Marquess'

One of Edwardian England's most colourful ornaments, Henry Cyril Paget was the son of Henry Paget, the 4th Marquess of Anglesey, and his wife Blanche. His mother died when he was two, and Paget went to live with an actor, Benoit-Constant Coquelin (believed by some to have been his biological father). He remained with Coquelin in Paris until the age of eight, when he was moved to the rather greyer climes of the Paget family seat of Plas Newydd, Wales. His childhood there was a lonely one, his principal companion an elderly Scottish nurse. A sickly boy, he was too ill to attend his own twenty-first birthday celebrations, which nevertheless carried on for a week without him.

In 1898, Paget's father died and he became the 5th Marquess, his annual income the then enormous sum of £110,000 a year. Over the next six years he squandered his inheritance in a manner that astonished his contemporaries.

Paget's great passion was the theatre. His first audiences were his tenants and neighbours, who were treated to free performances in the family chapel. He later formed his own theatrical company, which employed fifty people and toured England and Europe, putting on elaborately staged pantomimes and musical comedies. During intervals, Paget performed a 'butterfly dance' in the style of the celebrated modern dancer Loie Fuller. After each performance, he handed out photographs of himself wearing some of the dozens of fabulous costumes, usually featuring elaborate headwear, which he had commissioned (the costume for his favourite role of Pekoe in Aladdin was said to have been worth almost his entire yearly income).

Clough Williams-Ellis, the architect and creator of the supremely eccentric Welsh village of Portmeirion, described him as 'a sort of apparition — a tall, elegant and bejewelled creature, with wavery, elegant gestures, reminding one rather of an Aubrey Beardsley illustration'. He was famed for walking around

London with a poodle under his arm done up with pink ribbons, and for having his car modified so that the exhaust pipe sprayed perfume.

It all came crashing down in 1904, when Paget was forced to issue a statement to his many creditors. He sold off a vast amount of property, including numerous costumes, to pay his debts, which exceeded £250,000. After the sale, Paget was packed off to Monte Carlo where he lived in greatly reduced circumstances and, it seems, tried to play down his reputation. In 1904, he told a reporter from the *Daily Mail*, 'I must apologise for not appearing before you in peacock-blue plush wearing a diamond and sapphire tiara, a turquoise dog-collar, ropes of pearls and slippers studded with Burma rubies; but I prefer, and always have preferred, Scotch tweed.' He died in Monte Carlo the following year, aged twenty-nine. The obituaries in British newspapers barely concealed their contempt.

Paget was married once, to his cousin, but the marriage was annulled two years later. Many have assumed that he was homosexual, but there is no evidence that he ever had a physical relationship with anyone, male or female. As his family burned all his personal papers after his death, many mysteries remain.

PALMER, JOSEPH

(1788–1875)
Champion of the beard

Palmer came perilously close to being a martyr to his facial hair. In America and Britain, beards went out of fashion in the early eighteenth century, and remained so until well into the nineteenth. During these wilderness years for whiskers, a man who dared grow a beard was not just out of fashion, he was setting himself up for persecution.

Palmer was a bluff, sturdy Massachusetts farmer who fought in the War of 1812. In 1839, along with his wife Nancy and son Thomas, he moved to the town of Fitchburg. He was already sporting a full beard, and the good people of Fitchburg soon showed their displeasure. Palmer was jeered and pelted with stones, and women crossed the street to avoid him. The windows of his house were broken, and his son was bullied. The local pastor, Reverend George Trask, joined in the attacks, declaring in a sermon, 'Let us join in prayers for the vain Mr. Palmer. He admires only his reflection in the glass.' Palmer, a deeply religious man who defended his beard with biblical quotations, was not cowed by these attacks. He was also a practical man. When asked why he insisted on having a

beard, he replied that he would tell them if someone could tell him why others insisted on scraping the their faces from nose to neck up to 365 days a year.

Matters came to a head during a church service one Sunday. Palmer was kneeling, waiting to receive communion, when the minister passed him by. Incensed, Palmer strode to the altar, took a swig of communion wine and declared, 'I love my Jesus as well or better than any of you!' A few days later, he was set upon in the street by four men armed with shaving implements and soap. They threw him on the ground and prepared to remove the offending beard, but Palmer fought back with a jackknife, wounding two of them slightly in the legs and causing them all to flee. Palmer was arrested, charged with assault and fined. Refusing to pay the fine on principle, he was thrown into jail in Worcester, where he spent the next year. On three occasions, he was attacked by groups of prisoners attempting to shave him (once under the jailor's supervision) but each time managed to fight them off. He wrote letters which were smuggled from the jail and printed in newspapers, and his fame began to spread across the country. Tiring of their obstreperous prisoner, the authorities told him he could forget the fine and walk. He refused, saying

he would only leave if they carried him out on his chair, which eventually they did.

In 1843, soon after his release from prison, Palmer joined a utopian community called Fruitlands, founded by Amos Bronson Alcott (the father of Louisa May Alcott of *Little Women* fame) and Charles Lane. Situated on a farm near Fitchburg, the community was run along communal lines and aimed to be completely self-sufficient. Its members were strict teetotallers and vegetarians, swearing off all animal products as well as stimulants, like tea and coffee. While such strictures were common in the utopian communities of the time, Alcott and Lane went further, declaring they would not use animals to work their farm. Palmer, who contributed much furniture and farming equipment to the community, could see this would doom it to failure, and insisted on bringing oxen from his own farm for ploughing. It wasn't enough, and the community folded after seven months. Palmer bought the property and started his own commune, called Freelands, but it was not a success, and he was apparently living there alone when he died. By then, fashions had changed (Abraham Lincoln had become the first bearded president in 1861). A fine marble tombstone was erected over his grave, featuring a sculpture

of Palmer and the inscription 'Persecuted for Wearing the Beard'. ▣

PARSONS, JOHN WHITESIDE
(1914–1952)
Rocket scientist & occultist

The missing link between ☞ Aleister Crowley and Apollo 11, Parsons, known to his friends as Jack, was the son of Marvel and Ruth Parsons, and was born in Los Angeles. A few months later Ruth, having learned that Marvel was seeing a prostitute, kicked him out and eventually divorced him. She and Jack moved into a huge Italian style villa on Orange Grove Avenue, Pasadena, bought for them by her wealthy parents.

Parsons was a solitary child who loved science fiction stories and playing around with skyrockets with his best friend, Ed Forman, and he dreamed of inventing a rocket that would reach the moon. His first job, at the age of eighteen, was with an explosives company, and two years later he married Helen Northrup. His grandparents having lost their fortune when the stockmarket crashed, he could not afford to go to university, but became a brilliant, mostly self-taught chemist. In 1936, Parsons, Forman and a graduate student at the California Institute of Technology, Frank Malina, obtained permission to work at Caltech after hours on rocket experiments. Rocket science was still in its infancy, with most scientists dismissing the idea that rockets could have any practical uses. Parsons and his colleagues became known as the Suicide Club for the number of explosions they set off in their attempts to prove others wrong.

Parsons discovered Crowley's works during these years, and in 1941, he and Helen joined the Californian branch of Crowley's society, the Ordo Templii Orientis, or O.T.O. He saw no contradiction between his interests in rocketry and the occult — both were ways of leaving the mundane world behind — and Crowley, in England, was soon receiving glowing reports of this eager young recruit with movie-star good looks. Parsons persuaded the group to move to Pasadena, where they took up residence in a huge house at 1003 Orange Grove Avenue. Here, free love was practiced in the approved Crowleyan manner. Helen began sleeping with the lodge's leader, Wilfred Smith (she would eventually give birth to his son), while Parsons began a relationship with her younger half-sister, Betty. In 1943, with Crowley's backing, Parsons took over the leadership.

The Suicide Club made enormous advances in rocketry dur-

ing the thirties, and in 1941 was responsible for the first rocket-powered flight of an airplane. By the time America entered the war, the airforce was clamouring for rockets. Parsons' success was his downfall in the science, however. Rocketry had become big business, and there was little room for gifted amateurs. His increasing openness about his other life in the O.T.O. was also causing embarrassment (he had taken to chanting Crowley's 'Hymn to Pan' during rocket test flights). He was persuaded to sell his shares in Aerojet, the company that had grown out of the Suicide Club's work, for around $12,000 (later, they would have been worth millions) and used some of the money to buy 1003 Orange Grove Avenue. Thanks to internal disputes, many O.T.O. members had left by now, and Parsons advertised for boarders of an artistic, atheist and bohemian disposition.

Among those who came to live there was L. Ron Hubbard, pulp fiction tyro and future founder of the Church of Scientology, whom Parsons had met through science fiction circles. He sensed in Hubbard a natural magician, and wrote excitedly to Crowley about him. Betty was also impressed and took Hubbard as her lover. Parsons was upset but, as a loyal follower of Crowley, could not admit to jealousy. Instead he threw himself into a

series of rituals designed to produce a replacement for Betty in the form of an 'Elemental mate', with Hubbard acting as 'scribe', writing down messages from the astral plane. No sooner had these been completed when a red-haired woman named Marjorie Cameron turned up at the house. Parsons then began the next stage of the rituals, which involved him having sex with her. The object now was to create what Crowley called a 'Moonchild', a reincarnation of the biblical 'whore of Babylon' and a female Antichrist. Having completed the rituals, Parsons anxiously awaited the results. Crowley was not impressed when he heard about these goings-on. 'Apparently Parsons or Hubbard or somebody is producing a Moonchild,' he wrote to another American acolyte. 'I get fairly frantic when I contemplate the idiocy of these goats.'

Alas for Parsons, not only did the Moonchild fail to appear, but Hubbard and Betty did a bunk, taking with them a great deal of his money. The three had earlier set up a company with the idea of buying yachts on the east coast, sailing them to California, and selling them for a profit. Parsons sank nearly $3,000, virtually his whole savings, into the venture. With his permission, Hubbard and Betty went east to purchase a yacht, but it soon became apparent they weren't coming back.

ARTHUR UTHER PENDRAGON

Parsons eventually went to court and had the company wound up, but lost most of his money. He went on to marry Marjorie Cameron, but their relationship was a rocky one. After the war he lost his security clearance (partly because of his pre-war dabbling in communism, but mostly because of the rumours about his occult activities). In 1952, he was killed in a huge explosion in his laboratory after he dropped a can of fulminate of mercury. His mother, on hearing of his death, committed suicide a few hours later.

Aerojet, the company that Parsons co-founded, went on to provide the Command/Service Modules used in the Apollo space programme. Parsons, too, made it to the moon in a fashion — there is a crater (on its dark side) named after him. ▣

PENDRAGON, ARTHUR UTHER
(b. 1954)
'King Arthur'

This rambunctious modern-day monarch, born John Timothy Rothwell in Yorkshire, is the son of a long-serving British soldier who went by the name of Wilfred Rothwell, and his wife May. Leaving school at fifteen, he became a bit of a delinquent, messing around with

motorbikes and setting fire to things, then spent some time in the army, which he enjoyed, although it did nothing to change his innate distrust of authority. After his discharge, he had various jobs, including working for a construction firm, married a woman named Liz and settled down with a house and mortgage. Growing bored after a while, they made a mutual decision to simply walk away from the house. He formed a biker club and spent the next decade riding around England with his mates, attending rock festivals, fighting other biker clubs, getting drunk and generally raising hell.

He had many nicknames during these years, including Johnny Reb, Mad Dog, John the Hat and finally King John (the latter because he used to organise parties at a thirteenth century ruin called King John's Castle in Oldham). It was one night in 1986 that his closest friend, Kris Kirkham, known as 'the Whippet', suggested that his real identity was 'King Arthur, the Once and Future King', and handed him a book on the legendary British ruler. Flipping through it, Rothwell began to see parallels with his life. He had always had an interest in the occult, and a vague feeling that he was destined for greatness. When several signs seemed to confirm the Whippet's suggestion (including a passing raven brushing his face as he stood

in the middle of Stonehenge) he took the plunge and changed his name by deed poll to Arthur Uther Pendragon.

He needed a sword, of course, and acquired his own Excalibur. (It was actually the sword made for the 1981 feature film, *Excalibur*. When its maker told him he had vowed to only sell it to 'the real Arthur', Arthur only needed to hand over his passport.) He moved to Glaston-bury, the town in Somerset inextricably linked to King Arthur, where he began to adopt Arthurian dress, including a sackcloth emblazoned with a red dragon, later replaced by a white robe. He placed ads in biker magazines, announcing that King Arthur was back in action and seeking knights for a new Round Table.

It was only when he came in contact with the modern-day Druids that he realized what his cause should be. The Druids had recently been banned from carrying out rituals at Stonehenge by English Heritage, which owns the site. In September 1990, Arthur began a one-man picket outside Stonehenge. He maintained it for five months, turning up every day whatever the weather (it rained almost the whole time), urging tourists who had come to see the monument not to pay English Heritage's entrance fee. Having decided that, as King Arthur, he would accept no assistance from

the State, he survived on the generosity of friends and strangers, and slept in a nearby camp, in a hammock under a tarpaulin.

King Arthur's picket brought him his first media attention. He and his growing band of followers, whom he dubbed the Loyal Arthurian Warband (so he can say that he fights the law with the LAW) spearheaded the Druids' attempts to worship at Stonehenge, and were often arrested. (At one point, to give English Heritage a taste of its own medicine, his knights chained up the doors of its headquarters.) Arthur, always a man of action, also threw himself into numerous eco-protests, and in 1996, made a memorable appearance at a protest against the building of the A34 bypass through a forest in Newbury. He ended up high in a tree, armed with Excalibur, doing battle with a chainsaw operator in a cherrypicker, as police held back a crowd cheering him on. After over two hours he was dragged down and arrested yet again. During another protest, the London Metropolitan Police confiscated Excalibur, but Arthur eventually persuaded a judge to issue an order for its return, and he and his followers marched in triumph to Charing Cross Police Station to reclaim it.

Arthur, whose many titles include Battle Chieftain of the Council of British Druid Orders,

continued to fight for the right of worshippers to enter Stonehenge. In 1995, he took the matter to the European Court of Human Rights in Strasbourg. He lost the case but won the war when, in 2000, English Heritage again allowed access to the stones during the solstices and equinoxes. Today, King Arthur serves as the Druids' representative at English Heritage meetings, and even the police have been known to defer to him. He has run for Parliament as an independent, and is a seasoned media performer with many admirers (in 1997, the writer A.N. Wilson, with tongue only partially in cheek it would seem, recommended replacing the Prime Minister, Archbishop of Canterbury and the Royal Family with 'a single Royal, Spiritual and Political leader — King Arthur'). Arthur's capacity for drinking prodigious amounts of cider remains undiminished, however, so there seems little risk of this king becoming too respectable any time soon.

PERELMAN, GRIGORY

(b. 1966)
Mathematician

One of the most brilliant mathematicians of our time, Perelman made headlines around the world when he solved one of the greatest 'open' problems in mathematics, the Poincaré conjecture, then turned down a $1 million prize for doing it.

Perelman was born in Leningrad. He studied mathematics at Leningrad State University, and went on to work for a number of institutions in the U.S.S.R. and America. The paper in which he offered his solution to the Poincaré conjecture (first proposed by Henri Poincaré in 1904 and almost impossible for a non-mathematician to understand) appeared in 2002, but it was not until 2006 that several groups of scholars, working independently, confirmed that Perelman's solution was correct. In that year, he was awarded the highest honour in mathematics, the Fields Medal, but refused to accept it.

In recent years, Perelman has become critical of professional mathematics, citing what he sees as the ethical failings of some of his colleagues, and no longer works as a mathematician. He lives in a small flat in St. Petersburg with his mother and sister, and can sometimes be seen walking around the city with his eyes on the ground. He wears ragged clothes and rarely cuts his beard or fingernails. In 2010, it was announced that he had qualified for an award offered by the Clay Mathematics Institute for solving one of their 'Millennium Prize Problems'. Perelman turned down the prize, worth $1 million, saying that another mathematician was equally deserving of it. Reporters besieged his flat, but Perelman refused to come out. When one of them managed to reach him on his mobile phone, he said, 'You are disturbing me. I am picking mushrooms.'

PESSOA, FERNANDO

(1888–1935)
Writer

Pessoa (whose name means 'person' in Portuguese) was born in Lisbon. His father, Joaquim Pessoa, a journalist, died when Fernando was five. His mother, Maria, remarried and took him to Durban, South Africa, where his stepfather was the Portuguese consul. He studied English, becoming fluent in it, and began writing poetry in his teens. In 1905, he returned to Lisbon where he briefly studied literature, but abandoned this when his fellow students, who were mostly republicans, went on strike. Politically, Pessoa was a monarchist and Sebastianist (Sebastianism being the belief that the sixteenth century King Sebastian, who had died during an ill-advised crusade against the Moroccans, would somehow return to restore Portugal to its former glory). After receiving an inheritance from his grandmother, he set up a publishing company which soon failed, and collaborated on a literary magazine,

Orpheu, which folded after two issues.

As a child, Pessoa wrote letters to an imaginary friend, the Chevalier de Pas, who wrote back. The Chevalier was the first of many alter egos Pessoa would invent. His poems were published under a host of names, but these were much more to Pessoa than mere pseudonyms. Each 'heteronym', as he called it, was a fully fledged individual with his own history, appearance, beliefs and writing style. Thus, Alberto Caeiro had blond hair and blue eyes, wore a monocle, wrote poems in which he described what he saw spontaneously, without intellectualising, and died of tuberculosis. Ricardo Reis was a physician who lived in Brazil (having left Portugal in disgust after it became a republic), walked with a slouch, and wrote poems in a more formal style which display a pessimistic view of life. And so on. In all, it is estimated that Pessoa created around seventy-two of these heteronyms.

After his return to Lisbon, Pessoa rarely left it, and led a very quiet, celibate life. He supported himself by working as a translator and bookkeeper, frequented various bars, cafés and restaurants in the evening, then went home to write.

Having an interest in mysticism, Pessoa began to correspond with ☞ Aleister Crowley in the late 1920s. He translated Crowley's

'Hymn to Pan' into Portuguese, and invited Crowley to visit him if he should ever be in Lisbon. In 1930, Crowley arrived in the city with his latest 'Scarlet Woman', a young German artist named Hanni Jaeger. When Crowley learned that Jaeger intended to return to Germany without him, he and Pessoa cooked up a plan for Crowley to fake his own suicide to make her feel guilty. He wrote a suicide note and left it under a cigarette case with his initials on it near the Boca do Inferno ('Hell's Mouth'), a chasm on the shore near Cascais where the seawater surges in spectacular fashion. It was Pessoa's job to notify the press. The story was reported across Europe, Scotland Yard sent a detective to Lisbon to investigate, and Crowley was briefly reconciled with Jaeger.

After Pessoa's death from cirrhosis at the age of forty-seven, a trunk was found containing hundreds of disordered pages. This was the manuscript of a book he had been writing for decades, a semi-fictionalised diary entitled *The Book of Disquiet*. This was written by a 'semiheteronym', Bernardo Soares, who, wrote Pessoa, was exactly like himself 'minus ratiocination and affection'. It was pieced together — in an order assigned by its editors — and published in 1982.

Pessoa was almost completely unknown in his lifetime, but is today considered Portugal's foremost Modernist writer. ▩

PHILLIPPS, SIR THOMAS
(1792–1872)
Book collector

As a book collector, Phillipps had an admirably simple strategy. 'I am buying printed books,' he once wrote, *'because I wish to have one copy of every book in the world!!!!!'*

He was the illegitimate son of a Manchester businessman, also named Thomas Phillipps. When he was two, his father retired and moved to a house called Middle Hill, in Gloucestershire. Phillipps' book mania began early. At the age of sixteen, when he made the first catalogue of it, his library contained 110 volumes. He studied at Oxford, married Henrietta Molyneux in 1819, and was made a baronet in 1821.

Phillipps was a notoriously prickly fellow who always lived well beyond his means. He spent much of the 1820s on the continent to avoid his English creditors, but his acquisition of books and manuscripts only increased, and he bought from many libraries dispersed after the French Revolution. He bought anything and everything printed or written on paper — illuminated manuscripts, scientific treatises, Shakespeare quartos, household records, topographical studies, early Bibles, engravings, ballads, diaries, broadsheets. He craved material from all countries, periods, and in all languages. He was quick to buy and slow to pay, often infuriating his dealers, but they knew that if he wanted something, he would pay more than anyone else — when eventually he got around to paying.

By 1840, his collection consisted of 30,000 individual volumes and manuscripts, stored in large boxes which could be removed quickly in case of fire, and so haphazardly catalogued that Phillipps was often unable to find particular items.

After bearing him three daughters, Phillipps' wife died in 1832. He immediately set about looking for a new one, but stipulated that she would need to bring with her a dowry of at least £50,000. 'Do not suppose that I wish for money with the intention of swallowing it up in paying my debts only,' he wrote to one prospective bride, entirely unconvincingly. These high expectations made a new wife hard to find, and it was not until 1842 that he married Elizabeth Mansel, the daughter of a clergyman (after accepting a much reduced dowry).

By the mid-1850s, most of the rooms in Middle Hill were packed solid with boxes of books and the family was forced to eat meals in the housekeeper's room. In 1863, after protracted negotiations, Phillipps took out a lease on an enormous house, Thirlstaine in Cheltenham, and moved his collection there. In his last years, as his health deteriorated, he became even more bad-tempered, and was increasingly occupied with his other great passion, anti-Catholicism, but his collecting fervor only increased. At the time of his death, he owned some 50,000 books and 60,000 manuscripts, the largest collection ever amassed by any individual.

Phillipps often acted abominably, but he had his good points. He was always very generous to scholars who wished to visit him and examine his collection (although he barred Catholics in his later years). He was genuinely passionate about preserving the past, and in particular his acquisition of paper ephemera — which no one before him had ever seriously collected — ensured that an enormous quantity of valuable material survives which would otherwise have been lost. And while his long-suffering family bore the brunt of his obsession, it seems that they retained their affection for him.

Phillipps made strenuous attempts to ensure that his collection remained intact after his death, but his unreasonable demands meant that these came to nothing. In the 1880s, his grandson began the process of selling it off, and this continued for decades. In fact, it was not until 1977 that the residue of the Phillipps' collection was sold.

PHILP, ALAN

(1926–2007)
'The UFO Man'

For some twenty years, the bearded, impassive figure of Alan Philp could be seen standing by the Princess Highway in the Sydney suburb of Arncliffe, every morning and afternoon, bearing a colourful sign with the words 'UFO Chariots Isaiah 66:15 Christ Return'.

Philp, who was raised as a Christadelphian, served in the U.S. Army Small Ships Section during World War II. He was badly affected by his wartime experiences, and afterwards spent time in a mental hospital. Later, he worked as a journalist and industrial designer. He spent many years studying the Bible, and could speak Aramaic, Ancient Greek and Hebrew. In 1961, he was living in Revesby when he saw a UFO in the night sky. He connected this with the chariots mentioned in the Book of Isaiah — 'See, the Lord is coming with fire, and his chariots are like a whirlwind; he will bring down his anger with fury, and his rebuke with flames of fire.' He believed that Christ would return in such a chariot in 2018.

Philp began to hand-letter signs on old flour bags and attach them to telegraph poles. When a policewoman told him he needed council permission to do this, he took to wearing the signs. He spent years walking the streets of Sydney and became one of its most recognisable figures, although few knew his name. After moving to a council flat in Arncliffe during the seventies, he realised that the motorists who drove along the nearby highway were the perfect audience for his message. After that, he was there most mornings from 7 a.m. to 10 a.m. and a few hours in the afternoon, invariably wearing a hat and overcoat, his sign clutched to his chest.

If questioned by passersby, Philp was happy to discuss his beliefs, but he mostly let his sign do the talking. 'I try to follow the scriptures, all their rules and regulations,' he told a local newspaper reporter in 2003. 'But am I eccentric? Well, if people hold what the scriptures say as being eccentric, well, I guess I am.'

In 2007, Philp collapsed while crossing the street and was placed in an aged care facility where he died a few months later at the age of eighty-one.

POCKRICH, RICHARD

(1690–1759)
Inventor

Born in County Monaghan, Ireland,

'Projecting Pock', as he was called, was a prolific if often wildly impractical inventor. During his lifetime he was best known as the creator of the 'Angelic Organ', which consisted of a series of wine glasses filled to varying degrees with water, and played by rubbing a wet finger along their rims. While glasses had been used to produce music before this, Pockrich refined the technique and was the first person to give a public performance on them (in Dublin in 1743). The ethereal sounds produced by the Angelic Organ, also called the glass harp and musical glasses, quickly caught on, and concerts were common until the end of the nineteenth century. Gluck, Mozart and Beethoven all wrote music for the glasses, and Benjamin Franklin was so impressed when he heard them on a visit to London that he devised his own mechanised version, which he called an 'armonica'.

Pockrich's father was a member of Parliament. Pockrich inherited his estate at the age of twenty-five, and frittered most of it away on grand schemes, including a plan to grow grapes on reclaimed bogs, and another to transform large parts of County Wicklow into a huge goose farm. Some of his inventions were eminently practical (an unsinkable lifeboat made from tin); others less so (artificial wings for every man and woman in Ireland). He also believed he had discovered the means of prolonging life indefinitely by transfusing the blood of young people into the elderly. Realising an oversupply of old people might cause problems, he proposed that Parliament pass an act which stated that anyone 'attaining to the age of 999 years, shall be deemed to all Intents and Purposes dead in law'.

Pockrich himself stood for Parliament twice, without success. He died when the room in which he was staying in a London coffeehouse caught fire. ▣

PODBER, DOROTHY
(1932–2008)
Artist

Podber told people that her mother had thrown herself down a flight of stairs before she was born in an attempt to abort her. Her father, Joseph, worked in a New York speakeasy owned by the mobster Dutch Schulz. Podber went to Walton High School, where she gained a reputation for rebelliousness, once organising a student strike. During the fifties, she hung out with New York's avant-garde royalty, including Allen Ginsberg, Jasper Johns and John Cage, and later became part of an informal collective known as the 'amphetamine rapture group' or 'the mole people' (she was designated

as one of its 'witches'). In 1963, when 👉 Andy Warhol opened his celebrated Manhattan studio, the Factory, the mole people became regular visitors and appeared in many of his films.

One day in 1964, Podber arrived at the Factory wearing a black biker jacket and white gloves, accompanied by her Great Dane, known as Carmen Miranda (or possibly Ivan de Carlo). She was supposed to take part in one of Warhol's films, but when no filming eventuated, grew impatient. She noticed a stack of Warhol's silk-screened paintings of Marilyn Monroe lying against a wall, and asked him if she could shoot them. Warhol, perhaps not understanding what she meant, said he didn't mind, whereupon Podber peeled off her gloves, produced a small German pistol and fired, hitting Marilyn in the forehead. Warhol, hitherto blasé about violence, told Billy Name that Podber wouldn't be welcome at the Factory again. Everyone nevertheless took her act to be a fabulous piece of performance art. Her bullet had penetrated four paintings, which Warhol renamed 'Shot Red Marilyn', 'Shot Light Blue Marilyn' and so on, and eventually sold.

Podber helped manage the hip Nonagon Gallery in the mid-sixties. Her closest friend was Ray Johnson, an enigmatic pop artist who distributed his artworks mostly by mail. He and Podber collaborated on various pranks, including talking their way into people's homes where they would re-enact the shower scene from *Psycho*. Podber was an artist in her own right, producing collages and other works, but it would be fair to say these were overshadowed by her non-artistic antics, not all of them legal. She was arrested at one point for running an abortion referral service, while another scheme was an agency which hired out cleaners to doctors' surgeries (where they would have easy access to drugs).

Podber had many lovers, including a banker (she claimed that she would only have sex with him on the floor of his vault). She was married three times, most happily to a bisexual shipyard worker, Lester Schwartz. They gleefully shared lovers, male and female, until his death in 1986. In 2007, Podber was interviewed by Joy Bergmann in her small apartment in the East Village. She was living on welfare and in fragile health, but remained defiant and unapologetic. 'I've been bad all my life,' she said. 'Playing dirty tricks on people is my specialty.'

In 1984, 'Shot Red Marilyn' was sold at Christie's in New York for $4 million. At the time of Podber's death, each of the four paintings she had cheerfully punctured was estimated to be worth $17 million. ▣

PONSONBY, SARAH
see Eleanor BUTLER

POTOCKI DE MONTALK, COUNT GEOFFREY

(1903–1987)

Poet & pretender

Geoffrey Wladislas Vaile Potocki de Montalk was the eldest son of Robert Wladislas de Montalk, an Auckland architect, and grandson of Count Joseph Wladislas Edmond Potocki de Montalk, who migrated to New Zealand in 1868. The Potockis were (and indeed still are in these post-communist times) one of the grand old noble families of Poland. Joseph had dropped 'Potocki' from his name on his arrival in New Zealand, but his grandson reclaimed it, and after extensive genealogical researches undertaken with his brother Cedric, would claim to be the heir to the Polish throne.

The family lived in a large house with extensive gardens called Vallambrosa, and Potocki's early years were idyllic. His mother, Robert's first wife Annie, doted on him, dressed him in fancy clothes, and instilled in him the idea that he was special. This charmed life came to an end when Annie died, shortly before Geoffrey's fifth birthday, after giving birth to a daughter, Dulce. Robert married again in 1912. According to Geoffrey, his stepmother starved and whipped him, and made him wear drab clothes (which he found particularly galling). When Robert's architectural business declined, he moved the family to a rundown farm which was another failure. Potocki increasingly retreated into his own imagination, and into poetry, which he had been writing since the age of eight.

Potocki excelled at school, briefly studied law, then theology, and in 1924 married Lillian Hemus, with whom he had a daughter, Wanda. He proved far more adept at writing poetry than providing for a young family, and after filing for divorce in 1927, set off for London. He managed to survive there with the aid of a few benefactors, and by making trips to Paris where he taught English, and had two books of poetry published. He also mingled with Polish aristocrats for the first time, and learned the language.

In 1931, Potocki put together a small book made up of his translations of a ribald poem by Rabelais, a parody of another by Verlaine, and a few risqué verses of his own, one of them entitled 'Here Lies John Penis'. He took the manuscript to a typesetter, intending to print it himself and distribute it among

friends. The typesetter took it to the police, and Potocki was arrested and charged with publishing an obscene libel. Fully expecting to be acquitted, he arrived at the Old Bailey for his trial wearing what had become his habitual garb — a cloak and sandals, and with his hair long. The Recorder of London, who was presiding, made little secret of his contempt for Potocki and his work ('these filthy poems') when instructing the jury, and he was sentenced to six months in prison. There was a great outcry about this verdict (after all, the poems had not even been published), but Potocki was badly let down by his supporters and barrister during the appeal, which was rejected. He was sent to Wormwood Scrubs to complete his sentence.

Potocki was devastated by this manifestly unjust treatment. Having been enchanted by England on his arrival, he came to loathe it. He became much more serious about his claim to the Polish throne (which was based on his descent from the last elected Polish king, Kazimierz IV, who abdicated in 1668), and had a magnificent crimson robe made for himself in Poland. He also became much more right-wing politically, and (for more obscure reasons) anti-Semitic. He bought a printing press and published his own pamphlets and an anti-democratic, pro-monarchist political/arts journal

called *The Right Review*. He openly supported Germany during the war, calling it a lesser evil than the Soviet Union. In 1940, having failed to appear in court after being charged with a blackout offence, Potocki and his French wife Odile (whom he had married in a pagan ceremony the year before) barricaded themselves in their flat when police arrived to arrest him. Despite the best efforts of Odile, who sprayed the police with pepper, they were soon overcome and imprisoned Potocki for two months in Wandsworth. His most important act during the war was the publication of a pamphlet about the massacre of thousands of Polish officers in the Katyn forest in 1940. The British government denied that their then allies the Soviets had committed this, and the truth was not generally known for many years. Fearing the pamphlet would lead to official retribution, Odile left him.

In 1947, Potocki left England and settled in Dragiugnan, France. So great had his aversion to England become that he refused to speak or think in English for several years. He lived in a hut, then a house which he slowly restored, grew olives and taught himself Sanskrit. In 1959, he received a letter from Susan Powys, the adopted daughter of the novelist T.F. Powys, in which she revealed that she was his daughter (her mother, Minnie, had been one of his pre-war lovers).

Susan, who changed her name to Theodora de Potocki, travelled to Draguignan to meet him, and he accepted her invitation to visit her and Violet, T.F. Powys' widow, in Dorset. He found them living in a large, squalid house overrun by cats, dogs and other animals. Wanting to do the right thing by Theodora, he spent six years and much of his money cleaning and restoring the house with the intention of selling it. Things ended badly, with the house failing to sell and Potocki mired in litigation with the Powys family, which was not resolved until 1971. He had printing presses in both Draguinan and Dorset, and continued to work tirelessly into his late eighties, issuing a stream of poems and idiosyncratic pamphlets.

In 1983, Potocki returned to New Zealand for the first time since 1927, and visited his daughter Wanda, who had been just two years old when he last saw her. In his final years, he grew frail and forgetful. His house at Draguinan was broken into, his possessions stolen and his papers trampled. The year before his death in a French nursing home, his cousin Stephanie de Montalk, who later wrote a sympathetic biography of him, managed to save much of his extensive archive and have it transported to New Zealand.

PRATT, DANIEL

(1809–1887)
'The Great American Traveller'

Pratt was born in Prattville (named after a more illustrious relative) in Massachusetts, and as a youth worked as a carpenter's apprentice, but threw this in and disappeared from the community. He reappeared about ten years later, having somehow transformed himself into a self-styled 'travelling encyclopedia, a universal genius, a library of facts'. Some were less than impressed by the transformation, calling him 'maggot-brained' or 'brainsick', but Pratt was in no doubt about his own brilliance. 'I am in possession,' he wrote, 'of a vast fund of genuine, sound faith, belief, knowledge, wisdom, understanding and judgment that will be worth more to the American Government than all the administrations [in] the last 106 years of American history.'

He became an inveterate pedestrian and lecturer on matters scientific, political and philosophical. 'The Great American Traveller,' as he styled himself, later boasted that he had walked over 200,000 miles, visiting twenty-seven states and making numerous trips to Washington. In his lectures, he spoke quickly and vociferously, words and concepts tumbling over each other.

He could move between subjects within a sentence, and many of the words he used were of his own devising. His talks often concerned the laws governing the universe, and had titles like 'The Solar System', 'Equilibrium', and 'The Vocabulaboratory of the World's History'.

As he moved from town to town, Pratt would seek out meetings — regardless of their nature — in the hope of taking the floor. He often spoke at colleges, especially in New England (long known as an area accommodating to eccentrics), and was invariably a hit with the students. Sometimes college authorities attempted to eject him, but the students would rally to his defence. While they occasionally played tricks on him (a student once set fire to his notes which, written on the back of a voluminous roll of wallpaper, flared up impressively), they usually applauded him lustily, blew horns and shook rattles in his honour, and liked to nominate him for president. Pratt did run for president on occasion, but he also campaigned on behalf of other candidates including Abraham Lincoln. He was once extremely put out when, having delivered some of his writings to Lincoln in the White House, they were returned with instructions that he send no more.

Pratt published a periodical called the *Gridiron*, issued broadsides and poetry, and claimed to have distributed over 200,000 pieces of literature (very few of which seem to have survived). A tall, thin, sun-bronzed fellow, usually dressed in a dilapidated top hat and rusty black suit, he stayed in cheap hotels when on the road, surviving on the proceeds of his talks and the kindness of strangers. In his last years, his legs seem to have failed him somewhat, and he rarely left Boston.

'*I will challenge the western world, take me for all in all, to beat me writing or speaking on the saving properties of human life and the universe.*'

DANIEL PRATT

PRICE, DR. WILLIAM

(1800–1893)
Archdruid of Wales

William Price was a contrarian of the highest order. He was a practitioner of alternative medicine, a political radical, an advocate of vegetarianism and free love, and a worshipper of nature who declared himself the Archdruid of Wales. He was also the man who introduced cremation to the British Isles.

The son of a clergyman, he was born in Rudry, Wales, and demonstrated his contrariness as a young man by walking around the countryside naked. After studying medicine at the Royal College of Surgeons in London, he returned to Wales and worked as a doctor for mining companies. He was appalled by the working conditions of the miners, and became a local leader of the Chartist movement for social reform. After being involved in a confrontation between Chartists and soldiers in the Welsh town of Newport, known as the Battle of the Westgate Hotel, in which twenty Chartists were killed, he was forced to flee to Paris, where he remained for seven years.

Price had long been interested in Druidism, the ancient Celtic religion apparently based upon the worship of nature. On a visit to the Louvre one day, he noticed a precious stone engraved with a figure of a man calling to the moon, accompanied by an inscription nobody had been able to decipher. Price realised that it was Druid script, and moreover it was addressed to him, being a message from the last Archdruid of 2,000 years before, appointing him as successor.

Apart from fragmentary accounts by ancient Greek and Roman writers, including Julius Caesar, almost nothing is known about the original Druids, so anyone claiming to be a latter day Druid has considerable scope for formulating beliefs and rituals. As Archdruid, Price adopted a striking costume of white tunic, scarlet waistcoat and green trousers. He wore his long hair in plaits, and had a hat fashioned from a fox skin, so that the head was perched on top of his, the legs dangled in front of his face, and the tail hung behind. He usually conducted his rituals at a boulder known as the Rocking Stone in Pontypridd, providing considerable entertainment for the locals as he addressed Druidic incantations to the moon.

Price continued to practise as a doctor. While he had a reputation as a brilliant surgeon, he despised conventional medicine, favouring herbal remedies. He also refused to treat anyone who smoked. He disliked lawyers as much as doctors, and became quite litigious in his later years. During one court case, in which he was trying to prove that his late father had been of unsound mind when disposing of a portion of his estate, he had the corpse exhumed so that the skull could be examined for evidence of madness (which he duly found, although other doctors disagreed).

Marriage was another institution Price despised. He had many lovers during his long life, mainly young women, and fathered many children. When he was eighty-five, his mistress Gwenllian Llywelyn gave birth to a boy who was named Iesu Grist (Welsh for Jesus Christ). When he died at the age of five months, Price announced that he was going to have him cremated, a practice then unknown in Britain. A hostile crowd disrupted the ceremony, the baby's half-burned body was dragged from the fire, and Price was arrested. He later defended himself in court, arguing that burials were wasteful and polluted the land, and in any case there was no law against cremation. The judge agreed, and cremations were soon taking place throughout Britain.

Price and Gwenllian went on to have a daughter, and a second son, also named Iesu Grist. Two years later the Archdruid died at the age of ninety-three, after asking for a glass of champagne, his usual remedy when feeling ill. 20,000 people turned up to see him cremated. ▣

PYKE, GEOFFREY
(1893–1948)
Inventor

Pyke was the epitome of the eccentric scientist whose brilliantly original ideas were, alas, usually impossible to put into practice. He was the son of a Jewish lawyer, Lionel Pyke,

who died when he was five. He attended Wellington school, where he insisted on dressing as an Orthodox Jew and was bullied mercilessly. After two years of this his mother relented, and he was withdrawn from the school and given private tutoring. When World War I began he offered his services to the *Daily Chronicle* as a war correspondent. He managed to reach Berlin and began to compile reports, but after a few days was arrested as a spy. He was told he would be shot, but instead was interned. After almost a year, Pyke and an accomplice managed to escape and make their way back to England, where he was treated as a hero, gave lectures and wrote a book about his experiences.

Pyke married Mabel Chubb and they had a son, David. After the war, he made a fortune investing in commodities, and decided to use the money to start a school on progressive lines where David could be educated. Such schools, where children were treated with dignity and given the freedom to learn at their own pace, were popular at the time, with A.S. Neill's Summerhill being the best known. Pyke's school, Malting House in Cambridge, was one of the more radical in the freedoms it allowed, and was considered quite a success. Pyke had massively overextended himself in his investments, however, and in 1928 lost his

fortune almost overnight. He was forced to close the school, and soon after this Mabel left him.

Pyke spent the thirties dreaming up various schemes for the betterment of humanity. With war against Germany looming, he decided that a public opinion poll showing the majority of German people were against a war might make Hitler think again. As this poll would need to be conducted in secret, Pyke proposed sending students to Germany disguised as golfers, who could ascertain the views of the populace surreptitiously. Incredibly, about ten of these 'golfers' did make their way to Germany, but fortunately they were recalled before war was declared.

Pyke spent the war working as an ideas man for Combined Operations, a department of the War Office charged with taking the fight to the Germans in Europe. With his beard, scruffy attire and habit of working in bed, Pyke did not always endear himself to other military men, but he found a champion in Admiral Mountbatten, who became chief of Combined Operations in 1941. The schemes Pyke dreamed up included an invasion of Norway by soldiers in motorised sledges disguised as German officers' latrines, and a plan to transport men from ships to shore through pipes, but undoubtedly his wildest

idea, and the one for which he is most remembered, was Operation Habakkuk. This involved the construction of enormous ships made of frozen water mixed with wood pulp. This mixture, which Pyke dubbed 'Pykrete', was much more resistant to melting than pure ice, and as strong as concrete. Mountbatten was very taken with the idea, and (as he told the story at least) went to see Churchill about it. Finding him in his bath, Mountbatten tossed a cube of Pykrete into it, and Churchill was suitably impressed with its non-melting qualities. Roosevelt thought the idea had merit, too, and Pyke was sent to Canada to work on a prototype, but the war ended before any of the frozen battleships were deployed.

After the war, Pyke retired to a rented room in Hampstead. He continued to come up with ideas, and invested a lot of time working on pedal-powered trains, trucks and other vehicles, but it seems that he had become disillusioned with a humanity that had rejected so many of his ideas. One night, he shaved off the beard he had worn all his adult life, swallowed a bottle of pills and died. ✦

RACUYAL, PASCUAL

(fl. 1930s–1980s)
Perennial candidate

Racuyal, an engineer, ran as a presidential candidate in every election in the Philippines from 1935 to 1986. Among his policies were:

❖ The building of plastic roads to save on wear and tear and allow recycling.
❖ Manila encased in huge plastic bubbles to reduce the temperature and increase productivity.
❖ Adoption of a new thirty-day-a-month, thirteen-month-a-year calendar, with the thirteenth day of each month named 'Jehovah'.
❖ The United Nations General Assembly moved to Baguio City.
❖ The use of 'algebraic-geometric detection' to eliminate government corruption.
❖ Lightning helicopter raids against gangsters and other criminals throughout the Philippines, led by Racuyal himself.

Despite such policies, and the admirably hands-on nature of the last one in particular, Racuyal never gained more than a handful of votes. He was forced to abandon his last run for office, in the 1986 election that pitted Ferdinand Marcos against Corazon Aquino, when the electoral commission declared him a 'nuisance candidate'.

For other perennial candidates, see ☞ Mitsuo Matayoshi and ☞ Nicolás Zúñiga y Miranda. ▣

RAËL (CLAUDE VORILHON)

(b. 1946)
UFO contactee

The future Raël, messenger of the Space Brothers and founder of the Raëlian Movement, was born Claude Vorilhon in the village of Ambert, near Vichy, France. He was the son of a fifteen-year-old farm girl, Collette Vorilhon, and a French Jew, Marcel, from the Alsace region of Germany.

The young Vorilhon's great loves were music and car racing. Arriving in Paris in 1961, he sang in streets and cafés. He was picked up by a producer and had a hit record in 1966 under the name Claude Celler, but his pop career ended when the producer committed suicide. Vorilhon married, had two children, and started a car racing magazine, then began to race competitively. As with his singing career, he was moderately successful. However, it would be for travelling in another sort of vehicle that Vorilhon found fame.

According to the account in his first book, *Le livre qui dit la vérité* ('The Book That Tells the Truth'), on 13 December 1973, Vorilhon drove to the volcanoes overlooking Clemont-Ferrand in central France. Climbing to one of the craters, he saw a fog, and then a flying saucer descending silently. A figure 1.2 metres (four feet) high, with almond-shaped eyes and long black hair emerged. The alien invited Vorilhon into the spacecraft, and told him that he had been chosen to tell humans 'the truth about what they are, and what we are'. Over the next few days, he gave Vorilhon a radical reinterpretation of the Bible. He said that the Hebrew word 'Elohim', usually translated as God, is plural and means 'those who came from the sky'. The Elohim, who live on a distant planet, are much more advanced in science and technology than us. 25,000 years ago, they came to Earth and set up laboratories in which they created plants, animals and then humans.

The alien gave Vorilhon a new name, 'Raël', which means 'light of the Elohim'. His job is to spread the word about the Elohim and work for world peace and the elimination of nuclear weapons. Should sufficient progress be made, the Elohim will return and bestow on humans their scientific knowledge, including the secrets of immortality. In expectation of this happening, Raël's other task is to build an embassy where the Elohim will stay after their arrival.

Word of Vorilhon's encounter spread through French UFO circles. Hundreds wrote to him and attended his public meetings, and the Raëlian Society was founded in 1975. By then, Raël had experienced a far more dramatic encounter with the Elohim. In his second book (English title: *Extraterrestrials Took Me to Their Planet*), he describes how the alien from his first encounter appeared again, revealed that his name was Yahweh, and took Raël to his planet, where 8,400 resurrected humans from Earth were living, including Moses, Jesus, Elijah, Muhammad and Buddha. Raël saw that their life was an easy one, with all the work done by 'biological robots', and most went around naked. There were no families on the planet, Yahweh explained, and men and women lived in equal relationships (although some decided to live with robots designed to their specifications). Raël watched a clone of himself being made, then was shown six models of female robot, including a black woman and a Chinese woman. Unable to decide which one he liked the most, he ended up in a bath with all six.

Yahweh told Raël that the Jews were the product of the Elohim mating with Earth women, so the embassy to welcome them should be located in Israel. If Israel refused, Yahweh said, it would be destroyed. He also revealed that the man named Marcel had not really been Raël's father. In fact, his mother had been transported by the Elohim from her farmhouse to a spacecraft, impregnated, then had her memory of it erased. Yahweh was Raël's true father, and Jesus his brother.

Raël tells his followers that, if they are judged worthy, the Elohim will resurrect them after death by cloning. His teachings on morality are based on his experiences on the Elohim's planet. He advocates free love and sexual experimentation. Raëlian meetings are characterised by music, meditation, nudity, cross-dressing and overt displays of affection. Drugs, including caffeine, are banned, although the occasional glass of red wine is allowed — Raël is a Frenchman, after all.

After coming under attack by French anti-cult groups in the 1990s, Raël moved to Quebec. The Raëlians purchased an estate in Valcourt which houses UFOLand, a theme park with exhibits including a full-size model of the spacecraft that took Raël to the Elohim's planet, and a model of the proposed embassy, shaped like a donut with extensions. Building the embassy has proved problematic, however, with the Israeli authorities refusing Raël's requests for land to build it on, Yahweh's threats of destruction notwithstanding. In an attempt to appease them, Raël modified the original Raëlian symbol (a swastika inside a Star of David), but so far the Israelis have stood firm.

In 1998, Raël created 'The Order of Raël's Angels'. The women accepted into this will have the task of welcoming the Elohim and the prophets (Jesus, Buddha and the rest) when they arrive on Earth, and looking after their every need, including making love to them. The most attractive of them, the 'pink angels', are forbidden from having sex with anyone other than the Elohim or a prophet (which on Earth, for the moment, means Raël), although they are allowed to have sex with each other.

Raël has always courted publicity, and his biggest splash has been with cloning. In 1997, he started a com-

pany called Clonaid, headed by a French chemist, Dr. Brigitte Boisselier, which offered to clone embryos for $200,000, and announced that fifty Raëlian women had volunteered to become surrogate mothers. He was considered an important enough part of the human cloning debate to be invited to address a U.S. congressional hearing on it. He arrived wearing his trademark padded white suit, his thinning hair tied in a Samurai style top-knot, and spoke about the need for science to progress without hindrance from religion.

In December 2002, Boisselier held a press conference in Florida, and announced that a cloned baby named Eve had been born to an American woman. Bosselier promised that proof of this would be forthcoming, but by the end of January, she was back-peddling and saying she had lost track of the parents. That's the last anyone has heard of the cloned baby.

The Raëlians had ridicule heaped upon them, of course, but they had made the front pages of newspapers across the world. Raël had succeeded in the first half of his mission — to spread the word about the Elohim to anyone who might be interested.

Now he just needs to get that embassy built. ▣

RAMPA, T. LOBSANG
(1911–1981)
Mystic

In 1956, a remarkable book was published in England. *The Third Eye* was the autobiography of a Tibetan lama, one Tuesday Lobsang Rampa, who had entered a lamasery in Lhasa at the age of seven. It contained vivid descriptions of his spiritual training (which included learning how to astral travel), an encounter with a Yeti, and other incredible adventures. Its most startling chapter concerned a procedure Rampa underwent at the age of eight. A small hole was drilled in the centre of his forehead and a sliver of wood inserted into it. Rampa experienced a blinding flash and a searing pain. He was told that he would now see people as they really are. Looking around, he could see their auras, like golden flames. His 'third eye' had been opened.

It was certainly a wild story, but it was full of seemingly authentic detail, and the publisher, Secker & Warburg, was a reputable one. The book received mostly positive reviews, and became an instant bestseller. Inevitably, doubts were raised about its veracity. This was something that the publisher had clearly expected, for a note had been included in the book saying that the manuscript had been sent to twenty Tibetan experts

for verification, but their responses had been inconclusive. A group of Tibetan scholars hired a private detective, Clifford Burgess, to investigate the author and determine the truth. Burgess soon discovered that the author's real name was Cyril Henry Hoskins, he had been born in Plympton, Devon, and he had never been to Tibet in his life.

Hoskins was the son of a plumber, and helped with his father's business until his father's death in 1937. After that, he worked for a surgical instrument company, and as a clerk in a correspondence school. He had a deep fascination with the occult, and during the early 1940s, began telling people that he had been a flight instructor in the Chinese airforce. In 1948, he shaved his head, grew a beard, and changed his name to Dr. Carl Kuan-suo. He had delivered the first part of *The Third Eye* to publisher Fredric Warburg in person, telling him that he was also known as Rampa. The publisher was very suspicious, especially after Kuan-suo/Rampa failed a simple test in Tibetan, but he had an explanation for this. He said that during the war he had been interrogated by Japanese wanting information about Tibet, and in order to prevent himself from giving it, had used his psychic powers to block his knowledge of the language. Warburg eventually decided to accept the book.

Burgess tracked Rampa down to Dublin, where he was living with his wife San (or Sanya) and secretary Sheelagh Rouse. When his findings were printed in a newspaper, reporters besieged the house. But Rampa proved more than equal to this challenge to his integrity. Yes, he was the plumber's son from Plympton, and yet *The Third Eye* was also an accurate account, for what had really happened was that the lama's spirit had entered the body of the Englishman.

Rampa elaborated on this remarkable twist to the saga in his third book, *The Rampa Story* (1958). It seems that Cyril Hoskins had been deeply unhappy with his life, while Rampa, over in Tibet, was in need of a new body, his current one having been knocked about badly during the war. One day, Hoskins was up a tree attempting to photograph an owl, when a branch broke and he fell to the ground, hitting his head. While he was lying unconscious, an emissary from Tibet, travelling on the astral plane, arrived and put the idea of a swap to him. In return, Hoskins would be given a new body and have some of his karmic burden erased. After discussing the matter with his wife, Hoskins agreed, and a month later, Rampa and two assistants astral travelled to England.

The silver cord that connected

Hoskins' spirit to his body was cut and his spirit floated off (where it went, Rampa did not say). and Rampa entered Hoskins' body. He spent three days getting used to it, at which point the woman who was now his wife introduced him to the realities of life in postwar Britain — she told him to go down to the Labour Exchange and look for work.

The revelation that Rampa was actually Cyril Hoskins, or at least a resident in his body, had little or no effect on his book sales. *The Rampa Story* was followed by a further seventeen volumes, (including one, *Living With the Lama*, which was apparently the work of Rampa's cat, Mrs. Fifi Greywhiskers). They covered the gamut of what became known as 'New Age' beliefs — telepathy, UFOs, Atlantis, time travel, ancient wisdom.

In the late sixties, claiming continued harassment from the press, Rampa, his wife and secretary moved to Canada, where he spent the rest of his life. He continues to have loyal followers who believe that everything he wrote is true. ▣

REICH, WILHELM

(1897–1957)
Orgonomist

Reich was born in Galicia, then part of the Austro-Hungarian Empire. His father, Leon, who ran a cattle farm, was an authoritarian with a violent temper which his son inherited. His childhood was a sexually charged one. He recalled that, at the age of four, he watched his nursemaid having sex with her boyfriend, and asked her if he could 'play' at being her lover. He first had intercourse as early as the age of eleven, and shortly after this, discovered that his mother, Cecilia, was having an affair with one of his tutors. When Reich told his father about this, his mother committed suicide.

Reich served in the Austrian army during World War I. After the war he studied medicine and became interested in psychoanalysis. He met Freud in 1919, and began to practise as an analyst shortly afterwards. He rose quickly through the psychoanalytic ranks, and Freud remarked that he had 'the best head' in the Vienna Psychoanalytic Society. Some older analysts resented his success, and their enmity increased as Reich strayed from orthodox Freudian theory, particularly on the subject of sexuality. Freud, of course, traced many psychological problems in adults back to the 'Oedipus complex' and other sexual conflicts he claimed were common in childhood, but had comparatively little to say about what constituted normal sexuality in adults. Reich, on the other hand, developed the theory of 'orgastic potency'. He claimed that a healthy sex life — which he thought few people had — was essential to well-being, and achieving this should be the primary goal of psychoanalysis. Reich's fellow analysts mocked him as 'the prophet of better orgasms'.

During the 1920s, Reich became involved in left-wing politics, and joined the Communist Party. He believed that sexual and political oppression were inextricably linked, and devoted himself to what he called 'sex-political' work, giving talks on sexuality to working class groups and distributing sex education literature. Reich's efforts pleased nobody. The psychoanalysts disliked his political activities, the communists were suspicious of his calls for sexual liberation. In 1933, he was expelled from the Communist Party, and he was forced out of the International Psychoanalytic Organisation the following year. His marriage to another analyst, Annie Pink, with whom he had two daughters, also ended.

Since his days as a medical student, Reich had believed himself to be a man destined to make great discoveries. Settling in Norway, his researches took him far beyond conventional psychoanalysis. He became interested in the changes in electrical charge that occur in the human body in different states, especially states of anxiety and sexual pleasure, and broke a cardinal rule of psychoanalysis by insisting that his patients were nude or semi-nude during therapy. Despite his lack of experience in the natural sciences, he acquired a microscope and began to study microorganisms. He believed that he had discovered particles midway between non-living and living, which he called 'bions'.

Reich, as always, attracted a few devoted disciples, but he was ridiculed in the Norwegian press, and vilified after a (false) rumour went around that he was furthering his studies by observing mental patients having sex. He decided to move to America, and left Norway just before war broke out. He set up a laboratory in New York, but later moved his operations to an estate in Rangely, Maine, which he named Organon. In 1946, he married Ilsa Ollendorf, and they had a son, Peter.

Shortly before leaving Norway, Reich had made his most momentous discovery, the key, as he saw it, to life itself. While studying bions, he had noticed that some of them gave off a bluish light. From this, he postulated the existence of 'orgone energy', which permeates the universe and is present in all living things. It is orgone which makes the sky and the seas appear blue, and moves the planets and the stars.

Reich believed orgone was attracted to organic material and repelled by metals, and invented the 'orgone accumulator', a box constructed from alternating layers of organic and metallic material, which he claimed concentrated orgone energy from the atmosphere. He believed that short periods spent sitting in one had great benefits for many conditions and ailments, from burns to cancer (although he never claimed that the accumulator could cure cancer). He also believed that orgone density in the atmosphere is responsible for clouds and thunderstorms, and this led to 'cloudbuster' experiments, in which he used an orgone-generating device to create rain. When a panic over UFOs swept America in the early fifties, Reich decided that they were alien spacecraft powered by orgone energy.

Reich's colleagues noticed that he had become far more domineering after his arrival in America, and he grew increasingly infuriated when other scientists dismissed orgone energy as a fantasy. His state of mind can be seen in the title of a book intended for the general public, which he wrote during this period: *Listen, Little Man!*

In 1951, Reich began a series of experiments to determine whether orgone could counteract the effects of radiation. The results were not what he had expected. It seemed when orgone was exposed to radiation, it became what he called 'DOR' or 'deadly orgone energy'. Many of the workers at Organon became ill during the experiments (although each suffered different symptoms), and at one point the estate was completely evacuated. Reich had more to worry about than DOR, however. Since the late forties, the Food and Drug Administration (F.D.A.) had been investigating his activities, and in particular the orgone accumulators, which the Reichians had been renting out. After some perfunctory testing, and despite the fact that it could not find anyone who had used the accumulater who was dissatisfied with it, the F.D.A. declared it a fraudulent medical device, and in 1954, Maine's district attorney filed for an injunction preventing their distribution. When Reich refused to attend court, the injunction was granted, and in 1956, he was arrested and sentenced to two years in prison. F.D.A. agents invaded Orgonon, destroyed the boxes and burned Reich's books.

Reich died in his sleep in prison the following year. Since his death, few of his experimental results have been replicated, but then, very few people have tried to replicate them.

'*A person like me comes along
once every thousand years.*'
WILHELM REICH

RIDDING, ERNEST

(1927–2002)
'The Fridge Man'

Ernest (known to all as Ernie) Ridding was a bearded, gnomelike figure who lived in a ramshackle house in the Sydney suburb of Glebe. The house and front yard were perpetually filled with fridges and other electrical appliances that he had repaired, or was in the process of repairing, ready to give away to the poor.

Born in Victoria, Ernie never knew who his father was, and his mother died when he was very young. He was brought up in a Salvation Army boys' home. As a youth, he worked on farms around Victoria, honing his fixing skills on machines, vehicles, even animals. Ernie's methods as an amateur vet were unorthodox — he would anaesthetise horses by whacking them on the head with a lump of wood — but they got results.

In 1946, an altercation over a tractor with a farmer named Harben led to his being committed to Kenmore Mental Hospital. It only took a few weeks for Ernie's usefulness to be noticed, and he was put to work in the office. Here he was occupied filing and typing, and would greet new patients with a cheery 'Welcome to the Nuthouse!' He also set about trying to trace the relatives of his fellow patients, some of whom had not had visitors in twenty years. He was in the hospital for eighteen months, and while he remained angry at the police and doctors who had put him there, seems to have mostly enjoyed himself. When writing his name, he would add the letters 'L.L.M.,G.K.N.' to it — 'Legally and Lawfully Mad, Graduate of Kenmore'.

Ernie first became known to the public during the 1960s, when he began to work for the Reverend Roger Bush, who ran the Helping Hand Mission and had a newspaper column and radio show. Bush would request donations of appliances which Ernie would pick up, fix if necessary, then deliver to whoever needed them. Stories began to circulate about the irrepressible little man clad in shorts and barefoot all the year round. He said that some people would donate things just to get a look at him.

In 1972, Ernie set up his own 'mission'. Over the next thirty years he and a few volunteer helpers gave away over 3,000 fridges, as well as countless television sets, stoves and other household goods, and, in later

years, computers. A hand-painted sign at the front of the house read, 'Ernie's Charity Recycling. If you want to talk money — PISS OFF!' When his fame spread through newspaper articles and television reports, all sorts of people, not all of them poor, began turning up at his house looking for free white goods. All too often they rejected what was on offer (Ernie only worried about whether something worked, not what it looked like). He grew accustomed to such ingratitude.

Ernie ran for a seat in Parliament during the 1988 New South Wales state government election. He issued an eighteen-page manifesto which included policies such as 'RIDDING the land of poverty', 'RIDDING the State of Mental Institutions' and 'RIDDING our schools of backward pupils'. As Ernie said, even his name was useful. He only received 250 votes, but was pleased to have given people a choice. In the mid-nineties, he began to write an autobiography on a computer he had fixed. Reaching the present in 1997, he kept going, and the book, *Self-Portrait of a Nut*, became a stream-of-consciousness diary in which he recorded his auction purchases, the things he had given away, news events and philosophical musings. He distributed this ever-expanding memoir on computer disk.

Ernie was a proud lifelong

celibate, a vegetarian, and a firm believer in the value of fasting and imbibing one's own urine. In 1999, he was featured in an exhibition, 'Sydney Eccentrics, A Celebration of Individuals in Society,' held at the New South Wales State Library, and turned up for the opening night. In his last years, his eyesight was failing, and his doctor had prevailed on him to wear shoes for the first time in decades, but he remained admirably useful till the end. ▣

'Thank God for Madness, and the art is mastering it.'
ERNEST RIDDING

RIGAUT, JACQUES
(1898–1929)
Writer

It seems that Rigaut was a man who lived to die. A writer closely associated with the Dadaist and Surrealist movements in Paris, the theme of suicide is a constant in his writings, few of which were published in his lifetime.

Rigaut was the son of a department store buyer. As a young man, despite his poverty, he always dressed elegantly in well-cut suits. He projected an air of world weariness, and claimed that when his

ERNEST RIDDING

closest comrade was killed in front of him during World War I, he felt nothing. In one piece, he wrote, 'Try, if you can, to arrest a man who carries suicide in his buttonhole.' In another, 'Suicide should be a vocation. The blood circulates and demands a justification for its interminable journey.'

He kept a pair of dice in his pocket to help him make important decisions. Like ☞ Witkacy, he enjoyed disconcerting people in social situations. He never said hello or goodbye, and was known to scurry off in the middle of conversations.

Rigaut found employment as the secretary of Jacques-Émile Blanche, a fashionable portrait painter almost forty years his senior. It's hard to think of two more apparently different individuals than this pillar of the artistic establishment and the young and flippant Dadaist, but Blanche and his family had great affection for Rigaut, and he wrote a perceptive essay on him after his death.

Despite his claimed indifference to poverty, Rigaut was clearly fascinated by wealth. In 1924, he met a rich American divorcée in Paris. He moved to New York and they married in 1926, but the marriage only lasted a year. He stayed in America long enough to become an alcoholic and heroin addict, and returned to Paris in 1928. He sought treatment in a number of clinics, attempting to conquer his addictions, but failed.

'The General Suicide Agency', one of Rigaut's pieces published posthumously, is a prospectus for the eponymous 'state-run' company, giving the prices for various forms of suicide, from the most expensive (electrocution) to the most cost-effective (hanging). The Agency particularly recommends itself to those who have refrained from suicide for fear of 'making a mess of it'. The fastidious Rigaut was going to make no such mess. One day, having dressed immaculately, he placed a rubber sheet on the floor and a pillow against his chest to muffle the gunshot, and fired a bullet into his heart, using a ruler to ensure that his aim was true. André Breton, the arch-theorist of Surrealism, who also rhapsodised about suicide (although he would hardly have contemplated it for himself), saw it as a consummate Surrealist act. 'Jacques Rigaut sentenced himself to death at about the age of twenty,' he wrote 'and waited impatiently for ten years, ticking off the hours, for exactly the right moment to put an end to his existence.' ▣

RIZZOLI, A. G.

(1896–1981)
Dream architect

Achilles Rizzoli was one of five

children of Innocente and Erminia Rizzoli, who migrated to America from an Italian-speaking region of Switzerland in the 1890s. In 1915, Rizzoli's father disappeared (twenty-one years later his body would be found in dense woodland — he had apparently shot himself), and over the next few years, his siblings married or moved away. In 1933, Rizzoli and his mother moved into a small house in Marin County, California, where he would live the rest of his life. He slept in his mother's bedroom, in a cot at the foot of her bed, and continued to do so after her death in 1936.

As a teenager, Rizzoli studied engineering and joined an architect's club. He wrote stories about architects, which were rejected by magazines, and a novel, *The Colonnade* (under the pseudonym Peter Metermaid). He had 3,000 copies of this printed, but never distributed them. He worked at various jobs, and in 1936 found a permanent position as a draughtsman with a San Francisco architectural company, where he worked diligently for forty years.

Rizzoli was a shy individual, and after the death of his mother withdrew further into himself, rarely leaving the house except to go to work or Sunday mass. He began to spend his evenings and weekends creating a series of beautifully

executed, large scale architectural drawings. Some of these were 'symbolisations' of people he knew and admired, literally people drawn as buildings — his beloved mother, for example, was represented as a vast gothic 'Kathedral'. Other buildings were intended to be part of an imaginary exposition, an ideal city called the Y.T.T.E. (which stood for Yield To Total Elation). In conceiving this, Rizzoli had clearly been inspired by the Panama Pacific International Exposition, a remarkable world's fair held in San Francisco in 1915, which featured a number of temporary buildings including a Tower of Jewels forty-three storeys high.

At first glance, Rizzoli's drawings look like they could be of real buildings, albeit grandiose ones, exhibiting a mix of ancient and modern styles. They are meticulously drawn and decorated with official looking emblems and scrolls. A great deal of carefully lettered text has usually been added — descriptions, slogans ('Now there's no more any longer any reason for feeling lonely') — technical notes, poems, and the names of Rizzoli's (imaginary) sponsors and collaborators. Rizzoli's writings bristle with anagrams, odd constructions and invented words, so that his meaning is not always clear. He also drew up a number of 'plot plans' showing the layout of the buildings in the Y.T.T.E., which he imagined would be located on an island. At its centre would be a statue, the Tower of Life, surrounded by four buildings representing the four seasons, called the Eagerray, the Nevermine, the Roomiroll and the Tootlewoo.

Other buildings (of which there were almost a hundred) were the Fortress Moderne, the Vitavoile of Happiness, the Bug of Debauchery, the Laboratory of Experimentation, the Bossiroam and the Pen of Bestiality (where, a note informs us, 'the sordid and brutal is to be practised'). Rizzoli's work is not without conscious humour — one of the bathrooms in the complex is called the Acme Sitting Station (or A.S.S.). He was keen for others to see these creations, and between 1936 and 1940, opened his house for an exhibition on the first Sunday in August, called 'The Achilles Tectonic Exhibit'. Only a few local children and some of Rizzoli's friends and co-workers attended.

Rizzoli lived frugally, spending most of his money on art supplies. He was extremely naïve sexually, and did not see female genitalia until he accidentally glimpsed a neighbour's child at play when he was forty. This was a momentous experience for him, and was commemorated in a number of drawings, including one of an enormous phallic skyscraper entitled 'The Primalglimpse at Forty'.

Several subsequent drawings debate the virtues of 'phallism' versus virginity, but in the end, Rizzoli remained a virgin.

He stopped making plans for the Y.T.T.E. in 1945, and from then until 1957 laboured on a prose work now mostly lost. His head was increasingly filled with visions, and to record them he embarked on his third and last great project, the A.C.E. (which stood for, among other things, Acme of Christian Endeavor). This was a mixture of prose, poetry and illustration, executed on around 325 large sheets of vellum. His spiritual collaborators included Christian saints and saints of his own invention, historical figures, artists and eminent architects (some of whom offered criticism as well). He came to realise that the A.C.E. was nothing less than the third testament of the Bible. Sometimes he despaired that God had given him such a task — 'All this, expected of one man to do, is simply outrageous.'

He was working on a section of the A.C.E. entitled 'Rest in Peace' when he suffered a stroke that left him paralysed and speechless, and he died in a nursing home four years later. His works were fortunately saved by his family, and stored in a garage. Their discovery in 1990 caused a sensation in 'outsider art' circles, and a travelling exhibition organised by the San Diego Museum began in 1997. As with  Henry Darger, a strange, rich and comprehensive world had survived which could so easily have been lost. ▣

ROBERTSON, JAMES

(d. 1790)
'The Daft Highland Laird'

Robertson, of Kincraigie, Scotland, was a fanatical Jacobite. (The Jacobites supported the restoration of the Stuart line to the thrones of England, Scotland and Ireland, after the last Stuart king, James II, was deposed during the Glorious Revolution of 1688.) Robertson fought in the rebellion mounted by James II's grandson, Charles Edward Stuart, a.k.a. Bonnie Prince Charlie, in 1745, and was thrown into the Tolbooth jail in Edinburgh. Here he enjoyed himself so much, and was full of such extravagant praise for the pretender to the throne, that he earned the nickname 'the Daft Highland Laird'. His jailers judged him to be harmless though, and released him.

His family, deciding he was mad, arranged for his younger brother to take control of their estate. Robertson was more upset about being out of prison. His dearest wish was to be a martyr for the cause of Jacobitism — to be whipped, or hanged or, best of all, beheaded. He did his best to be

arrested again, spouting treason in the streets and drinking loudly to the health of Bonnie Prince Charlie, but the authorities merely looked on with amusement. Growing more desperate, he stopped paying rent to his landlady and urged her to bring suit against him. She obliged and he was arrested and imprisoned, but alas, his friends paid his debt. Robertson refused to budge until two soldiers of the Town Guard arrived at his cell one morning and told him they had come to escort him to the courthouse for his treason trial. Overjoyed, he followed them out of the prison, but once he was in the street the door was shut and the soldiers abandoned him to his unwanted freedom.

Frustrated in his attempts at martyrdom, Robertson took up other pursuits. Having a knack of carving in wood, he began to fashion the heads of notable persons of the day, painted them and stuck them on the ends of sticks. Those he disliked, including the King and his ministers, would be mercilessly caricatured. Sometimes he affixed more than one head to the stick in ironic juxtaposition, placing, for example, the noble features of some worthy gent beside the wizened face of that other notable Edinburgh character of the day,  'Bailie Duff'. Robertson would walk around the streets holding his

wooden heads aloft, and people would come up to him, eager to see who was being lampooned that day. A robust, handsome fellow, he could often be seen debating political issues in the lobby of Parliament House, and though many considered him feebleminded, he was also known for his biting wit. Children called him 'Laird o' Totums', due to his habit of giving them teetotums (spinning tops) and other toys that he had carved. ▣

ROCHE, JOHNNY

(d. 1884)
Builder of 'Castle Curious'

Roche, who was born in the early nineteenth century, was a native of Wallstown near Castletownroche, Ireland, and had a reputation for being able to make just about anything. A blacksmith by trade, he migrated to America with his wife around 1840, but returned to Ireland a few years later (minus the wife and the fortune he had hoped to make there). He built a mill (originally used to process flannel and later corn), sculpted busts of the local gentry, carved tombstones, made and repaired musical instruments like fiddles, and was a sought-after dentist (his specialty was false teeth fashioned from cow hooves). He also made his own clothes, shearing his sheep for the wool and even making the buttons.

Roche's greatest creation was the three-storey tower, forty-five feet (13.7 m) tall and complete with turrets and crenellations, which he built on a bank of the River Awbeg over three years from 1867 to 1870. 'Castle Curious,' as it became known, was constructed with stones and sand from the river and lime from nearby Mallow, and Roche is said to have built it single-handed, using only the most rudimentary tools and a donkey to haul the lime. He also sculpted gargoyles for the walls, carved the huge oak front door, and made all the interior fittings and furniture. On completion, Roche moved into his castle, which had numerous rooms laid out in haphazard fashion. He had his blacksmith's shop on the ground floor, and liked nothing better than to ascend to the top of the southern turret and blow a horn.

Roche wrote his own epitaph: 'Here lies the body of poor John Roche, He had his faults but don't reproach; For when alive his heart was mellow, An artist, genius and comic fellow.' He also built a tomb for himself. It was on a little islet in the middle of the river, across from the castle, and was in the shape of an aeolian harp. Apparently the local coroner put a stop to his plans though, telling him, 'Go, rest thy bones in Mother Earth and don't pollute the river.'

Castle Curious still stands, albeit in a dilapidated and roofless state. In 2009 it was put up for sale with an asking price of €160,000.

RODIA, SIMON (SAM)

(1879–1965)
Creator of the Watts Towers

'I was going to do something big and I did it,' said Rodia. His real name was Sabato Rodia, and he was born in a village near the town of Nola in southern Italy. He migrated to America in the 1890s, his elder brother having made the trip a few years previously, and held down various jobs, including labourer, logger and construction worker. He was usually known as Sam to his friends (the name Simon, which now seems inextricably linked to him, derives from an erroneous 1937 newspaper report). In 1902, while living in Seattle, he married Lucy Ucci, and they had two sons, and a daughter who died young. After a while, his heavy drinking proved too much for his wife, who left him, taking their sons with her, and they divorced in 1912. In 1917, he moved to Long Beach, California. Four years later he bought a triangular block of land in the Watts district of Los Angeles, and at some point in the 1920s

began the construction of his great work, which he called 'Nuestro Pueblo' ('Our Town'), but which is now known as the Watts Towers.

As its name suggests, Rodia's creation is dominated by seven towers, the tallest of which is 99.5 feet (twenty-nine metres) high. They were fashioned from steel bars and pipes which he joined together without the use of bolts or welding equipment, then covered with chicken wire and cement. He laboured on them whenever he had spare time from construction jobs, day and night and regardless of the weather. He used only simple tools, and worked without plans or even scaffolding, a greasy fedora on his head and his arms caked with cement. The design of the towers, although intuitive, is elegant and ingenious (the famed architect and designer Buckminster Fuller called Rodia 'a natural engineering sculptor'). The other structures he built in his 'town' include a gazebo, birdbaths, fountains, a ship ('the Ship of Marco Polo') and an outdoor oven. All are decorated with tiles and found objects — broken crockery, green and blue bottles, teapot spouts, seashells and china figurines. With their organic structure, and skin of tiles and broken crockery, the towers are reminiscent of the work of ☞ Antoni Gaudí. When shown a photograph of Gaudí's

SIMON (SAM) RODIA

Sagrada Familia once, Rodia asked, 'Did this man have help?'

The Watts district changed at the beginning of World War II. Most of the poor whites and Hispanics with whom Rodia was friendly moved out, and black workers moved in as industry geared up for the war effort. Rodia, an anarchist, hated the industrialisation and the war. There were rumours that his towers were being used to transmit radio messages to America's enemies in Japan, and his neighbours encouraged their children to vandalise his handiwork and throw garbage over his walls. After a while, Rodia was worn down by their attitude, and he was also growing old. He ceased to add to the structures in the mid-1940s, concentrating instead on refining their decoration. In 1954, after possibly suffering from a stroke, he gave the deed to his property to a poor neighbour, packed up his things and walked away. He never saw the towers again.

The neighbour soon sold the property to a man named Montoya, who had plans to build a Mexican restaurant on it, but these were thwarted when, in 1957, the City of Los Angeles issued a demolition order on the site, calling the towers a hazard. Two years later, without telling them about the order, Montoya sold the site to two men, Nicholas King and William Cartwright, who appreciated its significance and wished to preserve it. King, Cartwright and others formed a committee to save the towers. A hearing was held at which engineers testified to their structural soundness, and it was agreed that a test should take place. During the test, a lateral force of 10,000 pounds (4,540 kg) was applied to the tallest tower, but this did not even crack the cement on it (in the end, it was the testing equipment that buckled under the strain). The demolition order was cancelled and, after restoration, the site was opened to the public in 1960. The following year, Rodia, who was now living quietly with members of his family in Martinez, California, was persuaded to attend a conference on the towers at Berkeley University, and was given a rapturous reception.

For other DIY monument builders, see ☞ Ferdinand Cheval, ☞ Leonard Knight, ☞ Edgar Leedskalnin and ☞ Justo Martinez. ▨

ROKEBY, MATTHEW ROBINSON, (LORD)

(1713–1800)
Aquatic nobleman

Matthew Robinson developed his great love of being submerged when visiting the baths at Aix la Chappelle in France as a youth.

The son of a gentleman usher of King George II, he studied at Trinity College, Cambridge, and in 1754 inherited his father's estate, Mount Morris in Kent. He served as a member of Parliament for Canterbury, impressed many with his integrity and independence of mind, and was a great champion of personal liberty. He retired from Parliament in the 1880s, citing ill health as the reason, and thereafter spent most of his time indulging in aquatic pleasures.

At first he was satisfied by daily trips to the coastal town of Hythe, where he had a hut built for himself on the beach. He always walked the three miles (4.8 km) there and back, accompanied by a carriage and a liveried servant walking behind him (if it rained, Robinson would insist on the servant riding in the carriage, while he would continue to walk). On reaching the sea he would plunge into it, and often remain in it so long that he fainted and had to be dragged out. Convinced of the health-giving properties of water, he had a series of fountains built along the road between Mount Morris and Hythe. Whenever he saw anyone drink from them, he was so pleased he would drop a few coins in their hands.

Later, Robinson had a bath-house built adjoining his home, with glass ceiling and walls so that the water could be heated by the sun. Robinson spent much of his day in this bath, even eating his meals in it. His diet mainly consisted of beef tea — a suitably watery repast.

In 1794, after the death of his uncle, the Bishop of Armagh, he inherited the title Lord Rokeby. By now, he was known not just for his watery habits, but for his beard, which was then a great rarity. In fact, he was described as 'the only peer, and perhaps the only gentleman, in Great Britain, who has been distinguished in modern times by a venerable and flowing beard'. Rokeby's beard was, indeed, a magnificent thing. It reached to his waist and was so voluminous it could be seen from behind, while he could tuck the ends of his moustache behind his ears. Once, late in life, when Rokeby travelled to a nearby town to vote in an election, a crowd gathered around him after he was mistaken for a Turk. At least he did not suffer the persecution faced by ☞ Joseph Palmer in America, where beards were similarly out of fashion.

Rokeby was a nature lover who let the 800 acres (324 hectares) of his estate run wild. He never fenced the land or planted anything, but the black cattle and sheep that grazed on his land thrived nevertheless. He hated churches, believing the proper place to worship God was in the fresh air. He hated doctors too, refused to take medicine, and died at the age of eighty-nine.

ROLFE, FREDERICK (BARON CORVO)

(1860–1913)
Writer & fantasist

This would-be priest, dubious Italian nobleman, aesthete and homosexual had a prodigious fantasy life which he channeled into his best-known work, the remarkable novel *Hadrian the Seventh*. Born in Cheapside, London, Rolfe was the eldest son of a piano maker fallen on hard times. Although he left school at fifteen, he initially worked as a teacher, and after converting to Roman Catholicism, was sponsored by the Bishop of Shrewsbury to train for the priesthood at St. Mary's College, Oscott, in 1887. His fellow students found him an aloof character, fond of fine clothes and Meerschaum pipes, who seemed far more interested in painting than his religious studies. Having run up large debts (it would become a lifelong habit) he was expelled from the college after less than a year. Unwilling to relinquish his dream of the priesthood, he obtained another sponsorship in 1889 to study at the Scots College in Rome, but this too ended with his expulsion. Rolfe never did take holy orders, but later abbreviated his name to 'Fr. Rolfe' to suggest that he had.

Rolfe's time in Rome wasn't entirely wasted. He was befriended by an elderly, English-born Catholic woman, the Duchess of Sforza-Cesarini, who gave him an allowance and bestowed on him, or so he claimed, an estate which entitled him to call himself Baron Corvo ('corvo' is Italian for raven). He also soaked up enough Italian history and atmosphere to write a book about the Borgias a few years later. Returning to England in 1890, he painted fresoes in a Hampshire church, ran up more debts and left under a cloud after being involved in dodgy negotiations to buy a house. Moving to Aberdeen in Scotland, he worked as a tutor briefly, and concentrated on another hobby, photography, experimenting with colour and underwater photography, and claiming to have invented a new method of taking photos using artificial light. Attempts to solicit funds from various eminent Catholics failed, and he fell so far behind in his rent that he was physically ejected from his boarding house (while still in his pajamas).

He then turned up Holywell, Wales, where he adopted the name of Austin. He was commissioned to paint church banners, but fell out

with his employer, Father Beauclerk, when he demanded an exhorbitant fee for his work. These years culminated with two vitriolic articles attacking Rolfe's character which appeared in the *Aberdeen Free Press* in 1898 and were reprinted in various Catholic papers. Rolfe, who had a knack of making enemies, became convinced there was a full-blown Catholic conspiracy against him.

Having failed to make a living as painter and photographer, Rolfe focused his energies on writing. The first of his 'Toto' stories, in which a young Italian peasant tells folktales about the Catholic saints, appeared in the famed aesthetic journal *The Yellow Book* in 1895 under the name Baron Corvo, and were later collected in the book *Stories Toto Told Me*. He followed this with the highly idiosyncratic but evocative *Chronicles of the House of Borgia* (1901), while his masterpiece, *Hadrian the Seventh*, appeared in 1904. It opens with impoverished Englishman George Arthur Rose (closely based on Rolfe) receiving a visit from a cardinal and bishop, who tell him the church made a terrible mistake when it failed to accept him as a priest years earlier. Ordained by the cardinal, he is whisked off to Rome where a papal conclave is trying to decide who will be the next pope. Rose, proposed as compromise candidate, is elected, and takes the

name Hadrian VII. The rest of the novel records his attempts to reform the Church (which include selling off its treasures) and generally saving the world, and ends with his assassination by a disgruntled Irishman. Like Rolfe's other books, *Hadrian the Seventh* is written in a highly mannered style, with many words of his own invention, and contains numerous thinly veiled portraits of his friends and enemies. The book is, of course, inherently implausible, yet Rolfe's dream of finding glory within the Catholic Church was so heartfelt that it has an odd conviction. It failed to sell though, as did another novel, *Don Tarquinio*, and Rolfe made no money from either book.

With his debts mounting, Rolfe accepted an offer from a friend, R.M. Dawkins, to accompany him on a holiday to Venice. Dawkins left him in the city with a little money, which eventually ran out. Rolfe remained in Venice for the last five years of his life. He spent his time swimming, rowing (he unsuccessfully applied to become a gondolier) and writing caustic letters to former friends he now considered enemies (the fact was that Rolfe was his own worst enemy — and an implacable one). Having finally given up the idea of becoming a priest, he also abandoned celibacy. He eagerly seduced young boys, and wrote a

series of explicit letters to an acquaintance in England, extolling the pleasures that Venice offered a keen homosexual. When he had a little money he stayed in a hotel, but he also slept in a boat, or in the open, and often went without food for days. He died suddenly one evening, after suffering a heart attack while taking off his boots.

Rolfe was almost forgotten after his death, but interest in him revived after A.J.A. Symons published his brilliant 'experiment in autobiography', *The Quest for Corvo*, in 1934. Many of his unpublished works were located and issued. *Hadrian the Seventh* is now considered a minor classic, and a stage version became a hit in the 1960s, even reaching Broadway. Such posthumous acclaim dwarfed anything this strange, tormented man achieved in his lifetime. ◉

ROS, AMANDA MCKITTRICK
(1860–1938)
Writer

Amanda Ros has often been called 'the World's Worst Writer', but the fact is that the only really bad writing is boring writing, and Amanda was never boring, in her writing or in her life.

She was born Anna Margaret

McKittrick in Ballynahinch, Northern Ireland. In 1886, she took up a post as schoolteacher in Larne, and the following year married the town's stationmaster, Andy Ross. In 1897, as a tenth anniversary present, Andy funded the publication of her first novel, *Irene Iddesleigh*. The author was listed on the title page as Amanda McKittrick Ros (she had taken the first name from a favourite novel, and shortened Ross to Ros because she thought it looked more aristocratic.) Amanda's unique style is evident from the book's first paragraphs.

Sympathise with me indeed! Ah, no! Cast your sympathy on the chill waves of troubled waters; fling it on the oases of futurity; dash it against the rock of gossip; or, better still, allow it to remain within the false and faithless bosom of buried scorn.

Such were a few remarks of Irene as she paced the beach of limited freedom, alone and unprotected. Sympathy can wound the breast of trodden patience, — it hath no rival to insure the feelings we possess, save that of sorrow.

The novel tells the story of Sir John Dunfern and his unhappy relationship with the eponymous heroine. Although she is secretly in love with her tutor, Oscar, Irene agrees to marry Sir John. Their relationship soon breaks down,

however, and Sir John suspects that her affections lie elsewhere. He confronts her in the novel's most famous scene.

'Can it be that your attention has ever been, or is still, attracted by another, who, by some artifice or other, had the audacity to steal your desire for me and hide it beneath his pillaged pillow of poverty, there to conceal it until demanded with my ransom?

'Speak! Irene! Wife! Woman! Do not sit in silence and allow the blood that now boils in my veins to ooze through cavities of unrestrained passion and trickle down to drench me with its crimson hue!'

Irene denies all, but when Sir John finds one of Oscar's letters, he has her imprisoned in a chamber where many of his family's lunatics have been locked up over the years. Irene escapes and travels to America with Oscar, but he takes to drink and dies. Years later, she returns to Dunfern Mansion. Sir John has died but she is greeted by their son, Hugh.

'False woman! Wicked wife! Detested mother! Bereft widow!

'How darest thou set foot on the premises your chastity should have protected and secured!'

Irene beats a hasty retreat and is found dead the next morning.

The first person to appreciate the novel's unique qualities was a humourist, Barry Pain, who penned a review entitled 'The Book of the Century'. As he read Irene, Pain wrote, 'its enormities went on getting more and more enormous in every line, the book seemed something Titanic, gigantic, awe-inspiring.'

Amanda could be one of the most vicious writers ever to pen to paper when roused. The preface to her second novel, *Delina Delaney*, is taken up with a blistering attack on 'This so called Barry Pain', who 'has taken it upon himself to criticise a work the depth of which fails to reach the solving power of his borrowed and, he'd have you believe, varied talent'.

Amanda's second novel tells the story of the noble Lord Gifford, the virtuous Delina Delaney and the villainous Madame-de-Mane. After it appeared, a number of Amanda Ros societies were formed, and she had a card printed which read, 'Amanda M. Ros, author. At home always to the honourable,' and played up her celebrity status. Each Sunday she travelled to church in a carriage drawn by a pony, attended by a young man in livery.

Amanda's literary career slowed down after this, mainly due to her involvement in protracted legal battles over a lime kiln and

other properties she had inherited. Amanda became so frustrated by the process — and the lawyers making money from it — that she took to protesting outside their offices, equipped with a toy trumpet to blow 'raspberries' on, while her first volume of poetry, *Poems of Puncture* (1913) includes a number of furious attacks on lawyers.

Amanda's husband Andy died in 1917. Four years later she married a farmer named Thomas Rodgers, and resumed writing a novel she had begun earlier, *Helen Huddleson*, but never finished it. She published one more collection of poetry and invective, *Fumes of Formation* (1933). Her belief in herself survived until the end, and she once wrote, 'I expect to be talked about at the end of 1,000 years.' ◉

'*My works are all expressly my own — pleasingly peculiar — and not a borrowed stroke in one of them.*'

AMANDA MCKITTRICK ROS

SAGAWA, ISSEI

(b. 1949)
Celebrity cannibal

Sagawa, the son of a company president, was born in Kobe, Japan. His cannibalistic fantasies began at the age of four or five with a nightmare in which he and his brother were being boiled in a pot. As he grew older, he became obsessed with the idea of eating a western woman — Japanese women, he would later explain, held no attraction for him. His first attempt to enact this fantasy came when, while a student of English literature at Tokyo's Wako University, he attacked a German woman in her room (she was able to fight the diminutive Sagawa off). The incident was covered up. Sagawa graduated in 1977 and, with financial help from his father, was able to continue his studies at the University of Paris.

In 1981, Sagawa met a twenty-five-year-old Dutch girl named Renee Hartevelt who was also studying in Paris, and fell in love with her. He paid her to give him German lessons and on 11 June, invited her back to his apartment. He declared his love for her, but she told him that she thought of their relationship as purely intellectual. She was reciting a poem in German to him when he picked up a rifle and shot her in the back of the neck, killing her. He butchered the body, eating various parts of it and storing strips of flesh in his refrigerator for later. 'Finally I was eating a beautiful white woman,' he wrote later in one of his meticulously matter-of-fact accounts of these events, 'and thought nothing was so delicious.' Two days later he was observed clumsily disposing of the remains of the corpse, which he had stuffed into two cardboard suitcases, and was soon arrested.

His father flew to Paris and hired the best defence lawyer he could find. Sagawa was subjected to psychological tests, and in 1983 the case against him was dropped on grounds of insanity. He was committed to a mental asylum in a Paris suburb but had only been there a year when, having branded him an untreatable psychotic, French authorities bundled him onto a plane and sent him back to Tokyo. Held in Matsuzawa Hospital, he underwent further tests which persuaded the hospital's superintendent that he was fit to stand trial. The Japanese police were taking a less than considerable interest in the case, however, and he was never formally committed. At the bidding of his father, he was released from the asylum.

Sagawa's story attracted the interest of Japanese intellectuals. A prominent playwright, Juro Kara, corresponded with Sagawa during his stay in La Sante prison following the murder, and turned his story into a novel that became a bestseller. Sagawa wrote his own novel about Renee's murder, *Kiri no Naha* ('In the Fog') while in prison, and has since written several more books. After his release, he was interviewed on television and featured in magazine photo-spreads. Intellectuals vied with each other over the real meaning of Sagawa. His cannibalism, opined one commentator, psychologist Shu Kishida, 'is an extreme form of the inherent admiration of every Japanese for the white race.' In 1991, Sagawa was allowed to travel to Germany where he put Renee's German lessons to good use on a television chat show.

Sagawa lives in a small flat in Tokyo where he writes film and restaurant reviews, and executes oil paintings of naked western women (a typical work shows a homogenous expanse of pale buttocks and limbs,

ISSEI SAGAWA

with a knife and fork tucked unobtrusively in one corner).

He has acted in films, too. He is still occasionally visited by foreign journalists, keen to interview this peculiarly Japanese national treasure. ▨

SATIE, ERIK

(1866–1925)
Composer

Satie was born in Honfleur, France. He studied at the Paris Conservatoire for several years but failed to graduate, and his relationship with the musical establishment remained an uneasy one. He began to make a name for himself as a composer with three limpid piano pieces supposedly in the style of Ancient Greek music, the *Gymnopédies*, the first of which was published in 1888.

Interested in esoteric subjects, Satie joined the French branch of the Rosicrucian Order, for which he composed ceremonial music. In 1892, tiring of the Rosicrucians, he founded his own church, L'Église Métropolitaine d'Art de Jésus Conducteur, or the Metropolitan Church of Art of Jesus the Conductor. The church, of which he was the sole member, issued a number of spirited edicts blasting Satie's enemies, including several music critics, and advocating the spiritual benefits of a life of poverty for artists (a subject

then close to his heart).

In 1895, after inheriting some money, Satie abandoned his church and bought twelve identical grey velvet suits, thus inaugurating the period of the 'velvet gentleman'. The money soon ran out and he moved to a one-room apartment in the outer Paris suburb Arcueil, where he lived for the next twenty-seven years. He supported himself as a cabaret pianist and composer of popular songs.

Satie believed that composers should never bore the public, and most of musical pieces are very short. He liked to give them absurd titles like *Dessicated Embryos*, *Genuine Flabby Preludes (For a Dog)*, and *Three Pear-shaped Pieces*, and often added whimsical notations to his scores. In his last two decades, Satie flitted through the various avant-garde movements without ever really joining any of them, although he was particularly associated with the Dadaists and Surrealists. His 1915 ballet, *Parade*, on which he collaborated with Jean Cocteau, was staged by Sergei Diaghilev's famous Ballets Russes company, with designs by Picasso.

Satie adopted a new persona, the 'bourgeois functionary', complete with conservative suit, bowler hat and umbrella. He claimed to eat only white foods (including eggs, rice, coconuts, animal fat, white cheese

and fish). In private he indulged in a curious hobby, drawing imaginary metal buildings on cards which he filed away in a cabinet. Sometimes he advertised these buildings for sale or rent in newspapers.

It seems that Satie only had one serious relationship in his life, a brief affair with a painter and former trapeze artist, Suzanne Valadon, which left him devastated when it ended. He led a largely solitary, orderly life. On his death, his friends ventured into his apartment for the first time. Inside they discovered two pianos, one on top of the other and set up so they could be played simultaneously; about a hundred umbrellas; six velvet suits left over from the 'velvet gentleman' period; and a number of unpublished compositions. These included *Vexations*, a piece consisting of 180 notes which were to be repeated 840 times. (Before playing it, Satie wrote, 'it would be advisable to prepare oneself beforehand, in the deepest silence, by serious immobilities.')

Satie was largely forgotten after his death, but underwent a revival in the 1960s. His short, simple pieces are now hailed as the forerunners of ambient, minimalist and any number of other experimental musics which have come after him. *Vexations* had its first public performance in New York in 1963, when a relay team of pianists, including John Cage and

John Cale, played it over eighteen hours. Whether Satie actually intended the piece to be played, or whether it was just his little joke, is not entirely clear. ▣

'My expression is very serious. When I laugh, it is unintentional and I always apologise, very politely.'

ERIK SATIE

SEABROOK, WILLIAM

(1886–1945)
Writer & adventurer

Seabrook, one of the most remarkable and enigmatic literary figures of the twentieth century, was born in Westminster, Maryland. As a young man, he went into advertising and was a great success at it, but in 1915 threw it all in to fight in Europe as a volunteer with the American Ambulance Field Service. His first published work was a short book about his section's experiences in some of the fiercest battles of the war.

After the war, he and his first wife, Katie, moved to New York where he became a journalist, writing quirky stories for Hearst's King Features Syndicate. They mixed in bohemian circles and Katie opened a café, but Seabrook again grew restless. In 1921, he set off for Arabia to gather material for a book.

Seabrook was a writer who felt incapable of writing about anything he had not personally experienced. He fell in with a Bedouin tribe, the Beni Sakhr, and developed a close relationship with its leader, Sheik Mitkhal Pasha. Seabrook lived with the tribe for months, adopting Arab dress and experiencing every aspect of their lives. He even took part in a *ghrazzu*, an armed raid to steal a neighbouring tribe's livestock. Mitkhal asked Seabrook if he wanted to join the tribe permanently, and he was tempted, but the violence of their lifestyle eventually persuaded him against it. Instead, he returned to New York and wrote a book, *Adventures in Arabia* (1927), which sold quite well.

Seabrook's next journey was to Haiti, where his ability to empathise with other cultures was again evident. Befriended by Maman Célie, an elderly priestess, he gained entry into the secretive world of voodoo, took part in ceremonies involving animal sacrifice and worshippers possessed by voodoo gods, and encountered zombies — supposedly corpses revived by sorcerers to act as slaves. (His first sight of them gave him a hell of a fright, but he soon concluded that they were 'nothing but poor ordinary de-

mented human beings'.) Seabrook's book about his trip, *The Magic Island* (1928), which introduced the word 'zombie' to popular culture, caused a sensation and was a huge bestseller, making Seabrook one of the most famous writers of his day.

The Magic Island was a hard act to follow, but Seabrook was sure a visit to Africa would provide suitably striking material. He spent a year on the Ivory Coast and saw many strange sights, but his trip was curtailed when he caught a fever that almost killed him. Having separated from Katie, he went to Paris where he was joined by his new lover, Marjorie Worthington, an artist and writer.

Seabrook began to write his African book, but he had a problem. One of his goals in Africa had been to witness and, if possible, take part in a cannibal feast. He had spent time with a cannibal tribe, the Gueré (whose chief, Mon Po, wore a French fireman's helmet), but they had not let him take part in such a feast. Determined to write about cannibalism from firsthand experience, Seabrook managed to acquire through a journalist friend, who in turn knew an intern at a Paris hospital, a pound of flesh from the corpse of a young workman killed in a traffic accident. Seabrook took it to the house of a friend whose cook was happy to prepare a meal

from it (having been told it was wild goat). As the meal was being served, two women arrived who, despite being vegetarians, thought they might try some. Marjorie (who describes the scene in her memoir about Seabrook) persuaded them not to, then went outside to be sick.

Seabrook's *Jungle Ways* (1931) was generally received well, if not his indulging in cannibalism. He described human meat as tasting like 'mature veal or young beef', but if you read the book carefully, he never says that he ate it in Africa.

Seabrook was making a lot of money from his books, and he and Marjorie moved into a villa on the Mediterranean. His sadistic sexual impulses (his particular kink was tying up women) were proving a strain on their relationship, however. He was also drinking heavily for the first time, and had enormous difficulty finishing a book about a trip to the Sahara. Feeling himself on the edge of a breakdown, he took a typically drastic step, asking his agent in New York to arrange for him to be put into a mental hospital. His vivid account of his stay in Bloomingdale, *Asylum* (1935), became his most acclaimed book. In it, Seabrook discusses the rough treatment he received, which included being hosed down, and being immobilised for hours on end, with grim humour. Marjorie surmised that his sadism

had turned to masochism.

After his release from the institution, he wrote one more bestseller, a study of the occult, *Witchcraft* (1940), containing some fascinating anecdotes about ☞ Aleister Crowley and ☞ Gurdjieff, both of whom he had known. He eventually went back to the bottle though, and Marjorie, to her great sorrow, was forced to leave him. He married again and had a son, but his alcoholism only grew worse. He died in a New York hospital after swallowing a bottle of sleeping pills. ◾

SHAGGS, THE

Betty Wiggin (b. 1950),
Dot Wiggin (b. 1948)
& Helen Wiggin (1946–2006)
Rock band

The Shaggs were the most unlikely, unusual and unintentionally creative band of the 1960s. Many find their music unlistenable, but for famed rock critic Lester Bangs, they were 'better than the Beatles'.

The Shaggs began with a prophecy. When he was young, Austin Wiggin Jr.'s mother made three predictions: he would marry a strawberry blonde, have two sons whom she wouldn't live to see, and daughters who would play in a band. When the first two of these came true, Austin, a mill hand in the small

THE SHAGGS

town of Fremont, New Hampshire, decided that his daughters, Dot, Betty and Helen, would fulfil the third . (a fourth daughter, Rachel, occasionally joined them on bass). While they had no ambitions to be in a band, they liked music, and thinking that it might ease the monotony of life in Fremont, went along with the idea (although it's clear they didn't have much choice). Austin gave them their name, and Dot came up with some rudimentary songs. The girls' dreams of a more exciting life were soon dashed, however, as their

father imposed on them a rigorous daily schedule of hours of band practice in the concrete-lined basement of their house, interspersed with callisthenics. When he came home from work every night, they had to play him the song they had been practising that day. This went on for years.

Austin organised gigs for them at an old people's home, then a regular spot at a Saturday night dance in Fremont's town hall. The local teenagers greeted their performances with derision, but there was so little

to do in Fremont they turned up anyway. Then, in March 1968, about a year after the girls got their instruments, and ignoring their protests that they were nowhere near ready, Austin herded them into a recording studio. 'I want to get them while they're hot,' he told the bewildered studio engineer.

The resulting album, *Philosophy of the World*, was released a year or so later (it seems that no one can remember exactly when). All twelve songs on it are originals penned by Dot, and describing them is not easy. Dot and Betty sing weird, fractured melodies over a background of atonal guitar while Helen clatters away on her drum kit, and sometimes it seems like they are performing different songs simultaneously.

The album opens with the title track, which deals with the impossibility of pleasing people, a song no doubt born of the hours of practice in front of a never-satisfied Austin.

Oh the rich people want what the poor people's got
And the poor people want what the rich people's got
And the skinny people got what the fat people want
And the fat people want what the skinny people's got
You can never please
Anybo-o-dy
In this world.

Other songs deal with Dot's straying cat (the engagingly named Foot Foot), her love of the radio, Halloween and how wonderful parents are ('Parents are the ones who really care'). A mood of resigned melancholy pervades most of these songs. The Shaggs are aware of the smallness of their horizons and long to escape them, but cannot quite bring themselves to.

I turned around and headed for home
I learned my lesson never to roam...

A thousand copies of *Philosophy of the World* were pressed, but 900 of them went missing in mysterious circumstances, making it an extremely rare and valuable item today.

The Shaggs continued to play gigs, and became reasonably competent musicians. Austin never lost his belief that they would make it big, and continued to exercise a Svengali-like hold over them. When Helen married her first boyfriend, whom she met at one of the Saturday night dances, she was too scared to tell him, and continued to live at home for three months after the wedding. When he eventually found out, Austin went after her husband with a shotgun. Helen was twenty-eight at the time.

In 1975, Austin died of a heart attack at the age of forty-seven. The Shaggs put down their instruments

and got on with their lives.

And that would probably have been that had not Terry Allen, a member of an eclectic rock band called NRBQ, discovered a copy of *Philosophy of the World* in the late 1970s and arranged for it to be re-released. It had bewildered write-ups in *Rolling Stone* and other publications, gathered a cult following, and was released on CD in 1997. The Shaggs were astonished by their latter day fame, which culminated with Dot and Betty travelling to New York in 1999 to play two gigs organised by NRBQ.

'The Shaggs are real, pure, unaffected by outside influences,' wrote Austin Wiggin in the liner notes to *Philosophy of the World*. 'Their music is different, it is theirs alone.' And this is clearly the quality that has endeared them to a whole new audience. ◙

SHAVER, RICHARD S.

(1907–1975)
Visionary

Richard Sharpe Shaver, creator of one of the twentieth century's most remarkable alternative realities, was born in Pennsylvania. His father was a restaurateur, his mother a writer for popular magazines. As a young man he held down a variety of jobs, including slaughterhouse worker and crane operator. After two failed marriages, he married a woman named Dorothy. Throughout these years, Shaver immersed himself in pulp science fiction, occult and mystical works, and the books of ☞ Charles Fort.

Shaver traced the genesis of his mythology to 1932, when he was working as a welder in Michigan, and found there was something peculiar about a particular welding gun. Whenever he held it, he could read the thoughts of his fellow workers. More disturbingly, he could hear the screams of women being tortured, and the screams seemed to be coming from inside the Earth. Eventually he was forced to quit the job. Details of his next few years are vague, although it seems that he spent some time in a prison or mental hospitals, or perhaps both.

In 1943, Shaver sent a letter to the science fiction magazine *Amazing Stories* which was read by its editor, Ray Palmer. It contained what Shaver said was an 'ancient alphabet' that had originated in Atlantis. This was basically a code which assigned a meaning to each letter of the alphabet, so that 'A' meant 'animal', 'B' meant 'existence', 'C' meant 'to understand' and so on. According to Shaver, applying the code would reveal the true meaning of any word. Palmer, who was always open to wild ideas, published the letter, and

was intrigued when many readers wrote to say they had used the code and it had worked. He asked Shaver for more material and received a 10,000-word piece entitled 'A Warning to Future Man'. Palmer re-wrote this in a more pulp friendly style and published it under the title 'I Remember Lemuria' in the March 1945 issue, which quickly sold out.

According to Shaver, thousands of years ago Earth was colonised by a race of aliens called Titans, who were far more advanced than us. They communicated telepathically, lived for thousands of years, and continued to grow throughout their lives so that they ended up hundreds of feet tall. To serve them, the Titans created a number of beings, called 'robots' although they were of flesh and blood, and humans are descended from one of these 'robot races'. All was going well until one day the sun began to emit 'detrimental radiation' which caused the Titans to age prematurely. To escape it, they went underground, excavating vast caverns to live in. When the radiation penetrated these, however, they decided to move to another planet. They left behind a great deal of their machinery, and some of the robots. Under the continued influence of the radiation, many of these became stunted creatures called 'deros' (short for 'detrimental robots'). These malevolent beings wage a

constant, unseen war against mankind using the Titans' abandoned technology. They have a variety of rays that they can point at people — rays which can kill, or hypnotise, or induce illusions, planting thoughts in people's heads which they take to be their own. Basically, everything bad that happens in the world can be traced back to the deros. (Shaver later claimed that a dero ray had induced Lee Harvey Oswald to assassinate President Kennedy, which is, as hollow Earth historian Walter Kafton-Minkel noted, 'perhaps the ultimate conspiracy theory.') The deros are also sexual perverts, who like to shoot themselves with sexually stimulating 'stim' rays, and kidnap women from the surface and sexually torture them. (This accounted for the screams that Shaver had heard.) Fortunately there are some robots, the 'integrated robots' or 'teros', who have withstood the effects of radiation, and fight to help mankind. Shaver had actually learned the whole incredible saga from a beautiful tero girl named Nydia, who had fallen in love with him.

Palmer published more 'Shaver Mystery' stories and found the circulation of his magazine soaring. Hundreds of people wrote letters, some of them recounting their own experiences with the deros and teros. Shaver clubs were even formed in some cities. Many older *Amazing*

Stories readers were outraged by all this, however, and soon after the June 1947 issue appeared, featuring nothing but Shaver material, the magazine's owners made Palmer call a halt to it. He went off to found his own magazine, *Fate*, and over the next few years was instrumental in pushing the idea that UFOs are alien spacecraft. He remained faithful to Shaver, too, publishing a journal devoted to him, *The Hidden World*, in the early sixties.

Shaver's critics have labelled his tales the delusions of a paranoid schizophrenic. Yet those who knew him personally have said that he exhibited no signs of mental illness, and his marriage to Dorothy, a fundamentalist Christian, was a long and happy one. Shaver himself was a materialist who sought hard evidence for his stories, and thought he had found it in intricate pictures and texts which he believed the Titans had left behind in certain rocks. He called them 'rock books', and however you sliced one of them open, the pictures were there. When others failed to see them, he developed a technique of projecting the patterns from thin slices of agate onto a screen and painting the details — complex scenes showing Titans and other strange creatures intermingled — to make them more apparent. Palmer published a book about the paintings in 1975,

and Shaver also sold them by mail order.

Since Shaver's death (from lung cancer), aficionados of 'outsider art' have rekindled interest in his rock art, and several exhibitions have been held. 🔲

SHIELDS, ROBERT
(1918–2007)
Diarist

In 1972, Shields, a former Protestant minister and high school teacher, decided to keep a diary. But not just any diary. This diary would record everything that happened to him — every experience, everything he saw, or ate, or thought, or read, or heard, in five-minute instalments.

Shields, who lived in Dayton, Washington, typed his diary in a small office at the back of his house. He limited himself to two hours sleep at a time, so he could write down his dreams. He recorded his trips to the bathroom (in detail), and the dosage of medications that he took. He pasted food labels and other ephemera onto the pages, even samples of his nose hair (in case someone in the future wanted to reconstruct his DNA). He admitted that the diary made him reluctant to travel anywhere, because catching up on it on his return took so long. 'Sometimes I wonder why I impose

it on myself,' he said in an interview on National Public Radio in 1994, 'and then I say: "well, I'd rather do this than nothing."' To stop it would be like 'turning my life off'.

The entry for 21 April 1994 reads in part:

2:10–2:25 I rested on the couch.
2.25–2:35 I checked on whether our county tax payment had been received. It had.
We were shuffling back and forth between the ledger, the study and the telephone.
2:35–3:00 I rested on the couch.
3:00–3:25 I read the Walla Walla Union-Bulletin. Matthew Franklin Eaton [20] of 704 Irene Street, Walla Walla, tried to take a baby from Walla Walla General Hospital. He assaulted four of the nursing staff, who held him for the police…
3:25–3:35 I was at the keyboard of the IBM Wheelwriter making entries for the diary.
I drank two cups of orange juice.
3:35–4:30 I prepared a 10-ounce tin of Campbell's vegetable soup and ate it with saltines as I read Mr. Lincoln's Army by Bruce Catton. I washed out the soup pan and a frozen food tray left by Cordelia.
4:30–4:35 I was at the keyboard of the IBM Wheelwriter making entries for the diary.

A stroke in 1997 prevented Shields from continuing the diary (for a while he tried dictating it to his wife, but her enthusiasm for this quickly flagged). After his death, the diary was donated to Washington State University, with the proviso that it would not be read for fifty years. Occupying ninety-four cartons and with an estimated length of 37.5 million words, it is thought to be easily the longest diary ever written. ▣

SIBTHORP, CHARLES
(1783–1855)
Politician

Colonel Charles de Laet Waldo Sibthorp was perhaps the most perfect reactionary that politics has ever thrown up, in Britain or anywhere else. A member of an old landed family and veteran of the Napoleonic wars, he was the Member of Parliament for Lincoln almost continuously from 1826 to 1855. During those years, he was infamous — and endlessly caricatured — for opposing absolutely anything new.

Prior to his entry into Parliament, Sibthorp declared that he was against 'any attempts to subvert that glorious fabric, our matchless Constitution, which has reached its present perfection by the experience of

ages, by any new-fangled schemes which interested or deluded individuals might bring forward, and those who expect any advantages from such notions will find their visions go like vapour and vanish into nothing'. Sibthorp was a man of his word, and for decades he railed against numerous 'humbugs', as he called anything new and therefore undesirable. They included the Reform Act of 1832, Catholic emancipation, the building of the National Gallery, and the coming of the railways, or the 'steam humbug', which he was convinced was a dangerous and passing fad. Sibthorp's fulminations on these and other subjects were invariably greeted with delight by his fellow parliamentarians on both sides of the house, for he was a colourful and inventive orator. He also looked the part, dressing like a Regency buck in green frockcoat and white trousers long after they had gone out of fashion.

Sibthorp's greatest enmity was reserved for foreigners, whom he believed were incessantly plotting and scheming to undermine Britain's morals and institutions. He was incensed by the very idea of the Great Exhibition of 1851, which brought the finest arts and crafts from across the world together in London, and lamented the trees cut down to make way for its glittering centrepiece, the Crystal Palace.

For Sibthorp, the whole thing was a dastardly plot to bring a lot of foreigners into the country

Ironically, the only real enemy that Sibthorp seems to have made during his long political career was the figurehead of the society he wished so passionately to preserve — Queen Victoria. On the eve of her wedding to Prince Albert, Parliament debated the size of the annuity to be paid to him. The figure of £50,000 had been proposed, but Sibthorp argued that this should be reduced to £30,000 — seeing as Albert was a foreigner. Perhaps to his own surprise, his motion was carried. The Queen never forgave him for this, and refused to visit Lincoln as long as he represented it. ▣

SINCLAIR, DONALD

(1909–1981)
The original Basil Fawlty

Sinclair was born in Ireland, and had a long career in the British Navy which included coming under torpedo attack three times during World War II. A short, thin fellow, he married a much taller woman named Beatrice, who hailed from Aberdeen. It was at Beatrice's insistence that he left the navy and went into the hotel business in the British seaside town of Torquay. They managed the Greenacres Hotel

THE ECCENTROPEDIA

during the 1950s, before taking over the more upmarket Gleneagles. Sinclair was the sort of hotel manager who believes that hotels could be run perfectly smoothly if it weren't for the guests.

In May 1970, the Monty Python comedy team — John Cleese, Michael Palin, Graham Chapman, Terry Jones, Eric Idle and Terry Gilliam — checked into the Gleneagles. They were in Torquay for two weeks of outdoor filming. They first noticed there was something unusual about Gleneagles when Idle could not find the bag containing his squash gear. It turned out that Sinclair, thinking the bag might contain a bomb, had hidden it behind a wall. 'We've had a lot of staff problems lately,' he explained. Later, in the dining room, Sinclair proved highly critical of Gilliam's 'American' eating habits.

After a first night of filming, the team returned to the hotel at 12.30 a.m. Palin wrote in his diary that Sinclair greeted them with 'a look of self-righteous resentment, a tacit accusation, that I had not seen since my father waited up for me fifteen years ago'. Chapman's request for a brandy was curtly refused, and when Palin asked for a wake-up call, Sinclair raised his eyebrows and said 'Why?' Palin and most of the others decided to check out the next day (Sinclair was more than happy to

see them go, although his wife tried to force them to pay for the full two weeks). Cleese, however, was fascinated by the man's almost transcendental rudeness, and decided to stay on at the hotel to observe him. He was later joined there by his wife, Connie Booth.

In 1974, after Cleese had left Monty Python, he and Booth were casting about for ideas for a television show to write together, and remembered the fractious hotelier. The first series of *Fawlty Towers*, screened in 1975, became a huge worldwide hit, and was followed by a second series in 1978. When the inspiration for Basil Fawlty became known, many who had stayed at the Gleneagles or worked for Sinclair came forward with anecdotes, any of which could have slotted easily into a *Fawlty Towers* script. In addition to his various other duties, Sinclair acted as the hotel's barman, a role that often brought him into conflict with guests. He was known to close the bar abruptly whenever he grew sick of the people in there, and mutter darkly if anyone wanted a drink during the day. One couple who ordered a pre-dinner drink were told, 'You'd better drink up, my wife doesn't spend her life in the kitchen preparing good food to have it spoilt.' A mother who rang the night porter button to request hot water to warm her baby's bottle was berated by Sinclair — who was also the night porter — for making such a trivial request, while a guest who requested some more toilet paper was asked, 'What on Earth are you doing with it?'

Sinclair's widow Beatrice broke her silence in 2002, telling the *Daily Telegraph* that her husband was a disciplinarian who 'couldn't stand fools', but he was not the monster Cleese had portrayed. This only brought forth further anecdotes. Rosemary Harris, who had worked at the Gleneagles in 1973, recalled one breakfast where Sinclair was so slow making the tea — tea-maker being another one of his duties — that an impatient waiter put a teapot meant for four people on a table for two. Sinclair interrogated the wait staff about this, then marched into the restaurant and questioned the guests.

Sinclair and his wife left the hotel business in the mid-seventies, but he continued to exasperate people. On one occasion a couple of labourers he hired to do some work on his house were so insulted by Sinclair's criticisms that they spent a night painting everything in his front garden grey — including walls, doors, trees, bushes, swimming pool, garden furniture and car. ❧

SITWELL, DAME EDITH
(1887–1964)
Writer

Edith was the eldest child of ☛ Sir George Sitwell and his wife Lady Ida. They wanted a son, and did not take pains to hide their disappointment. Edith in turn had little affection for them, preferring the company of servants, birds and animals. She was a tall, thin girl, conscious about her appearance (she had deep-set eyes and a long nose) and her childhood was not happy, with her miseries increased by having to wear a brace to correct a curvature of her spine. She sought solace in music and poetry, and at fifteen visited the grave of ☛ Swinburne to pour honey on it. Her governess, Helen Rootham, later introduced her to French poets like Rimbaud and Verlaine.

Sitwell moved to London with Rootham in 1913, and published her first book of poetry two years later. Her poems were innovative, full of wordplay and striking imagery. Her brother Sacheverell suggested they would go well with a musical accompaniment and the result was *Façade*, a collaboration with the composer William Walton. For the first public performance, at the Aeolian Hall in 1923, Sitwell stood behind a backcloth on which was painted a large mask with a hole in the mouth, and

DAME EDITH SITWELL

recited her poems through a type of megaphone called a Sengerphone while a small orchestra played. The audience, which included Virginia Woolf and the painter Augustus John, tittered, and afterwards an old woman tried to hit Sitwell with an umbrella.

On a visit to Paris in 1927, Sitwell met a young Russian surrealist painter named Pavel Tchelitchew, who told her he was fascinated by her face because it reminded him of a Russian saint (a male one). Sitwell fell madly in love with him, spent as much time as she could in Paris to be near him, and began to support him financially, although she had little enough money of her own. Their relationship was doomed, for Tchelitchew was homosexual, and was in fact living with a man at the time. The artist caused her agonies for years. The thirties were also blighted for her by the slow and painful death of Helen Rootham from bone cancer.

Edith and her brothers Osbert and Sacheverell, who were also writers, had a knack for making enemies and were often dismissed as publicity seekers. Edith in particular could never tolerate bad reviews, and would fight back ferociously (although to her friends she was unfailingly warm, generous and loyal). As she could not support herself with poetry, she began to write books for money, including *The English Eccentrics* (1933), a work quite as eccentric as its subject matter. She also wrote two books about Queen Elizabeth I, a figure with whom she increasingly identified. She shared a birthday with her (and, as Elizabeth was reputed to have done, she died a virgin). She also claimed to have Plantagenet blood in her veins, which accounted for her long nose. As the years went by, Sitwell's friends noticed that she was becoming more 'queenly' in manner. She painted her face white and wore regal costumes — richly brocaded gowns and capes (often made from upholstery material), turbans and other elaborate headgear, and enormous rings on her long, slender fingers.

During the war, Sitwell published a number of new poems which were highly praised by the critics, cementing her reputation as a major poet. She first visited America in 1948 and was a great hit there, with thousands of people attending her lectures and readings. She declared her love of Americans (she got on terrifically with Marilyn Monroe) and often returned. On one visit, she was taken backstage at Ringling's Circus and introduced to a female gorilla twice her size. The gorilla took her hand, peeled the black glove from it, kissed it, then threw her arms around Edith's neck and kissed her on the cheek. Sitwell

thought the gorilla must do this with everyone, but the keeper said no, and perhaps she had done it because 'she thought you were her mother'. It became one of Sitwell's favourite stories.

In 1954, Sitwell was made a Dame of the British Empire, which delighted her. Her health began to decline in the late fifties, and she was consumed by worry about Osbert, who was suffering from Parkinson's disease. Beset by financial problems as usual, she was obliged to keep writing, and published her second book on Elizabeth I, *The Queens and the Hive*, at the age of seventy-five.

She made her last public appearance in May 1964, when she and Osbert (both in wheelchairs) attended a performance of *English Eccentrics*, an opera based on her book with music by Malcolm Williamson. ▣

'I am as highly stylised as it is possible to be.'
DAME EDITH SITWELL

SITWELL, SIR GEORGE
(1860–1943)
Aristocrat

Sir George Sitwell was only two-years-old when his father Sir Sitwell Sitwell died and he succeeded to the baronetcy. He took his aristocratic responsibilities seriously from the beginning, and when asked his name, once replied, 'I am Sir George Sitwell. I am four-years-old and I am the youngest baronet in England.'

Sitwell was a man of firm convictions. Outside his home, Renishaw Hall in Derbyshire, he had a sign posted which read 'I must ask anyone entering the house never to contradict me in any way, as it interferes with the functioning of the gastric juices and prevents my sleeping at night.' He had little time for contemporary life, and would have been far more at home in the Middle Ages. Indeed, he often operated as if he were in the Middle Ages, especially when it came to financial matters, and once tried to pay his son Sacheverell's fees at Eton in pigs and potatoes. Renishaw Hall remained without electricity until after his death, and guests found they had to make do with two candles in their rooms.

Much of his time was spent researching arcane subjects from the past, such as the histories of pig keeping, forks, beds and the cold, although few of the monographs he planned on these and other subjects were ever published. He was also an inventive fellow, his inventions including a small revolver for killing wasps, a walking stick that squirted vitriol on mad dogs, and an artificial egg made of smoked meat and rice coated with lime.

Sitwell's other great passion was for gardening on a grand scale. He spent endless time and money refashioning the gardens of Renishaw Hall, and later of his Italian Residence, Montegufoni Palace in Tuscany. He would raise or lower fully grown trees to improve the view, and once employed 4,000 men to create a lake. The results (which survive today) were much admired, and his book *On the Making of Gardens* was quite a success. He travelled extensively in Italy, always carrying an inflatable cushion, and although he was happy to stay at the cheapest inns and sleep in a dormitory, invariably wore evening dress to dinner. He was accompanied on these journeys by his unflappable valet, former seaman Henry Moat, the only man who could say what he liked to Sir George and get away with it.

The relationship between Sitwell and his three children, Edith, Osbert and Sacheverell, was fraught, to say the least, and he took a dim view of their literary careers. He warned Osbert that writing a novel would ruin his health, and when Edith won a prestigious poetry prize, told her there were far too many poets (she agreed).

With the exception of the money he splashed out on his gardens, Sitwell was always very careful with his finances. The same could not be said for his wife, Lady Ida, whose extravagance led her to accumulate massive debts. Afraid to tell her husband about them, she became involved with a crooked moneylender, Julien Field, foolishly signed papers he gave her, and ended up owing him £3,000. Field assumed that Sir George would pay the debt, but he refused as a matter of principle. Lady Ida was prosecuted and ended up spending three months in prison in 1915. This served to estrange him further from his children (Osbert was serving in the trenches in France at the time). When Ida died in 1937, Sir George said he was too tired to go to her funeral.

Sitwell spent most of the last two decades of his life in his Italian castle, and died in Switzerland. While they thought he was a monster, his children made good use of his peculiarities in their writings (especially Osbert in his various autobiographies), while Edith was no doubt inspired by them to write her classic work *The English Eccentric*.

STACE, ARTHUR

(1885–1967)
'The Eternity Man'

Stace was born in the Sydney sub-

urb of Balmain and had an awful childhood. His parents, immigrants from Mauritius, both drank heavily, as would his two brothers, his two sisters and Arthur himself. As a child, he slept on hessian sacks beneath the family home, scavenged in garbage cans for food, and received virtually no education. He was made a ward of the state at the age of twelve, and two years later was set to work in a coal mine. He later drifted into petty crime, carrying liquor to brothels and acting as a lookout during burglaries, and did regular stints in prison. In 1916, he enlisted in the army and served as a stretcher-bearer in France, where he was gassed and lost partial sight in one eye. On his return to Sydney, he began to drink more heavily than ever. Eventually he hit rock bottom, living rough and spending his last pennies on methylated spirits.

One night in August 1930, Stace attended a men's meeting at St. Barnabas Anglican church in Sydney, was converted to Christianity, and finally found the will to give up alcohol. The pivotal moment of his life came shortly afterwards. He was at the Burton Street Baptist church, listening to a famously fiery evangelist preacher, the Reverend John Ridley. 'I wish I could shout eternity through the streets of Sydney!' Ridley declared. The word 'eternity' rang in Stace's brain. 'Suddenly I

began crying,' he later recalled, 'and I felt a powerful call from the Lord to write "eternity". I had a piece of chalk in my pocket and I bent down there and I wrote it.' Without conscious effort on his part, the letters formed themselves into a beautiful copperplate script. Strangely, it was the only word that Stace could write like this — his normal handwriting was terrible.

The people of Sydney soon became aware of the enigmatic but thought provoking word which kept appearing on pavements all over the their city and its suburbs, and there was much speculation about who was responsible and why they did it. The mystery endured for over twenty years. Then, one day in 1956, the Reverend Lisle Thompson of the Burton Street Baptist Church noticed that the ubiquitous word had suddenly appeared near the church's cleaner, Arthur Stace. 'Are you Mr. Eternity?' he asked. 'Guilty, Your Honour,' Stace replied. Thompson, having persuaded Stace that his life story would be an inspiration to others, wrote a tract about him called 'The Crooked Made Straight', and the first newspaper interview with Stace appeared in the *Sunday Telegraph* on 21 June 1956.

Stace was a grey haired man, five feet three inches (160 cm) tall, with a nose broken in some drunken fight years before. He always

dressed impeccably in a grey felt hat, collar and tie and blue serge three-piece suit, and lived with his wife Pearl, whom he married in 1942, in a house in Pyrmont. He rose at 4 a.m. every morning and headed for a suburb that God had directed him to the night before. He would then get to work, writing 'Eternity' on the pavement at regular intervals in yellow crayon, and be home by 10 a.m. After retiring and going on the pension, he was able to devote himself full-time to his calling. He took to travelling by train, and 'Eternity' was soon appearing as far afield as the cities of Newcastle and Wollongong.

Stace's one-word message worked itself into the psyche of Sydney. He has been the subject of poems, songs, a documentary and an opera. In 1977, a brass 'Eternity' in the familiar script was inlaid in the pebbled pavement of Sydney Square. And during the fireworks which ushered in the year 2000, an enormous 'Eternity' blazed on the side of the Sydney Harbour Bridge, to the delight of Sydneysiders and the bafflement of international observers.

Of the 500,000 Eternity's Stace estimated he had inscribed in his lifetime, just one survives, inside the largest bell in the tower of the old General Post Office building in Martin Place, Sydney. 🖾

STANHOPE, LADY HESTER

(1776–1839)
Traveller

The redoubtable Hester was the daughter of Charles, 3rd Earl Stanhope, a scientist and inventor who supported the French revolutionaries. Ashamed of his aristocratic status, Charles went around obliterating the family crest whenever he saw it, and managed to disperse most of his fortune in the space of a few years. Hester was saved from poverty when her uncle, Prime Minister William Pitt the Younger, who was unmarried, appointed her hostess of his house. Sharp witted and self assured, Hester held her own with the politicians and other luminaries who came to dinner. She nursed Pitt through his final illness, and Parliament granted her a considerable pension of £1,200 a year after he died.

After several unhappy love affairs and the death of her brother in the Napoleonic Wars, she spent some time in Wales, then left Britain for good in 1810, travelling with a small party to Athens and Constantinople. Here she conceived the idea of going to France to meet Napoleon, a plan quickly scotched by the British authorities. She set off for Cairo instead, but her ship was

wrecked off Rhodes. Having lost all her clothes, she donned the dress of a Turkish gentleman, and wore male clothes — often of her own idiosyncratic design — for the rest of her life. She also learned Arabic and Turkish, and took to smoking a *narghila*, or water pipe. She became a celebrity in Cairo, and was received by the Pasha wearing a splendid outfit consisting of a cashmere turban, a purple velvet coat, and enormous purple pantaloons embroidered with gold. Continuing her travels, she visited Alexandria, Jaffa and Jerusalem, then set her sights on Damascus, despite being warned of its dangers. Christians were forbidden to ride on horseback in the city, and women to go unveiled. Stanhope, undaunted, rode into Damascus bareheaded, to the astonishment of the populace, and became as popular as she had been in Cairo.

Next stop was the Bedouin city of Parmyra, reckoned to be even more dangerous to the outsider than Damascus. Refusing the Pasha of Damascus' offer of a military escort, she made her way across the desert accompanied by two guides, and presented herself to the Bedouin Emir, who was as enchanted by her as the other rulers she had met. A tour of the old Roman town with its great temple was organised, with Stanhope leading a procession of the most important tribesmen, as

drummers beat an accompaniment. While her hosts were probably just exhibiting the hospitality for which the Arabs are famed — albeit on a grand scale — Stanhope was convinced to the end of her days that the whole thing was a ceremony in which she had been crowned 'Queen of the Desert'.

After this, the high point of her life, Stanhope lived in several towns in what is now Lebanon, and finally settled into a mazelike, thirty-six-room residence with gardens on the top of a conical hill in Joun. From here she ruled what she perceived to be her kingdom, and it seems that many of the surrounding tribesmen did indeed revere her (on one occasion, when a visiting Frenchman was murdered in the area, she called for retribution and 300 natives were killed, earning her the thanks of the French consulate). She became obsessed with the occult, alchemy and astrology, and dreamed that the Mahdi, the Arab messiah, would take her for his bride. Two sacred horses were kept at the ready for this momentous occasion.

Most of her English companions had returned home (her physician, Dr. Meyron, was the last to go in 1838) but she occasionally received curious visitors from Europe, whom she entertained lavishly. She ran up huge debts, and was outraged when the British prime minister, Lord Palmerston, cancelled her pension. Unable to stop her servants stealing from her, she dismissed most of them, and the house became disordered and overrun with cats. Towards the end, she rarely left her bedroom. After her death, the British consul arrived to find that everything of value had been removed from the house. ▣

STANSHALL, VIVIAN
(1943–1995)
Singer, musician & painter

The multi-talented but awfully un-disciplined Bonzo Dog Band singer was born Victor Anthony Stanshall. His father had been christened Vivian but, thinking this sounded sissy, had changed it to Victor. Stanshall Jr. did the opposite, changing his name to Vivian because he thought it sounded artistic. Victor was as nor-mal as his son was unconventional. He wore a pinstripe suit and bowler hat, worked for a finance company in London, and insisted that Vivian speak in upper class tones. Vivian later said he was 'downright terrified' of him. He was much closer to his mother, Eileen.

He was a precocious boy, speak-ing from the age of five months, and from the beginning his twin loves were art and music. He began to collect old 78 rpm records,

especially jazz and novelty songs, and taught himself to play a host of instruments from trombone to ukulele. When he was a teenager, the family moved to Leigh-on-Sea, and Stanshall's first jobs were working in a fun fair in the nearby resort town of Southend-on-Sea. He also joined a gang of Teddy Boys, swaggered around the streets wearing a top hat and frock coat, and got involved in 'fights, brawls and outrages'.

After a stint in the merchant navy Stanshall went to art school, and in 1962 formed a band with several of his fellow students. They were originally called the Bonzo Dog Dada Band (Bonzo being a car-toon dog created by George Studdy in the 1920s, and 'Dada' referring to the art movement), later the Bonzo Dog Doo-Dah Band, and later still just the Bonzo Dog Band, but were always known to their fans as the Bonzos. They played an anarchic species of trad jazz, with much of their repertoire deriving from Stanshall's collection of 78s. Their performances were charac-terised by Stanshall's inspired antics, outrageous costumes and props like 'Alma the dancing doll', with the songs punctuated by explosions. Upwards of forty musicians played with the band over the years, but the core was Stanshall, Neil Innes (who, along with Stanshall, wrote most of the songs) and 'Legs' Larry Smith (so named for his spectacular tap-dancing skills). Stanshall's offstage persona was almost as wild as when he was performing. When his future wife Monica first met him in an art school canteen (they were married in 1968) he was wearing a loud checkered suit, large rubber ears and octagonal glasses, with halved pink ping-pong balls over his eyes.

The Bonzos played regular gigs and, to their surprise, found they were making money from music. They became more professional, and introduced more pop songs into their set. Befriended by the Beatles, they appeared in the film, *Magical Mystery Tour*, while their first album, *Gorilla*, released in 1967, did well. The following year they had their only top ten hit, 'I'm the Urban Spaceman' (produced by Paul McCartney under the pseudonym Apollo C. Vermouth). They gained further exposure with regular appearances on the television show *Do Not Adjust Your Set*, a precursor to Monty Python featuring Michael Palin, Terry Jones and Eric Idle.

The hectic pace of touring and recording took its toll on the band, and Stanshall in particular. During their second tour of America in 1969, he began to suffer from stage fright and panic attacks. (Some of the other Bonzos suspected he had been experimenting with LSD; he denied this, and talked instead of

having had an out-of-body experience on stage one night.) Whatever the cause, he was prescribed Valium, to which he became addicted. On his return to England, he suffered a nervous breakdown, and at the end of that year the Bonzos announced they were splitting.

For all the craziness of the Bonzos, it's clear that the band gave some structure to Stanshall's life, and without them he floundered. He worked on various projects, including performing with different musicians, making humourous radio spots for the BBC, and providing the narration at the end of Mike Oldfield's mega-selling *Tubular Bells* album (for which he neglected to ask for payment). His heavy drinking and addiction to Valium and other tranquillisers made him erratic and unreliable, though. He lived with Monica and their son Rupert in a house in Finchley with very little furniture but a large number of tanks containing snakes, turtles, exotic fish (like piranhas) and various other creatures. Occasionally the snakes escaped, to the consternation of house guests. He once sent a note to his producer at the BBC, saying he could not make it to a recording session because 'We've got to get Rupert to a doctor. He's been in contact with a diseased parrot, we think it's psittacosis'. The producer was irate, but later learned that the

excuse was entirely true.

Stanshall had been an inveterate prankster since his school days, and his chief partner in crime was the Who drummer Keith Moon. Their most famous wheeze saw the two of them going into clothing shops and asking to see a pair of strong trousers. Taking hold of a leg each, they would tear the trousers in half, to the shop assistant's horror. This was the cue for a one-legged actor the pair had hired to enter the shop and declare, 'That's exactly what I've been looking for!'

After Stanshall's first marriage ended in 1975, he moved into a houseboat on the Thames. This was soon filled with the usual tanks full of creatures, along with various other oddities he had collected including African weapons and masks, a gorilla suit, and a mounted zebra's behind. His bedroom was an old garden shed fixed to the deck. He spent his time painting, writing, woodcarving, playing the tuba and shouting — Stanshall always loved shouting. He was eventually joined on the boat by his new partner, Pamela Longfellow, known as Ki, who was half Native American, and they had a daughter, Silky. His most substantial work during this period was a series of songs and radio skits revolving around the denizens of the seedy country estate of Rawlinson End, including the crapulous Sir

Henry Rawlinson, his brother Hubert and butler Old Scrotum ('the wrinkled retainer'). In 1980, this became a film, *Sir Henry at Rawlinson End*, with Trevor Howard in the title role and Stanshall as Hubert.

Ki and Stanshall then conceived the idea of fitting out a boat as a floating theatre. Backers were found, a boat acquired, and the Old Profanity Theatre opened in 1984. The following year saw a successful production of Stanshall's three-hour musical, *Stinkfoot*. By then, he and Ki had split up. Stanshall remained on his houseboat, which sank, was raised, then sank again for good six months later. He moved back to London and into a flat in Muswell Hill. His health was deteriorating and a bad case of tinnitus (a legacy of all those explosions during the Bonzo years) made it difficult for him to listen to music, but he did manage a tour of England in 1991, his first live performances in almost a decade. He also found a lucrative outlet for his verbal flights of fancy by writing and recording advertisements. Towards the end, Stanshall fell in with a group of itinerants who drank in his street. He allowed them to visit his flat, and they began to systematically relieve him of his possessions.

Stanshall died when a fire broke out in his bedroom, which also consumed the things that were dearest

to him — his paintings and musical instruments. Although it was an awful end, some of his friends, remembering how he had always wanted a Viking funeral, found it somehow fitting. ▣

STAWINOGA, JOSEPH

(1920–2007)
'The Ring Road Tramp'

The Polish-born Stawinoga lived for almost forty years in a tent inside a ring road in Wolverhampton, England, becoming a local legend and, later, an Internet phenomenon.

He arrived in England after the World War II, but the details of his life before then are murky. The most common story was that he served in the Polish army and had been imprisoned by the Russians, an experience that instilled in him a fear of confined spaces. According to his friend, Juliusz Leonowicz, after his arrival in England, he worked in a hospital and steelworks, and in 1952 married an Austrian woman. They lived in a boarding house, and Stawinoga apparently took to locking her in her room when he went to work. Not surprisingly, the marriage failed to last. Some time in the early 1970s, having been thrown out of a series of lodging houses and living on the streets for a while, with all his possessions in a pram,

he pitched a makeshift tent within the ring road and refused to budge. Wolverhampton council offered to rehouse him but he declined. Eventually it allowed him to stay put, and gave him a new tent every few years.

'Fred', as Stawinoga was known to people all over the Midlands, was a wizened and grimy old fellow with blue eyes, wild white hair and a long yellowish beard. (It was originally longer, but one day as he leaned over his gas fire it had caught alight. After that, he gave up the fire.) He rarely said anything apart from a few guttural words in Polish, and became all things to all people. Many admired him for his resilience and independence. The local Sikh and Indian community went further, revering him as a saint. An Indian woman who brought him tea every day told a reporter, 'We take our children to see him. We want to show them the man who does not have anything in this world but his relation with God.' Many others regularly brought food — more than he could eat — and tobacco — all of which he managed to smoke. At night Stawinoga would emerge from his tent to sweep the streets with a broom.

Stawinoga's fame grew exponentially in 2007, when a local student, Laura Croxford, created a page for him on Facebook entitled, 'We love you Wolverhampition ring-road

tramp.' It soon had 4,000 members who were making hundreds of posts a day. Stawinoga, certainly oblivious to it all, died a few months later. After his death, his friend Leonowicz caused some consternation among the tramp's fans by airing a story he said was told by some Poles, to the effect that Stawinoga had served in the German army during the war and been a member of the S.S. What evidence he had of this is unclear, although it must be said that Leonowicz's status as Stawinoga's friend is also unclear. He said he paid regular visits to the hermit to clip his fingernails and provide other services for him, but admitted that Stawinoga sometimes drove him away with his broom. ▨

STEAD, W.T.

(1849–1912)
Journalist & spiritualist

William Thomas Stead was the most famous British journalist of his time, as good at making the news as reporting it. A full-bearded, redblooded champion of many causes, he had a typically Victorian selfassurance and once confided to a colleague that he considered himself to be 'the man of most importance now alive'. He began his journalistic career as editor of a provincial newspaper, the *Northern Echo*, before

moving to London in 1881 to take up the assistant editorship of the *Pall Mall Gazette*. This had previously been a rather staid publication, but Stead, a journalist in the modern mode, changed all that. He was soon appointed editor, and began serving up to his readers a diet of sensational stories beneath lurid headlines.

In 1885, Stead took up the cause of virginal young working class girls being sold into prostitution and virtual slavery abroad (despite numerous attempts to raise it, the age of consent at the time was still twelve). Stead decided that the best way to demonstrate the ease with which a young girl could be procured was to procure one himself. With the help of an ex-prostitute, Rebecca Jarrett, Stead arranged to buy a thirteen-year-old virgin named Eliza Armstrong from her mother for £5. He then orchestrated a theatrical scene in which the hapless girl, having been examined to confirm her virginal state, was taken to a rooming house in London, chloroformed and subsequently packed off to Paris. Stead proceeded to expose the virgin trade in a series of ripe articles in the *Pall Mall Gazette* under the collective title 'The Maiden Tribute of Modern Babylon', and people were said to have rioted to get their hands on them. The articles were denounced as obscene in some quarters, and there was

outrage when it was discovered that Stead had engineered the purchase of Eliza Armstrong. When it was found that he had failed to obtain a receipt from Eliza's mother, he was charged with abduction and spent two months in Holloway Prison — which he thoroughly enjoyed. Stead's escapade seems to have had its desired effect, for later that year the age of consent was raised to sixteen and procuring was made illegal.

Always a deeply religious man, Stead became increasingly involved in spiritualism. Between 1894 and 1896, he edited a periodical, *Borderland*, devoted to psychic phenomena, and discovered he had a facility for 'automatic writing'. By sitting, pen in hand, and letting his mind go blank, Stead found that there were a great many spirits eager to enter his body and transcribe their thoughts through him. One of the journalistic techniques pioneered by Stead had been the extended interview. With automatic writing, he was able to extend this concept to the dead, thus achieving such journalistic coups as the late Mr. Gladstone's thoughts on the 1909 budget. But Stead found it was not just the dead who wished to use his writing hand. To his surprise, living friends and associates began communicating in this way (he noticed the interesting fact that, in their automatic communications, people were often a great deal more forthright than they were in person). While some objected violently to the whole idea, others agreed that Stead was getting their thoughts down well. Stead came to rely on this unique method of communication to such an extent that his hand became the equivalent of the modern businessman's mobile phone.

Stead's most frequent correspondent from among the dead was Julia, the spirit of an American actress whom he had briefly known. She was a remarkably ambitious spirit and urged Stead to put communication with the dead on a sounder business footing by setting up a bureau to regulate it. Stead eventually gave in and in 1909 organised what became known as Julia's Bureau. People wishing to contact their deceased relatives or friends sent requests to the bureau, which were vetted by Stead's daughter Estelle and a team of 'automatists'. Should all the necessary criteria be met, they would be invited to a séance with one of several mediums retained by the bureau, while Julia handled arrangements on 'the other side'. Stead lost a lot of money on Julia's Bureau, but considered the results well worth it.

Stead believed that he was clairvoyant and had foreseen several important events in his life — his editorship of the *Pall Mall Gazette* for one. This gift deserted him when

it came to the event that put a suitably sensational end to his life — he went down with the *Titanic*. ▣

STEWART, JOHN

(1747 – 1822)
Pedestrian &
natural philosopher

'Walking' Stewart, as he was known, acquired his nickname after spending some three decades traversing much of the world. Born in London, as a young man he went to India where he became a clerk with the East India Company. Disgusted by what he saw as the company's abuses of power, he resigned and shortly afterwards was captured by the troops of Hyder Ali, the Muslim ruler of Mysore. He ended up serving as a commander in Hyder Ali's army, and later worked for the Nabob of Arcot, his principal duties being to look after visiting dignitaries. In 1865, he set off for home on foot, in an extraordinarily circuitous route which took in Abyssinia, Persia, Arabia and parts of Africa, and arrived back in Europe in the early 1880s, able to speak eight languages. Subsequent walking tours took him through most of Europe, and to the United States and Canada, before he finally settled back in London, where he could be seen walking the streets in Armenian dress.

While doing all this walking, Stewart was formulating his philosophy, and eventually published some thirty philosophical treatises. It is not easy to summarise, or even fully understand, all of Stewart's ideas (many of his contemporaries found his books incomprehensible). An atheist, he believed that human beings are one with the natural world, and the most salient feature of our existence is that there is a constant exchange of matter between our bodies and everything around us. Given that parts of us will soon become commingled with other animals, and vice versa, the only logical conclusion is that all living creatures should be treated with respect and compassion. Stewart's ideas were a profound influence on Wordsworth, whom he met in Paris in 1792, and Thomas de Quincey said he was the most interesting person he had ever met.

Stewart himself had no doubts about his own intellectual importance. In the introduction to his *A New Practical System of Human Reason* (1796) he writes, 'Having travelled over the globe to detect the shades and gradations of human error, and the ignis-fatuus which mislead it, I now offer the following momentous work, which if it should carry the same conviction to mankind, as it possesses conceivability and truth in the mind of its author, must form an indelible epocha in human existence.' He once suggested that his name be engraved in gigantic letters on a 'projecting rock' in the Atlantic, so that people on passing ships would be curious enough to read his works. Fearing that his books might be lost to future generations, he urged people to bury copies of them deep in the ground (taking care to pass on the secret of their location before they died). De Quincey, at least, complied with this request.

Stewart had a mostly impecunious existence in London, relying largely on the generosity of his sister and her husband. In 1813, he came into a windfall when a claim he had made against the Nabob of Arcot for unpaid wages was upheld, and he received about £10,000. This enabled him to move into a new apartment, where he entertained friends with music and philosophical discussions (the former proved more popular than the latter).

Stewart always carried with him a quantity of poison with which he might kill himself, a precaution no doubt due to some of the barbarities he had witnessed on his travels. When he was found dead in his rooms with a bottle of laudanum beside him, some suspected suicide. His friend John Taylor doubted this, writing that Stewart 'thought his life of so much importance to man and all animals to which sensitive matter might be united, that he would have

been glad to have had it extended till he saw the triumph of his benignant principles'.

SUMMERS, MONTAGUE

(1880–1948)
Scholar & demonologist

Summers, born in Clifton, near Brighton, was the son of a successful businessman. He was a bookish young boy, drawn particularly to the literature of the seventeenth century, and liked to restage plays of the period in a toy theatre. He went to Oxford, where he acquired a veneer of eccentricity, dressing like a dandy in embroidered waistcoats, burning incense in his rooms, and writing a book of decadent poetry which one critic called 'the nadir of corrupt and corrupting literature'. At the same time, Summers was highly religious, and was briefly a curate in the Church of England until a scandal involving sex with young boys forced him to quit the diocese (he was eventually acquitted of the charges). In 1909, he converted to Roman Catholicism. Some thought this was because of Catholicism's belief in Satan, a belief shared earnestly by Summers. Later, he would claim to have been ordained as a priest, and while no record of this has ever been found, it is possible that he was (although the ordination, which could have taken place in Italy, was clearly somewhat irregular).

Summers spent the next fifteen years teaching in various schools. He adopted the garb of a seventeenth century clergyman — frock coat, purple stockings, buckled shoes — and had his hair cut so that it resembled a wig. He was popular with the boys he taught, and admired for his erudition and arcane knowledge. One of his favourite sayings was 'Tell me something strange.'

In the 1920s, he gave up teaching to concentrate on writing. He edited new editions of the works of various seventeenth century dramatists, and was acknowledged as one of the leading scholars in the field. But it was as the author of books on the supernatural, including *The History of Witchcraft and Demonology* (1926), *The Vampire: his Kith and Kin* (1928) and *The Werewolf* (1933), that he became famous. Summers firmly believed in the reality of witches, vampires and werewolves, just as he believed in the Devil, and fulminated against them with all the vehemence (and archaic language) of an old-time witchfinder. Yet some believed that Summers protested too much, that he was himself a practitioner of the black arts. There was a persistent story that he had conducted a black mass in his house in 1923, although the details of this are as murky as many other aspects of his life. Some

have suggested that, having delved into such things, he had been terrified by what he had found, and his zeal in denouncing witches and the like was the zeal of the reformed.

In person, Summers was a rotund, moon-faced fellow with a high-pitched voice and an impudent sense of humour. He had a wide circle of friends who clearly adored him. After the outbreak of World War II, most of his literary and social activities were curtailed, and he spent his last years living quietly in a house in Richmond with his secretary and companion, Hector Stuart-Forbes.

Summers was an acquaintance of ☞ Aleister Crowley and, given the interests they shared, it is not surprising that they got on well (at one point, they were planning to collaborate on producing, of all things, a perfume called 'It'). Crowley could be waspish about his fellow occultist, though. In a 1957 memoir, *The Eye of the Beholder*, Lance Sieveking describes a meeting with Crowley in 1928, during which he asked 'the Great Beast' what he thought of Summers.

'I haven't seen Monty Summers for years,' answered Crowley, knocking the end off his cigar with the air of an executioner.

'He takes care of that. He knows what would happen.'

'What would happen?'

'I should change him into a toad.' ▣

SUN RA

(1914–1993)
Jazz musician

Sun Ra did not believe he came from this planet (Saturn, maybe, but not this one) so did his best to obliterate the mundane early details of his life, but earthly records show that he was born Herman Poole Blount in Birmingham, Alabama. His father, Cary Blount, abandoned his mother, Ida, when Herman was very young. A quiet, studious boy who read everything he could lay his hands on, at the age of eleven he taught himself how to play piano and, more remarkably, how to read music. He began playing professionally while still in high school, going by the name of Sonny Blount. After a brief stint at a teaching college, where he excelled in every subject but business, he decided to concentrate on music, and gathered a band of musicians who rehearsed every day at his great aunt's house. He was already defiantly different. He barely slept, apart from brief naps at the keyboard, was a vegetarian and took vitamin pills (then almost unheard of), and could sometimes be seen walking the streets of Birmingham wearing a sheet and sandals. During the war, he was a conscientious objector, and spent time in prison for it.

In 1942, Blount moved to Chicago where he played with a series of bands, and continued to be an anomaly among jazz musicians. He didn't drink, smoke, take drugs or have sex (it seems he was a lifelong celibate) and was deeply religious, although not affiliated with any church. He studied the Bible and decided that its text had been tampered with, its real meaning hidden. He read books on numerology, etymology and the occult, and writers who argued that civilisation began in Egypt and the ancient Egyptians were black. He started to call himself Sonny Ra, after the Egyptian sun god. After some esoteric fine-tuning, this became Le Sony'r Ra, which he registered as his legal name in 1952 (Sun Ra for short). He devoured the works of ☞ Blavatsky and ☞ Gurdjieff, and believed the latter's theory that most people were effectively asleep. This applied especially to Negroes, who had forgotten their cultural and spiritual heritage. He thought that music was a way to rectify this. And he was just crazy about anything to do with outer space.

He increasingly saw himself as a moral and spiritual leader, and told of a strange experience. He had been contacted by beings from outer space, who transported him to their planet (which he took to be Saturn) on a beam of light. The aliens, who had antennae protruding from the ears and over their eyes, told him that the world would soon fall into chaos and hopelessness, and it would be his task to speak to people and reveal the truth. Transported back to Earth, he had a vision of himself in New York, looking up into the sky to see thousands of spaceships ready to land. Sun Ra dated this experience to 1936, which would have put him years ahead of other UFO contactees like George Adamski, but no one can recall him talking about it earlier than 1953.

Sun Ra formed a new band which had shifting personnel and shifting names, although they usually included the word 'Arkestra' (variations over the years included the Solar-Science Arkestra, the Intergalactic Myth Science Arkestra, the Omniverse Ultra 21st Century Arkestra and many others). He expected its members to devote themselves to music, as well as following his own strict moral code. Some found this impossible to do, while others found it impossible to play the extremely unconventional arrangements that he wrote. He had his musicians rehearsing endlessly, and urged them to stretch themselves, to play what they couldn't play. 'If you can't play it perfectly right,' he would say, 'then play it perfectly wrong.' The music was heavily percussive, and his bands of-

ten included several drummers. His musicians wore colourful costumes, while their leader was resplendent in robes and glittering capes, and wore a series of 'space hats' equipped with lights which grew more elaborate over the years.

Sun Ra moved to New York in 1961. He lived with some of his musicians in a house in the East Village which, with its walls painted orange, silver and gold, became known as the Sun Palace. Previously shunned by the jazz establishment (although championed by some musicians like John Coltrane and Charles Mingus), he began to garner a cult following, and released numerous records, many in small pressings with hand-painted covers. His music was increasingly experimental, and on albums like *The Heliocentric World of Sun Ra Vol 1* he dispensed with melody altogether. Word spread about his unique concerts and he played to packed houses, but continued to be oblivious to money, sometimes performing for little or nothing. In 1967, he played in Central Park accompanied by 100 musicians. He dreamed of performing with 1,000 musicians, or 10,000 — concerts that would transform the world.

Sun Ra toured the world extensively during the next two decades. His concerts, or 'cosmo dramas', were now full-on multimedia

SUN RA

events, featuring dancers, performers, costume changes, spectacular lightshows and films projected onto screens. The music would be interrupted by chants ('Space is the place!') or some of Sun Ra's cosmic philosophising. The musicians would leave the stage and walk among the audience as they played, and sometimes when the curtain went down they kept on playing, giving the impression that the audience had just been eavesdropping on them for a while.

Sun Ra kept up a Herculean touring schedule into his seventies. Even when he suffered a series of strokes in 1990 and was confined to a wheelchair, he kept touring. When his health continued to deteriorate, he returned to Birmingham where he was cared for by members of his family, who had seen little of him in decades. When he died he was buried wearing a white robe, with an Egyptian ankh symbol on his chest.

Sun Ra had been thrilled by the advent of the space age, which he had been predicting since the thirties. When the Voyager 1 space probe was launched in 1977, carrying a recording of representative Earth music from Beethoven to Chuck Berry, he didn't mind the fact that he wasn't included on it. 'The outer space beings,' he said, 'already know my music.' ▣

'I never felt like I was part of this planet.'
SUN RA

SUTCH, SCREAMING LORD
(1940–1999)
Singer and political candidate

David Sutch was born in Hampstead, London. When he was nine months old, his father William died in a blackout accident, and he was raised by his mother Annie, to whom he was very close. A born performer, he put on puppet shows for other children, and made his stage debut at the age of twelve, singing 'How Much is That Doggie in the Window?' at a Butlins holiday camp. During the late fifties, he worked as a window cleaner, which allowed him to grow his hair shockingly long for the time. If his contemporaries are to be believed, he was just about the only young man in Britain with shoulder-length hair. He was often jeered in the street.

Sutch fell in love with rock music and determined to become a rock star. He started performing around 1959, in a London coffee bar called the 2 I's. He could barely sing but he could scream, and he knew how to put on a show — his first

stage costume included a motor-
cycle helmet equipped with buffalo
horns and a leopardskin loincloth
made from his aunt's coat. Teaming
up with drummer Carlo Little he
formed the first version of his backing band, the Savages, which would
include a number of fine musicians
over the years (including pianist
Nicky Hopkins and future Deep
Purple guitarist Ritchie Blackmore).
He adopted the name Screaming
Lord Sutch ('Screaming' as a homage to U.S. shock rocker Screaming
Jay Hawkins, 'Lord' because of his
fondness for wearing top hats). He
began to receive a lot of publicity
for his increasingly theatrical shows,
and Sutch was a demon for publicity. He was obsessed with horror
movies, and for the song 'My Big
Black Coffin' had himself carried
onto the stage in a coffin borne by
men dressed as monks. After emitting some bloodcurdling screams
from inside it he would emerge,
resplendent in white face makeup
and evening dress, to wreak havoc,
spitting fake blood and green gunk
at the audience, chasing his fellow
band members with a huge fake
axe, setting fire to things, and toss-
ing worms at the girls at the front
(which always got a reaction). He
also liked to perform with a toilet
seat around his neck, for reasons not
so clear.

His earliest recordings were
produced by ☞ Joe Meek, whose
idiosyncratic production methods
meshed perfectly with Sutch's lurid
style. His first single, a version of
'My Big Black Coffin' (retitled 'Till
the Following Night') was recorded
in Meek's home studio, with Sutch
singing in the bathroom. It was
unanimously declared horrible
(though not in a good way) by
reviewers and banned by the BBC.
This was followed by what became
his signature tune, 'Jack the Ripper'.
It begins with footsteps, a girl's
screams, a burst of evil laughter and
dramatic chords. Sutch proceeds to
tell his story of murder and may-
hem, punctuated by an impossibly
cheery female chorus who trill 'The
Ripper! Jack the Ripper!' Other fabulous Sutch non-hits of the sixties
include 'Monster in Black Tights'
(co-written by Meek), 'Dracula's
Daughter' and the awesome 'Black
and Hairy'.

In 1968, Sutch embarked on
what became a two-year tour of
America. He was now dressing like
a Regency dandy in a gold brocade
coat and driving around in a Rolls-
Royce decorated from front to back
with a Union Jack, and many people
thought he really was a lord. While in
America, he recorded his belated first
album, *Lord Sutch and Heavy Friends*,
on which Jimmy Page and John Bon-
ham from Led Zeppelin played.

Back in England, Sutch had a

SCREAMING LORD SUTCH

son, Tristan, with his American girlfriend, Thann Rendessy, in 1975. They were living in a house in South Harrow, but Sutch's growing mania for collecting things put a strain on their relationship. He couldn't bear to throw anything away, and haunted secondhand shops and stalls where he bought all sorts of junk. By the time he died, he had filled his mother's house and several others. After Rendessy returned to America around 1977, Sutch had other relationships (and lived for a while with notorious brothel-keeper Cynthia Payne, although that relationship was apparently platonic), but never married.

Sutch first dabbled in politics in 1963 when, at the suggestion of his manager, he contested the by-election for Stratford-upon-Avon, the seat vacated by disgraced minister John Profumo. He stood under the banner of the Teenage Party, with the slogan 'Vote for the ghoul, he's no fool'. In the early eighties, Sutch and some friends formed the Official Monster Raving Loony Party. ('Vote for insanity. You know it makes sense.') Sutch became a fixture of British elections, running for Parliament thirty-nine times, usually scoring a few hundred votes and invariably losing his deposit. His finest hour was in the Bootle by-election in 1990, when he beat the candidate of the Social Democratic Party, leading to the party's dissolution. Sutch often infuriated the more conventional candidates (especially Margaret Thatcher, whom he stood against in 1983) but was admired by many for bringing humour — and some uncommon honesty — to the election process. It has also been noted how many of the proposals he made during his campaigns have come to pass, from lowering the voting age to eighteen, to passports for pets, to rebuilding the Cavern Club in Liverpool.

Sutch suffered terribly from depression in his last years. He was on medication but would sometimes take too much of it, or cut it out altogether. His diet was appalling, and his insomnia wasn't helped by his consumption of forty cups of tea a day. Always unable to keep to a schedule, he missed a lot of gigs, and was clearly sick of playing the pubs he had mostly been reduced to. Everyone who knew him agrees he was never the same after his mother died in 1997. Two years later, he hanged himself in her house with a skipping rope. He was discovered by his last girlfriend, Yvonne Elwood. When she let herself in the door and saw him hanging from a banister, she thought he was playing a joke and took a photo.

Sutch's death triggered genuine mourning across Britain. The *Times* gave him a respectful obituary.

SWAN, WALTER

(1916–1994)
Owner of
the One Book Bookstore

Swan was born into a poor family in Cochise County, Arizona. In 1940, he was living in Stockton, California, when he met Deloris Robinson at a Baptist Church social. They were married later that year, and went on to have eight children. Over the years, Swan held down many jobs including railway and ship-yard worker, farmer, plasterer and cement mason. He was a tireless worker despite various illnesses and accidents (he broke his back no less than four times), but it was always a struggle with eight children to support. At the age of seventy-one, he had a bad fall which forced him into retirement.

Swan had always been a great storyteller, regaling his children with tales of his early years, many of which involved his brother Henry. Some of these had been written down and published in a local news-paper. Now he and Deloris resolved to have them published as a book to be called *me an' Henry*. After the manuscript was rejected by twenty-nine publishers, they decided to publish it themselves. At the age of sixty-seven, Deloris taught herself how to use a computer, and pre-pared the text for printing. In 1988, she sent a flier out to everyone in the local phone book soliciting pre-publication orders, and the money that came in paid for the first 2,000 copies to be printed. They then mortgaged their house to pay for a further 5,000. It was when these proved harder to shift that Swan conceived the idea of opening a store that would sell his book and nothing else.

The One Book Bookstore was duly opened in a shopfront in Bisbee, Arizona. It soon came to the attention of the local press, then the national press, and Walter was suddenly famous. 'Even I can't believe what's happening,' he told a reporter. 'People peep in through the window and most come in out of curiosity. I show them my book and tell them it's a book with no big words — mainly because I don't know any. I let them know that the book is true and there are no bad words… And at least ninety per cent of the people who come in buy my book.' In the first two years, he sold 20,000 copies of *me an' Henry*, making him and Deloris financially secure for the first time in their lives.

Swan was inspired to write a second book, and to sell it opened — what else? — the Other Book Bookstore. ▣

SWINBURNE, ALGERNON CHARLES

(1837–1909)

Poet

Victorian England never quite knew what to make of Swinburne. The son of an admiral, at the age of twelve he was sent to Eton where he began to write the brilliant, musical poetry for which he would become famous. He was also flogged mercilessly by his tutor, which turned him into a confirmed masochist.

Swinburne was a peculiar physical specimen. He had a very large head perched upon a body which appeared too slight to bear its weight, tiny hands which fluttered constantly, and a great mass of flaming red hair. Despite his somewhat fey and fragile appearance, he had always been utterly fearless. Having failed to complete his studies at Eton, he went Oxford where he began to drink, which only added to his usual high spirits. He also met and became close to the painter Dante Gabriel Rossetti and other members of the Pre-Raphaelite Brotherhood.

The mercurial Swinburne failed to complete his studies at Oxford, leaving it with the consent of his parents. He went to live in London, where he met Richard Monckton Milnes, later Baron Houghton and a suitor of Florence Nightingale, who introduced him to pornography and the works of de Sade. In 1886, Swinburne published the first series of his *Poems and Ballads*, considered the first work of decadent poetry by a British writer. Brimming with not-so-subtle allusions to Swinburne's obsessions, chiefly sadism, lesbianism and incest, it outraged some of the critics. His work soon caught on with the younger generation, however, and he became immensely popular. His reputation for dissipation also grew, although some (including Oscar Wilde) believed he exaggerated his own achievements in the field. He is nevertheless known to have frequented an establishment in Circus Road, St. John's Wood, where two fair-haired women would whip gentlemen for a fee.

Swinburne's heavy drinking and dissolute lifestyle eventually caught up with him, and he had a breakdown in 1879. His friend, a lawyer and writer named Theodore Watts, fearing that Swinburne was about to die, whisked him away from the temptations of London to his home at No. 2 The Pines in Putney, and he stayed in this suburban cocoon for the remaining thirty years of his life. Watts kept a close eye on his charge, limiting him to one bottle of beer a day (and no floggings). His health returned and he continued to write, producing some highly respected critical works and much poetry, but

all agreed that this was not up to the productions of his decadent days.

In a celebrated essay, 'No 2 The Pines', Max Beerbohm described his visits to the household during the last years of the poet's life. Swinburne had become quite deaf, and the great dome of his head only had a few sparse grey hairs left on it, but he was as lively as ever, bounding up stairs three at a time, and excitedly describing his daily walks in his melodious, flutelike voice.

So respectable had Swinburne become that, on the death of Lord Tennyson, the Poet Laureate, Queen Victoria suggested that he might make a suitable replacement. It was left to Gladstone to tell her that his political views — he was a lifelong republican — precluded this. ▣

SYKES, SIR TATTON

(1826–1913)
Baronet

Sykes was a wealthy landowner who lived in Sledmere House in Yorkshire. His father, also Sir Tatton, was a popular fellow who bred racehorses. He had little time for his son, telling him he would amount to nothing. It was mainly to keep away from his father that Sykes spent years travelling abroad, going as far as Russia, Japan and Mexico. He loved his mother, but she too failed

to return his affections, and spent most of her time cultivating flowers. Upon coming into his inheritance after the death of his father in 1863, one of the first things he did was to order all the gardens on his lands and in the adjoining village dug up and purged of flowers. Henceforth, if he was out walking and noticed an errant bloom daring to show itself through the soil, he would take a swipe at it with his cane. 'If you want to grow flowers,' he told one of his tenants, 'grow cauliflowers.'

Sykes also had an intense dislike of front doors, and ordered his tenants never to use them. By way of example, he had several houses built with fake, painted front doors. Gravestones were another aversion, and he insisted on his relatives being buried in unmarked graves. Perhaps he resented the ornate 120 foot (thirty-seven metre) tower that the friends of his late father had erected in his memory.

One thing Sykes did like was milk pudding. He ate little else, saying it was the only thing his delicate stomach could tolerate. Wherever he went, even if he was staying at the Metropole Hotel in London, he took his cook, Mrs. Pember, so he could be certain of having his favourite dish. He also believed it was essential to keep his body at an even temperature, and whenever he went outdoors, wore six colour-

coded coats. If he grew too warm, he would peel off one or more of these coats and toss them away. The children of Sledmere knew that if they returned any coat they found to the house, they would receive a shilling from Sykes' butler. When travelling by train, Sykes was known to cool down by taking his shoes and socks off and sticking his feet out of the window. On one occasion, his son Mark was mortified when his father began to take his trousers off in a train station (not knowing that he had another pair underneath).

In 1874, Sykes married Jessica Cavendish-Bentinck, who was thirty years younger than him (her mother had forced her into the marriage). Jessica was a would-be novelist who liked to drink and gamble, and eventually ran up huge debts. The marriage inevitably broke down, and in 1896, Sykes became the first to take advantage of a new law stating that a man was no longer responsible for his wife's debts if he published them in a newspaper. The matter ended up in court, with the judge describing Sir Tatton as 'an obstinate and extremely whimsical old gentleman', while the press called him 'a man of helpless eccentricity, utterly unable to make any rational use of his vast wealth'.

In 1911, Sledmere House caught fire. Sykes refused to leave it until he had finished the pudding he was having for lunch, then sat in a chair in the garden, watching it burn. His only comment was, 'These things will happen, these things will happen.'

SYMMES, JOHN CLEVES
(1779–1829)
Champion of the Hollow Earth

In 1818, Symmes, a veteran of the war of 1812 who ran a frontier trading post in St. Louis, Missouri, issued a proclamation addressed 'TO ALL THE WORLD!' It read in part:

I declare the Earth is hollow, and habitable within; containing a number of solid concentrick spheres, one within the other, and that it is open at the poles 12 or 16 degrees; I pledge my life in support of this truth, and am ready to explore the hollow, if the world will support and aid me in this undertaking.

He went on to ask for 100 volunteers, with reindeer and sleighs, to embark on an expedition to the North Pole, where he vowed they would 'find warm and rich land, stocked with thrifty vegetables and animals if not men'.

He sent copies of his proclamation to schools, members of Congress and every town and city in the

United States. The overwhelming response was ridicule, and Symmes and his Polar Hole became the butt of jokes for years. An obstreperous fellow who was convinced that he had all the evidence he needed to convince any sensible person of the truth of his theories, Symmes was undeterred. Giving up his trading post, he began to work full time promoting his theory, writing letters to newspapers and giving lectures.

The idea that Earth is composed of a series of concentric spheres was first proposed by the respected British astronomer Edmond Halley in 1692. Symmes added a number of embellishments to it, most strikingly the polar openings. The northern opening, he said, was 4,000 miles (6,440 km) in diameter, with a sloping 'verge' or rim about 1,500 miles (2,415 km) wide. When people asked how explorers had failed to notice such an enormous hole — or indeed fall into it — Symmes argued that ships which had approached the northern opening had ended up sailing around the verge which, being magnetic, had upset their compasses, making it impossible for their true positions to be determined. He expanded on Halley's original ideas, declaring that spheres filled with concentric inner spheres were to be found throughout nature. Apparently empty space was filled with such spheres, too small to be seen, which

formed an 'aerial elastic fluid'. It was this fluid, pressing upon the larger planetary bodies, that caused gravity.

While Symmes was no orator and expressed his ideas in a notoriously haphazard manner, many came away from his lectures convinced that they should at least be tested by mounting an expedition such as he suggested. One of the great attractions of his theory was that the inner worlds represented a new frontier, possibly filled with riches and ripe for America to conquer. Several petitions signed by Symmes' supporters were presented to Congress, calling for an expedition, but all were rejected. The closest Symmes ever came to going on one came when the Russian government agreed to his request that he be allowed to accompany a Russian expedition to Siberia. Alas, Symmes could not raise the money for his fare to Moscow.

Symmes kept up a punishing schedule of lecturing which may have contributed to his death at the age of forty-nine. His son, Americus Vespucius Symmes, kept his father's ideas alive, while adding his own embellishments to them (he believed that the inner worlds were inhabited by the Lost Tribes of Israel). Since then, many others have expounded on the idea of a hollow Earth, not the least of them being the remarkable ☞ Cyrus Teed. ▧

SZUKALSKI, STANISLAUS

(1893–1986)
Sculptor & Zermatist

Szukalski was born in Warta, Poland, and while in his teens emigrated with his father to the United States. Settling in Chicago and setting up a studio in a loft, Szukalski soon began to attract attention with his sculptures — extraordinarily powerful, heavily symbolic evocations of gods and men locked in titanic struggle, works that owed precisely nothing to any prevailing art movement. Szukalski likened modernism to excrement smeared on a wall by an infant, and held all critics in contempt. The writer Ben Hecht, one of the first to befriend the sculptor, once saw him push a critic down the stairs after the latter had been so impudent as to poke his cane at one of Szukalski's creations. Hecht and other Chicago luminaries formed the 'Vagabond Club', the members of which gathered in Szukalski's loft to hear him expound his views on art and culture as he chipped away at huge blocks of marble.

In 1936, Szukalski returned to Poland with his wife and the bulk of his sculptures and drawings, and was hailed a national hero. The government gave him a large studio which became the Szukalski National Museum and commis-sions for statues poured in from around the country. The adulation was shortlived. The invading Nazis bombed the Szukalski Museum and toppled his statues. Szukalski fled back to America to start all over again.

Moving to Los Angeles, he supported himself by making ceramic tiles and, while continuing to produce sculptures at a prodigious rate, became increasingly preoccupied with anthropological research. His lifelong interest in the symbols and images of many cultures led to his discovery of the original, universal language of mankind, the proto-tongue or 'Protong', as he called it, which had been expressed in pictograms. This discovery became the basis of the science of Zermatism, essentially Szukalski's attempt to describe all of human history from the creation of the planet, without recourse to the so-called experts in geology, anthropology, etc, whom he considered no better than art critics.

Szukalski's complete rejection of conventional anthropology led to some wild notions. He postulated, for example, that the different facial markings found in various cultures commemorated ripples of mud on the faces of the first humans to emerge from the waters after the last deluge (the theory of the 'Tribal Flood Scumline'). His

STANISLAUS SZUKALSKI

most important discovery, however, was that there lived unsuspected among human beings another species, the Yetinsyny, who were the product of humans copulating with man-apes (Yetis, Sasquatch, the Pans of Ancient Greece). The Yetinsyny could be recognised by their small noses, large upper lips, short arms and torsos, big bellies and voracious appetites. They were, he wrote, typically the criminals, dictators, communists, trade union-ists and other destroyers.

Incapable of doing anything on less than a monumental scale, Szu-kalski produced thirty-nine volumes devoted to Zermatism, illustrated with tens of thousands of draw-ings. He took his failure to interest scientific institutions in his ideas philosophically — he had, after all, been exiled to the 'cultural Siberia' of Southern California. Excerpts from this vast work were published as *Troughful of Pearls/Behold!!! The Protong* in 1980.

> '*I put Rodin in one pocket and*
> *Michelangelo in another and*
> *I walk towards the sun.*'
> STANISLAUS SZUKALSKI

TCHAIKOWSKI, ANDRÉ

(1935–1982)
Pianist & theatrical benefactor

Tchaikowski was born Robert Andrzej Krauthammer in Poland. In 1942, he was smuggled out of the Warsaw Ghetto by his grandmother, who had obtained false papers for him. After the war, he studied piano at the Paris Conservatory, graduat-ing in 1950, then returned to Poland. A prodigiously talented musician and composer, he was accepted into the Polish Composers Union at the age of fifteen. He travelled extensively through Europe and America during the 1950s, playing with major or-chestras and making recordings, and was particularly known for his inter-pretations of Mozart and Chopin.

In 1960, he moved to England. Settling in Oxford, he continued to compose and perform. He was also

a great fan of the theatre, and often attended performances of the Royal Shakespeare Company in Stratford-upon-Avon. He was returning home after a performance of *Hamlet* (probably the 1979 production starring Derek Jacobi) with his manager, Terry Harrison, when he suggested that he might bequeath his skull to the company so that it could be used in productions of the play.

After Tchaikowski's death from cancer in 1982, Harrison read his will and found that he had followed through on his suggestion. It contained a clause in which he requested that his body be used for organ donation or medical research, then cremated 'with the exception of my skull, which shall be offered by the institution receiving my body to the Royal Shakespeare Company for use in theatrical performance'. The RSC accepted the bequest and the skull (after being allowed to air for two years on the roof of a building) was placed in the props department. It was depicted on posters for the RSC's 1984 production of *Hamlet*, then used in rehearsals for the 1989 production with Mark Rylance in the title role, but for various reasons the company decided not to use it during public performances.

Tchaikowski's skull finally made its stage debut as Yorick in 2008 when the RSC's director, Greg Doran, decided to use it in a production starring David Tennant (best known for playing Doctor Who on television). 'When I heard he had done this,' Tennant said, referring to the pianist's bequest, 'I thought, that's brilliant, that's what I'm going to do, but apparently you can't any more, the law's been changed.' ◉

TEED, CYRUS

(1839–1908)
'Koresh'

Though science is dead against it, the idea that the Earth is hollow and may contain vast unexplored lands has always had its champions. During the nineteenth century, the indefatigable ☞ John Cleves Symmes was the best known of them, but it was a physician, Cyrus Teed, who came up with the most novel variation on the idea. The Earth is indeed hollow, declared Teed, and we live inside it.

This unexpected state of affairs had been revealed to him, he said, by a beautiful, blonde haired woman who appeared to him in a vision. Teed, who practised 'eclectic' medicine (similar to homeopathy), was in his New York laboratory one night in October 1869, when the woman appeared. She was, he later wrote, the Universal Mother, the 'feminine face of God'. As well as revealing the secrets of the universe to him,

she told him he had been chosen to spread them to the rest of humanity.

Teed accepted his appointment as 'the Second Christ' with enthusiasm. He adopted the name 'Koresh' (Hebrew for Cyrus) and set about attracting followers. Progress was slow, but by 1892, Teed and about 100 followers were living in Chicago, in a luxurious mansion named Beth-Ophra and several adjoining cottages. His ultimate aim was to found a city, the 'New Jerusalem'. Like many of the other utopian communities that sprang up in nineteenth century America, this would be run on communist lines. And in recognition of the 'feminine face of God', men and women would be strictly equal.

Teed had a stroke of good fortune when a German immigrant who had chanced upon some of his writings offered 320 acres (129 hectares) of land in Estero Bay, Florida, to the cause. Teed and his followers moved there and set about building their community, eventually called the Koreshan Unity, with great industriousness. They built a huge meeting hall and numerous other buildings, and started a number of businesses which became very successful. The community grew to 200, and was by all accounts one of the happiest of the utopian experiments. It was run by Teed, his 'soul mate' Annie Ordway (known as Victoria Gratia) and seven other women. A

sign on the gate proclaimed proudly, 'We Live on the Inside.'

According to Koreshan cosmology, the Earth is a hollow sphere 8,000 miles in diameter, and the sun is a disk inside it a few hundred miles wide. We live on the concave interior of this sphere, and the rising and setting of the sun that we see is an optical illusion. While it may have come to Teed in a vision, he considered this a scientific theory that was testable, and one of his followers, Ulysses Grant Morrow, came up with an experiment to do just that. Morrow built a contraption of heavy wooden beams and steel that he called the 'Rectiliniator'. Its purpose was to draw an imaginary, horizontal, perfectly straight line in the air. This line would start some ten feet above the ground, but if Teed's theory was right and the Earth's surface is concave, it would eventually meet the ground. In 1897, Morrow and his assistants set the Rectiliniator up on a flat expanse of Florida beach and laboured with it for five months, creating an imaginary line that eventually, satisfyingly, plunged into the sea. The experiment (which no one seems to have ever bothered to replicate) was considered a resounding success.

The Koreshan Unity continued to thrive. It had an orchestra, an art gallery and a university — the Pioneer University of Koreshan

Universology. Teed had grand plans to transform it into a metropolis of ten million people. While it may never have reached these heights, it probably would have flourished a good many more years had Teed not decided to go into politics. In 1904, he founded the Progressive Liberty Party, and the local Democrats were not pleased when it proved attractive to voters. Shortly after this, Teed and his followers became involved in an altercation with some of their rivals. Teed received a head injury, and his health began to decline. After his death, his followers kept a vigil over the corpse, waiting for it to dematerialise in a flash of light, as Teed had predicted. Several days later, with the body rotting in the Florida heat, authorities made them bury it. Without its visionary founder, the community fragmented rapidly, although a few elderly survivors were still to be found there in the 1960s. Many buildings have been preserved, and the Koreshan State Historic Site was opened to tourists in 1967. ▨

TESLA, NIKOLA

(1856–1943)
Scientist

A brilliant inventor, almost a godlike figure to his most fervent admirers yet still unjustly neglected in the history of science, Tesla was a Serb, born in the Croatian village of Smiljan. An early fascination with mechanical problems and the properties of electricity led him to reject the priesthood, which his father had wanted him to enter, in favour of a career in engineering. He studied in Graz and Prague but could not afford to graduate, and remained basically self-taught. He possessed a remarkable eidetic memory which he said he had inherited from his mother. Until well into middle age he was able to visualise inventions in his mind in such detail and with such accuracy that he could, in effect, run tests on them before they were even built. In 1881, Tesla was strolling in a park in Budapest when the idea for his first great invention popped into his head — an induction motor running on alternating current (AC). The system of AC generation and distribution that he went on to develop was far more efficient than the direct current (DC) system then in use.

Obtaining a letter of introduction to Thomas Edison, Tesla sailed for the United States in 1884. Edison was impressed by him but would have nothing to do with alternating current, seeing in it the death of his own DC system.

Tesla looked for investors in AC, and found George Westinghouse. A 'Battle of the Currents' ensued,

NIKOLA TESLA

with Edison mounting a scare campaign about the alleged dangers of the new system. Reporters were invited to watch stray cats and dogs electrocuted with AC, while Edison's men even arranged to have it power the world's first electric chair in Sing Sing Prison. To counter such publicity, Tesla gave lectures illustrated with spectacular electrical effects. With tens of thousands of volts coursing through his body, the tall, elegantly dressed Tesla appeared to his audiences more like a wizard than a scientist. The clear superiority of AC over DC meant its triumph was inevitable, but not until Westinghouse had persuaded Tesla to sign away his royalties on the system. It is estimated that this cost him $12 million.

In 1893, Tesla gave the first public demonstration of radio transmission, an achievement still popularly associated with Marconi. He did pioneering work in fields as diverse as robotics and X-rays, but often neglected to patent his inventions, being more interested in moving on to the next problem. His greatest dream was the wireless transmission of electricity through the atmosphere, providing free energy for anyone who wanted it. He had found enough investors by 1899 to build an experimental transmitting station. An eighty-foot (24.4 m) tower was built in Colorado Springs, on

which was mounted a mast topped with a copper ball. As Tesla and his assistants worked each night, bolts of man-made lightning shot from the tower, and the desert for miles around crackled with electricity.

While he was often locked away in his laboratory for months at a time, unseen by his closest friends, Tesla would periodically emerge to make sensational statements to the press. He believed that while in Colorado Springs he had detected communications from another planet, and spoke of returning them. He boasted that, with a tiny oscillator set at just the right frequency, he could bring down the Brooklyn Bridge, and using the same principles, could split the very Earth asunder. While such statements were usually based on sound scientific ideas, he began to get a reputation as an impractical visionary, and his many personal eccentricities did not help. He couldn't bear the sight of pearls or the smell of camphor, would only put a spoonful of food to his mouth after calculating its volume, and was unable to touch the hair of another person. He seems to have remained celibate all his life.

In 1900, Tesla obtained the backing of J.P. Morgan and others to build a world broadcasting tower on Long Island. Six years later, with the tower incomplete and the money spent, he was forced to abandon it. He continued to do remarkable work, but was unable to fund it. In 1912, there were reports that he and Edison had jointly won the Nobel Prize, but in the end this didn't happen. (It was suggested that the two men — who still detested each other — had refused to share it.)

Tesla kept up appearances, dressing as finely as he had in his youth and living in hotels, but he was close to poverty. He fell out of step with science (he rejected Einstein's general theory of relativity) and became a fringe figure, largely forgotten. In his last years he devoted much of his time to feeding and caring for pigeons he found in the streets.

Tesla's reputation has undergone rehabilitation since his death. Later researchers have gone over his notes, maddeningly incomplete because of the amount of work he did in his head, and been amazed at the unforeseen applications of many of his patents. Some of his achievements, such as his creation of 'ball lightning' in the laboratory, have still not been replicated. ◙

---

*'One must be sane to think
clearly, but one can think
deeply and be quite insane.'*
NIKOLA TESLA

THAYER, TIFFANY
(1902–1959)
Writer

Thayer was, among other things, an author of outrageous bestselling novels, a fierce champion of ☞ Charles Fort and, in his later years, an inveterate crank. Born in Freeport, Illinois, he was the son of actors Elmer Thayer and Sybil Farrar, who divorced when he was five. Thayer became an actor, too, and as a teenager toured America in the Civil War play *The Coward*. Moving to New York in 1926, he worked in advertising, and in 1930 published his first novel, *Thirteen Men*, which deals with the lives of twelve jury members and the man whose trial they are serving on.

He followed this up with a string of big, bombastic and for the time quite risqué novels including *Call Her Savage* (1931) about a femme fatale (played in the movie version by Clara Bow); *Thirteen Women* (1932), in which a woman manages to persuade twelve of her college classmates to commit suicide; and *Little Dog Lost* (1938), a scathing satire on the movie business. Easily his strangest novel is *Doctor Arnoldi* (1933), which describes a world where one day, for no apparent reason, people cease to die, no matter how sick or badly injured they are.

As the still-pulsing, often uncon-scious bodies pile up, some are sent into space by rocket and others are dumped in the sea where they form islands, yet still they accumulate. ('Higher and higher the slimy piles grew, croaking, squealing and crawl-ing — all over the globe, like a solid sphere of maggots.') Thayer spent much of the thirties in Hollywood, writing scripts that mostly went un-filmed, and acting in one movie, *The Devil On Horseback* (1936), in which he played an excitable press agent.

Thayer first became aware of Charles Fort after reading his sec-ond book, *New Lands*, in 1924, and started to correspond with him. In 1930, he founded a Fortean Society in New York (which Fort himself refused to join). Its early members included Fort's friend, the novelist Theodore Dreiser, Ben Hecht and Alexander Woollcott. Thayer began to issue a Fortean Society magazine, later called *Doubt*, and continued to publish it until his death. Each issue featured some of Fort's unpublished notes of anomalous phenomena along with other items of Fortean interest, but Thayer also used it to push his hobbyhorses — and he probably had more hobbyhorses than any other man alive. He railed at governments, believing that both world wars had been the product of conspiracies. He thought that lie detectors, atomic power, higher

mathematics, the Sputnik, and Jonas Salk's polio vaccine were all hoaxes. He wanted marriage licences, fluori-dation of water, tonsillectomies and air travel abolished. He also insisted on using a new thirteen-month calendar, with year one being the year the society had been founded. Fort, the arch-sceptic, would prob-ably have been appalled by all this (then again, with his finely attuned sense of humour, he may have been amused as well).

Thayer's greatest obsession though, the one that dominated the last twenty years of his life, was the writing of a gargantuan sequence of novels set in Renaissance Italy, and built around the figure of the Mona Lisa. He worked for six months each year at an ad agency promot-ing Pall Mall cigarettes, then spent the rest of the year labouring on his magnum opus. He travelled to Italy for research, and had Italian books translated into English so he could read them. He eventually produced a handwritten manuscript of 46,000 pages. In 1956, the first three vol-umes (of a projected twenty-one) were published as *Mona Lisa, Part One: The Prince of Taranto*. All of the main characters in the book were historical figures, and Thayer, whose literary hero was Rabelais, declared, 'I don't want any reader to blame me for the sexual antics of these people. I didn't invent them. They behaved

like this.' He also had no doubts about his achievement, calling it 'a performance which stands alone and unmatched among the books of the world. It is as if Benvenuto Cellini had written "Decline and Fall"!' As it happened, these three volumes (in which Mona Lisa did not actually make an appearance) were the only parts of this vast work ever published. 🔳

THOMPSON, MARGARET
(d. 1776)
Snuff lover

Mrs. Thompson, who lived in London, was a great taker of snuff, or powdered tobacco which is inhaled through the nose. She left a celebrated will which began:

In the name of God, Amen. I, Margaret Thompson, being of sound mind, &c., do desire that when my soul is departed from this wicked world, my body and effects may be disposed of in the manner following: I desire that all my handkerchiefs that I may have unwashed at the time of my decease, after they have been got together by my old and trusty servant, Sarah Stuart, be put by her, and by her alone, at the bottom of my coffin, which I desire may be made large enough for that purpose, together with such a quantity of the best Scotch snuff (in which she knoweth I always had the greatest delight) as will cover my deceased

body; and this I desire the more especially as it is usual to put flowers into the coffins of departed friends, and nothing can be so fragrant and refreshing to me as that precious powder.

The will went on to stipulate further details of the funeral. Her coffin was to be carried by six men who were 'the greatest snuff-takers in the parish of St. James, Westminster', wearing snuff coloured beaver hats. They were to be accompanied by six women wearing hoods and carrying boxes of the best Scotch snuff 'for their refreshment as they go'. Sarah Stuart was to walk before the corpse, and at twenty-yard intervals fling handfuls of snuff upon the crowd, while a further two bushels were to be given away at the front door of Mrs. Thompson's house.

While Mrs. Thompson's requests were carried out to the letter, the amount of sneezing they caused was not recorded. 🔳

THORNTON, HAROLD 'KANGAROO'
(1916–2004)
Artist

The wildly colourful Thornton was born in the Sydney suburb of Enfield, and apprenticed to a signwriter at an early age. He ran a signwriting business during the

HAROLD 'KANGAROO'
THORNTON

war, did a year's formal training at art school, and became, as he put it, an 'artist of the people'. He first visited the Netherlands in the 1950s, and eventually became far better known there than in Australia. His artwork, which resembles traditional carnival or circus poster art and is rich in primary colours, appeared on numerous buildings and shopfronts in Amsterdam, most famously the exterior of the Bulldog Café, which opened in 1975. It was in the Netherlands that Thornton adopted the name 'the Kangaroo', saying that the Dutch found it hard to remember English names.

Thornton always had a fractious relationship with the art establishment in Australia, and had trouble finding galleries that would exhibit his works. He took to picketing outside the prestigious Archibald portrait prize each year (which he entered several times but, needless to say, never won), wearing his 'Sunday best', a suit painted with skeletons and scenes from Hell.

Thornton's painted clothes, hats and shoes became his trademark, particularly the coat which bore on its back the slogan 'Harold Kangaroo Thornton the Greatest Genius that Ever Lived'. He would paint anything, even, at one point, his false teeth (the paint eventually wore off, he explained, after he gave too many girls 'psychedelic lovebites').

He could often be seen in his gaudy attire, wheeling a shopping trolley around the innercity suburb of Darlinghurst. He was always short of money, mainly because he refused to sell any of his paintings. He fell in love with them all, he explained.

Declaring that Australians think football is more important than art (an indisputable assertion), Thornton spent his last years in the Netherlands, where a group of admirers called the Friends of Harold provided him with a house and living expenses.

THRING, FRANK
(1926–1994)
Actor

Thring was born into the cinema. His father, F.W. Thring, was a pioneer Australian film producer and founder of a cinema chain. One of Thring's first memories was the opening of the opulent Regent Theatre in Melbourne, which was decorated with antiques that Thring Snr. had brought back from Europe, and he made his screen debut as a toddler in *The Sentimental Bloke* (1919).

Thoroughly bored by school, Thring found work in the sound effects department of a radio station, then graduated to acting. There followed a brief, ill-advised stint in the

airforce, where he spent most of his time hiding in his hut and having gourmet food delivered to him from Melbourne. Discharged after six weeks, Thring returned to acting, toured Australia in several successful shows, then became manager of a repertory company. In 1954, he took his production of *Salome*, for which he had designed the costumes, to London. Theatre critic Harold Hobson was so impressed he wrote a glowing review featuring a photo of Thring as Herod under the headline 'WHO IS THIS MAN?' Thring later became friends with Laurence Olivier, and appeared with him in several Shakespeare plays in Stratford-upon-Avon.

Thring was a flamboyant homosexual, but when his mother died (has father having died years earlier), her will stipulated that he must be married to inherit her estate. He therefore married Joan Cunliffe, an actress, with Olivier giving the bride away and Vivien Leigh as maid of honour. Not surprisingly, the marriage only lasted nine months, and was annulled on the grounds of non-consummation.

Kirk Douglas caught Thring's performance in *Titus Andronicus*, and this led to his first Hollywood film role in *The Vikings* (1958). There followed a splendid career in epics. If you were a casting director looking for someone to play a louche, decadent historical figure, Thring was your man. Six feet two inches (188 cm) tall and heavily built, with a jowly face and a lugubrious manner of speaking, he projected an air of consummate oily malevolence in roles like Pontius Pilate in *Ben-Hur* (1959) and Herod Antipas in *King of Kings* (1961). 'You don't realise how boring it can be making a film, getting up every day at 4 a.m., waiting for hours for something to happen,' he said of these experiences. 'And there's always something wrong, the sun won't shine or the horses won't work…' There's a story, possibly apocryphal, that Thring once caused a take of a particularly elaborate scene to be aborted when a roast chicken he had concealed in his robes accidentally tumbled out.

Thring continued to spend half of each year in Australia, and lived in the lavish two-storey mansion his father had built in the exclusive Melbourne suburb of Toorak. He decorated it in black — black walls, carpets and furnishings — and the parties he held there were legendary. Many of the anecdotes told about him are unsuitable for a family friendly volume such as this. Perhaps one will suffice: Thring emerging from a bedroom, leaning over a balcony and calling out to other party guests, 'Bring me another boy. I've just burst this one.'

Always clad in black and adorned with chunky gold jewellery, Thring wrote a waspish column for a television magazine which made him many enemies. He was a fixture on Australian television for years, often appearing on chat shows, and was a memorable villain in *Skippy*, the series about an unfeasibly resourceful kangaroo which became a worldwide hit in the sixties. (On his first day on set, having spotted the animal playing Skippy tied up inside a hessian sack, he said, 'If that's the star's dressing room, I can't wait to see mine.') His later film roles included *Mad Dog Morgan* (1974), in which he played opposite Dennis Hopper, and *Mad Max: Beyond Thunderdome* (1985).

A final Thring story. One day, having been unable to contact him, Thring's agent went to his house, received no response to her knocking, and ended up breaking in. She found him in the kitchen, naked, gagged and tied to the table. When she tore the gag off, he declared, 'I've had the most marvellous weekend!' ◼

THYNN, ALEXANDER

(b. 1932)
The 7th Marquess of Bath

Alexander Thynn is today the foremost example of that great eccentric archetype, the dotty British aristocrat. Born in London, he grew up in Longleat, an extraordinary, 130-room Elizabethan house in Somerset built by his ancestor, Sir John Thynn, which he has called 'the only stage I have ever known'.

Thynn (who was born Thynne but later adopted the earlier form of the name) had a strained relationship with his father, the 6th Marquess, an authoritarian who collected paintings by Hitler and beat young Alexander with a riding crop. He went to Eton, did two years of national service in the lifeguards, and read philosophy at Oxford. It was at this point, while still in his early twenties, that he decided he was not cut out for a conventional life. He headed to Paris, where he studied painting and met a Hungarian girl, Anna Gyarmathy, whom he would later marry. He travelled extensively through Europe during the 1950s, kept a detailed journal of his life, and wrote the first of several novels.

Faced with the high costs of maintaining Longleat, Thynn's father had opened it to paying visitors in 1949, and later added a safari park to its attractions. In 1964, he made over the estate to Alexander, who moved back to Longleat and began to paint the first of the many murals that now adorn its walls. He paints in a colourful, swirly style,

TINY TIM

mixing his paint with sawdust so that it can be several inches thick.

The themes of the murals include the Ages of Man, Heaven and Hell, the Disco Mural and the mildly notorious Kama Sutra series. One of the spiral staircases in the house is decorated with portraits of Thynn's various lovers and mistresses over the years, around seventy-five at the time of writing, whom he famously dubbed 'wifelets'. (Anna, his long-suffering wife, whom he admits he married so as to obtain a legitimate heir, spends most of her time in Paris.)

Thynn ran for Parliament as a Wessex Regionalist in 1974 (Wessex being the old Anglo Saxon term for the area mainly encompassing Hampshire, Wiltshire, Somerset and Dorset), and later helped form a political party campaigning for autonomy for the region. In 1979, he was the party's candidate in the first European Parliament elections. Meanwhile, he has persisted with his literary endeavours. His fourth novel, *The Carry-Cot* ('a psycho-drama on the subject of baby-battering', as he put it), was the first of his works to be published, in 1972, and was followed by two more novels. Since then, he has concentrated on writing a vast, startlingly frank autobiography entitled *Strictly Private*. It is now said to be seven million words long, and contains

his unpublished novels as chapters. Although most of it will not be published until after his death, the sections dealing with his early years have appeared in book form and can be read on his website.

With his amiable, giggly personality, flowing grey hair and beard, and gaudy outfits (velvet trousers, embroidered waistcoats, oriental-style robes, etc), Thynn is one of the most recognisable figures in England, and often appears on television. Longleat remains a very popular tourist attraction, recording 360,000 visitors in 2006, and Lord Bath often comes out to meet them himself. It seems that these days only one thing rankles the 'loins of Longleat', as he is nicknamed (a play on the lions which roam its safari park) — he would like to increase the number of wifelets to 100 before he dies. ▣

TINY TIM

(1932–1996)
Singer

The unlikely sixties star and walking song repository known as Tiny Tim was born Herbert Khaury in New York. He was the only child of a Lebanese immigrant, Butros Khaury, and his Polish-Jewish wife Tillie. As a young boy, he was picked on and called a sissy by other kids, and

withdrew into himself, becoming obsessed with the popular songs of the early twentieth century. He spent endless hours in his bedroom playing old 78 rpm records on a wind-up gramophone, and developed an encyclopedic knowledge of the songs and the stories behind them.

Khaury's mother wanted him to have a steady job as an accountant or lawyer, but he dropped out of high school and embarked on a singing career. He let his hair grow long, plastered his face with white pancake makeup, and sang his repertoire of old, mostly forgotten songs in whatever seedy club or bar would have him. He accompanied himself on ukulele, and appeared under a variety of pseudonyms, including Larry Love, Emmett Swink, Rollie Dell and Judas K. Foxglove. At one point, he played in Hubert's Museum, a legendary establishment in a basement in Times Square, where his fellow performers included magicians, jugglers, human curiosities (i.e. freaks) and the fleas of Professor Heckler's Live Flea Circus.

During the early 1960s, Khaury settled on the stage name Tiny Tim, and became a fixture in Greenwich Village cafés. Standing just over six feet one inch (185 cm) tall, he was anything but tiny, but with straggly black hair falling over his shoulders

and ukulele clasped to his chest, he cut a suitably unconventional figure for the times, and the hippies loved him. In late 1967, Mo Ostin, a famously visionary executive with Warner Brothers Records who, during a long career, signed all manner of acts from the Beach Boys to the Sex Pistols, saw Tiny Tim perform and decided to take a chance on him. The result was his first album, *God Bless Tiny Tim*, which featured an eclectic mix of styles, from ukulele-driven ditties to lush psychedelic pop. Tiny's normal singing voice was a deep baritone, but on most of the songs, including 'Tip-Toe Thru' the Tulips' (originally a hit for Nick Lucas in 1929) he adopted a ludicrous yet strangely compelling falsetto.

In 1968, the same year as the album was released, Tiny made his first appearance on the hit television show *Laugh-In*. Many other television appearances followed, and sales of his album hit 200,000. Almost overnight he became one of the most famous recording artists in the world. Yet in an era of free love and radicalism, Tiny was as old-fashioned as the songs he loved. A devout Catholic and politically conservative, he spoke with elaborate formality, always referring to people as 'Mr' or 'Miss' such-and-such. He made no secret of the fact that he was attracted

to pretty girls, and the younger the better, but freely admitted to being a virgin. In fact, so prudish was he when it came to sex that he could not bring himself to say the word, or any words associated with it, and spelled them out instead. His other idiosyncrasies included obsessive cleanliness (he showered five times a day) and addiction to body lotions and hand creams. Journalists lapped it all up.

Tiny Tim released a second album (called *Tiny Tim's 2nd Album*), the cover of which featured a photo of him with his parents. His fame reached its peak in December 1969 when he married seventeen-year-old Vickie Budinger ('Miss Vickie'), whom he had met at a book signing, live on the *Tonight Show with Johnny Carson*. It attracted over forty million viewers.

After that, perhaps inevitably, Tiny Tim's novelty began to wane. There were no more hits, and the television offers dried up. His marriage failed (Budinger later told a tabloid newspaper that they had not had sex until six months after their wedding, although they did manage to produce a daughter, Tulip Victoria). Ripped off by various managers, Tiny had little money to show for his glory days. He kept plugging away, though, and toured with a circus for a while. In 1988, he gave a memorable performance at the

Brighton Festival in England which was billed as the 'World Non-Stop Singing Record'. Tiny sang over 130 songs from all periods of the twentieth century, and a recording of the event was later issued on three cassettes.

Tiny Tim's greatest champion in his last years was the Australian artist Martin Sharp, who put his iconic image on posters, designed costumes for him and spent over ten years making a documentary about him called *Street of Dreams*. Tiny began recording again, issuing his first albums since the sixties. Among these final recordings are several unexpected cover versions, including one of AC/DC's 'Highway to Hell'.

Tiny's second marriage, to Jan Alweiss, ended in 1995, and in the same year he married Susan Gardner. This third marriage was apparently a happy one, but it was not destined to last long. On 30 November 1996, Tiny was giving a performance for the Women's Club of Minneapolis when he suffered a heart attack while singing 'Tip-Toe Thru' the Tulips'. He was helped off the stage by Susan, and died in her arms.

TISHLER, JOSEPH

(1871–1957)
'Bellerive the Poet'

Tishler was born in Dunedin, New Zealand. His family moved to Victoria, Australia, when he was still a young boy, and he went to a state school where, he wrote, 'although a slow learner, I evinced poetic signs'. As a young man he worked in a jam factory, drove dray horses, and spent a while roaming the countryside as a swagman. Returning to Melbourne, he fell in with the Larrikins, the delinquents of their day, who appreciated his accordion playing. 'I attended their rowdy picnics and parties,' he recalled. 'I studied their sayings and style, was an eye witness to their Arguments and Brawls, and reconciled Em [sic] in trouble.' He joined a theatrical company, working mostly as a scene-shifter, although he occasionally had bit parts, including the role of a monkey in *Sinbad the Sailor*. Throughout these years, he spent his nights writing poetry. His favourite poet was Mrs. Hemans, best known for 'Casabianca' (or at least for its opening line, 'The boy stood on the burning deck'). He thought she was the greatest poet who had ever lived.

Using the pseudonym 'Bellerive', he began to send his poems to the *Bulletin*, the political-cum-literary magazine known as 'the Bushman's Bible'. The magazine printed them in its 'Answers to Correspondents' section, in which the more absurd contributions it received were held up to ridicule. Tishler didn't mind as long as they were being printed, and his poems would continue to feature there for over forty years.

Tishler was best known for his tales of low life, particularly bloodthirsty stories of murder. Idiosyncratic in spelling and metre his productions may have been, but they did not lack vigour.

A cold-blooded monster
His beautiful wife did slay
And from justice endeavoured
To hide he's foul play.
During the stillness of the night
Under a cellar's flagstones
He concealed he's poor
Victim's mutilated bones.

When he wasn't writing such bloodcurdling stuff, Tishler was a keen observer of everyday life. He wrote poems about bumping into 'a prowling cow' in the dead of night, and sitting on his favourite straw hat. He sang of a rat trapped on an airplane and an escaped pig, of fleas, flies, maggots, cockroaches and bedbugs.

Like the daring fleas –
They're a notorious pest –
Are loathsome bugs which
In old houses nest.
In worn ceilings and walls
They thickly about,
To revel they assemble
And prowleth around.

Tishler married late in life, and had a son. His wife was an amateur painter (she might have been a pretty good one, he said, but she had only been able to afford one lesson). They lived in a tiny cottage crammed with curios near the Victoria Markets in Melbourne.

Towards the end of his life, Tishler became disenchanted with the poet's lot. 'Writing poetry is a hard, cold life and you make more enemies than friends,' he told a journalist in 1950. Eighty-years-old and suffering from asthma, it seemed that the critics had finally worn him down. 'They're a hard lot, them critics, and there's some brains among them, too. They're up against you all the time.' Sadly, vindication of his art only came posthumously, when a collection of his poems, *The Book of Bellerive*, was published in 1961. Edited by the *Bulletin*'s former literary editor Douglas Stewart, it included some of Tishler's most evocative pieces, including this heartfelt paean to a pair of pants.

Dilapidated old pants,
You're beyond repair;
Through calm and storm
Like a board you did wear;
Made of tough cloth,
For work and its strain,
You cost me a pound
And I can't complain;
Too bursted and rent
For needle and thread,
You've got to come down
From the nail in the shed;
Out into the lane
Old pants you must go,
A gift from a poet
To a poor bottle-o.

TRAIN, GEORGE FRANCIS

(1829–1904)
Businessman, traveller & political candidate

The highly mobile Train was born in Boston, Massachusetts. His parents, Oliver and Maria Train, died of yellow fever when he was four, and he was raised by his Methodist grandparents who instilled in him the virtues of abstinence from alcohol and tobacco. He had his first experience of business working as a teenager in the Boston and Liverpool offices of his cousin Enoch Train's shipping company, the White Diamond Line.

Lured by reports of the Austra-

lian gold rush, Train and his wife
Wilhelmina set sail for Melbourne
in 1853. With his business partner,
Captain Ebenezer Caldwell, he
indulged in a flurry of activities,
including building warehouses,
importing goods and organising a
voluntary fire brigade. Train was
considered a breath of fresh air
in Melbourne's sometimes stuffy
commercial circles, and was known
for his enthusiasm, cheerfulness,
elegant dress sense and championing of republican values.

Train left Melbourne in 1855,
and travelled through Asia and the
Middle East before returning to
Boston, where he rejoined his wife
and daughter Susan. His accounts
of his travels were published in
a book, *An American Merchant in
Europe, Asia and Australia* (1857).
His next business venture was in
England, where he established a
horse-drawn tram company, but this
ran into opposition because the rails
his trams travelled on were above
ground level and interfered with
other vehicles. Back in America, he
worked for the Union Pacific Railroad, and established a construction
company called Crédit Mobilier of
America, which supplied services to
the Union Pacific. A great scandal
would later erupt when it was revealed that the owners and directors
of the two companies were the
same, and Crédit Mobilier had been

selling its services to the Union Pacific at greatly inflated prices (with
the bill then passed on to the U.S.
government).

In 1870, Train set out from New
York on a round-the-world trip. His
adventures included bathing naked
in a Japanese bathhouse, and being
arrested in France when mistaken
for a communard. Released after
President Grant and Alexandre
Dumas interceded on his behalf, he
made up time by hiring a private
train which got him to the Channel. Reaching Liverpool, he caught
a boat back to New York, arriving
eighty days after he had left. Train
was convinced he was the model for
Phileas Fogg in Jules Verne's *Around
the World in Eighty Days*, which appeared in 1873. (He would go on
two further round-the-world trips
in 1890 and 1892, on the latter trip
getting his time down to sixty days).

In 1872, Train stood for president as an independent. He was a
supporter of women's rights and
when he learned that ☞ Victoria
Woodhull and her sister Tennessee had been jailed after allegedly
publishing an obscenity in their
weekly newspaper, he came out in
their defence. He visited them in jail,
and to demonstrate the absurdity of
the charge, published a collection
of excerpts from the Bible relating to sexual intercourse. This saw
Train also charged with obscenity.

Held in the Tombs jail in Manhattan, he proved very popular with the other inmates, who elected him President of Murderers' Row. At his trial, he was acquitted on grounds of insanity and ordered to be institutionalised by the judge, but was allowed to leave the courtroom and immediately set off for England. He later put himself forward for the position of Dictator of the United States.

Train, who styled himself an 'aristocratic loafer', grew more eccentric in his later years. He refused to shake hands, believing that this led to a loss of 'psychic force', and instead, on meeting people, would clasp his own hands (a practice he had seen in China). He came out against the eating of meat and the wearing of underwear. He also stopped talking to people and communicated only by writing. At the end of his life, he could often be seen sitting on a bench in New York's Madison Square Park, feeding the pigeons and talking only to children.

URQUHART, SIR THOMAS
(1611–1660)
Scholar & translator

Urquhart was the eldest son of Sir Thomas Urquhart of Cromarty, Scotland, who ran up massive debts which would plague the younger Thomas for years. He was educated at King's College, Aberdeen, but failed to graduate, then spent several years touring Europe. A staunch royalist, he was knighted by Charles I after taking part in the battle known as the Trot of Turriff, in 1639. He published his first book, an undistinguished collection of epigrams, in 1641, and followed this four years later with a much more idiosyncratic work, a treatise on trigonometry, *The Trissotetras*, which, like all of Urquhart's writings, teems with words of his own invention

and is famously impenetrable.

After the execution of Charles I, Urquhart took part in royalist uprisings in Scotland. He was captured during the Battle of Worcester in 1650 and imprisoned in the Tower of London. Oliver Cromwell ordered his release the following year, but he was told he would have to forfeit his land unless he proved himself worthy of keeping them. He decided that the best way to do this would be by writing a series of books. The first of these, *Pantochronocanon*, was a work of genealogy in which Urquhart traced his ancestors back to Adam (among its revelations was the fact that the Pharoah's daughter, who discovered the baby Moses in the bulrushes, was named Termuth Urquhart). He followed this with *Ekskubalauron* (the title is one of his coinages meaning 'gold out of dung'), in which Urquhart outlined his ideas for a universal language. This was reissued in a revised form as *Logopandecteision*, with some added material in which he attacked his creditors and other enemies. Although in these books he describes what his proposed language will be like (rather than actually giving any examples of it), he leaves the reader in no doubt as to its benefits.

My Universal Language is a most exquisite jewel. It hath eleven genders, seven moods, four voices, ten cases, besides the nominative, and twelve parts of speech; every word signifieth as well backwards as forwards; and it is so compact of style that a single syllable will express the year, month, day, hour and partition of the hour.

Urquhart's last major work was a translation of the first three volumes of Rabelais' *Gargantua and Pantagruel*. For once he put his love of words to good use, and his version, in which he embroiders on the text but is faithful to its ribald, rambunctious spirit, is considered one of the greatest translations of a book into English.

Urquhart's last years are obscure. According to legend, he died during a fit of laughter brought on by the news that Charles II had been restored to the throne.

VAN BUTCHELL, MARTIN

(c.1735–1812)
Dentist

Van Butchell, the son of a tapestry maker to King George II, was a fashionable London dentist who later specialised in the making of trusses and the curing of fistulas and piles. While some considered him a quack, others swore by his skills, and he was able to command the highest prices for his services. On one point though he was firm — he refused to make house calls, his motto being 'I go to none'. He did not break this resolution even when an eminent lawyer offered him 500 guineas, an enormous sum, to attend him at his home.

He had a beard that reached to his knees, and sold strands of it for a guinea apiece (they were 'of use to the fair; that want fine children', he said in one of his advertisements). He could often be seen riding in Hyde Park on his white pony, which he liked to paint with black or purple spots, or stripes and circles of other colours. When walking in the streets, he always carried a large bone with which to attack impudent boys who insulted his appearance. He designed a costume for himself, a one-piece garment of elastic material that covered him from head to foot. He was something of an absolutist when it came to the colour of clothing, telling his wife that she could either wear all black or all white. She chose the former.

Van Butchell's fame reached new heights when his wife died in 1775. Enlisting the help of William Hunter, an eminent surgeon who had taught him anatomy, he had her body embalmed. Red dye was pumped into her veins, glass eyes were placed in her eye sockets, and she was put on display in a glass-topped case in Van Butchell's parlour, wearing her wedding dress. She proved a popular attraction, with so many of the gentry arriving to have a look that he was forced to put an announcement in a newspaper.

Van Butchell, not wishing to be unpleasantly circumstanced, and wishing to convince some good minds they have been misinformed, acquaints the Curious,

no stranger can see his embalmed wife unless (by a friend personally) introduced by himself, any day between nine and one, Sundays excepted.

Van Butchell's second wife, Elizabeth (who had opted to wear all white) eventually persuaded him to remove her predecessor from public display. She was taken to the Royal College of Surgeons, where she remained until the building was bombed during World War II. ▣

VAN DER ELST, VIOLET

(1882–1966)
Anti-hanging campaigner

The formidable Mrs. Van der Elst was probably more responsible than anyone else for the abolition of capital punishment in Britain. She was born Violet Dodge into a working class family in Feltham, Surrey, and at the age of seventeen married a civil engineer named George Nathan. After several years in Belgium, they returned to England in 1912, and bought a large house in Hampstead. Violet decided to start her own cosmetics business, and experimented with different formulas for face cream in her kitchen. She eventually hit upon a promising one, which she called 'Doge Cream' (after the former elected rulers of

Venice). She claimed it was based on a recipe used by Lucrezia Borgia, and sold it door-to-door from a carriage drawn by six horses. Among the other products she came up with were Shavex, a brushless shaving cream, and Zee-Kol toilet soap.

A determined businesswoman, Violet would turn up unannounced at stores, wearing a chinchilla coat and looking imperious, and demand to see the manager. She invariably left having secured a large order for her products. She spent a great deal of money on advertising, and always wrote her own copy. ('If Doge Cream is smeared around the eyes at night, every wrinkle will vanish as if a miracle has happened.') By the 1930s, her business had about 100 employees and was turning over £1 million a year.

George Nathan died in 1927, and soon afterwards Violet married a Belgian artist, Jean Van der Elst. The success in business enabled her and Jean to travel extensively throughout the world, picking up rare and curious works of art. Violet amassed a huge collection of jewels and furs, indulged in charitable works and mixed with high society (though she never completely lost her Cockney accent). She also amassed a huge library of books on the occult, demonology and witchcraft, subjects which fascinated her.

Jean Van der Elst died suddenly in 1934. Violet, who had loved him dearly, spent years trying to contact him in séances. She also decided to devote her life to a cause they had shared — the abolition of capital punishment. She was convinced that murderers were always in a state of insanity when they carried out their crimes, and that death by hanging was barbarous. Her campaign, modelled on the militant tactics of the Suffragettes, began in March 1935, when she protested outside Pentonville Prison against the execution of Charles Lake, who had killed a bookmaker in a fit of rage. For the next two decades, few executions in England were complete without a protest from Mrs. Van der Elst. These usually involved Violet arriving at a prison in her white Rolls-Royce, followed by a van equipped with a loudspeaker and dozens of men carrying sandwich boards with slogans like 'Mercy is Not Weakness'. Sometimes, one of the three planes that she owned flew overhead, an anti-hanging banner trailing from it. She was often arrested for blocking traffic and other misdemeanours.

Violet was a generally benevolent soul. If she was out driving and spotted a needy looking person in the street, she would despatch her chauffeur with money to give them. She treated her staff less well, pay-ing them the minimum wage and often suspecting them (sometimes correctly) of stealing from her. She was prone to sudden, violent rages during which, her former secretary recalled, 'The right side of her face would remain calm, with the eye closed, but the left one would glare and the nostril would twitch, and that side of her mouth would snarl.' (This asymmetric effect was no doubt the result of a less-than-successful face-lift she had in the thirties.) She could be calm again in seconds, though.

In addition to her anti-hanging activities, Violet composed concertos and symphonies (not being able to read music, she employed a man to write them down for her). She also wrote fiction, often with occult or mystical themes, and published a number of collections including *The Torture Chamber and Other Stories* (1937). She ran for Parliament twice, published a newspaper called *Humanity* in the 1930s, and at one point planned to start her own religion, but could not find a suitable church for sale.

In 1937, she bought Harlaxton Manor near Grantham in Lincolnshire. An extraordinary 100-room structure in mock Elizabethan style, built between 1837 and 1855, it boasts numerous turrets, gables and decorative flourishes. She renamed it Grantham Castle and spared no expense decorating it with paintings and statues, Louis XV furniture, tapestries from Buckingham Palace and the world's largest chandelier. When war broke out, she offered it to the government, and soldiers were billeted there. She spent the war years in London, and was courageous and defiant during the Blitz. After air raids, she drove through the streets with bundles of cash to give to people whose homes had been bombed.

Her fortunes declined after the war. She was presented with a huge bill for unpaid taxes, and was forced to sell her businesses and live in decreasingly grand houses. Her health and memory gradually failed. For all her wealth, she had essentially been without friends after her husband died, and spent her final years in a nursing home. She was cheered, however, when news came through in 1965, the year before her death from pneumonia, that capital punishment had been abolished in Britain. While some had disapproved of her methods of fighting for this outcome, no one ever doubted her sincerity. ▣

———————

'I have only one religion, and that is — Humanity.'
VIOLET VAN DER ELST

———————

VAN VLIET, DON

(1941–2010)
'Captain Beefheart'

Don Vliet (he added the 'Van' later) was born in Glendale, Los Angeles, the only child of Glen and Sue Vliet. He demonstrated artistic ability at an early age, attending sculpture classes at Griffith Park Zoo, and winning a prize at nine (for his elephant). The Vliets moved to Lancaster, on the edge of the Mohave Desert, where Don's neighbours included Frank Zappa. They shared a love of music, and spent hours together listening to blues, rock and doo-wop records. They began to record together during the early sixties, when Zappa briefly became the manager of a recording studio in Cucamonga, and planned to make a science fiction film in which Don would play a 'magic man' named Captain Beefheart. There are several different versions of the name's origin, with Zappa's the most evocative — he said that Don's uncle had a habit of going to the bathroom with the door open when Don's girlfriend was around, declaring as he did so that his member was as big as a beef heart.

In 1965, a Lancaster local, Alex Snouffer (later St. Clair), decided to form a band, and recruited Van Vliet who, despite his tender years,

DON VAN VLIET

could sing like a gravel-voiced old bluesman. Captain Beefheart and His Magic Band, as they were called, recorded a couple of singles, then an album, *Safe as Milk*. Released in 1967, it offered a mutated blues, soul and rock which only hinted at the strangeness to come. The band gained a cult following and played in the UK, but commercial success was elusive.

By the time their second album, *Strictly Personal*, was released in late 1968, Van Vliet was the only original member left. They had been dropped by their record company, but Zappa, who now had his own label, offered Van Vliet the chance to record an album with complete artistic control. Van Vliet decided that the others needed new names to go with the music he was envisaging, and so Bill Harkleroad, Mark Boston, Jeff Cotton, John French and Victor Hayden became Zoot Horn Rollo, Rockette Morton, Antennae Jimmy Semens, Drumbo and the Mascara Snake respectively. They lived together in a small house in Los Angeles, with barely enough money to buy food, and spent over six months rehearsing the insanely complicated songs Van Vliet had composed on piano, an instrument he could barely play, until they were note perfect. If ☞ Sun Ra and ☞ Joe Meek went to extraordinary lengths to convey to musicians the

ideas in their heads, and expected them to respond with extraordinary efforts, Van Vliet outdid them — the atmosphere in the house has often been likened to a cult. Many legends have grown up about the recording of what became *Trout Mask Replica*. One story which is true is that Van Vliet was worried about the effect the music was having on the trees surrounding the house, so had a tree surgeon come out and check them to make sure they were okay.

The resulting double album, which has a photo of Van Vliet with a carp's head strapped to his face on the cover, is not quite like anything else ever recorded. It contains twenty-eight mostly short songs full of unconventional rhythms, discordant guitars and passages reminiscent of free jazz, with the Captain growling his surreal, image-laden, semi-improvised lyrics over the top. While it strikes most listeners as an unholy cacophony, those who succumb to its peculiar charms are prone to calling it the greatest rock album ever made.

The album cemented the band's position as leading purveyors of avant-garde rock, especially in Europe, and Captain Beefheart always made good copy, confounding interviewers with gnomic utterances like 'There are forty people in the world and five of them are hamburgers.' Those who knew Don Van Vliet personally describe a man with a childlike sense of wonder at the world and a love of animals and nature. His conversation was almost as full of bizarre wordplay as his lyrics, and many were convinced he was psychic. There are numerous anecdotes about him reading minds, or doing things like getting up to answer the phone just before it rang.

The next album, *Lick My Decal's Off, Baby*, was almost as wild as *Trout Mask Replica*. The band was still broke though, and a series of more conventional sounding albums failed to bring commercial success. In 1974, Van Vliet quit music temporarily and moved back to Lancaster where he and his wife Jan, whom he had married 1969, lived in his mother's trailer. Zappa lured him back to music, and he toured with the Mothers of Invention (he spent most of his time on stage drawing in sketchbooks). He eventually put together a new version of the Magic Band and recorded several albums which were hailed as a return to form. Van Vliet's recording techniques remained as idiosyncratic as ever. He would ask a musician to play something as if it was a certain colour, or like 'a bat being dragged through oil'. He once told Cliff Martinez, the last drummer who worked with him, to play something 'like Fred Astaire

dangling through a tea cup'.

Sick of touring, Van Vliet quit music again in 1982, this time for good, and announced he would be concentrating on painting. He and Jan moved to a house on the northern Californian coast. As he had no formal art training, the art establishment was initially sceptical, but he secured exhibitions in some prestigious galleries and began to acquire a reputation. His paintings have been likened to the work of the abstract impressionists, although they usually include recognisable figures, most often animals.

Van Vliet last appeared in public in 1990, and gave his last interview in 1995. His reclusiveness was generally ascribed to ill health, and he died from complications from multiple sclerosis. ▨

VON MIERERS, FREDERICK
(1946–1990)
Male model from Arcturus

Von Mierers claimed to have been born into one of the oldest and most respectable of New York families. After his parents were killed in a car crash when he was four, he was looked after by his godmother, prominent society woman and arts patron Helen Kress Williams, who took him on trips to Europe where

FREDERICK VON MIERERS

he mingled with the aristocracy and even met Queen Elizabeth.

In fact, he was probably born Freddie Meyer or Meier in Brooklyn, and had an entirely unremarkable childhood. And while he was certainly a companion of Helen Williams in the 1960s and early seventies, it would seem his greatest interest in her was her money.

Von Mierers was an extremely handsome young man with piercing blue eyes. He had some success during the sixties as a model in New York, and greater success worming his way into high society. He frequented an exclusive club, had his name listed in the New York Social Register, and became an acolyte of the chic interior decorator Billy Baldwin. In the late seventies, he also developed an interest in astrology and 'New Age' spirituality, and began to charge people for astrological charts and psychic readings.

The pivotal moment in von Mierers' life, according to his own account, came in January 1978. He had a series of visions in which he saw his past lives, including one as a high priest in Ancient Egypt and another in India during the time of Buddha. Overnight he became an expert in 'Hindu astrology'. And most amazing of all, he realised that he originally hailed from the star Arcturus, where he had lived in 'a hydrogen-light body'.

Von Mierers attracted a small group of followers, and gave them 'life readings' at his Manhattan apartment. He put them on rigorous vegetarian diets and told them to abstain from sex. After the group featured heavily in a 1986 book by Ruth Montgomery, *Aliens Among Us*, sales of their tapes and books took off. Von Mierers also developed a lucrative sideline in gemstones, which he prescribed to his followers according to their psychic needs, and sold at vastly inflated prices.

His group, now called Eternal Values, grew to about 100 core members. There were two requirements for membership — you had to be good looking, and you had to have money. Many professional people, actors and models joined. Von Mierers taught that the end of the world was coming within ten years, and only his followers — his 'duchesses and lords' as he liked to refer to them — would survive to lead the New Age. 'Everyone I am training for leadership will have perfect features,' he said. 'I believe in the master race!' Not surprisingly, von Mierers held virulently anti-Semitic views, and was a great admirer of Hitler.

Von Mierer's apartment had walls of lavender, pink and turquoise, clouds painted on the ceilings, faux-Egyptian furniture and masses of artificial flowers. He

liked to entertain guests dressed in white with a parrot perched on each shoulder.

He dyed his hair blond and had plastic surgery so that by the end his formerly handsome face looked like a stretched mask. While he had once preached celibacy, he became increasingly obsessed with sex. New members of the group were expected to go through a multi-racial group sex rite known as 'the treatment', and von Mierers was said to have a large collection of photos of well-endowed black men which he had taken himself.

The group began to fragment in the late 1980s. Some members had paid over $100,000 for gemstones which they later found were practically worthless. The District Attorney's office began to mount a criminal investigation, but before he could be arrested, Frederick von Mierers died of AIDS. ▣

'It is true that our space brothers have arrived. And we are they!'

FREDERICK VON MIERERS

WARHOL, ANDY
(1928–1987)
Artist

Warhol was the youngest of three sons of Ondrej (Andy) and Ulja (Julia) Warhola, who immigrated to America from the Carpathian village of Mikova (then part pf the Austro-Hungarian Empire, and now in Slovakia). Warhol grew up in the smog-ridden, industrial city of Pittsburgh. His father was a stern workaholic who was often absent from home, and he was much closer to his chatty, storytelling mother. He was a shy, pale, sickly boy who preferred the company of girls to boys and loved going to movies. He collected signed photos of movie stars, and Shirley Temple was his first role model. At the age of eight he contracted chorea, also known as St. Vitus' dance, which causes involuntary shaking and slurred speech. He was confined to bed for a month, which he spent making drawings and collages with the assistance of his mother — a period he remembered as idyllic.

Warhol's father died when he was twelve. The money he had saved enabled Andy to attend college, and he studied art at the Carnegie Institute of Technology. After graduating in 1949, he moved to New York were he did the rounds of commercial art directors, armed with his portfolio. On his second day there, he showed up at the office of Tina Fredericks, art director of *Glamour* magazine, who told him she urgently needed some drawings of shoes. As Warhol (who dropped the final 'a' from his surname soon after his arrival in New York) was a confirmed shoe and foot fetishist, he eagerly accepted the assignment. He quickly became a sought-after graphic artist, turning out magazine illustrations and record covers for a host of clients. He worked tirelessly, and began to make a lot of money, but affected a proletarian look — work shirt, blue jeans — and was known as 'Raggedy Andy'. In 1952, his mother came to live with him in his dank basement flat on 75th Street, where they shared a bedroom and a rapidly growing collection of cats. (Later, he moved to a more luxurious apartment on an upper floor, while she remained in the basement.)

All of Warhol's efforts were directed to one end — he wanted to be famous, a celebrity like his childhood idols. He remained painfully shy, though, and convinced he was ugly. He had bad skin and was almost bald by his mid-twenties, so started to wear an assortment of wigs. He fell madly in love with various good-looking young men, but his self-consciousness meant he remained mostly celibate (sexually, Warhol was essentially a voyeur). And his efforts to break into fine art were going nowhere. He had a few exhibitions, but his work was dismissed by the art establishment, then still dominated by the champions of abstract expressionism.

He was saved by pop art. He didn't invent it — a group of British artists had first begun to appropriate images from popular culture in the fifties — but he saw it as the way to make his mark. He painted his first Campbell's Soup can in 1962, and soon after this discovered screen printing. Warhol had always enlisted the help of friends — even his mother — in producing his art. With screen printing he had the means to mass produce it, and was soon turning out his trademark multiple images of Marilyn Monroe, Elvis Presley and other celebrities. They were attacked by the media and older artists, but they made him famous. Warhol's image — the blond and silver wigs, the mono-syllabic answers to questions, the enigmatic statements like 'I want to be a machine', his whole alien demeanour — suddenly made sense. For many he *was* pop art.

In 1963, Warhol shot his first underground film — *Sleep*, a five-hour-plus record of his sometime lover John Giorno sleeping. (Warhol loved watching his friends sleeping, a trait he inherited from his mother, who had sometimes stayed up all night to watch him sleep.) Shortly after filming this, he moved into a new studio, an old factory space on East 47th Street. He hired Billy Linich (later Billy Name) to decorate it, which he did by painting the walls silver and covering every other surface in tinfoil. Linich introduced Warhol to the 'amphetamine rapture group', a flamboyant gang of mostly speed-addicted gay males, including Ondine, the dancer Freddie Herko, ☞ Dorothy Podber, and the evoca-tively named Sugar Plum Fairy. They virtually moved into the Factory, as it was known, and became the stars of Warhol's early films, including *Couch*, in which various permutations of them, along with anyone else who showed up, are seen having sex on the Factory's infamous couch.

Warhol abandoned painting during these years to concentrate on films, grooming new 'super-stars' including the waiflike socialite Edie Sedgewick, and mounting the multimedia event the Explod-ing Plastic Inevitable, featuring the band the Velvet Underground. The drug-fuelled madness at the Factory continued, with Warhol observing it all with his usual detachment. His friends warned him of the dangers of surrounding himself with such unstable people, and when a crazed friend of Ondine's burst into the Factory one day and held Warhol and several others at gunpoint, he decided to move to more business-like premises near 14th Street. This did not save him from Valerie Solanas.

Solanas was a lesbian and radi-cal feminist who had written *The S.C.U.M. Manifesto*, which called for the elimination of the male sex (S.C.U.M. being an acronym for the nonexistent 'Society for Cutting Up Men'). She also wrote a play, *Up Your Ass*, which she presented to Warhol, wanting him to produce it. He gave her a part in one of his films, but she continued to pester him about the play (which he had lost). Believ-ing that Warhol was persecuting her, she arrived at the Factory on 3 June 1968, with two guns in a paper bag. She shot Warhol and an art critic, Mario Amayo, and tried to shoot Warhol's manager, Fred Hughes, before escaping. Warhol suffered

terrible internal injuries and was briefly pronounced clinically dead at hospital, but surgeons managed to save him.

Warhol was never the same after the shooting. He spent a long time convalescing, during which he took to tape-recording his conversations with people. It was also during this time that he developed the habit of asking every man who turned up at the Factory to let him take a Polaroid of their penis.

Meanwhile, the business of Andy Warhol Enterprises was taking off. Some of the films, beginning with *Trash* and *Heat*, which were essentially directed by Warhol collaborator Paul Morrissey, became mainstream hits, and the value of his early paintings soared. Warhol developed a lucrative sideline painting portraits of the rich. He went out every night and became a fixture at Studio 54 and other fashionable nightclubs of the day, mingling with his beloved celebrities along with more dubious characters like the Shah of Iran's wife and Imelda Marcos.

With money pouring in, he could indulge his passion for collecting. He shopped every day, buying up vast quantities of antique furniture, folk art, ceramics, crystals, perfume — many of his purchases were never unpacked. The six-storey house he acquired in 1975 was so full of stuff by the time of his death that it was difficult to move through the rooms. But Warhol's collecting mania went further than this. During the sixties he developed the habit of never throwing anything away. He kept advertising flyers, receipts, magazine cuttings, artworks, party invitations and all sorts of other ephemera which were put into cardboard boxes and placed in storage. There are 610 of these boxes, which Warhol called 'Time Capsules', and the process of cataloguing them is ongoing.

For all the excesses of his life, and the lives of those in his orbit, Warhol remained a Catholic who went to mass every Sunday, and some of the last paintings he worked on were based on 'The Last Supper'. He died suddenly and unexpectedly after undergoing gallbladder surgery.

WARING, FRANCIS
(1760–1833)
Clergyman

The Reverend Francis John Waring was a busy man. Appointed Vicar of Heybridge in Essex, England, in 1786, he also held the curacies of St. Mary, Maldon and Mundon, and was expected to perform services in all three churches every Sunday. He achieved this by racing through services at lightning speed, allowing no time for responses from the congregation, and finishing with a sermon of a few hurried words. He would then run down the aisle, jump on his horse, and gallop to the next church on his list.

He was known for his peculiarities of dress, and often appeared in church wearing a straw hat and shooting coat, or dressed like a Quaker. Once, when a bishop commented on the fact that he was wearing a rather inappropriate costume of scarlet plush breeches and white stockings, he replied, 'That you should condescend to notice my breeches is an honour which I did not expect — there is my tailor's card.'

Waring insisted on living frugally. When invited to dinner, he refused to eat more than one dish, explaining that when he and his family dined at home they could only afford a single joint of meat. His house was furnished with logs instead of chairs, and he and his wife slept in an enormous wicker basket. He was hugely popular in Heybridge, and known for his quick wit and down to earth humour. One ecclesiastical historian records how 'Mr. Bugg, Mayor and Magistrate for Maldon, a huge pompous powdered man with overbearing speech not unlike the roar of a large mastiff addressed Mr. Waring rudely at a public dinner. Looking full in the face of the Mayor he gave a loud Bow-wow-wow-wow. The Mayor was effectually subdued amid the roar of guests.'

WATERTON, CHARLES

(1782–1865)
Explorer, naturalist
& conservationist

Waterton, who was centuries ahead of his time with his ideas about conservation and the evils of pollution, was the son of the 26th Lord (or Squire) of Walton Hall in Wakefield, Yorkshire. The Watertons were Catholics who had clung to their faith tenaciously in the face of years of religious persecution. Charles developed his passion for nature as a young boy, and took to climbing the tallest trees, towers and other structures in search of birds' nests. (His enthusiasm for climbing persisted. On a trip to Rome a few years later, Waterton climbed the dome of St. Peter's Basilica and left his gloves on the lightning rod.) He was educated at the Catholic college Stonyhurst, which he loved, and which indulged him by making him unofficial exterminator of rats and other vermin, all good training for the future explorer and collector of specimens par excellence.

In 1804, Waterton travelled to South America, and spent most of the next eight years managing three

plantations owned by his family in British Guiana (now Guyana). In 1812, he embarked on his first expedition into the interior of the country, returning to England the following year with samples of curare (the first to be brought to Europe), many birds preserved using a method of taxidermy he had devised (which left them hollow and lifelike) and a bad case of malaria. Three further expeditions followed. Waterton kept his hair cropped short, almost unheard of in his day, and insisted on travelling through the jungle barefoot. His adventures included wrestling with boa constrictors, dining on 'boiled ant-eater and red monkey', and suffering numerous accidents (he was as accident prone as he was fearless). One of his greatest disappointments was that he was never bitten by a vampire bat, although he slept with one foot hanging out of his hammock to encourage them. (Waterton believed that most ailments could be cured by bloodletting, so it would have been a match made in heaven.) He wrote it all up in a book, *Wanderings in South America* (1825), which sold well and has remained in print ever since. Some of his exploits raised contemporary eyebrows, and there was particular skepticism about his account of subduing a caiman (a species of alligator) with the help of several natives, during which he jumped on the creature's back,

grabbed its front legs and used them as a bridle. Such a feat was, however, certainly not beyond Waterton, who believed that no situation was so tight that one could not extricate oneself by 'presence of mind and vigorous exertions'.

Between expeditions, Waterton busied himself extending his estate at Walton Hall and turning it into the world's first nature reserve. At great expense he built a wall around it, some three miles (five km) long and eight feet (2.4 m) high, to keep out predators like foxes. Birds, needless to say, fared particularly well in his sanctuary, and Waterton counted no less than 123 species in it over thirty years. At one point, he noticed that trees on his property were dying and its waterways becoming polluted, and realised that a nearby soap and vitriol factory was to blame. He launched legal proceedings and the factory was eventually moved.

Waterton was not a scientist in the modern sense, or even in the nineteenth century sense. He had no proper scientific training, and spurned the use of Latin names for animals, which means that it is often impossible to identify which species he is referring to in his writings. He cheerfully described himself as 'daft as Dick's hatband', and indulged in pranks calculated to infuriate his more stuffy scientific colleagues. One of the specimens he brought

back from his last expedition was the preserved head of an 'Itouli' or 'Nondescript', which resembles a hairy faced old man, but which he actually fashioned from the backside of a howler monkey. (When an engraving of the Nondescript was used as the frontispiece of *Wanderings in South America*, many mistook it for the author.) He later used his taxidermic skills to create humourous tableaux, such as 'The English Reformation Zoologically Demonstrated', in which figures like John Knox were represented as frogs, toads, etc.

In 1929, Waterton married seventeen-year-old Anne Edmonton, the daughter of his close friend, Charles Edmonton, whom he had met in South America. Waterton had in fact been present at her christening, and always maintained that he knew he was destined to marry her. Less than a year later she died after giving birth to a son, Edmund. Waterton blamed himself for her death, and spent the rest of his life doing penance, sleeping on the floor with a wooden block for a pillow, and subsisting mainly on bread and weak tea.

In his last four decades, Squire Waterton's wanderings were confined to Europe, where he and his family sought out places of Catholic pilgrimage, saints' relics and the like — he remained a devoted and utterly unquestioning Catholic all his life. He loved receiving guests at Walton Hall, and loved to demonstrate his continued agility. Into his seventies, he was still shinning up trees, leaping over fences and scratching his ear with his big toe. He also had an unusual method of greeting guests. He would hide under a table in the entrance hall and, as they entered, leap out and bite at their ankles like a dog.

He died after a final accident, a fall which probably left him with a ruptured spleen, and was buried on his estate, which ceased to be a nature reserve soon after his death. Many of his taxidermic specimens can today be seen in the Wakefield Museum, looking as fresh as when he prepared them. ▣

WEST, MAE
(1893–1980)
Actress & writer

She was born Mary Jane West in Brooklyn, the daughter of John West, known as Battlin' Jack during his days as a boxer, and his wife Matilda, a German immigrant. By her own account, she first went on stage aged seven, and by 1910 was a regular in vaudeville (an unnamed reviewer in *Variety* the following year noted presciently, 'Miss West will develop.') She spent years treading

the boards in burlesque reviews, acquiring a reputation for the 'shimmy' (the risqué dance of the day), and began to write her own material. Her breakthrough came in 1929 with her provocatively entitled play *Sex*, in which she played a prostitute. Its successful off-Broadway run was interrupted by a police raid, and West, her manager and others were charged with producing an immoral play (she spent eight days in jail, which she milked for all the publicity it was worth). Other taboo-busting West plays of the twenties included *The Drag* (about homosexuals, cancelled after two performances), *Diamond Lil* (in which the wisecracking, sexually independent persona seen in her films was formed), and *The Constant Sinner* (in which she played the mistress of a black gangster).

West made the move to Hollywood in 1932 and caused a sensation with her first starring role in *She Done Him Wrong* (in which she uttered her immortal line, 'Why don't you come up and see me some time?'). Today it is hard to conceive just what an impact the sexually liberated (to use the terminology of a later era) West had at the time. By 1934 she was the highest paid star in Hollywood. By 1935 she was the highest paid woman in America.

In 1934, the censorship guidelines governing the film industry, known as the Hays Code, began

to be much more strictly enforced, and the movies West made after this were considerably toned down. She nevertheless continued to be the target for ferocious attacks by churchmen and self-appointed moral guardians. Yet, for all her success and notoriety, West's film career lasted little more than six years. Although she had officially cut seven years off her age, she was almost forty when she arrived in Hollywood, and had grown rather stout by the late thirties. Reviewers noted that audiences were starting to laugh at her love scenes. Advancing age was something that West would never acknowledge, however. In fact, she declared war on it, telling interviewers that she would never play anyone younger than twenty-six.

After her last major film, *My Little Chickadee* (1940), in which she appeared opposite that other larger-than-life personality W.C. Fields, West returned to the stage. Having failed to realise her dream project, a film about one of her idols, Catherine the Great, she turned her story into a play called *Catherine Was Great*. This was produced in lavish fashion by Mike Todd, with West wearing a series of fabulous costumes with elaborate headgear. She followed it with a successful revival of *Diamond Lil*, which included a tour of Britain.

West's taste in men ran to boxers and bodybuilders, and she

made sure that a large number of them were on stage for each of her productions. The imperial guard in *Catherine Was Great* was played by a number of bronzed L.A. beach boys squeezed into Russian costume. Unhappy with the leading man, West urged Mike Todd to consider taking on a local wrestler in his place. Todd gave him a screen test, and told her, 'He's a big, handsome brute all right, Miss West, but he seems incapable of reading difficult lines like "Yes" and "No".'

Mae West had by now become the extravagant, bejewelled seductress she played on stage and screen. She liked to give interviews in her Louis XV style bedroom, reclining on her enormous bed with white satin coverings and a mirror on the ceiling. In 1955, she began performing in Las Vegas, in a show which featured nine musclemen in loincloths. One of them, Chuck Krauser (who changed his name to Paul Novak), became her faithful companion and personal assistant, and was with her until the end.

West was ahead of her time in embracing the cluster of beliefs later dubbed 'New Age'. She was a keen spiritualist, attending séances where she chatted to Catherine the Great among others. She had her own yogi in the form of one Sri Deva Ram Sukul, consulted astrologers, and was great friends with the television psychic ☞ Criswell. She did exercises to increase her own psychic powers, until the spirits of the dead, which she called 'Forces', were appearing to her every night. They became so numerous they were interfering with her work, so she had to ask them to cut down on their visits.

As the years went by, West sailed on oblivious, secure in the knowledge that her strict health and beauty regime was keeping her as desirable as ever. She recorded two rock'n'roll albums in the sixties, and in 1970 made an unexpected return to the screen in the film version of Gore Vidal's novel about a transsexual, *Myra Breckinridge*, playing the sexually voracious Hollywood agent Leticia Van Allen. The film became one of the most critically reviled of all time (*Time* famously described it as 'about as funny as a child molester'). In the book that she wrote about her three favourite things, *Mae West on Sex, Health and ESP* (1975), West admitted that she didn't like a lot of the scenes either (the ones she wasn't in). This remarkable volume contains a number of startling revelations, including the fact that she first learned about sex at the age of thirteen, when she dreamed that a large, brown-black bear came into her bedroom and penetrated her ('... I saw the bear's sex organ spring forward from its fur...'). She also recalled her greatest ever lover, a member of the cast of *Diamond Lil* who, in the space of six hours one morning, made love to her no less than twenty-two times. When she asked him if that was normal, he said no, it was usually two or maybe three times, 'But I've been thinking about you for months.'

She had a final fling in front of the cameras in 1978 with *Sextette*, based on a play she wrote in the fifties. She plays the legendary star Marlo Manners, who has just married her sixth husband, Sir Michael Barrington (Timothy Dalton), but their honeymoon night is constantly interrupted by other men who want to sleep with her. Ringo Starr plays her fifth husband, and Keith Moon and Alice Cooper also put in appearances. The sight of a gym full of athletes drooling over the eighty-four-year-old West is certainly an arresting one, but if Mae does look a bit like a walking waxwork in her last role, the film is not quite the train wreck it is often said to be. It's even funny in parts, and you have to admire West's gumption.

West has been credited with inventing camp in her early movies, and acquired a huge gay following. At *Sextette*'s San Francisco premiere, she appeared wearing a diamond tiara, and was crowned 'Queen of the World'. She died two years later after suffering a series of strokes. ▨

WILLIAMSON, JOSEPH

(1769–1840)
'The Mole of Edge Hill'

Williamson is believed to have been born in Warrington in the northwest of England, and moved to Liverpool at the age of eleven. Liverpool was a booming city with a busy port at the time, and Williamson found employment with the Tate tobacco and snuff company. He ended up marrying the owner Thomas Tate's sister Elizabeth in 1802, and took over the company the following year.

Shortly after this, Williamson bought a house in Mason Street in an area named Edge Hill, and moved into it with his wife. He began to buy up the surrounding land, and built more houses along the street. Edge Hill was built on a sandstone outcrop, and the land behind the houses had been quarried, leaving a sheer drop of about twenty feet (sixty-one metres). As Williamson wanted the houses to have large back gardens, he engaged labourers to build brick arches where stone had been quarried, so that the land could be extended over them. It was at this point that the tunnelling began.

Williamson had his men dig into the sandstone beneath and around the houses. Between then and his death some thirty-five years

later, an extraordinary labyrinth of brick-lined tunnels and caverns was created.

The extent of them is still not known, for Williamson left no maps, was very secretive about them, and allowed few visitors into them during his lifetime. Charles Hand, a newspaper editor who explored some of the tunnels in 1916, when they were more accessible than they are today, gave this account:

They are grotesque beyond description; words fail to give an adequate idea of their appearance. Dungeons carved out of the solid rock, with no light and no ventilation, the only access being through a heavy wooden door; vaults with a roof of four arches meeting in the centre in a manner that present-day builders would not think of attempting; monstrous wine bins with many stone partitions for enormous quantities of bottles; massive erections of masonry and stone benches — all apparently without the slightest objective or motive.

Inside the tunnels, two houses were built with four rooms each, complete with spiral staircases carved from sandstone. There was also a tunnel leading from Williamson's house to his local church, and another to the pub.

When the Napoleonic Wars ended, Britain went into an economic recession, and many returning

soldiers could not find work. Williamson sold the tobacco company, expanded his tunnelling activities and took on many more men, becoming the biggest employer in the area. The tunnellers worked by candlelight, hacking away at the sandstone with pickaxes, with Williams directing them. After the death of his wife in 1822, he devoted almost his entire time to his tunnels, and was said to rarely emerge from them. Upon his death in 1840, the tunnelling stopped abruptly.

In the decades following, most of the tunnel entrances were closed. People whose houses stood above the tunnels dug openings into them and used them to dump their household refuse, so that some of them became clogged with rubbish. Construction work during the twentieth century saw some of the larger tunnels obliterated, while others were filled with building debris. Liverpudlians never entirely forgot about the tunnels, which were said to be the home of hordes of rats.

In 1995, an old stable yard where one of the two remaining entrances to the tunnels was located came under threat from developers. Williamson enthusiasts banded together and managed to save it. Today, some of the tunnels are open to the public for guided tours, and there are plans to open up more of them.

There continues to be much

speculation over why Williamson built the tunnels. The most popular explanation is philanthropy. The argument is that Williamson, having risen from poor beginnings, wanted to give something back to the working classes, especially during harsh economic times. This would explain why some of the work Williamson ordered appears to have been pointless — he would order his men to start digging a tunnel in one direction, for example, then tell them to brick it up. Alternatively, some have suggested that Williamson was a member of an apocalyptic sect, and the tunnels were intended to be a sanctuary when the apocalypse came. While Williamson was a devout man, and there were quite a few sects of this nature operating in Liverpool at the time, there is again no documentary evidence for this theory. Ultimately, no one can say what Williamson was thinking. ▣

WINCHESTER, SARAH

(1839–1922)
Builder of the
'Winchester Mystery House'

Sarah Pardee was born into a wealthy family in New Haven, Connecticut, and grew up to be a noted beauty and talented musician, fluent in several languages. In 1862, she married William Wirth Winchester,

the son of Oliver Winchester, who was busy making a fortune selling repeating rifles. The couple had a daughter, Annie, in 1866, but she lived for only a few days. After her death, Sarah fell into a deep depression which lasted almost ten years. She had not long emerged from it when, in 1881, William died.

Sarah, overcome by grief again, sought the consolation of spiritualists. She came to believe that the family was suffering a curse, placed on them by the vengeful spirits of people killed by Winchester firearms. One medium supposedly told Sarah that the only way to lift the curse was to sell her house, move west, and start building another one where the spirits could live with her — the only catch being that this house must never be completed. Whatever the truth of the story, this is what Sarah proceeded to do. Selling her New Haven mansion, she moved to Santa Clara, California, where she bought an uncompleted six-bedroom house from a doctor.

On the death of her husband, Sarah had inherited almost half the stock in the Winchester Repeating Arms Company, giving her an income of $1,000 a day. She began ploughing her fortune into building work. Workmen swarmed over the Santa Clara house day and night, and they would continue do so for the next thirty-eight years. Sarah

would present the foreman with a few sketches of what she wanted done each day, but there was no overall plan, and the house grew in a totally ad hoc fashion, room by room, tower by tower. Architectural anomalies abounded — rooms built within rooms, staircases that led nowhere, chimneys that weren't connected to fireplaces, doors that opened onto brick walls and, in one room, a window in the floor (some said these features had been added to confuse evil spirits). Sarah's obsession with the number thirteen was evident, with many of the staircases having thirteen steps, the windows thirteen panes, and so on. Despite its unfinished state, the house was lavishly decorated and furnished, and boasted three elevators and an elaborate heating system.

The house grew to over a hundred rooms and seven storeys. It was damaged in the San Francisco earthquake, which knocked the top three storeys off. These were not rebuilt, but the work otherwise continued as normal. Sarah lived in her constantly expanding house with a few servants. Her best friends were the spirits, with whom she communicated during séances at night.

Sarah Winchester died in her sleep at the age of eighty-three. The inside of her house was such a maze that it took workmen several weeks to remove the furniture and other

contents. Attempts were made to count the number of rooms in it, but the design is so extraordinarily complex that people kept coming up with different figures (160 is now the number usually given). Amazingly, this strange dream of a house survived its creator's death, and is today a tourist attraction. ▨

WINGATE, ORDE
(1903–1944)
Soldier & nudist

Born in Naini Tal, India, Wingate was the son of a British Army officer, George Wingate, and his wife Ethel, both members of the strict Plymouth Brethren sect. In 1905, after more than two decades in India and having attained the rank of colonel, Wingate Snr. retired from the army and returned to England, where he and Ethel devoted much of their time to missionary causes. The couple had seven children by 1911 — four daughters and three sons. They were educated at home to keep them from the evil influences of the outside world, and rarely encountered other children.

Wingate became a pupil at Charterhouse public school in 1916, and was later accepted into the Royal Military Academy in Woolwich, receiving his commission in 1923. His relative, Sir Charles Wingate,

who had been Governor-General of the Sudan and then British High Commissioner in Egypt, encouraged Orde to take an interest in the Middle East. He studied Arabic and, after taking time out for a bicycle tour through Europe, arrived in Khartoum in 1928. Attached to the Sudan Defence Force, he eventually commanded a force of 300 men, and acquired a reputation as a brilliant and unconventional tactician with an abrasive streak which did not always endear him to his fellow officers.

After a brief spell back in England (during which he married Lorna Patterson in 1935), he was posted to Palestine, then under British rule. Wingate's Plymouth Brethren background made him a staunch Zionist, eager to see Biblical prophecies fulfilled and the Jews returned to their Promised Land. The so-called Arab Revolt had begun, and Wingate led squads of British and Jewish volunteers, known as the Special Night Squads, who were instrumental in quelling the rebellion. Wingate eventually grew so outspoken about the Zionist cause that he was recalled to England.

After World War II broke out, he returned to the Sudan where he formed Gideon Force, composed of British, Sudanese and Egyptian troops, which had great success fighting the Italian forces in Ethiopia.

But it was in Burma, which fell to the Japanese in 1942, that Wingate made his name. A keen exponent of commando operations behind enemy lines, he was given permission to form a unit, dubbed the Chindits, which entered Burma at the beginning of 1943. Although the Japanese eventually forced them out, the operation was considered successful enough (by Winston Churchill in particular) that a much larger Chindit operation was mounted in Burma the following year, with many of the troops flown in by glider. In March 1944, Wingate was returning to India following an inspection of Chindit bases when the plane he was in crashed and he was killed.

If Wingate's military exploits were impressive, so too were his list of eccentricities. He wore an alarm clock on his wrist so he could time meetings, and when the alarm went off the meeting would be terminated — in mid-sentence if necessary. He was a great believer in eating raw onions and often wore one on a string around his neck. He was not a great believer in clothes, and would greet visitors — and even conduct strategy meetings — in the nude. Having decided that bathing was unhealthy, he used to clean himself with a toothbrush.

Four months after Wingate's death, Churchill addressed the House of Commons, calling him 'a

man of genius who might also have become a man of destiny'.

WINTLE, A.D.

(1897–1966)
'The Last Englishman'

The monocled and supremely stiff-upper-lipped career soldier Alfred Daniel Wintle was the son of a diplomat. He was born in Marioupol, Russia, and spent much of his childhood in France and Germany, becoming fluent in the languages of both countries. Visits to England were infrequent and much cherished, and it was perhaps because of this that his patriotism grew so fiercely. While still a boy he wrote in his diary 'There are two classes of insular Englishman — those who think no foreigner is as good as an Englishman, through sheer ignorance… and those who, like me, know it through experience.'

When World War I broke out, Wintle enlisted at the age of sixteen. After seeing much action on some of the fiercest battlefields of the war, he was badly injured by an exploding shell in 1917, losing his left eye, left knee-bone and most of his left hand, and was shipped off to England to recover from his wounds. Despite their severity, he contrived to soon be back at the front (he had attempted to escape the hospital where he

was being treated dressed as a nurse), and saw another year's fighting. Back in England after the war, he was surprised to find a Military Cross in the post one day. It was accompanied by a citation that noted two incidents of extreme bravery, during one of which he captured thirty-five enemy soldiers. Wintle had no recollection of either incident.

The day after the armistice was signed, Wintle wrote in his diary that he was declaring private war on Germany. 'I knew that the war with Germany was not over,' he wrote in his autobiography. 'They were merely lying low. The curtain would go up on Act Two when the blood thirsty Boche were ready.' He remained in the army during the interwar years, constantly chafing at the incompetence of the government and armed forces for failing to prepare for war.

War came, of course, and by June 1940 the situation in France was looking grim. Wintle had earlier made an agreement with a French general that, if such a time came, he would travel to France to help get as much of the French airforce to Britain as possible. Impersonating an airforce officer, he commandeered a plane, but the flight was cancelled by a superior. Incensed, Wintle drove to the Air Ministry, burst into an air commodore's office and demanded to be allowed to go to France. When the commodore refused, Wintle

waved a revolver at him and cursed him roundly. He was arrested and sent to the Tower of London to await a court martial. As soon as word got around about what he had tried to do, he became hugely popular with the officers garrisoned in the Tower, who took turns having lunch with him in his cell. At his court martial, Wintle began his defence by listing all the government ministers he thought should be shot. When it became apparent what an embarrassment Wintle posed for the authorities, most of the charges were dropped and he ended up being given a reprimand.

Returning to active duty, Wintle was posted to the Middle East, then sent on a secret intelligence gathering mission to France disguised as a French schoolteacher. Betrayed, he was arrested and imprisoned in a fort in Toulon. He escaped but was recaptured, and the guard on him was doubled. He went on a hunger strike, and took great delight in baiting his captors for looking slovenly and 'being traitors to France and the free world'. Eventually he escaped again in classic fashion, having laboriously sawn through iron bars with a bedspring, and made his way back to England. Wintle was not aware of the sequel to these events until 1959, when his exploits were celebrated in an episode of the television programme *This Is Your Life*. The

French commandant of the fort, M. Maurice Molia, a surprise guest, revealed that Wintle's behaviour as a prisoner had inspired him to join the Resistance, along with some 280 men of the prison garrison.

After the war, Wintle retired to the country with his childhood sweetheart, Dora, whom he married in 1944. He continued to rail against incompetence. On one occasion, having bought a first class train ticket and finding that there were no seats available on the train, he sat on the driver's seat and refused to budge until another carriage was added. His last great battle began in 1947, when his Aunt Kitty died. She had promised to look after her frequent companion, Wintle's sister Marjorie, in her will, but when the will was read, the vast bulk of her estate went to Kitty's solicitor, Frederick Nye. Wintle protested vociferously and consulted lawyers, but was advised nothing illegal could be proved. Taking matters into his own hands, he lured Nye to a hotel room, made him remove his trousers and took photographs. (The trousers were later displayed as a trophy in Wintle's London club). He was convicted of common assault and imprisoned. On his release, he managed to get the matter of the will heard in court, but lost, then lost the appeal. As a last resort, he appealed to the House of Lords. Ten years after his campaign began, the Law Lords unanimously found in his favour and Wintle cracked open the champagne.

Wintle's autobiography, *The Last Englishman*, was published posthumously in 1968. French and Germans do not get off lightly in it. ▣

'*I am never bored when I am present.*'

A.D. WINTLE

WITKACY (STANISLAW IGNACY WITKIEWICZ)

(1885–1939)
Artist, writer & philosopher

Witkiewicz, born in Warsaw, Poland, was the son of an eminent artist and critic (also named Stanisław Witkiewicz). Bitterly opposed to insitutionalised education, the elder Witkiewicz insisted that his son was educated at home. He grew up surrounded by artists, writers and musicians, while another major influence was his godmother, Helena Modrzejewska, a famous actress who instilled in him a love of theatre — he wrote his first play, *Cockroaches*, at the age of eight.

In 1905, to his father's disgust, he insisted on enrolling at the Academy of Art in Cracow, although he didn't last there long. He adopted a bohemian lifestyle, experimented with drugs, travelled around Europe observing the latest developments in painting, and wrote philosophical essays and his first novel. In 1913, he became engaged to a girl, but the following year she committed suicide. Distraught, Witkiewicz accepted an invitation from his childhood friend, the anthropologist Bronisław Malinowski, to join him on an expedition to New Guinea and Australia as an artist and photographer. The expedition was cut short by the outbreak of World War I. Witkiewicz returned to Europe and enlisted in the Russian army. He became an officer and fought at the front, and later observed the beginnings of the Russian Revolution in St. Petersburg. He was left with a horror of communism (but didn't think much more of capitalism).

Returning to Poland, he adopted the name Witkacy to distinguish himself from his father. He became associated with the first Polish avant-garde movement, the Formists, and divided his time between painting and writing experimental plays filled with images of sex and death (he would eventually write over thirty of them). In 1923, he married Jadwiga Unrug. With little money coming in from his formist paintings, he started a commercial portrait painting business. This

offered a variety of styles, from polished and flattering, to more objective, to a completely psychological interpretation. Whenever he did a painting, he would mark the canvas with a code to indicate which drugs he had been on when he painted it. These could be anything from cigarettes and beer, to cocaine and peyote. The portrait painting business was quite successful, and he was able to continue writing philosophical works and novels, including *Insatiability* (1930), which is today considered a Modernist classic.

Witkacy always lacked confidence in his own abilities, and like many essentially shy people, found freedom in playing roles. He painted and photographed hundreds of self-portraits in which he dressed in different costumes, from clown to workman to priest, creating a parade of personalities reminiscent of ☞ Fernando Pessoa. Philosophically, he was an existentialist who asked the basic questions: Why am I here? Why am I me and not someone else? For Witkacy, life was inherently strange, and much of his art, philosophy and everyday behaviour was designed to evoke this sense of strangeness. When talking to someone, for example, he might turn away suddenly, then turn back, revealing two halved ping-pong balls over his eyes, or he would suddenly pretend to be someone else, a po-

liceman for example. He walked the streets wearing garish clothes. When he knocked on a door, he liked to crouch down, then slowly rise up after the door was opened. He once ordered a veal cutlet in a restaurant, and when the waiter brought it to him, put it in his wallet.

One of the major themes of Witkacy's writing was that civilisation was about to be crushed by totalitarian forces. As the 1930s wore on, it seemed that his fears would be realised. In September 1939, the Nazis invaded Poland. Witkacy, whose health had been failing, fled into the countryside with a female companion, Czesława Korzeniowska. When word came through a few days later that the Russians were invading from the east, they decided to commit suicide. They both took poison and Witkacy slit his wrist. Korzeniowska survived, however, waking up the next morning beside Witkacy's body.

Despite his almost manic creativity, Witkacy was little known or appreciated in Poland in his lifetime, but the situation changed. His paintings now sell for large sums and his plays are regularly performed. In 1988, Poland's Ministry of Culture decided to bring his body back from Ukraine and give it a proper burial. The Russian authorities supplied a corpse which, despite doubts it was Witkacy, was buried with suit-

able honours. Later, DNA testing showed it was the body of an old woman. Witkacy, the compulsive impersonator, would have relished it all. ▣

WIZARD OF NEW ZEALAND, THE
(b.1932)
State-sanctioned sorcerer

Born Ian Channell in London, The Wizard's early life was uneventful — a brief spell in the airforce, marriage, a move to Australia where he took up academic posts in Perth and Sydney. Then came the magic year of 1968. At the time a member of the University of New South Wales's sociology department, Channell left his wife, moved into a communal house, and became a regular speaker in the Domain — a park in Sydney which has long been the haunt of soap-box orators. Letting his beard grow and planting a pointed hat on his head, Channell became 'the Wizard'. Thanks to a sympathetic vice chancellor and a show-stopping performance in front of the student union, he found himself appointed Wizard of the University (to the fury of the student radicals, who hated him even more than the conservative academics). He later moved to Victoria where he was made Wizard of Melbourne University and gave

lectures on a 'postmodern cosmology' of his own devising. Other activities during this period included offering his body to the Victorian National Museum as a 'living work of art' and standing as a monarchist candidate in the 1972 federal election.

In 1974, having decided that Australia was 'too urbanised, too serious and too Americanised for the likes of me', the Wizard moved to New Zealand. He took up residence in Christchurch's Cathedral Square, clad in an animal skin. A protracted dispute with the city council over his right to speak there followed, with the Wizard eventually emerging triumphant (and becoming a bona fide tourist attraction in the process). He went on to achieve national fame with his spell-casting at rugby games (not always successful) and rain dances (in one case — in Waimate in 1988 — spectacularly successful). He has also printed his own money (à la ☞ Emperor Norton) and mounted various campaigns such as an epic struggle to keep postboxes red. He is an ardent campaigner for polygamy, believing that monogamous relationships are emotionally crippling for men, who should instead have a number of female 'slaves'. It seems that, in the Wizard's case, the latter have proved hard to find. In 1990, in recognition of these tireless efforts, Prime Minister Mike Moore

THE WIZARD OF NEW ZEALAND

officially proclaimed him Wizard of New Zealand, and this is the name that appears on his passport.

The Wizard published his autobiography, *My Life as a Miracle*, in 1998. It's not the most modest memoir ever written (a typical sentence: 'The crowd were spellbound by my fluency and the extraordinary range and originality of my views on important subjects.'). Still, I don't suppose you get to be the Wizard of New Zealand by being coy. 🔲

WOOD, EDWARD D.
(1924–1978)
Writer & director

Wood, who was born in Poughkeepsie, New York, was the son of a postal worker, Ed Wood Sr. His mother Lillian, who had wanted a girl, used to put dresses on him as a child, and he became a lifelong transvestite. From the moment he was given his first movie camera on his 11th birthday, Ed Wood Jr. wanted to make movies. After serving as a marine in World War II (he claimed to have taken part in the invasion of Tarawa wearing a pink bra and panties beneath his uniform) and a stint in a travelling carnival, he went to Hollywood where he picked up work as a writer, bit player and stuntman. Befriending the ageing and drug-addicted Bela Lugosi, he

featured him as a godlike character ('Pull the strings!') in his first major film as a director, the autobiographical — and brave — *Glen or Glenda*, a.k.a. *I Changed My Sex* (1953). Wood played the title character/s, at ease in a blonde wig and his favourite angora sweater.

Wood spent years trying to break into the mainstream, but his career was destined to remain firmly in the world of exploitation. Gathering together a celebrated stock company of bona fide eccentrics including cadaverous television horror hostess Vampira (Maila Nurmi), television psychic ☞ Criswell ('Can you prove it didn't happen?!') and 400-pound (181 kg) Swedish ex-wrestler Tor Johnson, Wood somehow turned out a series of delirious low budget extravaganzas including *Jailbait* (1953), *Bride of the Monster* (1956), *Plan 9 from Outer Space* (1957) and *Night of the Ghouls* (1958). Many other projects went unrealised. Wood was a master of cost-cutting and improvisation. When Lugosi died during the filming of *Plan 9*, his masterpiece, Wood, undeterred, had the rest of his role played by a tall, thin actor (actually Wood's chiropractor) hiding his face behind a cape.

In the 1960s, Wood descended into alcoholism and poverty, and survived by writing pornographic paperback novels with titles like

Death of a Transvestite, *Drop-out Wife*,
The Gay Underworld and *Purple Thighs*.
Wood's brain worked faster than he
could type, and his grammatically
dodgy tales of transvestite hired killers, fierce biker girls and insatiable
hippy chicks are told with the same
overblown style that characterises
his films.

He was rediscovered in the
1970s, when a new generation
unearthed and embraced the trash
culture of previous decades, but
the acclaim came too late for Wood,
who died of a heart attack on 10
December 1978, three days after he
and his wife Kathy had been evicted
from their apartment, losing most
of their possessions. Wood was
dubbed 'the worst director of all
time', but among 'bad' films which
have developed cult status, Wood's
really stand out — inept and tawdry,
certainly, yet personal and hugely entertaining. Wood was a true naïve, as
uncomprehending of the world's realities as he was of the requirements
for a professional-looking motion
picture, and it is this that gives his
films their beguilingly illogical quality.
And no one else ever wrote dialogue
like Ed Wood.

He finally entered the mainstream, in a fashion, in Tim Burton's
1994 biopic *Ed Wood*, in which
Johnny Depp played the crazed but
ever-optimistic auteur. ▣

WOODHULL, VICTORIA

(1838–1927)
The first female
presidential candidate

Viewed as deeply eccentric by her
contemporaries, Woodhull now
seems more ahead of her time
than anything else, yet her oddities
have prevented her from receiving
proper recognition as the pioneering
feminist she undoubtedly was. Born
in Homer, Ohio, she was one of ten
children of Rueben 'Buck' Claflin,
a one-eyed petty thief and con-
man, and his wife Anna, a religious
maniac prone to ecstatic praying
and cursing. Victoria inherited some
of her mother's tendencies. She
believed that she possessed psychic
powers and, from an early age, that
she was destined for greatness.

Having had very little education,
at the age of fifteen Victoria married a doctor, Canning Woodhull,
with whom she had a son, Byron,
who was mentally impaired, and a
daughter, Zulu. After the wedding, it
soon became obvious that Canning
was far more interested in drinking
and womanising than practicing
medicine. Victoria, forced to be the
breadwinner, became a spiritualist
medium and healer, a profession
which her younger sister Tennessee
had taken up a few years earlier, at
the instigation of their father (who,

during this period, also began a new career as a bogus cancer doctor).

In 1865, a Civil War veteran and spiritualist, Colonel James Harvey Blood, visited Woodhull in her capacity as medium. She went into a trance and announced that they were destined to be married. Blood, like Victoria, was already married, but they would go on to divorce their respective spouse and marry several years later.

In 1868, a spirit named Demosthenes told Woodhull to move to New York. She was soon joined there by much of her extended family, who had been cheerfully living off Victoria and Tennessee for years. Woodhull's unhappy first marriage had left her an impassioned advocate for the rights of women, a stand supported by Colonel Blood, but realised she would need money for a campaign. This came along in the form of the ageing railroad tycoon Cornelius Vanderbilt, who engaged Victoria and Tennessee's services as spiritualists and healers (and possibly in other capacities — he came close to marrying Tennessee), and in return passed them stock tips. Victoria amassed a fortune playing the stockmarket, and in 1870 she and her sister became the first female brokers on Wall Street when they established Woodhull, Claflin and Co. In the face of great skepticism among the business community, the company flourished. Buoyed by its success, Woodhull announced she was going to run for the presidency in 1872.

To further her campaign, she started a newspaper, *Woodhull & Claflin's Weekly*, which was edited by Colonel Blood. The paper's masthead proclaimed, 'Progress! Free Thought! Untrammelled Lives! Breaking the Way for Future Generations!' It espoused women's suffrage and other radical causes, and attacked corruption in government and business. Many of its articles were written by the eccentric political philosopher ☞ Stephen Pearl Andrews.

In 1871, Woodhull became the first woman to address a congressional committee, arguing that the fourteenth and fifteenth amendments granted women the right to vote. Her activism saw her become the de facto head of the women's suffrage movement within months. Her detractors (including many women) denounced her advocacy of 'free love' and the fact that her first husband, Dr. Woodhill, continued to live with Victoria and her new husband, Blood — but they still turned up to her lectures. Among her staunchest supporters were, not surprisingly, spiritualists, for Woodhull made no secret of the fact that she was receiving help in her campaign from the 'other side'. She often lay

on the roof of her mansion communing with spirits, and claimed to receive daily revelations.

Woodhull also courted organised labour. She printed the *Communist Manifesto* in her paper, and gave speeches attacking Vanderbilt and other capitalists. None of this did her brokerage firm any favours, and Woodhull also suffered the indignity of being evicted from her house. Under pressure, she made a grave tactical error, publishing an attack in the *Weekly* on Henry Ward Beecher, a prominent clergyman (and brother of novelist Harriet Beecher Stowe), in which she accused him of having an affair with the wife of a fellow church member. At the instigation of morals crusader Anthony Comstock, Victoria, Tennessee and Colonel Blood were arrested and charged with sending obscene materials through the post. Woodhull spent 5 November 1872, the day of the presidential election, in jail.

The trio were eventually found not guilty on the obscenity charge. Woodhull had an acrimonious falling out with Blood and, after divorcing him, moved to England. Clearly battered by the controversies which had raged around her, she had also found religion, and stated that she had never advocated free love, which was patently absurd. She married a banker, John Martin, who was happy to ignore her scandalous past — and

the many letters he received about it from helpful strangers — and the marriage was a success. After largely disappearing from public view for a decade, Woodhull regained some of her old chutzpah and briefly returned to the U.S. in 1883 to mount a second campaign for the presidency, but this came to nothing. In 1885, she began to publish a new journal, the *Humanitarian*, which was quite as outspoken on social issues as the old *Weekly* had been, although it avoided personal attacks.

After her husband died in 1897, she inherited a considerable fortune, and went to live in the Martins' country seat in Bredon's Norton, Worcestershire. The village was very run down, and initially some of the villagers were not pleased by her efforts to modernise it — the street lamps she had installed were smashed — but she eventually won them over, acquiring the nickname 'Lady Bountiful'. She developed a late passion for motor cars, and spent much of her spare time in them, notching up several firsts — she was the first woman to drive though Hyde Park, and also went on a motor tour through France accompanied by her daughter Zulu (who had changed her name to Zula). Her last years were chiefly devoted to philanthropic work, and she died in her sleep at the age of eighty-eight. ▣

WRIGHT, ERNEST VINCENT

(1872–1939)
Writer

A lipogram is a text in which one or more letters of an alphabet, most commonly a vowel, have been ruthlessly excluded by the writer. The earliest recorded example is the 'Hymn to Demeter' by the sixth century Greek poet Lasus of Hermione, which does not contain the letter 'S' (or rather its Greek equivalent, sigma, Σ).

In English, the greatest lipogrammatical challenge is to write without using 'E', by far the most frequently used letter. This was the challenge risen to magnificently by the American writer Ernest Vincent Wright in his 1939 novel, *Gadsby*. It tells the story of the small town of Branton Hills, which was 'lazily snoozing among up-and-coming towns'. Enter one John Gadsby, 'a man of so dominating and happy individuality that Youth is drawn to him like a fly to a sugar bowl.' (Wright is very big on Youth, which he always spells with a capital 'Y'.) Having harnessed the power of the town's 'Youth', Gadsby brings about all sorts of civic improvements — a night school, a library, a hospital, etc. Eventually he is elected mayor.

As will be apparent, this is not the world's most exciting narrative. The real drama in the book, which runs to over 50,000 words, is Wright's tussle with the English language. Omitting 'E' places innumerable restrictions on a writer, from not being able to use the past tense of most verbs, to not being able to use the word 'the'. Wright jumped through some amazing verbal hoops to tell his story, resorting to all sorts of verbal stratagems to introduce elements (a fire truck, for example) which he could not actually name.

In his introduction to the book, Wright, whose other works included children's books like *The Fairies That Run the World and How They Do It* (1903), explained that he wrote *Gadsby* after being told that it couldn't be done. And it seems the effort may have been too much for him, for he died soon after (some accounts say on the day of) its publication.

Several other books minus the letter 'E' have appeared since *Gadsby*, most notably French writer Georges Perec's 1969 novel *La Disparation* (and its translation into English by Gilbert Adair, *The Void*). Taking a different tack, in 2004 another French writer, Michel Dansel, under the pseudonym Michael Thaler, produced a 233-page novel, *Le Train de Nulle Part* (*The Train from Nowhere*), which does not contain a single verb. ▨

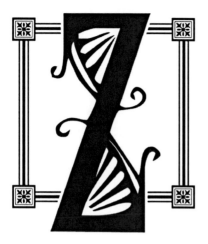

ZIOLKOWSKI, KORCZAC

(1908–1982)
Mountain sculptor

In 1948, Ziolkowski began to work single-handedly on what will be, if it is ever completed, the largest sculpture ever made.

He was born in Boston to Polish parents who both died when he was one-year-old. Raised in foster homes, he showed great artistic promise at an early age, but never had any formal training. He was working as a professional sculptor by the early 1930s, won several prizes, and assisted Gutzon Borglun in the creation of the monumental heads of Washington, Jefferson, Lincoln and Roosevelt on Mount Rushmore, in the Black Hills range of South Dakota.

In 1939, Chief Henry Standing Bear of the Lakota tribe sent a letter to Ziolkowski, in which he wrote, 'My fellow chiefs and I would like the white man to know that the red man has great heroes, too,' and proposed that a monument be erected in the Black Hills to Crazy Horse, the great Lakota warrior who had taken part in the Battle of the Little Big Horn. Ziolkowski was intrigued and did some preliminary research, but then World War II intervened. After the war, during which he served in the army and took part in the landing on Omaha Beach on D-Day, Ziolkowski moved to the Black Hills and staked a mining claim on the mountain which was to become the Crazy Horse Memorial. On 3 June 1948, at a ceremony attended by 400 Native Americans (including five Little Big Horn veterans), the first rock was blasted from the side of the mountain.

Zilkowski's design for the sculpture shows Crazy Horse mounted on a rearing horse, with one arm extended and a finger pointing imperiously ahead. When completed, it will be 563 feet (172 m) high, with the chief's head eighty-seven feet (twenty-seven metres) high (almost a third higher than the Mount Rushmore heads). The Little Big Horn survivors told Ziolkowski what Crazy Horse looked like (he had never been photographed), but the sculptor had always wanted a more idealised version, a symbol of all Native Americans.

In the first year, Ziolkowski worked by himself, using a jackhammer powered by a small generator, and slept in a tent on the mountain. After a few months, he was joined by twenty-one-year-old Ruth Ross, whom he had met before the war. Ruth initially came to help him build a staircase up the mountain, but she stayed on, and they married in 1950.

Progress was very slow in the first few years, and the project was deeply unpopular with the local white population. Ziolkowski began to raise money by charging admission to the site, but refused offers of federal government funding, fearing it would compromise his vision. This included, in addition to the sculpture, a Native American museum, university and medical school.

Ziolkowski worked on the mountain for thirty-four years, enduring broken bones, serious back injuries and two heart attacks. In 1982, when he died of acute pancreatitis, the site still bore little resemblance to his model of the sculpture. Ruth took control of the project after his death, and decided to concentrate on finishing Crazy Horse's head, which was completed in 1998, fifty years after work on the site commenced.

The Crazy Horse Memorial is not popular with all Native Americans, with some calling it a desecra-tion of the landscape which would have appalled its subject. Others have called it a monumental piece of kitsch. Work on it continues, however, although no one will venture to say when it might be finished. Ruth is still in charge, and seven of the ten Ziolkowski children continue to work with her. They know their father is watching them. He's buried in a tomb at the base of the mountain with a knocker on the inside of the door, so he can make himself heard if he becomes displeased with the progress. ▨

'Every man has his mountain — I'm carving mine.'

KORCZAK ZIOLKOWSKI

ZOZIMUS

(c.1794–1846)
Reciter

Zozimus, whose real name was Michael Moran, was a fixture on the streets of Dublin for many years. Blind from (or shortly after) birth, he was blessed with a phenomenal memory, and made his living by reciting poems and telling stories. His nickname came from one of his most popular poems, which described how Bishop Zozimus was

sent by God to hear the last confession of Saint Mary of Egypt.

He was a tall man who wore a long coat and cape with scalloped edges, an old beaver felt hat and corduroy trousers, and carried a stick attached to his wrist with a leather thong. He had a number of declarations which signalled a recitation was about to begin, including:

Ye sons and daughters of Erin attend
Gather round poor Zozimus yer friend
Listen, boys, until yez hear
My charming song so dear.

Zozimus was an animated performer, wringing every last dramatic possibility from his material, which usually had a patriotic or religious theme. He recitations were punctuated with topical jokes (he used to get his wife to read the newspaper to him every morning to keep him up to date) and humourous asides about his fellow Dubliners.

He composed some of the poems he recited himself, and a few were set down for posterity, including 'The Finding of Moses', which began:

In Egypt's land, contagious to the Nile
Old Pharoah's daughter went to bathe in
*   style*
She took her dip and came unto the land
And for to dry her royal pelt she ran along
*   the strand.*

A bull-rush tripped her, whereupon she
*   saw*
A smiling babby in a wad of straw.
She took it up and said in accents wild,
"Tare-and-ages, girls, which av yez own the
*   child?"*

Some of his poems were also set to music, including his splendid bit of doggerel, 'Saint Patrick was a Gentleman.'

Saint Patrick was a gentleman
He came of decent people
In Dublin town he built a Church
And on it put a steeple.

Zozimus fell ill around his fiftieth year and lost his voice, and thus his livelihood. He was buried in a pauper's grave, and had no tombstone until a traditional Irish band, the Dublin City Ramblers, bought one for him in the late 1960s. ▣

ZÚÑIGA Y MIRANDA, NICOLÁS

(1865–1925)
'The President of Mexico'

A participant in Mexican presidential elections for many years, Zúñiga was born into an aristocratic family in Zacatecas. He was a precocious child, and at the age of sixteen went to Mexico City where he studied law, geology, mathematics and other subjects. A tall, thin, foppish fellow with a drooping moustache who usually wore a frock coat and sombrero, he was never going to be content with a staid career in law, as his father had wanted. Instead he became interested in predicting catastrophes, like floods and earthquakes. He invented a seismographic machine with which he, apparently, predicted an earthquake which hit Mexico City in 1887. People therefore took much more notice of his next prediction, that on 10 August that year, the city would be destroyed by a volcanic eruption. On the evening of 9 August, a sense of panic swept through the city, heightened by false reports that smoke had been seen rising from the volcano Popocatépetl. On 11 August, with the city intact, Zúñiga was mocked and set upon with sticks by his fellow students at the National School of Jurisprudence, emerging with a crumpled sombrero and his frock coat torn to shreds.

When further predictions were no more accurate, Zúñiga decided to enter politics. Mexico was at this time ruled by President Porfirio Diaz, who maintained his grip on power with sham elections and by cowing (or killing) his opponents. Zúñiga decided to oppose him in the 1896 election, with his policies including land reform and reducing drunkenness by arresting the

producers of pulque (a fermented beverage made from the manguey plant). Diaz regarded Zúñiga as enough of a threat to have the police arrest him and throw him into jail for a short time, causing him to abandon the election. He came back swinging in the election of 1900, however, by which time Diaz had decided that he was a harmless way for people to let off steam. Zúñiga regularly contested elections after that, receiving a small vote each time, but was always convinced that he had really won. As with  Emperor Norton in San Francisco, the people of Mexico City embraced Zúñiga, and he was often invited to public events. He always dressed like a British gentlemen, with top hat, monocle and gloves, and one of his policies was that the government would buy western clothing for the peasants so they would look less backward. ▣

BIBLIOGRAPHY

ARTICLES

Allebone, Zoe, 'The Art Jester — Amsterdam Adopts Our Unseen Talent', *Sydney City Hub*, 21 March 1996.

Anon., 'The Gothic Belle', *People*, 7 November 1951.

'Bellerive, the Poet', *People*, 30 August 1950.

Berczeller, Paul, 'The man who lost his past', *The Guardian*, 6 September 2004.

Blumenthal, Ralph, 'A Man's 6-Pack Can Serve as His Castle', *The New York Times*, 7 March 2008.

Bradshaw, Paul, 'Voutie O Roonie O Scoodileroosimoe', *New Musical Express*, 19 January 1985.

Brenner, Marie, 'East Side Alien', *Vanity Fair*, March 1990.

Cadzow, Jane, 'Prince and the pawpaws', *The Good Weekend*, 20 February 1993.

Cooke, Rachel, 'The loins of Longleat', *The Observer*, 10 March 2002.

Dobner, Jennifer, 'Pup cloner is Joyce McKinney', *Desert News*, 10 August 2008.

Dutter, Barbie, 'I haven't had a meal in 5 years', *The Sun–Herald*, 1 November 1998.

Fidler, Richard, 'Frank Thring: Antichrist of the Menzies Era', *Strewth!*, Summer 2000.

Fowle, Farnsworth, 'Cultist Who Tried for 60 Days in 76 To Revive Follower Jumps to Death', *The New York Times*, 15 April 1977.

Gardner, Viv, 'Would you trust this man with your fortune?', *The Guardian*, 10 October 2007.

Garmon, Ron, 'The Boy from Out of this World: The authentic death of Tom Graeffe', *L.A. City Beat*, November 2008.

Gleaves, Rebekah, 'Interview with the Mongo', *Memphis Flyer*, 7 September 2000.

—, 'Mongo Loses Round Two', *Memphis Flyer*, 20 October 2000.

Gregory, Jason, 'Tarzan to jog the rest of days', *The Courier Mail*, 24 August 2003.

Gurt, Marat, 'Autocrat's death leaves void for Turkmenistan', *The Sydney Morning Herald*, 23 December 2006.

Helgalson, Gudjon, 'Master Bows Out: Chess star Fischer dies at 64', *The Sunday Telegraph*, 20 January 2006.

Holbrook, Stewart, 'The Beard of Joseph Palmer', *The American Scholar*, Vol 13 No 4, Autumn 1944.

Huck, Peter, 'Fun and Games with Bobby', *The Sydney Morning Herald*, 5 September 1992.

Jarvis, Robert M., 'The Curious Legal Career of Homer L. Collyer', *Journal of Maritime Law and Commerce*, October 2007.

Jefferis, Chris, 'Unrequited obsession', *The Sydney Morning Herald*, 11 October 2006.

Kelly, James and Rochell Girson, 'Juicy Medieval Morass', *Saturday Review*, 9 June 1956.

Kilgannon, Corey, 'Froggy's Last Story', *New York Times*, 10 September 2010.

Lazarus, David, 'Japan's Edison Is Country's Gadget King: Japanese Inventor Holds Record for Patent', *New York Times*, 10 April 1995.

Marshall, Steve, 'St. James the Janitor', *Fortean Times*, September 2001.

Martin, Douglas, 'Robert Shields, Wordy Diarist, Dies at 89', *New York Times*, 29 October 2007.

Melly, George, 'The Palais Idéal of Facteur Cheval', *Raw Vision 4*, Spring 1991.

Minkoff, Myrna, 'Glad to be Gaillard', *New Musical Express*, 21 October 1989.

Norman, Bob, 'The Alien Has Landed', *New Times*, 19 January 2006.

Moran, Jonathon, 'Jacko Expected to die "like Elvis"', *The Sunday Telegraph*, 28 June 2009.

O'Kane, Ruairi, 'Plop! A new king of bad poetry', *The Sunday Times*, 7 October 2007.

Pancia, Anthony, 'UFOs are chariots sent from heaven', *St. George and Sutherland Shire Leader*, 4 december 2001.

Papadakis, Marianna, '"UFO man" gone but not forgotten', *St. George and Sutherland Shire Leader*, 13 May 2009.

Perkins, Rodney and Forrest Jackson, 'Spirit in the Sky', *Fortean Times*, April 1998.

Perottet, Tom, 'Crazy Horse's revenge', *The Australian*, 12 April 2008.

Pitkin, Margot, 'King of eccentrics', *The Daily Telegraph*, 4 August 1919.

Pittenger, Peach R., 'The Cherry Sisters in early Vaudeville performing a failed femininity', *Theatre History Studies*, June 2004.

Reppion, John, 'The Undergound Empire of Joseph Williamson', *Strange Attractor Journal Three*, 2006.

Robson, Frank, 'The Outsider', *The Good Weekend*, 21 November 1998.

Rosemont, Franklin, 'All Things, All Men and All Animals: Arthur

Cravan', *Free Spirits, Annals of the Insurgent Imagination 1*, City Lights, San Francisco, 1982.

Rowe, Pearl, 'to nature boy, life needn't be capitalized', *Los Angeles Times*, 24 July 1977.

Russell, Hugh, 'His Holiness was not amused', *The Spectator*, 4 January 2003.

Savill, Richard, 'Fawlty hotelier was bonkers, says waitress', *The Daily Telegraph*, 18 May 2002.

—, 'My husband was not like Basil', *The Daily Telegraph*, 10 May 2002.

'Saparmurat Niyazov' (obituary), *The Guardian*, 22 December 2006.

'Saparmurat Niyazov' (obituary), *The Daily Telegraph*, 22 December 2006.

Schadewald, Robert J., 'The Flat-out Truth', *Science Digest*, July 1980.

Shlachter, Barry, 'Only 30 remain with UFO cult leader in new location', *Fort Worth Star-Telegram*, 21 March 1999.

'Sir Hugh Rankin, 3rd Bt.' (obituary), *The Daily Telegraph*, 2 May 1988.

Skinner, Doug, 'Doubting Tiffany', *Fortean Times, Special 200th issue*, 2005.

—, 'Visions of a Subterranean World: The Lost Art of Richard S. Shaver,' *The Anomalist 3*, Winter 1995–96.

Stewart, Cameron, 'Crazy dream', *The Weekend Australian*, 30–31 May 1998.

Stollznow, Karen, 'Coral Castle, Fact and Folklore', *Sceptical Inquirer*, January–February 2010.

Winterich, John T., 'The Life and Works of Bloodgood Haviland Cutter', *The Colophon 2*, 1930.

Woodford, Peter, 'After 30 Years Tarzan Found', *Sunday Telegraph*, 15 Deceember 1985.

Wyatt, Petronella, 'The Marquess of Bath — on the prowl for wifelet 76', *The Daily Mail*, 30 March 2007.

BOOKS

Amory, Mark, *Lord Berners: The Last Eccentric*, Chatto & Windus: London, 1998.

Anderson, Brooke Davis, *Darger: The Henry Darger Collection at the American Folk Art Museum*, American Folk Art Museum: New York, 2001.

Ashton, John, *Florizel's Folly*, Chatto & Windus: London, 1899.

Barnes, Mike, *Captain Beefheart*, Omnibus Press: London, 2004.

Benkovitz, Miriam J., *Frederick Rolfe: Baron Corvo*, Capricorn: New York, 1977.

Bird, John, *Percy Grainger*, Currency Press: Sydney, 1998.

Bondeson, Jan, *Buried Alive*, Norton: New York, 2001.

Booth, Martin, *A Magickal Life: A Biography of Aleister Crowley*, Hodder & Stoughton: London,

2000.

Brendan, Piers, *Hawker of Morwenstow*, Jonathan Cape: London, 1975.

Bridgeman, Harriet and Elizabeth Drury, *The British Eccentric*, Michael Joseph: London, 1875.

Brown, Peter Harry and Pat H. Broeske, *Howard Hughes: The Untold Story*, Da Capo Press: Cambridge, 1996.

Bubbett, Laurence W., *Biographical Sketch of Dr. Cyrus Read Teed (Koresh)*, The Koreshan Unity: Estero, 1951.

Burke, Carolyn, *Becoming Modern: The Life of Mina Loy*, Farrar, Strauss, Giroux: New York, 1996.

Burgess, *The Eccentric Ark: The Curious World of Frank Buckland*, The Horizon Press: New York, 1967.

Cavendish, Margaret, *The Blazing World and Other Writings*, Penguin: London, 2004.

Chambers, Robert (ed.), *Chambers' Book of Days*, W & R Chambers: London and Edinburgh, 1864.

Chambers, Robert, *Traditions of Edinburgh*, W & C Tait: Edinburgh, 1825.

Chidley, William James, *The Confessions of William James Chidley*, edited by S. McInerney, University of Queensland Press: St. Lucia, 1977.

— *The Answer, or the World as Joy*, Sydney D. Smith: Sydney, 1915.

Caufield, Catherine, *The Emperor of the United States of American and other Magnificent British Eccentrics*, Routledge & Kegan Paul: London, 1981.

Caulfield, James, *Portraits, Memoirs and Characters of Remarkable Persons*, H.R. Young and T.R. Whitely: London, 1819.

Churchill, Allen, *The Improper Bohemians*, Cassell: London, 1961.

Chusid, Irwin, *Songs in the Key of Z*, A Capella: Chicago, 2000.

Collis, Rose, *Colonel Barker's Monstrous Regiment*, Virago: London, 2001.

Davis, Richard Harding, *Real Soldiers of Fortune*, Scribner's: New York, 1906.

De Forde, Miriam Allen, *They Were San Franciscans*, The Caxton Printers Ltd: Caldwell, 1947.

Delano, Anthony, *Joyce McKinney and the Manacled Mormon*, Mirror Books: London, 1978.

De Montalk, Stephanie, *Unquiet World: The Life of Geoffrey Potocki de Montalk*, Victoria University Press: Wellington, 2001.

Dunmore, John, *Wild Cards: Eccentric Characters from New Zealand's Past*, New Holland: Auckland, 2006.

Dunstan, Keith, *Ratbags*, Sun Books: Melbourne, 1980.

Drury, Nevill, *The Witch of Kings Cross*, Kingsclear Books: Alexandria, 2002.

Dutton, Kenneth R. (ed.), *Kelver*

Hartley: A Memoir, The Hartley
Bequest Program: Newcastle,
1995.

Edginton, Brian, *Charles Waterton, A
Biography*, The Lutterworth Press:
Cambridge, 1996.

Elborn, Geoffrey, *Edith Sitwell, A
Biography*, Doubleday: New York,
1981.

Evans, Dr. Christopher, *Cults of
Unreason*, Delta Books: New
York, 1973.

Firbank, Ronald, *Five Novels*, New
Directions: New York, 1981.

Fountain, Tim, *Quentin Crisp*,
Absolute Press: Bath, 2002.

Fowler, Gene, *Minutes of the Last
Meeting*, The Viking Press: New
York, 1954.

Gabriel, Mary, *Notorious Victoria*,
Algonquin Books of Chapel Hill:
Chapel Hill, 1998.

Gardner, Martin, *Fads and Fallacies in
the Name of Science*, Dover: New
York, 1957.

Gattey, Charles Nelson, *The Incredible
Mrs. Van der Elst*, Leslie Frewin:
London, 1972.

Gibson, Ian, *The Shameful Life of
Salvador Dalí*, Faber and Faber:
London, 1997.

Graham, Harry, *A Group of Scottish
Women*, Duffield & Company:
New York, 1908.

Grey, Rudolph, *Nightmare of Ecstasy:
The Life and Art of Edward
D. Wood, Jr.*, Feral House: Los
Angeles, 1992.

Gwyer, Joseph, *Sketches of the Life
of Joseph Gwyer, (Potato Salesman);
with the Poems (Commended by
Royalty)*, J. Gwyer: Penge, 1876.

Hecht, Ben, *A Child of the Century*,
Simon & Schuster: New York,
1954.

Heming, Henry, *In Search of the
English Eccentric*, John Murray:
London, 2008.

Henry, Lyell D., *Zig-Zag-and-Swirl:
Alfred Lawson's Quest for Greatness*,
University of Iowa Press: Iowa
City, 1991.

Hernandez, Jo Farb, John
Beardsley, and Roger Cardinal.
*A, G. Rizzoli: Architect of
Magnificent Visions*, Harry N.
Abrams: New York, 1997.

Higham, Charles, *Howard Hughes:
The Secret Life*, Virgin Books:
London, 2004.

Holden, Robert, *Crackpots, Ratbags
and Rebels*, ABC Books: Sydney,
2005.

Hornadge, Bill, *Chidley's Answer to the
Sex Problem*, Review Publications:
Dubbo, 1977.

Houellebecq, Michel, *H.P. Lovecraft:
Against the World, Against Life*,
Believer Books: San Francisco,
2005.

Hughes, Robert, *Barcelona*, Harvill:
London, 1992.

Isay, David and Harvey Wang,
Holding On, Norton: Scranton,
1996.

Jay, Bernard, *Not Simply Divine*,

Virgin: London, 1993.

Jerome, Joseph (Brocard Sewell), *Montague Summers: A Memoir*, Cecil and Amelia Woolf: London, 1965.

Jones, Richard Glyn, *A Clutch of Curious Characters*, Xanadu: London, 1982.

Joshi, S.T., *H.P. Lovecraft: A Life*, Necronomicon Press: West Warwick, 1997.

Kafton-Minkel, Walter, *Subterranean Worlds: 100,000 Years of dragons, dwarfs, the dead, lost races & UFOs from inside the earth*, Loompanics Unlimited: Port Townsend, 1989.

Karasic, Paul, *I Shall Destroy All the Civilized Planets! The Comics of Fletcher Hanks*, Fantagraphics Books: Seattle, 2007.

—, *You Shall Die by Your Own Evil Creation!*, Fantagraphics Books: Seattle, 2009.

Karoly, Michael, *Hypnosis*, Paul Elek: London, 1961.

Keay, John, *Eccentric Travellers*, John Murray: London, 1982.

King, George, *You are Responsible!*, The Aetherius Press: London, 1961.

—, with Richard Lawrence, *Contacts with the Gods from Space*, The Aetherius Society: Hollywood, 1996.

Kirby, R.S. (ed.), *The Wonderful and Scientific Museum*, R.S. Kirby: London, 1803.

Klíma, Ladislav, *The Sufferings of Prince Sternenhoch*, Twisted Spoon Press: Prague, 2000.

Knight, Leonard, *Salvation Mountain*, with commentary by Leonard Knight, photography by Larry Yust, New Leaf Press: Los Angeles, 1998.

Koresh (Cyrus Teed), *The Cellular Cosmogony*, The Koreshan Unity Inc: Estero, 1951.

Kossy, Donna, *Kooks*, Feral House: Portland, 1994.

Lachmanm, Gary, *The Dedalus Book of Literary Suicides*, Dedalus: London, 2008.

Langdon, Paul, *Englishness Identified*, Oxford University Press: London, 2000.

Leedskalnin, Edward, *A Book in Every Home*, Edward Leedskalnin: Homestead, 1936.

Leslie, Desmond, and George Adamski, *The Flying Saucers Have Landed*, Werner Laurie: London, 1954.

Liberace, *The Wonderful, Private World of Liberace*, Harper and Row: New York, 1986.

Louvish, Simon, *Mae West: It Ain't No Sin*, Faber & Faber: London, 2006.

—, *Man on the Flying Trapeze: The Life and Times of W.C. Fields*, Norton: New York, 1997.

MacGregor, John M., *Henry Darger: In the Realms of the Unreal*, Delano Greenidge Editions: New York, 2002.

McCann, Graham, *Fawlty Towers*, Hodder & Stoughton: London, 2007.

McLoughlin, Dennis, *The Encyclopedia of the Old West*, Routledge & Kegan Paul: London, 1977.

McIntyre, James, *Oh! Queen of Cheese*, The Cherry Tree Press: Toronto, 1979.

McWilliam, Rohan, *The Tichborne Claimant*, Hambledon Continuum: London, 2007.

Merhan, Sir Alfred and Andrew Donkin, *The Terminal Man*, Corgi Books: London, 2004.

Michell, John, *Eccentric Lives and Peculiar Notions*, Thames & Hudson: London 1984.

Mielke, Hakon, *Let's See If the World is Round*, Hodge: London, 1940.

Montgomery, Ruth, *Aliens Among Us*, Fawcett: New York, 1985.

Morgan, Ted, *Literary Outlaw: The Life and Times of William S. Burroughs*, Avon: New York, 1990.

Munby, A.N.L., *Portrait of an Obsession*, Constable: London, 1967.

Munro, John M., *Selected Poems of Theo Marzials*, American University of Beiruit, Beirut: 1974.

Nash, Jay Robert, *Zanies*, New Century Publishers: Piscataway, 1972.

Onoda, Hiroo, *No Surrender: My Thirty-Year War*, New York: Kodansha International Ltd: New York, 1974.

Ostwald, Peter F., *Glenn Gould: The Ecstasy and Tragedy of Genius*, Norton, Scranton: 1997.

Page, Nick, *In Search of the World's Worst Writers*, HarperCollins: London, 2000.

Palin, Michael, *Diaries 1969–1979*, Wiedenfield & Nicholson: London, 2006.

Palmer, Susan J., *Aliens Adored*, Rutgers University Press: New Brunswick, 2004.

Parfrey, Adam, *Cult Rapture*, Feral House, Portland: 1995.

Parsons, Nicholas T,. *The Joy of Bad Verse*, Collins: London, 1988.

Paterson, James, *The Contemporaries of Burns, and More Recent Poets of Ayrshire*, Hugh Paton, 1840.

Pendle, George Pendle, *Strange Angel: The Otherworldy Life of Rocket Scientist John Whiteside Parsons*, Weidenfeld & Nicholson: London, 2005.

Pendragon, Arthur, with Christopher James Stone, *The Trials of Arthur*, Element: London, 2003.

Perkins, Kevin, *Bristow: Last of the Hard Men*, Bonmoat: Sydney, 2003.

Pessoa, Fernando, *The Book of Disquiet*, Exact Change: Boston, 1998.

Pyron, Darden Asbury, *Liberace*,

University of Chicago Press:
Chicago, 2000.

Raël (Claude Vorilhon), *The Message
Given to Me by Extra-Terresrtrials*,
AOM Corporation: Tokyo, 1986.

—, *Let's Welcome Our Fathers from Space*,
AOM Corporation: Tokyo, 1986.

Randall, Lucien and Chris Welch,
*Ginger Geezer: The Life of Vivian
Stanshall*, Fourth Estate: London,
2001.

Repsch, John, *The Legendary Joe Meek*,
Cherry Red Books: London,
2000.

Richmond, Keith, *The Occult Visions
of Rosaleen Norton*, The Oceania
Lodge of the Ordo Templii
Orientis and the Kings Cross
Arts Guild: Sydney, 2000.

Ridding, Ernest, *Self-Portrait of a Nut*,
(on disk), Sydney, 1999.

Ronson, John, *Them: Adventures with
Extremists*, Picador: London,
2001.

Ryersson, Scot D., and Michael
Orlando Yaccarino, *Infinite
Variety, The Life and Legend of the
Marchesa Casati*, Pimlico: London,
2000.

Scotto, Robert, *Moondog: The Viking
of 6th Avenue*, Process Media:
Los Angeles, 2007.

Seabrook, William, *Adventures in
Arabia*, Blue Ribbon Books: New
York, 1930.

—, *Asylum*, Harcourt, Brace and Co.:
New York, 1935.

—, *Jungle Ways*, Harcourt, Brace and

Co.: New York, 1931.

— *The Magic Island*, Harcourt, Brace
and Co.: New York, 1929.

Sharaf, Myron, *Fury on Earth: A
Biography of Willhelm Reich*, Da
Capo: New York, 1994.

Sharpe, Graham, *The Man who was
Screaming Lord Sutch*, Aurum
Press: London, 2005.

Sheeler, Jessie, *The Garden at Bomarzo*,
Francis Lincoln Limited:
London, 2007.

Sieveking, Lance, *Eye of the Beholder*,
Hulton: London, 1957.

Sitwell, Edith, *English Eccentrics*,
Penguin: Harmondsworth, 1971.

Skiles, Jack, *Judge Roy Bean Country*,
Texas Tech University Press:
Lubbock, 1996.

Smith, David Nicol, *Characters
from the Histories and Memoirs of
the Seventeenth Century*, Oxford
University Press: London, 1929.

Sommerville-Lang, Peter, *Irish
Eccentrics*, Lilliput: Dublin, 1990.

Stanley, Autumn, *Mothers and
Daughters of Invention*, Rutgers
University Press: New Jersey,
1995.

Steinmeyer, Jim, *Charles Fort*,
Tarcher/Penguin: New York,
2008.

Stern, Madeleine B., *The Pantarch: A
Biography of Stephen Pearl Andrews*,
University of Texas Press:
Austin, 1968.

Stewart, Douglas (ed.), *The Book of
Bellerive*, The Jacaranda Press:

Brisbane, 1961.

Stokes, Henry Scott, *The Life and Death of Yukio Mishima*, Ballantine Books: New York, 1974.

Sutch, Lord David with Peter Chipprndale, *Life as Sutch*, HarperCollins: London, 1996.

Summerscale, Kate, *The Queen of Whale Cay*, Fourth Estate: London, 1997.

Sutin, Lawrence, *Do What Thou Wilt: A Life of Aleister Crowley*, St. Martin's Press: New York, 2000.

Sykes, Christopher, *Orde Wingate*, Collins: London, 1959.

Symons, A.J.A., *The Quest for Corvo*, Penguin: Harmondsworth, 1960.

Szwed, John F., *Space is the Place: The Lives and Times of Sun Ra*, Da Capo Press: n.p., 1998.

Thayer, Tiffany, *Doctor Arnoldi*, Julian Messner Inc: n.p., 1934.

Thomas, Lately, *The Vanishing Evangelist*, Heinemann: London, 1960.

Thwaite, Joy L., *The Importance of Being Eve Langley*, Angus & Robertson: Sydney, 1989.

Timbs, John, *English Eccentrics and Eccentricities*, Richard Bentley: London, 1866.

Tomlinson, J., *Some Interesting Yorkshire Scenes*, Simpkin, Marshall and Co: London, 1865.

Topham, Captain, *The Life of John Elwes, Esq*, Ann Lemoine: London, 1802.

Treherne, John, *The Galapagos Affair*, Jonathan Cape: London 1983.

Trevor-Roper, Hugh, *Hermit of Peking*, Penguin: Harmondsworth, 1978.

Tumminia, Diana G., *When Prophecy Never Fails*, Oxford University Press: New York, 2005.

Turnley, Cole, *Cole of the Book Arcade*, Cole Publications: Hawthorn, 1974.

Van Hensbergen, Gijs, *Gaudí*, HarperCollins: London, 2002.

Washington, Peter, *Madame Blavatsky's Monkey*, Secker & Warburg: London, 1993.

Waters, John, *Shock Value*, Delta: New York, 1981.

—, *Trash Trio*, Vintage: New York. 1988.

Watson, Steven, *Strange Bedfellows: The First American Avant-Garde*, Abbeville Press: New York, 1991.

Week, David and Jamie James, *Eccentrics*, Phoenix: London, 1995.

West, Mae, *Mae West on Sex, Health and ESP*, W.H. Allen: London, 1975.

Wheen, Francis, *Who Was Charlotte Bach?*, Short Books: London, 2002.

Whitaker, Katie, *Mad Madge*, Chatto & Windus, London, 2003.

Whiteson, Leonard, *The Watts Towers of Los Angeles*, Mosaic Press: Oakeville, 1989.

Wilson, Colin, *Mysteries*, Granada:

London, 1979.

—, *The Misfits*, Grafton: London, 1988.

Wilson, George, *The Life of the Hon. Henry Cavendish*, The Cavendish Society: London, 1851.

Wilson, G.H., *The Eccentric Mirror*, James Cundee: London, 1807.

Wintle, A.D., *The Last Englishman*, Michael Joseph: London, 1968.

Wizard, The, *My Life as a Miracle*, Canterbury University Press: Christchurch, 1998.

Wolfe, Geoffrey, *Black Sun: The Brief Transit and Violent Eclipse of Harry Crosby*, Hamish Hamilton: London, 1977.

Woodruff, Douglas, *The Tichborne Claimant*, Hollis & Carter: London, 1957.

Wright, Ernest Vincent, *Gadsby*, Ramble House: Shreveport, 2004.

WEBSITES

John 'Mad Jack' Fuller, http://johnmadjackfuller.homestead.com/index.html

Beer Can House, www.beercanhouse.org/

Forestiere Underground Gardens, www.forestiere-historicalcenter.com/Forestierebio.html

The Parish of Heybridge, freespace.virgin.net/andrewandgeorge.heybridge/history0.htm

Lord Timothy Dexter, www.lordtimothydexter.com/index.htm

Nek Chand's Rock Garden, www.nekchand.info/

The Bock Saga, www.paulapeterson.com/Bock_Saga.html

Frank Chu Interview, www.starve.org/frank-chu.html

Tom Graeff, www.tomgraeff.com/

(Last accessed 6 October 2011)

ABOUT THE AUTHOR

Chris Mikul is a writer and illustrator based in Sydney, a city that has (mostly) welcomed its eccentrics. His books include *Bizarrism* (a compilation of articles from his long-running zine of the same name), *Tales of the Macabre and Ordinary* and *The Cult Files*. He's currently working on a book on impostors. ▦

ABOUT THE ARTIST

Glenn 'Glenno' Smith is an art mercenary, living in Sydney with his beautiful wife Gina and cats, Pishy and Cha-chi. His over-achievements can be seen on www.glennoart.com.au. He spends most of his illustration time making metal bands seem like powerful wizards, punk bands seem like earnest street-fighters while he himself is a humble conduit of pure creative energy lighting the mediocratic corners of the world with hope. ▦

A HEADPRESS BOOK
First published by Headpress in 2012

Headpress, Suite 306 The Colourworks, 2a Abbot Street, London, E8 3DP, UK
Tel 0845 330 1844 / +44(0)208 888 0781
Email headoffice@headpress.com

THE ECCENTROPEDIA
The Most Unusual People Who Have Ever Lived

Text copyright © Chris Mikul
Artwork © Glenn Smith
This volume copyright © Headpress 2012
Design, covers & layout: Mark Critchell
Headpress Diaspora: David Kerekes, Thomas Campbell, Caleb Selah,
Giuseppe Iantosca, Dave T.

The moral rights of the author have been asserted

CIP catalogue record for this book is not available from the British Library

This edition carries no ISBN number

Headpress. The gospel according to unpopular culture.

www.WorldHeadpress.com

Lightning Source UK Ltd.
Milton Keynes UK
UKOW041906041212

203146UK00002B/9/P